THE NEGRO IN THE NEW WORLD

BY

SIR HARRY H. JOHNSTON
G.C.M.G., K.C.B., D.Sc. Cambs.

Gold Medallist Royal Geographical and Royal Scottish Geographical Societies
Corresponding Member of the Geographical Society of Philadelphia, U.S.A.
and of the Italian Geographical Society, etc.

ISBN: 978-1-63923-869-9

Printed: March 2023

Published and Distributed By:
Lushena Books
607 Country Club Drive, Unit E
Bensenville, IL 60106
www.lushenabks.com

ISBN: 978-1-63923-869-9

THE NEGRO IN WEST AFRICA: LIBERIAN HINTERLAND

First Published in 1910

PREFACE

BOOKS are often synonymous with boredom nowadays. We have so much more to read through than our parents read before us [if we are to keep abreast of the ever-widening scope of world-interests] that the sight of the printed page is to many people almost a provocation to anger, suggesting a further strain on the already over-taxed eyes and over-stuffed brain. The literature of the almost immediate future may quite possibly be reduced to the pictographs from which writing began. A novelist, a traveller, an anthropologist, or an historian will be required to say what he has to say in a series of pictures—photographs and diagrams—and the letterpress will be confined to little more than descriptive titles and occasional verbal explanations.

In the year 1910, however, I have tried to tell in words as well as pictures the story of the NEGRO IN THE NEW WORLD, as much for my own education as for that of others. For those who are too busy to do more than glance at the pictures, and perhaps read through this preface (which is as much as fifty per cent of modern reviewers are able to accomplish, amid the rain of books in the English language), I will here summarise the conclusions to be deduced from my opinions and (I think) from my array of evidence.

In chapter I. I have set forth the theory that the Negro should be regarded as a sub-species of the perfect human type—*Homo sapiens;* that his sub-specific differences from the Caucasian or White man, the Yellow or Mongolian, are largely, but not entirely, in the direction of his being slightly more akin to the lowlier human stock which preceded in time and development the existing *Homo sapiens.* He is consequently in some features a little more primitive than are the non-Negro peoples of Europe, Asia, and America; and in others less so; or more highly specialised, more divergent from *Homo primigenius* than is the Mongol or the Caucasian. In any case he is distinctly superior in human evolution to the Australoid, the lowest in development of all existing divisions of *Homo sapiens.*

But although the Negro still possesses pithecoid characteristics long since lost by the Caucasian and the Mongol, although he comes of a stock which has stagnated in the African and Asiatic tropics for uncounted, unprogressive millenniums, he has retained dormant the full attributes of sapient humanity. He has remarkable and ungaugeable capabilities. It has been possible, over and over again, for individual Negroes to leap from a position of mental inferiority, such as the Caucasian's ancestors may have occupied fifty or even a hundred thousand years ago, to an equality in brain-power with some of the cleverest and ablest White men living at the present day. And it is always to be borne in mind (if we are not overrating the importance of the discovery of fossil negroids in Southern and Western France) that several branches of the Negro race may have known better days ten to forty thousand years ago, that the ancestors of the modern Negro in Africa may have pursued a downward course for many thousand years before their descendant was turned right-about-face by his Caucasian brother and compelled to take the ascending path which may lead him at some future period to a position of all-round equality with the white man.

At the present day the generality of negroes (leaving out of account exceptional individuals) are inferior in mental development and capacity to the peoples of Europe and their descendants in America, to the Eskimo, the Red Indian, the Japanese, the Chinese, the natives of India and of Tartary. The best types of Negro in bodily structure are almost as beautiful as the best types of European with (at present) the striking exception of the face. Morally, the Negro is nearly on an equality with the White race, and perhaps slightly superior to the Yellow. He is, however, more subject to disease, and is himself a hive of dangerous germs; perhaps has been the great disease-spreader among the other sub-species of *Homo sapiens.*

As regards chapters II. and III. I have arrived at the conclusion that the Spaniards did not exterminate the Amerindian peoples of tropical America with quite the degree of senseless ferocity attributed to them by historians, and that they were scarcely worse in this respect than the Anglo-Saxons of North America, or the French and British in regard to the Caribs of the West India Islands. Both the Spaniards and the Portuguese were to a great extent checked in their intention to destroy and dispossess many Amerindian peoples by the work of the Society of Jesus, of the Dominicans, and of one or two other orders of missionaries emanating from the Roman Catholic Church. In regard to the Spanish treatment of the *Negro* it was far *less* cruel than was that of the Anglo-Saxon or the Dutchman.

In chapter V. it is set forth that the Portuguese attitude towards the Amerindians (at any rate of Eastern Brazil) was better than that of the Spaniards towards the indigenes of Central and South America; the Portuguese treatment of the Negro in Brazil was a little less kindly than that of the Spaniards in Santo Domingo, Porto Rico, and eighteenth-century Cuba; but on the whole the Negro had, even in slavery, a less unhappy life and far greater opportunities for bettering his position and attaining his freedom in Portuguese Brazil than he had in North America before the year 1863, or in the British and French West Indies before 1834. The Dutch treatment (chapter VI.) of the Negro before the commencement of the nineteenth century was mainly atrocious. It is now as good as it is in the British and French West Indies. The Jews who settled and prospered so much under Dutch protection in Tropical America behaved no better to the negro than did the Christian. The Bush negroes who grew up as a powerful people during the eighteenth century in the forests of Guiana obtained and conserved their freedom and independence, not only as the result of gallant fighting against the Dutch forces, but equally because of the loyal way in which both parties respected the terms of peace which were embodied in the treaties that terminated this warfare.

In chapter VII. I have dealt with slavery under the French. I have attempted to show that in calling into existence a considerable number of half-breeds who were allowed to receive a good education in France, and yet in denying the ordinary rights of citizens to this educated class of mulattoes, the French had only themselves to thank (or their rancorous white planters of St. Domingue) for the insurrection that commenced with the mulattoes and was continued so tremendously by the negro slaves under Toussaint Louverture and other black generals. On the other hand, the Negro and the Negroid lost a great opportunity (owing to the class jealousy between the half-white and the wholly black) when all the leading insurgents of Hispaniola failed to support Toussaint Louverture—one of the greatest Negroes known to history—or, succeeding him, the intelligent mulatto politicians who ruled over the Republic of Haiti in its early days. Although the independence of Haiti was achieved mainly by the negroes, it is the negro majority that through several decades of misrule has well-nigh ruined Haiti, and has lost for ever the chances of bringing the whole island of Hispaniola under one Negroid Government.

On the other hand, though I maintain that the French planters and some of the French officials (and the Government of Louis Seize and his Ministers was no wiser) behaved so badly to the black man and the half-caste in St. Domingue as to merit the censure of history; elsewhere in tropical America France has treated the negro fairly well as slave and freeman, best of all, perhaps, as a free citizen, between whom and the white Frenchman there is little or no ill-feeling such as arises so often between the Anglo-Saxon and the Negro or Negroid. The impress of France on the negroes of Dominica, St. Lucia, St. Vincent, Grenada, and Trinidad has been so deeply implanted, has been so profound, that even after a hundred or a hundred and fifty years of British rule it still remains, moulding thought, language, religion, and social customs. Still more marked, of course, is the Frenchification of those islands of the Antilles that have remained under the French flag, or of the negroes of Cayenne. But this does not limit the influence of France over the Negro in the New World, or, still more, the Negroid. The patron country of Brazil is not Portugal, the United States, or Germany, but France. Because there is a very large negro or negroid element—perhaps over eight millions—in Brazil; and a large proportion of these dark-coloured Brazilians are educated, art-and-music-loving people, to whom France, and Paris above all, is a veritable Mecca. All the *rastaquouères* of South

America look to France for the finishing education of their children, for their own enjoyment, when they wish to touch the highest phase of our present civilisation, or to deal with the greatest developments of science, literature, and art. The Negroids of Central America and the West Indies are turning their steps more towards New York, Boston, Washington, and Chicago. But Paris is still the magnetic pole for the rest of the twenty-two millions of dark-skinned people in the New World.

An increasing number are going to Germany for education. Very few come to England, and the reason given recently in print is a simple one. If the man of colour goes to France or Germany, nowhere in these countries is he insulted or treated as an inferior being. No notice at all is taken of the difference between the colour of his skin and that of his hosts for the time being. Whereas if the negroid comes to England, or goes to any part of the South-Eastern United States, he is apt to be rudely treated. If he be a full-blooded negro, he will receive in England a kindly, half-contemptuous treatment, but he will be made to feel more at his ease about the docks of Liverpool and London than at university towns or in Bloomsbury. But the pure-blooded negro is a jolly person, not as a rule given to seeking or finding offence; whereas the negroid is a thousand times more touchy, more acutely self-conscious than either black man or white man. And this increasing type of American humanity finds in France a patroness which its sensitive nature warmly appreciates.

In chapters IX., X., and XI., dealing with Slavery under the British, I felt obliged to show with what terrible cruelties this institution was connected in the greater part of the British West Indies, and possibly also in British Guiana before 1834. Nor did these cruelties cease entirely with the Abolition of the Slave-trade and of Slavery. They were continued under various disguises until they culminated in the Jamaica Revolt of Morant Bay in 1865. Since 1868 the history of the British West Indies, so far as the treatment of the negro and the coloured man is concerned, has been wholly satisfactory, taking into consideration all the difficulties of the case. Much of the temporary ruin of the West India Islands during the middle of the nineteenth century was not directly caused by giving freedom to the slaves, but by a blunder perpetrated in 1849 in connection with the otherwise beneficent institution of Free Trade. After that year the sugar (and cotton) of the British West Indies raised by the paid labour of *free* negroes was obliged to compete in the British markets with the *slave*-grown sugar of the Southern States of the Union, of Spanish Cuba and Porto Rico, Dutch Guiana, and Brazil. If without interfering with the indisputable need of Free Trade in the United Kingdom a very legitimate differential duty had been placed on all slave-grown sugar, cotton, and tobacco, not only would the British West Indies have suffered little, if any, eclipse in their prosperity, but an end would have been put much sooner to the existence of Slavery in the Southern States of the Union, in Spanish, Dutch, and Portuguese America.

In chapters XIV. and XV. is traced the history of Slavery in the United States. It was here that the battle for human freedom was fought on the grandest scale and with the most tremendous results, and consequently the history of the Negro in this part of the world is so important that it requires a more ample treatment than is necessary for similar problems in Brazil or Spanish America. I have felt it advisable, as the result of reading a great many books (some of them little known), to give an explicit account of the exceptional cruelties attending Slavery in the United States. These cruelties, perhaps, were not greater than what went on in British Barbados or in the Bahama Islands, and certainly not more outrageous than the treatment of the negroes in Dutch Guiana; but the wickedness was on a far greater scale geographically and affected the welfare of a much larger number of human beings.

Even this may seem a thrice-told tale and an unnecessary raking-up of embers that have ceased to glow. I do not think so. I still believe that the bulk of my fellow-countrymen and the mass of my possible readers in North America have not realised [with our super-sensitive, twentieth-century consciousness] how bad was the treatment of the Negro in the South-Eastern States of the Union between, let us say, 1790 and 1860. This story should be re-written ever and again "lest we forget." Given the same temptations and the same opportunities, there is sufficient of the devil still left in the white man for the 300 years' cruelties of negro (or other) slavery to be repeated, if it were worth the white man's while, and public opinion could be drugged or purchased. Perhaps some day the white man's conscience may be universally educated up to the level of Christ's teaching and of the gospel according to Exeter Hall, and the subject of Slavery and the Slave Trade can be tacitly dropped.

So much for the past: the present is treated of in a series of chapters which to a great extent represent my own personal observations on the existing condition of the Negro in the New World. A visit to the United States in 1908 revealed to me the wonderful educational work which is being carried on at the Hampton and Tuskegee Institutes, and at the now-innumerable daughter-schools or sister-colleges; work which is (I believe) raising up the Negro and Negroid to play a great part in North America, the West Indies, Central and South America. If any efforts can bring the Negro mentally and physically to the best standard of the White man, it will be the work which was, for all practical purposes, initiated by General S. C. Armstrong, though foreshadowed by the prior enterprises of the Jesuits, the Moravian Brethren, the Society of Friends, the Baptists, and the Presbyterians. This work has since been continued in the States by such men and women as Dr. Frissell, Miss Laura W. Towne, Miss Ellen Murray, Dr. Booker Washington, Professor W. E. B. DuBois, Miss Rossa Cooley, Mr. Holtzclaw, and many other negro, negroid, and white Americans.

It is only right to remember, however, that the work of these prophets and teachers would have been a vain calling in the wilderness had it not been for the immense sums of money contributed (for the most part) by white millionaires of the Northern States, by one or two rich negroes or negresses who had gained their wealth in the North, and by a few white Southerners, the *avant-garde* of a great movement of reparation towards the Negro. One should also notice with gratification the increasing prosperity of those Southern States like Alabama, which are forgetting race prejudice in assisting the Negro to occupy a responsible position as a free and an educated citizen. Nowhere is the power of Money for good more strikingly shown than at Tuskegee. Andrew Carnegie, for example, by assisting to endow this Institute with a splendid income, has probably effected more change in the world's future than many a vaunted conqueror of the past, by land or sea.

Haiti, I have tried to show, is not quite so black as she has been painted. She has it in her to become a happy, wealthy, and respected negro community, if she will cut herself off from the preposterous traditions of her ridiculous past, cease to dress up in grotesque military uniforms, to be for ever marching to and fro to military music, and wasting her substance on warlike stores. For very shame she should cease to make the negro race a laughing-stock. She has no enemies, because the United States is her all-powerful friend.

In the British West Indies a much higher level of education should be aimed at by the people of colour. And just as the British Government has in a very munificent way taken in hand the agriculture of the West Indies, and grouped its teaching round a Central Institute, and thereby contributed greatly to the revival of prosperity, so in like manner some system of universal, British-West-Indian, *practical*, collegiate education should be brought into being. Otherwise, all intelligent negroes in these islands, and in British Honduras and Guiana, will look to receive their twentieth-century education at the hands of the United States. A great deal more should be done in the future to *unify* the British administration of these remarkable West Indian Islands, not merely in the interest of the Black and of the Yellow, but also of the White. So far as natural conditions are concerned, there is a considerable total area under the British flag in tropical America which might be colonised by White people without injustice to, or displacement of, the coloured race.

I do not think that there is any more reason for resigning the smaller West Indian Islands to the negroes than there is for excluding the negro from access to all parts of temperate America. The white people of the United States will have to get used to the presence of the negro in their midst as a brother, but not a brother-in-law. If the Imperial destiny of the English-speaking peoples of North America is to be achieved, they must expect to see their flag or flags covering nationally many peoples of non-Caucasian race, wearing the shadowed livery of the burnished sun. Already the Stars and Stripes float over the Isthmus of Panama. The influence of this same great nation keeps the peace and controls the destinies of all Central America and the northern half of South America, to say nothing of Cuba, Hispaniola, and Porto Rico, of Hawaii and the Philippines. Unless this Imperial progress is to be truncated and beaten back, the white citizens of this Republic must accustom themselves to accord rights of citizenship and of entrance into civilised society to men of all colours in all parts of their dominion. They—and we—may limit the franchise as we like, by conditions of education, physical fitness, property, or service to the State. But whatever may be the conditions restricting a franchise, they must be made to apply to all members of the human species without distinction of sex, race, or colour.

My book ends with a tabulation of the numerical importance of the Negro in the New World at the present day. As to the future of the black man in America or in Africa, it depends largely on himself. For many thousand years he has been a relatively idle creature as compared to the industrious European or Asiatic; who when not in slavery to each other were the slaves of ambition, of art and science, of gluttony, of lust, and of religion. In other words, they *worked*. The negro became constitutionally so lazy that he thought out very few problems for himself, but every now and again borrowed ideas from the Caucasian, who impinged on his territories in Northern Africa.

The rending of the veil which had shrouded him from the full gaze of the white man for thousands of years; the discovery of Negro Africa by the Arab, Portuguese, Hollander, British, and French forced the palæolithic or neolithic negro to gaze upon the full effulgence of the white man's civilisation—the civilisation of guns and gunpowder; of the Cross, the Mass, the translated Bible and hymnal; of schools and colleges, ships and wagons, distilled alcohol, railways and telegraphs, economic botany, modern rifles and artillery, canned food and corrugated iron. Probably for ten thousand years the negro of one type or another has been a slave or a servant to some kind of white man. Is that servitude at an end? Or will it be resumed in Africa under pleasanter terms more agreeable to the ingrained hypocrisy of the Christian European? Will the negro always occupy a lower social level in Brazil, in the West Indies, in North America?

If he is not content with a position against which the Jew has chafed and struggled from 300 B.C. to the Russian Pogroms of 1905 A.D. he will determine to do as the Jew has done: make plenty of money. Money solves all human difficulties. It will buy you love and respect, power and social standing. With money you can create armies and build navies, you can control the votes of your fellow-citizens, found and shape their educational institutes, conduct a Press, overcome disease, make actual the charity of early Christianity, achieve all purposes that are noble, and check the Devil at every turn; whether he crop up in the forms of alcoholism, disease, intestinal worms, religious intolerance, political oppression, waste of the earth's natural resources, or the misuse of corrugated iron. If you are rich you can roof your dwellings with tiles of the most beautiful, or stone slabs, or wooden shingles, marble terraces or leaden sheets; if you are poor you must content yourself with corrugated iron and know that your dwelling is a blot on the landscape.

The one undoubted solution of the Negro's difficulties throughout the world is for him to turn his strong arms and sturdy legs, his fine sight, subtle hearing, deft fingers, and rapidly-developed brain to the making of Money, money being indeed but transmuted intellect and work, accumulated energy and courage. And his leaders, his pastors and teachers, should direct his and their attention to the questions that are really vital: to theories and practices of disease-prevention and cure; to the correlation of intestinal worms and sanitary reform; to the inculcation of the chemistry of nature, of practical agriculture, beautiful horticulture, sound building, modern history, modern science, modern languages, modern religion, and modern temperance in eating, drinking, love-making, and public oratory.

Before proceeding to set forth the details in history and actuality on which these general conclusions are founded, I should like to express my acknowledgments to the many persons who have helped me in this task, either by facilitating my journeys or by supplying information or photographs. [Some names appear in the list of illustrations and the text of the book in relation to the source of illustration or notes, or services rendered. Those to whom I am more generally or signally indebted are enumerated here.]

The inception of the book was due to the invitation of Colonel Theodore Roosevelt, who was President of the United States when I made my journeys through different parts of the New World. Mr. Roosevelt indicated to me many lines of research which I have tried to follow up, and gave me considerable assistance by letters of introduction to persons in the United States, in Cuba, Haiti, and elsewhere. The Editor of the *Times* invited me to contribute a series of letters to that paper on the present condition of the Negro in America; and Messrs. McClure, of *McClure's Magazine*, secured the American rights in these letters, the composition of which was the starting-point of this book.

From the Right Honble. James Bryce and Mrs. Bryce I received the kindest hospitality at Washington and introductions to leading Americans which were of much value to me. Dr. Leander Chamberlain (brother of that Governor Chamberlain who worked at the reconstruction of the South after the War) was my principal guide and host in and through the wonders of New York—in some respects the most wonderful, most advanced, educative, interesting, and beautiful city in the world—certainly the one I should most like to live in, if residence in a town were obligatory. Dr. Chamberlain caused me to know many of the leading men in New York who are concerning themselves with the education of the Negro, amongst them Dr. Wallace Buttrick, who from the twenty-second storey of one of New York's Brobdingnagian palaces directs the affairs of that mighty institution the General Education Board.

Mr. Robert Ogden, a member of this Board and a Trustee of Hampton and Tuskegee, conveyed me to the last-named Institute and introduced me to Dr. Booker Washington.

(I had previously been the guest of Dr. H. B. Frissell, at Hampton.) What I have learnt from and through the Principal of Tuskegee and his staff (especially from Dr. Robert E. Park) is set forth in the chapters dealing with the Education of the Negro, as is also my indebtedness to Mr. J. O. Thompson and Mr. W. Thompson, well-known landowners in Alabama, whose acquaintance I made at Tuskegee, and who showed me so much of industrial and agricultural Alabama.

All Louisiana—the most interesting of the Southern States, as Alabama is the most beautiful—was thrown open to my inquiring gaze by the introductions of the Honble. Pearl White; and I shall long remember the hospitality of Mr. McCall on his estate by the banks of the Mississippi. Whatever it may have lacked in the "ante-bellum" days, the hospitality of the "South" is now a very delightful reality.

My sincere thanks are also due to Mrs. J. Perrin (to whom I was introduced by Mr. McClure), who resides for a part of the year on the Mississippi Delta, and who with one of her friends acted as my *cicerone* in visiting negro settlements in that region. Mr. Pearl White's introductions carried me through Florida to Cuba, where the Honble. R. Hawley [who supervises most of the great sugar estates of that island], together with the British Minister (Mr. A. C. Grant Duff) and the managers of the English railways, enabled me to see a good deal of Cuba at a minimum of time and expense. To Mr. Theodore Brooks, British Vice-Consul at Guantanamo, I feel exceptionally indebted.

In Haiti, thanks especially to the American Minister, Dr. H. W. Furniss, I was enabled to see more of the country and people in a relatively short space of time than any preceding traveller (I should think). I am also indebted to Captain Alexander Murray, the British Consul-General in that Republic, and to the courtesy and kindness of the Haitian officials; to Mr. C. Lyon Hall, a well-known British resident and banker at Port-au-Prince, and to Mrs. Lyon Hall; to the Messrs. Peters, British *concessionnaires* in Haiti; to the German Consul-General and the German residents at Port-au-Prince; and last, but not least, to the French priests and seminarists of the Haitian Church and Educational department.

[As showing the wide scope of the Roman propaganda, it was interesting to me to renew acquaintance in Haiti with Catholic missionaries whom I had last seen in East Africa and Uganda.]

In Jamaica Sir Sydney Olivier obtained for me every facility for sight-seeing and study which could save time and expense and procure for me the information I wanted. The kindly help of other Jamaican officials is acknowledged *in loco;* but I should like specially to thank Mr. W. Harris, Mr. H. H. Cousins, and Miss H. A. Wood for their initiation into the wonders and beauties of the Jamaican flora. Unfortunately I have only been able to use in the present work a fiftieth part of their information and pictures.

President Taft allowed me to accompany his tour of inspection over the Panama Canal zone in February, 1909. The facilities most kindly offered me by the Royal Mail Steamship Company enabled me to avail myself of this invitation and to visit the Spanish Main and the islands of Trinidad and Barbados. Other journeys to and through the New World were carried out under the ægis of Messrs. Thomas Cook and Son, to whose agent in New York I tender my sincere thanks.

Since my return to England in 1909 the further prosecution of my studies of the past and present of the Negro in the New World and his environment has been materially helped by Mr. Algernon E. Aspinall, Secretary to the West India Committee, to whom I have referred repeatedly in the body of the work; by Mr. Travers Buxton and the Library of the Anti-Slavery Society; by Dr. Robert E. Park, of the Tuskegee Institute; and by Professor W. E. Burghardt DuBois, of Atlanta University; by the Librarian of the Colonial Office, Mr. C. Atchley, I.S.O. (Colonial Laws on Slavery, etc.), and the Director of Military Operations (History of West India Regiments); Mr. Edward Heawood, Librarian of the Royal Geographical Society; Dr. J. Scott Keltie, LL.D.; Mr. Edgar Gardner Murphy (the well-known American writer on the United States Negro); Dr. R. T. Leiper, of the London School of Tropical Medicine; Dr. A. Keith, of the Royal College of Surgeons; H.S.H. the Prince of Monaco (illustrations of the skulls of negroid types found in the Grimaldi Caverns); E. H. Man, Esq. (late of the Andaman Islands) Mr. Roger Casement, C.M.G. (H.B.M. Consul-General, Rio de Janeiro); Mr. J. R. W. Pigott, H.B.M. Consul for Dutch and French Guiana; Dr. H. van Cappelle, an explorer of Dutch Guiana; Mr. D. O'Sullivan-Beare, H.B.M. Consul at Santos; Herr Walter Garbe and Dr. Max Schmidt (German travellers in Central Brazil); Mr. J. E. Devaux, Vice-Consul at Guadeloupe; The Right Rev. Wilfrid Hornby, Bishop of Nassau (Bahamas), and Dr. A. W. Holly, of the same place; T.E. The Governors of British Honduras (Col. E. J. E. Swayne, C.B.) and the Leeward Islands (Sir Bickham Sweet-Escott, K.C.M.G.); the Administrator of Dominica (Honble. Douglas Young, C.M.G.); H.E. Sir Everard Im Thurn, Governor of Fiji; Major Herbert Bryan, C.M.G., Colonial Secretary, Gold Coast Colony; the Commissioner of the Cayman Islands, G. S. S. Hirst, Esq., M.B.; H. E. Constantin Brun, Danish Envoy at the Court of St. James; H.E. J. P. Crommelin, Liberian Minister Plenipotentiary to Great Britain and France; Dr. Bumpus, of the American Museum of Natural History; Mr. Madison Grant, of the New York Zoological Society; Capt. T. C. Hincks (of the Royal Berkshire Regt., and formerly A.D.C. to the Governor of the Gold Coast); Capt. W. B. Stanley, a Travelling Commissioner of the Gambia Colony; Messrs. Hutchinson and Co., of 34 Paternoster Row; Mr. J. R. Henderson, of the Madras Government Museum; Mr. Francis Harrison, of the Natal Government Agency in London; Miss Alice Werner, of the African Society; Mr. H. S. Kingsford, of the Royal Anthropological Institute; the Royal Society of Arts (Brazilian photographs); the Religious Tract Society; Mr. C. W. Furlong, of Connecticut (an American explorer of South America and North Africa); Mr. William Aery, of the *Southern Workman*, Hampton, U.S.A.; Dr. Thomas Jesse Jones, a Professor at Hampton Institute; Messrs. James Rodway and J. van Sertima, of British Guiana; and Mr. R. Harold Paget, the representative in America of my literary agents, Messrs. A. P. Watt.

This long recital of names of so many eminent persons and authorities may arouse in the uninterested reader the feeling that their assistance and encouragement should have provoked a much better book. He will probably be right; but I have been actually embarrassed by the wealth of material in pictures and statistics collected personally or placed at my disposal by others. The attempt

volume the past and present of the Negro in the New World hose of encyclopædic instincts a disappointing result. One wish to make abundantly clear. The views and conclusions the evidence which has passed under my eyes are my own ily those of my friends and helpers, several of whom have, proofs, been inclined to dissent in some degree from my

H. H. JOHNSTON

1910

TABLE OF CONTENTS

LIST OF ILLUSTRATIONS

LIST OF MAPS

(IN ADDITION TO THE SKETCH-MAPS IN THE TEXT)

THE NEGRO IN THE NEW WORLD

CHAPTER I

THE NEGRO SUB-SPECIES

THE genus *Homo* has but one existing species: *Homo sapiens*. And this species (which according to the latest hypotheses of palæontologists may be two or three hundred thousand years old) is fairly divisible into four sub-species, all of which are so fertile in their cross-breeding with one another that they have in the course of time given rise to many transitional races and intermediary types: so much so that only about two-thirds of the living peoples of to-day can be decisively allotted to one or other of the definite sub-species. The remaining third comprises the long-established mongrel, hybrid races formed by the mixture of some or even of all of these four divisions of the existing human species. These distinguishable sub-species are—

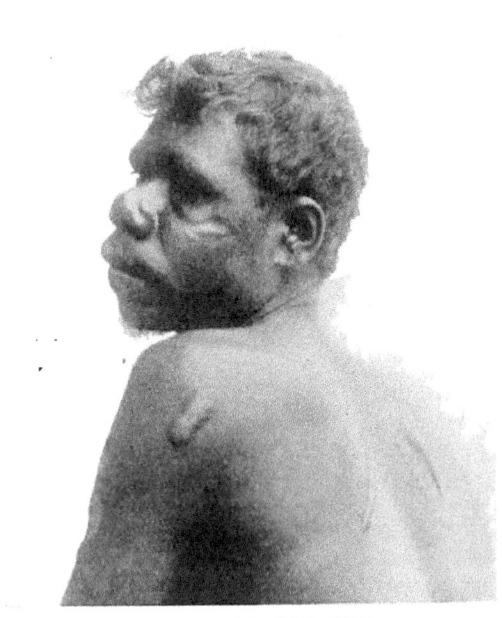

I. THE AUSTRALOID TYPE
A native of Gilbert River, Northern Australia

(1) The AUSTRALOID, nearest of all living men to the ancestral Human, to the palæolithic man of Europe and North Africa; and to the possible parent thereof—*Homo primigenius*, the man of Neanderthal and Heidelberg, of the Corrèze, of Spy, Krapina, and Gibraltar.

(2) The NEGRO.

(3) The CAUCASIAN or EUROPEAN, possibly descended in a direct line from the Australoid or basal stock, with which in any case it is closely allied.

(4) The MONGOLIC or ASIAMERICAN

An ancient mingling of (1), (2), (3), and (4) has produced the *Polynesian* type of (2), (3), and (4)—(4) predominating—the *Japanese*. The *Amerindian* peoples are mainly descended from an early branch of Mongolic mixed with Proto-Caucasian ; there are many tribes in the Malay Archipelago that are half Mongol, half Negrito (Asiatic Negro) ; the natives of Madagascar are a mixture of Mongolic-Polynesian and Negro. Negrito and Australoid in varying degrees of intermixture have produced the Tasmanian negroids and the Papuans. The aborigines of Ceylon (Veddahs) and India (Dravidians, Todas, etc.) are on the borderland between Australoid and Caucasian with (here and there) a touch of Negrito or Mongol. Some of the Central Asians or North Europeans are Caucasians crossed with Mongols, the two strains being either evenly balanced or one of them predominating. The proud peoples of Western and Southern Europe and of North Africa, of Syria, Arabia, and Persia are principally composed of Caucasian tinged very slightly or considerably with ancient or modern Negro, or Australoid (Dravidian) blood; the warlike tribes of North-East Africa are half Caucasian, half Negro. The very negro himself is scarcely of unmixed sub-specific rank, except in his extreme Bushman-Hottentot, Pygmy, and West African Forest types. Elsewhere a meandering rill of Caucasian—perhaps even of Australoid—blood permeates Negro Africa and Negrito Asia.

The AUSTRALOID is characterised by a dark skin, a hairy body, black, wavy head-hair, full beard, large teeth, a broad, *curved* nose, very projecting brow-ridges, prognathous jaws, and a hypsiloid[1] rather than a semicircular palate. In the configuration and development of the brain, the heavy brow-ridges, the proportions of the leg-bones, the spines of the neck-vertebræ, the lumbar curve of the vertebral column, and the shape and proportions of the foot,[2] the Australoid is slightly more ape-like than the other divisions of *Homo sapiens*.

The NEGRO probably sprang from the basal Australoid stock and thus inherited a dark-coloured skin, which in some developments of his sub-species —Asiatic and African—becomes almost brownish or greyish *black*. But in the very divergent *Bushman* branch of the Negro sub-species the skin colour is a brownish yellow—almost a light olive-yellow among the Cape Colony Bushmen—through which the mantling of the blood can be seen in the cheeks. It is possible that the lighter pigmentation of the skin in the Bushmen is a feature due to distinctive variation, and does not represent the original tint of the primal negro. But that this tint was not the sooty black[3] so characteristic of the modern negroes in Africa and Asia is probable from the fact that most negro babies are born with reddish-brown skins, and that this shade is the commonest skin-colour among the Congo pygmies. In the pale-skinned negroes

[1] i.e. shaped like a croquet hoop.

[2] The pithecoid foot is seen perhaps (so far as our very imperfect records go) in its most marked form amongst the Australoid-Negroid natives of the Solomon Islands, and occasionally among the Australian blacks ; while in a less extreme degree it is characteristic of the African pygmies and Forest negroes. In this pithecoid form of foot the greatest breadth is not from the second joint of the big toe to the second joint of the little toe, but across the tips of the toes. There is a distinct space between the big toe and the next, and instead of the big toe making a marked angle at the inner edge of its second joint and turning outwards towards the other toes, it is smaller in proportion (than the big toe of the European), and is placed either in a straight line with the inner side of the heel or even turns markedly inwards. The other toes are larger, longer, more separated, divergent, and projecting than with Europeans, and the instep is less arched.

[3] Elsewhere I have written on this subject : "The skin colour of the Nilotic negro is dark almost to blackness. That of the Forest negro tends rather towards chocolate-brown, while the skin colour of the Pygmies is more usually 'red' (in the estimation of their darker neighbours) : in reality a warm yellow-brown."

there is often a dark streak down the centre of the abdomen. The skin of the inner side of hand and foot is always paler—a pinkish yellow. Albinism is common among negroes, producing a pinkish-white skin, red iris to the eyes, and yellow-white hair. Another phase equally common is Xanthism, in which hair and skin are tinged with yellow, and the iris of the eye is a pale yellow like that of a lion.

The *Negro*, however, is most marked out from the other sub-species of *Homo*

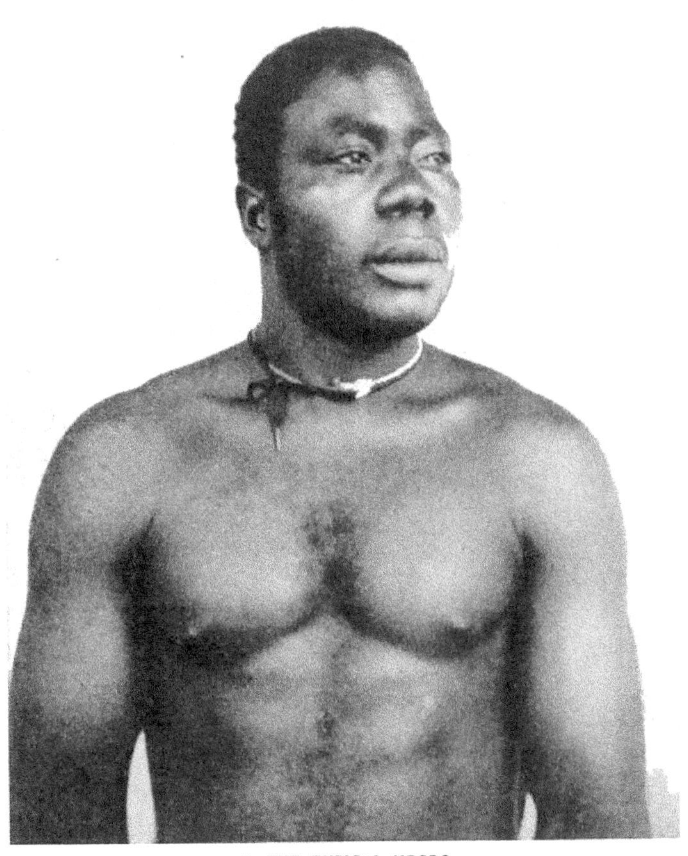

2. THE TYPICAL NEGRO
A Kru man from the Kru Coast, Liberia

sapiens by his *hair*. On head and body alike the adult hair is coarse, and tightly curled or kinky in spiral growths. It is without natural gloss or lustre, and is of a dull black colour. Occasionally in the Pygmy or Forest races the head-hair is brownish or greenish grey, or may even have a tinge of red.[1] In

[1] It is extraordinary how in North America and in the West Indies the crossing of the Negro with the "Nordic" (fair-haired) Caucasian brings out a tendency—deep-seated in the Human species—to *red hair*. Innumerable negroids in Anglo-Saxon America have bright red hair.

the Negro fœtus the hair-follicle is only slightly curved. The hair of the negro baby at birth grows almost straight and its transverse section is nearly round throughout the length of the hair; whereas after the child is a year old the hairs, curled in several spirals, emerge at an oblique angle from the plane of the skin surface, the hair-follicle in the epidermis is strongly curved, and a transverse section of the hair near its emergence from the skin would be in the form of a flattened ellipse. But the transverse section of the hair near its outer

3. THE CAUCASIAN TYPE
An Anglo-Saxon American (W. Plumer, an anti-slavery reformer of the middle nineteenth century)

extremity is almost circular. In the negro moustache the hairs are nearly if not quite straight, and the yellowish, fleecy lanugo-like body-pile present in so many adult male pygmies (and even in pygmy women and children) is either straight or only slightly crimped. There is a further peculiarity of hair-growth in the African negroes[1] and more especially in the Bushmen: both on the head and body the hair appears to grow in segregated groups, bands, or patches,

[1] This peculiarity is not observable in the Asiatic negroes and is very much diminished in the American types, partly no doubt because these are almost entirely derived from the hairy West African peoples.

separated by bald areas or zigzag streaks. I write "appears," because the hair-follicles are in actuality evenly distributed; but the hairs if short and very tightly curled converge to one another in little islets or tufts. This is most marked near the temples, and in the whiskers and abdominal hair of men. The Southern Bushmen possess to an exaggerated degree this feature of the tightly crimped, short head-hair growing in isolated tufts or rows; but their more northern examples scarcely differ in this respect from the normal negro type. The segregation of the hair-tufts is a fairly constant feature throughout *East* Africa, but is less observable (except on the body) among the Pygmies and *West* African negroes.

Body-hair is present among all types of Negro at the armpits and pubes, and is fairly abundant among the males of the West African and Pygmy groups on the chest, abdomen, and front side of thighs and legs No example has been recorded among negroes of hair on the *back*, a simian feature confined to sub-species (1) and (3).[1] Amongst the Bushmen-Hottentots hair on the body is entirely absent (except armpits and pubes), but beard and moustache grow in all men over thirty years of age. The East African and Nilotic Negroes are also rather hairless about the body.

The typical Negro skull is *long*[2] and very prognathous—only less so than in the Australoids. But with rare exceptions in the African negro and the Asiatic negritos there is no prominence of the brow-ridges These are unusually suppressed in the Bushman. In this point the Negro sub-species is less pithecoid than the Australoid or the European. The forehead bulges more than in other types of man. The nasal aperture is wide; the nasal bones are flatter and shorter than in Europeans.[3] The nasal spine which supports the septum between the nostrils is poorly developed or even absent. The nose itself is (in the pure negro) very flattened and depressed in the bridge, and the *alæ* or nostrils are thick and almost raised to the level of the nose-tip in extreme types. In this respect the Bushman is as primitive as other African negroes, but in some examples the nose is proportionately smaller, though even flatter than in the black negro; this peculiarly flattened aspect of the Bushman face is caused by the excessive prominence of the cheek-bones. In the Asiatic negroes, the nose is flat and "African" among the Aeta of the Philippines and the Samang of the Malay Peninsula; but has a better-developed bridge among the Andamanese and (extinct) Tasmanians, and also (but with many exceptions) among the Solomon Islanders. *In respect of nose development and shape* it may be said that *the Negro is more pithecoid* than any existing human race, except the lowest types of Australoids.

In typical negro skulls the width *across the brows* (through the temples) is markedly *less*—especially in women and children—than *across the cheek-bones*, while at the same time the under-jaw is retreating and the chin small. This configuration is (to our ideas of comely form) singularly unpleasing and gives the negro face an almost hexagonal or pentagon shape instead of the European oval. But it is a shape of face not at all uncommon in the inferior types of all the other sub-species, though particularly marked in the African Negro and the Bushman.

[1] Some Kafir men, however, are said to develop hair on the back. The western section of the Kafir-Zulu group is very hairy for negroes.

[2] The ordinary Bushman skull is less prognathous and is rounder (especially in the female) than that of the long-headed black negro. Yet there are types of Bushmen and even Hottentots which exhibit an extreme degree of prognathism. These may be survivals of the older "Strandlooper" race. See pp. 20-27.

[3] In several skulls from the Congo basin the nasal bones are fused into a single bone.

The *upper lip* in some Asiatic negroes, in the Congo pygmy and the West African groups (especially the people of the Niger delta, Abeokuta, and Benin) is long and even arched in outline, like the upper lip in the African anthropoid

4. THE CAUCASIAN TYPE
An Englishman: early twentieth century

apes. In such cases (where it is long and curved) its inner mucous surface is but little exposed; but in all African negroes and Bushmen the *lower lip* is much everted, and in the great majority of the sub-species, in Asia as in Africa, both lips are turned outward (exposing the mucous surface very considerably) in marked contrast to the thin-lipped, close-mouthed Mongol or North European.

Dark skin, squash nose, woolly hair, "blubber" lips, and "lark heel"—these are the principal taunts flung at the Negro. The dark skin affects not the sculptor's eye, but the other four points are the Negro's handicap in the competition for the Beauty Prize at some future Interracial Olympiad. Greater refinement of life will no doubt tend—is slowly tending—to modify or eliminate the elements of facial ugliness; but the most effective method of doing so is crossing with the Caucasian or even the Amerindian. Not, however, with the "Nordic" Caucasian, but with the already slightly negrified races of the Mediterranean countries, notably the Arab, Egyptian, and Berber.

The molar teeth of the Negroes are large, but the incisors and canines less so than in the Australoids and some Europeans. The white, even, uninterrupted teeth of the Negro races are one of their beauties. Only in certain types of Nilotic negro or negroid, like the Masai, Shiluk, and Dinka, is this rule broken by a tendency of the incisors to grow long and horse-like or with spaces between them.

The palate of the Negro is rather more hypsiloid than semicircular (as with the European and Mongol), but this simian feature is more marked in the Australoids.

In average height the African Negro (but not the Asiatic) is a taller type of man than any other sub-species except the Caucasian and its Polynesian hybrid. The tallest races (for tribal average) in the world are of the negro stock (Eastern and Equatorial Africa); but at the same time the Negro has produced (no doubt by partial degeneration) the smallest known human types—the Congo pygmies, southern Bushmen, and Asiatic negritos.

5. THE MONGOLIAN TYPE
A Chinaman from Eastern China

The Negro is proportionately *broader across the chest* than the other human races except the Caucasian and its hybrids, but decidedly *narrower across the pelvis*, though this condition is sometimes disguised by the excessive development of fat on the upper part of the thighs. The *lumbar curve* of the vertebral column is *less* marked than in the European and Mongol, but more so than in the more simian Australoid. The *sacrum* (coalesced, post-pelvic vertebræ) *is slightly narrower* in the Negro than in the European, but is not so narrow and pithecoid as is the sacrum of the Australoid. Negroes (Asiatic as well as African, also Bushmen) commonly possess the "*sacral notch*"—a simian feature very rare in Australoids and Europeans. (This is a space or notch opposite the second vertebra of the sacrum, due to its attenuation, which is particularly marked in the skeletons of apes and monkeys.) The *curvature of the sacrum* in Asiatic and African Negroes and in Bushmen *is very slight*, much less so, even, than in the Australoids. In this point and in *the broad shoulder-blade* the Negroes are *more pithecoid* than any other existing race, or even than the remains of *Homo primigenius;* for the Australoids have a narrow scapula like

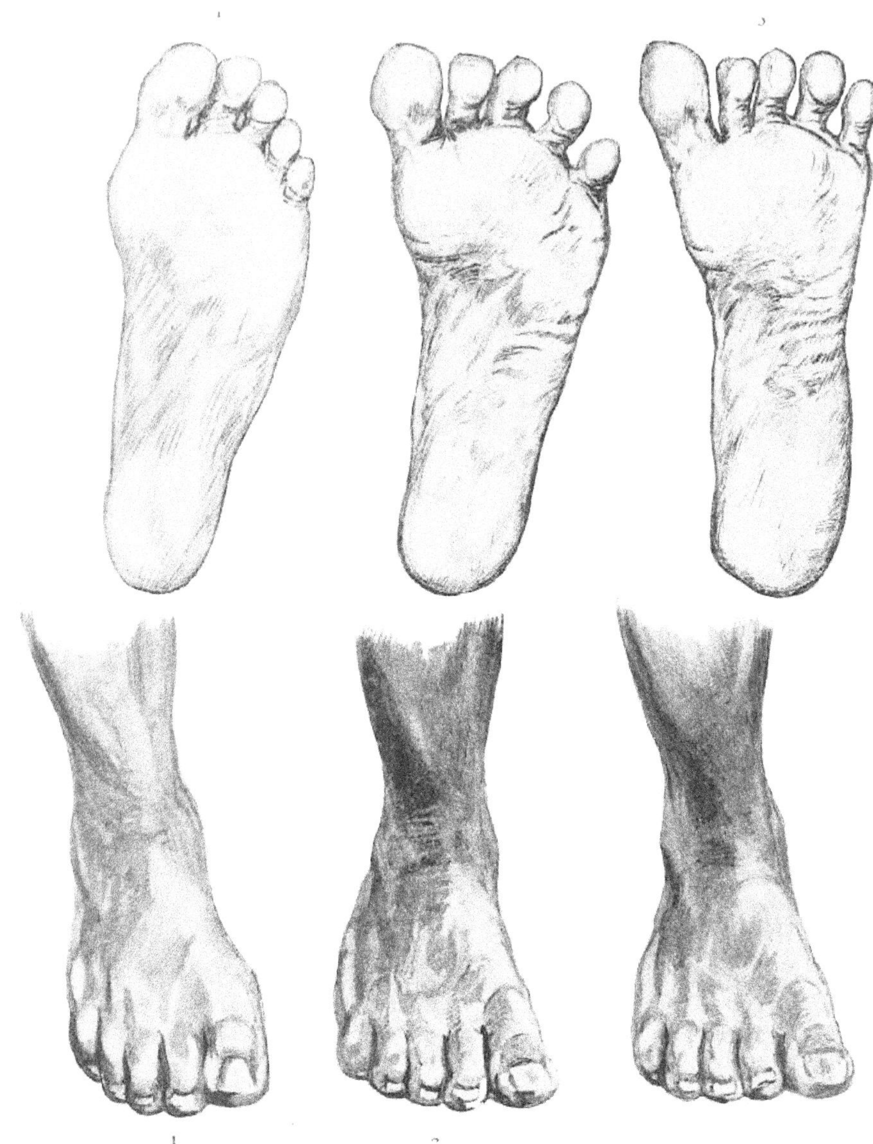

6. 1. FOOT OF EUROPEAN
2. FOOT OF FOREST NEGRO AND CONGO PYGMY (BUSHMAN FOOT IS SIMILAR)
3. FOOT OF AUSTRALASIAN NEGRO (SOLOMON ISLANDS)

that of Europeans or Mongols. The proportions of the pelvis and the *os innominatum* are very simian in the Bushmen; less so in Asiatic and African negroes and in Australoids. In the proportions of *the broad shoulder-blade* the Congo pygmy is the most ape-like of existing humans. In the angle of *humeral torsion* (motility of upper arm) the negro races are *inferior* to the European but superior to the Australoids. The *proportions of the leg-bones* in the African negro are slightly simian and in the Asiatic negroes those *of the arm-bones* also. (Namely, the *lower leg* is proportionately *longer* in comparison to the thigh and the upper arm *shorter* in relation to the lower arm.)

The negro hands are small and the fingers short. Both hands and feet in the Bushman are very small. Polydactylism (six fingers and six toes) is perhaps commoner among negroes (especially in West and South Africa and in the West Indies) than among the white or yellow peoples. In many cases the extra toe or finger is so well formed and complete that at first sight there is nothing abnormal in the appearance of the member; and the extra "seventh" digit (at the outer edge of the hand or foot: not the real "first finger," the "pre-pollex" or "pre-hallux") usually occurs on both hands and both feet in the same individual. [This feature is well illustrated in the Report on the Bahama Islands by the Geographical Society of Baltimore.] In the West African negro (and ancient European negroes) there is a considerable development of heel[1] (backward prolongation of the *os calcaneum*). This is *not* a simian feature but one that is ultra human. It does not seem to occur in the Asiatic negroes, Bushmen, or Congo pygmies, but is observable in the plain-dwelling natives of India. In the eastern Asiatic negroes the foot in the position and relative length of the toes is as pithecoid as in some Australoids (*vide* pp. 8 and 2). The same features occur among Congo pygmies and East and West Africans. Among the Bushmen, Hottentots, and less frequently the north-east African negroids a most distinctive and peculiar feature has been developed: steatopygia, or the accumulation of gluteal fat to a degree (more especially in the women) which makes the posterior jut out almost horizontally from the body. This development, so far, is seldom recorded among Asiatic negroes[2] or negritos (it is essentially *un*-simian) or among the typical negroes of Africa. There is a commencement of it among the Congo pygmies, in men and women of the Nilotic negroes or even the negroid Ba-hima, Somalis or Egyptians. It is occasionally observed in American negroes. Bushman or Hottentot children are born without any trace of it (ordinary negro children have an even slighter gluteal development than occurs in Europeans of the same age), and in adult Bushman or Hottentot males the development may be absent or in any case is far less pronounced than in the women, with whom it amounts to a positive monstrosity.

In the external male and female genitalia the Negro sub-species has developed peculiarities which are divergencies from the common human type but are not simian features. It is not necessary to redescribe them here[3] in detail, but it might be mentioned that the hypertrophy of the intromittent organ which is characteristic of male negroes (perhaps not male Bushmen)—with a corresponding exaggeration of the clitoris in the negress—is also met with in the Asiatic

[1] The "lark heel" is probably brought about by much walking on flat ground and is more observable in negroes living on the plains than in those inhabiting mountains.

[2] According to Carl Ribe (*Zwei jahre unter den Kannibalen der Salomo-Inseln*), steatopygia occurs among the Asiatic negroes of the northern Solomon Islands and in some examples is "hottentotenartig." E. H. Man records it among the female Andamanese, but leads one to infer that the deposit of fat is rather on the lateral side of the thighs and hips and not on the buttocks. This lateral accumulation of fat is characteristic of West African negresses.

[3] *Vide* for a sufficient summary of these points *Morphology and Anthropology: a handbook for students*, by W. L. H. Duckworth, M.A. My statements are also based on information available in the collections of the Royal Anthropological Institute.

negro (Andamanese and North Solomon Islanders) and is in contrast to the very moderate development of the same parts in the adjoining Australoids. Essentially characteristic of the women among the Bushman-Hottentots, and (sporadically) of certain tribes in the South Central Congo, in portions of the Nile Valley and East Africa is the "tablier Egyptien," a hypertrophy of the *labia minora* of the vulva.

The *cranial capacity* of the average negro is distinctly higher than in the Australoid (lowest of existing humans in that respect). The average is about *1260 cubic centimetres* in the Asiatic male negro, *1331 c.c.* in the *Bushman*, and *1388* in the *African male negro.*[1] In the male *Australoid* it is *1245 c.c.* In the *Caucasian* races the cranial capacity ranges in males from 1500 c.c. to 1600 c.c.; in the Mongolic group from 1500 to 1580 c.c.

The average Negro brain is larger than the Australoid but smaller than that of normal Europeans. The average weight of negro brains is about 1200 grammes. But the range of weights is extreme, from a recorded 974 gr. to 1445 gr. The American (U.S.A.) average would seem to be distinctly higher: about 1300 gr. (stated at 1331 by Parker in reference to Negro soldiers in the War of Secession.[2] The "sulcus lunatus," a fissure in each lobe of the hinder part of the brain (a feature very marked in apes and monkeys) is normally present in Negro (and Australoid) brains, but is very rare in the pure Caucasian race.

The iris of the Negro eye is dark brown, and the "white" or sclerotic is often (as in apes) pigmented—a dull reddish yellow. But this is rather a characteristic of the male, and of the lower types of negroes and Bushmen; it is rarely seen in women and never in children. Negro infants at birth and for a short time afterwards have not infrequently a dark, greyish-blue iris. The *plica*

[1] There is a considerable difference—from one to two hundred cubic centimetres—between the male and female skull capacities in all races, not excepting the Negro. The cranial capacity of the female Asiatic Negro falls as low as 1130 c.c. In a female Akka dwarf (Congo pygmy of Upper Welle River, Equatorial Africa), it was only 1070 c.c. In female Bushmen, however, it is usually about 1260 c.c. The lowest record among existing humans is a capacity of about 910 c.c. for a female Veddah. The skull capacity of *Pithecanthropos erectus* is estimated (now) at over 900 c.c.; of an adult male Gorilla (highest record among the anthropoid apes) at 573 c.c.

Among the American and Sudanian negroes (males) the record rises as high as 1450 c.c. But this is markedly exceeded in two Negroid skulls found in the Grottos of Grimaldi (Maritime Alps: see p. 26) and dating back to perhaps thirty thousand years ago, in which the skull capacity for the female was 1375 c.c., and for the male 1580 c.c.

Curiously enough, the cranial capacity of the Neanderthal Skull (*Homo primigenius*: presumably a male) was as high as 1500 c.c. (Dr. A. Keith, of the Royal College of Surgeons Museum, thinks it was even higher), very much above the Australian male average; and the "La Chapelle" Neanderthaloid skull, with an ape-like face, was 1626 c.c. in its cranial capacity. The lowest "prehistoric" record is the female Gibraltar skull, which was only 1080 c.c. (Dr. A. Keith.) But the *Hominidæ* required a rapid and enormous brain development in their evolution to compete with other large mammals in the struggle for existence and for world-wide distribution. Once the victory was won and Humanity acquired there could be here and there stagnation or even very slight retrogression in brain development, while the rest of the body was nevertheless being brought up to and maintained within the scope of the species *Homo sapiens*.

[2] The average weight of Australoid brains is guessed at 1185 grammes (Davis, quoted by Duckworth, p. 433, *Morphology and Anthropology*). The average among the European races (with a very large range) is probably 1400 gr. The extremes recorded are 964 gr. and 1842 gr. It is thought that Bismarck's brain would have weighed even more. His skull capacity was over 1900 c.c.! The average weight of the Asiatic and Eskimo-Mongol brain is probably very close to the Caucasian average, but that of Amerindians is said to be a little lower. Duckworth considers the Eskimo average *superior* to the Caucasian. The normal European range is between 1304 gr. and 1502 gr. Professor Waldeyer, of Berlin, gave in 1894 an average weight of only *1148* gr. for East African Negro brains. The Bushman brain would appear to weigh scarcely more than 1260 gr. In all races there is a marked difference in weight between male and female brains, that of the male being nearly 160 grammes heavier than the female. This difference—not quite so great—would appear to exist between male and female negroes.

semilunaris, a vertical fold of membrane immediately next to the lachrymal caruncle at the inner corner of the eye, is more developed in Negroes (especially Bushmen) and in Australoids than it is in the white races. It is the vestige of the third eyelid (nictitating membrane) and is often considerably developed in monkeys and other mammals, and is functional in birds and reptiles. In the negro this *plica semilunaris* is usually a reddish brown and lends a rather reddish tinge to the half-opened eye. The *retractor oculis* present in most monkeys and other mammals also occurs occasionally in negroes, and never in the white race.

A striking peculiarity in the African Negro is the musky or goat-like smell exhaled from the sweat, more especially from the axillary and inguinal glands. The odour is markedly characteristic of the African (it has not hitherto been recorded of the 'Asiatic negro); but also occurs to a much slighter degree in Europeans and East Indians as an exhalation from the armpits (more especially). Yet I would make bold to say that this skin odour is not as disgusting as that which proceeds from heated, unwashed Europeans and Asiatics. It is practically absent from many Africans who keep their bodies constantly washed. I mixed with many negro crowds and assemblies in the United States and scarcely once noticed any disagreeable smell, for the negroes, like the indigenous whites of the great American republic, seem to be an inherently cleanly people. I only detected disagreeable body odours proceeding from the offensively dirty Chinese travelling in the public cars, or from newly landed immigrants in New York.

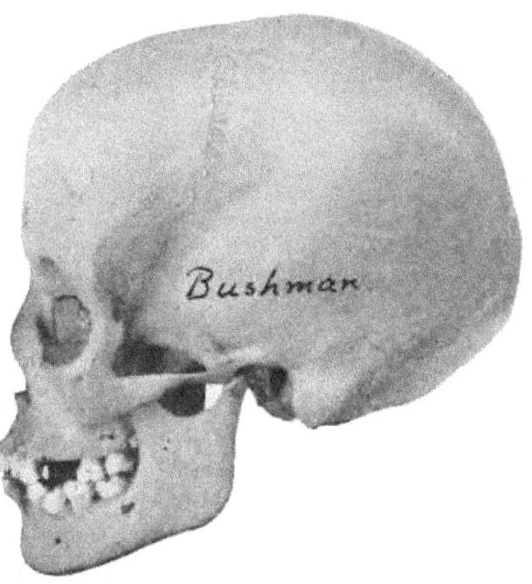

7. SKULL OF MALE BUSHMAN
Cape Colony

From this review of the physical features or peculiarities of the NEGRO sub-species it will be gathered inferentially that he is a distinct improvement on the Australoid in cranial development and is less simian in all other classificatory points, except in the shape of the shoulder-blade (which is very broad) and in the outline of the sacrum, which in all negroes is very much less curved than in Australoids, Caucasians, and Mongols.

In the retention of the brow-ridges and the tendency to the development of hair on the body (mostly in males) the CAUCASIAN has remained more generalised than the other sub-species, except the basal Australoid stock; and in the evolving of varieties (chiefly Nordic) with yellow, red, or brown hair, and blue or grey eyes, the Caucasian is most aberrant, stands alone: for all the other divisions of *Homo sapiens* have black or blackish-brown[1] hair and a brown iris to the eye. The Caucasian also is the only human race which in itself or in its hybrids with the other groups can produce perfect beauty of facial outline according to the æsthetic canons of the Negro, Mongol, and Caucasian. Facially, the unmixed Mongol (a term

[1] In some of the South American Amerindians, there is an underlying element of red in the hair-tint which produces an effect of colour like the pigment known as "warm sepia." Reddish hair occasionally appears in the Congo pygmies, to say nothing of Negro hybrids.

which includes the Eskimo but not the Amerindian) is as ugly as the Negro: uglier, indeed, to the eye of a European; for he has not the full, melting, long-lashed eye of the African, the rich bronze skin, the splendid physical proportions, and the frank, jolly look.[1] The Mongol has the hexagonal face, the exaggerated cheek-bone and low-bridged nose of the lower types of negroes, he has in some of the south-east Asiatics a prehensile great toe; and his want of brow-ridges deprives his moon-face of relief, expression, and the god-like majesty of the handsome European, Arab, or Panjabi, or the virile determination of the negro warrior. But the Chinaman, Tibetan, Japanese, Tartar, Samoyede, Amerindian, and Eskimo have the *brains* of a white man. Intellectually they are—let us say—twenty thou-

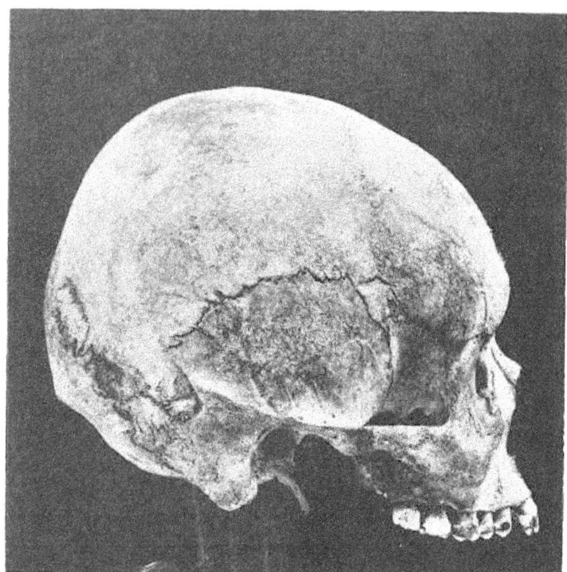

8. SKULL OF MALE OCEANIC NEGRO
San Cristoval, Solomon Islands

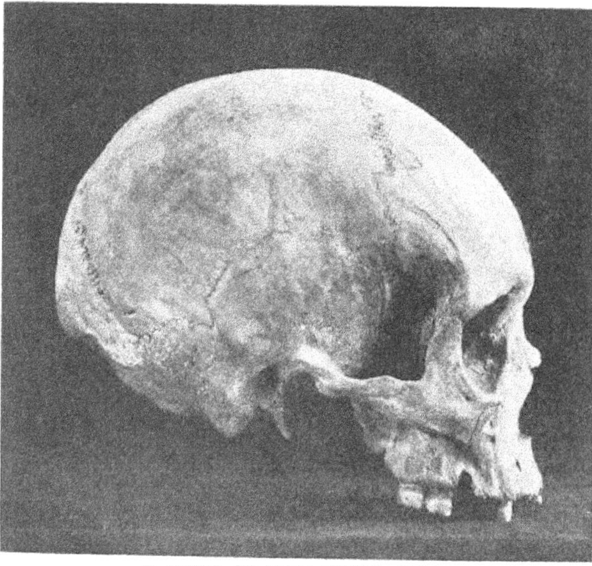

9. SKULL OF MALE NEGRO, U.S.A.

[1] "As to faces, the peculiarities of the negro countenance are well known in caricature; but a truer pattern may be seen by those who wish to study it any day among the statues of the Egyptian rooms in the British Museum: the large gentle eye, the full but not over-protruding lips, the rounded contour, and the good-natured, easy, sensuous expression. This is the genuine African model: one not often to be met with in European or American thoroughfares, where the plastic African too readily acquires the careful look and even the irregularity of the features that surround him; but which is common enough in the villages and fields where he dwells after his own fashion among his own people: most common of all in the tranquil seclusion and congenial climate of a Surinam plantation. There you may find, also, a type neither Asiatic nor European, but distinctly African; with much of independence and vigour in the male physiognomy and something that approaches, if it does not quite reach, beauty in the female. Rameses and his queen were cast in no other mould." (W. G. Palgrave, *Dutch Guiana*, 1876.)

sand years ahead of the average negro in cranial capacity, and in volume, weight, and convolutions of the brain. Physically (except for the aberrant Eskimo) they are classed by some anatomists with the White sub-species, from which they only differ in some slight facial deformity, in their relative hairlessness of body, and lank, round-sectioned head-hair.

But evolution does not always proceed slowly or at a uniform pace. Already individual Africans or Aframericans of unmixed negro blood; or Negroid hybrids with the Mediterranean White man or the Nordic rulers of the world, have shot far ahead of their grandfather the palæolithic savage, and (if they could be placed on the dissecting-table) would reveal an extreme of brain development which would rank them with the average European or Asiatic.

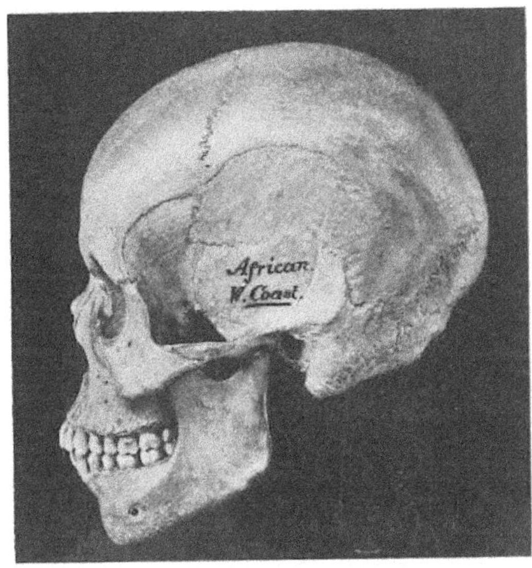

10. SKULL OF ASHANTI NEGRO
West Coast of Africa

The author of this book in his work on *British Central Africa*, written some years ago, ventured to make these remarks on the Negro sub-species:—"He is a fine animal, but in his wild state exhibits a stunted mind and a dull content with his surroundings which induces mental stagnation, cessation of all upward progress, and even a retrogression towards the brute. In some respects the tendency of the negro for several centuries past has been an actually retrograde one. As we come to read the unwritten history of Africa by researches into languages, manners, customs, traditions, we seem to see a backward rather than a forward movement going on for some thousand years past, a return towards the savage and even the brute. I can believe it possible that had Tropical Africa been more isolated from contact with the rest of the world and cut off from the immigration of the Arab and the European, the purely negro races, left to themselves, so far from advancing towards a higher type of

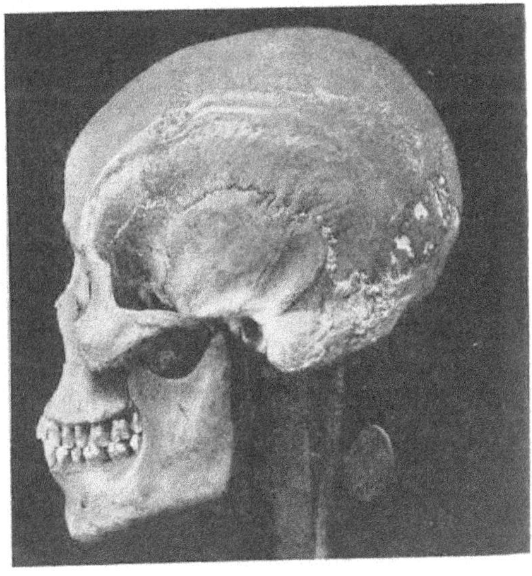
11. SKULL OF MAÑBETTU NEGRO
Northern Congo basin, Central Africa

humanity, might have actually reverted by degrees to a type no longer human, just as those great apes[1] lingering in the dense forests of Western Africa have become in many respects degraded types that have known better days of larger brains, smaller tusks, and stouter legs."

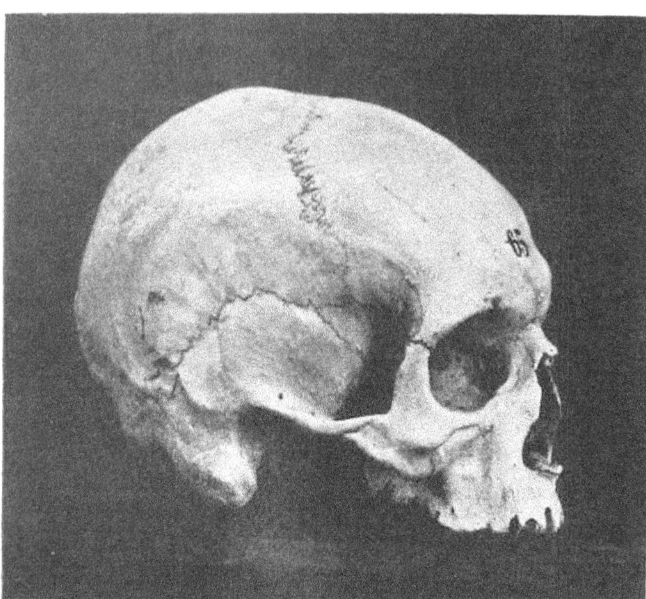

12. SKULL OF MALE MULATTO, U.S.A.

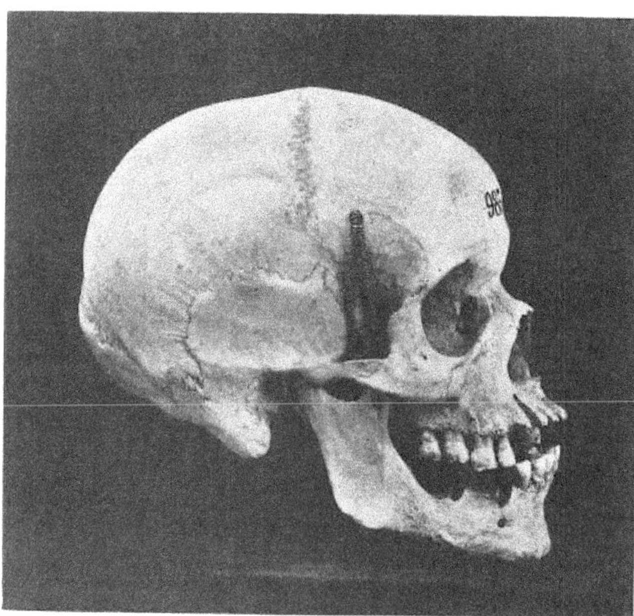

13. SKULL OF FEMALE NEGRO, U.S.A.

There is exaggeration in this view, no doubt, and sufficient emphasis is not laid on the much earlier regeneration of the black races of Africa by the influence spreading southwards of the prehistoric Caucasians of the Mediterranean and the historic Egyptian, the last-named being the foremost redeemer of the African. Yet it is significant that the ancient negroid remains of Southern France exhibit a cranial capacity much superior to that of the average wild African of to-day.[2]

Africa is the chief stronghold of the real Devil—the reactionary forces of Nature hostile to the uprise of Humanity. Here Beelzebub, King of the Flies, marshals his vermi-

[1] The allusion is to the gorilla.

[2] So do pygmy skulls obtained from old graves on the Middle Sanga River in the heart of French Congo, with a cranial capacity of 1440 c.c.

form and arthropod hosts—insects, ticks, and nematode worms—which more than in any other continent (excepting negroid Asia) convey to the skin, veins, intestines, or spinal marrow of men and other vertebrates the micro-organisms which cause deadly, disfiguring, or debilitating diseases, or themselves create the morbid condition of the persecuted human being, beast, bird, reptile, frog, or fish.

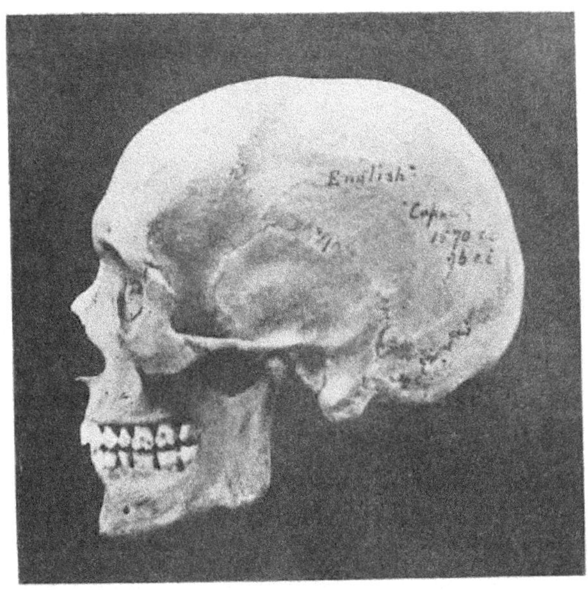

14. SKULL OF ENGLISHMAN

Africa and negroid Asia — India to the Philippines — seem to have been the great centres for originating and maturing the worst maladies which have afflicted, arrested, or exterminated mankind and his domestic animals. From India came dengue fever, small-pox, bubonic plague, cholera, Asiatic relapsing fever, beri-beri, dysentery, typhus, syphilis, the "surra" cattle-sickness, and some other zymotic diseases.

Africa on her part has originated "Sleeping Sickness" (*Trypanosomiasis*), which, though it has long existed in the Dark Continent, seems lately to have acquired fresh vigour, and to be about to depopulate much of West and West Central Africa.

In Africa has arisen the Nagana or "Tsetse" sickness among cattle and at least two other epidemic diseases among the beasts of the field, which, like Sleeping Sickness and Nagana, are caused by Trypanosome flagellates intro-

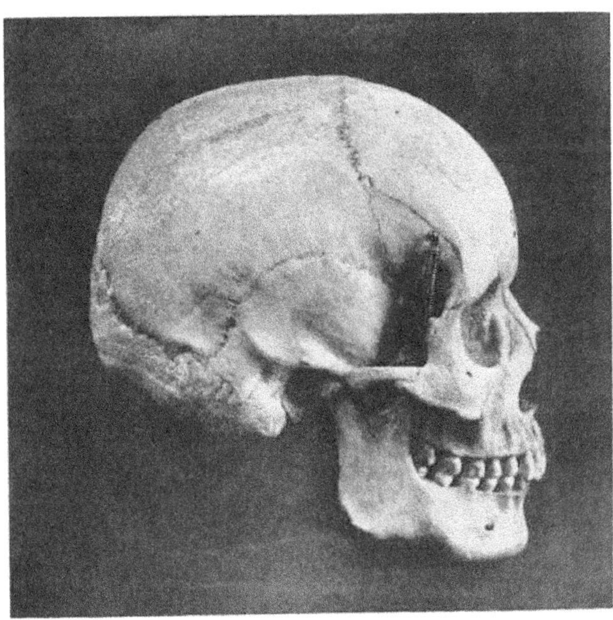

15. SKULL OF FEMALE MULATTO, U.S.A.

duced into the blood through the probosces of Glossina flies.[1] Malarial fevers caused by Sporozoa may be common to both Africa and Asia in their origin, but Africa alone seems to have generated the greatly dreaded Hæmoglobinuria (blackwater fever), which the Negro has recently conveyed to Central America. Among other African maladies are Zambezian "relapsing" fever, (carried by a poisonous tick), the "yaws" (*Frambœsia*, a terrible skin disease, akin to syphilis, and like it produced by a *Treponema* flagellate), and a number of dangerous illnesses due to the attacks of parasitic worms.

These are derived from the classes of Flat-worms, Tape-worms, and Thread-worms. A noteworthy Flat-worm of the Trematode order is the *Bilharzia hæmatobia*, which multiplies in the urinary bladder and causes a terrible form of hæmaturia among the negroes and negroids of tropical Africa and America. Elephantiasis is an African disease transported to America, and caused by the Nematode Thread-worm, *Filaria bancrøfti*. Another Nematode parasite is the well-known *Dracunculus medinensis*, or Guinea-worm, from which James Bruce, the eighteenth-century explorer of the Blue Nile, suffered so severely after his return to Europe This also has been carried to tropical America (Brazil) by Negro slaves.

But the worst Nematodes of all are the "Hook-worms" of the allied genera[2] *Ancylostomum* and *Necator*, now found to be cosmopolitan in their

[1] Treponemes and Trypanosomes are Flagellate *Protozoa*—excessively minute organisms of the basic sub-kingdom, the PROTISTA, which includes the *Protozoa* and the *Protophyta*—whose protoplasm develops a long whip-like process (*flagella*) which is used for moving and even for feeding the organism. The Flagellates resemble to a remarkable degree the male cells (*Spermatozoa*) of the Protozoa and of the Higher animals (the Metazoa); just as the Amœba, an even simpler form of Protist, resembles the female cells of animal organisms. The animalcule which causes Malarial fever is an Amœboid Sporozoon called *Hæmamœba malariæ*, conveyed to the human blood by Anopheline mosquitoes. An African form of dysentery is also due to a similar sporozoon, and so (it is thought) is blackwater fever. Zambezian relapsing fever is due to a *Treponema*. On the other hand, yellow fever (?), the bubonic plague, typhoid, dysentery (?), cholera, gonorrhœa, and tuberculosis (besides many other maladies) are due to *vegetable* micro-organisms—*Bacteria, bacilli*—introduced into the human system by various agencies, prominent among which are gnats (mosquitoes), flies, fleas, lice, bugs, and ticks. (The tick belongs to the Spider Class.)

"The common house fly, mosquito, and bed bug in all probability also transmit leprosy" (Extract from the Report on the Bahama Islands by the Geographical Society of Baltimore). Leprosy seems to be connected in some way with the eating of decayed fish. According to Mr. E. E. Austen, of the British Museum, the *Stegomyia* genus of mosquitoes conveys yellow fever in Africa and America, *Mansonia* transmits the filarial worms which produce filariasis and elephantiasis, *Culex fatigans* (a large gnat) is the carrier of dengue fever and filariasis. There are numerous species of *Anopheles* in America, Asia, and Europe ready to act as the transmitting agency for malarial (and blackwater) fevers; in Africa this purpose is effected by the allied *Myzomyia* and *Pyretophorus*. We therefore now know our enemies and should arrange to destroy them. Among other methods might be cited the recent recommendation by Captain J. A. M. Vipan, that the little fresh-water fish *Girardinus pœciloides*, of Barbados and northern South America (known by the negroes of Barbados as "Millions," from its numbers), should be distributed as widely as possible throughout the ponds and shallow streams of tropical America, because it lives on the larvæ of mosquitoes. One reason why there is so little malarial fever in Barbados is that *Girardinus* is almost the only fresh-water fish on the island, and therefore has no rivals. It is able consequently to devote itself to the destruction of the larvæ of gnats which pass the pupal stage in still, shallow water. *Girardinus* and other fish of similar tastes spread all over the world might in time rid humanity of the intolerable nuisance of gnats and midges.

[2] The Thread-worm class is styled scientifically *Nemathelminthes*. These almost exclusively parasitic worms are subdivided into three orders or sub-orders, of which one—the *Nematoda*—includes those forms more especially known as Thread-worms. This order is again subdivided into seven families, of which six contain some of the deadliest enemies of man and other mammals, of birds, reptiles, fish, insects, and plants, especially the plants useful to Man. When our Litany is brought up to date and Church services are made to appeal to intelligent people, there will be a clause: "From all Nematode worms, Good Lord deliver us!" One of these six families is the *Strongylidæ*, and in this group are placed the intestinal worms specially attacking Man: *Ancylostomum duodenale* and *Necator americanus*. Ancylostomum (under the name of *Agchylostoma*—a different rendering of the Greek words "Hook Mouth") was first described and named by an Italian investigator, Dubini, in 1843. He found it to be the cause of serious anæmia

range through the tropical and sub-tropical regions of the world (extending even into the temperate regions).

Both of these parasites, in a minute larval form, enter the human system directly through the skin by way of the pores or hair-follicles, and generally in the spaces between the fingers or toes, or on the wrists; perhaps also in drinking-water or dirty food, which carries them to the throat. They pass through the blood into the lungs and thence to the intestines, more especially that portion of the small intestine (below the stomach) called the duodenum. Here these dangerous Thread-worms burrow into and nip the capillary blood-vessels. Not only do they sever them, but they inject some poisonous saliva of their own which prevents the blood from coagulating, and so for hours the tiny veins go on bleeding internally. At last the human patient suffers from anæmia, takes to eating clay, dirt, filth, or incongruous food, becomes perpetually tired or insane, and unless cured by the expulsion of the worms dies of some disease induced by anæmia.

16. OCEANIC NEGRO TYPE
Negro mixed with Australoid, from New Ireland (New Mecklenburg)

Whilst the worms are feasting on the blood or tissue (it is not certain which) the females lay innumerable eggs, and these pass out of the human body in the fæces. The minute larvæ are soon hatched out, and infest the ground round the place where the exuviæ have been deposited. The larval worms must have moisture for further existence, and can live in water. But if after a certain stage in their growth they do not enter the human system, they die.

Seemingly the Negro race, in Asia as in Africa,—and in this connection it is interesting to note that the most infested parts of tropical Asia are those

among the poorer people of Milan and North Italy. The first discoverer of "Hook-worms," however, in a general sense, was Goeze, a German clergyman and biologist, who in 1782 found what he called "Hair" worms in the intestines of a badger. A later German investigator, Froelich, obtained similar worms from the viscera of a fox, and in 1789 named this parasite "Haaken-wurm," from the hook-like turn of its head-end. Scientifically he called it *Uncinaria vulpis*. Dr. Looss, whose investigations into these intestinal worms in Negroes and Egyptians succeeded those of Dr. F. Sandwith, refused to adopt Uncinaria as a generic name, as there was such uncertainty about the particular type of Hook-worm named by Froelich. *Dochmius*, applied to the Hook-worms by Dujardin in 1845, though long in use, has been dropped in favour of the revived *Ancylostomum* of Dubini, who first of all put his finger on the mischief this parasite was working on human beings (other species of *Ancylostomum* afflict other mammals).

Necator americanus was really discovered and named (in conjunction with Dr. Looss) by the great American pathologist Dr. Charles Wardell Stiles (now of the U.S.A. Marine Hospital Service), assisted by the investigations of Dr. Allen J. Smith, of Texas. *Necator* was originally thought to be a species of *Ancylostomum*, but, although nearly allied, the generic difference (according to Dr. R. T. Leiper, who has kindly supplied me with these notes) can be detected at once under the microscope by even an unlearned observer. Though styled "*americanus*," it is found all over the tropical world, even in Australia, and may have been brought from the Old World to the New by the Negro slaves. The most recent research into these intestinal parasitic worms has been carried out in Africa (North, South, East, West, and Central), and by deputy in tropical Asia and Australia by Dr. R. T. Leiper, of the London School of Tropical Medicine.

(India, Burma, Malay Peninsula, and Philippines) in which the Negroid element of the population is most apparent to an anthropologist—has in the course of ages habituated itself to the attacks of the Hook-worm, through an intense desire, almost a racial obsession, to purge the system with native or European drugs or by clysters. This practice may have partly helped the Negro in the struggle. Yet he suffers—racially—from Anæmia and Laziness. May not the Hook-worms have been the cause of both, have fettered the progress of the Negro for many thousand years?

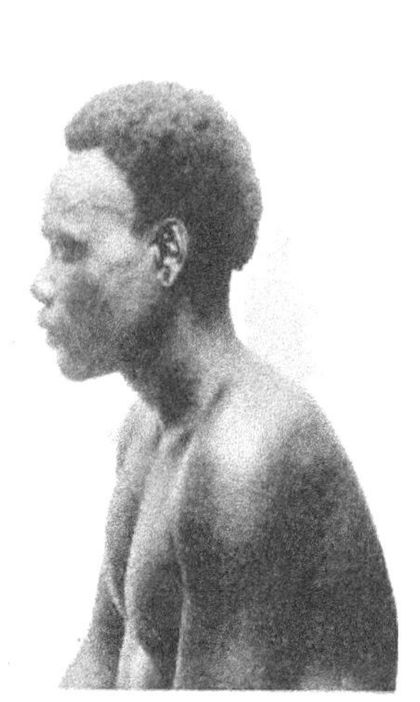

17. OCEANIC NEGRO
A man of Buka Island, northernmost portion of Solomon Islands group

He suffers, in Africa, Asia, and America, because he is, as a race, reckless about "sanitation." With some exceptions like the Baganda, the Ibo of the Niger Delta, and a few other peoples, the Negro and even Negroid in Africa and America (perhaps also in Asia) is heedless about the consequences of indiscriminate defecation: the men more than the women. It is rare in any uncivilised African centre of population to find places (as in Buganda) deliberately set apart for the deposit of exuviæ. Consequently the outskirts of African towns are noisome to a degree. In those unforested regions where there are many vultures, or in the rare districts in which pigs are kept (or in the desert where the sun dries up everything) there is not so much hook-worm and there is less laziness. But the Congo pygmies have it in their systems, and all Negro tribes in tropical Africa suffer from it more or less.

They imported this parasite into America[1] (no doubt) two or three hundred years ago, but it was not discovered nor did it attract attention until the beginning of the twentieth century. The Negro also (we may assume) conveyed the Hook-worm to Egypt.[2] From Egypt it travelled to Italy and Central—and no doubt other parts of—Europe. In fact it may be accountable now for some of the prevailing "laziness" and anæmia. But of course this Nematode worm affects far less the civilised populations of the world than it does the semi-civilised or savage, those who go about with bare feet, live filthily, ignore sanitation, and are careless about drinking-water.

Hook-worms first attracted the concentrated attention of scientific men about 1882, in connection with the terrible outbreak of "tunnel

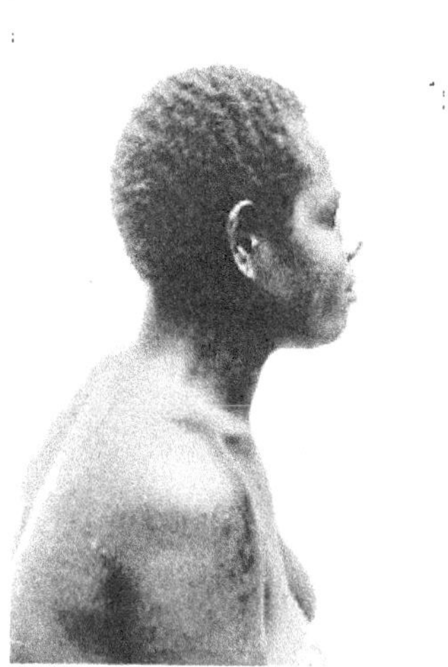

18. OCEANIC NEGRESS
Woman of Buka Island, N.W. Solomon Islands, Oceania

[1] An interesting article on the Hook-worms—especially *Necator americanus*, by Miss Marion Hamilton Carter, appeared in *McClure's Magazine* for October, 1909. It dealt specially with the ravages of this parasite among the two million "poor" whites in North and South Carolina, Georgia, and Virginia.

[2] Dr. Leiper has derived specimens of both *Ancylostomum* and *Necator* from the blood of Nyasaland and Moçambique negroes.

disease" among the Italian workmen excavating the St. Gotthard tunnel. After careful experiments (only possible by making use of dogs as subjects) Dr. Bozzolo of Turin, discovered—surely he deserves a Nobel prize?—that an unfailing cure—a certain means of expelling the worms—was the drug thymol (essence of thyme) followed by Epsom salts. So there is the remedy. It

19. ASIATIC NEGROES
Andamanese from near Port Blair, Andaman Islands

remains now only to diagnose the precise cause of anæmia, laziness, dirt-eating,[1] many cases of tuberculosis and diarrhœa, emaciation, and on finding it to be hook-worms to dose the patient (prudently) with thymol. Saul and David have slain their thousands and tens of thousands, and David has been beatified. What is to be done for Dr. Bozzolo, who has saved millions?

[1] We now understand why so many Negro tribes in the basin of the Congo have a craving for argillaceous clay as food. They are infested with hook-worms.

As before stated, the Negro is accused of having brought *Necator americanus* (perhaps also *Ancylostomum duodenale*) to America, thereby infecting millions of white Americans with the "Lazy disease." The charge is probably true. But, for the plagues which followed the whites are mainly to blame. They permitted or did not deter the Negro, under slavery or post-slavery conditions, from being as filthy in his sanitation as (according to the American doctors) are two millions of Southern whites at the present day (and I might add, at least ten millions of British landlords and peasantry who disdain to supply or to use earth closets). But the medical investigators of the United States, once they had tracked down the fell work of the "American Murderer," the Necator worm, rose to the same heights of heroism as were achieved by this noblest of professions in the suppression of Yellow Fever in Cuba and of Malaria in Italy. They—Drs. C. W. Stiles and A. J. Smith—made experiments on themselves, suffered from the blood-letting and anæmia, cured themselves, and then proceeded to restore to life, health, and civic validity two millions of sick and useless Southern whites.

20. THE WIFE OF A HOTTENTOT CHIEF, JAN JONKHEER

Actually an example of the underlying "Strandlooper" stratum of the Bushman race. Perhaps the most "simian" type of negro

[The pictures of African negro types given in this and succeeding chapters are selected to show the varied component elements which have gone to form the American negro, who by fusion will gradually become a new race]

And the effects of their epoch-making work will be felt in tropical America and the West Indies. Here the well-to-do whites live too carefully and cleanly to be easily infected by these parasitic worms. But the extraordinary anæmia and apathy among the "poor" whites of the Bahamas, Barbados, St. Kitts, Cuba, Porto Rico, Trinidad, and Central and South America is now probably accounted for by their being the prey of these blood-letting thread-worms derived mainly from their own carelessness, but also from the filthy surroundings still characterising centres of negro population. In Jamaica I noticed especially the insanitary condition of the soil around certain large negro schools, reformatories, and orphanages, or about the villages distant from large towns. Here there were rotting accumulations of human ordure sufficient to infect all bare-footed Jamaica with Hookworm disease.

21. A BUSHMAN OF CAPE COLONY

Of the "Strandlooper" prognathous type, similar to the woman shown above. These two specimens belong to the most prognathous known type of African

Why is not practical Biology taught in all elementary and secondary schools attended by all children of all colours and races? *Mens sana in corpore sano.* Teach them to be healthy and they will be good.

Amongst maladies caused by the more "vegetable" section of the *Protista* sub-kingdom, which have seemingly originated with the Negro sub-species and to which this type of man is peculiarly subject, are Leprosy, Tuberculosis, Craw-craw (a vile form of itch), and Ainhum (a disease of the toes leading to their amputation, which is very prevalent in West Africa, and has been carried thence to the West Indies). Leprosy may have originated with the Asiatic Negro—it is not a very obvious disease in untouched, interior Africa—but it has plagued Southern and Eastern Asia (and perhaps Polynesia) for thousands of years, and was carried by the Crusaders to all parts of Europe in the Middle Ages, while the African Negro conveyed it to America, where in the West Indies especially it is one of his worst afflictions.

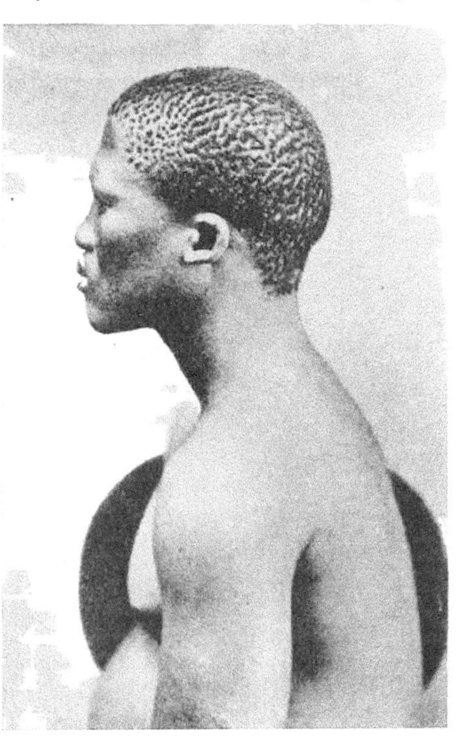

22. A BUSHMAN OF CAPE COLONY

The typical Bushmen are not so prognathous as the lingering vestiges of the antecedent "Strandlooper" type given in the preceding illustrations

It is a disease so closely allied to Tuberculosis that the *bacilli* causing both are hardly separable. Tuberculosis may have originated in Africa. Distinct traces of this disease have been found in Nubian negro and negroid skeletons buried at a period of at least four thousand years ago in the Northern Sudan; and at the present day Tuberculosis (with Pneumonia) is one of the chief causes of death in the Negroes and coloured peoples of America. Nearly five coloured people out of every thousand in the United States die of Tuberculosis in one or other of its manifestations, a rate about four times as high as it is for pure-blooded whites, but less high than for Amerindians in the same country. In the same region the death-rate for Pneumonia among the Coloured Race is about 3·5 per thousand, and among the Whites 1·8 per thousand.

Yellow Fever, said by the American doctors to be due to a vegetable micro-organism, was brought from West Africa to America in slave-ships at the end of the sixteenth and beginning of the seventeenth centuries (see note on p. 211).

It may be that to resist these fell agencies—these parasites which always attack a successful and pushing new species of plant or animal—the Negro's ancestors had to direct so much of their will-power to strengthening the body that they neglected the mind. Moreover, the Other Factor in the seeming duality of this world's government gave to the African negro (if not to the Asiatic) a vigour of genesic instinct which has been—in his struggle with an adverse environment and an appalling death-rate in young and old—a valuable counter-agent, a resource without which his attempts to people Africa would have been futile. But this virility, this lust for child-begetting and child-bearing, has left its mark on the negro's body and mentality, just as the primal dangers of starvation made him a born glutton. He has been so busy eating, drinking, marrying and begetting, that he has devoted little attention to the arts and industries, the astronomical and metaphysical speculations which have engrossed so much of the time and the vital force of the Eurasiatic peoples. The average individual of the uneducated, and, most of all, the savage negro type, is essentially unmoral. Men and women of this race are probably more inherently lustful, more eagerly addicted to sexual pleasures, than are the mass of Asiatics, Europeans, white Americans, and black Australians.

Transported to easier conditions of life, wherein the battle over nature has been at least half won, the Negro race finds itself burdened and held back by these tendencies and endowments. The Negro has no doubt a harder battle to fight against sexual lust than the Caucasian or the Mongolian. Education and refinement unquestionably help him in this struggle, as does hard work. White railway-labour-organisers in the United States and other contractors of labour at Panama have told me that in order to keep the men of their negro gangs from deserting, to retain them contented during their long months of work away from towns, they were obliged to engage in some way or another companies of negro prostitutes, who dwelt in camps or hastily constructed villages to which the men had easy access. In my visit to Panama nothing of the kind was apparent to me. I saw a great many Negro homes which seemed to be quite decently conducted, and in which the men and women had the demeanour of married couples; nor did I in my journeys to and fro about the States actually light on any of these camps of negro prostitutes. If they existed they were hidden away: and so far as outward decorum is concerned, there is no more to shock the observant traveller in the outside moral aspect of the negro's life in the United States than there is in that of the white man. In Africa one is well aware that if the Negro be incontinent in his own home, or in any temporary sojourn in an adopted home, he is fully as capable of chastity and abstinence as any particular lot of white men and Asiatics. His legends, his folk-lore, his social customs, inculcate a sort of elementary morality by teaching the unwisdom of sexual incontinence when men are engaged in great undertakings involving all their energies of mind and body—hunting, warfare, long journeys, agricultural operations, or religious exercises. Yet, when all is said on the Negro's behalf, he is still, racially, at a stage when he devotes too much of his attention to the procreative function.

23. A NAMAKWA HOTTENTOT HYBRID
Dutch-Boer and Hottentot

An amative disposition possibly gives to the Negro that expansiveness of character, that emotional unreserve which lead him to laugh or cry with equal readiness, to shout and declaim; and yet make him from the white man's point of view more easily managed, more sympathetic and likeable than many an Asiatic or Amerindian race. He is vain rather than proud, good-natured to a rare degree if his sensibility (always on the surface) is touched. He can be cruel; but his hate is short-lived, his gratitude vivid and sometimes the most lasting feeling in his mind. He has a keen sense of humour and is a natural wit. Singularly observant, yet too slothful to collate his facts and draw from them the deductions which have given the White man and the Yellow supreme power over men and nature: neat-fingered, deft, able to learn and to do almost anything that can be taught him by the White man, the Negro nevertheless has seemed up to the present time unable to originate. But that may come.

For three hundred years or so—especially during the nineteenth century—the White man has accused the whole Negro race of laziness. Of course the slave, the domestic servant, the factory child can never work too hard for the contentment of the slave-driver or the average employer. Down to ten or twenty years ago in many a household of the upper, middle, and "lower middle" class in our own country it was thought almost an infraction of some natural law for domestic drudges to want rest, relaxation, literature, lovers, and exercise in the open air. So if the negro got bored with monotonous and unending work for somebody else's main advantage he was stigmatised as so viciously lazy that it was really a moral obligation to flog, starve, or fine him into a Sisyphean routine.

24. A BERG-DAMARA (HAUKWOIN) NEGRO OF GERMAN S.W. AFRICA

The Haukwoin are a tribe of pure negroes in the mountains of Northern Damaraland. They speak a Hottentot dialect, but in physique are of the Forest West African negro type

Against the Negro man the charge, however, is *partly* true. He does not love work for the stimulus it gives to mental energy, for the joy of striving, of conquering obstacles. He has not the eager desire of the European and the Asiatic to conquer Nature and subdue the Devil of her reaction and recalcitrance. He is too easily satisfied with his surroundings.

In all the history of Africa and of the people of African race settled in the New World, the *negress* has probably never been idle. She is as unremittingly industrious as the average woman of the labouring and lower middle class in the United Kingdom. It is the negro *man* on whom the reproach lies—and justly lies—of being racially more lazy than perhaps any other human type. In the savage life of Africa if nothing more is aimed at than an existence of successful animalism, the male negro probably strikes an even balance with the female in the support of the community. On him falls the task of defending the family, the village, or the tribe against the attacks of wild beasts or of human enemies; he can be a strenuous hunter, a patient and arduous fisherman, he will also by fits and starts do all the rough work of felling timber and constructing the framework of houses. He is also the herdsman, the blacksmith, and the tailor, and by his successful forays in war or in the chase provides quite half the food supply of the community.

In return for these great dangers and excessive fatigues he expects to be allowed to spend the balance of his time in slothfulness. The women run far less danger than the men and are not required to undergo heart-breaking agonies of fatigue; on the other hand, they are expected to work steadily and monotonously; they are the great agriculturists, the cooks, the preparers of medicine, the producers of children, and the household servants.

But Asia and Europe with their greater infusion of divine energy, their loftier aspirations, have long left this state of existence behind from the close of the palæolithic period; and whereas this negro idea of life may have been good enough for the condition of Africa two thousand years ago, it is utterly out of keeping with the modern world.

Since I came to know something of the Negro it has occurred to me that there is more likelihood of an affinity of mind growing up between his race and the world of the Caucasian than between either of these divergent human types and the inscrutable Mongolian. (The very receptivity of the Japanese and the Polynesians may be due to the decided element of Asiatic negro which we know is infused through both these composite racial groups.) The negro mind compared to the Mongolian has very few unexplored recesses. It is largely an open book in which the white man, unless he wilfully spurns his opportunities, may write pretty well what he chooses at the present day. As yet the Negro is unhampered by racial or sociological prejudice, and still possesses an inherent admiration for his white cousin who has emerged within the last century from the long martyrdom of man: the heir of all the ages, the exponent of the most practical knowledge achieved by the human species through ages of experiment in Europe, North America, and Western Asia. Against this the Negro has no crooked science of his own to set up, such as still keeps China, Tibet, Hindu-India, Muhammadan Asia centuries behind the soaring Caucasian.

25. THE TYPICAL "BANTU" NEGRO
A Muhérero from S.W. Africa, near akin to the Kafir

In the past, with rapidity, the Negro has adopted the religions of the Caucasian: sacred animals and tribal totems, demigods and nature-spirits, the phallism, fetishism, and magic of the earlier Mediterranean faiths, conveyed to Negro Africa by the Libyan, Hamite, and Hima;[1] then, later, Muhammadanism; Christianity; freemasonry; faith-healing. Probably in the future we may induct him into a loftier faith and wiser practice, a Christian religion at one with science in a church which shall discard empiricism, useless metaphysics, and speculations starting from no material basis.

Where did the Negro sub-species arise? In what part of the Old World did

[1] The ancient Egyptians and their wild Gala relations carried their enterprise, their domestic animals and musical instruments, their religious ideas, folk-lore, and their neolithic and early metal-age civilisation almost to the sources of the Nile; and were received by the hopelessly savage, brutish negroes whom they found there as demigods. Their descendants (the Ba-hima) reign to this day as aristocracies or rulers in Equatorial Africa.

he specialise from the basal type of *Homo sapiens*, from the Australoid group, the outcome of early *Homo primigenius?* Possibly in Southern Europe, more probably in India. In the researches promoted by the Prince of Monaco, there were discovered in the caves of Grimaldi (Baoussé-roussé), near Mentone (French Riviera) two human skeletons, interred in a shallow grave ("une sorte de petit caisson en pierres") at a depth of about 27 feet from the present surface of the cavern floor; which, except in skull capacity, were obviously those of negroes. These remains were in all probability of great age, and *underlay* skeletons and other relics of the Cro-Magnon race, which last is regarded as an essentially "European" (Caucasian) type of man, and is associated in France with the later age of the mammoth, cave-lion, cave-bear, hyena, and reindeer, and a fauna and flora of a cold Glacial or post-Glacial age.

26. A ZULU BANTU NEGRO

The negroid skeletons of the Grimaldi grottos indicate a race of an average stature —men about 5 ft. 6 in., women about 5 ft. 1 in. —with poorly developed chins, a narrow pelvis, the fore-arm (humerus to elbow) very long in proportion to the lower arm, the thigh very short in comparison with the leg (simian and Australoid characteristics which are present—but not so markedly—in modern negroes); and generally with lower limbs much *longer* proportionately than the arms. This last is a feature that is very prominent in the Nilotic Negroes and sometimes in Hottentots, but not in the majority of modern negroes or in Australoids. The heel-bone (calcaneum) was even larger proportionately and more salient than in the modern negro (an ultra-human feature). These French negroes were very prognathous, had large teeth, and their palates were very hypsiloid. But the skull cases had a remarkable brain capacity: 1375 cubic centimetres for an old woman; 1580 for a male youth. The former figure is actually slightly *higher* than the average cranial capacity of modern French women, and the latter 21 c.c. *above* the average of modern French men. Both alike, as already stated, are far higher than the modern Negro average (say 1200 c.c. for women and 1388 for men). The age at which these Grimaldi negroes lived cannot be much less removed from the present day than thirty thousand years ago; it may have even been more remote, for they were contemporaneous in France with the Man of Corrèze (a lingering example of *Homo primigenius*, with a remarkable cranial capacity), with the mammoth, lion, African elephant, and hippopotamus. This negroid-type would seem (judging from skulls and skeletal remains) to have penetrated north-westwards as far as Brittany, and quite possibly to Britain and Ireland. Eastwards it is traceable to Switzerland and Italy, coming down through the neolithic to the historical period and fusing with the northern races. In modern times and at the present day it is obvious that there is an old Nigritic element in the population of North Africa, Spain, France, Ireland and West Britain, Italy, Sardinia, Sicily, and the countries bordering the Eastern Mediterranean, not entirely to be accounted for by the historical slave trade.

Yet the ancient negroid elements in these European populations seem to possess slightly more affinity with the Asiatic negroes or with those of North-Eastern Africa than with the typical African negroes or Bushmen of to-day.

In spite of these very interesting discoveries in the Grimaldi caverns, the deductions to be drawn from the rest of our limited knowledge point rather to *India*[1] as the original birthplace of the Negro sub-species; just as India or Central Asia may have been the evolutionary centre of the entire Human *genus* and of the *sapiens* species; and have witnessed the branching-off of the straight-haired, hairless-bodied, yellow-skinned Mongolian (who emigrated northwards through Central to Eastern and Hyperborean Asia, and to America; and southwards to Malaysia and the Pacific; and perhaps again to America, via the Pacific archipelagos). The only difficulty in adopting the theory that the Negro originated in India is the presumed absence at the present day of any pure negro type in Continental India; though there can be little doubt that the "pre-Dravidian" tribes of the Nilgiri Hills (the Kota, Kurumba, Irula, and Badaga) and of the forests south-west of Madras and of Maisur, Cochin, and Travancore (the Kader, Paniyan, Pulaya, Puliyar, and Kaniyan) have *a preponderating element* of negro blood. Many of these people are dark-coloured, with kinky or curly hair, are prognathous and flat-nosed, with thick, everted lips. The Andamanese are negroes.

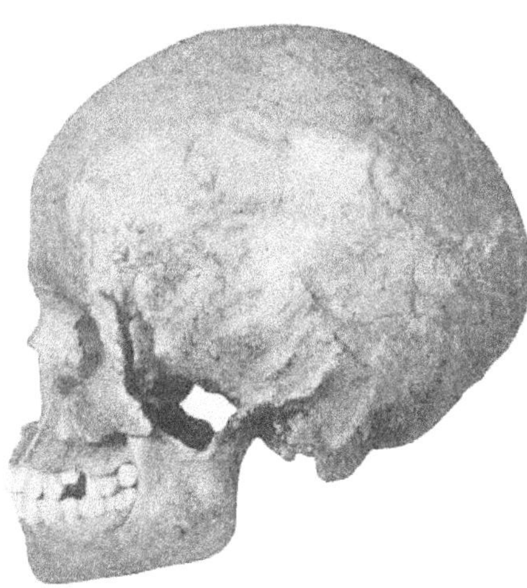

27. SKULL OF YOUNG MALE NEGROID
Of perhaps thirty thousand years ago, found in the Grimaldi Caves near Monaco

There is no indication as yet that any primitive negro type entered Ceylon. The Veddahs still lingering in that island are not negroid but either Proto-Caucasians or modified Australoids. But the negroid element permeates the low-caste or outcast "pariah" tribes of Western and Eastern India, and penetrates through the coast tribes of Southern Persia to Eastern Arabia.

Assuming, then, that the Negro sub-species was originated in the Indian Peninsula, we can in imagination see this type of dark-skinned, spiral-haired, flat-nosed man turning eastwards as well as westwards, invading Burma and the Malay Peninsula and Archipelago on the heels of the retreating Australoids, and securing as their exclusive home the Andaman Islands (they were probably exterminated in the Nicobars by the Mongolians that followed them). To this day dwarf negro people survive in the Far East—the Samang in the forests of the Malay Peninsula and the Aeta in the Philippine Islands. There

[1] Unless we revive Dr. Sclater's theory of a vanished continent in the Indian Ocean, a "Lemuria" which united Eastern Africa with the Malay Archipelago. It is, however, doubtful whether such a continent existed in any period of the Tertiary epoch; and highly improbable that it was still above water at the beginning of the human period.

are traces of the passage of a negroid people through Sumatra and Borneo, in the island of Timor, and markedly so in New Guinea, though here they have mingled with the Australoid and have produced the well-marked Papuan race. The existing populations of the Solomon Islands, of New Ireland, and of the New Hebrides are much more negro-like in physical characteristics; in fact, perhaps the people of New Ireland are the most nearly akin to the African negro of all the Asiatic or Australasian peoples. Asiatic negroes also seem to have entered Australia from New Guinea and to have passed down the eastern part of that continent till they reached the then peninsula of Tasmania, not, of course, without mingling with the Australoids. There is a negroid (Melanesian) element in Fiji, and as far west as the Hawaii Archipelago and among the Maoris of New Zealand; in a much less degree also, in Burma, Annam, Hainan, Formosa, the Riu-Kiu Islands, and Southern Japan.

28. KADER YOUTH
Negroid tribe of Southern India

The Elamites of Mesopotamia appear to have been a negroid people with kinky hair, and to have transmitted this racial type to the Jews and Syrians.[1] There is a curliness of the hair, together with a negro eye and full lips, in the portraiture of Assyria which conveys the idea of an evident negro element in Babylonia. Quite probably the very ancient negro invasion of Mediterranean Europe (of which the skeletons of the Alpes Maritimes are vestiges) came from Syria and Asia Minor on its way to Central and Western Europe.

29. PANIYAN WOMAN
Negroid bush-tribe of Southern India

It is possible that in or on the verge of Arabia the ancient basal stock of the generalised negro parted, divided into two great streams of divergent emigration: one to proceed to Europe via Syria, and the other to pass through Arabia[2] to Egypt and tropical Africa. In Arabia or in Egypt (it may be) arose the difference between the long-headed African negro and the rounder, shorter-headed *Bushman*, the last-named becoming more habituated than his congeners to a life in arid deserts or scrubby, open country.

The African Negro was again differentiated (probably in East Africa) into three main varieties: (1) the *prognathous* "*Strandlooper*" type, of whom vestiges living and

[1] The Jews are composed of three or four separate racial elements. The Asiatic negroid strain shows itself occasionally in the curly hair, the long eye, and proportions of the skull. The Jewish hybrids with the Negro in Jamaica and Guiana reproduce most strikingly the Assyrian type (*supra*).

[2] It is quite conceivable that the great peninsula of Arabia was once populated, as far as its natural conditions allowed, by a primitive negro stock, which may have been later on partially exterminated by changing and unfavourable conditions of climate and by the after-coming of the white man in his types

fossil are found in South Africa and the Sudan; (2) the *Forest Negro* and *Congo Pygmy*, of the Congo basin, Cameroons, West Africa, Uganda, and portions of the Bahr-al-Ghazal, with powerful torso, long arms, disproportionately short legs, very long head, considerable prognathism, prominent eyes and a long upper lip; and (3) the *Nilotic Negro*. This last (which is not without Australoid and European-Negro affinities) seems to proceed from an early intermingling between the Proto-Caucasian and the Forest Negro, but is a sufficiently ancient hybrid to have developed characteristics of its own, due, no doubt, to its original habitat having been the vast, flat, marshy regions of the Upper Nile Valley and the basin of Lake Chad. The *Nilotic Negro* has disproportionately long legs and is one of the tallest races of man. The facial features vary from the good looks of the straight-nosed Hamite to the prominent cheek-boned, everted-lipped negro of the Central Sudan, in whom there is a "Strandlooper" element.

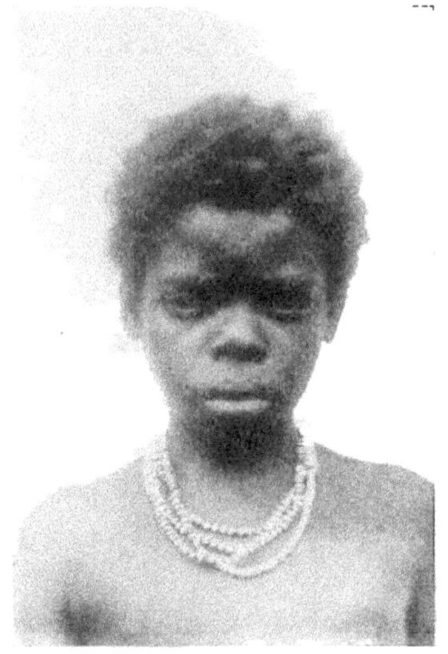

30. A PULIYAR BOY
Negrito tribe of Southern India

The *Forest Negro* may be seen in his more pronounced type of powerful chest, huge arms and short legs, and very prognathous face[1] in the denser forests of the Congo Basin and in the Niger Delta, and in a modified form along the west coast of Africa from the Gambia to the mouth of the Congo; but the physical type occurs sporadically in many parts of East, Central, South, and S.W. Africa. The mingling of Nilotic and Forest Negroes in past times has produced many tribes of black men with splendid, comely, and harmonious physical development; their limbs having much the same proportions as those of well-made Europeans, while the face also has acquired a certain refinement of feature. This is the physical type so much (but not exclusively) associated with the speaking of Bantu languages: the Upper Congo tribes, the people of Tanganyika and North Nyasa, the Swahili, Yao, A-Kamba, Baila, Batonga, Bakaranga, and Zulu.

It is of course possible that the Negro may not have

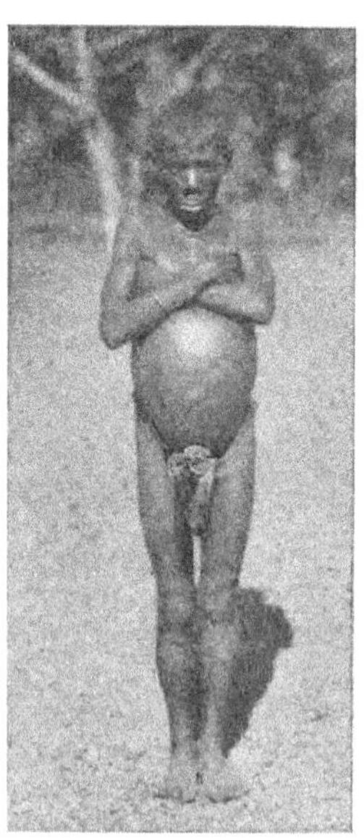

31. A CONGO PYGMY, BAMBUTE, ITURI RIVER
Even Congo pygmies have found their way as slaves from the Western Congo basin to the West Indies

of Hamite, Semite, and Iberian. The Hamites, or ancestors of the Egyptians, Galas, Somalis, etc., may even have been the result of intermixture in Arabia between the Mediterranean type of white man (Libyan, Iberian, Persian, etc.) and the bushman and negro savages of ancient Arabia.

Unless the Negro (and many other mammalian types of modern Africa) entered that continent from *Europe* (via Spain and Morocco; Sicily-Malta-Tunis; Syria-Sinai-Egypt) it is difficult to avoid the conclusion that Arabia must have been once an important half-way house to Africa from both Western Asia and India. The systematic exploration of this vast peninsula (which in existing fauna is slightly more African than Indian or "Palæarctic") would, no doubt, solve many enigmas in the geographical distribution and origin of mammals and of mankind; but it is, alas! rendered very difficult by the lava-beds and basalt, the shifting sands, heat, aridity, and most of all the fanaticism and superstition of the native tribes.

[1] See Illustration No. 2, p. 3.

been the first type of human being to enter Africa, from Arabia or across the isthmuses of habitable land between Mauretania and the Central Sudan: the Dark Continent may have been partially colonised by offshoots of *Homo primigenius*, or by the generalised "Australoid" form of *H. sapiens*, or even have received from Asia intermediate Anthropoids akin to *Pithecanthropos*. Traces of Australoid affinities in skull formation are not uncommon in the Equatorial belt of Africa from east to west, and there are remarkable resemblances in customs, weapons, and implements between the most primitive tribes of the Equatorial belt of Africa and the Australoids of Australia. Then again, the Negro was soon followed up in his appropriation of Africa by the Caucasian of an already negrified Mediterranean type: Libyans wandered across the Sahara, dispossessed the red-skinned pygmies of Western Nigeria, absorbed some of the Forest Negroes, and formed such hybrid stocks as the Songhai, Mandingo, Fula, and Nyamnyam; Hamites (Egyptian[1] and Gala) occupied Egypt from Arabia and pushed westwards across the Libyan Desert, mingling freely with long-legged or short-legged and prognathous negroes, and thus called into existence mixed races like the Tibbu, Nubian, Ethiopian, Masai, Andorobo, Hima, Gala, Somali, and Danákil.

32. THE TYPICAL ETHIOPIAN

A man of the Hadendowa tribe, near Suakin. These Ethiopians of the north-eastern Sudan are closely allied in blood and language to the Gala and Somali, and in a lesser degree (but not in language) to the Fula of Western Africa

There has been much infiltration of Caucasian blood from Europe and Western Asia in more recent, historic times. Pre-Islamic Arabs undoubtedly—notwithstanding the disputes as to the builders of Zimbabwe—were connected with and settled in South-East Africa perhaps more than two thousand years

[1] There are indications that the ancestors of the ancient Egyptians—themselves probably of Hamitic race coming from S.W. Arabia—found the Lower Valley of the Nile (then to a great extent cut off from Mauretania by gulfs, lakes, and deserts) in the occupation of a primitive negro or "Strandlooper" race. "Strandlooper" (shore-runner) was a nickname given by the Boers to the prognathous savages of the South African kitchen-middens.

ago. They must have taken to themselves concubines from the South African Negroes, and these last—possibly not yet "Bantu" in speech—may have already created the Hottentot hybrid with the Bushman in South-West Africa. Then from 1000 A.D. onwards came many Arabs, Persians, Baluchis, and Hindus to the East African coast. From out of the mingling of all these elements in different degrees arose the African peoples of to-day, very few of which are without some tinge of Caucasian blood due to the White man's persistent invasion of Africa from—let us say—12,000 B.C. to the present day.

CHAPTER II

AMERICA BEFORE THE NEGRO CAME

THE relative remoteness in time of the first human peopling of the two American continents is still an undetermined question. The present belief is that man had already permeated Asia and Europe and possibly parts of Africa before he invaded the North American continent from North-Eastern Asia; or if he reached North America in one of the inter-glacial periods (and thence spread to South America), he was killed off in the northern continent by the final triumph of the ice, while in South America he may have dwindled away to nothing before the supreme difficulties of endless swamps, pathless forests, and still vigorous wild beasts.

33. A SIOU AMERINDIAN, NORTH AMERICA

The human types which are indigenous to the Americas of to-day are divisible into two racial groups—the Eskimo and the Amerindian.[1] The Eskimo is a long-headed Mongolian, and in that respect is the most primitive form living of the yellow-skinned, straight-haired, hairless-bodied, narrow-nosed sub-species of *Homo sapiens*;[2] but in other directions this hyperborean race (originally from Northern Asia) is much specialised. The Amerindian would seem to be a mixture in varying degrees of a Proto-Caucasian type [like the Ainu of Japan], the Eskimo, and a Proto-Mongolian.[3] In some of his North American developments he stands very near to the Caucasian, from whom he differs mainly and only

[1] Additional information as to Amerindian aborigines is given in chapters IV., V., VI., XI., and XIV.

[2] The average cranial capacity of the male Eskimo is very high—1546 c.c. (W. L. H. Duckworth).

[3] It is always possible that from one to four thousand years ago the west coast of South America may have been reached by Polynesians coming by way of the Pacific Archipelagos. There may well have been islands or islets that have since been washed away or have sunk below the surface of the sea, which served to break the journey between Hawaii or Easter Island and the coasts of Mexico or of Chili. But if so, the physical type of American man would not have been greatly modified, since the Polynesians are a hybrid race composed likewise of Mongol and Proto-Caucasian, with an added element of Australoid or Melanesian (Asiatic Negro). Subtract the negroid or Australoid strain from the Polynesian, and you have an Amerindian. Many of the Mongoloid peoples of Borneo and Sumatra or Malaysia have a strong physical resemblance to the Amerindian. This generalised type (between Caucasian and Eskimo) may once have inhabited the whole Pacific coast of Asia, and have reached America by way of Japan, the Kuriles, Kamschatka, and the Aleutian bridge.

by the still marked prominence of the cheek-bones, the narrow eyes (sometimes with the epicanthic fold), the straight, coarse, round-sectioned head-hair, and the almost complete absence of hair on the body. In South and Central America the indigenes have a more Polynesian appearance, some of them resembling closely the Dayaks of Borneo (in culture as well as in physique). Here and there in Brazil and Peru there are suggestions of the survival of a long-headed and primitive human stock resembling slightly the Australoid. (The meaning of these indications, both existing and fossil, may well be exaggerated, and are due perhaps to local degeneration or deviation.) Perhaps on the whole the ancient dwarfish coast tribes of Peru and the modern Aymara group of the Peruvian highlands—with their pentagonal faces, short, flat noses, prognathous jaws, and short thighs—are the lowest in physical development known to exist in America.

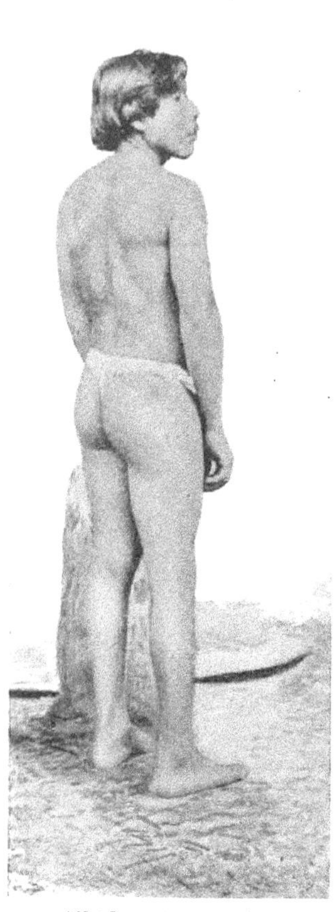

34. AN ARAWAK AMERINDIAN, BRITISH GUIANA

The Arawaks and the Caribs, as far as we know, were the only types of Amerindian inhabiting the West India Islands from Cuba and the Bahamas to Grenada and Tobago at the time of Columbus's discovery. Both peoples came from the Guianas

Why the Americas—which in food supply for man were perhaps more richly endowed by Nature than the Old World (in the elements of vegetable food, at any rate)[1]—were not as densely populated as Europe, Asia, and Africa, it is difficult to say. In Australia before the Island Continent was reached by Malays, and long after them by Europeans, the native races (Australoid and Negrito) had only attained a very low level of human culture, comparable to that of the lowliest stage of *Homo sapiens.* But in Australia man had to grapple with the increasing aridity of the centre and west, possibly was cut off from inhabiting part of the central regions by their being under water; and in the south-west, south, and east of this region had a poor food supply as compared with the rest of the world.

In North America the causes which kept man back from a rapid rate of increase were, firstly, the inclement climate which prevailed over two-thirds of the northern continent at the close of the Pleistocene; secondly, the destruction by insect agencies[2] and disappearance of many species of wild beasts which might otherwise have supplied the primitive Amerindians with ample food; thirdly, the density of the forests in other regions wherein at first man was unable

[1] Indeed it is difficult to see how in *tropical* America any able-bodied man or woman could starve even if they merely lived like the beasts of the field on the produce of the seashore, the shallow river, the forest, savannah, swamp, plateau, and pampas. There were land crabs and sea crabs, crayfish, prawns, fat beetle grubs, sea fish, river fish, manatis, iguana lizards (most succulent), toothsome game-birds, rodents innumerable, deer, tapirs, edible palms, nuts, pineapples, maize, papaws, and fruits, roots, tubers, and grains too numerous to catalogue, besides enormous quantities of wild honey. It was this native provender which enabled runaway negroes to live so easily in the backwoods.

[2] Two species of *Glossina* or "tsetse" fly have been discovered fossil in North America [Colorado]. *Glossina* may have reached America from West Africa, possibly before the complete disappearance of those

to procure sufficient sustenance and was attacked by jaguars, alligators, snakes, insects (ants, above all), and found his progress barred by appalling barriers of vegetation.[1] Then there was the utter inability to conceive a humanity common to all tribes and nations. Empires, late in the day, were, it is true, founded in Peru and Mexico, which united under a semi-civilised government several millions of human beings—perhaps ten millions in South America and four millions in Central America. But the population here was checked by infanticide, by endless human sacrifices and probably a heavy death-rate amongst children. This last would quite sufficiently account for the slow increase of the Northern Amerindians and of those living in a low, savage state in all South America to the east of the Andes. The inter-tribal wars, which, according to legends and traditions, raged all over the Americas between the ice sheet on the north and the Straits of Magellan on the south, and the frantic cannibalism practised by peoples of eastern tropical America, would, as in Africa, explain the constant depopulation or slow increase. Again, in many of the Amerindian tribes there was and is a certain lack of

35. CARIB AMERINDIANS, NORTHERN GUIANA

islets and archipelagos which almost connected the tropical regions of Africa and America as late as the Miocene period and after any actual isthmus had broken down. The *Glossina* in America may have, as in Africa, developed into the medium or the principal medium for transferring flagellate microbes into the blood of the wild horses, musk oxen, long-horned bisons, mammoths, and the relations of the pronghorn and of the South American camels, which still inhabited Northern and Central America after the advent of man.

[1] When considering the habitability of Africa and South America in earlier times—namely, the extent of the area which could be easily occupied by man—it must be borne in mind that probably fifteen to twenty thousand years ago, and farther back still in the Earth's history, the upper basin of the Niger, the region east and west of the Chad and the Shari basin, the Bahr-al-Ghazal, and above all the Congo basin; and in America the enormous area below a thousand feet in altitude, which is covered by the Amazon and its tributaries, besides the Orinoco basin, and the flats of modern Argentina and

virility; many of the Amerindian races lack that uxoriousness so characteristic of the Negro, that tremendous race fertility which over and over again repairs the ravages of disease and of human wickedness.[1]

36. AN AMERINDIAN OF SOUTH CENTRAL BRAZIL

Paraguay, were uninhabitable swamps interspersed with large lakes. All these modern plains through which huge rivers wind were then in a state of transition between the original condition of vast shallow, inland seas of fresh or brackish water and their present state of low-lying, flat, forested country or grassy pampas.

[1] Among the Amerindians of Western and Central North America, of the Antilles, of Northern and Eastern South America, a certain degree of race-suicide was and is going on through a persistent and perhaps ancient failure of virility among a proportion of the men, which leads to sexual depravity (homo-sexuality) among the males of the community. This tendency is strongly marked in the traditions,

When the Spaniards and Portuguese took possession of the West Indies, Central and South America, they found these new regions either sparsely populated or inhabited by peoples disinclined to hard and persistent work and of not very strong physical constitutions, so that they were fatally subject to epidemics of disease introduced or spread by the Europeans,[1] or easily killed by hard work or hard blows.

But another reason which prevented the Spaniards from making full use of the Amerindians as serfs lay in the intervention of the Roman Church and of such ecclesiastics or rulers in Spain as had any Christian humanity in their mental composition. It was ordained from time to time that Indians who accepted Christianity and joined the Church of Rome should be treated on an equal footing in America as Spanish subjects free in the eyes of the law. There is no doubt that some of the natives of Cuba and Porto Rico,[2] a few in Santo Domingo, and multitudes in Venezuela, Peru, and Brazil saved themselves from extermination by becoming Christians,[3] and also through the inclination evinced by both Europeans and Amerindians for a sexual union which has resulted in the many hybrid American peoples of to-day: half Spanish or Portuguese, half Amerindian in blood.

37. A WILD ONA "INDIAN" OF TIERRA DEL FUEGO

So that very early in the history of Europeanised America, the Spaniards first and the Portuguese later had to supplement their labour force in tropical America by immigrants who could work in torrid heat and yet need not be regarded as Christians. The problem was no sooner defined at the commencement of the sixteenth century than it was answered by the importation of Africans.

legends, and customs of certain tribes, and was so patent in Hispaniola and Mexico at the time of their discovery as to have at once attracted the attention of the Spanish explorers and historians. The vice exists still (according to official and scientific American publications) among the Amerindian tribes between Alaska and Northern Mexico, California, and the Mississippi. Its prevalence, past and present, among the Amerindians of Colombia, Ecuador, and Brazil is attested by many historians, missionaries, and explorers.

[1] Between 1550 and 1850 at least three million Amerindians must have died of small-pox in the West Indies, Central and South America.

[2] This island is of course known as Puerto Rico by the Spaniards. An excellent description of the aborigines, the Borinquens, is given in the *Twenty-fifth Annual Report of the Bureau of American Ethnology*, Washington, 1907.

[3] Especially under the decree entitled "Encomienda," published in 1512. Under this protection the indigenes of Porto Rico were henceforth classed as Spaniards, and now form the principal element in the peasantry of that island (the "Gibaros").

CHAPTER III

SLAVERY UNDER THE SPANIARD

AFTER the Spaniards had conquered finally the whole of the Canary Archipelago—an achievement which only preceded the discovery of America by a few years—they despatched to Hispaniola, Cuba, and Porto Rico Guanche slaves, the indigenes of the Canary Islands,[1] besides also recalcitrant Moorish Jews from Majorca, Jews and Morescos from Southern Spain.

The Turks and Arabs in the Crusades, and the Moors of Spain and North Africa had introduced to the mind of mediæval Europe the idea of negro slaves, of "black Moors"[2] who were strong, willing, and faithful servants to their white employers. Although Moor enslaved Christian and Christian attempted to enslave Moor from the eighth to the eighteenth century, neither found it a paying game. The two races were too near akin mentally and physically, too nearly equal in endowments to reign over each other.

When the Portuguese discoverers, urged on by Prince Henry of Portugal, had rounded Cape Bojador, and after reaching the Rio d'Ouro[3] in 1435, had, in 1441, captured some Moors on that desert coast and brought them back to Portugal to become slaves; the latter soon attracted the attention of Portuguese notabilities by their noble bearing. They explained that it was impossible for persons of their race and religion to pass into servitude; they would either die of a broken heart or commit suicide. On the other hand, there was a race cursed by God—the race of Ham and Canaan—the black-skinned people who were predestined slaves and who dwelt in enormous numbers to the south of the great desert. If their Portuguese captors would release them (the Moors of the Sahara coast) they would show the Christians the way to a river of crocodiles and sea-horses, to the south of which dwelt the black people who might justifiably and conveniently be imported as slaves into Portugal.

The offer was accepted, and at the close of the fifteenth century a brisk

[1] The Guanche in appearance must have been very like the white Moors of North Africa at the present day and not very dissimilar to the southern Spaniards. The names of some of these rather notable Guanche emigrants linger actually as the names of villages or plantations in Cuba, Haiti, and Santo Domingo at the present day. Thus Tinguarra, the name of an American sugar plantation managed by Englishmen in Cuba, is the name of a Guanche chieftain sent as a slave or prisoner of war to Cuba. The Canary Islanders in Spanish America are referred to as the "Isleños."

[2] This is the reason why *blackamoor* in English, *moriaan* in Dutch, *morian* in German, *moro* in Spanish, Portuguese, and Italian, and *moricaud* in French were early names for negroes. "Negro," a Spanish word, did not come into common use in England till the nineteenth century.

[3] "River of Gold," an inlet on the western Sahara coast, now part of a Spanish protectorate (Rio de Oro). It was here that the Carthaginians had a great trading depôt on the island of Kerne, where they exchanged the trade goods of the Mediterranean for the gold, ivory, and probably the negro slaves of West Africa.

trade in negro slaves was being carried on by the Portuguese between the Guinea Coast and Mediterranean Europe; Lagos, in Southern Portugal, becoming a great slave mart.[1]

38. A CANARY ISLANDER (GRAND CANARY)

This man resembles the type of New World colonists sent by Spain to people Porto Rico, Cuba, Santo Domingo, and the Spanish Main. They are constantly alluded to in the history of the Greater Antilles and Central America as the *Isleños* or "Islands' people"

[1] According to Bryan Edwards, the Portuguese obtained (about 1475?) a Bull from the Pope sanctioning the African slave trade. Earlier Popes had forbidden the traffic. A slave market was set up at Lisbon, at which from 10,000 to 12,000 negroes were sold annually in the sixteenth century. (*Historical Survey of Saint Domingo*, p. 220.)

The decision of Pope Alexander VI in 1493, followed by the Treaty of Tordesillas in 1494,[1] assigned to Portugal the west coast of Africa south of the Canary Islands, and to Spain the New World (of which, however, Portugal was soon afterwards able to claim Brazil as her share). It was therefore to the Portuguese possessions in Africa that Spain looked—since the Canary Islanders were not sufficient, or had already become Christians—for supplies of negroes to labour in the plantations, forests, and mines of the Antilles and of Eastern South America. By 1502 the first contingent of Africans had been landed in Hispaniola to work in the mines in lieu of the feeble-bodied Arawaks, or the fierce, intractable Caribs. They had been recruited from the negroes employed in the south of Portugal and of Andalusia as agricultural labourers, and were further supplemented in 1510 from the same source and in succeeding years by others obtained (through the Portuguese) direct from Guinea.[2]

The "Apostle of the Indians," Bartolomeo de Las Casas, Bishop of Chiapa, in Hispaniola, came to Spain in 1517 to protest at the court of the young King-Emperor Charles V against the harsh treatment which the West Indian indigenes were enduring at the hands of the Spaniards, who in twenty years had reduced an estimated million[3] of gentle-natured Arawaks to about sixty thousand. As an alternative to the forced labour of the survivors he proposed that the hardier negroes of West Africa should be imported into the Antilles, to furnish the unskilled labour in mines and plantations for which the native Amerindians had proved too weakly of constitution. (Later on, Las Casas himself records having regretted this proposal, when he learnt with

[1] The original decision of the Pope [the Bull of Demarcation beginning "Inter cætera"] drew the boundary line between the Spanish and Portuguese spheres at a distance of three hundred miles west of the Azores Islands. This limit discontented the Portuguese, and by the treaty of the following year at Tordesillas the boundary was shifted to an imaginary north-to-south line at a distance of 370 leagues (say 1110 miles) west of the Cape Verde Archipelago. This provision cut off much of Brazil from the Spanish sphere, and enabled the Portuguese to claim this portion of the New World when it was discovered by their navigators Pinçon, Cabral, and Amerigo Vespucci in 1499, 1500, and 1501.

In 1494, a Papal decision, followed by the Treaty of Tordesillas, had already divided Morocco into a Spanish and a Portuguese sphere of influence (as we should say nowadays). The Spanish half was the Moorish kingdom of Tlamsan (Tlemcen) or Eastern Morocco; the Portuguese division was the western portion of the country, the Moorish kingdom of Fez or Al-gharb (Algarve); and the boundary between the two spheres commenced on the north coast at Velez, in the Riff country. As the Portuguese domain in Morocco was that which was best supplied with negro slaves (because most accessible to the Senegal country and Western Nigeria), Spain was additionally dependent on Portugal for negro workers in Southern Spain as in America. Under this arrangement of Tordesillas, Melilla, first occupied in 1490, remained Spanish; Ceuta, on the other hand, was Portuguese, and was not garrisoned by Spain until 1580, or finally ceded to Spain until 1688. The long connection of Portugal with Morocco (not terminated territorially until the loss of Mazagan in 1770) resulted in a brisk trade in slaves for Brazil and the Spanish Indies, and was one of the routes by which Bornuese and Songhai slaves—many of whom were superior types of negroid—reached America. The Moorish conquest and occupation of Western Nigeria between 1590 and about 1730 greatly stimulated the slave trade with America through Saffi, Tangier, and Mazagan. But after 1590, the Moroccan oversea slave trade gradually passed into English hands.

[2] It is said by the American writer George Parker Winthrop that 300 negro porters and soldiers accompanied Cortes on his Mexican expeditions; negroes carried the loads of Balboa on his discovery of the Pacific Ocean in 1513, and went with Hernandez to Peru in 1530. Negroes assisted as servants and labourers in the founding of the Spanish city of St. Augustine in Florida in 1565, and were sailors on the Spanish ships which explored the coast of Virginia in 1528. A Spanish-negro explorer, Estevan, discovered New Mexico, the land of the Zuñi Indians, in 1539.

[3] A total which was probably an exaggeration. Modern opinion is occasionally inclined to the idea that Las Casas somewhat overstated his case. But the records of Porto Rico, Hispaniola, Cuba, Jamaica, the Lesser Antilles, Mexico, Colombia, and Peru make it clear that (in the West Indies, at any rate) the behaviour of the local Spanish authorities and settlers towards the Amerindian was extraordinarily bad; and this in defiance of the orders of the Spanish sovereign and his ministers and of the protests of the Church. The emissaries of the Roman Church, especially the Jesuits, got in time the upper hand and literally saved millions of Amerindians from destruction in Spanish and Portuguese America.

what cruelty and deception the Portuguese obtained their supplies of slaves from the West African coast). A year earlier, however (1516), in spite of the dogged opposition of Cardinal Ximenes, the first of anti-slavery prelates, Charles V had anticipated the idea, and had given licences to Flemish favourites to recruit negroes in West Africa for despatch to the West Indies. One of these patents issued by Charles gave the exclusive right to a Fleming named Lebrassa or Lebrasa to supply four thousand negroes annually to Cuba, Hispaniola, Jamaica, and Porto Rico. Lebrassa sold his patent to a group of Genoese merchants, who then struck a bargain with the Portuguese to supply the slaves.

These licences or patents were rendered necessary owing to the rigid monopoly of trade and traffic in Spanish America, which lasted till the end of the eighteenth century and confined all commerce to Spanish subjects and Spanish ships. But also in theory the slave trade was always an unchristian and illegal procedure in Spanish policy, and to engage in it required the special Assent ("Asiento") of the Spanish sovereign. In course of time this Asiento became a contract for supplying the Spanish Indies with negroes—an increasingly profitable enterprise which figures often in European and American history during the seventeenth and eighteenth centuries.

39. CAPTAIN SIR JOHN HAWKINS

During the closing years of his reign Charles turned against the principle of slavery for Indian or Negro. He promulgated the Code of 1542 for the better protection of the Amerindians of Spanish America and directed that all African slaves should be set free. Pedro de la Casca was sent out to carry this emancipation into effect: but one year after the retirement of Charles to the monastery of Yuste (1558) slavery and the slave trade were resumed.

Sometimes the contractors of the Asiento passed on a portion of their privilege to sub-contractors. Thus in 1562 a British sea-captain—John Hawkins, later Sir John[1]—took up a contract for the supply of slaves from Guinea to the Canary Islands, or direct to the Antilles. In 1562, '64, '67 he made three ventures on the west coast of Africa (Gambia, Sierra Leone, Western Liberia, and Gold Coast), in the course of which he purchased or

[1] Queen Elizabeth (like Queen Anne a hundred and forty years later) took shares in the British slave-trade, and lent Hawkins in 1564 one of her ships, named—ironically enough!—the *Jesus*.

kidnapped about eight hundred negroes for transport to the Spanish West Indies. Except for the interruptions of the Elizabethan wars with Spain, British and Portuguese shippers contrived as sub-contractors to convey several thousand negroes to Hispaniola, Cuba, Jamaica, and Porto Rico during the sixteenth century.

The Asiento passed to a Fleming in 1595, and was undertaken by the Portuguese governor of Angola in 1600; about 1640 it was conferred on the Dutch, and in 1701 on the French. In 1713 under the Treaty of Utrecht this much-desired contract was granted to the English (the South Sea Company), who held it till 1739, when it provoked the war of "Jenkins's ear." In 1748 the Asiento was abolished, after the Peace of Aix-la-Chapelle.

Contracts given to Portuguese, French, or British shippers to supply the Spanish Indies with slaves having proved unsatisfactory because of the excuse they gave for smuggling other goods into the closed markets of Spanish America, Spain resolved to acquire a recruiting-ground of her own in West Africa; and therefore in 1777 exchanged with Portugal a small piece of Spanish coast and an island in the south of Brazil for the (nominally) Portuguese island of Fernando Pô in the Gulf of Guinea, together with the islet of Anno Bom, and also the right to found a Spanish station on Corisco Island north of the Gaboon River (this last grew in time into the now large-sized territory of "Spanish Guinea" or the Muni River, about 9800 square miles). But the intentions of Spain were frustrated. The Bube tribes of Fernando Pô were doggedly opposed to serving as slaves, and besides resented so strongly the landing of white men on their beloved island that they harassed the Spanish garrison continually. Their attacks combined with the unhealthy climate led to the evacuation of the island at the close of the eighteenth century.

In 1827 the British naval authorities occupied the north coast of Fernando Pô as a base of operations for the suppression of the slave-trade; and although the British Government was obliged to recognise Spanish claims and eventually to witness in 1846 the resumption of direct Spanish control (the Spanish Dominican and the British Baptist—largely Jamaican—missionaries now intervening to protect the Bube natives), yet British intervention effectually prevented Fernando Pô becoming either a recruiting-ground or a receiving depôt for negro slaves, destined in the nineteenth century for the Spanish Antilles.

A good deal of slave-trading, however, went on at Corisco Island until the French occupied the adjoining Gaboon estuary and founded Libreville.

The slave-trade was declared illegal by the Spanish Government in 1820 after the receipt of a subsidy of £400,000 from Great Britain, but the prohibition so far as the Spanish authorities were concerned was a farce, and the trade in slaves from West Africa to Cuba and Porto Rico was only checked by the vigilance of British and French cruisers.

Debarred from using these Spanish settlements on or off the Cameroons coast, the slave-traders of nineteenth-century Cuba directed their attention to the Rio Pongo, a no-man's land north-west of Sierra Leone. Hither came the Fula traders from the mountainous interior bringing great "coffles"[1] of slaves from the Mandingo and Upper Niger countries. It was from the Rio Pongo that so many Mandingoes (and even an occasional Fula) reached Cuba and Brazil. The adjoining rivers and islands of Portuguese Guinea fed a similar slave-trade. Englishmen from Liverpool and English half-castes like John Ormond[2]

[1] The Arabic *kafilah*

[2] See for details the author's work on *Liberia*, Vol. I.

took an important part in this traffic with Cuba and Brazil, but at length these Rio Pongo and Bolama slave-depôts were broken up by the joint action of British and French gunboats.

The Cuban ships then found their way to the eastern side of the Sierra Leone colony, to the Gallinas or Gallinhas lagoon, and the River Sulima. Here there had settled in 1821 "Don" Pedro Blanco, a native of Malaga, originally the mate of a sailing-vessel. Gradually he had built up a large slave-trading business along the unclaimed Grain Coast (now Liberia) from the Sulima to the vicinity of the Cestos River, and from 1822 to 1839 he contrived to ship to Cuba, Porto Rico, South Carolina, and Georgia, the Bahamas, and Brazil an average five thousand slaves annually, some of whom were intercepted by the British or French cruisers. Blanco employed Spanish, Portuguese, American, or Russian ships for his slave-transports. One of his principal lieutenants was Theodore Canot, a French seaman.[1]

40. A FULA FROM THE WEST AFRICAN HINTERLAND NEAR THE UPPER NIGER
Of the type so often found in Spanish America

Blanco was said to have been a man of cultivated mind "not naturally cruel" (as is always said about the Robespierres and Neros of this world). He lived near the Gallinas lagoon in an establishment (with a large harem) "surrounded by every luxury which could be imported from Europe." His bills were as promptly cashed as a bank-note on the West African coast, in Cuba, London, or Paris. He employed large numbers of negroes as paid servants, watchers, spies, and police. From a hundred look-outs on the Gallinas beach and the islands of the lagoon these men, trained to use telescopes, watched the horizon for the arrival of British cruisers. By their signals they repeatedly saved incoming or outgoing ships engaged in the slave-trade from detection and capture by the British.

Pedro Blanco and his agents obtained their slaves chiefly from the Gallina, Mende, Gora, Busi, Vai, and Kpwesi tribes, from the Gibi, Sikong, and other peoples behind the Basã and Kru coasts.

In 1839 Pedro Blanco retired from the trade with a fortune of nearly a million sterling. At first he lived in Cuba, but here he got into some political difficulty and lost some of his money. He then moved to Genoa, and ended his days quite pleasantly on the Italian Riviera.

The Spanish slave-trading depôts on the coasts of Sierra Leone and Liberia had all been destroyed by the British or the Americo-Liberians by about 1847. If any slaves reached Cuba or Porto Rico after that date it must have been through American or Brazilian slave-ships; for the protests of the British Government in 1853 practically closed the Spanish slave-trade.

In 1873 the status of slavery was finally abolished in Porto Rico, but in

[1] See *Liberia*, chap. x., Vol. I.

Cuba not till 1886. Already the Moret law of 1870 had given freedom to all slaves in Spanish colonies aged sixty years and over, and to all children of slaves born after 1870.

The Spanish treatment of slaves down to the stress of the busy nineteenth century seems to have been much better than that accorded by the same nation to the indigenous Amerindians.[1] It was regarded as an act of piety, much encouraged by the Spanish priests, to emancipate one's slaves as a death-bed atonement by declaration or by testament; or at any time and for any reason. Contrary to the local laws in British and Dutch possessions (where manumission was either restricted, forbidden, or heavily fined), the Spanish laws of 1540, 1563, and 1641 (though the Royal Ordinance of 1789 omits these passages) provided that any male or female slave who could tender his or her master 250 dollars (about £56) was able to purchase liberty, and with it, in the case of a woman and for an extra twelve dollars, that of her unborn child. In selling the children of a female slave, the Spanish father thereof was to have preference over any other purchaser. The Spanish Government ratified and registered the freeing of a slave *gratis*. Slaves might not absent themselves without their master's permission in writing; if convicted of striking a white man they might be punished with death; and they were forbidden to carry arms. But they were fed on much the same food as their masters, and almost as well lodged;[2] and as the cost of their redemption was not too prohibitive, masters treated their slaves well lest they might be induced to save, steal, or beg the amount of money necessary to their redemption.

Once free, the Spanish laws took no note of differences of race or colour, only of conformity to the Roman Catholic religion. Yet custom excluded the freedmen (negro and mulatto) from employment as military officers or to civilian posts of importance.[3] Mulattoes were admitted without difficulty in the priesthood, but not negroes.[4]

The result of this comparatively kindly treatment was that Spanish slaves seldom revolted. There was a rising of negroes in 1522 on the plantation of Diego Columbus in Hispaniola, and later on another in 1555; and a few years afterwards the escaped negroes ("Symerons," i.e. Cimarrones—*vide* p. 240) on the coast of Mexico and Panama joined the English adventurers against the Spaniards. But from the beginning of the seventeenth century, one hears of no trouble between the Spaniards and their negro slaves until well into the nineteenth century, when there was a black revolt in Cuba in 1823 and 1844.

The 1540, 1563, and 1641 laws of the Spanish Indies regarding slavery were summed up in 1789 by a Royal Ordinance or Cedula proclaimed at Aranjuez on May 31st in that year.[5] In Cuba, Santo Domingo, Porto Rico, Louisiana, Florida, New Andalusia, and Venezuela there remained, no doubt, the additional or anterior laws, rules, and regulations alongside this Royal

[1] "Les Espagnols euxmêmes maltraitaient moins leurs esclaves que ne le firent plus tard les planteurs des Antilles ou de l'Amérique du Nord." (P. Chemin-Dupontès, *Les Petites Antilles*, 1908.)

[2] Monsieur de Saint-Méry, in his work on Spanish Santo Domingo, writes of the Spanish slaves: "Ils sont plutôt les compagnons de leur maitre que ses esclaves."

[3] In the earlier edicts or local laws of the seventeenth century, freed men were forbidden in the Spanish possessions to serve as notaries or police officials, to have themselves waited on by Indians, to carry arms, wear jewellery, silk, or a mantle reaching below the waist. But these laws had become a dead letter long before 1789.

[4] The Portuguese, on the other hand, made no difficulty about admitting pure-blood negroes not only to the priesthood, but to the episcopate. There have been several black bishops in Brazil.

[5] I quote from the English translation of May 31st, 1811, printed for the House of Commons.

Ordinance which were not annulled thereby; but if not, then the 1789 proclamation was less favourable to the slaves than the pre-existing legislation, for it makes no definite provision for emancipation either by the master's action or the slave's self-redemption.

41. THE ENTRANCE TO THE CATHEDRAL AT PANAMA
One of the oldest churches (in portions) of Spanish America; largely built by negro labour

The substance of the 1789 edict is this:—

(1) Every one who has slaves is obliged to instruct them in the principles of the Roman Catholic religion and in the necessary truths in order that the slaves may be baptized within the (first) year of their residence in the Spanish dominions. On every holiday of the Church (excepting at the time of the crop) they

are not to be allowed to work either for themselves or for their masters, but are to receive instruction in Christian doctrine. On these and other days when they are obliged to hear Mass, the owner of the estate on which they work is to be at the expense of providing a priest to administer to the slaves the Holy Sacrament and explain Christian doctrines to them. Every day as soon as their work is finished the slaves are to say the Rosary in the presence of the master or the steward "with the greatest composure and devotion."

(2) The justices of the districts in which the estates are situated, with the approbation of the magistrates and the syndic or recorder (as protector of the slaves)[1] shall fix upon and determine the quantity and quality of the food and clothes which are to be supplied to the slaves by their masters daily, according to their ages and sexes, and conformable to the custom of the country—like those commonly given to (free) day labourers; "and linen the same as the work-people have who are free." Which determination, after having been approved by the Court of the district, shall be fixed upon the door of the town-hall, and of the churches of every place, and of the oratories or hermitages of the estates, that every one may know it and that no one may plead ignorance.

(3) The first and principal occupation of slaves must be agriculture and not those labours which require a sedentary life. . . . The justices of towns and villages . . . shall regulate the work to be done in the course of the day, and the slaves shall have two hours to themselves to be employed in manufactures or other occupations for their own advantage. Neither the masters nor the stewards are to oblige slaves to work when they are sixty years old or before they are seventeen. Women slaves were not to be employed in business unsuited to their sex, or to be employed in work which would bring them into promiscuity with the men. The women were to receive two dollars yearly from their masters for domestic service.

(4) On holy days, when masters cannot oblige or permit their slaves to work, after they have heard Mass and the Christian doctrine explained to them, the said masters or their stewards shall allow the slaves to divert themselves innocently in their presence, but they shall not allow them to be amongst those of the other estates, nor even with the females; hindering them from excess in drinking and taking care that their diversions are ended before prayer-time.

(5) This chapter provided (very properly) for the lodging of slaves [a separate bed to each slave, not more than two slaves in one bedroom], an infirmary for their use when sick, treatment at the hospital, and decent burial when dead.

(6) Slaves who on account of old age or illness are not able to work, as likewise the children of both sexes, must be maintained by their masters; and these cannot give them their liberty in order to get rid of them, except by giving a sufficient stock (of goods or money) which must be approved by the justices and syndic (protector of slaves), to maintain them without any other assistance.

(7) The master of slaves must not allow the unlawful intercourse of the two sexes, but must encourage matrimony. Neither must he hinder them from marrying with slaves of other masters; in which case, if the estates were distant from one another, so that the new-married couple cannot fulfil the object of marriage, the wife shall follow her husband, whose master shall buy her at a fair valuation set upon her by skilful men who shall be nominated by the two parties; and in case of disagreement a third shall be appointed by the justice to

[1] Elsewhere the "protector of slaves" is referred to as the "Attorney-General" in the English translation of the Spanish word *procurador*.

fix a price. If the master of the husband does not agree to the purchase the master of the wife shall have the same faculty.

Chapters (8) and (10) allude to the obligation of masters to "educate" their slaves, but this probably means only in suitable industrial work. In (8) it is laid down that slaves must obey and respect their masters and the stewards, perform the work given them to do (conformably with their strength), and venerate master and steward "as the heads of the family." Failing to perform their obligations, slaves must be punished by the master of the estate or by his steward [according to the nature of the offence] with prison, chains, or lashes, which last must not exceed the number of twenty-five, and those must be given them in such a manner as not to cause any contusion or effusion of blood: which punishments cannot be imposed on slaves but by their masters or the stewards. In chapter (9) it is provided that in all grave crimes the slave is to be tried before an ordinary court of justice just as a free person would be; except that any fine levied on the slave is to be paid by the master, and that (apparently) the master of the slave is to carry out any sentence of corporal punishment, mutilation, or death, which may be awarded by the court on the guilty slave.

(10) The masters or the stewards who do not fulfil all that is ordered in the chapters of this Ordinance in regard to the education, food, clothes, diversions, habitations, etc., of the slaves, or who forsake the slave children or the old and sickly slaves, are to be fined 50 dollars for the first offence, 100 for the second, and 200 for the third, and these fines are to be paid by the master, even in the case where the fault has really been committed by the steward, supposing the latter not to be able to pay the fine. Of this fine, *one third* will belong to the *informer* who has drawn attention to the offence, *another third* to the *judge*, and the *last third* is to be put into the "*Fines Chest*." If these fines do not have the required effect and the Ordinance continues to be broken or not observed, a somewhat vague threat is uttered, that "I (the King) will take my measures accordingly." When masters or stewards are guilty of excess in punishing slaves, causing them contusion, effusion of blood, or mutilation of members, besides paying the above-mentioned fines, they are to be prosecuted as criminals and receive punishments suitable to the crime they have committed, while the injured slave is to be confiscated and sold to another master (if he is able to work), the selling price being put into the Fines Chest. If he is too injured to work he is to be practically free, whilst his former master is obliged to make him a daily allowance (to be fixed by the justice) for his maintenance and clothes during the remainder of his life, paying this allowance every three months in advance.

(11) All persons not being the master or steward who chastise slaves, injure, wound, or kill them, shall incur the same punishment as would be enacted by the laws against those who committed similar excesses towards free people. The prosecution is [illegible] be initiated by the master of the slave who has been injured, chastised, [illegible] killed, and the Attorney-General of the Colony as Protector of the slaves is [illegible] conduct the case.

(12) Masters o[illegible]ves are obliged every year to deliver to the justice of the town or village ir[illegible] district in which their estates are situated a list, signed and sworn to by t[illegible] of all the slaves which they have, giving particulars as to sex and age, in o[illegible]hat the notary of the Court may take account of them in a separate boo[illegible]ch is to be kept for this purpose, together with the lists presented by the [illegible]rs. Whenever a slave dies or runs away the justice is to

be informed of this fact within three days, in order that the Attorney-General may have this fact noted in the book; otherwise the master will run the risk of suspicion of having killed his slave and of being prosecuted for such a crime.

(13) In order that every possible means may be taken for ascertaining and checking the treatment of slaves by their masters or stewards, it is directed that the priests who go round the estates giving Christian instruction and saying Mass are to obtain information from the slaves as to how they are treated by their masters and stewards, so that if there is any wrong-doing the priest may give a secret and reserved notice of it to the Attorney-General, who will order the case to be investigated whether or not there is any truth in the complaint. The priests who by reason of their ministry give the said secret notice are not to be answerable for anything, even if the complaints of the slaves are not just. The priests are required to render this service so that the Attorney-General may cause the justice to nominate some individual of the municipality or other person of approved conduct, who shall investigate the business and give a report to the justice, who shall determine whether to take further proceedings or not.

In addition to the priests the justices and magistrates shall appoint other persons of good character to visit the estates three times a year, to make inquiry whether all the chapters of the Ordinance are observed, and if not, to inform the justices of this default. "It is likewise declared to be a popular action, that of informing against a master or his steward for not having fulfilled one or the whole of the said chapters, as the name of the informer shall not be made known, and he shall have the (third) part of the fine which he is entitled to without being responsible in any other case than in that where it is proved that the information is false. And lastly, it is likewise declared that the justices and Attorney-General, as protectors of slaves, will be made answerable for any neglect of theirs in not having made use of the necessary means to have My Royal Resolutions put into execution."

(14) The Chest of Fines is to be established at the Court of Justice in all towns and villages, to be provided with three keys, one of which will be held by the justice of the peace, another by the governor of the province, and the third by the Attorney-General. The produce of the fines stored in this Chest is to be used to meet the expense of carrying out the regulations of this Ordinance. Not a "single maravedi" is to be taken out of it for any other purpose, or without an order signed by the three who keep the keys, setting forth the destination of the money. Accounts as to this expenditure are to be submitted yearly to the Intendant of the province.

Although this Spanish Slave Code of 1789 was not in many respects so explicitly benign towards the slaves as the Edict of Louis XIV in 1685, it was intended to be put in force (while the other had become a dead letter). The French planters complained of it in Haiti as likely to lure slaves over the border into Spanish Santo Domingo; the American set ers in Georgia protested as it caused many slaves from the United States scape to Florida or Cuba; and when the British acquired Trinidad in 1797 a ritish West Indian capitalists proceeded to invest their money in the island, as expressly stipulated (in 1811) that the Spanish Slave Code (in force th rom 1789 to 1797) should be abrogated.

In the seventeenth century the negro slaves of t paniards did not welcome the British as deliverers either at the town of Domingo or in

Jamaica. They fought gallantly with their Spanish masters to keep out the English, already acquiring a bad name as slave-drivers.[1] On the other hand, the Spaniards treated their Indian slaves with the greatest harshness, and all the arrangements made about bloodhounds tracking runaway slaves and being fed (to make them fierce) on human flesh had rather to do with fugitive or rebellious Arawaks or Caribs than Negroes. Indeed, down to the nineteenth century the Spanish as compared to the other European nations in America were not large holders of negro slaves. In Santo Domingo at the close of the eighteenth century there were only about 10,000; in Cuba (1792) 84,000; in Porto Rico about 50,000; in Trinidad, Venezuela, New Andalusia, and Central America about 60,000; in Florida and Louisiana about 60,000.

It was not until the second quarter of the nineteenth century that, in commercial rivalry with the now independent Hispaniola and the enfranchised British West Indies, the Spanish planters in Cuba (to whom had been added in 1795 French refugees from Haiti) began to overwork their slaves in the rush to get rich quickly out of sugar and tobacco; and in the greater cost of servile labour due to the British stoppage of the oversea slave-trade.

In spite of the mildness of the Spanish Slave Code the condition of their slaves during the nineteenth century—especially after 1853—became almost unendurable; the death-rate among them was very high, and those that succeeded in escaping took to the forests and mountains and became some of the most dangerous fighters in the two great Cuban insurrections, from 1868 to 1878, and from 1895 to 1898. The slaves were fed on coarse, unwholesome food, were subjected to exhausting, unremitting toil, and numbers of them died or went mad from the slow torture of overwork, insufficient rest, and want of sleep.[2] The Catholic Church in Cuba in the nineteenth century, unlike the emissaries of the same Church in Haiti and Brazil, seems to have been utterly indifferent to the condition of the negro slaves. Many of these remained fetish-worshippers and believers in nauseous forms of sorcery; and it was not till the American brought with him freedom of religion to misgoverned Cuba and with it came missionaries and teachers from the United States, Jamaica, and France that the negroes of Cuba—in some respects a fine, vigorous race—obtained any insight into the more reasonable aspects of Christianity.

As regards the continental dominions of Spain in the two Americas, the slave-trade was prohibited soon after the various republics had proclaimed their complete independence. There had never been much demand for negroes on the mainland of Spanish America, except in the coast lands of Honduras, Costa Rica, Colombia, and Venezuela.

The status of slavery was abolished in Guatemala by 1824, and in Mexico by 1829. The remainder of the Central American States started "free" by ignoring the status of slavery in framing their constitutions. In Argentina, Peru, Chili, Bolivia, and Paraguay slavery ceased to be recognised in law about 1825. It lingered longest in Colombia, Venezuela, and Ecuador, scarcely coming to an end until from 1840 to 1845. Of all parts of Spanish continental America perhaps the most negrified was the Panamá isthmus, owing to the

[1] Intelligent European travellers in Africa and America during the last half of the eighteenth century recorded opinions of their own and answers to their questions from negroes which went to show that in the opinion of the negroes themselves the slave-holding nations stood thus in order of merit as regards kind treatment of slaves: the *Portuguese first*; then the *Spaniards*, the *Danes*, the *French*, *English*, and *Dutch*.

[2] John E. Cairnes, *The Slave Power, its Character, Career, and Probable Designs*, 1863.

need for transport and the traffic from sea to sea. Even before the making of the canal attracted many thousand West Indians, the Panamanian population had a considerable negro element.

In the regions of Northern South America, however, numbers of negroes had obtained their freedom by serving in the armies of Bolivar and other revolutionary leaders. Indeed, the independence of Venezuela and Colombia was partly won by the bravery of negro and mulatto soldiers fighting under Bolivar, Paez, and Sucre. And Bolivar was helped most materially during the critical years of his struggle (1814–16) by the assistance in men, arms, and money—two expeditions in all—granted to him by General Pétion, who was

42. NEGRO GANGS OF LABOURERS AND SKILLED ARTISANS CONSTRUCTING THE DRAINAGE OF COLON (PANAMA)

then ruling the southern part of the negro republic of Haiti. Twice did Bolivar, the Liberator of South America, find a secure refuge at Aux Cayes in Southern Haiti when all other neutral ports were closed to him. Yet at a later date he showed himself most ungrateful to the Haitians: affecting to ignore the existence of their republic and omitting to send to them as well as to all the other recently enfranchised states any diplomatic representative of his new government.

In Santo Domingo—the Spanish portion of Hispaniola—slavery came to an end (more or less) in 1801, when Toussaint Louverture had made himself master of the whole island. The Spanish authorities had quitted San Domingo soon after the Treaty of Bâle (1795) had transferred to France all Spanish rights over Hispaniola. In 1808, however, the Spaniards returned to the eastern part of the island to resume possession of their old colony, and the English assisted them by taking the town of Santo Domingo from the French, who thenceforth were without a foothold on the island.

Occasional attempts were made by the Spaniards between 1809 and 1821 to coerce the enfranchised negro settlers; and the Spanish officials of the restored régime of Ferdinand VII (whose ashes should be exhumed and scattered, for he was the worst foe to the glory and greatness of Spain that ever existed) made themselves so odious to the native inhabitants, without distinction, that the intervention of negro Haiti was sought, the Spaniards were expelled, and from 1822 to 1843 the whole of Hispaniola was united under one government, that of Haiti.

But the Spanish-speaking Domingans were mainly of mixed Amerindian-Spanish or nearly pure Spanish descent: only about a third were negro, and these negroes had long absorbed and adopted the gravity and stateliness of Spanish manners. The French negroes and mulattoes of Haiti with their incomprehensible Créole speech, their extravagances of words and actions, their frequent changes of government, civil wars, and murderous courts-martial disgusted the quieter people of Santo Domingo. So in 1843 Haitian rule was shaken off and in 1844 a separate Dominican Republic proclaimed. During the "twenties" of the nineteenth century a small number of United States free negroes had settled on the Samaná peninsula of San Domingo as farmers and their descendants (now nearly a thousand in number) remain there to this day, still talking a broken English.

43. NEGRO QUARTERS AT RIO GRANDE, PANAMA CANAL

From 1844 to 1861 the Dominican Republic had a very chequered existence, dreading negro invasions from the west or revolutions from within. The United States—here as in Haiti—were disliked because they still upheld humiliating social distinctions of colour. The thoughts of the Spanish-speaking Domingans turned once more towards Spain, and Queen Isabella II was invited to send troops to occupy their country and reorganise Santo Domingo as a Spanish colony. But a tactless archbishop and fanatical Spanish clergy were sent with the expeditionary force, and quarrelled with the natives on the subject of religion. The Spanish officials, civil and military, were equally stupid, and after two years' vain endeavours to win over the Domingans to the same style of colonial government as that which was ruining Cuba the Spaniards quitted Santo Domingo and the Dominican Republic was restored. Then followed more than thirty years of financial chaos and indiscriminate loans; revolutions; assassinations; yellow fever; and a stationary population in a land as near the Earthly Paradise in climate, soil, fruits, scenery, and inherent healthfulness as one can expect to find in the known world. The enunciation of the Monroe Doctrine prevented the intervention of any European Power to restore order in the Dominican government and finance. So, however reluctantly at first, the Domingans were obliged (1905) to place themselves in the hands of the United States, whose intervention has been of much the same type as that of Britain in Egypt and with the same happy results. Santo Domingo is now going ahead, but mainly in the direction of the White man's interests.

The white race preponderated even at the end of the eighteenth century,

44. DOMINICAN TYPES: AMERINDIAN-SPANISH AND NEGRO-SPANISH

though it was compounded of a nearly equal mixture of Spanish and Amerindian blood. Spanish interest in Hispaniola had languished after the first eager development of the sixteenth century. The enormous mineral wealth of continental America, the less mountainous character of Cuba and Porto Rico drew the stream of Spanish migration elsewhere than to the first metropolis of "the Indies." At the same time, the enormous increase of wild cattle in Hispaniola (due to the depopulation) attracted to this island—especially to the western part—the pirates and "Buccaneers";[1] who from their base (the little island of Tortuga, off the north-west coast of Haiti) harassed the sparse Spanish population of San Domingo. Although San Domingo was the first portion of the New World in which the sugar-cane was cultivated and there were many mills for cane crushing at work there in 1550, the Spaniards preferred after the sixteenth century to carry on their sugar production in Cuba, Porto Rico, and on the South American mainland. So the import of negroes into derelict Santo Domingo dwindled until a slight revival of industries occurred again in the middle of the eighteenth century.

45. AN AMERICAN CUSTOMS OFFICER, SANTO DOMINGO

The Spanish Domingans were racially stricter in morals than the French. They did not so readily mix their blood with that of the negro. The dark olive complexions of so many of the people are rather due to the Amerindians (Arawak, Lucayan, Carib) so freely espoused by the early Spanish immigrants, than to sexual union with the Negro. Yet there is a negroid element in the modern Domingans, but this rather comes from the Haitian mulattoes, many of whom settled in the Spanish portion of Hispaniola and intermarried freely with the Domingan *mestizo*. This mingling of the three strains in San Domingo has produced some vigorous types in mentality and physical energy, even if they lack the often remarkable beauty of facial outline to be seen in those Domingans—half Spanish, half Amerindian—in whom there is no negroid intermixture. (See for further information regarding the Domingans, p. 183.) Of the tripartite mixed types General José Miguel Gomez, the President of Cuba, is a good example. General Gomez is a native of San Domingo who migrated to Cuba and took a leading part in the war against Spain (1895–8).

46. A PORT AND CUSTOMS HOUSE ON THE DOMINICAN-HAITIAN FRONTIER
An American customs officer is in charge

Yet some of the direct Spanish-Negro hybrids are handsome men and women in regard to facial features and bodily shape, offering a remarkable resemblance sometimes to the good-looking negroids of North and North-East Africa. But there is also a subtle difference between the Hispanicised negro and the other blacks who have grown up under Anglo-Saxon, French, or Portuguese tutelage;

[1] From the Créole word "Boucanier." The Boucaniers were men, mostly French and English, who hunted the wild cattle and then smoke-dried, sun-dried, or baked the meat on or in *Boucans*. A *boucan* was a wooden gridiron, an invention of the Caribs for partially cooking and preserving human flesh; or some say really meant a clay underground oven applied to the same purpose.

a difference not always attributable to an infusion of Spanish blood: he is prouder, more reserved, more self-respecting; shows better taste in dress, has no servility of manner, is quietly courteous and astonishingly brave.

Poor Spain! Her people have such splendid qualities that mere contact with them has improved the often hostile races which have ranged themselves alongside—the Arab and Berber; the Irish, English, and Anglo-Celtic American; the Frenchman and Italian; the Jew; and the Negro. She ought to have been the premier nation of the world, combining the best of racial

47. A VIEW IN THE MOUNTAINS OF SANTO DOMINGO, NEAR HAITIAN FRONTIER

strains or mental influence: of the Celt-Iberian, Carthaginian, Roman, Goth, Jew, Arab, Libyan and Provençal, German and Italian. Yet her every purpose has been baulked: her valour and religious zeal; her shipbuilding, gun-casting, fortress-construction; her mastery of the art of painting and appreciation of the value of colour in the church, the home, the city, and the landscape; her magnificent literature written in the simplest, noblest, most logical development of the Latin speech; her people's unflagging industry: all these have availed her nothing in that three hundred and thirty years' long struggle with the Anglo-Saxon for supremacy in the New World which began by the attack of

Sir John Hawkins and Francis Drake on the Spanish fleet at San Juan de Ulúa[1] off the coast of Mexico in 1568 and ended in the surrender of Cuba to the Americans in 1898.

The slave-trade with America, and the introduction of the Negro into the New World, were, as we see, directly due to the rulers and ecclesiastics of Spain, though with no evil intention. The very word "Negro" is Spanish in form, for the Italian rendering of the Latin adjectival-stem *nigro* is *nero*, and

48. IN SANTO DOMINGO

the Portuguese by the fifteenth century had let "negro" fall into disuse, preferring to employ in the sense of "black" the obscure adjective *preto*.

[In the old French of the Crusades—1100–1300 A.D.—the term for "negro" is *nigre*, afterwards lost in more modern French; or *la neire gent*. In 1400–1500 French it is generally *moricaud*.]

To the Spanish language or to Spanish slang (rather than Portuguese) we are indebted for all the words in use to indicate the various shades and degrees

[1] The first European nation to defy the Pope's Bull and impinge on the Iberian monopoly of the New World was France, not England—Norman, Breton, and afterwards Protestant North-Western France; who in 1541 built the first European fort in Canada, in 1542 attacked Cartagena, in 1555 occupied Havana for a month, in 1558-67 colonised Rio de Janeiro, and in 1562–5 founded "Arx Carolina" near the mouth of the St. John's River (Mayport), in Northern Florida.

of hybridism between the Negro and other races. As these words will recur in the course of this book, it may be as well to enumerate and explain them here:—

A MULATTO (Spanish, *Mulato* or "muled") is the cross between *a pure-blood white man* and *a pure-blood negro*. (*Pardo* is an equivalent sometimes used by

49. CEREUS TRIANGULARIS
A tree cactus of Santo Domingo (forming much of the scrub there)

the Portuguese.) MESTIZO is the Spanish term for the hybrid between *a white man* and an *Amerindian*. MAMELUCO is the Portuguese (Brazilian) equivalent for Mestizo.

CREOLE (Spanish, *Criollo*, corruption of *criadillo*, "a little educated child") is a term which originally meant and still most frequently means *a white colonist* born in tropical America or Asia, but of pure European descent. But in Brazil and Peru it is applied to half-castes, or even (in Brazil) to absolute negroes of Brazilian birth and descended from negroes long settled in Brazil. In Sierra Leone the negroes who are freed slaves, or are descended from freed slaves not indigenous to the country, call themselves "creoles." Nevertheless, "Creole"

50. A NEGRO OF SANTO DOMINGO

is in the West Indies, Louisiana, and Spanish America (also in the Seychelles, Mauritius, and Bourbon), a native inhabitant of the White race.

The children of Mulattoes—mulatto father and mulatto mother—are styled CASCOS in Spanish America.

Quadroon (French, "Marabou"), *Quinteroon*, *Octoroon* (Spanish, *Cuarterón*, *Quinterón*, and *Octorón* or *Octarón*) are the designation of negroids mingled in increasing degrees with pure whites: thus a quadroon has *one-fourth* of negro blood, a quinteroon *one-fifth*, and an octoroon *one-eighth*. To these distinctions the Anglo-Saxon American adds another—the *Near White*, sprung perhaps from the union of an octoroon with a pure white. In most countries outside the United States, and perhaps Jamaica, the "near white," with one-sixteenth or less of negro blood, is reputed white and treated accordingly. (Alexandre Dumas—possibly even the Empress Josephine—was a "near white").

A ZAMBO or SAMBO (Spanish, *Zambo*, "bandy-legged") is a cross between a *Negro* and an *Amerindian* (sometimes this name is given to the cross between a pure Negro and a mulatto, which the French call "griffe.") In Brazil the offspring of a *Zambo* or *Caburete* (half negro, half Amerindian) and a *pure Negro* is called *Zambo preto* or *Cafuso*, between a *Mestizo* (half European, half Amerindian) and a Negro, *Chino*. The descendants of Zambos are sometimes called *Cholos*. A very common Brazilian term, CABOCLO or *Cabocolo*, means a civilized pure-blooded Amerindian.

CHAPTER IV

CUBA

IN the latest official census of Cuba (1907-8) there is a native population of 2,049,000; of which no less than 609,000 are classed as Negroes. 242,382 of these "coloured" people are unmixed negroes, of very black complexion: the balance of the 609,000 are mulattoes of varying tints. The

51. A GROUP OF "INDIOS"
Descendants of Cuban aborigines, East Cuba

colour line in Cuba is obviously not drawn with unkind precision; octoroons and people with only a slight evidence of negro ancestry may be classed officially as whites. And it is evident to any observant traveller penetrating into the country districts of Cuba that the Spanish peasantry of ancient settlement (as contrasted with the new Spanish immigrants since 1898) are considerably mixed in blood with the Amerindian, and that the "Indian" aboriginies of Cuba, instead of becoming extinct in the middle of the sixteenth century, have as half-breeds lingered in Central and Eastern Cuba to the present day. Pure-blood "Indians" are said to have existed in the East Cuban mountains down to the early part of the nineteenth century, and I have seen "Indian" reservations of land which were only finally broken up and thrown open to general settlement (mainly by Amerindian half-breeds) by the Spanish Government forty years ago. It is evident (to me) that a large proportion of the Cuban aborigines were not exterminated, but became absorbed into the Spanish-speaking community.

Thus in Cuba at the present day—Cuba with a superficies of over 44,000 square miles—there are three main elements of population: a million pure-

52. THE "BOHIO" OR HUT OF AN "INDIO" (DESCENDANT OF CUBAN ABORIGINES) IN EAST CUBA

blooded whites (mainly Spanish, but with an American, Canadian, and a French admixture not to be overlooked); half a million yellows (mixed Indian and Spanish); and over half a million negroes and negroids, the quadroon and octoroon members of which class being always eager to desert the negro camp and fuse with the yellow Cuban middle-class.[1] Gradually the three or four hundred thousand negroes or dark-skinned negroids of Cuba are segregating into a racial group apart from the whites and yellows, but a group to which it is incorrect to apply any derogatory classification as regards industry or intellect. Many Cuban negroes are wealthy citizens, dwelling in good town houses, and possessing flourishing country farms; their wives are well dressed, and their children are being well educated. Negroes or dark mulattoes are to be found in all the professions and in nearly every branch of the government

[1] There has also been a slight intermarriage with the Chinese where these people (coming from Jamaica to the extent of three or four thousand) have settled in the coast towns or along the railways.

service, notably in the police, army, post office, and public works. While the negroes are inferior in many qualifications to the pure-blood whites of Cuba, they may certainly be ranked next to them in physical efficiency and in mental vigour. They are a more potent factor in this country than the oldest section of the population, the yellow-skinned Spanish-Indian hybrid.

Yet Cuba is more a white man's country[1] than a future realm of the black man. The Cuban aristocracy and the town bourgeoisie are quite free from negro intermixture, are, in fact, very much like the population of Southern Spain. This white element has been re-enforced during recent years by a strong contingent of Spanish immigrants, numbering in 1908 185,398. These peasant settlers come mainly from Galicia, the Asturias, and the Basque provinces, and constitute a most valuable addition to Cuba's resources: for they are indefatigable workers, are sober, quiet, thrifty and moral. Wives have accompanied husbands and Spanish children are constantly raising the Cuban birth-rate. The success of these new Spanish colonists is attracting other immigrants from Spain and the Canary Islands, and if this continues for a few more years Cuba bids fair to become an independent Spanish-speaking Republic.

53. A SPANISH CUBAN

But for this movement (since 1898) Cuba had a considerable chance in the near future of developing into another Haiti or a San Domingo. The birth-rate among the "white" Cuban peasantry was low, that of the negroes high. Many families of the Spanish planting aristocracy had been ruined by the War of Independence and had retired to Spain. The negroes were brave fighters and had been the backbone of the revolt, supplying the insurgents with their stubbornest fighting force. They, in common with all Cuban citizens, without distinction of race or colour, had received the franchise under the new Republican Cuban Constitution. In an independent Cuba without outside interference the "coloured" vote would soon have amounted to a third of the total, and before long to a half, and finally have preponderated over the white element—with what effect on public order or efficiency it is difficult to say, since the Cuban negro differs in many characteristics from the dark race in the United States and in Haiti, and has not yet been sufficiently tried in positions of responsibility and public trust to have established a racial character, good or bad.

But the recent Spanish immigration has decided the balance in favour of a White Cuba, and this idea will be strengthened by the several thousand Americans and the hundreds of Canadians, Englishmen, Frenchmen, and Germans who are settling in this truly beautiful country in charge of great interests and developments of industry and commerce.[2]

[1] Few people who have not visited Cuba are aware how emphatically "white" is a considerable proportion—at least one half—of its population of 2,049,000. The people of the large and ancient town of Camagüey (for example), in Central Cuba, are entirely of white Spanish descent, and their women are justly renowned for beauty.

[2] The great landed proprietors—Spaniards in the past, now mainly Americans—dwell often in marble palaces near their sugar plantations, which recall the most sumptuous dwellings of Andalusia.

The black man who fought so bravely to establish Cuban independence from the crippling, choking régime of Nineteenth-Century Spain, runs some risk of being shouldered to one side by the rising White interests. For this reason a "party of colour" came into existence during the election period of 1908. It is under the leadership of an officer in the long War of Independence—General Morua Delgado—and will proceed to watch politics in the special interest of the negro voters.

But up to the present time the negroes of Cuba (since 1898) have had no

54. A SPANISH CUBAN WITH TWO CUBAN LADIES

subject of complaint against the Cuban or American administration of the island or against White "society." There is as yet no "colour line" in public conveyances, resorts, or places of entertainment. There have been negro mayors of towns and even negroid candidates for the government of provinces. Several members of the recently installed Cuban Government are persons tinged with negro blood.

Yet the negro is losing ground, politically and socially, and unless he is content with his present status of farmer, labourer, petty tradesman, minor employé, and domestic servant, there will arise a "colour" question here as in the United States.

At present, I repeat, there is none. Negroes and negresses travel alongside white Cubans in trains or street cars, sit next them in cafés, theatres, and churches, and the men match their birds against each other at those cock-fights which are still the most important pastime in Cuban life. The negro or negress merits this liberality of treatment on the part of White Cuba by being always well dressed, clean, and well mannered in public life. A larger proportion of the coloured people here[1] can read and write than is the case in most of the Southern States of the Union. They speak as good Spanish as do the white Cubans, and struck me as being industrious, quiet, sober, and prosperous. I noticed especially the good taste and good quality of the negro costumes in town and country. There was no overdressing, no ridiculous ostentation of patent leather boots at inappropriate seasons by the men, nor the perpetuation of the outworn horrors of European taste—chimney-pot hats and frock coats. The women seemed "just right" in their costumes—so elegant often that after studying with interest the shape and colour of the dress, one glanced with a start at the dark brown or yellow face of the wearer, surprised (unjustly enough) to find so much taste and gracefulness conjoined with the negro physiognomy. There was no blind copying of European fashions, whether or no they were suited to a person of dark skin and woolly hair; but a certain originality in the colour and cut of garments, the shape of hats and the arrangement of the *chevelure* which betokened thoughtfulness and innate good taste. If I were asked how the civilised negro and negress should dress in a warm climate I should reply "as in Cuba."

55. A CUBAN LADY OF SPANISH-FRENCH PARENTAGE

The country negroes of course clothe themselves more after the fashion of peasants—Spanish peasants: yet even here there is a self-respect, an eye for suitable colours and shapes, an appropriateness to the tasks to be performed, superior to the slovenly dress of the United States negro country-folk or the occasional nudity of the male Haitian peasant-proprietor. The children in the country (white, even, as well as black) are most sensibly allowed to run about

56. A CUBAN MULATTO

[1] Perhaps only 25 per cent are illiterate.

in warm weather with scarcely any clothes. In the towns the negro children—especially the little girls—are prettily dressed, and never in bad taste or with ostentatious finery.

Altogether, socially and materially, in Cuba the American negro appears at his best, so far as an *average* can be struck. Nowhere of course is there the intellectual development of the United States negro in his higher types: on the other hand, I did not see any real squalor, stupid barbarity, aggressive noisiness, or ill manners. The country homes seemed better and neater than

57. A NEGRO OVERSEER, CUBA

the worst class of negro habitation in the Southern States; the town dwellings might not always be sanitary, but they had about them the dignity of Spain.

The dwellings and surroundings of the Cuban negro peasantry are often attractive to the eye of a painter. An invariable feature in every household, where there is a man, is the gamecock. The Cubans, black and yellow, are passionately fond of cock-fighting, and although the Americans have tried to suppress this (they have completely done away with bull-fights), they have not succeeded. The beautiful game-fowl bred for this sport are certainly a further episode of picturesqueness in Cuban life—as are the magnificent long-horned cattle, the gaily caparisoned mules, and the barb riding-horses.

In Cuba the ever imitative negro race has acquired the pride of bearing, the good taste in dress and demeanour of the Castilian. The bad points in the negro population of Cuba are described to me by Cubans and Americans as (1) the tendency to form secret and Masonic societies which are more often than not leagues for the committing of crimes and foul practices; (2) gross immorality; (3) petty dishonesty. Their ardent love of gambling is so completely shared by their white and yellow fellow-citizens in Cuba, as also their overbearing demeanour and dishonesty when employed as petty officials, that it would be pharisaism on the part of white critics to add these charges to the list.

The country negroes of Cuba are imperfectly converted to Christianity. The Spanish branch of the Church of Rome has not taken them to its bosom

58. NEGRO TEAMSTERS, CUBA

with any cordiality since the early nineteenth century, and they are now, with real political freedom, steadily turning away from that church towards a vague and vicious heathenism—the fetishistic religions of West Africa—or, with decided moral improvement, towards the Methodism, even the Anglicanism, of the United States and Jamaica. The growing influence of Jamaica over the negroes of Cuba (Eastern Cuba, mostly) and of Haiti is so marked as to constitute almost a political factor in the future development of the Negro problem in America. Certainly the black Jamaicans who spread far and wide over the vast archipelago of the West Indies and the territories of Central America seem to be intelligent missionaries of a practical type of civilisation and enthusiastically "British."

In Haiti, the Church of Rome, as directed by a French clergy and French seminarists, is seen at its best: in the forefront of scientific research and imparting a sound education in practical matters. Here the Methodists and Baptists, or the Episcopalians of the States, make little progress in religious propaganda, and the influence of Jamaicans and Bahamans is mainly commercial. But in Cuba—perhaps also Santo Domingo—the Jamaican and the American bishops, pastors and teachers are rapidly drawing the negro population within the Protestant fold, certainly to the advantage of their moral and material value. Any religious influence which can sap and finally destroy these odious (and at their best, silly) secret societies—against which Rome has always set her face—cannot but benefit the Cuban negroes (for example). Moreover, missionary teaching—of any branch of the Christian faith—invariably breaks down racial prejudices and instils the love of a good and orderly government.

59. A CUBAN NEGRO

One direction in which Rome is losing negro adherents in Cuba and Anglo-American protestant Christianity gaining, is in the matter of marriages and baptisms. According to various informants the Roman Church in this island (as represented not only by the Spanish clergy, but by the recently established French priests whom the religious troubles of the Congregations have driven to Cuba and elsewhere) makes marriage so expensive a ceremony that Cuban negroes—or Cuban whites—prefer living in a state of concubinage to paying the fees demanded. (I asked, however, in one small town what was the minimum fee, and was told "five dollars"—£1—which does not sound very prohibitive even to a Cuban negro.) On the other hand, the Baptists, Methodists, or Episcopalians marry and baptise for nothing. The greatest attraction, however, which these younger churches offer to the negro all over America is a larger individual participation in the service. Hymn-and-psalm-singing is enormously attractive to this emotional, music-loving race. "A Jamaican Baptist came here last year with a portable organ and interested the people in his services," said an English resident to me in Eastern Cuba, "and there you see the result: the Catholic church is abandoned and shut up, while over there is the new meeting-house where the people assemble to sing hymns." In another part of Southern Cuba three thousand Cubans, mostly negroes, had gone over to American Episcopalianism, mainly owing to the genial services provided "in which they themselves could take part." I glanced at the hymns used, and noticed they were all in Spanish translations.

The white Cubans charge the negroes with still maintaining in their midst the dark Vudu or Hudu mysteries of West Africa.[1] There seems to be no doubt that the black people of Cuba (not the mulattoes) do belong to a number of secret or Masonic societies, the most widely-heard of being the NYAÑEGO; and it is possible that these confraternities or clubs are associated with immoral

60. NEGROES AT WORK IN A CUBAN SUGAR PLANTATION

purposes. They originated in a league of defence against the tyranny of the masters in the old slavery days. Several of them (as described to me) sounded as harmless as our United Order of Buffaloes. But those seeking after scientific truth should discount much that may be read on Vuduism. This supposed Dahomean or Niger Delta cult of the python or big serpent (monitor,

[1] See pp. 193-4, 196, and 253

lizard, crocodile or leopard), with which are associated frenzied dancing, mesmerism, gross immorality, cannibalism or corpse eating really exists (or existed) all over West Africa, from Sierra Leone to Tanganyika, and no doubt was introduced by Inner Congo, Niger Delta or Dahomé slaves into Haiti, Cuba, Louisiana, South Carolina, Jamaica, the Guianas and Brazil. Where Christianity of a modern type has obtained little or no influence over the negro slaves and ex-slaves, these wild dances and witchcraft persist. They are fast becoming a past phase in the life-condition of the American negro, and much

61. CUBAN NEGROES PLAYING DOMINOES DURING THEIR MIDDAY REST

of the evidence to the contrary is out of date, or is manufactured by sensation-mongers for the compilation of magazine articles.

The last vestige of noxious witchcraft lingering among the Cuban negroes is (said to be) the belief that the heart's blood or the heart of a white child will cure certain terrible diseases if consumed by the sufferer. The black practitioners who endeavour to procure this wonderful remedy are known as "Brujos" or "Brujas" (i.e. male or female sorcerers). At the time I was in Cuba (December, 1908), there were four or five negroes awaiting trial on this charge at Havana. Other cases—said to have been proved beyond a doubt—have occurred in Eastern Cuba within the last two or three years. But all these stories and charges are vague hearsay, and during the short time at my disposal I was not able to get proof of one. There is little doubt that occasionally in the low quarters of the old Spanish towns little white girls do disappear. It is too readily assumed that the negro is at fault.

I was informed by every resident or official whom I questioned that cases of negro assaults on white women were practically unknown in Cuba. On the other hand, young coloured or negro women and girls were never safe with men of their own race, that rape, or indecent assault, was the commonest charge on which negroes were arraigned. But further inquiry elicited that these attacks were generally made by young unmarried men on young unmarried women: were in fact a rough-and-ready courtship which would be more frequently followed by a formal marriage were it not that marriage fees (of State or Church?) were too high. The girl generally only brought the charge to compel the man to marry her. The Cuban courts in such instances

62. THE HOUSE OF A SPANISH SETTLER IN CUBA

are ready to waive punishment if the culprit and his victim are unmarried and are ready to go through the form of marriage in court. But it is said that many a young negro husband afterwards deserts the woman he has wronged.

Before quitting the subject of the Negro in Cuba I might perhaps give some description of the beautiful island—nearly as large as England—which would quite conceivably have become in time an independent Negro or Negroid State, but for the intervention of the American Government in 1898; an intervention which, with its results, made it possible and tempting for white emigrants to come here in such numbers as to turn the balance of potency.

In the first place—from the Negro's point of view, as well as the White man's—it ought at once to be said that not only are the Cubans of all colours greatly indebted to the courage, genius, and high-mindedness of the United States for the character and achievements of their intervention, but that the whole of Tropical America should give thanks for seven years of Twentieth-

Century Anglo-Saxondom in this island; a splendid property which Spain misunderstood and misused.

(Anglo-Saxondom, be it understood, means in the United States very often —as in modern Britain—the co-operation of Irish energy, Huguenot genius, and German-Jewish shrewdness with English courage and Scottish tenacity.)

63. A TYPICAL AMERICAN IN CUBA
Assistant on great sugar plantation

The Americans have completely extirpated Yellow Fever; have got rid of a good deal of Malaria in the same way (by draining, and by protecting dwellings against the mosquito with wire-gauze windows.) They have made the Press, speech, and literature absolutely free. Before they came the Bible in English or Spanish was contraband, and the embargo on modern literature what it was in Turkey under the Hamidian régime. They have endowed the

Cuban towns with magnificent public works, paved streets, and pure water; they have turned brigands into politicians (at any rate harmless to life), barracks into hotels, prisons into libraries, and hospitals into schools. They founded a great, secure National Bank; they established primary education on a well-equipped basis, and made education compulsory. Religion was freed from every trammel. Passports were abolished. Tourists increased from about ten per annum to a yearly thirty thousand. The beauty of the Spanish towns was not only left undisturbed, but was repaired and enhanced. The railway system under English, Canadian, and American management was extended throughout the length and breadth of the island. Good sanitation was introduced everywhere, together with up-to-date hospitals, new-style doctors and dentists, and scientifically trained nurses.[1]

64. THE ENTRANCE TO THE HARBOUR OF HAVANA, CUBA

This endowment (much of it paid for with American money) was Uncle Sam's send-off to the Cuban Republic; and it now rests with the white, yellow, and black Cubans to show that they can govern themselves in a manner suited to twentieth-century ideas and ideals.

The following extracts from my travel notes may give some idea of what a beautiful home the negro—as well as the white man—has in Cuba:—

The dominant note in the scenery is certainly struck by the royal palm (*Oreodoxa regia*). This is possibly the most beautiful and stately member of a princely order of plants. It is especially characteristic of Cuba, for although found also (sparingly) in Hispaniola and in Porto Rico, it is not native to the other Antilles or to tropical America. The stems of the royal palms are absolutely smooth, rounded like columns,

1 The other side of the medal is the much-increased cost of living which has prevailed since the American occupation. The dearness of comfortable living in Havana and most other Cuban towns is the only deterrent which can be quoted—besides the sea voyage—to explain why Cuba should not be the principal winter resort of civilised America.

and a uniform grey-white. The fronds as they wither fall off cleanly, leaving no perceptible roughness or scar; the result is that a row of royal palms looks like a colonnade of white marble pillars crowned with a copious but neatly arranged *gerbe* of glossy green fronds. The greenish—and when ripe, creamy white—blossoms (followed by small, shining, reddish fruit) grow out with prim neatness below the sheaf of fronds, just where the white marble column of the stem changes, without transition of tint, into the smooth emerald-green midribs of the ascending plumes of the fronds. Nearly every residence or even farmstead in Cuba is approached by an avenue of these palms, and although they do not precisely grow in forests, still the royal palms permeate Cuba with their stately influence, redeeming the landscapes from any meanness, even where industrialism has aimed at substituting the prosperous sameness of sugar-cane, cotton, or tobacco for the variegated colour and outline of forest, bamboo thicket, and prairie. Other noteworthy features in the landscapes of the plains and foothills are the brakes of glaucous green palmetto (*Sabal* and *Inodes*) and clumps or actual forests of two other types of tall, smooth-stemmed fan-palm, belonging to the genera *Coccothrinax* and *Thrinax*.

Huge bamboos (besides dwarf species) grow all over Cuba. The smaller bamboos of the genus *Arenaria* (similar to those of the Southern States) are obviously indigenous, as in Haiti. But a good many botanists maintain that the tall bamboos of Cuba, Haiti, and Jamaica, Trinidad, and other West Indian islands are of an introduced East Indian species. If so, this imported bamboo has spread everywhere in these lands till it has become an essential—and very beautiful—feature in the scenery.

An indigenous plant which arrests one's attention in Cuba from its striking appearance is the cycad, which grows so commonly by the roadside or at the thresholds of the cottages, no doubt planted by the natives for its handsome appearance.

Above 2000 feet (ordinarily) the Bahama pine makes its appearance, where it has not already been destroyed by reckless wood-cutting under the Spanish régime. In the Island of Pines this handsome and valuable conifer grows as low down as 500 feet altitude above sea-level.

Where the land has not been cleared for plantations, or its elevation (above 3000 or 4000 feet)[1] does not induce a temperate climate, the surface of Cuba is still clothed with dense tropical forest, in which the Cuban mahogany and ebony trees and a good many examples of the flora of Central America are met with. These forests mostly linger in East-Central and Eastern Cuba. They are being somewhat ruthlessly cut down by lumber *concessionnaires*. The Government of the Cuban Republic is not yet sufficiently awake to the importance of preserving forests in due measure for the climate and the amenities of scenery. There is a feature in the Cuban woodland which at once attracts the attention of the tourist coming from the north, and new to the American tropics, namely, the large number of aerophytic or epiphytic growths on the branches and trunks of big trees. These consist of lizard-like fig trees, which eventually strangle their host; of members of the pineapple family (*Bromeliaceæ*); of cacti, aroids, orchids, and ferns. In Cuba the commonest growth on the trees is a pretty aloe-like *Tillandsia*, with a spike of reddish-yellow buds, disappointing in that they barely open their petals. This epiphytic growth begins in the forests of the Southern States in the form of the celebrated "Spanish moss." Few people seem to be aware that this extraordinary growth is not a "moss" or a lichen, but belongs to a genus (*Tillandsia*) of the pineapple family!

The moister climate of the Antilles makes them less suited to cactus growth than the arid regions of the United States and of Mexico. Still cacti enter considerably, and picturesquely, into the scenery of Eastern Cuba, especially on sandy flats, which are the recently raised beds of former estuaries or lakes. Here the tall cacti, especially

[1] The really lofty Cuban mountains are in the south-eastern part of the island, where the Sierra Maestra range rises to 8400 feet abruptly from the sea-coast. Its appearance is majestic. Elsewhere, though the island is hilly (and the hills gave the Cuban insurgents many impregnable retreats), the altitudes seldom reach 3000 feet.

65. AN AVENUE OF ROYAL PALMS (OREODOXA REGIA) AT A CUBAN PLANTATION

of the genus *Cereus*, offer a striking parallel in appearance and rôle to the euphorbias. Like them they rise up out of the barren, sun-smitten waste, and serve as a shelter and a nucleus for other vegetation, thus in time creating oases of forest.

The rivers of Cuba, though seldom offering much facilities of navigation (except, perhaps, the case of the Rio Cauto of Eastern Cuba, which has a navigable course inland from its mouth of about forty miles for small boats), are remarkable from the point of view of scenery. Their upper courses are a succession of boiling rapids and snowy falls, as they tear down through the splendid forest of the hills and plateaus. The bed of each river (away from the alluvial plains) being usually bare limestone, the

66. CEREUS CACTI IN THE CUBAN LOWLANDS

colour of the water is a lovely greenish blue. Sometimes they flow over a long series of abrupt steps in the rocks, exactly like the formal descents of artificial cascades. When they have reached sea-level they meander through swampy forests of South American luxuriance, or create vast swamps which are jungles of reeds, rushes, and "water-hyacinths," and the home of countless herons, tree-ducks, pelicans, darters, rails, and jaçanás. The south coast of Cuba, away from the eastern prolongation, possesses more swamp lands of great extent than the northern part of the island. Zapata swamp, in the south of Cuba, is over 2000 square miles in area. This region is, or was, the breeding-ground of myriads of white herons (egrets); and here, in spite of native and American gunners, urged on a career of abomination by the misplaced taste of forty millions of unthinking American and European women, the beautiful white *Ardea egretta* is sufficiently numerous to be quite a feature in the landscape. The parrots in Cuba are becoming scarce, but the little green todies (with crimson breasts) are still as tame as robins, and the humming-birds will continue to buzz round the blossoms until they are finally extinguished by the plumage-hunters. It is supposed that Cuba possesses the smallest humming-bird in the world—*Calypte helenæ* (named after Princess Christian); but this may have a rival in tininess in a Peruvian species of *Acestrura*. The

67. A RIVER IN EASTERN CUBA

Calypte helenæ is an exquisite little creature not quite 2½ inches long with a forked crimson gorget. Its nearest relations are in Southern California.

No one visiting the forests of Eastern Cuba can readily forget his first sight of the trogon peculiar to Cuba—the *Prionotelus temnurus*. It is not difficult to watch it at close quarters in its favourite resorts, sitting on a bough with upturned head, displaying its white shirt-front and gorgeous crimson scarlet stomach, and uttering at intervals a low and singularly musical cry. The Cubans call it tocoloro.

Other prominent birds in the Cuban landscapes are the bold *Polyborus* hawks (*P. cheriway*) stalking about after their prey like the African secretary bird (the *Polyborus* type is not found in Hispaniola or Jamaica, and possibly reached Cuba from Florida); the prettily coloured kestrels (found also in Hispaniola) of vivid orange-chestnut, dove-grey, and black barrings; the very numerous black cuckoos (*Crotophaga*) with parrot beaks; and the Turkey buzzards (*Cathartes aura*). These last are only found in Cuba, the Bahamas, and Jamaica; not in Hispaniola.

In Cuba, as in Hispaniola, the domestic pig has run wild, and developed into a lean long-legged, miniature wild-boar. The forests, moreover, of Cuba and of Haiti are full of deer. These I found to be simply roebuck, with, in the male, rather fine antlers. The history of this introduction is that the French first of all brought the roe from France to Martinique; then, as they throve there, the roe deer were carried on to Haiti and San Domingo, whence the French refugees in 1794 brought them to Cuba.

68. THE PAVEMENT OF CUBAN STREETS BEFORE THE UNITED STATES CAME ON THE SCENE

Cuba, Hispaniola (Haiti), Porto Rico, and Jamaica (besides the Bahamas, Virgin Islands, the northern Leeward Islands and Barbados) are entirely without poisonous snakes. In the swamps and river estuaries of Cuba there are two species of harmless crocodile—*C. rhombifer* (peculiar to Cuba) and the widespread *C. americanus* (*acutus*). There is no alligator.

Not one of the old Spanish towns of Cuba but is a source of inspiration to a painter. No towns in Spain are more "Spanish" or more picturesque, with their narrow streets, projecting balconies screened by carved wood or iron grilles, tiled roofs, thick walls, *patios* glowing with sunlit vegetation, their sixteenth and seventeenth century cathedrals, churches, chapels, monasteries, and convents. The steeples and doorways of some of these churches (and of a good many Cuban buildings generally) almost suggest the Moorish influence in architecture which prevailed in Southern Spain down to the period of Columbus's voyage. Several of the ecclesiastical buildings still contain magnificent altar-pieces and shrines of hammered silver.

69. "SINCE THE AMERICANS CAME"

A street in a Cuban town beautifully paved and asphalted, drained, yet more picturesque than before

In Santiago, the eastern capital of Cuba, and now one of the most beautiful places in the world, the solidly constructed houses (the Spaniards, among many great qualities, had that of building appropriately and permanently) were painted in tempera almost every attainable tint, combined with white copings, window-frames, doorways, parapets, and skirtings. One house is ultramarine-blue (and white), another dull mauve (and white), or pale green, maize-yellow, pink, terra-cotta, sky-blue, greenish blue, apricot, grey-brown. The effect, combined with the fronds of palm trees and bananas, the dense foliage of figs, evergreen oaks, mimosas, orange trees, and giant laurels, the brilliant flowers of bushes and creepers, the brown-red tiled roofs, the marble seats and monuments, the graceful balconies, the white stone colonnades, the blue waters of the harbour, and the magnificent encircling mountains, is daring, but eminently successful. One might undergo at Santiago de

70. A PORTION OF THE GREAT ESPLANADE OF WESTERN HAVANA
One of the most splendid and healthful public works executed by the Americans

Cuba a colour cure for melancholia. But in pre-American days the streets were utterly neglected and the drains stank (as was also the case in all other Cuban towns). There was either a pavement of rough cobble-stones, with a filthy-smelling gutter on either side, or there was no pavement at all—merely the dust, mud, and rock of the pristine pathway. The city was almost impassable for carriages; rough carts groaned and rattled over its uneven surfaces.

The Americans, represented by a deputy or provisional governor, changed all that. The steep streets were asphalted, tram lines were laid along the principal thoroughfares, and neat side-walks of stone or brick were constructed, while at the same time a modern system of drainage was created. The cool grey or white of the asphalt, stone, or encaustic brick is an admirable accompaniment to the riot of colour above and around; the town is odourless, save for the scent of flowers, and its streets are accessible to all types of carriages; while poor people can for five cents travel this way and that, across the town and out into the country in pretty little electric tramcars proportioned and painted to suit the narrow streets and gay colours of this fairy-tale city.[1]

[1] Before quitting the subject of Cuba, I should like to acknowledge here the information and hospitality I received from Mr. Theodore Brooks, British Vice-Consul at Guantánamo.

CHAPTER V

SLAVERY UNDER THE PORTUGUESE: BRAZIL

ALTHOUGH the Portuguese may have slightly forestalled the Spaniards in bringing Negroes from Africa to work in Europe, the Spaniards were the first to transport negroes as a labour force to America. The Portuguese discovered Brazil[1] in the last year of the fifteenth century, but it was not until 1531 that they began to turn their discovery to any account.

71. THE COAST OF BRAZIL

[1] It was a dye-wood which gave a permanent name to the country of Brasil. Apparently pieces of "Brasil-wood" (from Leguminous trees of the genera *Cæsalpinia* and *Peltophorum*) carried by the Gulf Stream had been washed up on the shores of Western Europe, and the deep red colour of the wood was thought to resemble the glow of embers, and therefore derived from some Romance dialect the name of *Brasil*. This wood was called by the Portuguese, *Pao Brases*, and they had no sooner discovered the coast of Brazil and named it "The New Land of the True Cross" than they made acquaintance with the forests of *Cæsalpinia* and *Peltephorum* trees and sent a cargo of billets of this timber (yielding a crimson; scarlet dye) from Pernambuco to Lisbon as early as 1515. The wood was then called "Fernambuc" (which was the old name of Pernambuco), but soon afterwards it resumed in commerce its old European name of "Brasil-wood," and the country which produced it in such quantities was known as *A Terra do Brazil*.

During the remainder of the sixteenth century they utilised the indigenous Amerindians almost entirely in working these territories, which were at that period confined to the coastal region and the shores of the great eastern affluents of the Rio de la Plata. Some of the earliest arrivals among the Portuguese adventurers mingled with the Indians in patriarchal[1] fashion, and their descendants, together with the well-disposed Amerindians and the fairly numerous Portuguese immigrants, sufficed during the first hundred years of Brazilian history to till the soil.

Sugar was introduced into Eastern Brazil about 1540.[2] The oldest centre of continuous Portuguese colonisation, however, is São Paulo, in the south. Two European nations attempted to dispute the possession of Brazil with the Portuguese, in defiance of the Pope's mandate: the French (chiefly at first the Huguenot section of that nation) and the Dutch. The town of Rio de Janeiro was actually founded by French Huguenots in 1558, though captured by the Portuguese in 1567. But these foreign attacks on the rapid growth of Portuguese colonisation did not take much effect until Portugal and her possessions became in 1578 part of the Spanish Empire. Then the nations of North-Western Europe saw alike an opportunity to gratify their hatred of Spain and their longing for a share of, or at least a foothold in, the wonderful New World, so jealously closed against their commerce and enterprise by the two kingdoms of the Iberian peninsula. The Dutch attempted to settle in Guiana—the debatable land between Spanish and Portuguese America—as early as 1585; from 1612 the French and from 1624 the Dutch made determined efforts to establish plantation colonies in North-Eastern Brazil, and began to introduce negroes from West Africa to assist them; for they were received with hostility by

[1] The story of "Caramarú," the noble Portuguese who was shipwrecked near Bahia, adopted by the Tupinamba Indians, elected to be their chief, and who by his numerous native wives created a whole clan of vigorous half-castes, is typical of the early relations between the Portuguese and the indigenes of Brazil: a much happier section of American history than the Spanish dealings with the Antilles and Peru. Great credit is, however, due to the Jesuit missionaries of the sixteenth and seventeenth centuries, who intervened most masterfully to save the native tribes of Brazil from unjust treatment at the hands of the incoming Europeans.

[2] According to Mons. L. E. Moreau de Saint-Méry [who in his work on Saint Domingue (1796) quotes Herrera], the Sugar-cane was first introduced into America by a Spaniard named Aguilon, in 1505. He brought it from the Canary Islands and planted it in Hispaniola. Another Spaniard, a surgeon named Vellosa, applied himself assiduously to the cultivation of the cane introduced by Aguilon, and by 1530 there were at least twenty prosperous sugar-mills at work in the eastern half of Hispaniola. The Portuguese brought the sugar-cane from Madeira to Brazil about 1540, and thence it spread northwards to the Guiana settlements. From Hispaniola it was borne to Jamaica (about 1570). Its culture was pursued with some vigour during the greater part of the sixteenth century; then it languished. But cacao or chocolate was coming into favour as a drink and confectionery getting more and more popular in Europe. Coffee beginning to be used in 1640 further increased the demand for sugar, so that from the year 1640, more or less, arose a renewed interest in cane cultivation in tropical America—the "Sugar Age" commenced which was to enhance enormously the value of the West Indies, Guiana, and Brazil, and also increase a hundredfold the need for Negro slaves. The sugar-cane was brought from Brazil to Barbados in 1641, from Guiana to Martinique and Guadeloupe in 1644, the French settlements in Haiti in 1640 (?), and was reintroduced into Jamaica from Guiana in 1675.

Humboldt at the close of the eighteenth century distinguished three varieties of sugar-cane in cultivation in tropical America: (1) the "Créole" cane, with deep green leaves, brought originally from India to Sicily and Spain and thence to Madeira, the Canary Islands, Hispaniola, Brazil, and Guiana; (2) the "Otaheite" cane with light green leaves, brought from the Pacific to Mauritius and thence to Cayenne and Martinique; (3) the Batavia cane with purplish-green, broad leaves, introduced from Java into Guiana by the Dutch and thence spread over Venezuela and the Antilles for its rum-producing qualities. Of all these varieties he considered the Otaheite the most valuable, as it produced more juice than the others and its refuse made better fuel.

The edible *Banana* or plantain (*Musa sapientum*) was likewise introduced from the Canary Islands to Hispaniola (thence to Brazil, etc.) by the Spaniards early in the sixteenth century.

the Amerindians, who sided with the Portuguese.[1] In spite, however, of the opposition offered by indigenes and Portuguese settlers, the Dutch managed to secure a hold over the north-east coast of Brazil which lasted until 1654, and in 1637–41 captured from the Portuguese several footholds on the west coast of Africa and a portion of the colony of Angola. Their slave-trade with North-Eastern Brazil probably introduced the first negroes into that region.

The Portuguese, when they replaced the Dutch in Brazil, took over such of their negro slaves as had not escaped to the bush and mingled with the wild Indians. They, the Portuguese, had not ceased to be slave-traders since they brought negroes from the Moorish coast and Senegal River to Portugal and Spain in the middle fifteenth century; but hitherto they had chiefly purveyed them in small numbers to the Spanish Antilles,[2] themselves preferring in Brazil the labour of Amerindians or of Portuguese immigrants—genuine colonists. But after the recovery of Portuguese independence and the expulsion of the foreign settlers, the cultivation of sugar, begun by the French and Dutch, was taken up with vigour; and Negro slaves (better suited to this work than Amerindians) were brought over in large numbers from Angola and the Congo, from Dahomé, Lagos, and Old Calabar.

73. THE ANGOLAN ELEMENT IN THE BRAZILIAN NEGRO POPULATION

The left-hand figure illustrates the Kongo type; the right hand, the fine-featured Holo people of the Angola hinterland

But it was not till about 1720–30 that the great importation of negroes into Brazil began. This was occasioned by the discovery of diamonds and the eagerness to work the gold-mines of Minas Geraes (South-East Brazil).

At this time the seaboard towns of Brazil between Pernambuco on the north and Santos on the south became swollen with a slave population, as well

[1] In fact the "Indians" and the Portuguese-Indian half-castes materially assisted to expel the Dutch from Bahia in 1625.

[2] In 1600 the Portuguese governor of Angola undertook the "Asiento" or contract for supplying slaves to the Spanish Indies. The adventures of Andrew Battell, given in *Purchas: His Pilgrimes*, published in 1625 (book VII. p. 983), throw a very interesting light on the early Portuguese slave-trade in Angola. Battell was an Essex fisherman who, seized with a love of adventure so common at the commencement of Elizabeth's reign, shipped in some British vessel making a daring voyage to the Forbidden New World, and got shipwrecked on the coast of Brazil somewhere about 1580. (There is a great discrepancy in dates and geographical points in Purchas's narrative, suggesting misunderstanding and printer's errors; but I think Battell's story substantially true, and that he wandered in South-West Africa between 1589 and 1606.) Battell was rescued from the Brazilian Indians by the Portuguese, but only to be held a prisoner on their ships so that he might not reveal the secrets of Brazilian geography to his fellow-countrymen. He was taken over to Angola and eventually left as hostage among the savages, with whom he lived for years. At last he again reached the coast (perhaps near the Congo mouth), and another slaving ship enabled him to get back to England after moving adventures. He accompanied the Portuguese seamen in an extraordinary journey they made in the Benguela country with the Jaga (Giaga) marauding tribe. These dreaded "Jagas" (Jaga was the title of their leaders) were probably the modern Ba-jok, or Ba-kioko, now living on the Upper Kwango River. Assisted by the Portuguese, they ravaged the Benguela district, bringing the captives whom they did not eat to sell as slaves to the Portuguese ship, which ever and again would pass over to America, land her cargo of negroes, and return for more.

as the mining settlements of Minas Geraes. The majority of the people of Rio de Janeiro (the capital) were negroes at the beginning of the nineteenth century, and that race is still almost predominant in the suburbs of the capital city.

The Slave-trade was theoretically abolished by Portugal, *north* of the Equator, in 1815 (south of the Equator it was to continue till 1830); Brazil took the same measures in 1826, and declared the trade piracy in 1830. Nevertheless, it was during the second quarter of the nineteenth century that negroes were most numerously imported into Brazil—as many as 1,350,000, it has been

74. BRAZILIAN NEGRO WORKERS IN DIAMOND-MINING EXCAVATIONS
Lençóes district, Eastern Brazil

computed, and this in spite of the activity of British and French cruisers. The British Government by the Convention of 1826 had the right of inspecting suspicious ships in Brazilian waters, and of condemning them if found to contain slaves fresh from Africa. But the local authorities (though not the Imperial Brazilian Government) winked at and even encouraged the traffic until after 1850. The slaves recruited for Brazil during the nineteenth century came almost entirely from the Lower Congo, Dahomé (Whydah, where there grew up quite a Brazilian colony), Lagos, Bonny, and Old Calabar. The Lagos slaves were of the Yoruba, Egba, Jekri, and Sobo (Benin) tribes, but also included people from the Central Niger and Hausaland. A few (but influential) negroes came from Portuguese Guinea, and were mostly of the Mandingo or "Malé" stock.

Some of the Africans introduced into Brazil during the first quarter of the nineteenth century were of splendid physique. They are described by English travellers as being the most vigorous and athletic-looking persons that it is possible to contemplate, models for a Farnesian Hercules, with muscular frames hardened and improved by exercise, magnificent pictures of strength and activity, and as such strongly in contrast to the flabby Brazilians of Portuguese descent, who at that period looked the very personification of indolence and inactivity. The best-looking slaves at that time were said to come from the Gaboon and Angola, and the ugliest from Moçambique (the Portuguese seem even to have introduced Hottentots and Bushmen, obtained probably from the region south of the Kunene River). A considerable number of slaves seem to have come from the Upper Congo above Stanley Pool. They were classed as Anzico, the old Portuguese name for the Bateke people, who were the intermediaries generally in passing on the immense supply of slaves from the Upper Congo to the coast regions.

75. NEGRO TYPE FROM UPPER CONGO (BANGALA)

Judged by the extent of time and space covered by their operations the Portuguese were perhaps the greatest of all slave-trading nations. But the effect of their commerce in negroes was not entirely evil, so far as Africa was concerned. It introduced to the innermost parts of the Congo basin, as well as through almost all West Africa from Mossamedes on the south to the Senegal on the north, much wealth in brass and silver, guns and gunpowder [with which the natives could successfully overcome the ravages of wild beasts and procure supplies of ivory for their own enrichment], large supplies of distilled spirits [harmful, indeed, but provocative of energy], many industries and arts in weaving cloth, carving ivory, casting and working metals. The bronze art of Benin is almost entirely due to the inspiration of the Portuguese (who visited that country mainly for the trade in slaves), also the designing of pottery (especially in the southern basin of the Congo), and many other arts and industries which have distinctly raised the level of the Western negro's culture. Then as regards food-stuffs, the Portuguese slave-trade has indeed enriched negro Africa. The Portuguese slave-traders brought with them to the west coast (as also to the east) the sugar-cane, sweet potato, onion, tobacco plant, maize, pineapples, tomatoes, Chili peppers, guavas, wheat, rice, manioc, the domestic pig, the Muscovy duck, and European cattle. These introductions were repeatedly made with the deliberate object of arresting famines such as in the historical period have devastated Africa to a degree scarcely realised by European historians, whole tribes disappearing every now and then when a failure of the rains, a blight, or a disease has killed their indigenous food crops or driven away the wild game. Undoubtedly the influence of the Portuguese—attracted to Africa mainly as a source of labour supply for Portuguese America—wrought some surprising movements all along the coast regions of West Africa and in the southern basin of the Congo, by which organised kingdoms arose which created or stimulated commerce, and which in their general effects on the people were perhaps less drearily horrible than the anarchy of cannibal savages.

In the dim recesses of the Congo basin, naked savages began to realise that there was a world outside their encircling ring of gorilla-haunted forests, a world which would barter for war-captives or social derelicts beads, brass, iron wire, guns, gunpowder, bells, scarlet cloth, and rum. Hitherto they had made war for gluttony, to obtain victims for their cannibal feasts; now they started forth in their war-canoes to raid for slaves which might be bartered for trade goods with the intermediary tribes at Stanley Pool or on the River Kwango.

The wars between one native tribe and another, which were carried on for the ultimate purpose of supplying slaves for America, had existed previously (though not on such a large scale). Eunuchs, concubines, and servants were required for the Moslems (the Eastern Slave-trade) and victims for the human sacrifices and cannibal feasts of bloody West Africa (Ashanti, Dahomé, Benin, and the Lower Niger, Western Congoland, and the empire of the Mwata Yanvo; Liberia of olden times, the Ivory Coast, Southern Nigeria, the Cameroons, and the inner basin of the Congo). So far as the sum of human misery in Africa was concerned, it is probable that the trade in slaves between that continent and America scarcely added to it. It even to some extent mitigated the suffering of the negro in his own home; for once this trade was set on foot and it was profitable to sell a human being, many a man, woman, or child who might otherwise have been killed for mere caprice, or for the love of seeing blood flow, or as a toothsome ingredient of a banquet, was sold to a slave-trader. Criminals who would have been executed for serious or for trivial offences were spared for the same purpose.

76. A BAHIAN NEGRO
Probably from Lagos, West Africa

But it was in the sea transit to America under conditions several times referred to in this book, and in the after treatment of the slave when he or she reached the New World, that the unpardonable cruelty occurred.

Portugal (after preliminary restrictions in 1815 and 1823) abolished the Slave-trade in Portuguese African possessions from 1830 onwards, and received as a solatium a sum of £300,000 from Great Britain. In 1836 it was forbidden to export a slave anywhere from a Portuguese colony. But the actual *status* of *Slavery* was not abolished in Portuguese Africa until 1878. As a matter of fact, the export of slaves from Portuguese East Africa did not really come to an end until the Federal power got the upper hand of the Confederate South in the United States in 1863; and from Portuguese Guinea, Dahomé, and Angola, until Brazil abolished slavery in 1888. Even after that date a modified form of slave-trade has continued in the Angolan interior to supply the cacao plantations of São Thomé.

The first Emperor of Brazil as early as 1814 drew up regulations to alleviate the sufferings of the negroes in their passage from the coast of Africa, by enforcing far more commodious space for them and better provisions on the slave-ships; but it is to be feared that later on in the nineteenth century these regulations were but little observed, after the commerce had become contraband, for here is a description of a Brazilian slave-ship seen in the year 1829 by the Rev. R. Walsh (*Notices of Brazil in 1828 and 1829*, London, 1830).[1]

77. AN OLD BRAZILIAN EX-SLAVE, BAHIA

"The first object that struck us was an enormous gun, turning on a swivel, on deck, the constant appendage of a pirate; and the next were large kettles for cooking, on the bows, the usual apparatus of a slaver. Our boat was now hoisted out, and I went on board with the officers. When we mounted her decks, we found her full of slaves. She was called the *Veloz*, commanded by Captain José Barbosa, bound to Bahia. She was a very broad-decked ship, with a mainmast, schooner-rigged, and behind her foremast was that large formidable gun, which turned on a broad circle of iron on deck, and which enabled her to act as a pirate, if her slaving speculation had failed. She had taken in, on the coast of Africa, 336 males and 226 females, making in all 562, and had been out seventeen days, during which she had thrown overboard fifty-five. The slaves were all enclosed under grated hatchways, between-decks. The space was so low that they sat between each other's legs, and stowed so close together that there was no possibility of their lying down, or at all changing their position, by night or day. As they belonged to and were shipped on account of different individuals, they were all branded, like sheep, with the owners' marks of different forms. . . . These were impressed under their breasts, or on their arms, and, as the mate informed me, with perfect indifference, 'queimados pelo ferro quento'—burnt with a red-hot iron. Over the hatchway stood a ferocious-looking fellow, with a scourge of many twisted thongs in his hand, who was the slave-driver of the ship. Whenever he heard the slightest noise below, he shook the whip over them, and seemed eager to exercise it. I was quite

[1] The Rev. R. Walsh, LL.D., whose *Notices of Brazil* is a classic, was a man quite remarkable for his scholarship and breadth of view. He accompanied the British Minister to Brazil as chaplain and tutor to his family. Walsh was on board a King's ship at the time; and as the slaves came mainly from Dahomé the captain of the man-of-war wished to arrest the slaver and set the slaves free at Sierra Leone. Unfortunately the Portuguese captain of the ship showed that he had come last from Kabinda, *south* of the line, a region not yet excluded from a permissible sphere of slave-trading of the Anglo-Portuguese Convention: so the poor wretches passed on to their doom.

pleased to take this hateful badge out of his hand, and I have kept it ever since, as a horrid memorial of reality, should I ever be disposed to forget the scene I witnessed.

"As soon as the poor creatures saw us looking down at them, their dark and melancholy visages brightened up. They perceived something of sympathy and kindness in our looks, which they had not been accustomed to, and, feeling instinctively that we were friends, they immediately began to shout and clap their hands. One or two had picked up a few Portuguese words and cried out, 'Viva! viva!' The women were particularly excited. They all held up their arms, and when we bent down and shook hands with them they could not contain their delight; they endeavoured to scramble upon their knees, stretching up to kiss our hands, and we understood that they knew we were come to liberate them. Some, however, hung down their heads in apparently hopeless dejection; some were greatly emaciated, and some, particularly children, seemed dying.

78 A NEGRESS (OF ANGOLA ORIGIN), EASTERN BRAZIL

"But the circumstance which struck us most forcibly was, how it was possible for such a number of human beings to exist, packed up and wedged together as tight as they could cram, in low cells, 3 feet high, the greater part of which, except that immediately under the grated hatchways, was shut out from light or air, and this when the thermometer, exposed to the open sky, was standing in the shade, on our deck, at 89 degrees. The space between-decks was divided into two compartments 3 feet 3 inches high; the size of one was 16 by 18 feet, and of the other 40 by 21 feet; into the first were crammed the women and girls; into the second, the men and boys: 226 fellow-creatures were thus thrust into one space 288 feet square; and 336 into another space 800 feet square, giving to the whole an average of 23 inches, and to each of the women not more than 13 inches, though many of them were pregnant. We also found manacles and fetters of different kinds, but it appears that they had all been taken off before we boarded.

"The heat of these horrid places was so great, and the odour so offensive, that it was quite impossible to enter them, even had there been room. They were measured as above when the slaves had left them. The officers insisted that the poor suffering creatures should be admitted on deck to get air and water. This was opposed by the mate of the slaver, who, from a feeling that they deserved it, declared they would murder them all. The officers, however, persisted, and the poor beings were all turned up together. It is impossible to conceive the effect of this eruption—517 fellow-creatures of all ages and sexes, some children, some adults, some old men and women, all in a state of total nudity, scrambling out together to taste the luxury of a little fresh air and water. They came swarming up, like bees from the aperture of a hive, till the whole deck was crowded to suffocation, from stem to stern; so that it was impossible to imagine where they could all have come from, or how they could have been stowed away. On looking into the places where they had been crammed, there were found some children next the sides of the ship, in the places most remote from light and air; they were lying nearly in a torpid state, after the rest had turned out. The little creatures seemed indifferent as to life or death, and when they were carried on deck, many of them could not stand.

"After enjoying for a short time the unusual luxury of air, some water was brought; it was then that the extent of their sufferings was exposed in a fearful manner. They all rushed like maniacs towards it. No entreaties, or threats, or blows, could restrain them; they shrieked, and struggled, and fought with one another, for a drop of this precious liquid, as if they grew rabid at the sight of it."

Out of this slaving ship during the first seventeen days of their voyage fifty-five slaves, dying or dead from dysentery, had been thrown overboard. Though there was a large stock of medicines displayed in the cabin with a manuscript book containing directions how they should be used, the so-called doctor on board was a negro who was unable to read! On many of these slave-ships the sense of misery and suffocation was so terrible in the 'tween-decks—where the height sometimes was only eighteen inches, so that the unfortunate slaves could not turn round, were wedged immovably, in fact, and chained to the deck by the neck and legs—that the slaves not infrequently would go mad before dying of suffocation. In their frenzy some killed others in the hopes of procuring more room to breathe. "Men strangled those next to them, and women drove nails into each other's brains."[1]

As long as the slave-trade was recognised in Brazil the Imperial Government derived from it a revenue of about one million sterling per annum, the town of Rio de Janeiro alone producing £240,000 per annum. For every slave landed in Brazil there was levied about £8 in duties, imperial or municipal. When the slave-trade was ostensibly abolished in 1830, this revenue was sacrificed.

When a cargo of slaves arrived in Brazil it was usually purchased by a class of people called "ciganos" or gipsies, and who seem to have been actually of gipsy origin, with dark olive complexions, black eyes and hair, and a rather sinister expression of countenance. It is supposed that they descend from the gipsies who were expelled from Portugal in the seventeenth century and despatched to Brazil. Dr. Walsh gives the following description of a cigano slave-driver:—

He was a tall, cadaverous, tawny man, with a shock of black hair hanging about his sharp but determined-looking visage. He was dressed in a blue jacket and pantaloons, with buff boots hanging loose about his legs, ornamented with large silver spurs. On his head he wore a capacious straw hat, bound with a broad ribbon, and in his hand was a long whip, with two thongs; he shook this over his drove, and they all arranged themselves for examination, some of them, particularly the children, trembling like aspen leaves.

[1] What the survivors may have looked like when they were landed at their destined port, Bahia, may be surmised from this description of Captain Stedman's (written in 1798):—

"They were a drove of newly imported negroes, men and women, with a few children, who were just landed from on board a Guinea ship, to be sold as slaves. The whole party was such a set of scarcely animated automatons, such a resurrection of skin and bones as forcibly reminded me of the last trumpet. These objects appeared at that moment to be risen from the grave or escaped from Surgeons' Hall; and I confess I can give no better description of them than by comparing them to walking skeletons covered over with a piece of tanned leather." (From J. G. Stedman's *Surinam*.) These words, though applying to Guiana, north of Brazil, and to an earlier date than 1829, almost exactly summarise the scattered references to the condition of recently landed slaves at Brazilian ports in the works of English and German authors between 1820 and 1848. Much the same description is given by Bryan Edwards of slaves just landed in Jamaica. But the recuperative power of the Negro is extraordinary, and after ten days' or a fortnight's good feeding many of these physical wrecks were in prime condition for the slave-market.

At the sales of slaves conducted by the ciganos in huge warehouses usually near the sea-shore, the negroes and negresses were exposed for sale, nude or nearly nude. They were handled by intending purchasers—Brazilian men or women—without the slightest regard for decency or delicacy, exactly as though they were animals being purchased for their physical qualities. According to the Rev. R. Walsh, it was quite a fashionable thing for white Brazilian ladies in the early part of the nineteenth century to go shopping for slaves just as an Englishwoman might visit Bond Street. The elder slaves were usually allowed to sit on benches while the young ones squatted on the floor.

I was particularly attracted by a group of children, one of whom, a young girl, had something very pensive and engaging in her countenance. The ciganos observing me look at her, whipped her up with a long rod, and bade her with a rough voice to come forward. It was quite affecting to see the poor, timid, shrinking child standing before me, in a state the most helpless and forlorn, that ever a being, endued, like myself, with a reasonable mind and an immortal soul, could be reduced to. Some of these girls have remarkably sweet and engaging countenances. Notwithstanding their dusky hue, they look so modest, gentle, and sensible, that you could not for a moment hesitate to acknowledge that they are endowed with a like feeling and a common nature with your own daughters. The seller was about to put the child into all the attitudes, and display her person in the same way, as he would a man; but I declined the exhibition, and she shrunk timidly back to her place, and seemed glad to hide herself in the group that surrounded her.

The men were generally less interesting objects than the women; their countenances and hues were very varied, according to the part of the African coast from which they came; some were soot-black, having a certain ferocity of aspect that indicated strong and fierce passions, like men who were darkly brooding over some deep-felt wrongs and meditating revenge. When any one was ordered, he came forward with a sullen indifference, threw his arms over his head, stamped with his feet, shouted to show the soundness of his lungs, ran up and down the room, and was treated exactly like a horse, put through his paces at a repository; and when done, he was whipped to his stall.

The heads of the slaves, both male and female, were generally half shaved; the hair being left only on the fore part. A few of the females had cotton handkerchiefs tied round their heads, which, with some little ornaments of native seeds or shells, gave them a very engaging appearance. A number, particularly the males, were affected with eruptions of a white scurf, which had a loathsome appearance, like a leprosy. It was considered, however, a wholesome effort of nature, to throw off the effects of the salt provisions used during the voyage; and, in fact, it resembles a saline concretion.

Many of them were lying stretched on the bare boards; and among the rest, mothers with young children at their breasts, of which they seemed passionately fond. They were all doomed to remain on the spot, like sheep in a pen, till they were sold; they had no apartment to retire to, no bed to repose on, no cover to protect them; they sit naked all day, and lie naked all night, on the bare boards, or benches, where we saw them exhibited.

A sale of slaves at a country village is thus described by Walsh (writing in 1828). The cigano driver has gone round arousing buyers and inviting them to the market outside the village inn.

The slaves, both men and women, were walked about, and put into different paces, then handled and felt exactly as I have seen butchers feel a calf. He occasionally lashed them and made them jump to show that their limbs were supple, and caused them to shriek and cry, that the purchasers might perceive their lungs were sound.

Among the company at the market was a Brazilian lady, who exhibited a regular model of her class in the country. She had on a round felt hat like an Englishman's, and under it a turban, which covered her head as a night-cap. Though it was a burning day, she was wrapped up in a large scarlet woollen cloak, which, however, she drew up so high as to show us her embroidered shoes and silk stockings; she was attended by a black slave, who held an umbrella over her head, and she walked for a considerable time deliberately through the slaves, looking as if she was proudly contrasting her own importance with their misery.

These are Dr. Walsh's first impressions of the Negro in Brazil:—

I had been but a few hours on shore, for the first time, and I saw an African negro under four aspects of society; and it appeared to me that in every one his character depended on the state in which he was placed and the estimation in which he was held. As a despised slave, he was far lower than other animals of burthen that surrounded him, more miserable in his look, more revolting in his nakedness, more distorted in his person, and apparently more deficient in intellect than the horses and mules that passed him by. Advanced to the grade of a soldier, he was clean and neat in his person, amenable to discipline, expert at his exercises, and showed the port and being of a white man similarly placed. As a citizen, he was remarkable for the respectability of his appearance and the decorum of his manners in the rank assigned to him; and as a priest, standing in the house of God, appointed to instruct society on their most important interests, and in a grade in which moral and intellectual fitness is required, and a certain degree of superiority is expected, he seemed even more devout in his orations and more correct in his manners than his white associates. I came, therefore, to the irresistible conclusion in my mind that colour was an accident affecting the surface of a man, and having no more to do with his qualities than his clothes, that God had equally created an African in the image of His person, and equally given him an immortal soul, and that an European had no pretext but his own cupidity for impiously thrusting his fellow-man from that rank in the creation which the Almighty had assigned him, and degrading him below the lot of the brute beasts that perish.

As regards their general treatment of the negro slave, male or female, the Portuguese and Brazilians *by no means* occupy a bad position in the scale of international morality. On the contrary, they rival the Spaniards for the first place in the list of humane slave-holding nations, and even in Africa their treatment of their slaves (or slave-like apprentices of more recent date) was far less cruel than that of the Dutch, the British, or the French. Slavery under the flag of Portugal (or Brazil) or of Spain was *not* a condition without hope, a life in hell, as it was for the most part in the British West Indies and, above all, Dutch Guiana and the Southern United States.

Towards the close of the eighteenth century an official Protector of slaves was instituted in most of the great centres of slave labour in Brazil to intervene between bad masters and ill-treated slaves. But the most substantial hope of all for the Brazilian slave, as for the Spanish (prior to the nineteenth century), was that at any time *he could purchase his own freedom*. At all times, from the sixteenth to the nineteenth century, the slave in Brazil could compel his master by law to liberate him if he or she could repay to the purchaser the sum of the original purchase price. And in Brazil a slave (male or female) who was the parent of ten children could *demand* his or her freedom.

As to the means of getting money for this purpose, the law obliged a slave-owner or overseer to give liberty to his slaves on all public and ecclesiatical holidays, together with all Sundays. This meant, including Sundays, eighty-five days out of the year of 365. On such days the slave was not forbidden to work (as he was by characteristic Anglo-Saxon hypocrisy in British and British-

American slavedom), but might hire his labour to whom he chose, or go hunting, fishing, and money-making on his own account. When the slave had by great industry amassed sufficient *milreis*, he would not only purchase his own freedom, but next set up as a slave-owner on his own account! Slaves who had grown wealthy and had succeeded in freeing themselves would often invest their further savings in the slave-trade and send money to West Africa to purchase slaves to be forwarded to them in Brazil, or even, if they were very rich, send funds, arms, and trade-goods to African connections of potency, and by these means get up raids in their old homes or amongst neighbouring tribes to supply the Brazilian slave-market; for the Negro is scarcely yet altruistic. At no time until quite recently was he particularly shocked at the slave-trade and slavery as it affected other people. He might be broken-hearted on his own account, or on that of his wife, mother, brother, sister, or child, but cared not the least about the abstract right or wrong in this traffic or the sufferings of other negroes not related to him.

Of course this indifference on his part was no excuse for the better-educated white man, any more than because a person might have a depraved taste for spirits it would palliate his being urged by example to dipsomania.

Various writers on Brazil between 1820 and 1850 relate instances of Portuguese masters or mistresses whipping their slaves to death. But these cases seem to have been rare, and the facility with which negroes could escape into the woods and live with the aborigines or by themselves (subsisting on wild produce) must have restrained slave-owners from driving their slaves to desperation.

When a slave ran away and was recaptured, or returned of his or her own accord, it was usual to invoke the intercession of some local personage of rank or standing, who became the *padrinho* or sponsor of the slave, and usually intervened to prevent excessive punishment.

Flogging with a whip or lithe cane was not so common a punishment in Brazil as in the other slave-holding countries. And in most cases where "flogging" is alluded to by English writers the use of the *palmatorio* is really meant. This is a curious-looking instrument, like a battledore in shape, or a large lemon-squeezer with a long handle. Its oval, thick, flat "business" end is pierced with round holes. The palms of the hands (or the soles of the feet) are slapped with the *palmatorio* and the suffering to the hands is said to be frightful. That may be so; but apparently the power of using the hands is soon recovered and the *body* of the slave remains uninjured and unscarred.

The Jesuits, before they were expelled from Brazil (and expelled for being so very solicitous about the treatment of the Amerindian aborigines and the negro), did much to raise the condition of their black wards, especially in religion. In Brazil the Roman Catholic Church (as in Haiti, only more so) showed a rarely modern attitude towards the negro. Even as early as the eighteenth century there were not only black clergy, but even black bishops. And in Brazil the *negro* clergy seem from the end of the eighteenth century onwards to have been more reverent, better living, more earnest than the Portuguese clergy, and it is a question whether this distinction does not still exist.

Louis Agassiz wrote about 1865:—

The other day, in the neighbourhood of Rio, I had an opportunity of seeing a marriage between two negroes, whose owner made the religious, or, as it appeared to me on this occasion, irreligious ceremony, obligatory. The bride, who was as black as jet, was dressed in white muslin, with a veil of coarse white lace, such as the negro women make themselves, and the husband was in a white linen suit. She looked, and I think she really felt, diffident, for there were a good many strangers present, and her position was embarrassing. The Portuguese priest, a bold, insolent-looking man, called them up and rattled over the marriage service with most irreverent speed, stopping now and then to scold them both, but especially the woman, because she did not speak loud enough and did not take the whole thing in the same coarse, rough way that he did. When he ordered them to come up and kneel at the altar his tone was more suggestive of cursing than praying, and having uttered his blessing he hurled an amen at them, slammed the prayer-book down on the altar, whiffed out the candles, and turned bride and bride-

79. A BRAZILIAN LANDSCAPE IN THE VICINITY OF RIO DE JANEIRO

groom out of the chapel with as little ceremony as one would have kicked out a dog. As the bride came out, half crying, half smiling, her mother met her and showered her with rose-leaves, and so this act of consecration, in which the mother's benediction seemed the only grace, was over. I thought what a strange confusion there must be in these poor creatures' minds if they thought about it at all. They are told that the relation between man and wife is a sin, unless confirmed by the sacred rite of marriage; they come to hear a bad man gabble over them words which they cannot understand, mingled with taunts and abuse which they understand only too well, and side by side with their own children grow up the little fair-skinned slaves to tell them practically that the white man does not keep himself the law he imposes on them. What a monstrous lie the whole system must seem to them, if they are ever led to think about it at all.

"The funeral service was chanted by a choir of priests, one of whom was a negro, a large, comely man, whose jet-black visage formed a strong and striking contrast to his white vestments. He seemed to perform his part with a decorum and sense of solemnity which I did not observe in his brethren." (Dr. Walsh, 1828.)

Brazilian negroes are usually very religious, and with the exception of those (mostly Mandingoes) who still profess Muhammadanism, are the willing adherents of the Roman Catholic Church. And there is no doubt that this Church exercises a wholesome discipline over their lives. The pity of it is that the Roman Church is—with some notable exceptions—so badly served still in Brazil by careless, brutal, and licentious Portuguese priests.

The existence of slavery warped the minds and morals of the white people inhabiting Brazil. The knowledge that you could do almost anything you liked towards your slave, male or female, and the laxity of public opinion with regard to sexual morality induced a state of affairs to prevail during the first seventy years of the nineteenth century which has been referred to in no measured terms by certain bishops of the Roman Church of European origin, and by (Sir) Richard Burton[1] and numerous British and German travellers, to whose works the reader who is curious in human depravity is referred.

Here is a printable instance, taken from the volume of the Revs. J. C. Fletcher and D. P. Kidder.[2]

These writers, reviewing the morals of slavery, refer to the case of an Englishman settled in Brazil, who purposely had as many children as he could by slave women because he found that his children were generally pretty, even with "light, curling hair, blue eyes, and a skin as light as that of a European," and he was consequently able to sell them at a good price when they were old enough to leave their mothers.

This description of a Luso-Brazilian patriarch and his incestuous slave family may be thought incredible; but those who like myself visited Mossamedes in Southern Angola in the "eighties" of the last century will be able to recall a precisely similar instance in the household of a retired medical man who resided in the vicinity of that pleasant city.

"My host was a white Brazilian, more pleasing in his aspect and manners than most others I had met with. He showed me into a comfortable *quarto*, newly plastered with white clay, with beds and mats of green bamboo, which were fresh and fragrant, and formed a strong contrast with the mouldering filth I had left. When supper was ready, he took me kindly and courteously by the hand, to an apartment where it was laid out on a clean cloth, and well and neatly dressed; a stewed fowl with *pão de trigo* (wheaten bread), accompanied by green vegetables—a species of *Brassica* which he cultivated.

"When I had finished, he invited me to his porch, where he brought me some excellent coffee, and set a mulatto of his establishment on an opposite bench, to play on the guitar for my amusement. He then called forth and introduced me to his whole family. This consisted of two mothers, a black and a white, and twelve children, of all sizes, sexes, and colours; some with woolly hair and dusky faces, some with sallow skins and long black tresses. In a short time they made up a ball, and began to dance. It was opened by the youngest, Luzia, a child about four years old, with dark eyes and coal-black hair. She was presently joined by a little black sister, and they com-

[1] Burton was consul between 1865 and 1869 at Santos, and wrote an admirable description of Eastern Brazil in his *Highlands of Brazil*.

[2] *Brazil and the Brazilians*, by the Rev. James C. Fletcher and Rev. Dr. D. P. Kidder, who travelled in Brazil at different times between 1857 and 1866.

menced with a movement resembling a Spanish bolero, imitating admirably well the castanets with their fingers and thumbs. The movement of the dance was not very delicate; and the children, when they began, showed a certain timidity and innate consciousness that they were exhibiting before a stranger what was not proper; but by degrees they were joined in succession by all the children, boys and girls, up to the age of seventeen and eighteen, and finally by the two mothers of the progeny. I never saw such a scene. It was realising what I had heard of the state of families in the midst of woods, shut out from intercourse with all other society, and forming promiscuous connexions with one another, as if they were in an early age of the world, and had no other human beings to attach themselves to. I had personally known some, and I had heard of others, brothers and sisters, who without scruple or sense of shame lived together, supporting in other respects the decencies of life; but here it was carried beyond what I could have supposed possible, and this precocious family displayed among themselves dances resembling what we have heard of the Otaheitan Timordee." (Dr. Walsh.)

The dances to which negro slaves were trained were not always of the blameless quality described by Mad Margaret in *Ruddigore*. They usually began with a slow movement of two persons, who approached each other with a shy and diffident air, and then receded bashful and embarrassed. By degrees, the time of the music increased, the diffidence wore off, and the dance concluded with "indecencies not fit to be seen nor described." Sometimes it was of a different character, attended by jumping, shouting, and throwing their arms over each other's heads, and assuming the most fierce and stern aspects. The indecent display was a "dance of love," but the shouting dance was a mimicry of war.

Dancing in Brazil, as elsewhere in America, was the great passion of the negro, and the one consolation which made his slavery tolerable. Whenever a group of them met in the street or on a country road, or at the door of an inn or wineshop, they got up a dance; and if there was no instrument in the company, which rarely happened, they supplied its place with singing. On all the estates where there was a number of slaves, Saturday night would be usually devoted to a ball. A fire of wood or maize cobs would be lighted up in the biggest shed, and the slaves would continue dancing till daylight.

Walsh, Fletcher and Kidder, H. W. Bates,[1] Burton and other writers on nineteenth-century Brazil all give instances of the good behaviour of slaves living under favourable conditions. Here is a typical case quoted by Walsh:—

"I now found that she was the widow of a gentleman, who had been proprietor of the estate all round. He had died a few years before, leaving her with two little girls, her daughters, and twenty-four slaves, fourteen males and ten females. The former were located in huts up the sides of the hills, and the latter lodged with her in her house. With this large family of slaves, she lived alone in the mountains, having no white persons but her little children, within several leagues of her. Yet such was the moral ascendency she had acquired, that her whole establishment moved with perfect regularity, and cultivated an estate of several square miles."

Slaves, negro and mulatto, were often trusted by their masters with large sums of money or supplies of trade goods and sent away to trade in rubber or other produce. They very seldom betrayed their trust.

[1] *The Naturalist on the Amazons*, by H. W. Bates. A fascinating study of Man and Nature in Northern Brazil.

Nevertheless, the relatively beneficent laws regulating slavery in Brazil during the eighteenth and nineteenth centuries were frequently evaded by slave-owners, and slaves ran away to the woods to escape ill-treatment, or to obtain remission from incessant hard work. Whenever they were recaptured they were flogged, and in addition an iron collar was firmly riveted round their necks. From this collar a long bar projected at right angles, which terminated either in a cross or in a broad twisted curve. The bar was intended to impede them if they took to flight again, as it would soon become entangled in the bush. Slaves thus decorated were very common objects in all the Brazilian towns in the early part of the nineteenth century. British and German travellers also note the frequency of suicide amongst the Brazilian slaves before Emancipation came.

Adult negroes in Brazil seldom became reconciled to slavery, especially if they had been born in Brazil, and consequently born to unending servitude. If they could not secure their freedom in one way or another, they frequently committed suicide: usually when a master before death had promised manumission and had forgotten to state his intentions in a will properly executed.

80. A FULA
Of the type trading between Scarcies River, West Africa, and Brazil

During the first quarter of the nineteenth century there grew up a considerable aggregation of Muhammadan negroes in the Brazilian towns of Pernambuco, Bahia, and Rio de Janeiro. These people called themselves *Musulmi* (Moslems), but the non-Muhammadan negroes styled them *Malé*, and under that name they are recorded in the history of Brazil.

Malé, or Mali, is an interesting name which throws some light on the origin, at any rate, of the leading spirits of the Muhammadan confraternities throughout Brazil. It is obviously the race name of the Mandingo peoples of Senegambia. We know that through Portuguese Guinea many Mandingo and even Fula slaves were brought to Brazil, and owing to their superior type of physique and character were generally notable people. But the Abbé Ignace Étienne,[1] who has written two interesting articles on this subject, ascribes the Muhammadan negroes of Brazil for the most part to the Yoruba (Nago), Hausa, and Bornu (?) peoples of the Lagos hinterland, and also alludes to the Gege, Gruma (? Gurma), Kabinda, Barba, Mina, Calabar, Ijebu, Mondubi, and Benin, as Muhammadans. The Barba people of Borgu, and the tribes of Bornu, are certainly more or less Muhammadans, but the others mentioned (as far as they can be identified) are pagans in their home of origin, and can only have become Muhammadans by contact with these influential Yoruba and Hausa people since their arrival in Brazil. I cannot help thinking that the Abbé Ignace Étienne, and other writers on the subject, have overlooked the important Mandingo element in the slaves of Brazil. Mr. Consul O'Sullivan Beare in a letter to the writer

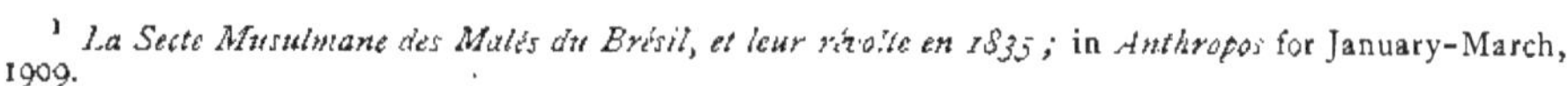

[1] *La Secte Musulmane des Malés du Brésil, et leur révolte en 1835*; in *Anthropos* for January–March, 1909.

of this book mentions the interesting fact that Fula people of the Gambari[1] tribe or district come backwards and forwards now to Bahia to trade. From allusions in the works of earlier writers, it would seem as though in the early nineteenth century Fula or Mandingo slaves who had obtained their freedom had opened up a considerable commerce between Portuguese Guinea and Brazil, just as other Brazilian negroes did between Brazil, Lagos, and Dahomé.

At the present day the Musulmi of Bahia speak a dialect of Yoruba (the Nago); formerly (says the Abbé Ignace Étienne) they could read and write Arabic. To-day their priests and holy men (*Alufa*) no longer understand the Arabic of the Koran and use a Portuguese translation.

As early as 1694 the negroes working in the palm forests of Pernambuco coalesced into a tribe of revolted slaves which for a long time resisted any attempts at subjugation by the Portuguese. In 1719 the negroes of the Minas Geraes province had made a far-reaching conspiracy to massacre all the whites on Holy Thursday, but like so many of these negro plots it failed of effect through premature revelations, and the bulk of the negroes to avoid punishment

81. BAHIA, EAST BRAZIL, FROM THE HARBOUR

escaped into the forests, where they lived with the Indians (whom they had joined in a revolt seven years previously). In 1828, at Bahia, more than a thousand negroes had risen against the yoke of slavery, but they were vanquished by Brazilian soldiers at the Pirajá River. Another attempt at a rising was made at Bahia on the 10th April, 1830, but also was suppressed without difficulty by the authorities; but for six years, between 1831 and 1837, the negroes all over Brazil were simmering in insurrection. The Imperial Government of the country was disorganised owing to the abdication of Don Pedro I and the long minority of his son which followed. There were attempts at revolution amongst the whites, so it is hardly surprising that the blacks, having far more serious grievances, were ready to strike for independence, between Maranhão on the north and Santos (São Paulo district) on the south.

But the Malé insurrection which broke out on the night of January 14th, 1835, at Bahia, had a distinctly religious as well as a racial character: it was mainly confined to the Muhammadan negroes, who were determined if successful to found a Muhammadan state in the north-east of Brazil, which was to be under a negress queen. A good number of the insurgents were not even slaves,

[1] From the Great Scarcies River (Western Sierra Leone). *Gambare* or *Kambare yaji* is the Fula name for the Great Scarcies River (F. W. H. Migeod).

but free men and wealthy. The total number of Muhammadans or "Malés" was probably not more than 1500, but they believed they had obtained the adhesion of large numbers of pagan or Christian negro slaves who were disgusted with their condition of servitude. As usual, however, warnings and denunciations had reached the police officers, and to a certain extent Bahia was not taken by surprise. In spite of furious fighting, the Malés were vanquished and took to flight. Large numbers of prisoners were taken. Some were shot, others were flogged ("two hundred, five hundred, and even one thousand strokes," which could not have left many of them living!) others were sent to

82. A NEGRESS OF BAHIA

convict establishments, and a few were deported to Africa. The Abbé Ignace Etienne is of opinion that if the movement had been more ably directed by its promoters, and had been better armed, it might, with the furious, reckless courage displayed by the insurgent negroes, have overwhelmed the Portuguese and have actually succeeded in establishing—at any rate for a time—a Muhammadan negro government in the province of Bahia.

Negro slaves were apparently introduced into the State of Matto Grosso[1] at the beginning of the eighteenth century, when the mineral wealth of this region began to be first exploited and when the intervention of the Jesuits had checked

[1] In the south-centre of Brazil, on the rising ground of the southern basin of the Amazon.

the enslavement of Amerindians. In 1718 the capital of the State of Cuyaba was founded by Pascoal Moreira Cabral de Leme. From that date the importation of negroes grew considerably, and it was entirely due to their labour that the mines received such development. The negroes were, of course, brought from the São Paulo district. Apart from those that were regularly introduced, many of the runaway negroes from the regions nearer the coast

83. VISCONDE DO RIO BRANCO

An opponent of slavery in Brazil, who as premier of the Brazilian ministry in 1871 carried through a partial emancipation and improved the position of the remaining slaves

made for Matto Grosso and existed alongside the slaves as a free population giving its labour for wages.

By 1872 the free negroes largely outnumbered the slaves. In the first half of the nineteenth century negroes and negroids were twice as numerous as the whites, and the Amerindian population had shrunk to very small proportions. At the present day there are about fifty thousand negroes and negroids in this important State. Here, as elsewhere in Brazil, there was no great shock or interruption to industry caused by the sudden emancipation of 1888, for the growth of the free negro element has been so considerable, and white Brazilians so accustomed to treating it with consideration and paying it wages for its service, that the emancipated slaves (where they were not aged pensioners) joined the ranks of the free coloured people without difficulty.

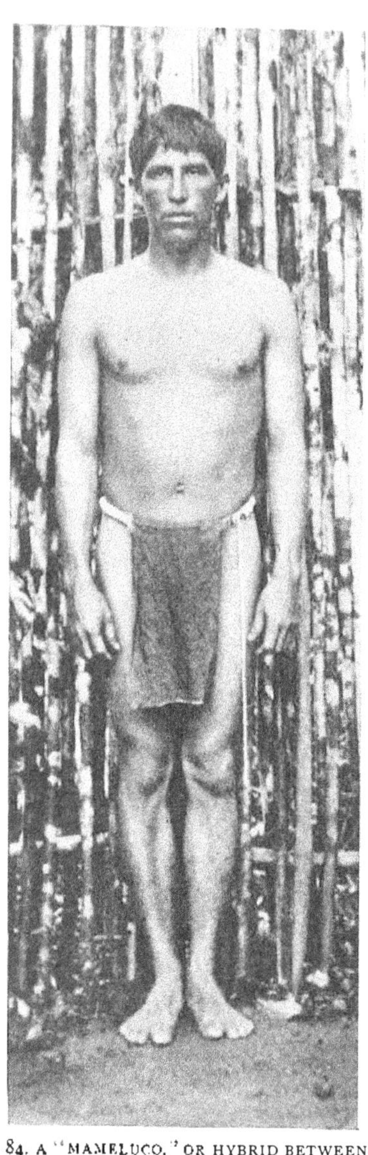

84. A "MAMELUCO," OR HYBRID BETWEEN AMERINDIAN (CARIB) AND EUROPEAN

Although this individual was a native of Guiana, to the north of Brazil, he resembles very closely the better types of Brazilian mameluco

Semi-independent, pagan Bush-negroes, Muhammadan "Malés," and Christian "emancipados" have, in the later history of Brazil, once or twice given trouble to the authorities in the interior (the eastern and southern provinces chiefly) by their independent demeanour. Before the complete emancipation in 1888 there were attempts made to send the more turbulent back to West Africa.[1]

In 1835 there were 2,100,000 slaves in Brazil; in 1875 the number had dropped (after the partial emancipation of 1871) to 1,476,567. But there was a recrudescence of demand for slave labour (or official estimates were wrong), for in 1884 the total number of slaves was computed at nearly 3,000,000. In 1888, however, slavery was abruptly abolished by Imperial decree (under the regency of the Princess Isabella), and the discontent caused by this final blow to servitude (just as railway and rubber developments were giving it a new value in the eyes of the entrepreneur), coupled with other causes of political unrest, cost the dynasty of Bragança the Brazilian throne.

After emancipation the movement towards a fusion of races between the ex-slave and the descendants of his Luso-Brazilian masters went on more rapidly even than during the three centuries of mild servitude. The Portuguese are at heart an essentially kind, good-natured people, and least of all Christian European races have a contempt for the coloured races. Possibly this may spring from these two facts: that there is a strong Moorish, North African element in Southern Portugal, and even an old intermixture with those negroes who were imported thither from North-west Africa in the fifteenth and sixteenth centuries to till the scantily populated southern provinces; and also that Brazil, the Azores, and Madeira were rather colonised from the Moorish southern half of Portugal than from the Gothic north.

[1] Between 1850 and 1878 about four thousand to six thousand Brazilian "emancipados" settled at Lagos and Whydah, and a few went to Angola.

Arrived in Brazil, the Portuguese—prolific breeders outside Portugal[1]—another paradox!—mixed eagerly with the *Amerindians* and raised up a great, proud, and warlike intermediary race of Mamelucos.[2] Then in the late seventeenth century they and the mamelucos began to mix maritally with the imported negresses. Unlike the British and British-Americans, and like the French and Dutch, they did not spurn or neglect their offspring by slave concubines. On the contrary, they educated them, set them free (usually), lifted them above servitude, raised them socially to the level of the Whites; and at the present day it may be truly said that among two-thirds of the Brazilians speaking Portuguese there are no colour distinctions in society or politics. The co.our problem is only beginning to appear slightly in the expanding German and Swiss settlements, and more markedly in the centres of pure white Portuguese colonisation in the south.

The growing-up of a huge empire of mulattoes, of mixed Caucasian-Negro-Amerindian blood, impressed very unfavourably Louis Agassiz when he explored Brazil in the later sixties. In his book[3] he writes as follows:—

> This mixture of races seems to have had a much more unfavourable influence on the physical development than in the United States. It is as if all clearness of type had been blurred, and the result is a vague compound lacking character and expression. This hybrid class, although more marked here because the Indian element is added, is very numerous in all the cities; perhaps the fact, so honourable to Brazil, that the free negro has full access to all the privileges of any free citizen, rather tends to increase than diminish the number.[4]

But it may be that Agassiz took a too pessimistic view, and that the new Brazilian race, though it may have for centuries an unchangeably yellow-brown skin and undulating hair, may develop into a vigorous human type able to hold its own against the Nordic or the Mediterranean White man, the pure negro (if

[1] The area of Portugal, the Azores and Madeira is 35,290 square miles, more than two-thirds the size of England; and England, not so completely habitable as well-nigh-perfect Portugal, supports a population of thirty millions. The total population of Portugal and the Islands is only six millions.

[2] "The product of European and Indian is a fine type; handsome, well-built, and nice in character. I believe further that the Indian blood once introduced tends to eat up the other blood and to reproduce itself again and again. There is more than mere blood in this. One cross of Indian blood will show in many generations, often stronger in the son than in the father who was nearer the original Indian strain—in the clear-cut, sensitive lips and mouth, the straight nose, clear, clean, olive skin, and the extraordinary, straight, black oily hair—blue-black, and exuding a natural oil which is clean and sweet and keeps the hair abundant and glossy. The Indian possesses the "Spirit of the Soil," whatever that is, because he has been evolved through so many ages where he now lives. The same influences of food, climate, air, forest, hills, and a thousand imperceptible influences which are at work on the new-comer, causes any drop of Indian blood in his children to bring out the Indian type peculiarities and cause his descendants, if the mother have the least tinge of Indian about her, to look more like the aboriginal of Brazil than is warranted by racial descent." (From a correspondent.)

[3] *A Journey in Brazil*, by Louis Agassiz, 1868.

[4] Agassiz adds this note: "Let anyone who doubts the evil of this mixture of races, and is inclined, from a mistaken philanthropy, to break down all barriers between them, come to Brazil. He cannot deny the deterioration consequent upon an amalgamation of races, more widespread here than in any other country in the world, and which is rapidly effacing the best qualities of the white man, the negro, and the Indian, leaving a mongrel nondescript type, deficient in physical and mental energy. At a time when the new social status of the negro is a subject of vital importance in our statesmanship, we should profit by the experience of a country where, though slavery exists, there is far more liberality toward the free negro than he has ever enjoyed in the United States. Let us learn the double lesson: open all the advantages of education to the negro, and give him every chance of success which culture gives to the man who knows how to use it; but respect the laws of nature, and let all dealings with the black man tend to preserve, as far as possible, the distinctness of his national characteristics, and the integrity of our own."

How can Agassiz dogmatise on the laws of Nature? May he not, like Mrs. Partington, be trying to sweep out the Atlantic?

any survive in the New Brazil of the twenty-first century), or the regenerated Amerindian.[1]

The liberated negro slave has, like every other Brazilian citizen, the vote. The franchise is extended to all male citizens over twenty-one years of age who are *literate*, not beggars or vagrants, not in active service as soldiers, or monks in a monastery. The negro or negroid is equally eligible for holding all public, municipal, and political offices.[2] He enjoys the same protection of the laws as his white or yellow fellow-citizen. He is now a "Homem Brazileiro," and the word negro, even when applied to one of pure negro race, has come to be used only as a term of abuse, which may be made still further offensive by supplementing it with the words "de Africa." This has come to be one of the most offensive terms one can apply to a Brazilian citizen, even though he be of unmixed negro descent. If you must discriminate as to colour in conversation, you speak of a "preto" [*preto* in Portuguese = black].

"All colour distinctions in the population of Matto Grosso have fallen away, and with them all distinction between the white race, the Amerindian, and the Negro. In Matto Grosso, indeed, the apparently irreconcilable social disparity between the three races seems to have found a satisfactory solution."[3] Nevertheless, the white race still holds an ascendancy throughout Brazil as the foremost exponent of modern civilisation; nor is this ascendancy likely to be lost, in spite of the climatic advantage possessed by the African race. This is due, in the opinion of modern writers, to *the supreme influence of capital.* The white race has *capital* behind it: the negro has *not.*

The conditions regarding the acquisition of land (more especially Government land in new districts) require the possession of more or less ready money. The white man, therefore, acquires the land and surveys it at his own expense. Before he casts his eye over this likely estate it may already have been squatted on by negroes, negroids, or "Indians" (these squatters are called "Moradores" in Brazil), or after the estate has been acquired and surveyed, the Moradores drift thither and settle on it with or without permission. But before long they are obliged to come to terms with the real owner of the estate, who has acquired these rights by a legal contract. So far from the estate owner desiring to evict the squatter, he is anxious to come to terms with him, because if he be harsh, the squatter with his invaluable labour will move off to an unclaimed piece of land or to a more considerate employer. The unwritten law which all parties believe in and observe is that the Morador shall pay for his rent and for other benefits in labour, and this he is quite ready to do, provided the demands on his time are not unreasonable. But the estate owner generally keeps a store, and is in a small way a banker. The result is that the Moradores—Negro and Indian—are generally more or less in debt to the proprietor they serve; and the latter, if need be, has recourse to the law to compel the payment of debt by a reasonable amount of labour. Usually quite patriarchal conditions arise between the white Padrão and the coloured "Camarada." This last receives in theory small monthly wages, which are not always adequate to the payment of the rent and the purchase of goods; but then he has a right to

[1] A well-informed correspondent in Brazil writes to me on this topic: "The Brazilian negro is fast disappearing. The future Brazilian will have very much negro blood in him, but he will be a *yellow* man, and will regard Paris as his Mecca. He does already!"

[2] "All negroes are 'citizens of Brazil'—entirely equal, legally, socially, and by democratic sentiment or instinct. In that respect, Brazil is a true republic." (A correspondent.)

[3] Dr. Max Schmidt in *Koloniale Rundschau* for April, 1909.

share the two principal meals of his Patron, to whose family he considers that he belongs. The Padrão is usually the godfather—and his wife the godmother—of the Camarada's children. The Padrão conceives himself obliged by the requirements of good feeling to give occasional entertainments to the tenants with singing, dancing, and fireworks, usually on saints' days.

Until the negro acquires capital, which he invests in land and in the

85. IN THE FORESTS OF SOUTH CENTRAL BRAZIL

development of estates, so long will the white man hold the political and social ascendancy in Brazil. And it should be noted once again that negro tenants very much dislike settling down under *negro* landlords (where there are such). They infinitely prefer to associate themselves with the development of estates owned by *white men*, or, at any rate, by such persons who endeavour to conceal the slight element of the negro or the Amerindian in their bodies by behaving with the liberality and justice attributed to the white man.

It is obvious[1] that the capabilities of the negro imported from Africa must have been of the greatest value to the early settler in Brazil, as he possessed just those qualities which were lacking in the Amerindians, even if the latter race had furnished all the skilled and unskilled labour demanded by the development of this vast region. The Negro, for example, displayed a remarkable knowledge of cattle-breeding and an inherent skill in the working and forging of minerals—the blacksmith's art in particular. As the Amerindians of Brazil were practically unacquainted with the care of domestic animals at all (since, except near the frontiers of Bolivia and Peru, they did not even know the llama or the guanaco), they were of no use in cattle-breeding. Indeed, as

86. TREE FERNS IN A BRAZILIAN FOREST

late as 1901 all attempts to induce them to raise live-stock have been fruitless. The climate over much of Brazil made it difficult or impossible for a people of European descent to take charge of cattle, sheep, goats, or horses. In this respect, in Matto Grosso the negro has been particularly useful, has displayed remarkable gifts as a cattle-keeper, and has even imparted those gifts to his hybrids with the Amerindians and with the white man. It is said that many useful practices in connection with the breeding and keeping of cattle were learnt by the early Portuguese settlers from the negro, and not taught by them to him.

The almost exclusive monopoly of blacksmith's work which the negro population holds in Matto Grosso is quite remarkable. With the exception of the peoples along the frontiers of Bolivia and Peru, the working of metals was

[1] These observations are founded on an article by Dr. Max Schmidt in the *Koloniale Rundschau* for April, 1909.

practically unknown to the Amerindians of Brazil in the sixteenth century; and even at the present day most of the iron implements in their possession (such as lance-heads, arrow-heads, iron rings for striking fire with flint) have been made for them by negroes living amongst them or in their neighbourhood. Dr. Max Schmidt observed that the negro in making great lance-heads for the Guato Indians, imitated very closely the shape and pattern of the old Guato lance which had a bone point.

Quite a million of the Amerindians are still pagan; twenty or thirty thousand of the negroes are Muhammadan (more or less) or actually preserve their fetishistic beliefs brought from Africa. These pagan negroes have fetish temples in their villages in which they house the rude figures of gods similar to

87. A SCHOOL TEACHER AND PUPILS, SOMNO RIVER, MINAS GERAES

those of Dahomé and the Niger delta. I have seen a collection made in Brazil (by Dr. H. W. Furniss, U.S.A. Minister to Haiti) of these wooden painted idols which might have come from the west coast of Africa. But Christianity is rapidly spreading among all classes and races. All the Brazilian Christians, except two hundred thousand (mostly Germans, British, and a few negroes), belong to the Roman Catholic Church; though there is no State religion, and all reasonable faiths may be freely held.

Education is *not compulsory* in Brazil; and the negro peasantry at the present time are very poorly educated, few of those who have reached middle age being able to read and write. These faculties are much more common amongst the present young people of between ten and fifteen years of age. In the towns, however, the standard of negro education is much higher and scarcely differs from that of the white population. Very few negroids are unable to read, write, and cipher.

The average negro house in the country is built of wood and clay and covered with tiles. The dwelling usually consists of two fair-sized rooms, with a shed or lean-to which serves as a kitchen. There is no window, and the house door, which generally stands open, is the one means of admitting light. The hammock is universally adopted as a bed. There are a few wooden chests for clothes, and a table on which usually stands a glass case containing images of the saints.

The dress amongst the peasants in the case of the men is usually a shirt and trousers, a leather belt, leather shoes or slippers, and a broad-brimmed hat made of felt or straw. The women wear a cotton skirt and blouse, but very

88. BRAZILIAN NEGROES (AND LUSO-BRAZILIANS) ENGAGED IN WASHING RIVER-SAND FOR DIAMONDS

often in the country only a skirt. The small children run about naked, but on approaching puberty the girls wear a short cotton frock and the boys a tattered shirt.

All the well-to-do negroes and negroids are dressed like Frenchmen of good standing, in garments devised by Anglo-French tailors, hosiery usually from England or the States. Homburg hats, and *chapeaux de haute-forme* (on appropriate occasions). "Their ladies of course go to Worth, or imitation Worth. Clothes are a perfect mania with all classes and colours in Brazil, except the peasants; it is their first and last thought. But one must admit that they usually dress in good taste,"[1] writes a correspondent in Brazil.

[1] He adds: "The curious thing is that the cross between the clumsy negro slave and the not particularly 'fringant' Portuguese—with a dash of the wild Indian thrown in—should present such a contrast to the parents or grandparents in the way of cleanliness and smartness. The coloured Brazilian is the greatest

Of course in general mode of life, social customs, etc., the educated coloured people of Brazil are scarcely distinguishable from the Portuguese middle or upper classes, according to their means and social status. The peasants, however, away from the towns lead a more African existence, and except that the house or hut may be a little superior to the average negro home in Africa, manners and customs in domesticity are little changed from the standard of the Gold Coast or Dahomé—not a very low standard, by the by.

At their meals the negro men and boys eat with spoons and sit at a table, but the women and girls (in the country) employ nothing but their fingers in helping themselves to food, and usually eat apart from the men.

89. BRAZILIAN NEGROES STARTING ON A SAILING VOYAGE ON THE UPPER SAÔ FRANCISCO RIVER

The country negroes and many of those who dwell in towns do not trouble themselves very much about contracting a legal marriage. Negro men and women simply live together in what is called locally the *companheira* system. A woman with or without children simply takes up her abode with a man who pleases her and shares his home as his wife at the pleasure of both parties. Yet these unions are sometimes as permanent as if they were consecrated by the Church or contracted under the law. There is, however, a good deal of unrecognised polygamy, and many negroes are husbands of more than one wife.

dandy you can imagine, and the vainest fop. Every man and boy without exception carries a pocket mirror and a comb; and in the streets, trams, ferry boats, etc., he constantly uses both. His curls are as dear to him as is—or was—the 'quiff' to Tommy Atkins. The Neo-Brazilian has a good conceit of himself. One thing I must say in his favour: he is clean."

The irrepressible negro and negroid—you may dislike their physiognomy, call them fop, gorilla, and other disagreeable names, but they always come up smiling and bear little malice—enters all careers, serves in all trades, professions, and employments in Brazil, from the humblest to nearly the highest, from the scavenger and sewage collector to the priesthood, college professorships, party-leadership, even perhaps to the presidential throne. At least it is said that more than one of the chief magistrates of the "United States of Brazil" has had a tricklet of Ethiopia in his veins.

90. H. E. NILO PEÇANHA, PRESIDENT OF BRAZIL (1908-10)

Negroes constitute a large proportion of the Brazilian standing army of 19,000 men, of the police[1] and navy (with a personnel of 6000). They furnish in like manner the bulk of the recruits for military bands and civilian orchestras. Some of the best music in Brazil is produced by half-caste negroids or pure-blooded negroes.

The total area of Brazil is enormous: including the recently purchased Acre territory it amounts to 3,293,000 square miles.[2] The population for 1908 is approximately 20,000,000, divided roughly under the following racial types: 8,000,000 *whites*, 1,700,000 *mamelucos* (Caucaso-merindian); 2,000,000 *Amerindians*; 5,582,000 negroids (mulattoes, etc., Cafuzos, and hybrids between the three racial stocks of America); and 2,718,000 more or less pure-blood Negroes.[3]

As regards the *rate of increase*,

91. A "CAFUZO"
Hybrid between Negro and Amerindian

[1] The military police force of Rio and most other big towns is pure Negro, or Cafuzo (Negrindian); the civil police are almost all white men or Mamelucos. The General commanding the Rio Police is (or was) a Mulatto. The senior Admiral in the Navy and the present Minister of Marine (1909) are also Eurafrican in race. As a rule, however, the officers in the standing army and in the police force are white, or white tinged with Amerindian blood.

[2] Nearly as large as the United States and Alaska.

[3] Counting Negroes and Negroids there are approximately *8,300,000* people of more or less African descent in Brazil, as against 8,000,000 of European race. If the 8,000,000 whites joined with the 1,700,000 Caucaso-merindians and the 2,000,000 Amerindians, there would be a White-Yellow majority of 3,400,000 over the Browns and Blacks. But this is an idle speculation, as Fusion is the key-note of Brazilian Government.

recent statistics published by Dr. Pires de Almeida (in the Rio *Jornal do Commercio* during September, 1909) show that it is greatest (4·4) not among the pure whites or the absolute negroes, but in marriages between civilised "Indians" (Caboclos) and *Mamelucos* or Caucaso-merindian hybrids. The average number of children produced in a marriage between a white man and an Amerindian woman is *four*; between an Amerindian man and a white woman 3·8. Negroes married to negresses give a proportion of about *three* children per marriage, and the unions of pure-blood whites, 3·5.

There are no statistics concerning uncivilised Amerindians, but the average increase, i.e. number of *live* children born to their women, is guessed at *under one*. Great stress is laid by Dr. de Almeida on *living* children, because he points out what a large proportion of the children in Brazil are born dead. The *death-rate* among young children is *very high* among negroes, negroids, and Amerindians. Civilised Amerindians in Brazil (*Caboclos*) have a proportionate increase of *three* children per marriage and a less heavy infant death-rate. Negroids intermarrying with Negroids show a birth-rate of 3·3. White men uniting with negresses, and negroes with white women have a birth-rate in Brazil of only 2·9. On the other hand, Amerindians married to negroes and leading a civilised existence in cities have a high birth-rate: 3·9.

92. A BOTOCUDO AMERINDIAN OF EASTERN BRAZIL (RIO DOCE)

Dr. Bulhões Carvalho considers the *Amerindian* the most fecund stock in the country; especially when mingled with an infusion of white or negro blood. But the Amerindian element is lowering the stature of the Brazilian people, which, except in the pure white or unmixed negroes, is sensibly shorter than it was at the beginning of the nineteenth century, before the great intermingling of the racial types began.

The geographical distribution of Negroes and negroids in Brazil is approximately as follows:—They inhabit all the coast region for one or two hundred miles inland, from Pará (near the mouth of the Amazons) to the frontier of Uruguay; the provinces of Minas Geraes, São Paulo, and Matto Grosso. They are particularly numerous in the towns of large size, and in the vicinity of Rio de Janeiro, Santos, Bahia, Pernambuco, Ceará, and Maranhão. A few are found in the coast region of Brazilian Guiana. But although they are scattered sporadically all over Brazil, and as traders and chance workers penetrate the most remote Amazonian regions, they really only count as the *preponderating element* of the population in the coast-lands of Eastern Brazil, in Minas Geraes, and in the mining districts of Matto Grosso. The rest of Brazil is given up to a sparse one and three-quarter millions of Amerindians, civilised[1] and uncivilised, to Mamelucos, and to whites. Of course a good many whites and Caucaso-merindian hybrids inhabit the same parts of Brazil that are (otherwise) mainly populated by negroes and negroids. The "whitest"

93. ON THE BANKS OF THE AMAZONS RIVER

[1] The wild, naked—and most of the wild Amerindians of Brazil go absolutely naked, men and women—aborigines are called by the Portuguese, *Indios bravos*; the civilised and clothed, *Caboclo*, fem. *Cabocla*. It has already been mentioned that the name for the hybrid between Portuguese and Amerindian—perhaps the coming race in Brazil—is *Mameluco* (a fanciful term derived from the Arabic Mamluk); that of the hybrid between Negro and Amerindian is *Cafuzo*, "a very rake-helly type," writes a correspondent, "but a vigorous one and very prominent in the Brazilian army and military police." "As to the Indians of the Amazons, they are very fine chaps mostly, but differ greatly according to tribe and locality, both in physical form, strength, and skin-colour. Some are copper, others olive, yellow, or brown; and some are nearly white. Some are handsome tribes; others repulsive in the extreme. There is one extraordinary tribe, the *Paratintins*, exceedingly tall and abnormally developed in a manner precisely recalling those strange descriptions gathered by the missionaries of the sixteenth century from native legends in Northern South America; descriptions of an awful tribe of cannibal, licentious giants which appeared from the Amazon valley and committed frightful ravages on the civilised peoples of Colombia and Ecuador." (From a correspondent.)

The present Amerindian population of Brazil can scarcely be less than 2,000,000. They may not have increased very much since 1890, when they were last counted, but in that year no attempt was made to include in the census many tribes in North-West, Central, and East-Central Brazil. The number of mamelucos or Caucaso-merindian hybrids is approximately 1,700,000. They are a type that is increasing faster than any other race in Brazil.

portions of Brazil are the Rio Grande do Sul, Santa Catherina, Paraná, São Paulo, and south-eastern Matto Grosso.

As regards the *white* population the Portuguese element is overwhelmingly large, not only from the pre-independence days, but by the steady Portuguese immigration since 1850, amounting in all to quite 2,000,000. During the last fifty years about 230,000 Spanish or Spanish Americans have entered Brazil, and about 1,000,000 Italians have remained there; and these "Latin" elements have easily fused with the nearly related Portuguese, especially in language. For some reason the German element in the population has been much exaggerated, and "a million Germans" are often attributed to Brazil by the American Press. As a matter of cold fact, there appear to be about 150,000 Germans, Austrians, Baltic Russians, and German Swiss in Brazil; but owing to their energy and increasing wealth they and the four to five thousand British wield an influence quite out of proportion to their numbers.

Yet the coloured man administers, even if he does not rule! Especially since the commencement of the Republic. At the present moment there is scarcely a lowly or a highly placed Federal or Provincial official, at the head of or within any of the great departments of State, that has not more or less Negro or Amerindian blood in his veins. I am not putting this forward as a reproach: quite the contrary. It is an interesting fact, and an encouraging one.

CHAPTER VI

SLAVERY UNDER THE DUTCH

THE Dutch were hard taskmasters; as slaveholders disliked perhaps more than the British or the British Americans. They threw themselves into the slave-trade and the establishment of slave-worked plantations with a zest exceeding that of any other nationality: in the Malay Archipelago, at the Cape of Good Hope, in North America, Guiana, and Northern Brazil.

The Dutch made their first trading voyage to the Guinea Coast in 1595, sixteen years after throwing off the yoke of Spain. On the plea of warring with the Spanish Empire, which then included Portugal, they displaced the

94. ELMINA CASTLE, GOLD COAST

Elmina—Edeña in native parlance—was the first stronghold of the European slave trade on the West Coast of Africa. It was held by the Dutch from 1637 to 1872

latter power at various points along the west coast of Africa: at Arguin (north of the Senegal), at Goree (purchased in 1621 from the natives), Elmina (captured from the Portuguese in 1637), and at São Paulo de Loanda about the same time. They also threatened Moçambique on the east coast, and possessed themselves of the island of Mauritius. From the Moçambique coast they brought slaves to the Cape of Good Hope, some of which were transferred later to America.

On the Gold Coast, in addition to Elmina the Dutch established sixteen other forts, some of them alongside British settlements, which last the Dutch West India Company regarded with the keenest jealousy. The Dutch Gold Coast Possessions—like the British—were governed by a Chartered Company, that of the Dutch West Indies.[1] Goree and Arguin were lost to the French in

[1] Reconstituted as the New Dutch West India Company in 1674 and chartered to control the Guiana Coast in 1682.

1677-8, and Angola was only held for about eight years; therefore the Dutch during all the great period of American colony-making in eastern tropical America—the "sugar age," from 1660 to 1840—were obliged to rely on the Gold Coast for their slave supply. As they purveyed for other nations in addition, it is mainly the Dutch (but also the British) who are responsible for the introduction of so many Gold Coast slaves into the West Indies, South Carolina, and the Guianas. These were usually called "Koromantis," from the Dutch fort of Cormantyn or Koromanti near Cape Coast Castle, or "Minas" from El Mina; and they were probably derived from the Ashanti and the warlike tribes of the Black and the White Volta. The Koromanti slaves were always the prominent or the sole fighters in the great slave revolts of the West Indies and Guiana during the seventeenth and eighteenth centuries.[1]

95. A KORMANTYN OR KOROMANTI
Free negro bush-soldier of Dutch Guiana, eighteenth century

The Dutch fixed on Guiana first of all as a region of tropical America where they would meet with least opposition from Spaniard or Portuguese. They visited the coast as early as 1580, and continued to send ships thither on trading expeditions, until in 1614 the states of Holland granted local monopolies of trade to any Dutchman who would found settlements in Guiana. Thus encouraged, Essequibo was established in 1616 and Berbice in 1624. Surinam (Paramaribo) was acquired from the British by treaty in 1674. But Guiana was also an attraction to the English and French. Sir Walter Raleigh sailed up the Orinoco River in search of the legendary "El Dorado" country and revisited the Orinoco region again in 1617. Although he scarcely entered the real Guiana country eastward of the Orinoco basin, he drew attention to its gold-bearing possibilities from 1595 onwards, and British adventurers attempted and partially succeeded in founding settlements at the mouths of the many parallel rivers flowing northward through (what are now the separate colonies of) British, French, and Dutch Guiana.

In 1621 the first Dutch West India Company was established, and afterwards took the slave-trade in hand as a monopoly in Guiana and the Dutch West Indies. This company took possession of the island of Santa Cruz, which commands the passage between the Greater and Lesser Antilles, in 1625. [Santa Cruz was captured by France and eventually sold to Denmark in 1733.] Shortly afterwards the Dutch occupied the islands of Curaçoa, Bonaire, and

[1] They were also called "Koffies," from Kofi, a common Ashanti name.

Aruba off the north coast of Venezuela, which have remained Dutch down to the present day. In 1640 the little island of Saba, and at a later date the southern half of St. Martin and the island of St. Eustatia (all in the northernmost group of the Lesser Antilles) were added to the Dutch West Indian possessions, and became mainly peopled by negroes, besides, like Guiana, affording a refuge to many Jewish traders.

In 1630 and in 1651–2 British adventurers built small trading towns on the Surinam coast, particularly at Paramaribo; and in 1662 Charles II granted the whole of Guiana to Lord Willoughby of Barbados, who brought with him a number of English and negroes and established his head-quarters at Paramaribo.[1] Here his colony was strengthened by several hundred Jews anciently

96. ON THE COPPENAME
In the land of many rivers, Dutch Guiana

of Spanish origin, who had first come to America under Dutch protection, but who fled from one of the temporary Dutch settlements—Cayenne—when it was recaptured by the French in 1664.[2]

[1] The long stay of the British in Surinam [really only terminated in 1674] implanted English so firmly amongst the Negro slaves that even to this day their dialect is a jargon much more compounded of English than of any other language.

[2] An important element in the colonisation of Dutch Guiana were the Jews, mainly of Spanish and Portuguese origin, who had migrated to the Dutch settlements from French Cayenne in 1664 (led by the heroic Samuel Cohen Nassy), or who came there when expelled from Spain and Portugal, or proceeded direct from Holland to Surinam. They brought to or created in the colony great wealth, and under the Dutch flag they enjoyed peculiar privileges, which were not terminated till 1825, when they became merged without distinction in the rest of the free citizens of Dutch America. When Lord Willoughby's Guiana colony was withdrawn in 1675, the Spanish and Portuguese Jews who had settled there migrated to Jamaica and Barbados. The Jamaica Jews, bearing for the most part Spanish names, have been from time to time very notable persons in the development of the West Indies. Many of the Jews with the Spanish or Portuguese names whom one encounters in English society have derived their fortunes from the West Indies. Lord Beaconsfield's "fairy godmother," Mrs. Brydges Williams (*née* Cordova), whose fortune went so far to establish his position and power in British politics, had derived her money from the West Indies.

The West Indian Jews played a considerable part as brokers in the slave-trade, and had representatives at the Gambia, Sierra Leone, and elsewhere on the West African coast until the slave-trade was finally extirpated.

But in 1667, by the Peace of Breda, and by the Treaty of Westminster in 1674, the Dutch secured all Guiana (except the French portion—Cayenne) and governed it as a number of separate colonies under the direction of the New West India Chartered Company.[1] Sugar-cane cultivation became their most lucrative industry, and to work this large numbers of negroes were brought to Guiana. Many of the slaves, however, ran away to the thickly forested interior, mingled slightly with the Amerindians and formed warlike savage tribes, which by the beginning of the eighteenth century were at war with the Dutch.

Owing to dissatisfacton with negro slave labour the Dutch in 1714 attempted to introduce natives of the East Indies—"kulis"—into Guiana, thus forestalling the "coolie" traffic of the nineteenth century. But the experiment was a failure; the East Indians were badly treated, many died, and a few ran away and joined the "bosch negers" in the forests. Therefore as there was an ever-increasing demand for sugar from Essequibo, Demerara, Berbice, and Paramaribo, and as also the cultivation of the coco-nut palm had been introduced (in 1688) and of cacao (1725), the demand for negro labour in Guiana once more became a great impetus to the slave-trade.

97. BREAKING THE JOINTS AND MUTILATING NEGRO SLAVES CONDEMNED TO DEATH BY TORTURE

From a drawing by Captain J. G. Stedman, at the close of eighteenth century

During the eighteenth century the Dutch in their Guiana possessions inflicted shocking cruelties on their negro slaves. They probably fed and housed them better than did the British, and took more trouble to educate their half-caste children; but otherwise they certainly hold (comparing all the records) a sad pre-eminence over their contemporaries of all nationalities in the eighteenth century for extravagant torture and even reckless massacre in their dealings with negroes free and enslaved.

In Guiana married and unmarried Dutch women had no tenderer hearts towards their domestic slaves than had their men relations to field-hands, town servants, or labourers. It is recorded of a certain Miss S——n that she always had her female slaves flogged across the breasts because it caused them greater pain. Negresses in Surinam,[2] it is stated by Captain Stedman, frequently

[1] To whom Guiana was handed over in 1682.

[2] Some of these statements and the accompanying illustrations are derived from the *Narrative of an Expedition to Surinam*, by Captain J. G. Stedman (London, 1796). Stedman was an officer in the British Navy, but there being no war on hand and he unable to live without pay, joined the Scottish Brigade in the service of Holland and was sent with a variety of officers and men of mixed nationality to Surinam, where they were to combat the Bush or Maroon negroes who gave that colony such trouble and anxiety. The principal commandant of the force was a French Swiss. He relates an incident on the way out to show the heartlessness of the Dutch captain of the transport on which he was travelling. A boat-

received two hundred lashes—sometimes for nothing more serious than breaking a cup; they were flogged till their intestines were exposed, and pregnant women till they aborted. "A young female slave—having proved unequal to the task given her to perform—was sentenced to receive two hundred lashes and to drag during some months a chain several yards in length, one end of which was locked round her ankle while the other was affixed to a weight of at least one hundred pounds." At some of the plantation houses the Dutch ladies were waited on at table by absolutely naked female slaves, the reason given (to Stedman) being that unless these young women went about absolutely bare they might conceal signs of pregnancy, a condition which their mistresses wish to avoid or avert, as "bearing children would spoil their shape." The husbands of similar ladies on their part preferred that their barge-rowers should likewise remain nude: "Being healthy, young, and vigorous, they looked extremely well, and their being naked gave us a full opportunity of observing their skin, which was shining and nearly as black as ebony."

98. A MULATTO WOMAN OF DUTCH GUIANA

"Walking out on the 1st of May, I observed a crowd of people along the waterside, before the house of Mr. S—lk—r, where appeared the dreadful spectacle of a beautiful young mulatto girl floating on her back with her hands tied behind, her throat most shockingly cut, and stabbed in the breast with a knife in more than eight or ten places. This was reported to have been the work of that infernal fiend Mrs. S—lk—r from a motive of jealousy, suspecting that her husband might fall in love with this unfortunate female. This monster of a woman hàd before drowned a negro infant merely for crying—nay, she was accused of still greater barbarity. Arriving one day at her estate to view some negroes newly purchased, her eyes chanced to fall on a fine negro girl about fifteen years old who could not even speak the language of the country. Observing her to be a remarkably fine figure, with a sweet engaging countenance, her diabolical jealousy instantly prompted her to burn the girl's cheeks, mouth, and forehead with a red-hot iron; she also cut the tendon Achilles of one of her legs, thus rendering her a monster of deformity and a miserable object as long as she lived; the poor victim not knowing what she had done to deserve so severe a punishment."

This female fury, for whom no imagined hell is hot enough, but who, alas! can be matched here and there in the eighteenth-century record of Dutch Guiana—nay, even in the Southern United States and one or two British West India Islands and in French St. Domingue—was supplicated by her slaves for a more merciful treatment; whereupon she at once—to assert her authority—knocked out the brains of a quadroon child and caused two young negroes, its

swain—a fine young seaman—fell overboard into the sea from the fore-yard-arm. "His presence of mind in calling to the captain as he floated alongside, 'Be not alarmed for me, sir,' in the confidence of meeting with relief, attracted peculiar compassion, and even caused some murmuring, as no assistance was offered him; in consequence of which, after swimming a considerable time within view, the unfortunate young man went to the bottom."

relations, to be beheaded. Some of her slaves afterwards picked up these bloody heads and went in to Paramaribo to lay them before the Governor, pleading for his intervention. His only answer was to order them to be flogged severely round the streets of Paramaribo.

As in the British and French colonies of the period, a slave *could not bear witness*, could not be heard in a court of law. But had a white person witnessed these atrocities and given evidence on the subject, the utmost penalty that would have been inflicted was a fine of £50.

There seem to have been a number of Dutch women in the Guiana settlements of the eighteenth century, and they stood the climate much better than the men as regards vitality; but something in the air, the food, the life seems to have made them as energetic, passionate, and vicious as their husbands tended to become languid and *ramolli*. It was no uncommon thing for a Dutch lady of Surinam to have buried four European husbands and to be on the look out for a fifth; whereas no Dutch man was known to have been widowed (of a white wife) more than twice. The Dutch women had often good cause for jealousy, because their husbands after a short residence in Guiana preferred the society of quadroons and mulattoes and even Indian girls. Yet the men seem to have been too limp to intervene to save their wretched mistresses from the vengeance of the lawful wife.[1] According to Stedman and several other writers of the late eighteenth century, the British Leeward Islands at this period made a profitable business out of rearing quadroon and octoroon girls and sending them to Dutch Guiana to be sold for the harem.

99. AN OCTOROON GIRL
Dutch Guiana, eighteenth century

The Jews were as bad as the so-called Christians. A Jewess of Paramaribo, impelled by groundless jealousy, killed a young and beautiful quadroon girl by "plunging a red-hot poker into her body." She was only punished by a trifling fine and banishment to a country village. Another young negro woman, having her ankles chained so close together that she could scarcely move her feet, was knocked down with a cane by a Jew and beaten till the blood streamed out of head, arms, and sides.

For disobedience or anything approaching mutiny (mutiny being often the refusal of sexual intercourse with a white overseer) women were broken

[1] With the curious inconsistency of the Saxon, local society in the eighteenth century was very severe on Dutch women who were unfaithful to their Dutch husbands with white men, and expelled such women from the colony; but winked at less avowable amours between white women and negro slaves.

alive on the rack with iron bars, decapitated, flogged till their flesh was in ribbons, and hung up by the thumbs to a branch, or tortured in ways that are unprintable.

If this treatment of the women slaves was as bad as is represented, what is to be said about the sufferings of the men slaves in Dutch Guiana between the close of the seventeenth and the end of the eighteenth century? Men were hung up to gibbets by means of a hook inserted under the ribs, being left to revolve thus in the blazing sunshine till they died; they were bound to stakes and slowly roasted to death;[1] they were covered with wounds (partly self-inflicted, so as to escape torture by suicide) and then heavily loaded with chains and fastened close to the fierce, spirituous heat of rum-stills—a process thought to entail a specially painful and lingering death. Negro criminals were sometimes executed by being torn asunder, each limb being fastened to the saddle of a restive horse.

100. ONE OF THE ATROCIOUS METHODS OF KILLING SLAVES PICTURED BY STEDMAN
Hanging them up by a hook to die of thirst and famine

The slaves were compelled to work every day in the week if the master wished it.[2] As in the Bahamas and the Southern States, it was thought a smarter commercial policy to work a strong slave to death in ten years than to let him live to old age and then be pensioned off.

There were of course exceptions to this general rule of insane or thoughtless cruelty. Free persons of colour were better treated than in the British possessions or the French colonies. Some of these lived to be centenarians. A few Dutch masters and mistresses were kind-hearted employers and even philanthropists, employing their spare money in redeeming slaves that interested them or manumitting their own slaves; and it was distinctly easier and cheaper in these Dutch possessions for a slave to purchase his freedom or to be redeemed than in the British American dominions of the eighteenth century.

Here is the portrait of a typical Dutch planter-magnate of Surinam

[1] As late as 1832.

[2] "With some masters their tasks can never be performed, as they must toil on, day and night, even Sundays not excepted. I recollect a strong young negro, called *Marquis*, who had a wife he loved, with two fine children; he laboured hard, and generally finished his task of digging a trench of five hundred feet by four o'clock in the afternoon that he might have some time to cultivate his little garden and go to catch fish or fowl to support his beloved family: hard did Marquis strive to earn this additional pittance; when his *humane* master, apprised of his industry, for his encouragement informed him that if he could delve five hundred feet by four o'clock, he could certainly finish six hundred before sunset; and this task the unfortunate young man was condemned from that day ever since to perform." (Stedman.)

in the last quarter of the eighteenth century, as delineated by Captain Stedman:—

"A planter in Surinam, when he lives on his estate, gets out of his hammock with the rising sun and makes his appearance under the piazza of his house, where his coffee is ready waiting for him, which he generally takes with his pipe, instead of toast and butter. There he is attended by half a dozen of the finest young slaves, both male and female, of the plantation to serve him; in this *sanctum sanctorum* he is next accosted by his overseer, who regularly every morning attends at his levee, and having made his bows at several yards' distance with the most profound respect, informs his Greatness[1] what work was done the day before; what negroes deserted, died, fell sick, recovered, were bought or born; and above all things which of them neglected their work, affected sickness, or had been drunk or absent. The prisoners are generally present, being secured by the negro-drivers, and instantly tied up to the beams of the piazza or a tree, without so much as being heard in their own defence, when the flogging begins, with men, women, or children, without exception. The instruments of torture on these occasions are long hempen whips that cut round at every lash and crack like pistol-shots, during which they (the slaves) alternately repeat, 'Dankee, massera' (Thank you, master). In the meantime the owner stalks up and down with his overseer, affecting not so much as to hear their cries till they are sufficiently mangled, when they are untied and ordered to return to their work without so much as a dressing.

101. A TYPICAL DUTCH GUIANA PLANTER OF THE EIGHTEENTH CENTURY (STEDMAN)

"This ceremony being over, the 'dressy' negro (a black surgeon) comes to make his report; who being dismissed with a hearty curse for allowing any slaves to be sick, next there makes her appearance a superannuated matron, with all the young negro children of the estate, over whom she is governess; these being clean-washed in the river clap their hands and cheer in chorus, when they are sent away to breakfast on a large platter of rice and plantains; and the levee ends with a low bow from the overseer as it began.

"His worship now saunters forth in his morning dress, which consists of a pair of the finest Holland trowsers, white silk stockings, and red or yellow Morocco slippers; the neck of his shirt open and nothing over it, a loose flowing nightgown of the finest India chintz excepted. On his head is a cotton night-cap, as thin as a cobweb, and over that an enormous beaver hat that protects his

[1] Or *Achtbaarheid* = Respectability. The full form of address to a planter of good standing was *Edele Achtbaar Heer* (Noble, Respectable Sir) —H. H. J.

meagre visage from the sun, which is already the colour of mahogany, while his whole carcase seldom weighs above eight or ten stone, being generally exhausted by the climate and dissipation. To give a more complete idea of this fine gentleman I, in the annexed plate, present him to the reader with a pipe in his mouth, which almost everywhere accompanies him, and receiving a glass of Madeira wine and water from a female quadroon slave to refresh him during his walk.

102. A BUSH-NEGRO OF THE SARAMAKA TRIBE, DUTCH GUIANA

"Having loitered about his estate or sometimes ridden on horseback to his fields to view his increasing stores, he returns about eight o'clock, when if he goes abroad, he dresses, but if not remains just as he is. Should the first take place, having only exchanged his trowsers for a pair of thin linen or silk breeches, he sits down and holding one foot after the other, like a horse going to be shod, a negro boy puts on his stockings and shoes, which he also buckles, while another dresses his hair, his wig, or shaves his chin, and a third is fanning him to keep off the mosquitoes. Having now shifted he puts on a thin coat and waistcoat, all white; when under an umbrella carried by a black boy, he is conducted to his barge which is waiting for him with six or eight oars, well provided with fruit, wine, water, and tobacco, by his overseer, who no sooner has seen him depart than he resumes the command with the usual insolence of office. But should this prince not mean to stir from his estate he goes to breakfast about ten o'clock, for which a table is spread in the large hall, provided with a bacon-ham, hung beef, fowls, or pigeons broiled; plantains, and sweet cassavas roasted; bread, butter, cheese, etc., with which he drinks strong beer and a glass of Madeira, Rhenish, or Mozell wine, while the cringing overseer sits at the farther end, keeping his proper distance, both being served by the most beautiful slaves that can be selected; . . . and this is called breaking the poor gentleman's fast.

"After this he takes a book, plays at chess or billiards, entertains himself with music, etc., till the heat of the day forces him to return into his cotton hammock to enjoy his meridian nap, which he could no more dispense with than a Spaniard with his siesta, and in which he rocks to and fro like a performer on the slack rope, till he falls asleep, without either bed or covering; and during which time he is fanned by a couple of his black attendants, to keep him cool.

"About three o'clock he awakes by natural instinct, when having washed[1] and perfumed himself, he sits down to dinner, attended as at breakfast by his deputy governor and sable pages, where nothing is wanting that the world can afford in a western climate of meat, fowls, venison, fish, vegetables, fruits, etc., and the most exquisite wines are often squandered in profusion; after this a strong cup of coffee and a liqueur finish the repast.

"At six o'clock he is again waited on by his overseer, attended as in the morning by negro-drivers and prisoners when the flogging once more having continued for some time and the necessary orders being given for the next day's work, the assembly is dismissed and the evening spent with weak punch, *sangaree*, cards, and tobacco. His worship generally begins to yawn about ten or eleven o'clock, when he withdraws, and is undressed by his sooty pages. He then retires to rest, where he passes the night in the arms of one or other of his sable sultanas (for he always keeps a seraglio) till about six in the morning, when he again repairs to his piazza walk, where his pipe and coffee are waiting for him; and where with the rising sun he begins his round of dissipation, like a petty monarch, as capricious as he is despotic and despicable.

103. BUSH-NEGROES OF THE AUKAN TRIBE, DUTCH GUIANA

"Such absolute power indeed cannot fail to be peculiarly delightful to a man, who in all probability, in his own country, Europe, was a—nothing."

Captain Stedman goes on to relate that when, from accumulated miseries, disease, melancholy, or home-sickness slaves became unfit for work, the plantation owner or manager decided to put them to death; and to avoid incurring the penalty of fifty pounds which might be inflicted if by chance any white man testified to such an action, they had various ingenious ways of getting rid of the slaves they wished to kill. One would be to take the slave out to shoot game and "accidentally" put a bullet through him; another, to fasten the slave to a stake in an open plain under the burning sun, and supply him (or her) "with one gill of water and one plaintain a day" till the slave dies of hunger or sunstroke; or to fasten him (or her) naked to a tree in the forest with arms and neck extended under pretence of stretching the limbs. Here the slave is regularly fed, but is actually stung to death by mosquitoes and ants. Or unwanted slaves can be drowned "accidentally." One Dutch woman-owner of slaves used to fasten any one or two she did not want and could not sell inside

[1] The utmost washing these gentlemen underwent (we are told in other works) was having water poured over their faces and hands.—H. H. J.

a square of piled-up faggots. These were set fire to as though by accident and the slaves consumed in the flames.

"As to the breaking of their teeth, merely for tasting the sugar-cane cultivated by themselves, slitting up their noses and cutting off their ears from private pique, these are accounted mere sport and not worthy to be mentioned."[1]

In fact, in Dutch Guiana during the eighteenth century, as in South Carolina, Georgia, and Tennessee during the nineteenth century, slaves in their desperation often committed suicide to escape unendurable tortures. They would leap into the cauldrons of boiling sugar, drown themselves, take poison, or throw themselves from a height.

104. A EUROPEAN VOLUNTEER IN THE SERVICE OF THE DUTCH WEST INDIA COMPANY (ABOUT 1780)

This corps of about 800 Dutch, Swiss, British and Germans was employed against the Bush negroes of Guiana

Sometimes they would take revenge on their cruel owners before killing themselves. A case is quoted by Stedman of a negro who had been very badly treated by his master. The latter went away on a short journey with his wife, and on his return found that the negro had shut himself up in his owners' dwelling-house together with their three young Dutch children. Seeing his master and mistress approach, the negro ascended to the roof of the house with the children, whom he threw over one by one on to the pavement below, flinging himself over the parapet immediately afterwards, all four having their skulls smashed in front of the horrified Dutch couple. Another negro, whose wife had been taken from him and sold by the wife of his Dutch owner, shot the owner (against whom he had no grievance) and before shooting himself said to the widow, "I thought if I killed you, your suffering would be at an end; whereas if I killed your husband whom you love, you would suffer as I have done in losing my wife."

It may be imagined that this bad treatment of the slaves—which seems to have commenced so far as the Dutch were concerned from about 1650—was the cause of many of them deserting and taking refuge with the Bush negroes. This was certainly the case down to the middle of the eighteenth century. But this was not so after 1761, and still more after 1786, when agreements and treaties were entered into with the Bush negroes similar to those made between the British and the Maroons of Jamaica. Under these arrangements runaway slaves were sometimes returned to their Dutch masters to suffer horrible tortures and finally death.

[1] Captain J. G. Stedman.

In those plantations or estates where the negroes were well treated[1] a pleasant picture has been drawn by Captain Stedman.

Under a mild master and an honest overseer, a negro's labour is no more than a healthy exercise which ends at the setting sun. The remaining time is his own, which he employs in hunting, fishing, cultivating his garden, or making baskets and fish nets for sale; with this money he buys a hog or two, sometimes fowls or ducks, all of which he fattens upon the spontaneous growth of the soil, without expense and very little trouble, and, in the end, they afford him considerable profit. Thus pleasantly situated, he is exempt from every anxiety, and pays no taxes, but looks up to his master as the only protector of him and his family. He adores him, not from fear, but from a conviction that he is indebted to his goodness for all the comforts he enjoys. He breathes in a luxurious, warm climate, like his own, which renders clothes unnecessary, and he finds himself more healthy, as well as more at his ease, by going naked. His house he may build after his own fancy. The forest affords him every necessary material for the cutting. His bed is a hammock, or a matting called *papaya*. His pots he manufactures himself, and his dishes are gourds, which grow in his garden. He never lives with a wife he does not love, exchanging for another the moment either he or she becomes tired, though this separation happens less frequently here than divorces do in Europe. Besides the regular allowance given him by his master weekly, his female friend has the art of making many savoury dishes, such as *braf*, or hodge-podge of plantains and yams boiled with salt meat, barbacued fish, and Cayenne pepper. *Tom-tom* is a very good pudding, composed of the flour of Indian corn, boiled with flesh, fowl, fish, Cayenne pepper, and the young pods of the *ocro* or althea plant. Pepper-pot is a dish of boiled

105. MAAGDEN STRAAT
An important street in Paramaribo

[1] Not all the masters of slaves were monsters of iniquity, and one or two cruel slave-owners were Scotchmen, for there were quite a number of Scotch settlers, or officials in the Dutch service, in Guiana during the eighteenth century. On the other hand, some of the kindly and even benevolent slave-owners were British Americans who settled in Guiana under the Dutch flag both before and after the American Revolt against Great Britain. Some of the higher Dutch officials, owing allegiance rather to the States-General or their nomination to the Stadhouder (Prince of Orange) than to the Dutch Chartered Company which administered the Guiana settlements down to 1792, were men of kindly disposition who frequently attempted to better the condition of the slaves. On the other hand, the spirit animating the Chartered Company was usually pitiless to the last degree. The general condition of the slaves, it is true, improved after 1786, when peace was finally made with the Bush negroes, and through the influence of the Prince of Orange, who received and conversed with representatives of the Bush negroes.

fish and capsicum, eaten with the roasted plantains. *Gangotay* is made of dried, and *afofoo* of green plantains. *Acanfa* and *doquenoo* are composed of the flour of maize, and the latter is eaten with molasses. His common drink is the limpid stream, sometimes corrected by a little rum. If he is accidentally wounded or indisposed, he is cured for nothing; but it is very seldom he troubles the faculty, being tolerably skilled in herbs and simples, besides scarifying and puckering the skin, which serves instead of bleeding. The inconvenience of vermin he remedies with a comb, by plaistering up his hair with clay, which being dried on the head, and then washed with soap and water, makes him clean beyond conception; his teeth are constantly kept as white as ivory; for this purpose he uses nothing but a sprig of orange-tree, bitten at one end, until the fibres resemble a small brush; and no negro, male or female, is to be seen without this little instrument, which has besides the virtue of sweetening the breath.

So much for his body; and with regard to his *soul*, he is seldom troubled with qualms of conscience, or fear of death, as I have stated, being firm and unshaken in what he was taught to believe, which is indeed little, but plain; and when he is no more, his

106. NICKERIE
An important town in Western Surinam, Dutch Guiana

companions or relatives carry him to some grove of orange-trees, where he is not interred without expense, being generally put in a coffin of the very best wood and workmanship, while the cries and lamentations of his surviving friends, who sing a dirge, pierce the sky. The grave being filled up, and a green turf neatly spread over it, a couple of large gourds are put by the side, the one with water, the other with boiled fowls, pork, cassava, etc., as a libation, not from a superstitious notion, as some believe, that he will eat or drink it, but as a testimony of that regard which they have for his memory and ashes; while some even add the little furniture that he left behind, breaking it in pieces over the grave. This done, every one takes his last farewell, speaking to him as if alive, and testifying their sorrow at his departure; adding, that they hope to see him, not in *Guinea*, as some have written, but in that better place, where he now enjoys the pleasant company of his parents, friends, and ancestors; when another dismal yell ends the ceremony, and all return home.

The Bush negroes, or "Bosch negers" of the Dutch, were derived, in part, from the ex-slaves of the English, abandoned on the Guiana coast or along the rivers of Guiana, when the British by degrees were expelled or withdrew from this region. These English-speaking negroes greatly disliked their new Dutch masters, and fled from them into the trackless forests of the interior, where they maintained themselves without much difficulty so far as the indigenous Amerindians were concerned. Except in regard to the coast tribes of Caribs, the Amerindians of all Guiana were a gentle, peaceable race, very well inclined towards the white man, not liking the negro (nor mingling their blood much with his), but, on the other hand, no match for him as warriors. The Bush negroes when hard-pressed by the Dutch settlers or their Indian allies, would take refuge within the limits of French or Spanish Guiana. With the French they were much associated, and when the French forces invaded the Surinam territories in 1711–12 under Cassard, all the Dutch slaves that could manage to

107. THE WORKADAY COSTUME OF THE COLOURED WOMEN OF DUTCH GUIANA

escape joined the Bush negroes and with them assisted the French forces to inflict the most damaging attack on the Dutch settlements, many of which were thus destroyed.

From 1715 to 1775 there was an almost unending warfare between the Dutch, the Bush negroes, or their own slaves for the time being. There was a great rising of ill-used slaves on the Upper Surinam River in 1730, beginning on one of the plantations of the Chartered Company. This war, which extended to fighting with the already emancipated Bush negroes, did not come to a close till 1749, when a formal treaty was made in the name of the Dutch Government with 1600 victorious negroes. These 1600 (it is observed by W. G.

Palgrave[1]) scrupulously observed the conditions of their treaty afterwards; but many of the revolted slaves joined with other bands of Bush negroes and retreated to the forests at the head-waters of the River Komowain (Commowijne). Here they defied the Dutch under a leader named Sam-sam.

108. NEGRO ROWERS, DUTCH GUIANA

In 1757 Sam-sam was succeeded by a Muhammadan negro named Arabi, who may quite possibly have come from the Northern Senegal coast[2] and have been of half Moorish or Arab extraction. So considerable was the influence gained by Arabi and his victories over the Dutch troops, that he might have succeeded, had he desired, in overwhelming and destroying the white settlers throughout this region, but he chose instead to open negotiations for permanent peace with the Company's Government, and succeeded in obtaining for himself and his followers not only liberty and independence, but also a considerable tract of territory stretching between the Cottica and Commowijne Rivers on the west and the French frontier at the great Marowain (Maroweyn) River on the east. This important group of Bush negroes was henceforth known as the Auka, or, in the old Dutch spelling, the Oucans, from the fact that the treaty of peace between them and the Dutch was signed in 1761 at a plantation called Auka (Ouca) in the Upper Surinam River. Immediately after this, the runaway negroes (mostly from the Luango coast) who had settled along the banks of the Upper Saramaka River, also arose in rebellion and obtained peace from the Dutch Governor on similar terms to those accorded to the Aukans. In this way the immediate hinterland of the Surinam settlements was secured, so far as hostility from the Bush negroes was concerned, between the Korantain or Corantyn River on the west and the Maroweyn (French frontier) on the east. In what is now British Guiana—then the Dutch settlements of Berbice, Demerara, and Essequibo, there was no very great development of Dutch interests and

109. NEGRO WOMEN, DUTCH GUIANA

[1] *Dutch Guiana*, London, 1876.

[2] There were many "Poregoedoc" (Poregudok) negroes or negroids in Dutch Guiana who seem to have been derived from the Dutch trading stations of Goree and Arguin, north and south of the Senegal. Poregudok probably = Portendik.

prosperity, and no particular need to take action against such runaway negroes as had escaped from the settlements to the interior.

But in 1763 nearly all the slaves of the coast region revolted against their masters, and for a time almost the only places in Dutch hands were the capital, Paramaribo, and the plantation of Dagerrad. The Bush negroes of the interior held fast to their treaty engagements and gave no aid to revolted slaves, who were led by two able chiefs, Bonni and Baron, who established their headquarters on the Maroweyn River, from which they obviously received succour at the hands of the French settlers of Cayenne. In 1770 the Dutch Governor, Louis Nepveu, organised a corps of enfranchised negroes under a Dutch officer, Colonel Stoelman. These "Bonni" negroes, as they came to be called, were tackled with desperate determination by the Government of the Dutch Company in 1773. In addition to the negro corps already organised, the Company obtained from Holland eight hundred soldiers—Dutch, Scottish, English, German, and Swiss, under the command of a Swiss officer, Colonel Fourgeoud. This was the expedition accompanied, as one of its officers, by Captain J. G. Stedman, the Englishman who wrote such a vivid account of Dutch Guiana on his return to England at the close of the eighteenth century. Though the Bonni negroes fought desperately, they had at last to acknowledge themselves defeated. Bonni himself took up his residence with some of his followers in the French colony of Cayenne; but the greater number of the insurgents made terms with the Dutch and settled down in the interior regions between the Maroweyn and Surinam Rivers. Their descendants either still exist under the clan name of Bonni (derived from the now-British settlement of Bonny or Obani, in the Niger delta), or have fused with another clan known as Musinga,[1] or Bekau (also called Matrokan).

110. A CHINAMAN OF DUTCH GUIANA MARRIED TO A NEGRESS

By 1786 all warfare was over between the Dutch and the Bush negroes, and by 1792 the Government of the Chartered Company was replaced by the direct rule of the States-General, a rule which was to last four years before the British swooped on this country, and during those four years to effect great improvement in the condition of such negroes as remained in slavery. As to the Bush negroes, they were so completely satisfied with their treatment once peace was concluded with the Dutch, that they fought bravely and determinedly against both French and British to save Guiana for the Dutch nation. In 1814 the Netherlands definitely lost the larger western half of Guiana[2] to Great Britain,

[1] These seem to have been Gold Coast negroes.

[2] This had always been much less "Dutch" than the Surinam region, east of the Corantyn River. Many British and a few French planters were settled at Demerara, Berbice, and Essequibo.

who had occupied all the coast region of this great province at intervals since 1781, and who in 1814 restored Surinam to the Dutch but purchased what is now British Guiana. Great Britain abolished the slave-trade in all this region in 1807, but the Dutch Government did not condemn the slave-trade until 1814 nor abolish *slavery* in Surinam and the Dutch West India Islands until 1863. The retention of slavery in this colony when in the adjoining British possession steps were being taken to give freedom to the blacks caused great discontent to arise among the Surinam negroes in 1832, and an insurrection of slaves in that year resulted in the capital, Paramaribo, being partially destroyed by fire. The reprisals were savage: negroes identified as incendiaries being burnt alive in public.

III. THE "GRANMAN" OR CHIEF, OSESI, OF THE AUKAN TRIBE OF BUSH NEGROES
Accompanied by his two ministers or "adjutanten," Dutch Guiana

In 1845 the colony of Surinam was separated from that of the Dutch West Indies, and in the same year came out a Dutch Governor of Surinam — Baron van Raders — who remodelled the administration of the colony, improved the treatment of the slaves, and declared the ports open to the commerce of the whole world without discrimination. After careful preparations slavery was declared at an end in 1863, about the time when in spite of free trade the affairs of Surinam had reached the lowest depth of depression. But instead of growing worse after abolition they began slowly to improve.

The political constitution was changed in 1865 to what it now is. There is a House of Assembly, of which four members are nominated by the Sovereign, and the remainder—from five to nine—are elected by the people on a low property franchise, open to all citizens, without distinction of race or colour. But the powers of this House are only deliberative. It cannot initiate legislation, and the Governor if he wishes may pass a law over the head of its adverse vote, but in so doing must furnish the Assembly with his reasons in writing. Such as it is, the constitution appears to give complete satisfaction to the multi-coloured inhabitants of this Dutch State.

East Indian kulis were introduced into Surinam in 1873 and now number nearly 20,000. Their advent, as elsewhere in tropical America, has been a great boon. It has enabled the European capitalist to carry on his productive planting work and has put the local negro on his mettle. The Surinam negroes imitate the East Indians in many things, even if there is no intermingling of races.

There are some 400 Chinese; the whites number about 2500, including the Dutch soldiers, sailors and officials, and 1050 Jews. The settled negroes and half-castes amount to about 55,000 and the Bush negroes to nearly 30,000. The Amerindians have diminished much since the eighteenth century owing to alcoholism and small-pox. There may be as many as 4000 left in the far interior

112. A CEIBA TREE (BOMBAX)
Worshipped or respected by peasants or Bush-negroes in the West Indies and South America

of Dutch Guiana. They are being pushed into Brazilian territory by the vigorous Bush negroes.

These latter are aptly described by W. G. Palgrave[1] as "ranking among the best specimens of the Ethiopian type. The men are often six feet and more in height, with well-developed limbs and pleasing open countenance; and the women in every physical respect are, to say the least, worthy of their mates. Ill-modelled limbs are in fact as rare among them as they are common among some lighter-complexioned races. Their skin colour is in general very dark, and gives no token of the gradual tendency to assume a fairer tint that

[1] *Dutch Guiana*, London, 1876.

may be observed among the descendants of negroes residing in more northern climes. Their hair, too, is as curly as that of any Nyam-nyam or Darfuri chief, or native of Senegal."

The Bush negroes are free from taxation, and govern themselves under their own head-men and chiefs, the more important of whom receive investiture from the Governor at Paramaribo. The jargon they talk—which is corrupt English mixed with Portuguese, French, and a little Dutch—is gradually giving way to Dutch amongst those who go to work in or who frequent the white man's towns and settlements. But it is doubtful whether Dutch will ever be popular as the speech of negroes whose ancestors came from Equatorial Africa and used many broad, distinct vowels and (ordinarily) no faucal gutturals or abruptly collocated consonants.

113. THE LATEST FASHIONS IN SURINAM (1910)

The ancestors of the Bush negroes were scarcely Christians, for at the time they escaped from servitude the Moravian missionaries had not got to work in Guiana. Some, however, escaping from Brazil, brought distorted fragments of Christian beliefs. A few were Muhammadans by tradition ; and an attenuated belief in sorcery remained everywhere amongst them.

But except for notions of a curious trinity of two gods and a goddess, obviously derived from Christianity, they are—or were until the Moravian Brethren settled amongst them in the nineteenth century—pagans ; and worshipped a number of divinities, such as Gran Gado (the "great God"), Jesi Kist, Maria (a goddess), Ampuka, or Amuku, or Banko—the god of the forest, usually worshipped in the form of a tall ceiba or silk cotton tree (*Bombax*)—Buemba, or Toni, the god of water, and Hiari, a demon, associated with poisonous trees.[1]

[1] Much information regarding the Bosch-negers, their habits, customs, beliefs, and language, is given in the works of the Moravian Brethren, published at Herrnhut, Moravia—such as *Die Buschneger Surinames*, by H. G. Schneider, Herrnhut, 1893; *Bij de Indianen en Bosch-negers van Suri-*

Dutch Guiana (and for the matter of that, the Dutch West India Islands), which began in the seventeenth century by being a hell for the negro slave, has ended in becoming, at the commencement of the twentieth century, a negro paradise. "The combined discipline of Dutch rule and Moravian teachership have trained the African native into the Surinam créole, the cannibals of the Gaboon into the peasants of Munnickendam."[1] The teaching and example of the missionaries have checked the excessive licentiousness of the once-savage Bush negroes; their marital unions are more regular (as are those of the civilised negroes), and in consequence their families of children are larger and the infant mortality is less. Nor are the Moravians the only agency for good: there are the Roman Catholic schools and institutes, and some fifteen thousand of the negro and negroid population of the Dutch colony belong to that Church. The Dutch Government has set on foot practical tuition in agriculture and horticulture; and in many ways the Surinam negro is rising in the social scale: and as he rises he finds in the men who come and go from the Netherlands none of that *morgue*, that quiet (and consequently more unbearable) insolence of disdain which occasionally checks the loyalty of the negro or the negroid towards the colonial administration of the Anglo-Saxon.

name, De Binnenlanden van het district Nickerie (Suriname), and other works by Dr. H. van Cappelle, published in the Netherlands between 1903 and 1908. Dr. H. van Cappelle's writings give valuable bibliographical references as well as much original information on the Bush negroes and Amerindians of Dutch Guiana.

[1] Palgrave.

CHAPTER VII

SLAVERY UNDER THE FRENCH

THE Norman French of Dieppe are said to have been the first European people to trade with the West African coast. According to the stories and traditions gathered into a book by Villault de Bellefonds (in 1666), between the years 1339 and 1412 French ships from the Norman ports had visited most parts of the West African littoral from the Senegal River to the Gold Coast.[1] Their inducement was the trade in ivory and gold. Negro slaves were not thought of in those days.

The French also were the first of the European nations to attack the Iberian monopoly of commerce with the New World. Their assaults on the Spanish settlements in Mexico and Cuba, their attempts to colonise Florida and Brazil in the middle of the sixteenth century, are enumerated on pages 53 and 78. For the remainder of that century they were too much occupied with domestic feuds to give much thought to America. But when Henri Quatre was well seated on his throne, charters were given to explorers and officials who laid the foundation of Canada and visited the coast of Guiana (in 1604).

In 1617 there was formed in France a company of adventurers to explore the "Isles of America," and its agents prospected the Guiana rivers and visited the Lesser Antilles, then abandoned by the Spaniards and peopled by fierce Caribs. Through the patronage of Richelieu, Louis XIII granted a charter to the Compagnie des Iles d'Amérique in 1625, and by 1626 its agent, d'Esnambuc, had secured, by arrangement with the English, half the island of St. Christopher. By 1635 the French Company had occupied Guadeloupe, Martinique, and St. Lucia, after several repulses and much hand-to-hand fighting with the Caribs, whom in these three islands they exterminated. By the year 1648 they had also acquired the island of Grenada.

In 1626 a small body of Norman traders from Rouen settled at the mouth of the Sinnamary River in what is now French Guiana; and in 1634 other Normans founded the town of Cayenne, on an island at the mouth of a small river (Cayenne is but the French rendering of the widespread Amerindian geographical term "Guiana" or "Guayana").

Between 1643 and 1652 three Norman companies were founded to develop Guiana, which was then called "La France Equinoxiale." They all failed, and between 1650 and 1664 Cayenne was occupied by the Dutch.

But in 1664 a chartered Compagnie des Indes Occidentales was formed under the patronage of Colbert, and entrusted with the management of the

[1] This theory of the early voyages of the Dieppois ships to West Africa is very strongly combated by C. Raymond Beazley in his *Dawn of Modern Geography*, Vol. II. It has been equally strongly upheld in the recent writings (1905-6) of Mons. L. Binger, the great French explorer and administrator.

French West India Islands (including Montserrat), and with the Guiana settlements. In 1674 this company was dissolved, and all its possessions were placed under the control of the French Crown.

Great activity was now displayed by the French Government in encouraging the emigration of French settlers to French America, which gradually spread from the St. Lawrence and the Great Lakes down the Missouri and Mississippi to the Gulf of Mexico, included much of Western Hispaniola, part of St. Christopher and St. Martin, the islet of St. Bartholomew, Guadeloupe, Martinique, St. Lucia, Grenada, and the eastern part of Guiana. Dominica, St. Vincent, and sometimes St. Lucia and Tobago, were, in times of lassitude—weariness of

114. THE TOWN OF CASTRIES, ST. LUCIA, BRITISH WINDWARD ISLANDS
Founded by the French about 1674

war with the doggedly-fighting Caribs, or the persistent British Navy—set aside as "neutral," a neutrality which was merely regarded by both Britain and France as a breathing-space during which "unauthorised" colonists of both nations settled on these disputed lands. Still, through treating the Caribs and the negro slaves more sympathetically, French influence became so profoundly implanted in Dominica, St. Lucia, and even St. Vincent, that the Caribs of the eighteenth century and the negroes of to-day might well have been French subjects, judged by language, religion, and sympathies. And all the geographical features of the Windward and most of the Leeward Islands bear French names.

During all the seventeenth century the French were justifying their appearance in the Antilles by their vigorous encouragement of tropical agriculture. Owing to their connection with Guiana and attempts at seizing portions of

Brazil, they were able to bring to their West India islands various useful plants and trees. Further, they imported roe-deer and peacocks from France and let them loose on Martinique and Guadeloupe, from which islands they were transported to Haiti, Cuba, and many other parts of the Antilles. The roe-deer now running wild in Cuba, Haiti, and one or two of the Lesser Antilles are derived from the stock imported from France in the seventeenth century; so are the wild peacocks of Haiti and Antigua.

The first idea of the adventurer-concessionnaires, the noblemen-proprietors, or of the chartered companies when they got hold of the Antilles or of Guiana was colonisation by Europeans, and Europeans who would devote themselves to agriculture and stock-rearing. Difference of climatic conditions had hardly been realised; and perhaps to men and women coming from sunny France, agricultural work on a breezy West India islet seemed not beyond their strength. But the first colonists of the French islands were Normans, Bretons, and people from the west of France; Flemings and Picards, later on Rhenish Germans and Alsatians: men and women of the Nordic race, who were well able to fight or to sail ships, to carry on sheltered industries or trades, but who could not bend their backs to tillage without getting sunstroke and fever. Some came at their own expense and received grants of land; others were apprentices who for the cost of their voyage and a very poor annual salary bound themselves as contracted labourers for a term of three years. During this term of apprenticeship they were little better than slaves, but at the end of their three years they received small grants of land.

115. A MULATTO WOMAN, MARTINIQUE

But for sugar-planting and all forms of tropical agriculture they were no use, and as early as 1642–5, at the beginning of the sugar and coffee boom, negroes were introduced into Martinique to work on the plantations. By 1645 the trade in slaves with the French West Indies and Guiana was in full swing.

The plantations of Cayenne (Guiana) were cultivated during the seventeenth and eighteenth centuries by a few negro slaves obtained from the Dutch and Portuguese; by such of the Amerindians as could be induced by the Jesuit missionaries to settle down to agriculture; and above all by French colonists.[1] French Guiana made no great demands on the Slave-trade until the early nineteenth century.[2] It was to St. Christopher, Haiti, Martinique, Guadeloupe, St. Lucia, Grenada, Dominica, and Trinidad[3] that the French despatched the negroes they obtained from Africa: as also to Louisiana, which colony along the lower course and delta of the Mississippi (and the adjoining territory of Alabama) was founded by the French in 1700–18.

Though possibly the first of European nations to visit the west coast of Africa, the French were practically the last to establish slave-trading depôts there. The ships of Dieppe and Havre, of Nantes and Bordeaux began to trade at and examine the Senegal River early in the seventeenth century—from 1604 to 1637—but no real settlement of a lasting character was made in this region till the founding of Fort St. Louis du Sénégal in 1662. This became the head-quarters of the French West African slave-trade, and to it were added in 1677–8 the Dutch possessions of Rufisque, Portudal, Joal, and Goree Island (off the modern Dakar) between Cape Verde and the Gambia; and in 1717–24, Portendic and Arguin Island off the Sahara coast. During the eighteenth century the French ships traded for slaves with Sierra Leone, Liberia, the Ivory Coast, and Dahomé;[4] and the Loango coast immediately north of the Congo mouth. This last region indeed became so important as a slave-recruiting ground for Saint Domingue (Haiti) that the Portuguese were sternly warned off it at a time (1786) when they had thought of bringing it under the Government of Angola.

Owing to the frequent wars with the British during the close of the seventeenth and greater part of the eighteenth centuries, the direct French slave-trade from Africa—especially Senegal—was much interfered with; and a good deal of the slave-supply to the French West Indian Islands, Haiti, and Louisiana was undertaken by the Dutch, Danes, and Portuguese. Nevertheless in 1701 the Spanish Government passed on the Asiento Contract to the French

[1] From 1674 to the middle of the eighteenth century was the golden age of French American colonisation, and of Cayenne in particular. The adjoining Dutch colony of Surinam was several times overwhelmed, and many of the revolted Dutch negroes joined the French as free fighting men and assisted to open up the forests of the interior. But "La France Equinoctiale" was still thought a possible home for a European population. In 1763, the prime minister, the Duc de Choiseul, obtained for himself and a relation, the Duc de Praslin, a concession of the country between the rivers Kuru and Maroni (Maroweyn), in Western Guiana. They then sent out some 12,000 colonists from Alsace-Lorraine, who were landed at the mouth of the Kuru, in a swamp where even fresh water was lacking! It was the rainy season of the year, no waterproof dwellings were ready to receive the settlers, and many of the necessaries of life in the tropics were wanting: although, *mirabile dictu!* a supply of *skates* was sent out amongst the equipment deemed necessary for Guiana colonists. No doubt the ignorant bureaucrats who organised the expedition confused Guiana with "les quelques arpents de neige," Canada. By 1765 only 918 of the Alsatian colonists were living. In spite of this disaster other attempts at French colonisation were made between 1784 and 1788. In the Revolutionary period and under Napoleon many political offenders were sent here, in most cases to die. Six hundred Royalists were landed at Sinnamary in 1796 and in a few weeks four hundred of them were dead Not that the climate of Guiana or any other part of Equatorial America is so deadly, but that the white man requires to be most carefully screened from sun, rain, cold sea-breeze, and damp; and at the same time to obtain good and suitable food.

[2] Lafayette, the hero of French intervention in the North American rebellion, and a great Anti-slavery champion in France between 1790 and 1793, possessed a large plantation near Cayenne which was worked by negro slaves. These slaves (according to Bryan Edwards in his *History of the West Indies*) Lafayette sold to the number of seventy in 1789 "without scruple or stipulation," not even giving them a chance to purchase their own freedom.

[3] Trinidad was almost a French colony (under a Spanish Governor) from 1783 to 1797. Creole French is still the most widely spoken language in that island among the negroes of the countryside.

[4] Dahomé through Hwida (Whydah, Ajuda) sent many slaves to the French and British West Indies, especially from its western frontiers from the "Popo" (often pronounced and written "Pawpaw") country. From this region came the ancestors of Toussaint Louverture and President Barclay of Liberia. In the eighteenth century Dahomé was written on the French maps "Dauma," which no doubt is the right pronunciation.

"Royal Senegal Company," in whose slave-trade enterprise Louis XIV (unconsciously copying in this the English queens Elizabeth and Anne) held a large number of shares.

It was the possession of St. Domingue (Haiti)[1] however that involved France most deeply in the slave-trade and in the condition and history of the Negro in the New World: to an extent more important in its ultimate effects than the operations of any other European Power save only Britain and her daughter, the United States. France was the first nation to ridicule the idea of an Hispano-Portuguese monopoly of the New World. England was a good second; and in these splendid piracies the seamen of Southern and Western England and of Northern and Western France often acted in union and partnership. Together they had got hold of the island of St. Christopher (St. Kitts) in 1625, at a time when many of the smaller Antillean and Bahaman islands were to be had for the taking[2] or at worst a tussle with the Caribs. A Spanish naval force descended on St. Christopher in 1629 and drove out nearly all the French and English pirate-settlers. These smoked-out hornets circled round several likely points of vantage (such as Antigua) and finally established themselves on the island of Tortuga, off the north-west coast of Haiti.

There were Dutchmen and North Germans at first, as well as English and French, among these West Indian pirates; and to this mixture we owe the few Dutch words in the vocabulary of negro seamen in the West Indies and in the Negro patois of Haiti, besides the term "freebooter" applied alternately with "buccaneer" to the settlers of Tortuga. ["Freebooter" comes from the Dutch *vrijbuiter*, "free plunderer," and was corrupted by the Spaniards into *filibuster* and the French into *flibustier*.] The Dutch buccaneers of Tortuga chiefly came from the island of Santa Cruz, whence they had been ejected by the Spaniards.

From Tortuga the pirates were wont to resort to the opposite coast of Haiti to kill the wild oxen which were the descendants of the cattle introduced into

[1] It may be convenient at this stage (at the risk of repetition) to explain the nomenclature of this French possession. The whole island was called "Española" or "Little Spain" by Columbus (who spelt the word in semi-Italian fashion, "Espagnola"). He had previously applied to it the Amerindian names of *Bohio* (really meaning a village or settlement) or *Babeque*. He landed first at the north-western extremity (Mole St. Nicholas), December 6th, 1492. This western part of the island was called by the natives *Haiti* or "the mountainous country," and the whole island seems to have been known by these Arawaks as *Kiskika* (Quisquica) or the "vast country," or, as some wrote it, *Quisqueya*.

Later on Española was latinised into HISPANIOLA; and this word remains to this day the most convenient general name for the whole island. In 1494 Columbus's brother, Bartolomeo, founded a new capital for the Spanish colony, in place of the unhealthy "Isabella" which Christopher had established in the previous year on the north coast of the island, at the mouth of the little river Bahabonito. This new capital was named at first "Nueva Isabella," but after Columbus visited it in 1498 he changed the name to "Santo Domingo," to commemorate the patron saint of his father, Dominico Colombo. After Columbus left the place its site was changed from the east to the west side of the River Ozama. Gradually Spanish interest in this neglected island centred round its capital city, and the name *Hispaniola* was forgotten except by pedants, and SANTO DOMINGO adopted instead. From this arose the French rendering *St. Domingue*, which was applied to what we now call HAITI until 1804. But it is interesting to note that the Amerindian name Haiti, proper to Western Hispaniola, was preserved by the negro slaves, who no doubt had picked it up from the last of the Arawaks, with whom their runaways sought refuge. Already in the latter part of the eighteenth century *Haiti* was once more in use for North-Western St. Domingue, and after 1804 it was adopted as the official name of the Negro republic. *Santo Domingo* or *La Republica Dominicana* is the official designation of the Spanish part of Hispaniola.

[2] The explanation of the apparent indifference which Spain at first showed to the doings of British, French, and Dutch in the Lesser Antilles lay in the fact that finding no minerals of value in these smaller islands and having almost entirely denuded them of Amerindian inhabitants (to supply the plantations and mines of Cuba, Porto Rico, Hispaniola, and Jamaica with Arawak and Lucayan slaves), she had completely abandoned them and only awoke to their strategic importance when they became the homes of pirates.

Hispaniola by the Spaniards. Many herds of these had made their way to the depopulated western portion of the great island. To dry the beef of these slain cattle they erected wooden frameworks from which the chunks of meat were suspended over a fire. Such arrangements were called *Boucan*,[1] the users of them, who made a profitable commerce of this grilled or smoked beef, were nicknamed *boucaniers*, or buccaneers. Gradually the French[2] preponderated in the community of buccaneers which had its head-quarters on Tortuga (in fact, in 1641 the island was declared to be French territory and the English were driven out), and by 1663 the French King had definitely extended his protection to the north coast of Haiti and had placed it under the control of a French commandant (Deschamps-de-la-place).

By 1680 the Spaniards had commenced to recognise the principle of dividing the island of Hispaniola with France. It was not till 1777, however, that a definite treaty fixed the limits between the French and the Spanish portions of Hispaniola (Santo Domingo). The full authority of France over this colony was thus not completely determined until less than twenty years before the loss of it by the negro insurrection (1804–8).

116. CATTLE OF NORTHERN HAITI
Descended from the wild oxen possessed by the Buccaneers

By 1680, there were quite a number of negro slaves in the French West Indies, more especially in the Lesser Antilles. And the French were not chary of mingling with the negresses, so that the problem of the position of the half-caste—was he slave or free?—had already presented itself to French legists and ecclesiastics. Louis XIV and his advisers gave very serious consideration to the whole question of negro slaves in America, their condition and prospects, their rights and wrongs; and in 1685 promulgated the famous "Code Noir," as the edict was commonly called, the most humane legislation in regard to the unhappy negroes which had been devised until the repeal of slavery; and far superior to any laws in force in the British slave-holding territories.

The Edict of 1685 ordained that all slaves should be baptised and instructed in the Apostolic Roman Catholic religion; that slaves should never be called upon to work for twenty-four hours, on Sunday, or on any festival of the Church; that free men who had children from their concubinage with women-slaves, together with the master of such slaves (if he consented to such concubinage) should be punished by a fine of two thousand livres of sugar, but if the man so erring was himself the master of the slave, then, in addition to the fine, the slave-concubine and her children should be taken from him, sold for the benefit of the hospital and never be allowed to be freed; excepting, that is, unless the man was not married to another person at the time of his concubinage, in which case he was to *marry* the woman slave, who, together with her children, should thereby become free. Masters were forbidden to constrain

[1] See note on page 51. *Boucan*, by George Sylvain, a Haitian writer, is said to have been applied more correctly to an underground oven wherein the Caribs baked their meat.

[2] Nearly all Normans or Bretons.

slaves to marry against their will. Children of a slave father and a free mother were born *free*; of a free father and a slave mother, they were the property of the owner of the female slave. Christian slaves were to be buried in consecrated ground. Slaves were forbidden to carry arms (except at the command of their master), to gather in crowds, to sell sugar-cane (even with their masters' permission) or anything else without their masters' sanction and knowledge. For contravening the regulation as to assembling in crowds they might, if often repeated, be killed.

They were to be well nourished and clothed at the expense of their masters, and if not so treated might complain to a magistrate and the case would be inquired into and justice done without expense to the slave. The same course would be taken if a slave was cruelly injured or abused by his master. Slaves, however, were incapable of holding property or of inheriting it. Everything they might acquire was the property of their master. They could not serve in any public office, act as agent for any free man, or be valid witnesses in a court of law, civil or criminal. Their evidence might be taken down to furnish the court with information without (illogically enough) the judges drawing therefrom any presumption, conjecture, or proof. The slaves themselves could have no recourse to the law (except in regard to complaining of their masters' treatment) or seek for reparation for any outrages or deeds of violence committed against them; but on the other hand they could be pursued in justice and punished "avec les mêmes formalitiés que les personnes libres." If a slave struck his master, mistress or their children in the face, or elsewhere, his blow drawing blood, he would be punished with death; and the same sentence was to be inflicted if a slave committed a violent assault on any free person. Thefts were to be punished with death, branding, or whipping; and any loss of property due to a slave's theft was to be made good by the slave's master; failing which the slave became the property of the person whose goods had been stolen. Runaway slaves were (after a month's absence) to be punished for the first offence by having the ears cut off and the shoulder branded with a fleur-de-lys; for the second offence they were branded on the other shoulder and hamstrung (!); and the third time they ran away they were to be killed. Any freed man who sheltered a fugitive slave was fined three hundred pounds of sugar for every day he retained the slave. Masters were to be allowed to put a slave in chains and to whip him or her with rods (*verges*), but were forbidden to torture, mutilate, and still more to kill, slaves under pain of judicial proceedings and severe penalties. A slave family—husband, wife, and children under age—belonging to one master might not be sold separately.

117. FRENCH NEGROES DANCING ON A FÊTE DAY
Eighteenth century

Finally—and for a century, at least, these last provisions of the French Code were thought to be inconveniently liberal in the British-American colonies—*any slave-owner of twenty years old and upwards might during his life or at his death give freedom to his slaves without assigning any reason or* (if a minor) *asking the opinion or consent of relations or guardians; any slave appointed under his master's will universal legatee, executor, or guardian of the master's children became* ipso facto *free; and all slaves once freed—by any process that was lawful—had precisely the same position, privileges, and civil rights as any French man or woman born free.*

These last words are important to remember, because in this respect, as in others protecting the rights of the negroes or "coloured" people, the "Code Noir" was never properly applied in Haiti; and thus in course of time arose the sense of a bitter injustice among the freed men and slaves—near-whites, mulattoes, and negroes—of this important French colony.

118. QUIET INDUSTRY
A French-speaking negress-seamstress in Louisiana

The Spanish had firmly opposed by arms the colonisation of Florida by French or British, and had equally stoutly defended Mexico; but their resistance to foreign intrusion between Florida and Texas died away during the seventeenth century, and the French pioneers coming down from Canada in the far north by means of the Mississippi and its great affluents (leaving ineffaceable evidence of their passage and their colossal exploits in the geographical names between Chicago and New Orleans) took possession of the Mississippi delta in 1682. In 1700 the colony of Louisiana was founded; by 1711 the French had occupied the Alabama coast and commenced to build the town of Mobile. In 1719 an instalment of five hundred negro slaves "from Guinea" was landed at the just-commenced settlement of Nouvelle Orléans and in 1721 nearly fourteen hundred more. In 1732, when Louisiana reverted to the Crown of France (these settlements had hitherto been under Chartered Companies), there were only two thousand negroes, but thenceforth a steady importation went on till 1803, when Louisiana became part of the United States, by whom the slave trade had been forbidden.

France had lost interest in her colonies of New Orleans and Mobile when obliged to withdraw from Canada in 1760–3, and so, by a secret arrangement transferred Louisiana to Spain (in 1762), and withdrew from Alabama in favour of Britain in the following year. Neither the French settlers nor their negro slaves approved the transfer to Spain, and managed to stand out against it until 1769, in which year Spain took possession with an overwhelming force; and punished severely by many executions the first serious attempt in America to dispute the will and disposal of the mother country in Europe. Between 1770 and 1800, the Spaniards introduced many more negroes (the descendants of whom speak Spanish to this day) into Louisiana. Some of them escaped to the marshy forests of the south-west and lead still a quasi-wild existence there.

Although the French flag has not flown over Louisiana or Alabama (Mobile) since 1769, except for a few months in 1802–3, the vitality of the French tongue, religion, manners, customs, and cookery among the negroes and

119. A FRENCH-SPEAKING LOUISIANA NEGRO AND HIS GRANDCHILD

"coloured" people in Louisiana, Southern Mississippi, and the Alabama seaboard is remarkable and from many points of view is not to be regretted. Whatever they may have done in Haiti, here the French settlers seem to have treated their slaves with kindness and to have applied faithfully the Code Noir of 1685.

In Haiti—or Saint Domingue, as the colony was called—French colonisation, under the stimulating profits of sugar cultivation, flourished exceedingly after the Peace of Ryswick in 1697 had confirmed Louis XIV in the possession of Western Hispaniola. But the great "essor" of this remarkable colony dates from 1722, when the wisely inspired government of the Regency[1] removed certain restrictions imposed on the trade of Saint Domingue with France. Since 1713 there had been peace with Great Britain; the seas were safe; the slave-

120. AN EARTHLY PARADISE: HAITI AT ITS BEST

recruiting-grounds in Senegambia were organised; large numbers of colonists came from France to Haiti, and there was no stint of negroes to work under them.

Perhaps nowhere in America was existence made more delightful for the White man; and this small territory of ten or eleven thousand square miles produced during the eighteenth century more sugar, coffee, chocolate, indigo,

[1] Wisely inspired perhaps only in regard to its foreign and colonial policy, in taking broader views of which last it owed much to the ideas of the remarkable Scottish adventurer, John Law, who before his fall in 1720 had a good deal to do with the development of Louisiana.

timber, dye-woods, drugs, and spices than all the rest of the West Indies put together. But the French seem to have treated their slaves at times with a wanton, almost tigerish cruelty which left a deep impression on the Negro mind and tradition. Yet they were less proud racially than the Spaniards and freely begat half-breed children with their negress-concubines, thus bringing into existence several thousand notable mulattoes, quadroons, octoroons, and near-whites.[1] By the provisions of the Code Noir these half-breeds were all practically free persons and many of them possessed considerable property. The more intelligent and lightest coloured were sent to France by their French fathers to be educated (this in the first half of the eighteenth century rather than later).[2]

121. A WATERFALL IN THE GROUNDS OF AN OLD FRENCH PLANTATION IN HAITI, FORMING A NATURAL SHOWER-BATH

But the intentions of the Code Noir were not carried out to their logical conclusion. Though these half-castes and "near whites" were in the eyes of the law free citizens, they were frustrated in the exercise of their civic rights.

Before 1744 the position of the black and the coloured people in Haiti was not so bad.[3] Owing to the provisions of the Code Noir, many of the white settlers had married their negro mistresses and thereby set them and their half-caste children free, some of whom had become very wealthy by inheriting the property of their white

[1] Forty thousand in numbers in 1789.

[2] Because of the ferment arising in the minds of the free persons of colour [who went to France for their education and then on their return to Haiti began to agitate for the recognition of their civic rights] the white planters through their agency or club at Paris brought strong influence to bear on Louis XVI to issue an edict forbidding the free men of colour of St. Domingue to come to France for education or for any other purpose. This was done in 1777.

In vain was it pointed out by those who pleaded the cause of the free mulattoes that the Code Noir of Louis XIV, still unrepealed, distinctly proclaimed the complete liberty and "civisme" of all freed slaves.

[3] Nevertheless there were serious slave revolts in 1679, 1691, and 1718. In the middle of the eighteenth century there arose a negro named Macandal, who by his clever poisoning of a few white planters or officials and numerous negro overseers and guards created quite a panic.

father. Consequently there were many mulatto heiresses. About 1749 there was a great increase in the white emigration from France to Haiti, and a large proportion of the immigrants were needy young French women, *des filles à marier*, and without dot. These—and their mothers—were disgusted to find they were but little in demand, for the young Frenchmen of St. Domingue preferred mulatto girls with large dowries. From this arose a bitter jealousy between the white Frenchwomen and their coloured fellow-citizens. The prejudice against colour grew in intensity and was rendered more acute when, after the Peace of 1763, a large number of mulattoes who had been sent to France for their education returned thence to Saint Domingo and wished to play a part in the affairs of their own country.

They—the mulattoes and octoroons—were then forbidden to hold any public office, trust, or employment however insignificant; they were not even allowed to exercise any of those professions to which some sort of liberal education is supposed to be necessary. All the commissioned posts in the naval and military departments, all degrees in law, physic, and divinity, were appropriated exclusively by the whites. A mulatto could not be a priest, a lawyer, a physician, or a surgeon, an apothecary, a schoolmaster, or a goldsmith. He was not permitted to undertake any public charge or commissioned office either in the judiciary or in the army;[1] nor to assume the surname of the white man to whom he owed his being.[2] Neither did the distinction of colour terminate, as in the British West Indies, with the third generation. The privileges of a white person were not allowed to any descendant from an African, however remote the origin. The taint in the blood was incurable, and spread to the latest posterity.

122. A TYPICAL HALF-BREED OF DISTINCTION

General Alexandre Pétion, the first President of Haiti, 1806–18

"L'interêt et la sûreté veulent que nous accablions la race des noirs d'un si grand mépris que quiconque en descend, jusqu'à la sixième génération, soit convert d'une tache ineffaçable," wrote Hilliard d'Auberteuil in 1775 in a book in two volumes (*Considérations sur la colonie de Saint Domingue*) which he published a year afterwards. In this passage he reflected faithfully contemporary white opinion.

This book was suppressed in 1777 by order of Louis XVI, not on account

[1] This was a later development more characteristic of the southern provinces. Down to the middle of the eighteenth century, freed men of colour or blacks served occasionally as officers in the French armed forces. Early in the history of the eighteenth century, two of these North Haitian negroes—Vincent Ollivier and Etienne Auba, had, somehow or other, become captains in the black militia of the parishes they inhabited (the troops called "Les Suisses Noirs"), and consequently had the right to "porter l'épée du roi." Vincent Ollivier even went to Europe and fought as an officer in the German wars under Maréchal Villars, and as he was an exceedingly tall man—almost a giant—was presented to Louis XIV. He died in Haiti at the extraordinary age of a hundred and twenty years. Etienne Auba lived to be ninety-eight.

[2] Whatever might be their virtues or their wealth, they were never admitted to the parochial meetings. At shows, theatres, etc., they were pushed on one side and had separate and inferior places assigned to them in the churches. The prohibition, however, to bearing European names was very seldom enforced. "Sang-mêlés," or mulattoes, were forbidden to eat with white people, or to dance after nine o'clock in the evening, or to use the same stuffs for their clothing as the whites. To enforce this last regulation, policemen were entrusted with the execution of this decree, and it was not an infrequent sight in Haiti to see them even at the doors of churches tearing off the clothes from mulattoes of both sexes, "qu'ils laissaient sans autre voile que la pudeur."

of its rigorous views as to the "colour question," but because "il attaqua l'administration des chefs de Saint Domingue." Hilliard d'Auberteuil dared to point out the intolerable tyranny of the military government[1] under which Saint Domingue was groaning; he illustrated the chafings of the white colonists against the insolent and wasteful administration of French generals, colonels, and captains; chafings which enlisted the planter element against the "ancien régime" and in favour of constitutionalism, *until* in 1789–92 the great men of the Revolution espoused the cause of the man of colour.

Even under Louis XIV the "Code Noir" had been modified by local ordinances which received Royal Approval; further modifications were introduced under Louis XV and XVI, sometimes by royal decree, sometimes by resolutions of the Conseil Supérieur of Cap Français. But Article 59 of the 1685 Edict (that which declared that all freed slaves enjoyed the same liberties and rights as other free men) was left untouched.

It is noticeable (point out one or two writers of the late eighteenth and early nineteenth centuries) that the infractions of the "Code Noir" and the increased maltreatment of slaves and free mulattoes did not take place until the Jesuits had been expelled from Saint Domingue about 1766-7.[2] Here, as in Brazil and Paraguay, they had exasperated the white colonists by standing up for the natives or the negro slaves; and in Hispaniola they had endeavoured to exact from the local government a full application of the various slave-protecting edicts. Whatever faults and mistakes they may have been guilty of in the nineteenth century the Jesuits played for two hundred years a noble part in acting as a buffer between the Caucasian on the one hand and the backward peoples on the other.

In their intense desire to obtain recognition of "white" citizenship some of the wealthy or influential men of colour of Saint Domingue (quadroons, octoroons, "near-whites") would declare themselves to be of partly "Indian" descent, thus accounting for their dark complexions. On this plea they would ask for "letters patent" from the local government officials establishing their freedom from any negro intermixture. Down to about 1760 this certificate was rarely refused, and in this way numbers of "sang-mêlés" entered white society and melted finally into the bosom of the French nation; they or their descendants often becoming the most "acharnés" enemies of the negroid freed man, or the most pitiless masters of slaves.[3]

But after 1770 the White planters of the West Indian colonies and French society at home became so sensitive to the purity of their Caucasian blood (not knowing that all France and much else of Western and Southern Europe is saturated with an ancient negroid element indigenous to Europe many, many thousand years ago) that their influence reacted on the Court and the Secretaries of State. In 1771 the Minister of Marine and the Colonies thus expressed the Royal views as to the granting of patents of "white" citizenship to Domingans of rather dark complexion:—

"Sa Majesté n'a pas jugé à propos de la leur accorder; Elle a jugé qu'une

[1] There were not infrequently good-hearted governors-general such as M. de Bellecombe and M. d'Ennery. But they could not stand up against the soldiery on the one hand and the arrogant planters on the other.

[2] Les Jésuites . . . prêchaient, attroupaient les nègres, forçaient les maitres à retarder leurs travaux; faisaient des catéchismes, des cantiques, et appelaient tous les esclaves au tribunal de la pénitence: depuis leur expulsion les mariages sont rares. . . ."—*Hilliard d'Auberteuil.*

[3] Just as the bitterest enemies and cruellest detractors of the Jews in France, Belgium, Germany, Austria and Russia have often been Jews that have changed their name and their religion.

pareille grâce tendrait à détruire la différence que la nature a mise entre les blancs et les noirs, et que le préjugé politique a eu soin d'entretenir comme une distance à laquelle les gens de couleur et leurs descendans ne devaient jamais atteindre : enfin, qu'il importait au bon ordre de ne pas affaiblir l'état d'humiliation attaché à l'espèce dans quelque dégré qu'elle se trouve ; préjugé d'autant plus utile qu'il est dans le cœur même des esclaves, et qu'il contribue principalement au répos des colonies. S.M. approuve en conséquence que vous ayez refusé de solliciter pour les Sieurs —— la faveur d'etre déclarés issus de race indienne ; et Elle vous recommande de ne favoriser sous aucun prétexte les alliances des blancs avec les filles de sang-mêlés.

"Ce que j'ai marqué à M. le comte de Nolivos, le 14 de ce mois, au sujet de M. le Marquis de ——, capitaine d'une compagnie de dragons, qui a épousé en France une fille de sang-mêlé, et qui par cette raison ne peut plus servir à Saint-Domingue, vous prouve combien S.M. est déterminée à maintenir le principe qui doit écarter à jamais les gens de couleur et leur posterité de tous les avantages attachés aux blancs."

The northern part of Haiti having been earliest and most completely colonised by the French, and being far ahead of the south in commerce, there was greater luxury and refinement of manners amongst the French colonists, and these traits were also characteristic of the 9000 free mulattoes and even of the 170,000 slaves which the northern province possessed at the time of the insurrection (1791).[1] There were even a number of pure-blooded negroes amongst the "Affranchis" of the northern province, who were "Chefs de familles respectables presque tous liés en légitime mariage." Many of these free negroes were educated, enlightened, quiet and dignified in their manners, and even "ayant des inclinations aristocratiques."

But in the western and southern provinces, it was amongst the mulattoes (who were very numerous) that the most enlightened men and respectable families were to be found. These mulatto families sent many of their children to France to receive a liberal education. But in consequence of the injustice with which these mulattoes or educated negroes were treated by the white colonists, so far from their ideas being aristocratic, they were democratic, even revolutionary, especially among those who had obtained their education in Europe and who returned to Haiti to find a grinding tyranny afflicting their brothers.

The influence of the modern spirit which arose in France under the teaching

[1] According to Hilliard d'Auberteuil, between 1680 and 1776 there were introduced into Saint Domingue more than 800,000 negro slaves, of which only 290,000 remained in 1776. Their constant decrease was not due to disease nor to unwillingness to marry and beget children. But many of them were literally worked to death by unremitting labour, while the masters discouraged the women from child-bearing because they could not spare them from field-labour during the last month or two of their pregnancy, or while they were suckling the child. So they frequently forced women who were with child to abort, and then even grudged the day or two's absence from work while they recovered from such an operation.

Yet if well treated by kind masters of humane instincts (and of course there were such in St. Domingue) the negroes would be most prolific. Hilliard saw an old Senegalese negro who had been eighty-seven years in slavery and had married three wives. These had given him twenty-two children, who in turn had bred ; and the ultimate result was that this patriarch of over a hundred years old was surrounded by fifty-three of his descendants to the fourth generation.

In 1789, according to Moreau de Saint Méry, besides the 170,000 slaves in the north province, there were 168,000 in the west, and 114,000 in the south, making 452,000 in all. Then there existed at the same time several thousand "maroon" negroes—ancient and modern runaways—who were mostly living on the Bahoruco mountain in the north-eastern part of Haiti. These, after eighty years of guerilla warfare with the French and Spaniards, had won respect from both and had concluded peace with the French in 1780.

of men like Rousseau, Condorcet, and Mirabeau led, about 1776, to the discussion of slavery as an institution and to the rights of free men of colour. The decision of Lord Chief Justice Mansfield in England (1772) and the first motion brought against the slave-trade in the House of Commons (1776) were not without their effect on contemporary French opinion, and from that time onwards the harassed mulattoes of St. Domingue (forbidden after 1777 to come to France) had a body of sympathetic friends and advocates in Paris which by 1788 had crystallised into the "Société des Amis des Noirs." This was at one and the same time an Anti-slavery and Anti-slave-trade organisation; its president was Condorcet; Mirabeau, Lafayette, Pétion, the Duke de la Rochefoucauld, Robespierre, and Brissot were among the members; but the most eager advocate among them all of the rights of the free mulatto and the negro slave was the Abbé Henri Grégoire, Curé of Emberménil, afterwards Bishop of Blois.

123. IN THE BACK YARD OF AN OLD FRENCH COUNTRY HOUSE, DIQUINY, HAITI

He, indeed, in 1789 presented to the National Assembly a petition in favour of the free mulattoes of Saint Domingue, setting forth all their disabilities and deprivations. Soon afterwards the Declaration of the Rights of Man (in August, 1789) seemed, if it were logically applied to the French oversea possessions, to accord full civic rights to the already free "sang-mêlés" of St. Domingue, and also inferentially to discountenance slavery.

These steps in advance infuriated the strong White Planter party, the thirty thousand French settlers of more or less pure blood, whose representatives and members when on leave of absence had their rendezvous in Paris at the Hotel Massiac, and gradually constituted themselves into a "Club Massiac" to watch the interests of the planters in St. Domingue. Out in the colony at this time (1789–90) any attempts on the part of coloured people to claim the position accorded to them under the Decree of 1685 or even to hold political discussions, were repressed by the white planters with the utmost cruelty and much loss of life, even white Frenchmen being killed brutally for pleading the cause of the mulatto. Children and women were massacred who were in any way, even accidentally, connected with the freed man who had expressed a desire to possess full civic rights without distinction of colour.[1]

In Paris the Club Massiac devoted itself to influencing the members of the National Assembly against any interference with slavery or explicit recognition of the rights of the "sang-mêlés." Too much philanthropy in this direction, they hinted, might lead to the declaratiom of the local independence of Saint Domingo, the white residents of that colony having already displayed "des velléités d'indépendance" in 1788. In that year in fact an irresistible movement had taken place among the white planters towards the establishment of local constitutional government, and commissioners had been elected and despatched to Paris in 1789 to place the views of the White colony before the French Government.

But the free mulattoes simultaneously desired a consideration of their claims and grievances, and somehow, notwithstanding the futile law of 1777, they managed to be represented in Paris by two delegates—Julien Raymond[2] and Vincent Ogé, envoys who at once enlisted the sympathies and help of Grégoire and Brissot.

124. THE QUIET GARDEN OF AN OLD FRENCH TOWN HOUSE, HAITI

But virtually the text of the new Constitution of Saint Domingue was drawn up at the Club Massiac. This Constitution provided for absolute self-government on the part of the colony, but resembled the Act of Union of to-day in South Africa in ignoring the right of freed coloured citizens to have any voice in the government of their own country. It also inferentially maintained slavery as an institution. But Grégoire and Brissot were reconciled to the enacting of this Domingan constitution by the text of the "covering despatch" which would go out with it to the Governor-General of Saint Domingue. In this there would be a paragraph (Article 2) from which might be deduced the non-existence of any colour bar in the formation of the Colonial Assembly.

Vincent Ogé, disgusted at the surrender of the National Assembly to the planter interest, returned quickly to his native land to plead the cause of the free mulattoes there and to see that the Governor (Count Peinier) carried out his instructions as regards non-recognition of the colour bar in the elections which took place in 1790–1. He conferred first with a friend, a mulatto named Jean Baptiste Chavannes, who advised him to incite the negro slaves of the northern province to revolt, and then at their head to demand from the local government justice for the coloured people, but Ogé shrank from this step.

[1] For a detailed account of the atrocities committed by the whites of Haiti on the yellow and black freedmen, inquiring only as to their political rights, see pp. 115–19 of Ardouin's *Études sur l'Histoire de Haïti.*

[2] Raymond had reached Paris in 1784, enabled to do so by the backing and sympathy of a noble-minded Governor-General of St. Domingue—M. de Bellecombe—who thoroughly sympathised with the "affranchis." Raymond, like Ogé, was a mulatto of wealth and of high education.

10

He confined himself to writing rather bombastic letters to the Governor-General (Count Peinier).

The Governor replied evasively and later attempted to arrest Ogé and Chavannes, who now raised a force of nearly three hundred armed mulattoes and with this band disarmed some of the planters in their vicinity. This action they carried out with very little bloodshed: only one white man was killed. Doubtless Ogé thought the negro slaves would rally to his support, but these latter were given no time for deliberation. The rising was nipped in the bud by energetic military measures, and Ogé and his officers were obliged to fly across the Spanish frontier and give themselves up to the Spanish authorities.

Ogé's enterprise at the moment met with but little sympathy from the mass of the negoes and even of the coloured people. So far, he and the rest of the forty thousand "sang-mêlés" had not concerned themselves much with the four hundred thousand negro slaves. They had seldom attempted to plead much for the condition of the slave or to advocate the abolition of slavery.

In January, 1791, the Spanish Governor of Santo Domingo very meanly surrendered Ogé and his companions to the French,[1] and they were all killed under circumstances of shocking brutality.[2]

"The blood of martyrs, etc.!" The news of these fiendish excesses of the planter government aroused horror and shame in Paris—so soon to be plunged into far worse horrors—and the Abbé Grégoire succeeded on May 15th, 1791, in carrying a motion to the effect that "the people of colour resident in the French colonies, born of free parents, were entitled to, as of right, and should be allowed the enjoyment of all privileges of French citizens and among others those of being eligible to seats both in the parochial and colonial assemblies."

The enforcement of this precept in 1791 in any case was likely to precipitate Saint Domingue into civil war, because the planter element was determined never to admit equality of political rights with forty thousand men of colour. But apart from this, when the resolution of the National Assembly became known in the island some of the mulattoes of the north rose in arms to avenge Ogé, and their deeds were soon after thrown in the shade by a black rebellion which was to prove more awful in its results than any movement of the Negro in America before or since. The insurrection broke out on August 22nd, 1791, and was confined to the long northern province of Haiti. Its first leader was a negro called Bouckman, but its guiding spirit was Toussaint Louverture, though for several years he kept in the background as a secretary of one of the negro

[1] Asking in return that he might be given the decoration of the Cross of St. Louis.

[2] The trial of Vincent Ogé, Chavannes, and their companions before the Conseil Supérieur of Cap Français lasted two months. The accused were not allowed any counsel for defence. They were sentenced to death. Ogé and Chavannes were executed (February 25th, 1791) in the following manner, as were most of the "officers" of Ogé's troop): Their arms, legs, thighs and backbones were broken (with clubs) on a scaffold. They were then fastened round a wheel in such a manner that the face was turned upwards to receive the full glare of the sun. "Here," ran the sentence, "they are to remain for as long as it shall please God to preserve them alive": after which their heads were to be cut off and exposed on tall posts.

There are a good many references to God during the trial. Needless to say He was assumed to be entirely on the side of the planters and as anxious as they that the coloured man should not get the vote, and equally horrified at Ogé's mad appeal to force. What sickens the decent reader of the record of the White man's dealings with the Black—and if he were not a philosopher, would turn him into an atheist—is the hypocrisy of the White man, who is constantly cloaking greed, injustice, chicanery, bloodshed and fiendish cruelty towards some coloured race by invoking the Deity as his partner, Managing-Director, aider and abettor. The Negro has been to the full as cruel as the White man; he can cheat and rob quite as well. But he is not an odious hypocrite; he is often a criminal for the sheer pleasure of being cruel or of taking somebody else's property, but never "ad majorem gloriam Dei."

generals. The revolted blacks and mulattoes killed without pity even masters and mistresses who had treated them well; not, in some cases, sparing their own white fathers. They outraged a few white women, ripped up others who were pregnant, impaled infants on pikes, and even used an impaled white child as a banner of defiance. One of their leaders—a hideous creature called Jeannot—drank the blood of the whites whom he massacred, and several other negroes relapsed into actual cannibalism.

It is only fair, however, to state that Jeannot was shot for his atrocities by Jean-François, one of the first great leaders of the revolt, that Toussaint Louverture nearly always interposed when he could to save lives and to treat prisoners with clemency—so much so that he was often accused by other negroes of undue partiality for the whites. Also it must be remembered that nearly all these horrors, with the doubtful exception of the blood-drinking and eating of human flesh, could be paralleled among the contemporaneous wickedness of the French planters and soldiers, who, moreover, had taken the lead in the perpetration of atrocities on defenceless negroes and half-castes for over a hundred years.[1] No impartial reader of the records dealing with the period 1680–1791 can feel over-much pity for the one to two thousand whites who lost their lives in the first outbreak of the Haitian rising. Simultaneously—or soon afterwards—the whites, whenever they got any temporary advantage over the negroes, beheaded, hanged, burnt alive, broke on the wheel, ripped open, and impaled men, women, and children with a gusto fully equal to that shown by the most brutal African. It was a shocking time and a shocking system, if there be any validity in our present ideas of right and wrong.

The French settlements of the west and south were menaced by a small army of mulattoes (about 4000) under Beauvais, the brothers Rigaud, Marc Borno. Pétion, and Boyer (to mention a few who subsequently became famous in Haitian history). They had collected on the Artibonite River near Mirebalais, and had summoned the Governor-General of St. Domingue in a respectfully worded letter to give effect to the pronouncement of the French National Assembly of May 15th. The Governor (Blanchelande) replied evasively; there was further correspondence (the mulattoes received a certain support from the French planters who held republican ideas); and at length war broke out between the bulk of the French planters (with the civil and military authorities on their side) and the mulattoes. In the skirmish or battle of Pernier, however, the mulattoes were victorious; and by October, 1791, an understanding had been reached between the belligerent, "ancien régime"

[1] Bryan Edwards, in his historical survey of Saint Domingo, gives the following description of the manner in which captured negro insurgents were executed: "Two of these unhappy men suffered in this manner under the window of the author's lodgings, and in his presence, at Cape François, on Thursday, the 28th of September, 1791. They were broken on two pieces of timber placed crosswise. One of them expired on receiving the third stroke on his stomach, each of his arms having been first broken in two places; the first three blows he bore without a groan. The other had a harder fate. When the executioner, after breaking his legs and arms, lifted up the instrument to give the finishing stroke on the breast, and which (by putting the criminal out of his pain) is called *le coup de grâce*, the mob, with the ferociousness of cannibals, called out 'Arrêtez!' (stop) and compelled him to leave his work unfinished. In that condition the miserable wretch, with his broken limbs doubled up, was put on a cart-wheel, which was placed horizontally, one end of the axle-tree being driven into the earth. He seemed perfectly sensible, but uttered not a groan. At the end of forty minutes some English seamen, who were spectators of the tragedy, strangled him in mercy."

At a later date, when a French army under General Leclerc was endeavouring to reconquer Haiti, an occasional amusement with the officers at Cap Français was to make a small arena, fasten in the middle of it a negro prisoner, and then let in several famished mastiffs, which proceeded to devour piecemeal the living, shrieking man.

whites of Western and Southern Haiti and the mulatto forces, which now reached a total of four or five thousand men, and in addition were to some extent allied with the negro insurgents of the north.

At this juncture arrived the text of the decree of the Constituant Assembly of Paris of September 24th, 1791 (inspired by the Club Massiac and the panic caused in France by the rising of the negroes). Article 3 of this new colonial law placed the political status of free coloured people and negroes (as also of slaves) completely at the mercy of existing colonial assemblies, subject only to the eventual sanction by the King of laws which might be passed and made operative by the colonial assemblies (then entirely composed of white men). Already—besides the vacillating treachery of the French Parliament—another betrayal of the negro cause was in contemplation amongst the planters of the "ancien régime" school of thought in St. Domingue, and that was to hand over the colony to the English on the understanding that the "ancien régime" was to be restored and all the slaves brought back under the yoke. In August, 1791, the Government of Jamaica had been actually asked by some of the Domingan officials if it could arrange to send over the Jamaica maroons (wild negroes) to help subdue the revolted slaves in Northern Haiti.

To restore order and proclaim a general amnesty in Haiti three commissioners (one of whom was M. Roume) were sent by the French Government in the autumn of 1791, bearing with them the decree of September 24th, which once more annulled the liberties of the coloured people. But they were impotent to effect any improvement. On account of this decree the "contre-révolutionnaires," the aristocratic planter party of Port au Prince and Cap Français, had once more refused to carry out the promises of equal civic rights to the coloured men, and the war between the two parties broke out afresh, mainly in the south of Haiti. Frightful atrocities were committed on both sides, the whites being fully as bad as the mulattoes, and generally initiating the horrors.

In the spring of 1792, the new Legislative Assembly at Paris, again anxiously considering the "colour question" (the arguments and counter-arguments delivered before it read so very modern), came round once more to the sentiment that there should be no colour-bar to civic rights on French territory, so it rendered the famous decree of April 4th, 1792, subscribed by a constitutional monarch before whom was already yawning the abyss, and drawn up by a minister—Roland—who lived and died a hundred years before his appropriate time.

Three new commissioners—Polvérel, Sonthonax, and Ailhaud (together with a new Governor-General, d'Esparbès)—were appointed to proceed to St. Domingue to put this decree in force and to reorganise the colony on a new base if necessary. With them went a force of six thousand troops of a kind more penetrated by the new spirit of liberty than the older garrisons.

Before their arrival, the Colonial Assembly had passed a decree affirming the absolute necessity of maintaining slavery as an integral article of the colony's constitution, and when the commissioners arrived, this was quoted to them. Both Polvérel and Sonthonax (Ailhaud never counted in these conferences, and soon went home) solemnly assured the members of Assembly that the French Government had not the slightest intention of abolishing slavery. This declaration they made repeatedly with almost humiliating asseverations, but did not succeed any the more in securing the adhesion of the "contre-révolutionnaires"—the extreme planter majority in the Colonial Assembly. The rock on which they split was the determination of the new Commissioners to enforce the decree of April 4th, and oblige the Colonial Assembly to grant the fullest possible suffrage held by white men to the free mulattoes and negroes.

Though at one with the armed mulattoes, the three commissioners were not successful in securing altogether the allegiance of the black army camped in the north-east of Haiti under the orders of Jean-François, Biassou, and the

125. TOUSSAINT LOUVERTURE, ABOUT 1795

ever more important Toussaint Louverture. This was partly due to the suspicion with which Toussaint and his associates regarded both the whites of any party and the mulattoes. Yet Toussaint Louverture had not at this juncture demanded the unconditional emancipation of the slaves; merely of a few hundreds among them. His brother generals (if not he himself) frequently offered slaves for sale to the Spaniards as a means of raising revenue. The mulattoes were many of them slave-owners. The utmost demands down to the spring of 1793 was the recognition of full political rights on the part of all mulattoes and negroes already free.

If the situation was already complicated by the intrigues between the "contre-révolutionnaires" and the British in Jamaica and in England, it was rendered increasingly difficult for Sonthonax and Polvérel by the intervention of Spain (through the Spanish Government of Santo Domingo) and the execution of Louis XVI. This last event is supposed to have shocked Toussaint and the rebellious negroes profoundly. A hundred and more years ago, negroes in Africa and America were entirely monarchical in their ideas. All their conceptions of government centred in a chief—elected, or more often hereditary. From their own chiefs they would endure much cruelty and oppression before they deposed or assassinated. On several occasions between 1788 and 1792 the negroes in insurrection in this French colony had wished to lay their grievances before the French monarch directly, thinking he might prove to be a real father of his people without distinction of colour. And now to learn that he had been beheaded by his own subjects increased their utter distrust of the French.

So Toussaint, Jean-François, Biassou, and others enlisted under the banner of Spain, accepted military grades in the Spanish army and decorations of Spanish orders: all these compliments offered them by the Spanish Governor of Santo Domingo being in pursuance of the dynastic war declared against France on the morrow of Louis XVI's execution. They swore "to die in defence of the Bourbons."

Events were precipitated by the attack on the two Commissioners at Cap Français (Northern Haiti) and on Rigaud and other mulatto leaders in the southern province. This revolt against their authority was headed by the French Governor-General (Galbaud) and most of the military and naval forces of the "ancien régime," and of course enlisted the sympathies and support of the planters.

To save the colony for republican France, Sonthonax and Polvérel released the negro gaol-prisoners at Cap Français, drafted many negro slaves into their armed forces, and made full use of the mulattoes (in addition to such French troops as remained faithful to the Republic). Cap Français was burnt down and about three hundred whites—many of them women and children—were killed by the negro allies of the two Commissioners, who were commanded by a ferocious Congo negro named Makaya.

On September 20th, 1793, British forces, at the invitation of the French planter party, were landed at Jérémie in Southern Haiti, and by May, 1794, the Mole St. Nicholas, Tiburon, and Port-au-Prince were in British occupation.

But republican France was victorious in Europe, and at the Peace of Bâle in 1795 compelled Spain to cede to her the whole of Hispaniola, so that in 1796 the Spanish forces and officials had withdrawn from all the eastern part of the island except the town of Santo Domingo.

The desperate Commissioners, Sonthonax and Polvérel, when the descent of the British from Jamaica seemed imminent, had by a series of proclamations and solemn functions between June and September, 1793, proclaimed *the final and universal emancipation of all slaves* in Hispaniola.[1]

Toussaint Louverture was won over to the French cause by the emancipa-

[1] Their action was confirmed by a decree of the National Convention at Paris dated *February 4th, 1794*. This confirmation had, however, been opposed by Robespierre, but supported by Danton. It is said that Danton's advocacy of the emancipation of the slaves greatly angered Robespierre and was one of the causes that led to his sending his great rival to the guillotine. Napoleon when First Consul revoked this decree in 1802 and reinstituted slavery in Hispaniola, the French Antilles, and other possessions.

tion of the slaves. He had begun to doubt the sincerity of the Spanish Governor of Santo Domingo in espousing the cause of the black man. He therefore somewhat abruptly threw off his allegiance to Spain and transferred it to republican France. No doubt, if he could have been called upon to justify his action he would have said that he was only loyal to one cause, that of the negro, and that he was ready to serve under the banners of the government which gave his fellow-negroes the full rights of man. Jean-François and Biassou did not agree with him, and eventually passed over to the Spaniards altogether. Still, Toussaint Louverture and the other negro leaders who made

126. PORT-AU-PRINCE FROM THE SHORE, ON THE COAST ROAD TO LÉOGANE

terms with the Commissioners confined their military action principally to the northern parts of Haiti.

In the south the cause of the French Republic (and of the coloured man) was defended by the mulatto forces under André Rigaud and other mulatto generals. But although the mulattoes fought very bravely (they displayed extraordinary ferocity towards such whites as fell into their power) they could not succeed at first in dislodging the British, and after the fall of Port-au-Prince in May, 1794, Sonthonax and Polvérel made their way across the mountains to Jacmel and left that port in June, 1794, to return to France and to present themselves under a Decree of Accusation before the bar of the National Convention. They would certainly have been beheaded by the order of Robespierre but that fortunately they reached France after the Revolution of Thermidor had put an end to the bloodthirsty tyranny of that perverted creature.

General Laveaux, an officer inducted into the principal military and civil commands as Governor, by the two Commissioners, kept on friendly terms with Toussaint; and when a mulatto rising at Cap Français made Laveaux temporarily a prisoner, Toussaint Louverture entered Cap Français, suppressed the revolt, and as a reward was promoted by Laveaux to be Lieutenant-General of the Government of Saint Domingue on the 1st April, 1796. Thenceforth the negroes were supreme in all the northern part of Haiti, while André Rigaud was at the head of the mulatto forces and dominated all parts of the south and west not in British possession.

At this time Sonthonax returned from France as Commissioner and promoted Toussaint to be General of Division in the armies of France and later Commander-in-Chief in Saint Domingue. All this time Toussaint was steadily drilling his troops, and a deep-seated jealousy was growing up between him and Rigaud, the Commander of the mulattoes in the south. A new Commissioner came out from France to replace Sonthonax, who had been practically expelled by Toussaint in 1797. This Commissioner—General Hédouville—called a conference between Rigaud and Toussaint at Cap Français, affecting to desire to bring about an agreement between them. But Toussaint, having good reason to fear treachery and arrest, made his escape from Cap Français and returned to the head-quarters of his army.

By 1798 the British were sick of their futile attempt to conquer Haiti. They had lost the greater part of their white soldiers and sailors from yellow fever,[1] and they found over and over again that their mulatto or negro allies were faithless. It only remained for them to secure reasonable terms for the French planters, who had invited the coming of the British and who had often fought gallantly under the British flag. Brigadier-General Maitland, who conducted the negotiations for evacuation, tried at first to treat with General Hédouville, but the latter was a stupid fanatic and attached more importance to the death or the expulsion of the French planters who sympathised with the "ancien régime" than to anything else. Consequently, Brigadier-General Maitland negotiated with Toussaint alone and made over to him the last British stronghold in the island—the Mole St. Nicholas.[2] Toussaint Louverture treated the French colonists with kindness and honour and enabled many of them to return to their homes and plantations. Hédouville actually instigated Toussaint's own nephew, General Moïse, to murder some of these white colonists who had settled again near Cap Français, then took fright at his own action and embarked for France, meantime authorising Rigaud to consider himself the Governor of the Southern Department and not to obey Toussaint. Yet Rigaud, whenever he had the power, murdered the whites in the south of Haiti without pity or hesitation, though at least half-white in his own extraction, and employing many "poor" whites in his army of 12,000 men.

Meantime, one of the first Commissioners sent out by France in 1789—Roume—was residing at the town of Santo Domingo to represent French authority in the eastern part of the distracted island. Toussaint, who seemed to be loyal to France, invited Roume to take up his abode with him as Commissioner. Roume did so, and then tried to effect a reconciliation between Rigaud and Beauvais (on behalf of the mulattoes) and Toussaint Louverture,

[1] Out of over 15,000 troops landed between 1795 and 1798 only 3000 survived to leave Hispaniola. At least 11,000 died of tropical diseases. The total cost of British intervention in Haitian affairs was £5,000,000.

[2] Toussaint had at this time a well-drilled army of 18,000 infantry and 1000 cavalry, almost exclusively negro.

the great negro Commander-in-Chief, but with no ultimate effect. Later on, in 1799, Toussaint sent a large force of negroes under Dessalines and Christophe to conquer the south of Haiti. The French Government intervened when the conquest was almost complete by sending another Commissioner, who confirmed Toussaint in his position and persuaded Rigaud to leave for France.

127. TOUSSAINT LOUVERTURE, ABOUT 1799
From Captain Marcus Rainsford's *History of St. Domingo*

Finding that Commissioner Roume had been organising without his knowledge a negro revolt in Jamaica, Toussaint ultimately compelled that French representative to leave Hispaniola, after giving him permission to occupy the eastern part of the island. Consequently, by the close of 1800 Toussaint Louverture was the undisputed master of the whole of Hispaniola. He now promulgated a Constitution which for some time past he had been elaborating. Saint

Domingue was to be a self-governing colony of France under a Governor to hold power for five years. Negroes, white men, and mulattoes were to be absolutely equal before the law, and to hold posts under the new government without distinction of colour. Trade was to be practically free, with a slight preference in favour of France. General Toussaint Louverture was, however, to be President for life, with power to name his immediate successor. This Constitution was sent to France in 1801 to be submitted to the approval of the First Consul. Meantime, Toussaint established a civil administration of some effectiveness. The island was divided into districts, and in each district there was to be an inspector to see that all the ex-slaves returned to their work at the plantations and factories on the understanding that they were to be paid for their services. A fifth part of the produce of each estate was to be divided amongst the labourers. Friendly arrangements as regards commerce were concluded with the United States and even with England; both the finances of the island and agriculture made distinct progress towards recovery during 1801.

But his dream—which in its fulfilment might have had such a great effect on the future of the black man in America—was not to be realised. Napoleon Bonaparte determined to reduce Haiti once more to the position of a white man's colony, and at the close of 1801 despatched to the island a force of twenty-five thousand French soldiers under the command of his brother-in-law General Leclerc. With Leclerc returned Rigaud, Pétion, and Villatte, three leading mulatto generals eager to serve with the French against their black fellow-countrymen. Once more the unfortunate town of Cap Français[1] was set on fire and again destroyed, by Toussaint's general, Christophe, who was commanding there and was unable to resist so huge an armament as that brought out by General Leclerc.

The negro troops under Toussaint, Christophe, and Dessalines retreated from the coast to the mountains after some very stiff fighting in which they proved their quality. Thousands of the French soldiers died of yellow fever, among them their commander, Leclerc; but the war and the sufferings entailed wore out the patience of Toussaint's generals, notably Christophe, who began to make terms with the French. Toussaint, wishing to save his country from further disasters, wrote to Leclerc and tendered his submission. An interview followed in which he was treated purposely with great distinction, and he then issued orders to all his officers to acknowledge the authority of France and disarm their soldiers. Having done this, Toussaint retired to his own estate at Ennéry. One day he received a letter from a French officer asking for an interview at a place near the plantation. Toussaint kept the appointment, but was immediately arrested and bound with ropes. His family (wife, children, and brother) were then collected and all of them despatched to the coast, whence they were sent on a French ship to France. Toussaint, on his arrival in that country, addressed a dignified appeal to Napoleon, just about to be made Emperor, but received no answer. He was separated from his family, who were left at Rochefort, while he himself was interned at the Château de Joux in the French Alps near Besançon. Here he died soon afterwards from privations

[1] Since the declaration of Haitian independence, the name of this place, which for a hundred years was practically the French capital, has been changed to Cap Haitien. It was rebuilt once more under the rule of Christophe, but was again destroyed by a terrible earthquake in 1842. Its present condition bears but few traces of its magnificence during the eighteenth century, though in its surroundings and port it has the making of one of the great sea cities of the world.

128. THE SPLENDID MOUNTAINS OF HAITI WHEREIN THE FRENCH SOLDIERS FOUND THE HAITIAN NEGROES UNCONQUERABLE

and the effects of the extreme cold, and under such suspicious circumstances that it was alleged poison had hastened his end—an allegation, however, that was probably untrue. His body was thrown into the common grave of prisoners of no distinction. Altogether, the treatment of this man by the French is *a lasting blot* on French honour. He was undoubtedly a very fine creature.

Toussaint Louverture was born in 1746 at the plantation of the Comte de Bréda, on the mountains just behind Cap Français, the son of a negro slave named Gao-Ginu. In the faint traditions preserved about his father's descent, the father was said to have been a native of the Zaire country, to have come from a district between the main Zaire (Zaire = Congo) and the "Posambo" River, from a tribe known as the "Arada." Gao-Ginu was believed (as is said in all such occurrences) to have been the son of a king. The River Posambo is not identifiable in the modern maps of Africa, but the "Arada" tribe or country is obviously "Alada," in Southern Dahomé. There is practically nothing to confirm the story that Toussaint Louverture was of Congolese origin, i.e. from the vicinity of the Zaire; whereas the name of his father and other fragmentary indications make it very probable that he came from Southern Dahomé. If so his father and the grandfather of President Barclay of Liberia were practically fellow-countrymen. The portraits of Toussaint Louverture show a decidedly Negro face, but one of a not uncommon type, such as might come from Dahomé or the Gold Coast.

The baptismal names of this Negro hero were Pierre Dominique Toussaint, to which as he grew up he added the name of Bréda, from the plantation on which he was born. Soon after the Negro insurrection of 1791 he acquired and adopted the nickname of Louverture [which he always spelt Louverture, and not L'Ouverture]. Various explanations are given of this nickname: the favourite being that it was applied to him because he always made "an opening" in the ranks of the enemy wherever he charged; but the more probable derivation is that of the marked gap in his mouth when he spoke. Toussaint had lost most of his front teeth early in life, and when he spoke it was with a whistling, lisping sound. As he grew up from being a mere herd-boy to becoming his owner's coachman, he managed to learn to read and write, and was always noteworthy for his admirable conduct and honesty. Unlike most of his fellow-slaves, he would not live in concubinage, but insisted on marrying his wife in church. She had had a son by a former husband, whom he adopted. She gave him two sons of his own, but they died before or just after their father. He had at least one brother—Paul, and there are collateral descendants of Toussaint at the present day in the north of Haiti, one of whom is Dr. Enoch Désert, an LL.D. of the Faculty of Paris.

Toussaint all through his life seems to have been sincerely religious, and as a zealous Catholic was strongly opposed to the African ideas of fetish and sorcery, which were so prevalent amongst his fellow-slaves. Though his handwriting was bad he composed excellent French, and was really quite as much of a statesman as a warrior. His private life seems to have been absolutely above reproach, and that in a country which was described by contemporary French writers as rather worse than "the cities of the Plain." He was not of very strong physique, but had trained himself to something like athleticism and was a magnificent rider. He was exceedingly fond of animals and treated them with a kindness and consideration which are, alas! too rare in the Negro nature. He was invariably tender to women and children of no matter what colour, especially wretched fugitives whom he could assist. He could deal pitilessly with men who opposed his plans or who displayed the slightest treachery, and he certainly did not make war with rose-water.

But the characteristic of Toussaint which most forcibly struck the Europeans who had to deal with him, notably the English, was his loyalty to his pledged word. He is never known to have been false to his promise, or to have departed not merely from the letter, but even the spirit of his engagements. The only exception which might be pleaded by an *Advocatus diaboli* would be his treason to Spain. He had accepted a high rank in the Spanish army and had enrolled himself as a subject of the King of Spain, yet after the promise of Sonthonax that the slaves should be set free in Haiti, he abruptly renounced all Spanish engagements and even (it is said) attempted to secure the person of the Spanish Governor. It may be that he considered the threatened British attack on Haiti a sufficient excuse—for the British were then the most determined opponents of emancipation and the close allies of the tyrannical French planters. It may also be that he had reason to suppose that Spain would be equally hard on the Negro if the French power was expelled from Haiti.

129. TOUSSAINT LOUVERTURE, ABOUT 1802

His loyalty to his word probably cost him his life and his chance of reigning as an uncrowned king: for if he had gone back on the French in 1800 and made a treaty with the British (as he was invited to do), and perhaps also a treaty with the United States, it is unlikely that the First Consul would have ventured to despatch an overwhelming expedition to reconquer Haiti.

Toussaint certainly lived luxuriously whenever he had the opportunity, so far as splendid surroundings, good food and wine, and general comfort were concerned: and he amassed large sums of money. But of these, again, he seems to have lent voluntarily a great proportion to the French Treasury in Haiti, and, needless to say, his widow and children recovered none of it at his death.

One French planter—the Marquis d'Hermonas—said of Toussaint that "God in this terrestrial globe could not commune with a purer spirit"; Roume, the first and last French Commissioner of the island, wrote of Toussaint that he was a philosopher, a legislator, a general, and a good citizen. The English officers, military and naval, who had to deal with him recorded with something like enthusiasm his probity, his perfect manners, simplicity, and bravery. Very different were the impressions they recorded of the feline Mulattoes, who might be astute, audacious, heroic sometimes in their bravery (abjectly cowardly at others), but who seemed in contrast with the grave deportment, calm courage, and reasonable talk of Toussaint Louverture representatives of a really inferior brand of man.

It is a *disgrace* to Haiti that amidst all her monuments, good, bad, and indifferent, none has been raised to commemorate the character and the achievements of Toussaint Louverture, whose record is one of the greatest hopes for the Negro race. No doubt this is partly due to the long political preponderance of the mulattoes, who hated and despised their mothers' race, and who, though they fought a gallant fight with the domineering planters for the rights of the coloured man to be treated as a citizen, still in their heart-of-hearts desired to maintain the status of slavery for the Negro. It is one of the sad features of the great problem attending the relations between White and Black that this scission between Negro and Mulatto is perpetuated even to the present day in Haiti.

General Leclerc died at the close of 1802. He was succeeded by General Rochambeau (notable for his frightful cruelties to negro prisoners, to whom he gave no quarter). Something like forty thousand French soldiers died of yellow fever in 1802 and 1803. The kidnapping of Toussaint Louverture had not brought peace but a renewal of war, for in spite of the inexcusable treachery of Christophe, Dessalines, and other Negro generals to their great leader, the mass of their soldiers resented the abduction of Toussaint and took up arms once more to attack the French. The British were blockading the coasts, and Rochambeau to save the remainder of his army—eight thousand men—was obliged to surrender to the British at discretion. Accordingly by the end of

Votre très humble et obéissant serviteur Toussaint Louverture

130. THE HANDWRITING AND SIGNATURE OF TOUSSAINT LOUVERTURE

1803 there was no French soldier left in the western part of the island, and only a few in Santo Domingo (who withdrew soon afterwards and were replaced in 1808 by Spaniards).

On the 1st January, 1804, General Dessalines[1] declared the independence of "Haiti" at Gonaives, in the western part of the island. All the members of his staff who surrounded him swore for ever to renounce France and to die rather than live under her dominion. Then followed under the decree of Dessalines a massacre of almost all the French planters remaining in Haiti, even to their wives and children. A good deal of the slaughter was carried on under the eyes of Dessalines himself. He was, in fact, an abominable monster of cruelty, the Negro at his very worst, and equally unscrupulous in regard to public finance. In August, 1804, he proclaimed himself Emperor of Haiti, yet was unable to expel the French from the city of Santo Domingo, a failure which lessened his prestige. In June, 1805, after publishing a Constitution which dissatisfied his generals, the mulatto power (temporarily crushed by Dessalines and Toussaint) raised its head, united with the Negro notabilities who had grown to hate Dessalines, and this first Emperor of Haiti was shot in an ambuscade at Pont Rouge in the northern suburbs of Port-au-Prince.

[1] This pure-blood Negro soldier was born on a plantation in Northern Haiti called Des Salines. His name originally appears to have been Jean Jacques, to which he afterwards added the name of the plantation on which he was born.

After his death General Henri Christophe took the first place amongst the negroes, whilst General Pétion[1] was at the head of the mulattoes and commanded in Port-au-Prince, where he proclaimed another Constitution defining Haiti as a republic. To conciliate the Negro element, Christophe under his directions was elected as President of the Republic. But Christophe wanted absolute power, and attempted to crush the mulattoes and capture Port-au-Prince. Failing this, he made Cap Haitien (formerly Cap Français) his capital, and declared himself (1806) President of Haiti, but at a later date (1811) King of Haiti. Pétion, however, was elected President by the Senate at Port-au-Prince in 1807; in 1810 Rigaud returned from France, having escaped from prison, and was allowed by Pétion to command in the south. The western extremity of the long Southern Province had become an independent chieftainship under a negro named Goman; the Spaniards had reoccupied the eastern part of Hispaniola, and Christophe (1811) had proclaimed himself King Henri I, ostensibly of Haiti, but in reality only of the Northern Province. So that at the close of the great Napoleonic Wars the island of Hispaniola was divided into five more or less independent states. A menace of French reoccupation in 1814 procured a temporary truce between all these elements. General Pétion, the mulatto President at Port-au-Prince, died in 1818. In many respects he was a good man and a clement ruler. He did much to assist Bolivar in his struggles against the power of Spain. He was succeeded by another mulatto, General Boyer. Boyer was energetic and honest and an able commander in warfare (as is shown all through the insurrectionary struggle) as well as an administrator. He conquered the negro chieftain, Goman, in the south-west, resumed full control over the Southern Department, and then prepared to try conclusions with the

131. JEAN-JACQUES DESSALINES
Governor-General of Haiti, 1804; Jacques I, Emperor of Haiti, 1804–6

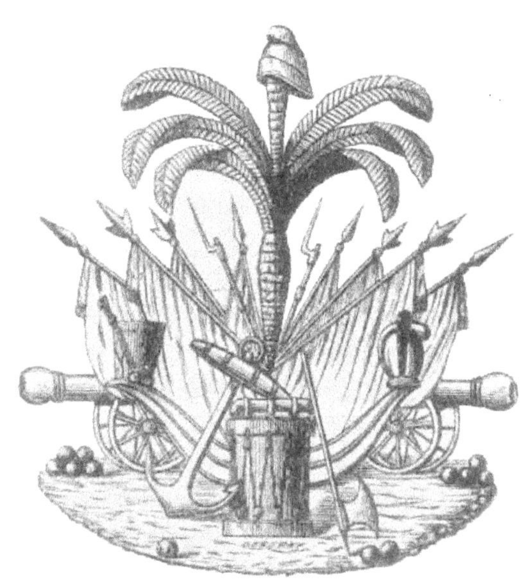

132. THE NATIONAL EMBLEMS OF HAITI
Cap of Liberty, caricature of a palm tree, banners, bayonets, cannon, war drum, anchor, and executioner's axe

[1] Rigaud had been sent back to France by Leclerc and was actually confined in the Château de Joux at the same time as Toussaint.

savage King Henri I,[1] who evaded this issue by committing suicide in 1819. Boyer then entered Cap Haitien, and three years later (1822) occupied Santo Domingo and reigned over the whole of Hispaniola as President for twenty-five years.

133. GENERAL HENRI CHRISTOPHE
Afterwards Henri I, King of (Northern) Haiti, 1811–20

Between 1822 and 1843 was the Golden Age of Haiti.[2] For the greater part of the time the mulattoes were politically in the ascendant and the affairs of state were conducted with some ability. France, who had in 1817 manifested an intention of re-conquering Haiti, was gradually brought to adopt a less hostile attitude and at last induced to recognise Haitian independence subject to an indemnity equivalent to £6,000,000, which was to be distributed among the dispossessed planters or their heirs. This indemnity crippled Haiti for perhaps seventy years. In fact France could hardly have thought of a subtler revenge. The country could not always pay the instalments (£80,000 a year!) out of revenue, and so until the issue of the American Civil War (say in 1867)—after which all European aggression in the New World became a dangerous enterprise—Haiti went in constant dread of an attack by France, or by Spain acting with the permission of France: therefore the military party in Haiti had the excuse for keeping up an enormous standing army.[3] This system imposed on the country that curse of Military Government which has so delayed the progress of all the Central and South American republics. The army makes and unmakes the Presidents and baulks any effective measures of reform. At the present day Haiti only requires a standing army of 2000 men in addition to a country constabulary and town police; but for nearly two-thirds of the nineteenth century this negro republic dared not disarm for fear of immediately falling a prey to either France or Spain.

134. JEAN-PIERRE BOYER
President of Haiti (ruler of all Hispaniola after 1822), 1818–43

But during Boyer's Presidency the French indemnity was reduced from a total of £6,000,000 demanded by the Government of Charles X to the £3,600,000 asked for by Louis Philippe's Cabinet. Louis Philippe in 1838 acknowledged the complete

[1] Henri Christophe was born in the island of Grenada, October 6, 1757, and became a waiter at an hotel, where by amassing a large sum from tips, he managed to purchase his freedom. He migrated to St. Domingue, and eventually joined the forces of Toussaint Louverture, in which through his superior attainments he soon rose to be a general. He was talented and ambitious, but extraordinarily cruel. His wonderful palace of Sans Souci and his extraordinary fortifications near Cap Haitien have been well described by Mr. Hesketh Prichard and other writers. These buildings were to a great extent shattered and destroyed in the earthquake of 1842. Though an ignorant man himself, Christophe strongly favoured education and started a number of schools among the people of Northern Haiti.

[2] Sir Spencer St. John does not altogether confirm this. He writes in his *Hayti, or the Black Republic* (quoting Haitian writers) that the country was in a state of ruin, without trade or resources of any kind; with peculation and jobbery paramount in all the public offices.

[3] The army during General Boyer's Presidency was fixed in the budget at 45,000 men; yet, subsequently, it tended to be a "skeleton army" with a full cadre of officers, but the men only enumerated on paper for the most part and the appropriations for their pay and rations divided among the officers.

independence of Haiti. Great Britain and the United States had done so by 1825.

135. GENERAL PIERROT
President of Haiti, 1845-6

A concordat with the Pope in 1836 established Haiti definitely as a Christian country, though it is true that it was only superficially so; and the incoming priests, under little or no control, were often Europeans of evil lives and a source of profound scandal. In 1860 a new concordat was signed with Rome, and the Haitian Church reorganised by a French hierarchy. Since then, though the Roman Catholic Church has become to a very great extent a foreign body, it has through its French priesthood done a great deal for Haiti in religion and education.

Boyer's prestige was weakened with his fellow-countrymen by the exactions of France and Spain and was brought still lower by the terrible earthquake of 1842, which destroyed the town of Cap Haitien and affected unfavourably all the north of Haiti. There were several hundred deaths, and many people lost all their property. Boyer "had ceased to please" the sovereign people, and upon the outbreak of an insurrection in the north abdicated and brought to a close an unprecedentedly long tenure of power in restless Haiti—a Presidency of twenty-five years. In spite of some mistakes he was by far the best President Haitian history has known and remarkably honest. He left more than a million dollars in the Treasury when he abdicated. A new Constitution was promulgated, but Boyer's immediate successor—Hérard-Riviere, a light mulatto—only reigned four months. The Spanish portion of the island secured by Boyer was lost after Boyer's fall, and for many years the condition of the country was steadily retrograde.

136. GENERAL SOULOUQUE
Afterwards Faustin I, Emperor of Haiti, 1847-59

Between 1843 and 1847 there were no less than four presidents, two of whom, Hérard-Riviere and Pierrot, were mulattoes. The last of these, Riche, a negro, was a good ruler, but died after only a year's administration. Then the Ministry brought about the election of Soulouque, a captain of the Presidential guards, who had been born a slave and was an ignorant, heathen creature; bloodthirsty and cruel.

137. FABRE GEFFRARD
President of Haiti, 1859-67

Soulouque organised a terrible massacre of the mulattoes in 1848, and proclaimed a new Constitution in August, 1849; with himself as Emperor, and a military nobility of four princes, fifty-nine dukes, and a large number of marquises, counts, and barons. In 1852 (as if purposely to annoy and forestall Louis Napoleon) he was crowned at Port-au-Prince as Faustin I, Emperor of Haiti. His imperial reign of seven years was unparalleled in its political murders and financial waste. His attempts to reconquer the Spanish portion of Hispaniola were attended with crushing disasters. A mulatto general, Fabre Geffrard, at length placed himself at the head of popular discontent. The Emperor Faustin, finding his army deserting him, abdicated in January, 1859, and was only able to leave Haiti alive by the intervention of British men-of-war and artillerymen. He retired to Jamaica in a British ship.

138. SYLVAIN SALNAVE
President of Haiti, 1867–9

General Geffrard's Government did some good for Haiti, but was hampered throughout its eight years of existence by incessant negro insurrections, the worst of which were headed by a negro named Salnave, who after Geffrard's resignation in March, 1867, marched on Port-au-Prince and seized the Government. Like several of his successors, he was hastily voted President, "l'épée à la gorge." Constitutional government ceased to exist, and his Presidency was one long civil war, punctuated by some remarkable feats of arms on the part of mulatto generals, massacres ordered by Salnave, powder explosions, the landing of British and French marines, and the intervention of the Dominican Government, which arrested Salnave and handed him over to the revolutionary generals of Haiti to be tried for his crimes. He was deservedly shot.

139. MICHEL DOMINGUE
President of Haiti, 1874–6

His successor, Nissage-Saget, a mulatto, ruled as President for four peaceful years. Unfortunately, his Government for some inexplicable reason favoured as next candidate for the Presidency a creature called Domingue, whom Sir Spencer St. John justly characterised as "an ignorant and ferocious negro (born in Africa)." Domingue succeeded Nissage-Saget, and placed at the head of his ministry his nephew, Septimus Rameau. This last individual was one of the many evil geniuses of Haiti; perhaps the most evil, since he did not *merely* kill (he caused the leading mulatto generals to be assassinated), imprison, banish; but he plundered to such an extent that Haiti is still impoverished by his financial operations. President Domingue was entirely governed by his nephew, Septimus Rameau, and therefore must bear the blame for his iniquities. Septimus Rameau caused Domingue's Government to raise a loan in Paris of £2,500,000. The loan was raised at a considerable discount, and the bulk of the money never reached the Public Treasury of Haiti at all, but was divided amongst the friends and partisans of Domingue's Government. A small balance of this amount remained in the National

140. GENERAL BOISROND-CANAL
President of Haiti, 1876–9

Bank of Haiti, and it was in attempting to remove this and fly with it to Jamaica that Rameau was killed by the populace. France insisted that this loan should be recognised by the Haitian Government, so that it is a part of the financial burden which the modern Haitians have to bear.

141. GENERAL SALOMON
President of Haiti, 1879-88

Domingue, "the ignorant and brutal negro," was succeeded as President by a mulatto general of eminence and education, Boisrond-Canal, but the latter's honest government of the country was made impossible by the intrigues and insurrections of another mulatto politician. About this time the Mulattoes became identified with the name or idea of a Liberal (Progressive) Party in Haiti, whilst the Blacks were more or less Conservatives and haters of the foreigner and of white civilisation.

Naturally, the negroes were enormously in the ascendancy as regards numbers—more than ten to one—but had the mulattoes remained united and possessed something like real patriotism so as to subordinate personal ambitions and greed, they might have been able to remain in power and gradually raise Haiti by universal education to a great position in the West Indies. But every man thought and worked for himself only, and so after the brief intervals of sweetness and light under enlightened mulatto administration would follow terrible periods of negro misrule.

142. GENERAL F. D. LÉGITIME
President of Haiti, 1888-9

One such period began with the election to the Presidency (by the mob of Port-au-Prince) of General Salomon in October, 1879. Salomon was a negro general and minister who had made himself notorious during the reign of Soulouque as a murderer not only by implication but as an actual assassin of mulatto notabilities. During one of his long exiles he had married a white Frenchwoman, and at the commencement of his Presidency in 1880 he seemed to be making some effort to reconcile the opposing parties representing various degrees of colour and to show that Haiti was not adverse to White enterprise interesting itself in her development. But these good intentions did not last long, and Salomon's reign was characterised, like that of all his negro predecessors, by innumerable political murders, insurrections, incendiary fires, reckless issue of paper money, and foreign humiliations. Eventually in 1882 he abdicated to save his life, and fled to Cuba. His successor, General Légitime (who, of course, had led the revolt against him) was a dark mulatto. His tenure of power also ended in flight—to New York. Then came General Hyppolite, who

143. GENERAL HYPPOLITE
President of Haiti, 1889-96

was a negro, and whose rule was a period of relative tranquillity and some slight recovery. He, moreover, died peaceably during his Presidency. He was succeeded by another negro as President—General Tirésias Augustin Simon Sam, whose daily life seemed, to Mr. Hesketh Prichard,[1] "to be chiefly passed in playing draughts near the window of a room opening upon a balcony which overlooks the Champ de Mars."

144. GENERAL TIRÉSIAS A. SAM
President of Haiti, 1896–1902

At the end of General Sam's Presidency some movement was made to elect General Firmin, a mulatto; and one or two other mulatto candidates for the Presidency were in favour. But somehow or other the negro General commanding the Haitian army in the Northern Province marched down from Cap Haitien on Port-au-Prince and arrived there just as the election was coming on. His troops permeated the streets, shouting "Vive Nord Alexis, President d'Haiti," and half unconsciously, without anybody knowing that he was a candidate for power, he was elected to the supreme post by the Legislature.

145. GENERAL NORD ALEXIS
President of Haiti, 1902–8

Under Nord Alexis the reign of terror began again. Every mulatto (more especially) possessing any independence of character and presuming to criticise the mistakes of the Government was punished, or, if they could get at him, surprised at night and summarily shot. In this way occurred the political murders of March, 1908, the remembrance of which was vivid when I reached Haiti at the close of that year. Whether the murders were dictated or not by the household of the President little matters so far as his responsibility was concerned. Yet Nord Alexis is living peaceably in Jamaica at the present day, no doubt very well off. As to the allegations of State plundering attributable to him, his wife, or his Administration, it is preferable to refer my readers to the Haitian Press of 1908–9.

The actual cause of his downfall was the following. Considerable losses to the State (which derives much of its revenue from the export duty on coffee) were occurring through merchants at the seaports getting the General in command (or some civilian official in charge of the customs) to charge them only half the export duty due on large consignments of coffee; on the understanding that this 50 per cent fraud on the Haitian Government was shared between

[1] *Where Black Rules White*, by Hesketh Prichard, 1900.

exporter and official. In other words, the exporting merchant would pay only 50 per cent of the export duties actually due to the Government on his coffee and would give in specie or notes 25 per cent of the export duty to the fraudulent official. It was believed by General Nord Alexis that frauds on a very large scale of this kind (I cannot say if they *did* exist—I am told not) were going on in the Southern Province of Haiti, which was under the strong local government of General Auguste Simon. Simon was very popular throughout the south of Haiti, which he had governed (and governed reason-

146. H. E. ANTOINE SIMON, PRESIDENT OF THE HAITIAN REPUBLIC

ably well and with great clemency) for over twenty years. He was a pure-blooded negro, but a person held in high esteem locally on account of his kindliness and peaceable ways. Public attention was more and more directed to Simon in preference to the noisy General Firmin, who was the oft-recurring adversary of Nord Alexis. It occurred to the late President of Haiti (after he had burnt down a third of Port-au-Prince in his search for "Firministe" arms and ammunition) that General Simon wanted looking up and punishing for permitting these frauds on the customs-house. He summoned him, therefore, in October, 1908, to Port-au-Prince to give an account of his stewardship. Simon anticipated only too surely the perfunctory court-martial and fusillade. Therefore, he wisely marched on Port-au-Prince at the head of his better-disciplined troops, and proclaimed the downfall of Nord Alexis. The army of the latter melted away on the approach of Simon, or joined his force.

The only recourse of the hated Nord Alexis was to drive down to the beach with the French Minister, covered with the French flag, and embark on a French war-vessel which landed him in due course in Jamaica. The hurried election of General Simon to the Presidency followed, and I must say that although he had only been in office for less than two months before I reached that disturbed country, the effects of his new administration seemed highly beneficial. Practically a political amnesty was declared and at most two or three murderers were executed. It would be ungracious to say that the merit for this clemency lies with the unpublished exhortations of the American Government, though these may have had some effect on certain of the politicians who had gone over to General Simon and were now eager for revenge on the instruments of Alexis's tyranny. But General Simon himself seems to be an essentially humane person with a horror of bloodshed.

He has the chance to render his tenancy of the Presidency illustrious by abating the military power, which is the scourge of Haiti; and for the first time in the history of that distracted negro republic, allowing the Constitution to have fair play, and its provisions to be enforced and administered by the ordinary processes of the law.

After this résumé of the history of Haiti, any further description of French dealings with the Negro in America and Africa must come rather as an anti-climax. But France has not done with the question in America. She still rules—and now rules well—some 370,000 negroes and negroids in the New World, in Cayenne (Guiana), which has an area of 30,500 square miles, and in the French Antilles (the islands of St. Barthélémy, St. Martin, Guadeloupe, and Martinique), with a superficies of 1069 square miles. Thus she possesses 31,570 square miles of tropical America, with a very considerable commerce (an approximate annual value of £3,656,000), and not without political importance.

In 1802 the First Consul restored the status of slavery in French America, and thereby lost Haiti indefinitely. During the Hundred Days, Napoleon (perhaps hoping to conciliate Great Britain) theoretically abolished the slave-trade with Africa as a lawful commerce for French ships, but legislation on the subject was not in force till 1818. Between 1830 and 1848 (under Louis Philippe) Libreville was founded on the estuary of the Gaboon River in Equatorial West Africa, as a place of refuge for freed slaves taken by the French cruisers from the slave-ships captured off the West Coast of Africa. American Protestant missionaries were encouraged to settle in this Gaboon region, and that is how the Gorilla was discovered.

In 1848, after several partial emancipations, the status of slavery was *abolished* throughout the French dominions.

The island of Martinique—the birthplace of the Empress Josephine and the early home of Françoise d'Aubigny [Madame de Maintenon]—passed through a period of remarkable prosperity between 1713 and 1762. During this time its slave population rose to a total of something like 85,000; and conjoined with this were about 3000 free negroes and negroids, and 7000 whites.[1] The introduction of the coffee shrub in 1726[2] (by Desclieux, from

[1] Including the descendants of 300 Portuguese Jews from Brazil.
[2] Apparently, two years earlier coffee plants had been sent to Martinique from Surinam.

the Jardin des Plantes at Paris, where it had been received from Arabia) added greatly to the wealth of Martinique and the rest of the French West Indian possessions.

Between 1794 and 1802, and 1809 and 1815, Martinique was in British hands (as it had been for short periods once or twice before). The British, who much wished to possess it permanently, always called it punctiliously "Martinico,"[1] preferring to think of its distant Spanish discovery rather than its long prosperity under French development. Like St. Domingue, it was handed over to the British in 1794 by the Royalist Planter party, who were infuriated at the abolition of slavery by the French Assembly in that year. As the British retained the institution of slavery till they had re-transferred the island to the French Government in 1802, or more definitely in 1815, it was not till 1816 that the French authorities had to face the growing demand for emancipation from the French negroes, here and in Guadeloupe; the more insistent, since many of the slaves were in touch with the free citizens of Haiti who had successfully thrown off the yoke of France. In 1816, 1822, and 1824 there were serious slave-risings in Martinique; and in 1831 "a veritable civil war."[2] This last arose because of the bitter disappointment that the French Revolution of 1830 was not followed by emancipation. As a matter of fact, so serious was the attitude of the negro population in Guadeloupe and Martinique in 1831, that a partial emancipation was at once decided on, and measures were taken in succeeding years which increased the numbers of free persons of colour by leaps and bounds, so that in 1848, when slavery was definitely abolished by the French Parliament, there were only a few thousand slaves in the French Antilles remaining to be liberated. Compensation was granted in this year to the owners at the rate of 500 francs per slave.

147. A FRENCH NEGRO
Martinique

Guadeloupe had much the same eighteenth-century history as Martinique. Whenever France was at war with England, England seized and held these two (and other) West Indian islands. In 1789 Guadeloupe reached (like Martinique) the apogee of its prosperity under the régime of slavery. In that year there was a population of 14,000 whites, over 3000 free negroes and mulattoes, and over 90,000 slaves. Its annual trade amounted to nearly £1,300,000. The decree abolishing slavery, of February 11th, 1794, initiated the same civil war here as elsewhere in the French West Indies, and the Royalist party admitted the British troops.

[1] The Créole-negro name for the island is "Mantinino."
[2] *Les Petites Antilles*, by P. Chemin Dupontès.

But here Guadeloupe history followed a line of its own. Soon after the British had garrisoned Guadeloupe with 20,000 soldiers arrived one of the giant personalities of the French Revolution to whom nothing was impossible, Victor Hugues, sent as Commissioner of the French Republic to put the slavery abolition decree of February 11th, 1794, in operation. He brought with him a force of 1100 French soldiers. Realising the situation as soon as he had landed, he appealed to the negro slaves whom he had come to enfranchise. They sprang to arms, and in the course of a few months he had not only forced the British to evacuate Guadeloupe with their 20,000 men, but had carried the war into several British West India islands, ravaging, ransoming, burning, and arming negroes against the white man. Unfortunately for his ultimate success he hated a French non-republican more bitterly than an Englishman, and

148. LYCÉE CARNOT, POINT À PÊTRE, GUADELOUPE

slew many of his fellow-countrymen with the guillotine. In 1802 he was passed on to Cayenne, where he *radoucissait* his fury, and before the British and Portuguese turned him out in 1809 he did much to improve the conditions of French Guiana and of its negro slaves.

After 1848 and the Abolition of slavery the French Antillean negroes absolutely refused to work on the plantations, and the trade of Guadeloupe and Martinique fell in annual volume from £4,160,000 to £2,120,000. A labour force was necessary—under the system then and now prevailing, of large properties under European control. Whether at that juncture indeed [just following on abolition, when the negro after two centuries of forced labour wanted a rest] it would have been possible or wise to adopt a new land scheme at great expense and turn all the ex-slaves into petty proprietors is a question of some interest: it may be that a subdivision of the land and a system of *petite culture* will be the eventual solution of the commercial decline of the French

Antilles. But as the big sugar-growing properties were still maintained after 1848 it was necessary to obtain for their working a supply of certain and uncapricious labour. A new "slave-trade" was started with Africa, but under improved conditions of transport. Through a Marseilles commercial house connected with the Loango coast and the Lower Congo about 16,000 negro slaves of the Congo-Gaboon regions were "ransomed" and then liberated, to be immediately afterwards inscribed as labourers contracted for work in the Antilles for a term of five years, at the end of which time they had a right to be repatriated.[1]

149. A MARTINIQUE NEGRESS

Simultaneously from 1852 to 1862 over 10,000 Indian kulis were imported from French India and over 2000 Chinese. But the redemption-liberation-and-apprenticeship of the Loango and Congo negroes was fast degenerating into a bad form of slave-trade and excited many remonstrances from England. A convention between Britain and France in 1861 put a stop to the "redeemed apprentice" system, and in place of this the British Government threw open to France all British India as a kuli-recruiting ground. As a result, at least 60,000 East Indians were brought to the French Antilles between 1862 and 1884, in which year all further foreign immigration was stopped. The kulis gradually dwindled in numbers (by disease, intermarriage with other races, and a return to India) until there are scarcely more than 15,000 at the present day, of whom most are to be found in Guadeloupe (in Martinique, about 600).

This foreign labour, however, enabled the French Antilles to maintain their export trade to a great extent after the abolition of slavery; though East Indian—still more so, Chinese—labour proved to be inferior in vigour[2] to that of the Negro. After a lapse of thirty or forty years the coloured population descended from the slaves began once more to seek for work. But it is the descendants of the Loango-Congo negro contract-labourers and of the kulis and Chinese which remain the best agriculturists. The Martiniquais or

[1] As a matter of fact, they never availed themselves of this right, or if they claimed it, there was none to hear and defend their rights. But they obviously liked their treatment in the French Antilles and proved altogether superior to the old-time slaves. About 9300 went to Martinique and 6700 to Guadeloupe.

[2] "Whilst an Indian gives about 220 days' work out of the 365, and a Chinaman only 150, an African is good for 280 days' work in the year. . . . The constitution of the Indian lends itself badly to the hard work of agriculture." (P. Chemin Dupontès, *Les Petites Antilles.*) But it is freely stated that East Indian kulis in Cayenne and the French Antilles have not been well treated by their French employers.

Guadeloupiens of the old slave stock prefer to go in for professions and trades. Education is at present badly given, or is of an inappropriate character for a peasantry mainly agricultural. "There is a 'Lycée' or public college in Guadeloupe and Martinique at which teaching (without any 'colour' distinction) is free and of first-class character: but 'first-class' from the point of view of the middle-class population of an important French provincial town. It has but little relation to life in the West Indies" (*from a correspondent*). But here as in Haiti the French have known how to communicate to their coloured people the French genius for cooking. Martinique and Guadeloupe turn out the best cooks in the New World. And these Martinique and Guadeloupe negroes are usually of polished manners, even if they do not conform to the ideal morality of the Anglo-Saxon. The present negro and negroid population of the two dependencies is about 330,000.

At different times during the nineteenth century the constitutions of Martinique and Guadeloupe (the last-named includes the two little French Windward Islands, St. Barthélémy and St. Martin) were shaped with increasing liberality in popular representation. They now possess considerable powers of self-government, except in fiscal matters. Each island has a Governor and a Privy Council, and an elective Council-General or Assembly of thirty-six members. These thirty-six councillors are elected on a universal male suffrage, distributed without distinction of race or colour.

Each island also elects two deputies and one senator to represent the colony in the French Parliament,[1] and it is not prescribed that these citizens of the French Antilles should be white men.

150. A GUIANA NEGRESS

It will be long before the stately matrons of Cayenne adopt the Directoire style.

After the definite abandonment of Haiti in 1825, French interest in Cayenne revived. This colony had been in Portuguese occupation from 1809 to 1817; and despite the 1815 abolition of the slave-trade in the French possessions, a good many negroes found their way as slaves to work in the sugar plantations and to search for the gold which had been first discovered by a French settler in 1819.[2]

The Portugo-Brazilian occupation of Cayenne from 1809 to 1817 brought with it a considerable addition to the slave population, but conferred benefits on the Brazilian Empire and on the French colony, for while on the one hand the Portuguese found in the plantations and gardens of French Guiana valuable spice trees and other vegetable products of tropical Asia and Africa—carefully brought to Cayenne by French navigators and governors

[1] It would be a very satisfactory step towards the effective federation of the British Empire (which we talk so much about and make very few sacrifices of constitutional pedantry to effect) if the British West Indies and East Indies and other regions under the direct rule of the United Kingdom could likewise have their elected representatives (of all shades of colour) in the Imperial Parliament expressing the wants and aspirations of the coloured people through the mouths of coloured men, and not the cold or unconvincing deputy of a white man.

[2] About £550,000 worth of gold—chiefly worked by negro labour—was exported from Cayenne in 1907. This is the average annual output.

and now carried back by the retiring Portuguese to their Brazilian Empire—the French learnt from Portuguese Indians where and how to look for alluvial gold.

In 1852 Cayenne had been again adopted by the French Government as a region to which criminals or political prisoners might be sent as convict settlers. In the following year it was decided that convicts of African or Asiatic race might also be transported to Guiana; and after 1864 it was mainly from the prisons of Algeria, Senegal, Pondichéry, and Indo-China that the penitentiary settlements were recruited. The preponderating races among these "récidivistes" were Arab and Negro. A good many Algerians and Senegalese have in course of time found their way as freemen or runaways into Dutch and British Guiana, and into Northern Brazil. Occasionally they have proved themselves desperate criminals, but more often the climate and discipline of French Guiana have tamed them. They have been popular as husbands—one might almost say as "sires"—among the Guianan negresses, and have during the last fifty years sensibly modified for the better the physical type of the negro in these regions.

CHAPTER VIII

HAITI

I SAID good-bye to Cuba under a sunset of crimson and gold, a reminder of the old Spanish colours which eleven years ago were still waving over the island—the red and yellow that the Cubans might well have retained (with a different device) in their national flag instead of the inept red, white, and blue, which two-thirds of the world now adopt, without reason, as national colours.

151. A WEST INDIAN SUNSET

After a rough passage across the sixty or seventy miles of strait between the two islands, Haiti received me in the blue and silver of placid water girdled with lofty ranges of mountains wreathed or crowned with white clouds. The open arms of Haiti are two peninsulas of alpine heights that enclose a vast gulf of sheltered sea screened from rough winds and vexing currents; a gulf which would make the safest and amplest naval station in the world.

Port-au-Prince, the capital of Haiti, is placed near the south-westernmost edge of a broad plain, the *cul-de-sac* of the old French colonists; but its suburbs are over the spurs of the southern mountains. In daylight, viewed from steamer deck in the outer harbour, it does not present a poor appearance. This is largely due to the magnificent new cathedral, which is placed so as to give a focus to the town. Without this cathedral (of French design and Belgian construction), Port-au-Prince, two or three years ago, must have presented a somewhat paltry aspect for a capital city. The other notable buildings are seldom remarkable for stateliness of design or prominence of position, though there are some handsome churches. Behind the actual shore-line (to the south and east) the land rises rapidly into green highlands, studded with fantastic palaces, and the highlands enlarge into mountains of almost Alpine character. On the sky ridges of these may be seen from the shipping in a harbour of intense tropical heat, the silhouettes of the tall pine trees, which indicate a land of cool, invigorating temperature within half a day's climb.

152. THE NEW CATHEDRAL
Port-au-Prince, Haiti

I first saw Port-au-Prince in the late evening, and the effect, after the brilliant, variegated lighting of Cuban and American towns, was disheartening. We might have been approaching some sullen, pirate capital of Haiti two hundred and fifty years ago, desirous of offering no attraction or assistance to the inquiring stranger. A few dull yellow lights blinked from the dense foliage of the suburbs. Here and there a glowing red lamp seemed to indicate danger. Although Port-au-Prince, with its suburbs, is a city of 104,000 inhabitants, and is the capital of an independent state of some 10,500 square miles in area, it possesses no system of public illumination.

When one lands here in the morning (steamers may not communicate with the shore after sunset) the impression is more favourable, though docks and wharves are absolutely non-existent, and landing from or boarding the steamer means a long and weary row. But it is obvious that Port-au-Prince—thanks to German, American, and Haitian enterprise—has made considerable strides of late towards the amenities of life. It is true that in dry weather the streets near the seaside are intolerable with their clouds of malodorous dust, that there is no continuous side walk along any of the streets, and that, with the exception of about half a mile of recently macadamised roadway, the paving of the streets is monstrous in its grotesque imperfections. But the houses are by no means uncomely, nor is the town nearly so dirty as it was described by various writers down to the year 1900. Either they exaggerated, or their criticisms stirred up the civic authorities of Port-au-Prince to effect considerable improvements in the cleanliness of the streets. There are shops for most purposes and at least two decent hotels, where the cooking is *superior* to the *average* cuisine in Jamaica, Cuba, or the Southern United States.

A welcome surprise which greets the visitor to Port-au-Prince who goes from any other part of America (not excepting Jamaica and the other British

West India islands) is the greater cheapness of living. European luxuries are perhaps rather dear, but not the essentials of life—good bread, meat, fish, eggs, vegetables, fruit, coffee, and milk. In fact in Port-au-Prince it seemed to me that one returned to the prices and the comforts of Europe, especially in so far as good food, well cooked, is concerned. Any one not content with Haitian beef, mutton, fowls, turkeys, eels, sea fish, lobsters, vegetables, oranges, grape fruit, mangoes, pineapples, guavas, coffee and chocolate must indeed be hard to please.

The President's palace, situated with its surrounding garden on one corner of the extensive Champ de Mars, is a turreted, verandahed erection, apparently roofed and faced with corrugated iron, or with some cold grey glistening metal.

153. IN THE STREETS OF PORT-AU-PRINCE

The general appearance is not unpleasing, though a little "baroque," especially when in times of festivity it is extravagantly decorated with the blue and red Haitian colours. But the so-called garden which surrounds it is a dreary trampled waste perpetually paraded by soldiers. Not far away is the range of Government offices, all in one building. In front of this, painted a gaudy red and blue, is one of those extraordinary rostrums found in every town in Haiti, large or small, whether dating or not from the time of the French colonisation I do not know. From these open-air pulpits addresses are made to the populace, and laws are proclaimed. The Champ de Mars has, no doubt, been much improved of late, and may even in time be made an open space of agreeable appearance. At present it consists of irregular patches of turf, crossed in many directions by roads authorised and unauthorised. Some of the former are macadamised.

The houses in the suburbs of Port-au-Prince are for the most part built by Germans, and are really tasteful in their architecture, cool, comfortable, and surrounded by beautiful gardens. The public cemetery, on the other hand, is a staggering mixture of beauty (vegetation and the old tombs), grotesqueness (the modern miniature houses and goblin huts erected to house the deceased), and horrors.

Port-au-Prince possesses market buildings which are worthy of Paris in size and design, but the interior is nauseously filthy, so much so that the mass of the country people prefer to establish themselves in open-air market-places away from the great buildings erected for their use. In these open-air markets there is endless material for the painter or photographer. The sellers are mainly women, who have journeyed into Port-au-Prince from the country,

154. THE PRESIDENT'S PALACE, PORT-AU-PRINCE

riding sideways on donkeys, horses, or mules, situated, it may be, on the top of enormous panniers of provisions. Nearly every woman wears a large and picturesque straw hat, fastened by a leather band under the chin that ends in little twiddles of leather so absurdly resembling the pointed chin beard of the negro man that the market-women look like men dressed in women's clothes. These clothes are always ample and picturesque, usually blue cotton, or else gay prints with many flounces. Some of the women in the market-place are selling fish which an artist would purchase for their colours alone. They look like the *poissons d'Avril* in Eastertide shop-windows—such combinations of blue and orange, scarlet and mauve, yellow and black, pink and green. Other vendors are surrounded by a troop of tethered turkeys, fine plump fowls, or Muscovy ducks. Goats, sheep, cattle, and pigs wander where they please. Pigeons and an occasional green parrot lend variety to the immense crowd of humans, beasts, and birds.

One curious point about Port-au-Prince and the whole of Haiti and Santo Domingo is that the turkey buzzard (*Cathartes*) is entirely absent, a strange contrast to all the other West India islands and the Southern United States. Haiti has no other scavengers but pigs and dogs.

The water-supply of Port-au-Prince is grumbled at by the residents, but though it may not be as perfect as tradition relates it was under the French Government, it seemed to me to be very much better than in many other West Indian towns I have visited. Some of the fountains are very picturesque, and obviously date from the French period of over a hundred years ago. All over this large town there is an abundant supply of good, fresh water for the poor as well as the rich, and the drinking-water usually served in hotels and private houses seemed to me pure and good.

155. THE STATUE TO DESSALINES ON THE CHAMP DE MARS, PORT-AU-PRINCE

He is represented as the declarer of Haitian independence in 1804. [This statue, which is of hollow metal with a flag of painted tin, is an ugly object, and ought to be removed]

Port-au-Prince is always hot, often dusty, and a good deal afflicted by mosquitoes; it has many other faults, no doubt, and yet it is not without attractions. Ice is abundant and cheap. There are at least two good newspapers, one of which gives a very ample supply of European cablegrams. It is a noisy place; the dogs are perfectly sickening in their midnight howlings, alarums, and excursions; there is too much military music, and on festivals people let off guns and fire crackers. And yet it is one of those towns that by a strange inconsistency one is sorry to leave and glad to return to. The educated Haitians, however they may mismanage their public affairs, are most agreeable people to meet in society—witty, amusing, well read, except in the natural history and botany of their own country. There is a very pleasant club where the European and American residents meet the natives of Port-au-Prince, and a delightful friendship seems to exist amongst all the foreign residents.

I have referred to the German suburban residences of Port au Prince, especially those which lie on the south-east of the main town. But perhaps the most beautiful district within easy reach of the capital is round about Diquiny and Bizoton. The railway runs along the shore road from Port-au-Prince to the vicinity of these outlying bourgs, and there is as well a fairly good carriage-road, with picturesque old bridges over the innumerable streamlets that come tearing down from the mountains. Here, between Port-au-Prince and Léogane, many of the beautiful country seats are little more than modernised reconstructions of the estates of the French planters. The district is musical with a never-absent ripple of falling water, and the extravagant tropical vegetation is reduced to orderly pictures by masonry runnels and conduits of the old French irrigation systems. Probably nowhere else can one see such a complete riot of brilliant colour. The clouds, attracted by the high mountains, are always a feature in the landscape—dazzling white cumulus at noonday, becoming flamingo-red in reflection of the sunset. The high mountains are purple-grey. The sea of the Gulf of Haiti is the most brilliant blue-green. The distant town of Port-au-Prince is pink and white and grey. Around the many-coloured houses are groves of crimson-scarlet *Poinsettia* or smalt-blue *Petræa*, together with roses, oleanders, allamandas, hibiscus, and a hundred and one flowering shrubs and creepers of the tropics. As to the foliage trees, there are royal palms and fan palms, trees unknown to me with large glossy leaves like magnolias, the primly perfect mahogany trees, orange trees loaded with fruit, the Haitian oak, mimosas, flamboyants. This region is indeed an earthly paradise,

156. INSIDE THE CEMETERY, PORT-AU-PRINCE

with the Delectable mountains behind, up which, if you choose, every morning you may ride to the pine-ridges and the air of North America.

Every square mile of Haiti (I should think) is beautiful, or at least is interesting. The greater part consists of ranges of incredibly tortured mountains. No doubt in the far distant past it has been the scene of volcanic energy. Yet there is not much of its area covered with igneous rock. For the most part the formations seem to be of limestone, a limestone which in places is such a pure, cold white as to look like snow. In the very high mountains—nearly nine thousand feet—the hasty observer might well be excused for believing that he saw vestiges of snow in the crevices or deep clefts of stream valleys. In reality it is due to the rush of water from the summits, which tears away the surface soil and reveals the limestone. In the dry season many a river valley is blazing white with its tumbled masses of chalky stones and pebbles.

The plains of Haiti occupy but a small portion of its area, and they are usually fertile, or could be rendered so by irrigation. Where they are uncultivated they are overgrown with a low scrub of very thorny mimosa and logwood, but even this is rendered tolerable by the highly scented yellow blossoms and by the clumps of weird-looking cacti. Here in this low-lying country are specimens of arboreal cactus worthy of Mexico. A form of prickly pear (*Nopalea*) grows to a height of about thirty feet in a solid stem, and pushes out in all directions great pudgy hands of flattened leaf-stalk, studded (as though with giant rubies) by red flower-buds or blossoms, and having a strange resemblance to some Hindu god or goddess with innumerable hands. A species of *Cereus* (bristling with white thorns) grows in erect columns. A thornless type of *Cereus* is so grotesque in the pointing of its fat, gouty fingers that it, together with another writhing, snake-like arboreal cactus, might be the fit surroundings of an enchanter's cave in a stage féerie. Perhaps, however, the most beautiful item in the vegetation of the plains and mountains of Haiti (ranging from sea-level to seven thousand feet) is the agave with its basal cluster of immense, bright green lily leaves and its flower stalk twenty to thirty feet in height tufted with clusters of golden-yellow blossoms. In and out of the corollas of these golden flowers dart woodpeckers of crimson, black, and gold, starlings of black and silvery yellow, metallic humming-birds, and innumerable small quits of variegated tints. Hovering over these and occasionally making a successful dart are small kestrels of bright chestnut orange and dove-grey, with bars and splotches of deep black. Columbus noted the abundance of bird-life when he discovered this great island, and referred especially to the songs of the "nightingales." [These were really mocking birds, apparently the same as the American species.]

157. THE PRINCIPAL MARKET, PORT-AU-PRINCE

The scenery of Lake Azuey (beyond the Cul-de-sac plain) is very beautiful. Its salt waters are of an intense blue-green, and the surrounding mountains, clothed with forests of *lignum vitæ*, glaucous green fan-palms, and straight-stemmed pine-trees rise to altitudes of six to nine thousand feet. At its eastern, Domingan end is a colony of the scarlet American flamingo. Miniature wild boars (domestic pigs run wild two or three hundred years ago; see p. 187) come down to its clean sandy beaches to search for stranded fish or other water offal.

And what may not be said in detail about the Haitian mountains? The highest (Mont de la Selle) is a few feet under 9000, but the ridges rise so abruptly from sea-level or from the tremendous gorges which separate one *massif* from another that you get the full value of their height. They have been carved by water, sun, and wind into the most exaggerated relief, and many of their crevices are illuminated by the fissures of limestone. Here and there is a curious intrusive hummock of bright red clay, only partially revealed because of the exuberant vegetation. This again assumes so many tints owing to the season or the sunlight that the Haitian hill-sides frequently resemble a turkey carpet with their scrub of scarlet fuchsia, rose-pink honeysuckle, intensely green bracken and maidenhair ferns, and the mauve-and-white of certain *Compositæ*, the purple of many labiates, the yellow-and-silver of everlasting flowers. The large white blossoms of the local blackberry (which has a most delicious fruit

158. AN OPEN-AIR MARKET, HAITI

the size of a mulberry) should not be omitted in describing this mountain scenery.

In the dells of the mountains, about 4000 feet, are handsome jungles of tree ferns. Everywhere grows the glossy green agave, with its lofty column of gold flower-clusters. The aromatic scent of the pine woods is indescribably good to the jaded white man exhausted with the tropics.

And nearly everywhere, except on the highest peaks and ridges, may be seen the picturesque and happy peasantry—happy if dwelling far enough away from the oppression of the town governments. Wherever there is a fairly level patch or plateau there is a collection of thatched huts surrounded by an emerald grove of bananas, and by fields of maize, sorghum, cabbages, and sugar-cane. The country swarms with domestic birds and beasts—horses, donkeys, pigs, dogs, cattle, goats and sheep, turkeys, fowls, and guinea-fowls. The peasants usually wear clothes of blue-dyed cotton and huge straw hats.

The dress of the men is a blue gaberdine and trousers; that of the women is a loose robe not unlike the Egyptian costume.

The scenery of such parts of the Republic of Santo Domingo (Republica Dominicana) as I was enabled to have a glimpse of, naturally resembled that of Haiti. I am informed by Americans that the landscapes of the auriferous Cibao range of mountains (highest peaks averaging 10,000 feet) were surpassingly grand, and the pine forests of *Pinus bahamensis* more abundant than in Haiti. The highest point in the whole of the Antilles seems to occur in Santo Domingo—the Loma de la Tina. This apparently has never been ascended, and its guessed-at altitude (10,300 feet) has not been as yet confirmed by the

159. A CHURCH AND SEMINARY, PORT-AU-PRINCE

American surveys. In the more northern part of the Cibao range is the striking peak of Yaqui, about 9700 feet.

The Spanish civilisation of the Dominican Republic (which has an area of nearly 18,000 square miles) gives a picturesqueness to town or village life which is quite different to the colonial French or purely Negro aspect of inhabited Haiti. The game-cock is everywhere much in evidence. There are some negroes in San Domingo, but the mass of the population is of Spanish or mixed Spanish-Amerindian origin—a handsome, well-set-up, grave, virile-looking people of olive or pale yellow complexion. The Americans, who are giving a general direction and advisory control to Dominican affairs, are effecting wonders of happy and wise development in the exploration, communications, industries, and commerce of Santo Domingo. Their customs officials and surveyors are of the best American pioneer type.

The area of the entire island of Hispaniola is computed to be about 28,250 square miles. The area of the Dominican Republic may be stated approximately at 17,750, and that of Haiti at 10,500 square miles. These computations at present satisfy neither Santo Domingo nor Haiti. The Spanish republic claims the old French frontier as being the eastern limit of Haiti, and would assign to the Haitians a total area of about 9200 square miles, equivalent to the extent of the old French colony. The Haitians, however, claim at least 1300 square miles between the Artibonite River and the Cordillera, more especially the districts of Banica and Hinche, and base their claims on the fact that this land has been in Haitian occupation since the time of Toussaint Louverture, and that the natives of the disputed land speak French and are negroes.

The limits of the old French frontier have nothing to do with the question. Between 1825 and 1844 the Haitian Government ruled the whole island, and when in 1860 it admitted the independence of the Spanish-speaking portion, it

160. A RESTAURANT BY THE SEASHORE, NEAR PORT-AU-PRINCE

naturally attributed to Haiti the regions remaining in Haitian occupation and distinct ethnographically from the Spanish-speaking portion of Hispaniola.

The United States will take care that this frontier argument is settled amicably, and if it goes by the abstract justice of the matter will see that Haiti emerges from the dispute with at least 10,500 square miles of territory.

The actual figures as to the population of Haiti given in the latest returns for 1908 are 2,794,366, of whom 1,118,000 are men and 1,676,366 are women (there are about 250 white and 6,000 coloured foreigners). The Government publishes no statistics on the subject, but allows journalists to collect them from the local authorities. According to the aforesaid Haitian journalists or publicists, the rate of increase of births over deaths in the towns is very high; but in the country districts a serious mortality occurs amongst children under the age of five, which sensibly lessens the national increase, reducing it from about 25 per cent per annum to about 5 per cent.

From my own inquiries, researches, and glances at the country I should think 2,700,000 a modest estimate of the Haitian population, if by "Haitian" is meant the negro race in Western Hispaniola speaking Creole French. I should be inclined to put it at 3,000,000; and Americans who have travelled over both Haiti and the Dominican Republic agree with me on this point. But it must be remembered that during the last thirty or forty years the warlike half-Spanish population of San Domingo has made marked aggressions on

161. THE MOUNTAINS AND PINE WOODS (7500 FEET ALTITUDE) OF HAITI

the original French frontier, thus extending the Spanish (Domingan) influence over that portion of the island still inhabited by Creole-speaking negroes.

The population of the Dominican Republic is either more carefully estimated at the present day or has risen markedly since the Government of the United States imposed peace on that distracted country. It is now computed at 900,000, and offers a marked contrast physically and mentally to the

Haitians. There are Spanish-speaking negroes in parts of the Dominican State, but they are not numerous. Large negro communities in this region are limited to the region of the Haitian frontier, and obviously represent former patches of French influence or rule which have been wrested from the Haitian Government since its decline in warlike power sixty years ago.

The real Domingans, that is to say, the non-negro, half-Spanish, half-

162. A NOPALEA TREE CACTUS, HAITI

Indian[1] population of the State of Santo Domingo (now officially styled the Dominican Republic), are a good-looking race, with Castilian manners; as

[1] It is believed that pure-blooded Amerindians lingered in the unexplored and densely wooded parts of Haiti down to within the memory of persons now living. In hybrid types a few are said to exist at the present day on portions of Domingan territory, and it is evident that they are perpetuated in a mixed form in the Domingan population, some members of which resemble very much the "Indios" of Eastern Cuba, and are evidently of mixed Spanish or Amerindian blood. But a naked Amerindian woman was seen in the mountains of Haiti about twenty-five years ago by Monsieur Espinasse, who, I believe, picked up the clay water-pot that the woman had left behind in her flight. A number of them, moreover, seem to have mingled their blood with that of the French pirates and colonists and the negro slaves of these last in the latter part of the seventeenth and beginning of the eighteenth centuries.

a rule, extremely honest and very hospitable, moral (at any rate as regards their relations with foreigners), and intelligent. Their chief drawbacks hitherto have been a certain sleepy idleness and a passionate love of gambling, the vehicle of this being cock-fighting (as in Cuba, and, to a much slighter extent, in Haiti). They are as quiet and reserved as the Haitians are noisy and expansive. When they go to war—politically or as a matter of private vendetta—they mean business. Nevertheless without American support San Domingo a few years ago ran the risk of being eventually absorbed by Haiti through sheer weight of numbers.

Until quite recently it is probable that Haiti had developed a good deal

163. A PACHYCEREUS CACTUS, HAITIAN LOWLANDS

more culture and civilisation in her towns than was the case with San Domingo. The Haitians were far more prolific than their neighbours, and probably much harder workers. It is not necessary to compare the one people with the other to the disadvantage of either; it is sufficient to state that, although on the map the island looks as though it should be unquestionably one political entity (just as is the case with the Iberian Peninsula), in reality no two American peoples are more unlike and naturally separated than the Haitians and the Domingans; and the union of the two divisions of the island under one executive is as improbable as the union of Portugal and Spain.

It is scarcely correct to write of "French-speaking" negroes in referring to the Haitians. As far as I can ascertain, out of the nearly 3,000,000 negroes who may be described as Haitians, only about 200,000 (a generous estimate) are able to talk and to understand the French language. The remainder, who are more especially of the peasant class, speak what is described as "Creole French," but which is an entirely new language, far more different from French than is "pidgin" English from the language of the United Kingdom or the United States. It is possible for any Englishman or American to understand in a very short space of time even the corrupt English of the west coast of Africa, to say nothing of the very much better negro English of the West Indies or of the greater part of the United States. It is true that in some islands and isolated peninsulas of Virginia, South Carolina, and Georgia, there may be a mixture of English and African spoken among the negro fishermen or peasants, which is quite incomprehensible to an Englishman or an American; and it is also possible that similar jargons may have arisen in parts of the British West Indies of which I

164. THE SANTO DOMINGO END OF LAKE AZUEY

know nothing. But in a general way there is no linguistic barrier whatever between the white and the coloured people in the whole of English-speaking America.

In Louisiana, however, in Haiti, Guadeloupe, Martinique, St. Lucia, Dominica Island, and Trinidad, the Creole French which is spoken by the negroes is essentially a language by itself, differing from French in grammar, voçabulary, and pronunciation. It is, to my thinking, a barbarous and clumsy jargon; but this opinion would be received with indignation by the English, German, French, and Haitian people who speak it as a second language, having picked it up from negro servants in their youth. Creole, especially the dialect of Haiti, has been so aptly illustrated by Haitian and French authors that I need not describe it further here. It still preserves archaic French terms, some words of Breton, a certain element of the Indian languages still lingering in the island of Hispaniola at the time of the arrival of the French buccaneers, a little Spanish, and more than a little English, together with a few words of African origin. Of course, the bulk of the vocabulary is garbled and abbreviated French.

The Dominican Republic, on the other hand, emphatically belongs to the Spanish-speaking world, and any European acquainted with Spanish can get on without difficulty with the Domingans. On the other hand, to deal easily with the Haitian people it is essential to master this entirely new language—Creole. Away from the principal towns French is not more useful than English.

Large sums of money are appropriated annually in the Haitian budget for the maintenance of schools in all the communes of Haiti. This appropriation

165. A WILD BOAR, LAKE AZUEY

is one of the many cruel tricks played on the Haitian people by its Government. In the beautifully printed "Budget Général" (which is published annually at Port-au-Prince), under the head of the Department of Public Instruction, there is a *cadre* providing for the education of Haiti—primary, secondary, and advanced—with a detail and completeness worthy of Switzerland or Germany. Yet much of this organisation exists only on paper, and the funds appropriated for this splendid purpose find their way into the pockets of Government officials, or possibly never leave the Treasury. There are fairly good schools in Port-au-Prince and in the eleven or twelve principal coast towns of Haiti. I doubt if there are any rural schools at all, in spite of the fact that 500 are provided for in the budget; or, if they exist, they do so as a means for providing a petty sustenance for some totally incompetent person. The plain fact remains that something like 2,500,000 out of the 3,000,000 of Haitians cannot read or write, and are as ignorant as unreclaimed natives of Africa.

Haiti is a country of extremes; and you may meet Haitians in Port-au-Prince or in one or two other big towns on the coast so highly educated, so clever with tongue and pen, so witty and well read, such men of the world, that their society makes even Jamaica and Cuba seem provincial and out of the movement. Take, for example, such a writer as Fernand Hibbert. His essays are worthy of the pen of Anatole France or Pierre Loti, and of course he is only one amongst a dozen or more contemporary Haitian men of letters. But, although much of this culture is derived from local educational institutions, it is essentially Parisian. In many parts of Haiti a good and sound education is given by the French seminary priests, as to whose general civilising work in Haiti it is pleasant as well as just to tender a tribute of praise. Science in its most modern forms and developments has its Haitian abode in the Catholic Seminary of St. Marcel at Port-au-Prince.

166. PINUS BAHAMENSIS
The fragrant pine of Florida, the Bahamas, Hispaniola, and Cuba.

The Government of Haiti subsidises a college in France for the education of Haitian priests, but as far as I can ascertain only four or five priests in the whole of Haiti are of the Negro race; the others are Frenchmen of France. It also gives general scholarships to Haitian youths for a final education abroad, mainly in France. Unhappily, the weak point in all this superior education of the Haitians is its utterly unpractical relation to a useful and profitable existence in the West Indies. How this comes about I cannot see. The France of to-day shows herself able to educate and send to her empire in Africa and Asia hosts of young men supplied with the most practical instruction in modern science and in all such learning as may be turned to material use in countries wholly different from France herself. But the education which she gives to the youth of Haiti is perversely useless in its nature. It is apparently only adapted to life in Paris or in a French provincial town, and the adepts thus trained show a singular tendency on returning to Haiti to cast off their European learning. Young doctors, sent to France for education in medical science, come back and discard any modern aseptic or antiseptic theories in their practice, in fact almost revert to the position of negro charlatans. Lawyers can think of nothing but the meticulous intricacies of the Code Napoléon, and seem incapable of devising a simple civil and criminal jurisprudence applicable to the essentially African race which inhabits Haiti. As to other branches of modern science—agriculture, forestry, zoology, botany, mineralogy, bacteriology—not a single Haitian interests himself in such pursuits. There are the magnificent pine forests of Alpine Haiti being recklessly destroyed year after year by ignorant peasants or hasty *concessionnaires.* The Government of Haiti, from the President down to the lowest "buraliste" in Port-au-Prince, does not care an iota.

Haiti possesses one of the most magnificent floras in the world and a wonderful display of bird-life. Do you suppose any Haitian knows or cares anything about the trees, flowers, or fruit, beautiful or useful, of his own country;

167. A HAITIAN PEASANT ON HIS WAY TO MARKET

the birds, the fish, the butterflies, the rocks, minerals, rainfall, or wind force? Not one. And yet these same men amongst the two hundred thousand educated people know a good deal about the landscapes of France, England, Germany, and Italy; can quote with appreciative delight the nature studies of Tennyson; admire the art of Corot and Daubigny; and have even heard of Turner. The amazing beauty of their own country is only apparent to them when their attention is called to it by utter strangers; and then they put forward quotations from foreign writers on Haitian scenery as an excuse for their political shortcomings or financial defalcations. They know all about the nightingale and nothing of the Haitian warblers. In their poetry they refer to the eagle and swan (completely absent from their sphere), but never to the frigate-bird or flamingo.

That they have a sense of beauty, from the highest to the lowest—the peasant to the president of the Cercle de Port-au-Prince—is evident from the choice of sites for their villas or villages, the arrangement of trees and flowering shrubs around their habitations, the breeding of peacocks (these beautiful birds are abundant in many Haitian towns and hamlets), and the dress and adornments of the peasantry. As to the dress of the two hundred thousand educated people, though less exotic than it was, it is still, as in Liberia—a worship of the tall hat and frock-coat. In the streets of Port-au-Prince, as of Monrovia, in a temperature 95 degrees in the shade and something under boiling-point in the sun, you may see Haitian statesmen cavorting about in black silk hats of portentous height and glossiness, with frock-coats down to their knees, and wearing lemon kid gloves. The peasantry show originality, taste, and a real sense of appropriateness in their costume. The educated people in their passionate admiration of France do not even dress as do the very sensible French colonists of the French West Indies or of Africa, but wear what they believe to be the last fashion of Paris.

168. "JOSEPH," MAÎTRE D'HÔTEL
An excellent type of Haitian

In fact it is the attachment to France which is the great bar to Haitian progress. If the Monroe Doctrine did not exist and was not supported by eighty-nine million of people in the United States, I should say the best thing which could happen to Haiti would be a French direction of their country on much the same lines as the American intervention in the affairs of the Dominican Republic. But the United States will not permit France, England, or Germany to play such a rôle in Haiti. France, in fact, has ceased to be a great American power, however important may be her rôle in the other three-quarters of the globe.

Haiti must learn English or Spanish if she wishes to advance and to hold her own in the American hegemony. In conversation with one of the Haitian leaders I suggested that, inasmuch as their young men could get no practical education in tropical agriculture in France, they should be sent instead to learn that and other essentially useful things at Booker Washington's Tuskegee Institute in Alabama. He agreed as to the value of Tuskegee training, but put forward the language difficulty as a reason for not sending Haitians to be educated in the United States. Yet according to statistics Haitians in the Government schools are supposed to be taught English, Spanish, and German, in addition to French. (This, of course, is not the fact, except in the seminaries of the French priests.)

And so, while the Dominican Republic, Cuba, Mexico, and all the rest of Spanish-speaking America are interchanging ideas and at the same time strengthening in a marked manner their commercial relations with the United States, Canada, and Jamaica, Haiti remains aloof from all these movements,

170. A WELL-TO-DO FARMER, HAITI

a little black China in the midst of the Antilles, regarding all the rest of the world, except the far-off France, as uninteresting barbarians. Yet with extraordinary inconsistency their historians continue to harp on the terrible cruelties inflicted by the French on the slave ancestors of the Haitians, and on the way in which France for thirty years after their declaration of independence obliged them to maintain great military forces to resist reconquest, and at the same time crippled their finances by the imposition of an indemnity of £6,000,000,[1] which it took them half a century to pay.

At least two out of the three millions of Haitian negroes are only Christians in the loose statistics of geographers. They are still African pagans, with a vague recognition of the Cross as an unexplained but potent symbol. They believe in a far-off, scarcely heeding Deity and a multitude of spirits, ancestral and demiurgic. Magic or empirical medicine ("wanga") is, of course, believed in; and ranges in scope from genuine therapeutics to sorcery, mesmerism, and poisoning.

171. A HAITIAN COUNTRY HOUSE OF THE MIDDLE-CLASS TYPE

As to "Vuduism," much exaggeration and untruth have been committed to

[1] Reduced by Louis Philippe's Government to £3,500,000.

paper on this subject, so far as it affects Haiti. Snake-worship is of doubtful occurrence, owing to the rarity of snakes in Haiti. Such harmless snakes as do exist[1] are tolerated in some villages or fetish temples for their rat-killing propensities. The idea has therefore got abroad that they are "kept" as sacred animals by the Vudu priests or priestesses. Sacrifices of eggs, rum, fowls, possibly goats (white fowls or white goats preferred) are offered to ancestors or minor deities presiding over the fertility of crops, rainfall (nature-forces, in fact), and various small animals (perhaps even human remains) are deemed useful in sorcery. To obtain human bones, and also for the more materialistic purpose of robbing the dead of their clothes and ornaments, graves are sometimes violated; but not with the loathsome intent to eat the dead body. This ghoulish practice still survives in the Congo basin, but has never been traced to Haiti on trustworthy evidence. Isolated instances—about four or five—of cannibalism (the killing and eating of children) have occurred in the criminal records of Haiti during the last twenty years, but the convicted were, in nearly all cases, punished with death; the one or two not executed had been proved to be mad, and were confined in prison or asylum. These acts of cannibalism were mostly examples of mad religious exaltation. Haiti "Vuduism" has absorbed elements of Freemasonry and Christianity. It predicts the future, investigates crime, arranges love affairs. Presidents of Haiti have consulted the oracles of Vudu priests and priestesses as to their coming fate, as an occasional British statesman might half-laughingly submit his hands to a Bond Street palmist. (See note on p. 253.)

172. A "VUDU" HOUSE, HAITI

The 2,500,000 Haitian peasants are passionately fond of dancing, will even sometimes dance almost or quite naked. And following on this choregraphic exercise is much immorality. It is for these dances and not for mystic "Vudu" purposes that the drums may be heard tapping, tapping, booming, rattling at night. No secret is made, nor is any shame felt about these village dances, in which many young people take part.

In most of the country districts polygamy is openly practised. The rite of marriage—civil and religious—is probably confined to about an eighth of the total adult population. In fact, in almost all features of their lives, except in dress, language, and rudeness of manners, the Haitian peasantry has returned to African conditions. But so far as placid acceptance of a bad government is concerned, and in their perfect courtesy and absence of truculence towards

[1] Haiti (Hispaniola), like the rest of the Greater Antilles, has *no* poisonous or dangerous snake. It possesses one or two species of Tree Boas (*Epicrates*); a species of Water Boa (*Ungalia*); colubrine snakes of the genera *Dromicus* and *Liophis*, *Uromacer*, and *Hypsirhynchus*; the last two *peculiar* to Hispaniola. All are small except the Tree and Water Boas, and they are not at most more than six or seven feet long.

foreigners, the Haitian people may be regarded as civilised. In small things they are thievish; in large concerns law-abiding and honest.

Four-fifths of the Haitians—the peasantry of the country, that is to say—are hard-working, peaceable country people. These four-fifths of three million are entirely negro in race, and probably represent a mingling of West African types from Senegambia, Dahomé, and the Congo. It is a race which exhibits, away from the towns, a fine physical development; its skin colour is much darker and the negro type more pronounced than in the United States. Owing

173. "VUDU" DRUMS, HAITI

to causes at present obscure (locally it is attributed to the consumption of bad salt codfish) leprosy has obtained a considerable hold over certain districts, especially in the plains, and syphilis is still answerable for terrible ravages amongst the coast and town population. Still to the tourist, glancing in a cursory way, the people of the interior—the peasantry—seem an essentially healthy, vigorous negro race.

The tourist observer is conscious of another fact about them: that they are mostly hard-working, the women especially. As the employés of Europeans they are disheartening, owing to the irregularity of their work. For a day or so, if amused or interested, they will labour like veritable heroes, then the men will get drunk or decide on an inopportune spell of rest. Put to piece-work they would probably get through more labour than the European in the same period of time; but here, as in Africa, they tend at first to resist regularity of industry.

174. THE BASE OF A FETISH TREE, ON WHICH VOTIVE OFFERINGS ARE PLACED. HAITI

They are ready to work when the rest of the world wants to rest. They may decide to repose when it is the regular time for exertion. They are noisy, slightly quarrelsome amongst themselves, and some are inclined to drunkenness.

175. THE REAL ARTICLE!
A priestess of the Obia with a tame snake. Lagos Hinterland

The women are the best part of the nation. They are splendid, unremitting toilers. In the face of all discouragements with which a bad Government clouds their existence the women of Haiti remind one of certain patient types of ant or termite, who, as fast as you destroy their labour of months or days, hasten to repair it with unslackening energy. The market-women that descend from the country farms to the Haitian towns know that on their way to the market-place, and in that market-place, they will be robbed by soldiers and officers until the margin of profit on the sale of their wares has practically disappeared. Yet they continue to toil, to raise poultry and cattle, till the fields, see to their gardens, make pottery and mats. They cannot stop to reason, but must go on working from three years old to the end of their lives. Such industry (which is almost equally supplemented by that of the peasant husbands) protected should make Haiti one of the richest countries in the world for its size and population; but so long as it is cursed by its present military despotism the utmost that the women of Haiti can do is to keep their country just above the waters of bankruptcy and their households from complete despair.

The curse of Haiti from the day she established her independence in 1804 to the present time is this tyrannical and wasteful government of the military party. *Plus ça change, plus c'est la même chose!* Scarcely a President in the history of Haiti has not been a military man, and the favourite leader for the

176. HAITIAN CATTLE

time being, of the major portion of the army. It seems impossible for a really civilian Government of Haiti to come into existence. The country possesses a pedantically perfect Constitution, providing every possible safeguard for civil liberty and freedom of elections. Yet President after President calmly ignores the precepts of the Constitution, and either governs Haiti despotically or allows the country to be misruled and shamefully robbed by a camarilla of

177. THE WAY THE HAITIANS RESTRAIN THEIR DOMESTIC PIGS FROM WANDERING

Ministers. Whenever some intelligent Haitian politician attempted in the past to point out acts of unconstitutional government, he was either taken out and shot, then and there,[1] by order of the President, or was flung into prison and perhaps made to undergo tortures.

That President Antoine Simon will follow in the bloody footsteps of his Presidential predecessors is very improbable. He is a man of obviously kindly nature, with a record of twenty-two years' essentially clement government of the

[1] As late as 1908.

great southern province of Haiti; but he is an old man of imperfect education, and though he may turn out a complete surprise, yet so far he has done nothing to improve the conditions of political elections. The whole power of the country is still entirely based on the soldiers.

The theoretical standing army of Haiti is 30,000 men, of whom perhaps there are 10,000 at this moment under the colours. According to the Constitution of the country conscription is in force, and every able-bodied man must serve for a certain period in the national army. In the case of any country of great magnitude pursuing a world policy universal military service is, or is going to be, a practical necessity. But countries in the position of Haiti should be happily exempt from such a tax on industry. Whom has Haiti to fear as

178. A FIFE-AND-DRUM BAND, HAITI

regards exterior enemies? Aggressions from any European Power? No. The United States forbids that, and equally restrains the Dominican Republic from any policy of conquest. The United States is the only Power which could with any success or justification interfere with the independence of Haiti; and what could 10,000 or 30,000 Haitian troops do against the forces of the United States? Consequently, Haiti needs no army for other purposes than the maintenance of public order within the limits of the Republic. For this purpose a well-disciplined, well-armed force of 2000 men would be quite sufficient, together with a constabulary of 1000 rural police. Of the irregular army, 1000 men might be employed as frontier guards to assist the customs officers all along the inland frontier between Haiti and the Dominican Republic, 500 might serve as the President's guard in Port-au-Prince, and the remaining 500 be stationed in small detatchments in the leading coast towns. The law of conscription need not be abolished; it might be allowed to become a dead letter under present circumstances, not to be revived save by the vote of a free Assembly.

At the same time that the army is reduced, the President might dismiss and pension off the horde of generals, at present the curse of the country There are generals who are delegated viceroys for each of the five great departments or provinces, which they really rule as despotic satraps. There

179. A HAITIAN POLICEMAN

are "generals of arrondissement" and "généraux de place"; there are generals of division and unattached generals; in fact, though the term "general" is not always used in official designation, it has come to be the common address of respect to any official of any importance in Haiti.

It is very rare to meet with any general officer who has any modern education. They live away from the capital like semi-independent African chiefs, ruling the people with a rod of iron and plundering them mercilessly of their hard-earned subsistence. The chief weapon they wield is, "Give me this woman for my concubine; give me this horse to which I have taken a fancy; send me so many bushels of maize, so many bunches of bananas, so many fowls, or so many labourers to work on my estate, or I shall force you to serve in the army." If the peasant or the village head-man refuses such a request, he is arrested by the general's soldiers and leaves his home, perhaps for ever.

One reason why in Haiti one sees scarcely any other people than women coming to the markets is because the men are afraid to leave their hidden villages or mountain eyries and come down into the cities or bourgs, in case they may be impressed into military service or reimpressed; for it matters nothing if they have served before or completed their full term of service.

Under the accursed military despotism of Haiti home life is constantly broken up; in fact, it is the old slave-trade again under another form. Once the men are snatched from their homes and enrolled in this preposterous army, with its Second Empire costumes, its out-of-date artillery, and its assorted rifles and mixed ammunition (the soldiers' really effective weapons being the club

180. A RAMSHACKLE HAITIAN DWELLING DEFENDED BY CACTI

and matchet), with the usual negro *insouciance* they dry their tears, tend their weals and bruises, and resign themselves to a city life of laziness, thieving, debauchery, drunkenness, untidy squalor, and impudent begging. Some of them become licensed bandits, robbing the stranger as well as the native. But, since there are decent folk amongst them (as there are in every collection of negroes), some of them try, during the long periods of military inaction, to earn a living "by licence"—that is to say, with the permission of their commanding officer they hire themselves out as servants, labourers, or muleteers. In such cases quite 50 per cent of their miserable gains have to be paid to their officers, from the colonel (possibly) down to the sergeant.

Any one who has followed my argument can see how this blighting army prevents the putting into force of the constitutional Haitian government. If you are a Haitian and attempt a pacific revolution by appealing to the reason of your fellow-citizens, the Executive of the day arrests you arbitrarily and throws you into prison without a trial, using the ignorant army as its force and remaining victor so long as the army supports its favourite general as

President. If another general can win over or arm better a larger proportion of the standing army than the man in power, then there is another revolution and another military President. But what about the Legislature? That, under the existing circumstances, is the creature of the military Executive. This is how elections are at present managed in Haiti. Voters are registered between October and December in every year; but no respectable citizens attempt to go and vote, because they know they will be hustled by the soldiery and that every form of chicanery and violence will be adopted to prevent their recording their suffrage (except for the official candidate). The persons told off by the Executive to register voters finally draw up a more or less nonsensical list (which, contrary to the law, is never posted up), consisting either of bogus names, or else the names of soldiers put forward as voters by officers in the

181. PEASANTS' HUTS, HAITI

confidence of the Executive; for the fact that *soldiers on active service are allowed to vote in all political and municipal elections* is a flaw of the otherwise immaculate Haitian Constitution.

Once in three years the elections take place for the Chamber of Deputies (which itself elects the Senate). Unless you are a candidate on the special list of the Executive—that is to say, the nominee of the military President—your election is hopeless. First of all, the Election Tribunal is a farce; if there has been sufficient support of public opinion to elect on to that tribunal independent persons not the creatures of the Executive, the said Executive persuades or bribes two or three of its agents on the Election Tribunal to resign on some pretext or another. It then quashes the whole constitution of the tribunal, nominates instead a committee of citizens to superintend the elections, and naturally takes care to appoint its own partisans or employés in that capacity.

The soldiers next come forward and vote for the names written down for them by their officers; and these names, of course, are those of the Government candidates. Even supposing that, in spite of violence or chicane, some independent electors have been registered and do put in votes for non-Government candidates, this matters little; for the Government-appointed Judge of the Election Tribunal calmly ignores such votes and declares the Government candidate elected unanimously.

And, as I say, any loud or sustained protest against this despotic military rule (and, unhappily, the military element in Haiti is usually of an uneducated negro type) is met by *peines fortes et dures*, or at any rate by severe ostracism from anything that is going in the way of Government employment.

Will it be so under the rule of Antoine Simon? Will the truth be allowed to reach his ears? Will he be allowed by his camarilla to read anything that is written on the subject? He has a magnificent opportunity. He is President for six years. He is the head of the army and a military officer of long and distinguished service. He could do what no civilian in Haiti could accomplish. He could reduce the army to two thousand men and make it no longer an instrument of tyranny. He could restore that freedom of the Press which has not existed in Haiti for over fifty years.

182. A HAITIAN MASON

Under the free discussion of a freed Legislature and an independent Press other reforms could then be carried out which would right what is wrong in the finances and institute public works for the development of Haiti, a country of remarkable resources, perfect climate, and inherently hard-working population.

But a few more years of wastefulness and fraud in the collection and administration of public revenues, which has been characteristic of the Haitian Executive since 1870, will make the country bankrupt, rich as it is, or provoke the emigration of the peasantry in large numbers to Cuba and San Domingo.

The present External Debt of Haiti, consisting of the 1875 and 1896 loans, amounted at the end of 1908 to a total of $11,996,355, or £2,499,240. Of this £752,000 bears interest at 5 per cent, and £1,747,240 bears interest at 6 per cent. There is said to have been no amortisation of the bonds of this foreign loan since 1903. Sums for this purpose are attributed annually in each budget, but apparently do not reach the French Bank of Haiti.

The Internal Debt of this Republic amounts to about $13,030,184, or, approximately, £2,714,622. This is the least valuation which can be assigned to it. It is probably much larger, and in its origin is mainly traceable to unpaid salaries and other emoluments due to Haitian officials. The employés of the Government, except those that really form part of the Executive or the officers of the army who have to be kept faithful to the Executive, are usually paid in "obligations" (bonds), which the Haitian Government is never able to cash. These Treasury bonds (so to speak) were once intended to bear an interest of 12 per cent until the Government could redeem them. The Haitian official to whom these pieces of paper were given, being obliged to maintain himself and his family, took them to foreign bankers and merchants, who bought them for cash at a great reduction from their face value. Thus a good deal of this Internal Haitian Debt (divided mainly into "pink" and "blue" bonds and "consolidated") came into the hands of foreigners, who expected to receive the 12 per cent per annum interest promised by the Haitian Government. After a time the Haitian Executive, finding that these bonds had been purchased at possibly only 25 per cent, or 40 per cent, or 50 per cent of their face value, decided to reduce the annual interest to an amount ranging from 3 per cent to 6 per cent. This act excited a great deal of clamour, but the dispute was eventually settled on the above terms of interest.

In addition to the indebtedness already tabled, the Alexian Administration

183. THE GOVERNMENT SECRETARIATS AND OFFICES, PORT-AU-PRINCE

issued paper money to the face value of £1,978,176 ($9,495,248), and circulated nickel coins of little intrinsic worth to the nominal value of £1,561,510 ($7,495,248). Consequently the national debt of Haiti amounts in all to £8,753,548, of which £5,213,862 is interest-bearing and secured, and £3,539,686 is worthless paper money and nickel coin unsecured.

The natural result of all these measures was the immense rise in the rate of local exchange, so that Haitian money and products became very cheap and foreign money and foreign products very dear. Trade and intercourse were hampered by a thousand expensive *tracasseries*, greatly to the profit of jacks-in-office, and much to the hindrance of honest trade and profitable intercourse. None of this national debt of 8¾ millions sterling is represented by any public works. Quite four million pounds of it is nothing but plunder taken by Presidents and Ministers.

The revenue of Haiti is raised partly on a burdensome tariff of high import duties, but mainly on the export duties levied on coffee, cacao, dyewoods, timber, hides, fibre, copper, and other minerals. What keeps the country going practically is *coffee* derived from the plantations originally planted by the French colonists. If all the coffee that left the Haitian ports for France and the United States paid export duty according to the tariff, the Haitian revenue would be much higher than it is; but at nearly every port there is a private scheme in force by which the exporting merchants largely understate the weight of the coffee they are sending out of the country, and share the profits of this swindle with the local and Executive officials of the day.

184. OUTSIDE THE CEMETERY, PORT-AU-PRINCE
Here are the graves of political martyrs killed summarily without trial during 1908 by orders of President Nord Alexis because they criticised his administration

In addition to the rescue of Haiti from the throttling grasp of the military party, it will be necessary to institute absolute honesty and thrift in the conduct of public affairs. Officials—from the highest to the lowest—must be paid adequate—let us say even handsome—salaries, scaled according to responsibility and efficiency; but in return the country must exact from them ruthlessly an honest administration of public moneys.

But what use is it talking of the "country" doing this or willing that when no more than 200,000 out of 3,000,000 Haitians have the slightest approach to education? The masses in Haiti only realise that they are plundered at every turn by the authorities, and are just beginning to ask themselves whether they would not be better off as free settlers in Cuba, Jamaica, or the Dominican Republic.

This eastern division of Hispaniola has grown strong enough to keep the Haitians at bay, and has found settled peace, prosperity, and the certainty of a bright future by wisely placing itself under the wing of the United States. Such, no doubt, is the predestined fate of Haiti: to accept United States advice in the management of its home concerns (retaining its governing powers to the full) and to leave its foreign affairs entirely to the State Department at Washington.

185. A PORTION OF THE TOWN OF PORT-AU-PRINCE BURNT DOWN BY INCENDIARY FIRES IN AUGUST, 1908

CHAPTER IX

SLAVERY UNDER THE BRITISH

(BERMUDAS, BARBADOS, TURKS AND CAICOS ISLANDS, LEEWARD ISLANDS, AND DOMINICA)

THE ENGLISH first entered into the African slave-trade through the adventures and contracts of Sir John Hawkins (1562–7). Previous to his visits to Senegambia and the Gold Coast for cargoes of slaves, British ships had from about 1553 (if not earlier) found their way to the west coast of Africa to trade in pepper, spices, perfumes, ivory, and gold.

186. CAPE COAST CASTLE (CABO CORSO), GOLD COAST
First a Portuguese and then a British depôt (founded in 1626) and shipping-place for the slave trade

It is suggested by one or two historians[1] that although Queen Elizabeth lent two ships to Sir John Hawkins and invested money in his enterprise, she believed in so doing she was merely engaging in the procuring of such products as those already mentioned; and that when she realised Hawkins was applying his or her ships to the kidnapping of negroes and their transportation to the Canary Islands and the West Indies, she censured him and withdrew her support.

But no great development followed Hawkins' attempts. He became a

[1] Especially Thomas Clarkson, in his *History of the Abolition of the African Slave Trade*, etc., Vol. I.

pirate himself towards the Spaniards in the New World, and after his death in 1595 (near Porto Rico) the Spanish West Indies were closed against British ships, while the Portuguese on the west coast of Africa, both before and after the union of their country with Spain, were very hostile to any infringement of their monopoly and impartially attacked the Dutch, French, and English ships which sailed along the West African coast or ascended some of the rivers.

It was not, therefore, until the middle of the seventeenth century, when Portugal was once more independent and seeking alliances against Spain, that the English were able to set up in a permanent fashion slave-trading establish-

187. NEGROES FROM NORTHERN TERRITORIES OF GOLD COAST

A good many of this type found their way to America as "Koromanti" slaves because they were shipped from the British and Dutch coast stations of Coromantyn or Koromanti near Cape Coast

ments on the Gambia River (1618, 1664) and on the Gold Coast (1618, 1626, and 1668). Before that, they generally bought the slaves they required from the Dutch; or exported them from Morocco.

The Sharifian Empire in that country had felled the Portuguese dominion of Al Gharb by the Battle of Kasr-al-Kebir (1578), and soon afterwards (1590–5) had conquered Timbuktu, Jenne, Gao, and the Upper Niger, thus affording a great impetus to the overland slave-trade between Nigeria and Morocco.

The English began to establish a trade with Morocco in 1577, owing to the embassy sent in that year by the canny Elizabeth, who saw her way to building up a Mediterranean trade for England by allying herself in friendship with the

Moors and Turks. In 1588 a patented or chartered company—the Company of Barbary Merchants—was founded and included on its "Board" the Earls of Warwick and Leicester. From that time to the middle of the eighteenth century the British had almost the monopoly of Morocco trade, and exported numbers of slaves thence to British and Spanish America.

The BERMUDAS, or Somers Islands, were definitely settled by the English from 1612. They were possibly the second portion of British America (Virginia coming first in 1619) on which negro slaves were landed;[1] and the Bermudas were the focus from which radiated much of the early English colonisation of the Bahamas, St. Kitts, and Antigua. They are narrow curved islets (rarely more than a mile broad) about 580 miles east of the North Carolina Coast, of limestone formation, partially covered with coral reefs and sandbanks, with a total habitable area of little more than nineteen square miles. At first they served more as a depôt, both for trade, piracy, and colonisation, than as a plantation ground; though tobacco grows wild there and was industriously cultivated by negro slaves (obtained through the Dutch) from about 1660 to 1707. During the last part of the seventeenth century, throughout the eighteenth and early nineteenth centuries, the English colonists of the Bermudas and their negro slaves developed into a fine bold race of seamen. They built sailing ships of from two to three hundred tons from the timber of the Bermuda "cedar" (a red juniper), and in these vessels brought the fish from the Newfoundland banks to the coasts of Portugal and the Mediterranean, or waited at the islands of Madeira, Ascension, or St. Helena for the returning Indiamen, from whom they obtained cargoes of tea, spices, porcelain, silks and other wares of the Far East. They carried back port wine to Newfoundland, and Madeira wine to New England and the Carolinas; and distributed all along the eastern seaboard of North America the products of the East Indian trade. The Navigation Acts[2] which did so much to alienate the loyalty of the North American colonies built up a great prosperity for the Bermudas, both for the privileges they conferred on ships under the British flag and the profits to be obtained by hardy seamen from smuggling in defiance of the regulations intended to operate only in the selfish interests of Great Britain.

After the war of the American rebellion the great value of the Bermuda archipelago as a naval station in the Western Atlantic became obvious, and from about 1783 a fresh development took place in the islands' industries, and the value of their twelve thousand acres of exploitable ground became greatly

[1] There were probably negroes here as early as 1620, and by 1630 there were several hundred on the "still vexed Bermoothes."

[2] As the Navigation Acts, of which the first was passed in 1651, have much to do with the slave-trade and the development of the West Indies they may be briefly described here: They were laws of the British Parliament which restricted the carriage of colonial produce to English or Colonial-owned ships with an English captain and a crew at least three-quarters English. And goods destined for the American colonies and West India Islands could only be conveyed in ships similarly owned and manned, and loading in English ports. Moreover, the greater part of the products grown or manufactured in the American colonies or plantations could only be shipped to England. Other closely-related laws fettered and prohibited Colonial (just as they did Irish) manufactures; to such an extent as to outdo the illiberal policy of Spain towards Spanish America.

The Navigation Laws, of course, were initiated by Cromwell in order to create a great commercial marine for England and to deal a blow at the Dutch, who had become the world's great carriers in slaves as in everything else. Supplemented by similar legislature under Charles II they effected their purpose; but in the latter half of the eighteenth century cost us our original American colonies and hampered the commercial development of the British West Indies. These Navigation Laws were almost abolished by Huskisson's legislation in 1823 and completely disappeared in the sunrise of Free Trade in 1849.

enhanced. While on the one hand it was sought to ameliorate the conditions of slavery, it was not desired (then) to make it easy for a class of free negroes and men of colour to grow up and seek a position of equality alongside the whites.

In 1789 the Legislature of Bermuda passed an Act to make obsolete a much older Act of the same Legislature, which forbade the forfeiture of the life and estate of any white man who killed a negro "or other slave." But in 1806 an Act of the Bermudan Legislature pronounced the rapid increase of the number of free negroes and free persons of colour "to be a great and growing evil," and

188. A NEGRO HOMESTEAD IN THE BERMUDA ISLANDS

laid down that no slave under forty years of age should be emancipated, except on the condition that he left the islands within three months. If a slave was more than forty years of age he might be emancipated upon the owner paying £50 into the public treasury. No free negro or person of colour was to be capable of acquiring or being seized of any real estate whatever. No house was to be leased to any free negro for a longer term than seven years.

But about 1828, at the instances of the British Government, legislation was carried through the Bermuda House of Assembly conferring on free negroes and men of colour the same privileges as their white fellow-citizens; and in 1834 the status of slavery was abolished. The Bermudan slave-owners received for some reason only about £12 compensation for each slave: a less amount than was granted anywhere in the West Indies.

This House of Assembly, for which negroes and mulattoes may now elect members and in which, if elected, they themselves may sit, dates almost from 1620: certainly from 1684, in which year the Bermudas became a colony directly governed by the Crown. The Government consists now of an Executive Council on which there may be two unofficial, nominated members; a Legislative Council with six unofficial nominated members; and the House of Assembly with thirty-six members, all *elected* by the people of Bermuda on a franchise granted to all resident males having freehold property not less than £60 in value, or an equivalent in annual income. The only qualification necessary to a *member* of the House of Assembly (besides British nationality) is the possession of freehold property of a minimum value of £240. There are about 1320 electors out of a population of 19,000;[1] and there are no political disabilities whatever connected with race or colour. Out of these 19,000 about 12,500 are negro or coloured and 6500 are white.

The remarkable shipping business of the Bermudas has died down since the abolition of the Navigation Laws and the short spell of profitable blockade-running during the American Civil War. But for the last forty years the Bermudans—black and white—have made an increasingly profitable pursuit out of market-gardening and horticulture for their special trade with the United States.

Connected in original history with the Bermudas are the TURKS[2] and CAICOS Islands (about thirty in number, but only eight inhabited), lying some seven hundred miles to the south-south-west of the Bermuda group. They are scarcely the south-easternmost prolongation of the great Bahama bank (as is often stated), for between them and Inagua and Mariguana (easternmost of the Bahamas) lies a narrow but very deep strait of water, equally separating them from Hispaniola. In addition, they have never had any political affinity with the settlers of the northern and most inhabited Bahamas, and at the close of the eighteenth and beginning of the nineteenth centuries the two or three thousand whites, mulattoes, and negroes of the Turks and Caicos were constantly in conflict with the tyrannical and odious white man's House of Assembly at Nassau. In 1848 their petition to be severed from the Government of the Bahamas (to which they had been attached in 1799) was granted, and since that date they have been an almost separate colony under the general direction of Jamaica.

The total land-area of this group is 166 square miles, and the present population is 6000, mainly negroid. There are few pure-blooded negroes in this colony, and barely 100 whites who are free from a negroid strain. The ancestors of the white "Turks" and Caicans migrated from Bermuda during the seventeenth century, bringing their negroes with them but not allowing these slaves to marry and settle down. For a long period they only visited the Turks and Caicos "cays" to conduct the annual "salt-raking."[3] The Spaniards expelled them in

[1] This total refers to residents and does not include the garrison of five or six thousand soldiers and seamen.

[2] The name is derived from the stumpy, turban-like "Turk's head" cacti which grow on these wind-swept islands. The largest of the islands—Grand Caicos—is twenty miles long by six broad. Grand Turk is seven miles by two.

[3] Salt-raking, to which one sees so many references in studying the history of the West Indies, is an industry limited mainly to the Southern Bahamas, Turks and Caicos, and some of the outer islands and islets of the Lesser Antilles. Advantage is taken of the low flat lands practically at sea-level, perhaps cut off from the sea by dunes or beaches. Canals are dug and these natural reservoirs are flooded with sea-water. When sufficient has been admitted, the canal mouth is closed by wooden gates and the shallow sea-water left to evaporate. When the water has been turned into salt by the action of the fierce sun, the salt is raked into heaps and left to bleach. Salt thus made is particularly good for fish and meat curing.

1710, but some returned and others joined them. Colonisation was reinforced by "loyalist" white settlers from Georgia in 1784-5 who brought negro slaves with them. Many slaves also were obtained from the ships wrecked on these coral islets on their way to Jamaica or Cuba.

Latterly there was no strict slavery on this group, owing to the lack of a regular government and to the partial fusion of the races. Moreover, many of the negro slaves escaped into the bush and for a time relapsed into savagery. A handsome, muscular, sturdy seafaring race[1] is growing up here, which with some continued further isolation may develop a very interesting local type of Caucaso-negroid not unlike in aspect to some of the Southern Mediterranean peoples.

They are governed by a Commissioner, aided by a Legislative Board, the four unofficial members of which are nominated by the Governor of Jamaica. Laws passed in Jamaica may by special announcement be made to apply to the Turks and Caicos.

Salt-raking is still the principal industry, and salt to the extent of about £15,000 is exported annually. Sponges also are obtained and cured locally and exported to the value of several thousand pounds annually. Grand Turk —the most inhabited island of these two little archipelagos—derives some importance from being a landing-place and station of the British Direct West India Cable Company.

Education down to the close of the 'eighties was lamentably backward, but is now well attended to by the local government. The seven elementary schools are unsectarian, free, and have about 580 children on the roll. There is an admirable public library at Grand Turk.

The first negroes to reach BARBADOS[2] arrived in 1626 in the same ship with the first party of English settlers. The English and their ship had proceeded from London, but they made use of their "letters of marque" on the way to capture a Portuguese ship near the Bermudas, and out of her they obtained a few negro labourers.

The British Barbadians next proceeded to the Dutch colonies in Guiana, and thence recruited Amerindians under solemn covenant with the Dutch Governor to return them after two or three years of indentured work; but they shamefully broke their contract and enslaved the Indians, most of whom eventually died, while a few succeeded in escaping. More negroes therefore were brought from some quarter, possibly supplied by the Dutch. By 1636 a regulation was passed by the Governor's Council in Barbados to the effect that all negroes or Indians landed there must be considered as slaves, bound to work on Barbados for the rest of their lives. By 1645 there were no less than 6400 negroes in Barbados, brought from Guinea and also from Bonny (Niger delta), presumably by the Dutch.

In 1647 Yellow Fever made its first appearance at Bridgetown in Barbados, and in 1692 there was a bad epidemic. Apparently the first outbreaks of yellow fever spread to Barbados from Porto Rico,[3] but later on in the eighteenth

[1] "Calm, sober, and contented," writes of them their former Commissioner, Dr. G. S. Hirst. But the same authority points out the still serious mortality in these naturally healthy islands from Tuberculosis. This disease is encouraged by the horror of fresh air in the houses of the poorer people.

[2] "Seven or eight"—*Captain John Smith's Travels*, etc., London, 1630. Barbados had been prospected by the English in 1605.

[3] Yellow fever was not heard of in America until the slave-trade was in full swing. Apparently it was first observed in Porto Rico at the close of the sixteenth century, in the French island of Guadeloupe in 1635-40, at St. Kitts in 1648, and Port Royal, Jamaica, in 1655. Its first appearance in the

century the disease broke out afresh when slaves were transported direct from West Africa to Barbados in British ships. Yellow fever was the first scourge which was evolved by the slave-trade as a punishment to the white man for coercing his black brother into forced labour and expatriation.

In 1674 the number of slaves in the island is said to have exceeded one hundred thousand, and a large proportion were Koromantis from the Gold Coast—a class of negro much in demand for working capacity, but foremost in all the slave revolts and movements towards freedom which were so common in

189. BRIDGETOWN AND "THE BRIDGE," CAPITAL OF BARBADOS
Founded early in 1629. Also a Barbados policeman of 1909

Barbados during the last quarter of the seventeenth and throughout the eighteenth century.

In 1667 an Act was passed for "the better ordering and governing of negroes." It commences, "Whereas the plantations and estates of this Island

United States was at Charleston in 1693. We now know that it is carried from the blood of one human being to that of another by a mosquito of the genus *Stegomyia* (*S. calopus*).

It would seem to have been an African disease in origin, since negroes and even negroids are practically immune, while Amerindians and Europeans are particularly susceptible. But it is not known to exist in Africa except on the coast region of Senegal, the Gambia, Sierra Leone, and very occasionally in Liberia and the Gold Coast. In these parts it occurs sporadically, and of course must be carried from one human being to another by *Stegomyia* mosquitoes, which exist in West Africa as well as in tropical America. According to H. W. Bates (*The Naturalist on the Amazons*), yellow fever did not reach the Amazon Valley and Northern Brazil till the middle of the nineteenth century.

At the time of my visit to Barbados in February, 1909, yellow fever had broken out in the western towns. It is time this disease was altogether suppressed in the island by the scientific destruction of the *Stegomyia* mosquitoes. As regards *malarial* fever, it is almost non-existent here, mainly because the shallow streams and ponds swarm with a tiny fish (*Girardinus*), which devours the *Anopheles* mosquito's larvæ. See note on p. 16.

cannot be fully managed and brought into use without the labour and service of great numbers of negroes and other slaves. . . ."[1] The negroes are described as "barbarous, wild, and savage natures . . . wholly unqualified by the laws, customs, and practices of our nations"; and the Act speaks of the disorders, rapines, and inhumanities to which they are naturally prone and inclined, and trusts that from these "this Island through the blessing of God may be preserved and the lives and fortunes of the King's subjects secured, besides at the same time providing properly for the negroes, and other slaves, and guarding them from cruelties and insolences." No negroes or other slaves are to leave on Sabbath days, holy days, or any other time, to go out to their plantations, except such as are domestic servants and wear a livery, or unless they carry a ticket under the master's or mistress's hand, or some other person by his or her appointment. They are forbidden to carry clubs, wooden swords, or other mischievous or dangerous weapons, or to use or keep drums, horns, or other loud instruments; or to give sign or notice to one another of their "wicked designs or purposes." Any negro or slave offering any violence to a Christian by striking or the like is to be severely whipped by the constable, and for his second offence of that nature, not only to be severely whipped and burnt in some part of his face with a hot iron, but to have his nose slit: unless, of course, such striking of a Christian be in the lawful defence of a master or mistress, or of their goods. The Act refers to the many heinous and grievous crimes such as murders, burglaries, highway robbery, rape, and incendiarism committed "many times by negroes and other slaves," as well as their "stealing, killing, or maiming horses, mares, gelding-cattle, or sheep." The owner of any slave executed judicially for his crimes is to be compensated by the State for the loss of the slave, "which value shall never exceed the sum of £25 sterling."[2] No person "of the Hebrew nation" was allowed to keep or employ more than *one* negro or other slave. The Act also provided for the chase of the runaway negroes who had taken to the woods and other fastnesses of this island, fifty shillings sterling being given as the reward for every negro taken alive or dead. "If any negro or other slave under punishment by his master or at his order unfortunately shall suffer in life or liberty, which seldom happens," no person whatsoever shall be liable to any fine therefrom. But if any man shall of wantonness, or only of bloody-mindedness, or cruel intention, wilfully kill a negro or other slave of his own, he shall pay into the public treasury £15 sterling; but if he shall so kill another man's, he shall pay the owner of the negro double the value, and into the public treasury, £25 sterling; and he shall further, by the next justice of the peace, be bound over to good behaviour during the pleasure of the Governor and Council, and not be liable to any

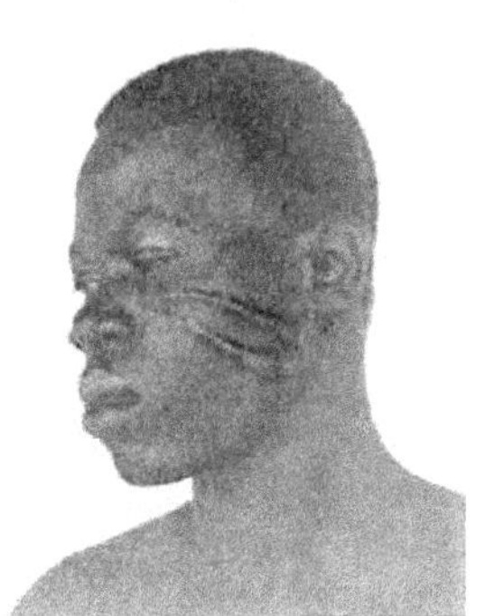

190. A KANJAGA NEGRO, FROM GOLD COAST HINTERLAND
A "Koromanti" negro in slavery parlance

[1] All through the second half of the seventeenth century there were of course many English, Irish, and Welsh indentured apprentices (practically slaves) and political prisoners who were sold as slaves by the British Government and were worse treated than were the negroes.

[2] In the eighteenth century the value gradually rose to £60 and £100 here and elsewhere in the West Indies.

other punishment or forfeiture for the same; neither is he that kills another man's negro or other slave by accident liable to any other penalty but the owner's action at law. "But if any poor small freeholder or other person kill a negro or other slave by night, out of the road or common path, and stealing, or attempting to steal his provision, or other goods, he shall not be accountable for it."

In 1668 an Act was passed declaring the negro slaves of Barbados to be real estate. In 1676 an Act forbade "people called Quakers" from bringing negroes to their meeting. "Whereas of late many negroes have been suffered to remain at the meeting of Quakers as hearers of their doctrine and have been taught in their principles, whereby the safety of this island may be much hazarded, various penalties shall ensue if such proceedings continue."[1] Amongst these, was six months' imprisonment and a fine of ten thousand pounds of

191. AN OLD-TIME ENGLISH PLANTER'S MANSION IN BARBADOS, SURROUNDED BY A GROVE OF TREES: SUGAR PLANTATION IN FOREGROUND

Muscovado sugar to be inflicted on any person not an inhabitant and resident of this island who shall hereafter publicly discourse or preach at the meeting of the Quakers.

With the law of 1708 all negroes employed in selling milk, meat, or firewood on account of their masters shall have at all such times that he, she, or they are selling the same, a metalled collar locked about his, her, or their neck or necks, leg or legs, with the name of the master or mistress engraved thereon, and the name of the parish wherein they live. Slaves, or any white person on their behalf, who removed the "hooks, and rings, or collars round the negroes' necks and legs," without leave of their master, mistress, or overseer, were to be punished; the white persons by being fined "the sum of £10 current money to Her Majesty (Queen Anne), her heirs and successors, and the negro or negress by receiving forty lashes on his or her bare back by order of any one of Her Majesty's Justices of the Peace."

In 1688 the laws of Barbados obliged slave-owners to provide their slaves

1 In 1709 Barbados had got so accustomed to the Quakers, that they brought in an Act to allow them to give evidence by affirmation instead of on oath.

with clothes once a year—drawers and caps for the men, and petticoats and caps for the women, regulations ignored by the planters, whose male slaves frequently went quite naked.[1]

Immediately after the accession of Charles II an Act had been passed in Barbados, commencing: "Whereas divers opinionated and self-conceited persons have declared an absolute dislike to the government of the Church of England, as well as by their aversion and utter neglect or refusal of the prayers, sermons, and administration of the sacraments and other rites and ordinances thereof used in their several parish churches, as by holding conventicles in private houses and other places, scandalising ministers, and endeavouring to seduce others to their erroneous opinions upon pretence of an alteration of Church government in England," etc. This Act went on to impel all persons to give due obedience to the government of the Church of

192. A WINDMILL AND SUGAR FACTORY, BARBADOS

England, and another Act passed in the same year (1660) ordained that all masters and overseers of families shall have prayers openly said or read every morning and evening "with his family," upon penalty of forty pounds of sugar, the one half to the informer, the other half to the public treasury of this island; that all masters of families should regularly attend their parish church "with their families." "If a servant make default of repairing to the church according to the true intent of this Act, and if the fault be in his master, then his master is to pay ten pounds of cotton for every such default; if the neglect be in the servant, he is to be punished at the discretion of the next justice of the peace. Servants and children are to be instructed in the fundamentals of the Christian religion. The churchwardens of every parish are to be provided with a strong pair of stocks, to be placed near the church or chapel, and the constables, churchwardens, and sidesmen shall in some time of

[1] The negro fishermen of north-east Barbados at the present day are frequently quite nude when engaged in fishing.

divine service every Sunday walk and search taverns, alehouses, victualling houses, or other houses where they suspect lewd or debauched company to frequent, and if they shall find any drunk, swearing, gaming, or otherwise misdemeaning themselves, that forthwith they apprehend such persons and bring them to the stocks, there to be by them imprisoned for the space of four hours, unless every such offender pay five shillings to the churchwardens of the said parish for the use of the poor. If a master or free man swears or curses, and thereby blasphemes the name of God, he is to forfeit for every such offence four pounds of sugar; if a servant, two pounds of sugar. If the servant have no wherewithal, he is to be put into the stocks."

These pietistic laws and regulations were almost a dead letter as soon as

193. THE WHITE ROADS OF BUSY BARBADOS

published. From after the middle of the seventeenth century until the close of the eighteenth century the treatment of the Barbados negroes and mulattoes was increasingly brutal, their British and even Spanish Jew[1] owners seeming to be obsessed by a lust of cruelty such as later in history arose in Surinam and in the Southern States of the American Union, an expensive gratification of wild beast instincts, since after all the slave was valuable property, and it was waste of good money to maim or kill him.

But the evidence collected for the House of Commons through the exertions of Thomas Clarkson, William Wilberforce, and others (as well as retrospective research) gave the circumstances of Barbadian slavery a place in infamy fully equal to the worst records of St. Domingue, South Carolina, and

[1] A number of Spanish and Portuguese Jews settled in this island and in Jamaica between 1660 and 1700. By local petty tyranny they were only allowed to keep one slave each, and were not enfranchised until 1831.

Georgia. Here are two examples culled from many attested episodes of horror:—

Captain Cook and Major Fitch, passing in the night a plantation-house in Barbados, heard the shrieks of a woman in agony; they broke open the door and saw an unfortunate negress chained to the floor while her white master was flogging her within an inch of her life. The two officers protested against his inhumanity. The white monster cried out that he was well within the law: he had only given her "thirty-nine lashes"[1] at any one time; this punishment had been repeated already three times that night and he would give her another thirty-nine before morning, would in fact (and probably did) flog her to death in spite of what any one might do, if he pleased; and he would certainly prosecute the two officers for breaking open his door. (I have summarised this quotation from William Wilberforce's speech in the House of Commons on April 18th, 1791.)

194. A SEVENTEENTH-CENTURY CHURCH (? ST. MARY'S) IN BRIDGETOWN, BARBADOS

In supporting Wilberforce's motion on this same occasion Mr. William Smith quoted the following from the evidence of General Tottenham: "In the year 1780 in the streets of Bridgetown, Barbados, I saw a youth about nineteen, entirely naked, with an iron collar about his neck, having five long projecting spikes. His body both before and behind was covered with wounds. His belly and thighs were almost cut to pieces with running ulcers all over them; and a finger might have been laid in some of their weals. He could not sit down because his hinder part was mortified; and it was impossible for him to lie down on account of the prongs of his collar." On inquiries it was found that this wretched boy had been nearly whipped to death by a savage master and then abandoned to starve. No one in Bridgetown took any notice of the incident and the master went unpunished.

195. "BUSY BARBADOS"
Going to market

For a hundred years slaves in Barbados were mutilated, tortured, gibbeted alive and left to starve to death, burnt alive, flung into coppers of boiling

[1] The legal limit.

sugar, whipped to death, overworked, under-fed, obliged from sheer lack of any clothing to expose their nudity to the jeers of the "poor" whites. It is little to be wondered at therefore that there were frequent slave revolts and projected (alas!—one feels inclined to exclaim—seldom accomplished) massacres of the whites.

196. FREEDOM AND INDUSTRY
A woman worker in the fields, Barbados

The first of these risings took place in 1649, but was abortive, for as usual one tender-hearted negro could not bear to think of his white master (a judge) being murdered, so revealed the plot in time for measures of repression to be taken. In 1674 the warlike Koromanti slaves plotted to rise and overwhelm the white people, intending to murder the men and espouse the white women. But the scheme was discovered by a negress house-servant, and the leading conspirators were arrested, tried, burnt alive, or beheaded. In 1692 another organised revolt was discovered and averted, and the same thing occurred in 1702. In the latter half of the seventeenth century many badly-treated Barbados slaves escaped from the island in boats and canoes and took refuge with the Caribs or the French in the Windward Islands.

During the eighteenth century, however, Barbados was the rendezvous of such large naval and military forces engaged in the frequent wars with France and Spain that the Barbadian slaves seem to have given up as hopeless any notion of a rising against the white man. Moreover, the negro being heart and soul a warrior, often fought alongside his English or Scottish master to repel the French, attack the Spaniards or the Dutch, and pursue wild bands of Irish rebels who attacked some of the West India Islands after the Treaty of Limerick set them free to rove the world and defend the cause of the exiled Stuarts. Then too, in between episodes of Barbadian glory (for both White and Black Barbadians were splendid fighters[1]) there

197. A BARBADIAN PRIVATE OF THE WEST INDIA REGIMENT, JAMAICA

[1] So many Barbadians have served from first to last in the "West India Regiments" (there is now one West India Regiment divided into two battalions, one in Jamaica and the other at Sierra Leone), that it may be appropriate to give a short account of these famous negro troops here, though they have been withdrawn from Barbados since 1906.

The 1st West India Regiment started with the enrolment of white Loyalists and negro slaves at Savannah, after its capture by British troops in 1779. The body of fighting-men then brought together under the British colours was called the South Carolina Regiment. (To-day the West India regimental march is, "South Carolina is a Sultry Clime," with the refrain, "O! so early in the morning," etc.)

On the conclusion of the war, the regiment was moved to Jamaica in 1782, and then consisted partly of white, partly of black men.

The whites became Jamaican planters; the negro soldiers could not at that stage of Jamaica history, so they were drafted off to the Leeward and Windward Islands, and employed again as soldiers. In 1795 the remainder of them, together with other negro recruits and white officers, were amalgamated

were intervals of blockade and famine when many of the negroes died of starvation. And thousands perished in the recurrent hurricanes

with various militia corps (such as "Malcolm's" or "the Royal Rangers"), and became the first of the twelve "regiments raised to serve in the West Indies."

These regiments were registered in the Army List of 1798 as "West India Regiments."

The second of these (afterwards the "2nd West India Regiment") grew in 1795 out of a local militia corps called the St. Vincent Rangers. All the twelve regiments took part with the navy in the capture of the French, Dutch, and Danish possessions in America. After the Napoleonic wars were over, the West India regiments (one or more of which had been qualified as "Royal," so that their direct descendant of to-day has royal emblems in its insignia) were reduced and reorganised. After the abolition of slavery in the 'thirties, they became more especially a body of negro troops, only the officers of which were white, and included many Barbadians in their midst. In the middle of the nineteenth century, the one or other of the two regiments (now two battalions of *the* West India Regiment) were stationed at Freetown, Sierra Leone, and from 1850 onwards they fought many battles for the British Government on the Gambia River, in the interior of Sierra Leone, and in Ashanti. At the present day the 1st Battalion is stationed in Jamaica and the 2nd Battalion in Sierra Leone. The total strength of the two battalions is 1175.

Their present uniform, so picturesque, yet business-like, and so attractive to recruits, was practically the invention of Queen Victoria (I am informed by Colonel A. R. Loscombe). It was introduced in 1858. The Queen had been much struck with the uniform of the French Zouaves, and suggested to the War Office that her West India regiments might have a uniform like them. But I have ascertained from the Director of Military Operations that the first proposal to relieve the West India Regiment of its inappropriate and uncomfortable British uniform in favour of a more African dress came from Major Ord in 1856. His proposal was approved and signed by the Queen, but as his suggested style of uniform was not adopted it is permissible to suppose that the Queen may have then put forward the idea of a Zouave uniform.

198. A BANDSMAN: WEST INDIA REGT.

199. "A STAKE IN THE COUNTRY"
Most of the Barbadian negroes at the present day own their small holdings

The late Colonel A. B. Ellis (well known for his ethnographical studies of West Africa), and more recently Colonel A. R. Loscombe and Mr. A. E. Aspinall, have written on the history and qualifications of these remarkable negro soldiers, who could, if we wished, play a considerable part in maintaining the British position in tropical America, if it were ever menaced.

For the employment of negro soldiers (mainly West Indians) by the *French* in Europe during the Napoleonic wars, see a very interesting article in *Questions Diplomatiques et Coloniales* for October 16th, 1909. From hints given here and there, it is evident that France looks upon Senegal and Southern Algeria (where the oases contain a more than half negro population) as valuable recruiting grounds, and intends thence to reinforce her home army should she again be invaded by a foreign enemy.

which pious people ascribed to the wrath of the Almighty at the iniquities perpetrated by the slave-holding whites (though they seem to have overlooked the fact that His punishment fell mainly on the poor wronged negro).

One way and another, the Barbadian negroes diminished in numbers during the eighteenth century from the (no doubt exaggerated) estimate of 100,000

200. "BUSY BARBADOS": GOING TO MARKET WITH POULTRY

at the end of the seventeenth century to the approximate 65,000 of 1800. The excess of deaths over births was a constant feature, and the deficit had to be supplied from Africa annually to the extent of an average five hundred per annum out of the approximate thirty-eight thousand annually exported from Africa in British ships. In 1764 there were 70,706 negro slaves in Barbados; in 1780, 68,270; in 1786, about 62,115; at the end of the century about 65,000.[1]

[1] But it must also be borne in mind that Barbados exported hundreds, even several thousand negroes to the British Windward Islands and to Trinidad between 1797 and 1800.

The abolition of the slave-trade in 1808 effected a slight amelioration in the condition of the Barbadian slaves, since owners now began to care more for the physical and moral welfare of their negroes. At the same time it checked a process of manumission which had been going on for a long time, prompted by conscience, kindliness, or shirking of responsibility. Before the commencement of the nineteenth century it had become a frequent practice on the part of owners to turn adrift or grant freedom to slaves who were sick, aged, or mutilated, and these starving people were becoming an inconvenient burden on the rates. To check this, and also the increase of the politically-inconvenient class of free blacks and mulattoes, the House of Assembly passed a law (similar to those in force in Jamaica, the Bahamas, and most other West India islands) obliging every person manumitting a slave to pay £300 into the Treasury for a female and £200 for a male, so that the freed woman might receive £18 and the freed man £12 a year for their maintenance.

201. THE HOUSE OF ASSEMBLY IN BRIDGETOWN, BARBADOS
One of the oldest parliament houses in the world

Emancipation was in the air. The abolition of the slave-trade was obviously only preliminary to the abolition of slavery. The Barbados blacks became impatient. Though better treated they were harder worked than ever. A free mulatto, Washington Franklin, in 1815 went about among the slaves quoting the speeches denouncing slavery which were being delivered in England, and pointing to the success which had attended the Negro rebellion in Haiti. On April 14th, 1816, the slaves rose in the parish of St. Philip in South-Eastern Barbados and commenced burning cane-fields, windmills, houses, and stores. They did not apparently kill many (? or any) of the white settlers, who were mostly "quittes pour la peur." The militia and soldiery promptly dealt with the rising, which was subdued in two or three days with only one soldier killed on the British side, but with great loss of life to the negroes. A number of prisoners were hanged on the estates they had ravaged, and a hundred and twenty-three were deported as convicts to British Honduras.

But this slave revolt shook up the callous Barbadian Government. The slave laws of the colony were consolidated and ameliorated in 1817. In 1823 an association was formed, with the Governor at its head, for the purpose of giving instruction in religion to the slaves. In 1831, however, a step was taken of a far-reaching importance almost greater and more beneficial at that period than the actual emancipation of the slaves [which followed in 1834–40]; and this was the carrying through the House of Assembly by Mr. Robert Haynes a bill *repealing the political disabilities* of *free negroes* or *men of colour*. From 1832 all free male negroes or mulattoes have had the same electoral and civic privileges as white men; in fact, "colour" distinctions in politics among free people ceased from that date to exist in Barbados, and when slaves and slave-like apprentices all became free men by 1840, Barbados assumed—and has retained—the distinction of being a portion of the British Empire with a Constitutional Government based on popular representation which ignores differences of race-origin or skin-colour in its citizens.

The House of Assembly consists of twenty-four members elected on a

202. CODRINGTON COLLEGE, BARBADOS

popular suffrage, which is higher than that of the Bahamas and lower than in Guiana.[1]

The elections take place annually, and the present number of registered voters is not quite two thousand. There is, besides the Executive Council and the Legislative Council of nine members (a Senate nominated by the Crown),

[1] For *voters* the qualifications are: to be male subjects of the British Crown over twenty-one years, and possessed of an estate or rents from an estate of an annual value *of at least* £5, or the occupier of a house, etc., parochially *assessed at* £15 *per annum*, or to have paid town-taxes at Bridgetown of £2 per annum, or country-town-taxes of £1, or in receipt of a salary or pension of not less than £50 (unless he is a "domestic or other menial servant." Why? This seems petty!), or who is in receipt of a clear income of £15 a year from "real estate," or is a bona-fide lodger in a £50-a-year house in which he himself pays £15 a year rent, or who is a barrister, solicitor, physician or surgeon or holds a British or Codrington College degree. To some of these qualifications there is a condition of six months' previous residence attached.

The qualifications for *members* are to be a male British subject of over twenty-one; who owns thirty acres of land with a house on it worth £300, or a totality of estate valued at £1500, or to be in receipt for life of £120 a year from lands, etc., or to have a clear annual income from any source of £200.

an *Executive Committee* which really carries on the government of the island and initiates legislation, leaving to the popular Assembly the voting of supplies and of the laws, which last must be approved by the Legislative Council and be subject to a veto from the Crown. The British Government appoints the principal public officers (except the Treasurer, who is an official selected by the House of Assembly). The Executive Committee is composed of the Governor, his Executive Council, one member of the Legislative Council, and four members of the House of Assembly nominated by the Governor. On this Executive Committee there is at present

203. "BUSY BARBADOS": SELLING ISLAND POTTERY

one negro, and there are seven coloured men or negroes in the House of Assembly.

Education in Barbados is not compulsory, but about 75 per cent of the negroes and coloured people born since 1860 are able to read and write. The educational system of the island is under a Board appointed by the Governor. The Bishop of Barbados presides over this Board of Education at the present time, and the district control of the primary schools is vested in the Church of England clergyman of the parish.

At present there are 166 primary schools with a roll of 25,178 scholars (15,300 in average attendance), costing the Barbadian Government £11,000 per annum. Another £7000 to £8000 is spent by the same Government on higher-grade education at Harrison College,[1] Bridgetown; at The Lodge; and (for girls) at Queen's College. There are also two fine second-grade schools for boys and one for girls. The colony provides four scholarships annually (through the Education Board), each of the handsome value of £175 annually for *four* years. These are tenable at an English University, or at an Agricultural or Technical College in America—a broad-minded provision. The Government of Barbados also places four Island scholarships of £40 a year each at the disposal of Codrington College, to be reserved for natives of the Island.

Codrington College was founded in 1712, on the bequest of Colonel Christopher Codrington, who died in 1710. He had bequeathed to the Society for the Propagation of the Gospel 763 acres of land, with buildings, mills, 100 cattle and 315 slaves. The Society was to keep up the sugar plantations with 300 slaves, but was to found a college wherein "physic, chirurgery and divinity" were to be taught. Of course during the eighteenth century instruction was only given to white students, and at first theology (of a very barren type) was the only thing taught; but later on law and medicine were added. Candidates were prepared here for holy orders.

204. "BREEZY BARBADOS"

The College was at first much hampered by debt (in spite of the generous contributions of its founder's son, William Codrington). The income derived from the sugar estate was about £2000, but the cost of the buildings saddled the Trust with debt.[2] Even after it was in full activity (1748 and onwards), mismanagement and continual disasters from hurricanes abated its usefulness. By 1813 the number of scholars had fallen to twelve; but in this year a minister was obtained to give *oral* instruction to negroes (as much as might be imparted under the slavery laws). Improvements were effected in 1825, and in 1830 the institution was solemnly opened as a college, well equipped with hall, library, chapel, etc. The very next year nearly everything was blown to the ground by a hurricane! Once

[1] Harrison's Grammar School or College was founded in 1733 by Thomas Harrison, a merchant of Bridgetown, for the education of twenty-four indigent (white) boys of the parish. They were to be taught reading, writing, arithmetic, Latin and Greek, without fee or charge. Outside these twenty-four, paying scholars might be received also into the school. After 1840, more or less, coloured or negro boys were also admitted and now form the preponderating element. The teaching in this school has been reported as excellent by several visitors, and it must be so from the number of its students, white and coloured, who have distinguished themselves at Oxford and Cambridge.

[2] By the latter part of the nineteenth century the sugar estate had become so depreciated in value that an appeal for funds became necessary. Subscriptions raised in England by the West India Committee saved the College from closing its doors.

more a financial effort was made—verily the White Man does not acknowledge defeat in the West Indies (Talk about languor! Where else does he stand up so bravely to the Devil of Reactionary Nature?)—and the limestone walls of the College rose anew. Its present appearance has been compared to New Buildings of Magdalen College, Oxford.

From about 1840, negro or coloured students began to appear among the alumni; now they form the large majority of the students at what is the oldest university in the West Indies. Since 1875 Codrington College has been affiliated with Durham University; but on visiting Durham a year or two back it struck me that the graduates of Codrington [though they appreciated the distinction of being associated with the most picturesque cathedral town in England] found neither the teaching of its sleepy University nor its northern climate attuned to the requirements of West Indians or the West Indies.

205. "BREEZY BARBADOS"
The person despoiled of his hat by Barbadian zephyrs is Mr. A. Greaves, the author's photographic and general assistant throughout his American journeys

The bulk of the modern Barbadians (over 156,000) belong to the Church of England. There are some 15,000 Wesleyans, 7000 Moravians, and 816 Roman Catholics. Very little superstition remains among the coloured people; but occasionally there are proceedings in the police-courts against *Obia* men and women for malicious poisoning of animals or plants. Sexual morality is perhaps better than in the other West India islands. Serious crime is very rare (among the natives); out of a negro and coloured population of about 180,000 there is a daily average of only 217 in prison. 315 negro constables and white officers suffice to maintain order. I found these Barbados policemen as civil, obliging, spruce, and intelligent as their comrades of Jamaica—which is high praise; for the Jamaica constabulary is only to be matched by the police of the United Kingdom.

About 74,000 acres of Barbados—a little less than two-thirds of its area—are under cultivation; 35,000 in sugar-cane, and nearly 20,000 in cotton. The greater part of these sugar and cotton plantations belong to white men, resident and absentee, and the coloured inhabitants do not own much of the soil of the island. As a rule they work for fair wages on the white planters' land.

The coloured Barbadians seem to the passing tourist to be a most industrious people, both men and women.[1] They make rather picturesque pottery out of porous clay; quarry stone; fish; breed poultry, pigs, goats, and other live-stock; cultivate kitchen-gardens; ride as jockeys at the races; fill all the

[1] Here is a brief pen-picture of Barbados taken direct from my note-book (February, 1909):—
Busy Barbados! Every one is civil—excellent policemen—the bright, clean, picturesque city of

trades and most of the professions (for there are no Indian or Chinese competitors here), and occupy most of the minor posts in the Administration. Special attention should (I think) be called to their taste and skill in ornamental work, made out of brightly coloured sea-shells, fish-scales, feathers,

206. BUST OF SIR CONRAD REEVES, FORMERLY CHIEF JUSTICE OF BARBADOS

wood, dried plants, which is sold to eager tourists in the form of artificial sprays of flowers for dress embroidery or table decoration; doyleys, necklaces, filigree

Bridgetown—its slightly pompous, late-Georgian House of Assembly and substantial Government buildings of whitish stone.

The port—blue-green water, white schooners, with chains painted red like necklaces of coral.

The curiosity shops . . . ornaments from fish-scales . . . stuffed toads and strange fish . . . the comfortable, cheap public carriages, with their well-dressed, well-spoken coachmen.

The country roads—blazing white . . . busy Barbados! women going to market with turkeys, fowls, bananas; men and women working in the fields . . . the teams of many mules dragging plantation carts. The windmills . . . fields of cotton coming sparsely into flower with large red-and-lemon-yellow blossoms; the emerald-green sugar-cane and its plumes of purple-grey. The "great house," in style something like a Ramsgate verandahed villa of 1830; buried in trees. The factories with their chimneys and windmills. The stumpy, wind-blown fan palms. Eastern-looking goats and African sheep. The bold, *white*-eyed, glossy-black "starlings," *the* bird of Barbados (*Quiscalus fortirostris*). Pigs everywhere, but not dirty or lean.

brooches, etc. etc. I know it is the fashion to laugh at such arts at present as not to be dissociated from the 'forties and 'fifties of the last century; but personally I think this modern work in Barbados is often beautiful, and instances a remarkable taste in colour and design which possesses an originality of its own. I shall not live to see it, nor will most of my middle-aged readers; but I am sure that the Negro Race some day, or its hybrid with the White man, is going to astonish the world in the arts of Design and Music.

207. H. E. PRESIDENT ARTHUR BARCLAY, OF LIBERIA
A native of Barbados, but derived two generations back from Pōpō, Dahomé

Since the abolition of slavery the general progress of Barbados towards established prosperity and well-being has been steady, except for the unpreventable ravages of occasional hurricanes. The total negro and negroid population in 1834 was about 100,000 (in that year there were 83,176 slaves who were emancipated at an average compensation of £20 14s. each). This with some fluctuations has risen since to about 180,000 at the present day, in spite of the considerable migrations from the island to other parts of America—sometimes 18,000 persons in a year. Barbados is to the seas of Central America what Malta is to the Mediterranean, a hive

208. "BUSY BARBADOS": THE HARBOUR OF BRIDGETOWN

of industrious people swarming out from their tiny island home (Barbados is about the size[1] of the Isle of Wight, and Malta half that area) to colonise, trade, teach, preach, serve the British Government, work in all careers, and labour with their hands and heads. A poor mulatto boy of Barbadian birth—Reeves—rose to be Sir Conrad Reeves and Chief Justice of Barbados, winning in that capacity the universal regard of black, white, and coloured. A negro boy born in Barbados in 1854 migrated to Liberia in 1865, entered the public service of the State in 1878, and ascended through many different grades of office till he became the President of this negro republic in 1904, showing himself through six recent years of difficult and critical work to be a statesman, a diplomatist, and a highly educated man of the world.

The present commercial value of Barbados is approximately *£2,140,000* per annum, of which *£1,200,000* represents imports and *£940,000* exports In the palmiest days of Slavery in the eighteenth century the exports were valued at scarcely more than *£600,000* and the imports at *£450,000*. So that under freedom and free labour the population and commerce of Barbados have more than doubled.

The BRITISH LEEWARD ISLANDS—now associated in one Federal Government of five presidencies and including a total area of 714 square miles—have only shared the same unity of administration since 1832. At present they consist of the Virgin group, Anguilla, Barbuda, St. Christopher (called for short St. Kitts), Nevis, Antigua, Montserrat, and Dominica. St. Christopher vies with Barbados in being the oldest British West India colony, having been first settled by Englishmen in 1623.[2] All the other islands mentioned except Dominica were included in the "Leeward Charaibee" Government (the centre of which was Nevis Island, near St. Christopher) in 1672, during the reign of Charles II. Antigua afterwards became the seat of government, and from 1816 to 1832 St. Christopher and the adjacent islands and Virgin group became a separate government. Lovely, reluctant, Frenchified Dominica did not till 1756–63 become a British possession, nor was it grouped with the Leeward Islands till 1832.

Into all these islands (except Dominica) negro slaves had been introduced during the middle of the seventeenth century, experiments of a treacherous nature having first been made with Amerindians. To St. Christopher, Antigua, and Montserrat a good deal of white convict labour was directed between 1650 and 1700. Many Irish rebels were sent here (or came after the battle of Limerick expressly to annoy), and it is stated by all who have visited Montserrat that the negro population of that island speaks English with a strong Irish brogue and in a very interesting dialect (preserving old English and some Irish words), derived from the several thousand Irish settlers or convicts inhabiting Montserrat two hundred years ago.

As early as 1661 exception was taken to the doctrines of the Quakers as likely to inspire both white and black slaves with discontent and a struggle for freedom. In that year Quakers were forbidden access to the island of Nevis, and in 1677 any master of a vessel bringing a Quaker to Nevis was to be heavily fined. Quakers were similarly driven away from Antigua and the Bermudas.

[1] Its area is 166 square miles.

[2] The first colonising expedition in that year was fitted out by Mr. Ralph Merrifield, of London, and led by Sir Thomas Warner, and the first English name given to the island was "Merwar's Hope," from the first syllables of the two founders' names.

There was considerable forced and free white colonisation, even though the valuable Quakers were kept out, but negro labour proved to be the only way of cultivating sugar in the Leeward Islands, and by the close of the eighteenth century there were some forty thousand negro slaves in St. Kitts alone. It was here that the Rev. James Ramsay lived for nineteen years as chaplain and studied the condition of the slaves. After his return to England, and when vicar of Teston in Kent, he wrote the celebrated book *An Essay on the Treatment and Conversion of the African Slaves in the British Sugar Colonies*, which was of such use to Clarkson and other reformers. He was also one of

209. A SUGAR MILL AND OX-TEAM WITH SUGAR CANE, ST. CHRISTOPHER, LEEWARD ISLANDS

the witnesses whose evidence was laid before the House of Commons in the debates of 1791.

The round, mountain island of Nevis lying close to the attenuated extremity of St. Kitts was during the eighteenth and early nineteenth centuries a favourite health resort in the summer time for the white planters of the West Indies, and all the year round a great slave-mart and rendezvous of the slave-trading ships.

The treatment of slaves in the Northern Leeward Islands (Dominica was not associated with the Leeward Islands until 1832) was somewhat better than in Jamaica or Barbados, British West India.

Antigua was the first of the Leeward Islands to amend the position of the negro slaves in the eye of the law by passing an Act (about 1787) which gave accused negroes trial by jury for all serious offences, and allowed in the case of capital convictions four days between the time of sentence and execution. The Government of Antigua also permitted, even encouraged the Moravian Brothers to establish missions amongst the negroes in Antigua from 1760 onwards. By 1787 the Moravian Brethren had converted to real practising Christianity 5465 slaves and free negroes in Antigua, 80 in St. Christopher, 100 in Barbados and Jamaica, 10,000 in the Danish Antilles, and 400 in Dutch Guiana.

The Northern Leeward Islands further modified their legislation in favour of their slaves in 1798. Under the Act of this year, the weekly food allowance for every adult slave was to be nine pounds of corn or beans [or eight pints of peas, or wheat, or rye flour, or Indian corn meal, or nine pounds of oatmeal, or seven pounds of rice, or eight pints of cassava flour, or eight pounds of biscuit, or twenty pounds of yams or potatoes, etc., or thirty pounds of plantains] and a pound and a quarter of herrings (or various other salted fish), or three pounds of fresh fish, or other fresh provisions of good quality. In case of being unable to supply provisions in kind, the owner of the slave was to pay commutation at the rate of four shillings a week to every slave, and allow two half-holidays in each week for the slave to go to market and lay out to the best advantage such commutation money. But these allowances in money or provisions might be reduced in proportion to the amount of garden land allotted to the slaves for raising their own food crops. In any case, each capable negro slave was to receive an allowance of forty square feet of garden land. Every slave in the Leeward Islands was to receive twice a year, if a male, one jacket made of good sound woollen cloth and one pair of woollen trousers of good sound Osnaburg linen; and if a female, one wrapper of such woollen cloth and one petticoat of such Osnaburg; but if he so willed, the owner might give the slave, instead of goods, a sufficient blanket and a hat or cap (with the consent of the slaves), the same to be in lieu of such clothes as aforesaid. Every slave within the Leeward Islands employed in field or plantation work was to have at least one complete half-hour for eating his breakfast, resting and refreshing himself, and two hours at "noon or dinner-time." After the publication of this Act, owners of slaves were to endeavour to induce or oblige their slaves to practise monogamy, and women bearing children to their chosen husbands were to be rewarded by four dollars for the first child and one dollar for each succeeding child, and to every male and female slave who lived together faithfully and peaceably as man and wife was to

210. A NEGRO SAILOR OF ST. KITTS (TALL MAN ON LEFT HAND) AND A COMRADE FROM NASSAU, BAHAMA ISLANDS

be paid a dollar a year as long as they so lived together. As in Jamaica (after 1798) and most of the other islands of the British West Indies, a female slave who had six children living, born in regular cohabitation, was to be relieved of all but light work. Any owner of slaves or overseer, or other white man who should attempt to induce any female slave to be unfaithful to her husband was to be fined £100. No slave was to be prevented by his or her master from receiving religious instruction, or attending church or chapel on Sunday at any place of worship held by the regularly established clergy, or any Christian sect tolerated in the Leeward Islands. Nevertheless, very strong opposition was shown to the creation or increase of a class of free negroes who might ask for civic rights. In 1802 a law was passed for the Northern Leeward Islands requiring the owner who wished to register the manumission of his slave to pay

211. IN LOVELY DOMINICA

into the public treasury the sum of £500 (in the case of a slave not native to the Leeward Islands, £1000). Any one who willed the freedom of his slaves after his death must provide from out of his estate £500 in current money, to be paid into the public treasury for each manumitted slave. [The Legislature of each island might, however, if it saw fit, forego these conditions.] In 1828 the free negroes and men of colour were admitted to the same civic and political rights as the whites in all the Northern Leeward Islands, and Antigua liberated all its slaves in the autumn of 1833 without waiting for compensation or asking for apprenticeship.

After the slaves were emancipated they were in time possessed of sufficient property or employment[1] to qualify in some cases as voters for the elected members of the different Legislatures of Antigua, St. Kitts, and Dominica. But between 1877 and 1898 the elective principle was done away with (through the influence of the white colonists and largely to avoid the problem of the

[1] The qualification for electors was a freehold valued at £10 *per annum*, and for members of the House of Assembly, forty acres of land or a house worth £40 a year.

coloured voter); and now all the members of the five separate island Councils[1] are nominated by the Governor, and the non-official councillors themselves co-opt representatives on the central Legislature for the entire colony.

The island of DOMINICA is one of the most remarkable in the long chain of the Lesser Antilles. It is extremely mountainous, though the highest point of its mountains (Grand Diablotin) is barely 5000 feet in altitude. Active volcanic agencies are still observable throughout the island; there are numerous hot sulphur springs, and there is a boiling lake. The total area of the island is about 304 square miles,[2] but of this, even at the present day, barely a third is under cultivation. The rainfall appears to be of an average 118 inches per annum, varying from 182 inches on the eastern side to a bare 50 inches on the western shore. The innumerable streams which descend from the rugged mountains in beautiful cascades are remarkably well supplied with edible fresh-water fish and with crayfish. Land-crabs, apparently of three kinds, swarm in

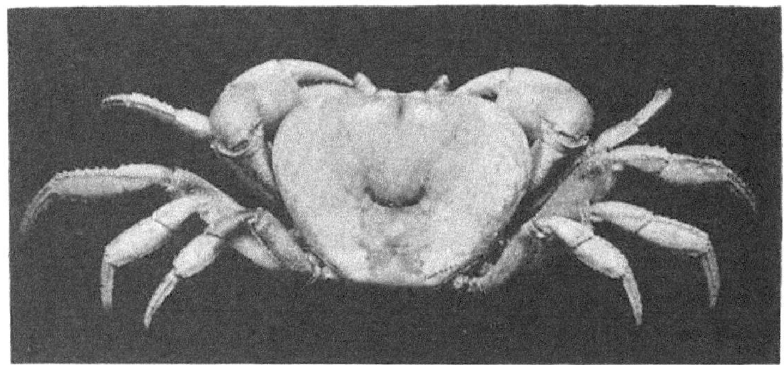

212. THE PRINCIPAL LAND-CRAB (GECARCINUS LATERALIS) OF THE WEST INDIES
Specially common, and sought after as a delicious article of food, in Dominica

the mountain forests and on the coast-lands, and in former times iguana lizards were very abundant.[3] There appear to be no venomous snakes in Dominica

[1] (1) The Virgin Islands of Tortola, Virgin Gorda, Anegada, Sombrero, etc.; (2) St. Christopher (St. Kitts), Nevis, and Anguilla; (3) Antigua, Redonda, and Barbuda; (4) Montserrat; (5) Dominica.

[2] It has until recently been understated at 291. The total acreage is 192,140 acres (The Honble. Douglas Young).

[3] The land-crabs of Dominica are classed by the natives in three sorts, the white, the black, the red. [These are two varieties of *Gecarcinus lateralis*, and *Pseudothelphusa dentata*.] The White land-crabs are regarded as poisonous because they feed—or have fed quite recently—on the blossoms and leaves of the Manchineal (*Hippomane mancinella*). This is a tree growing in the marshy districts along the coasts of the West India Islands and of Central America. Its leaves, bark, and blossoms are extremely poisonous. The tree grows sometimes to as much as forty feet in height. The water below it is rendered poisonous by its decaying leaves. The flowers are a sickly yellow colour, something like those of poppies, but rather larger, and the poison is derived from the milky juice or sap of the branches, leaves, and flowers. All other creatures but these land-crabs seem to find the Manchineal a deadly poison But the bark of this tree is fibrous and makes excellent rope, and the trunk and branches are very similar to cork wood, as light, durable, and useful for floats and buoys.

The Black crabs are said to be excellent and quite safe for food, if taken from places far away from the Manchineal trees. They are very fat when in season (this is during the winter months when they are in their burrows and moulting their shells), and the females are full of a rich, glutinous spawn which is described as "perfectly delicious." The Red crabs are much smaller, but are also wholesome and delicious to eat, especially when full of spawn. A pepper-pot is made by the negroes of Dominica with the flesh of the black crabs as its basis, mixed with a kind of cabbage and capsicum pods, and eaten with rice or a pudding made of maize flour.

Another negro dainty throughout the Leeward and Windward West India Islands is, or used to be,

—a curious contrast to Martinique and the Windward Islands farther to the south. The tropical vegetation is magnificent.

Dominica was originally so strongly occupied by Carib Amerindians [who had concentrated their forces here when they were forced to leave St. Christopher, Guadeloupe, and Martinique] that both France and England hesitated to colonise it. At length the French at the close of the seventeenth century won over the Caribs to allow a certain number of French settlers to establish themselves on the island. In the early eighteenth century the French planters introduced several thousand negro slaves. The British followed the French, but both nations repeatedly agreed to consider the island as neutral; until it was captured by a British force in 1759 and annexed at the Peace of 1763. During the long "neutral" period Dominica had become thoroughly Francicised. The negroes at the date of British annexation may have amounted to 10,000.

213. TWO WOMEN AND A CHILD OF DOMINICA
Showing various degrees of intermixture between Carib, Frenchman, and Negro

They had conceived a great liking for their French masters and were not at all pleased at coming under British taskmasters. The French naturally were outraged at finding a British island separating Guadeloupe from Martinique.

They consequently recaptured it in 1778. Nevertheless a good many English colonists remained on their plantations, depending on the guarantees of the Treaty of Capitulation made between Governor Stuart and the Marquis de Bouillé; but neither the spirit nor letter of this treaty was fairly observed by the new French Governor, Duchilleau, who, not satisfied with making the position of the English generally intolerable, armed many of the slaves, and still more the maroon negroes of the mountains, who attacked and destroyed some of the British plantations and killed a few of the planters. Although the

the Iguana lizards (*Iguana tuberculata* and *I. delicatissima*). The uneatable Iguana of Jamaica, Cuba, and the Bahamas is *Cyclura carinata;* and that of *Hispaniola* is *Metopoceros cornutus* (G. A. Boulenger) Europeans as well as negroes find the flesh of the large, handsome lizards of the Iguana genus (which are also found in Central and South America) extremely good. Its taste is a blend of turtle and chicken. The eggs of the Iguana are considered great dainties by the Dominican negroes, who also eat large bull-frogs and the grubs of the big boring beetles.

English regained possession of Dominica in 1783, this ferment amongst the negro population continued. The latter, though many of their ancestors had deserted from Martinique owing to the oppressive regulations in force there, were exceedingly French in sympathies, and belonged as well to the Roman Catholic Church. They combined under a leader named Farcel in 1791 and 1794, murdered a number of English planters, and gave cause for much anxiety to the British authorities in Dominica, who had great difficulty in subduing the insurrection. Curiously enough, by so acting the Dominican negroes were the principal cause of the arrest in England of the Anti-Slavery and Anti-Slave-Trade movement. The news of this negro war in Dominica (together with the anxiety caused by foreign affairs) brought the Anti-Slave-Trade proceedings in the House of Commons to a temporary close, and delayed for something like fourteen years any drastic reforms in this direction.

214. A COLOURED WOMAN OF DOMINICA
Showing mixture of French, Carib, and Negro blood

In the eighteenth century and down to 1898, the white settlers of Dominica (and later on all persons possessing the requisite qualifications) enjoyed representative institutions, and in 1863 these were consolidated into a single Chamber combining the Council and House of Representatives, nine of the twenty-eight members of this Chamber being nominated by the Governor and nineteen elected by the people. In 1865 it was attempted by the British Government to abolish the electoral franchise and to make Dominica a Crown Colony. But this attempt roused such bitter opposition on the part of the populace that it was abandoned in favour of a reduction of members of the Legislative Chamber and the bare provision for a Government majority. This was further altered in 1871, when Dominica and the other Leeward Islands were more closely united in a single Federal Colony. The seat of Government was transferred to the far more English Antigua, and eventually a Commissioner (instead of a Governor) was placed at the head of the Dominican Administration. The island Legislature still persisted, but many of the affairs of Dominica were now dealt with by the Federal Executive and Legislative Councils for all the Leeward Islands. These last were modified by the Act of 1899, which did away with the directly elected element in the composition of the Federal legislative body, substituting eight members elected by the non-official nominated members of the Councils of Antigua, St. Kitts, and Dominica. As regards the partly elective Legislating Assembly of Dominica, this in 1898 was abolished and a Crown Colony system substituted, in which the six non-official members (two or three of them negroes or negroids at the present time) were nominated by the Governor and not elected by the people, who have now no franchise in legislation. There is representative administration of municipal affairs at the capital, Roseau (the Town Board); all the elective members are coloured. When employed in positions of trust they do *not* prove more dishonest than their white fellow-citizens.

The present acting assistant to the Attorney-General is a full-blooded negro (a native of Barbados). A dark-coloured man (a Dominican) was Registrar and Provost Marshal from 1886 to 1891, and also acted as Chief Justice of the island in 1873, and as Solicitor-General and Attorney-General of the Leeward Islands on several occasions from 1881 to 1886.

215. A LANE IN DOMINICA

There is no doubt that the deep impression made by the French on the character and manners of the Dominican negroes in the first half of the eighteenth century led to their being, until quite recently, very discontented British subjects. The island was a second time invaded by the French under Victor Hugues in 1795, and fresh encouragement was then given to the maroon negroes to continue their attacks on the British residents. Another serious French invasion occurred in 1805. The capital, Roseau, was burnt by negroes and French soldiers, and the latter were only persuaded to leave the island by the payment of a large sum of money. By 1813, however, after indescribable difficulties in a country where transport, even at the present day, can only be effected on the shoulders of men or the backs of sure-footed mules, the strength of the maroon negroes was overcome. This struggle between the British and the runaway negroes of Dominica had lasted for forty years, and had completely exhausted the resources of the island and arrested its commercial development.

In 1844 a rebellion known as "La guerre nègre" broke out as the result of an attempt on the part of the British Administration to take a census. The real cause was the irritation of the negroes, many of them recently emancipated from slavery, at the attempt to reserve for the Government a strip of land about a hundred feet in width all round the shore of the island. The negroes thought that they were to be driven inland away from the sea-coast, and then to be once more enslaved by law. In 1847 there were again riots, this time caused by the quarrels between the British settlers, who were mainly Protestants, and the French Creole planters and French and Irish Roman Catholic priests, together with the mass of the negro population, who were all Roman

Catholics. It is observable, in fact, down to the very close of the nineteenth century, that the Roman Catholic Church in Dominica was steadily anti-British in sentiment, and seems to have worked up the feeling of the negro population of the island in the direction of a possible reunion with France. This impression gave great acerbity to the debates in the Legislative Assembly, as the Protestants became ultra-Protestant in their desire not to weaken the British connection, while the Catholics became passionately Catholic and exaggeratedly French. More trouble connected with land occurred in 1853, and again in 1863, 1869, 1886, and finally 1893; when in a serious riot (also due to the attempt of the local Administration to uphold the right of the Government to vacant land) four or five negroes were killed by police or blue-jackets. Much bitterness also had arisen between the Governor of the Leeward Islands and educated people of all parties in Dominica as to the application of public funds to road-making and other public works. It is difficult to say who was in the right, because it was really Nature that was in the wrong, terrible floods having wrecked much of the road and bridge work.

The British Government sent out in 1893 a Royal Commission under Sir Robert Hamilton to inquire into the cause of these disturbances and the friction between the Administration and the people. This Commission produced an excellent and instructive report; and many of its recommendations were carried out by the Imperial Government. Since the close of the nineteenth century Dominica has been far more contented and peaceable throughout its diverse population than in any former period of its long and troubled history. It is interesting to note that it still retains an indigenous Carib population numbering about 300, and dwelling in specially allotted land in the north-eastern portion of the island. The population of the island at the present day (33,000) consists of about 500 whites, 400 Caribs (mixed with negro, but also of pure blood), 100 East Indians or Chinese, about 24,000 negroes, and 8000 negroids, nearly the whole of these speaking a French-Creole language (similar to that of Martinique and Haiti) and only a small proportion understanding English.

The "colour question" exists, as in other West Indian colonies, though not perhaps to such a marked degree, because of the paucity of whites in Dominica. There have been no marriages between black and white during the last twenty-seven years, but white men (chiefly Englishmen) have occasionally married coloured girls, and a small section of the best born and educated coloured people have always moved in good society with the whites.

The criminal statistics of Dominica are evidence for the good character of its people. Sexual crimes, murder, burglaries, or other grave offences against property or person are of very rare occurrence. But the marriage rate is low, and the proportion of illegitimate births is nearly fifty-nine per cent (1908). Illiteracy is very marked, in spite of the fact that there is a *compulsory* Education Act and that the Government maintains elementary schools throughout the island which afford free education to all children between the ages of five and twelve. It is stated that only ten per cent of the adult negroes can read and write. The coloured people send their children to England (mostly) to be educated.

The principal avocations of the negroes are agriculture (many of them are peasant proprietors), mason's work, carpentry, petty trading, shop-keeping, school-teaching, and medicine. There are four negro doctors in Dominica, one of whom is a Government District Medical Officer. The police force is composed entirely of negroes, with white officers. The mulattoes and octoroons furnish the island with mechanics, engineers, shop-keepers, clerks, druggists, and merchants; and nearly all the civil service (except the highest posts) is recruited from this class. The faith of the people is that of Rome.

The *total population* of the Leeward Islands at the present time is about 180,000. In some of the islands population is decreasing owing to commercial stagnation and the attractions of Porto Rico, Panama, and the Danish Antilles; in some like Dominica, Montserrat, Anguilla, and the Virgin Islands it is markedly or slowly increasing. Out of the 180,000 about 5000 are White (Virgin Islands, Antigua, Dominica, and St. Christopher, mainly);

216. MARKET SQUARE, ROSEAU, DOMINICA

104,000 are negroes; 25,000 are mulattoes and "near-whites"; and the remainder are Caribs, East Indians, Chinese, etc.

Except in Dominica the predominant form of Christianity is Protestant, and the negroes and negroids belong chiefly to the Church of England, the Moravian Brethren's Church, and the Wesleyan Church. [The adherents of the Baptist Church of Great Britain seem chiefly to be confined to Jamaica.] In all the Northern Leeward Islands education is denominational and is carried on (assisted by important Government grants) by the Anglicans, Moravians, Roman Catholics, and Wesleyans. There are, however, two Government schools in Antigua. Except in Antigua and the Virgin Islands, education is free. Secondary education is provided by the denominations in St. Kitts and Antigua, and is partly supported by Government funds. There are in all throughout the Leeward Islands 124 schools with an attendance of 12,222 pupils. Agricultural and technical instruction is imparted in the Virgin Islands, Dominica, and perhaps elsewhere by the Imperial Agricultural Department, which has its headquarters in Barbados. This work has created or revived an interest in the planting of Sea Island cotton among the whites and the coloured people in the Virgin Islands, and cotton has almost completely ousted sugar in Montserrat. In Tortola (the largest of the Virgins) there is a singular abundance of fibrous plants —agaves, tillandsias, bromelias, etc. (relations of the pineapple). Cacao and lime-juice (from the small green lime, *Citrus medicus*) are the chief growths and exports of Dominica and Montserrat; Dominica also sends coffee, nutmegs, spices, sugar, vegetable oils, timber, and fruit. Pineapples are exported from Antigua and Montserrat; sugar, molasses, rum, arrowroot, and tobacco from St. Kitts and Nevis; the tiny islet of Sombrero (only added to the British dominions in 1904) exports valuable phosphate of lime, so also does Barbuda; salt is "raked" and exported from Barbuda, St. Kitts, and Anguilla; cattle and horses are bred in Barbuda—the last of the undeveloped, proprietary islands. Anguilla also breeds and exports cattle, ponies, and turkeys. There are wild peacocks in Antigua and wild fallow-deer (or roebuck?) in Barbuda.[1]

So that surely the negro and negroid should find enough to occupy them profitably in these paradisiacal Leeward Islands, without going elsewhere to earn a livelihood; and the population, instead of decreasing in the Antigua and St. Kitts groups, should increase steadily and wax in comfort, wealth, and intelligence? Where does the weakness lie? The five or six thousand whites seem to be languid, and the "poor" whites to have inbred too much and lost their stamina (so, at least, one is told). But the 175,000 vigorous negroes and negroids of the Leeward Islands should become a million in number and still have plenty of room and plenty to do. What is lacking in the Leeward State? Want of a compulsory and appropriate education, I suspect.

[1] The island of Barbuda within the government of the Leeward Islands is peculiar in that it is *private property*, ostensibly belonging to the English family of Codrington, whose rights descend from the seventeenth century. Actually, it is administered, not by the British Government, but by two *concessionnaires* in whom are vested the rights of the Codringtons. It is rather a large island compared to some of its neighbours, having an area of about 140 square miles, with a negro population of 770, and a handful of whites. Its surface is low (the highest point being below 200 feet in altitude), but it is remarkably fertile and well watered, and a good deal of its area is covered with fine forests. It is, indeed, described as being one of the most beautiful islands of the Antilles, but its *concessionnaires* do not favour immigration, and only encourage cattle-breeding and the exportation of phosphates of lime. A French authority estimates Barbuda could easily sustain 100,000 inhabitants. If this is true, it seems irreconcilable with the policy of the twentieth century that the agents of the Codrington family should continue to lock up in a condition of uselessness one of the best islands of the Leeward group. They ought to be all expropriated at a fair valuation by the Leeward Federal Government, and Barbuda be thrown open to general settlement.

CHAPTER X

SLAVERY UNDER THE BRITISH—*Continued*

JAMAICA

JAMAICA occupies an important place in the past history and in the future prospects of the Negro in the New World. This island of 4207 square miles, lying nearly in the middle of the Mexico-Caribbean Sea, almost equidistant from the north coast of South America and the south coast of North America, between Central America and the outer ring of the Lesser Antilles, was discovered by Columbus in 1494, and was apparently first called by the Spanish "Isla de Sant' Iago," but afterwards by its native name of Xaymaca.[1]

The island was then well populated by Arawak Amerindians of the same race as those of Cuba, Hispaniola, and the rest of the Antilles, but by degrees the indigenes perished at the hands of the Spaniards, or were transported elsewhere, or fled in their canoes to Yucatan. Negroes were introduced into Jamaica perhaps as early as 1517. The Spaniards, beginning at St. Ann's Bay, confined their settlements principally to the north coast regions and to that splendid tract of park-like country in the very middle of Jamaica, round about Moneague. No minerals of value having been found in the island, Spanish efforts were chiefly confined to sugar cultivation, while the amazing beauty of the island seems to have so impressed them that they colonised it partly from that point of view. In those days there was no yellow or malarial fever; there were no ticks; live-stock throve amazingly; a hot sun, abundant rainfall, and rich soil produced a remarkable abundance of food.

Jamaica was aimed at once or twice by the bold seamen-pirates of Queen Elizabeth's time; but the Spaniards remained masters of the island until 1655, when it was captured by an expedition sent out by Cromwell to seize the large island of Hispaniola. This expedition was beaten off by the Spanish at San Domingo, and not daring to return home and report a failure, it contented itself with the much easier conquest of Jamaica.

When this took place the greater part of the negro slaves belonging to the Spaniards fled to the mountains. Even before this date those negroes who disliked the mild servitude under the Spaniard (who never maltreated his African slaves as he did his Amerindian subjects) were constantly running away and living in the dense forests of the mountain peaks, where they made

[1] Said to mean in the Arawak language of the Greater Antilles "(the land of) wood and water." The name Xaymaca, or Jamaica, recurs in the geography of Eastern Cuba, and perhaps under slightly different forms in Haitian place-names, and in the Lesser Antilles. Xaymaca was probably at the time of Columbus's discovery pronounced Shaimaka, for it is possible that at that period the letter *x* in Castilian (as in Portuguese, Catalan, and most of the other Romance dialects of Spain) represented *sh* and not χ (= *kh*), as at present.

common cause with the persecuted Arawaks. To these escaped slaves was given the name of "Cimarrones," or mountaineers—from *Cima* (a peak)—a term soon shortened into Marrones (English, Maroons). The earlier Maroons of Jamaica absorbed into their midst a small remnant of the Amerindian indigenes, the remainder of whom, from disease and Spanish oppression, had become extinct by the middle of the seventeenth century. Several thousand negroes, however, settled down comfortably under the Spanish colonists, and when Jamaica was invaded by a British force in 1655 many of the negro slaves fought valiantly on the side of the Spaniards. When the Spanish

271. THE DISTRICT OF MONEAGUE IN THE CENTRAL PARK-LANDS OF JAMAICA, 2000 FEET ABOVE SEA-LEVEL

Government was finally eradicated from the island (by the defeat of Governor Sasi at Ocho Rios in 1657), most of the Spanish-speaking negroes took to the mountains and fused with the Maroons.

The hostility of these escaped negroes was partially allayed in 1663 by the tacit acknowledgment of their freedom and the grant of twenty acres to every man who settled down under the British Government, and by the formation of a "black regiment" out of the more civilised young men, who agreed to serve under a negro head-man named Juan de Bolas. This leader was given the rank of colonel in the Jamaica militia.

But Juan de Bolas was killed, and his regiment deserted or perished in the bush warfare, which began again in 1664, and lasted almost without intermission until the pacification of 1738. During this long period the Maroons (seldom

218. A TYPICAL LANDSCAPE IN BEAUTIFUL JAMAICA

more than three thousand in number of fighting-men) seriously hindered the settlement and prosperity of Jamaica. They were at home in the pathless forests of the mountains, lived in the caves and among the precipices of the Cockpit country in North-West Jamaica, carried on a little furtive agriculture, and were dependent for their food on the wild pigs with which Jamaica then abounded, on land-crabs, pigeons, and fish; besides such vegetables as they stole from the white men's plantations or found in the forest.

A small band of them would creep up to some planter's house at dead of night, and if the place was insecurely guarded and the planter could be taken by surprise, would murder all the whites and burn down the buildings. White women were scarcely ever outraged; they and their children were contemptuously killed.

219. THE TREATY OF PEACE BETWEEN THE BRITISH AND THE MAROON NEGROES OF WEST JAMAICA, 1738

A special police was organised—white and black—and the example of the Spaniards was followed in the employment of dogs to hunt down these bush thieves and assassins. (These dogs are described by Bryan Edwards in 1791 as "much resembling the shepherds' dogs in Great Britain, and being no larger, but possessing the keen scent of the bloodhound, the greyhound's agility, and the bulldog's courage.") In addition to the special bush constabulary with their fortified posts and packs of savage dogs, the Assembly of Jamaica decided in 1737 to import two hundred Mosquito Indians from Nicaragua to track down the enemy.[1]

These measures wore away the resistance of the Maroons, whose chiefs, "Captain Cudjoe, Captain Accompong, Captain Johnny, Captain Cuffee, Captain Quaco," accepted the overtures of peace proposed by the Governor, Sir William Trelawney, in 1738. In the articles of pacification they were granted 1500 acres of land at Trelawney town (twenty miles inland from Montego, N.W. Jamaica), and 1000 acres at Accompong town and elsewhere in the Cockpit country. Their personal freedom was recognised, and they were to be paid thirty shillings in

[1] In 1741 a Jamaica law laid it down very positively that all Indians arriving in Jamaica were to be regarded as free people, that any attempt to sell them was punishable, and would be null and void. And a further law of George III inflicted the penalty of death on any one who kidnapped or stole an Indian.

future (afterwards increased to three pounds) for every fugitive slave they brought back to his owner.

From 1738 to 1795 the Maroons remained at peace with the British Government, and even in 1760 were allied with the British forces in putting down a serious rebellion of the Koromanti slaves in St Mary parish. But in 1795 (on a very frivolous pretext, probably because they had heard of the successful rising in Haiti) they broke out into rebellion and endeavoured to provoke a general rising of the slaves. In this they were nearly successful (but for the prompt action of Governor the Earl of Balcarres). A few surrendered to the British at the commencement of the trouble, but the remainder—only some five hundred fighting-men, all told—inflicted several reverses on the British troops,

220. THE MAROON SETTLEMENT OF TRELAWNEY TOWN, IN NORTH-WESTERN JAMAICA

retired into the difficult Cockpit country and thence sent out marauding expeditions resulting in the murder of numerous white men and women. The only thing which had any effect on them was the threatened employment of dogs. Forty Cuban hunters and one hundred Cuban dogs were imported, and soon afterwards the whole of the Maroons had surrendered to the authorities. Those who gave themselves up before January 1st, 1796, were allowed to remain in Jamaica, and from them are descended the Maroons of to-day,[1] settled at Moore Town (N.E. Jamaica) and at various places in their old haunts round the Cockpit country. But of the most recalcitrant nearly six hundred were transported to Nova Scotia and eventually to Freetown, Sierra Leone. Here they gave more trouble and were generally at the bottom of any rows or riots occurring in the early days of that once dreary settlement and now model colony.

[1] Whom Governor Eyre employed in suppressing the alleged negro revolt of 1865.

221. IN A MAROON TOWN, JIM CROW COUNTRY, EASTERN JAMAICA

There was a remarkable spirit about the Maroons which, in spite of occasional episodes of cowardice or treachery, seems to have inspired a liking and respect in the minds of the British officers fighting against them, the sympathy felt for the "first-class fighting-man." So much so, that when the Assembly of Jamaica decided to transport a third of the Maroons to Nova Scotia (and thereby rid the colony of the terror they had inspired for a hundred and forty years) Major-General Walpole, the principal officer commanding the troops engaged in suppressing the Maroon rising, declined to accept the sword of honour voted him by the House of Assembly.

The Maroons can scarcely be said to have "reverted" to savagery, since they had never known civilisation. They went almost naked, and frequently became cannibals in the excitement of warfare or revenge. They were principally derived from the tribes of the Gold Coast—some unusually warlike strain—and did not among themselves speak English, but a jargon composed (it is said) of two or three Gold Coast languages, some Spanish, and a little English. Of the very few African words which survive in the negro dialects and folk-lore of Jamaica it is certain that the majority are derived from the Chwi language of the Ashanti and Fanti. The word for "white man"—*bakara* (buckra) is, however, from the Bantu or semi-Bantu languages of the Cross River and Western Cameroons (*Mu-kara*, singular; *Ba-kara*, plural).

222. MAROONS OF EASTERN JAMAICA

In 1673 the cultivation of sugar was systematically commenced in Jamaica by twelve hundred (mainly English) settlers who arrived from Surinam (Dutch Guiana), where they had been placed by Lord Willoughby in 1663. They colonised Westmoreland parish (westernmost Jamaica). The last quarter of the seventeenth century saw an enormous demand for sugar arising throughout Europe. No longer content with the niggardly and costly supplies received from the Spanish Antilles (through the trading houses of Seville and Barcelona) or from Madeira or Egypt, the awakening world of Northern and Central Europe saw in the undefended portions of Brazil, of the Guianas, and of the lesser West Indian islands splendid opportunities for the unlimited production of sugar from the sugar-cane; the only rival to which as a saccharoid being the analogous sweet Sorghum or Holcus reed of Asia and Africa (also introduced into America), or the honey of antiquity; for beetroot as a source of sugar was not to be called into existence till the beginning of the nineteenth century. The cultivation of sugar-cane could only be carried on by negro labour; consequently it produced a great development of the African slave-trade.

In 1673 there were 9504 negroes in Jamaica (apart from the Maroons) as against 7768 whites. In 1690 the number of negro slaves had risen to

40,000, while the whites had decreased to a slight extent. Coffee was introduced into Jamaica (from Surinam) in 1721[1] and increased the need of servile labour for its cultivation. Pimento or Allspice[2] was a wild Jamaican product which only patient negroes could gather.

Apart from the needs of Jamaican agriculture, large numbers of slaves were imported into Jamaica from the West African coast, in order to keep the Spanish Antilles supplied with black labour under the Asiento. This contract with the Spanish Crown had been assigned to a French company in 1701, though apparently a British company had been formed for the purpose in

223. THE STATELY GEORGIAN BUILDINGS OF SPANISH TOWN, SANTIAGO DE LA VEGA

The original capital of Jamaica after the earthquake at Port Royal in 1692 until 1872, when the seat of government was removed to Kingston

[1] The genus *Coffea* grows naturally in the densely forested regions of tropical Africa and Asia, a closely allied genus also being found in tropical America. The twin seeds of the Asiatic *Coffea* are useless for making the beverage: they are too bitter. In Africa the genus *Coffea* develops sixteen or seventeen distinct species, of which the Liberian coffee is remarkable for its large berry and resistance to fungoid diseases, and *Coffea arabica*—the first type to become known to the civilised world—for its delicious aroma and small berry. *Coffea arabica* probably grows wild in the forested part of Southern Abyssinia and Galaland, Uganda, and the well-watered regions of Equatorial Africa. It was first of all valued by the Gala and Gala-like negroids for the sweet pulp of its berries, but the Abyssinians and later the Arabs of Yaman and Aden (the shrub was early introduced into the well-watered mountains of Yaman) took to roasting the beans and making from them a stimulating beverage. The vogue of this decoction reached Constantinople and thence Europe through the French and English merchants trading with the Levant. Coffee-drinking was well established in France by 1650 and in England by 1660. Some Arabs who traded between Mokha and Java gave a few coffee beans to the Dutch Governor-General of that island, who forthwith commenced the cultivation of coffee in Java, and further sent *one* plant to the Dutch East India Company at Amsterdam. This one plant produced the seeds and plants which were sent out to Surinam (Dutch Guiana) in 1718; and from Surinam the coffee shrub spread to Jamaica (1721), Martinique (1724), Haiti, and Brazil. In Jamaica the coffee shrub flourished so greatly that it gave rise to distinct varieties of value, such as the "Orange" and the "Blue Mountain," and these have been sent to stock the plantations of Nyasaland in South-East Africa.

[2] Pimento is the berry of a tree about thirty feet high, which grows exclusively in the West Indies and particularly in Jamaica on the limestone hills near the sea-coast. It is the *Eugenia pimenta* and might almost be adopted as the national tree of Jamaica. Apparently it is impossible to transplant or to cultivate the Pimento tree. All that can be done is to clear the ground around the trees, saplings, and bushes to encourage their natural growth.

Jamaica in 1689, and the profitable privilege having been transferred to French hands was one of the grievances which provoked the great war of the Spanish succession in 1702.[1] By the Treaty of Utrecht in 1713 the monopoly of the Spanish slave-trade fell to Britain, and the South Sea Company was founded (1711) to carry slaves from Jamaica to Spanish South America.

224. THE GOVERNMENT BUILDINGS IN SPANISH TOWN

In the foreground is one of the guns captured by Rodney from Count De Grasse on April 12th, 1782, in his decisive naval victory

In 1732 occurred the first hint of better times for the Jamaica slaves: the Moravian missionaries settled in the island.[2] But the maltreatment of the slaves was considerable. They were constantly running away to the wild

[1] Another was that in June, 1694, a French fleet under Du Casse, the Governor of St. Domingue, had landed soldiers on the south-east coast of Jamaica near Kingston and ravaged the country as far as Port Morant, attempting to raise the negroes against the English; burning the white settlements, and cruelly torturing the white planters or officials whom they captured. By a refinement of wickedness, *dans le vrai esprit gaulois* they (the French soldiers) forced these captive planters to witness the violation of their English wives by their own negro slaves (Bryan Edwards).

[2] Also in Antigua and radiating from St. Thomas. See p. 230 and chapter on Danish West Indies.

Maroons in the western part of the island, and when this outlet to their feelings was checked by the agreement with the Maroons already referred to, the slaves broke out into serious insurrections in 1746 and 1760.

In 1764 there were 140,454 slaves in Jamaica, but public attention in Britain was becoming interested in the ethics of slavery.[1] The Methodists of England began in 1760 (in Antigua) to preach to the slaves; in 1783 a negro Baptist preacher was actually addressing slave congregations in Kingston (Jamaica).

225. THE PIMENTO TREE OF JAMAICA

The American War found negroes fighting in the British armies, and these black soldiers had virtually been emancipated by this service to the Crown. Some of these men of the South Carolina Regiment were eventually merged in the 1st West India Regiment, raised in "Martinico" in 1795, under Major-General Whyte; others drifted to Jamaica, settled in the towns, and added to the number of the embarrassing free negroes.

In 1787 the Wesleyan Mission was founded in Jamaica.

In 1777 the first motion was made in England against the Slave-trade.

In 1787–8 the growing agitation in England against the slave-trade and slavery, and the return to Jamaica of released slaves, excited a ferment among the Jamaica negroes (quite distinct from the Maroon movement) which culminated in a slave insurrection in Trelawney parish, early in 1798.

Prior to this uprising of the Jamaica slaves an attempt had been made in March, 1792, to amend and consolidate the local laws dealing with slavery and the slave-trade. As early as 1735 a law had been passed ordaining that slave families put up to auction on their arrival from Africa were as far as possible to be sold as one family to a single master, but this rule had fallen into disuse.

[1] Amongst other harsh regulations in force about this time and for long afterwards was the following: No mulatto, "Indian," or negro whatsoever was allowed in Jamaica to hawk or carry about, to sell any sort of goods, wares, merchandise whatsoever, except provisions, fruits, fresh fish, milk, and poultry; but these again could only be sold provided the mulatto, "Indian," or negro had a ticket from the master or owner of such goods. Mulattoes, "Indians," or negroes were entirely confined to retail trade in these articles. If they bought up provisions, etc., "to re-vend or engross," they were to be flogged with not more than thirty-nine lashes. This regulation applied to free negroes and mulattoes as well as to slaves.

It was now revived in the Consolidated Slave Act of December, 1797, which further provided that it should be part of the duty of each rector or curate in Jamaica to appoint and appropriate a certain portion of time in each Sunday, either before or after the performance of Divine worship, for the instruction of every free person of colour and of every slave who may be willing to be baptised and instructed in the doctrines of the Christian religion.[1] By this time there were about 4000 free negroes or half-castes in Jamaica. Their position was very miserable as they were not provided for in the Constitution. In 1799 Commissioner Roume of Haiti sent agents and funds to Jamaica to try to stir up a rebellion among the free men of colour and the slaves in order to embarrass the British Government, but his efforts failed and a number of incriminated blacks and mulattoes were shot or hanged.

226. AN OLD MANSION OF SLAVERY DAYS, NORTHERN JAMAICA

Nevertheless, in spite of simmering discontent among the slaves, Jamaica exported in 1803 her record crop of sugar, and the island was very prosperous, though it required an average annual consignment of 6000 slaves to keep up the requisite labour supply. In 1807, when the slave-trade was abolished by the British Parliament (to take effect the next year), there were 323,827 negroes in Jamaica. In 1814 Jamaica exported 34,045,585 lbs. of coffee, the largest annual crop ever despatched from the island.

In 1810, in the jubilee year of George III, the Jamaican Assembly laid down the law that no slave by becoming a Christian thereby became free; but since the abolition of the slave-trade the treatment of the slaves had improved. And though the House of Assembly refused to adopt Canning's House of Commons Resolutions of 1823,[2] for the improvement of the conditions of slavery, they had already passed in 1816 an "Act for the protection, subsisting, clothing and better order, regulation and government of slaves."

According to the terms of this Act, slaves were to be religiously instructed,

[1] This Act, I believe, or one somewhat later, dealt with the right to export—expatriate—slaves from Jamaica or the other British West India colonies—except as a punishment ordered by law. The misery often entailed on Jamaica slaves by the death or bankruptcy of their master was extreme.

"In a few years a good negro gets comfortably established, he has built himself a house, obtained a wife, and begins to see a young family rising about him. His provision ground, the creation of his own industry and the staff of his existence, affords him not only support but the means also of adding something to the mere necessaries of life. In this situation he is seized on by the sheriff's officer, forcibly separated from his wife and children, dragged to public auction, purchased by a stranger, and perhaps sent to terminate his miserable existence in the mines of Mexico; excluded for ever from the light of heaven, and all this without any crime or demerit on his part, real or pretended. He is punished because his master is dead or has been unfortunate." (Bryan Edwards, *History of the West Indies.*) Edwards adds in a foot-note that it was he himself who carried through the British House of Commons in 1797 a Bill making it illegal to sell negroes so as to expatriate them.

[2] See page 312.

fitted for baptism, baptised, and "made sensible of a duty to God and the Christian faith." They were to be allowed one free day in every fortnight besides Sundays, except during the crop season (though the Sunday was not of much use to them owing to the compulsory closing of shops!). But even during the crop season the slaves were to have an absolute remission from work

227. NEGRO PEASANT WOMEN, JAMAICA

between Saturday night and Monday morning. When not provided with a piece of land to cultivate on his own account a slave was to be allowed 3s. 4d. a week for his maintenance. They were also to be supplied with proper and sufficient clothing. Every female slave who had six children living, either born to her or adopted by her and brought up, was to be exempted from all hard labour in the field, and the owner of such female slave was to be exempted from all taxation on account of such female slave. No master was to turn away slaves on account of sickness or infirmity, but was to maintain them in food, clothing, and lodging for the rest of their lives. Manumitted negroes without means of support were to be maintained by the parishes, who were to recover their expenditure from the master, unless he had made sufficient provision for the freed slave. By this law also it was definitely laid down that any person wantonly, willingly, or bloody-mindedly killing, or causing to be killed, any negro or slave, should be adjudged guilty of felony without benefit of clergy, and suffer death accordingly. Imprisonment was also to be inflicted on any person who mutilated, cruelly treated, or confined without sufficient support any slave; and in the case of atrocious cruelty the slave might be given his freedom and receive a sum of £10 a year for his or her maintenance and support. It was also forbidden to load the body or limbs of a slave with chains or weights, or to fix an iron collar about the neck without the directions of a magistrate.

Manumission of slaves by will was facilitated. But if the deceased's estate was in debt, the manumission might not hold good, as the slaves would have first of all to be sold in satisfaction of such debts. Any slave going under the appellation of "Obeah," man or woman, and pretending to have communication with the Devil and other spirits, and attempting to use their influence to excite rebellion or other evil purposes, or to endanger the life or health of any other slave, were upon conviction to suffer death or transportation. A slave was also "by flagellation or imprisonment with hard labour" to be punished if found guilty of preaching and teaching as an Anabaptist or otherwise, without a permission from the owner and the quarter sessions. Transportation was to be inflicted "on any slave found in the possession of poisonous drugs, pounded glass, parrot beaks, dogs' teeth, alligators' teeth, or other materials notoriously used in the practice of witchcraft."[1]

In 1824 free negroes and people of colour were admitted to the Courts to give evidence on oath.[2]

[1] *Obia* (misspelt Obeah) seems to be a variant or a corruption of an Efik or Ibo word from the north-east or east of the Niger delta, which simply means "Doctor." The system embodied in that word (say also "medicine") is, like all European medical practice before the eighteenth century and many of the rites of Christianity in its healing formulæ, largely empirical. It is at once fetishism and magic, sorcery, hypnotism, faith-healing, thought-transference: in short, that royal road to results in a command over natural forces that humanity constantly hopes to achieve: not by patient study of cause and effect, and the employment of the proper physical agencies, but by blind guesswork, by wild supposition; hoping through some hundredth chance to stumble, without many years of preparatory study, on some wonderful new law which like the X-rays may make light of matter.

Obia is like Hudu or Vudu a part of the fetishistic belief which prevails over nearly all Africa, much of Asia, and a good deal of America. It would have been quite at home in the England of Elizabeth. In its "well-meaning" forms, it is medical treatment by drugs or suggestion, combined with a worship of the powers of Nature and a propitiation of evil spirits; in its bad types it is an attempt to frighten, obsess, and hypnotise, and failing the production of results by this hocus-pocus, to poison.

From the fiss-fass-fuss which is made by writers on American subjects relative to Obia and Vudu, one would think that this mixture of nonsense, of empiricism, of nauseous superstition, malignity, kindly sympathy, pathetic "feeling after God," positive knowledge of genuine therapeutics, glimmering of the possibilities latent in the human brain was peculiar to the mental composition of the Negro. Whereas it is (or was yesterday) just as evident in the white man's religion, freemasonry, medicine, quacks and quackery, Mrs. Eddys, Cagliostros, peasant witchcraft, and ex-voto offerings: it is equally sublime and not much more ridiculous.

The negro police of Jamaica are now (no doubt by order) very much—and very rightly—"down" on those who practise *Obia*. In *The Gleaner*, the principal newspaper of Jamaica, there was correspondence during 1909 which complained that the police dealt too harshly with men and women whose utmost crime was little worse than that of some of the new, ostensibly religious, sects in Jamaica—the obtaining money under false pretences. Severe floggings (it is alleged) "until the blood runs from the wounds" are inflicted on so-called *Obia* men who have merely attempted to tell fortunes by palmistry or crystal-gazing.

[2] About the same period (as part of the reforms encouraged by Canning in the British Parliament of 1823) similar concessions—the admission of slave evidence on oath against their master or any one else

In 1831, however, the negroes of North-West Jamaica, impatient of the slow progress of the emancipation movement, broke out into rebellion and destroyed property to the value of £666,977, and the British Government had to come to the relief of the wellnigh ruined planters with a loan of £200,000.[1]

1834 saw the definite abolition of slavery in Jamaica and the rest of the British possessions in America. The slaves then existing in Jamaica on whom compensation was paid (£5,853,975 altogether) only numbered 255,290. These were to continue to serve as apprentices for another four years.

In 1838, therefore, the white and coloured Jamaica planters found themselves with no certain labour force at their disposal, for many of the ex-slaves declined to do any work when they had provided for their immediate sustenance. An attempt was made by some of the planters to recruit more "free labourers" from West Africa, but this was opposed by the British Government as likely to renew slavery under another name. Indian coolies were imported in 1845, the experiment having already been successfully tried in British Guiana in 1838. But the Honourable East India Company imposed such expensive restrictions on this enterprise that it was abandoned and not renewed until 1868.

During this interval of time—between 1845 and 1868—the condition of Jamaica was discouraging. The adoption of Free Trade by the Mother Country actually ruined the island and made it bankrupt, however splendid

in the British Courts of the West Indies—removed a great hindrance to the administration of justice. Hitherto as no slave could testify (at any rate against a white man), very few owners in British America or in the Southern United States were ever convicted of heinous crimes against their slaves.

[1] No honest-hearted person can wonder that the negroes rose in rebellion against the cruel planters of this time who delves into the annals of the years between 1816 and 1833. When the anxieties of the Napoleonic wars and of the Haitian conspiracies were over the treatment of Jamaican slaves again became unbearably bad, especially in the north and west of the island.

Charles Buxton, the son of Sir Thomas Fowell Buxton, quotes the following instance (of which at least a hundred similar are recorded in other books and Government Reports) of the flogging of women in Jamaica occurring as late as 1832. It is recorded by a Mr. Whiteley, who was bookkeeper on the New Ground Plantation near St. Ann's Bay in Jamaica.

"The twelfth instance (he has quoted other cases of the same atrocious character) was that of a married woman, the mother of several children. She was brought up to the overseer's door one morning, and one of the drivers who came with her accused her of having stolen a fowl. Some feathers, said to have been found in her hut, were exhibited as evidence of her guilt. The overseer asked her if she could pay for the fowl. She said something in reply which I did not clearly understand. The question was repeated, and a similar reply again was given. The overseer then said, 'Put her down.' On this the woman set up a shriek, and rent the air with her cries of terror. Her countenance grew quite ghastly, and her lips became pale and livid. I was close to her, and particularly noticed her remarkable aspect and expression of countenance. The overseer swore fearfully, and repeated his order, 'Put her down!' The woman was then extended on the ground, and held down by two negroes. Her gown and shift were literally torn from her back, and, thus brutally exposed, she was subjected to the cart-whip. The punishment inflicted on this poor creature was inhumanly severe. She was a woman somewhat plump in her person, and the whip being wielded with great vigour, every stroke cut deep into the flesh. She writhed and twisted her body violently under the infliction, moaning loudly, but uttering no exclamation in words, except one, when she cried out entreating that her nakedness might not be indecently exposed, appearing to suffer from matronly modesty even more acutely on account of her indecent exposure than the cruel laceration of her body. But the overseer only noticed her appeal by a brutal reply, and the flogging continued. Disgusted as I was, I witnessed the whole to a close. I numbered the lashes, stroke by stroke, and counted *fifty*, thus exceeding by eleven the number allowed by the colonial law to be inflicted at the arbitrary will of the master or manager. This was the only occasion on which I saw the legal number of thirty-nine lashes exceeded; but I never knew the overseer or head bookkeeper give less than thirty-nine. This poor victim was shockingly lacerated. When permitted to rise she again shrieked violently. The overseer swore roughly, and threatened if she was not quiet to put her down again. He then ordered her to be taken to the hot-house, or hospital, and put in the stocks. She was to be continued in the stocks for several nights, while she worked in the yard during the day at light work. She was too severely mangled to be able to go to the field for some days."—From *The Memoirs of Sir Thomas Fowell Buxton, Bart.*, by Charles Buxton (John Murray, 1877).

might be the results of cheap food and raw material in the United Kingdom. Before 1846, the sugar of the British West Indies was protected in British ports by a heavy differential duty, levied on non-British sugar (from Cuba, United States, etc.). As this "foreign" sugar was *slave-produced* and that of Jamaica had now to be worked with uncertain and expensive *free labour*; yet as both received equal treatment in the British custom-houses; Jamaican and other British American sugar soon ceased to yield any profit.[1]

Cholera ravaged the island in 1850 and there were periodical outbreaks of yellow fever. The enfranchised negroes were restless and dissatisfied with their meagre allotment of land. Hurricanes destroyed the crops, and through one cause and another the mass of the people were frequently on the verge of starvation.

Although with freedom came the removal of all ostensible colour distinctions in the exercise of the franchise, yet as a matter of fact the greater part of the coloured population of Jamaica was on various specious pretexts kept out of the franchise which was legally its due. The Jamaican House of Assembly all through the first half of the nineteenth century seems to have been singularly arbitrary and corrupt. The Governor was little more than a cipher, and the white planters, for good or ill, completely swayed the Government of Jamaica. No regard whatever (according to the testimony of Governor Eyre) was paid to the fitness in character, education, or morals of the various white officials of the island whose appointment did not lie directly with the British Government; it was sufficient that they should be *white*. Consequently law and justice were not infrequently administered most unfairly—even cruelly—by white magistrates and J.P.'s to negro or mulatto subjects. Even as late as 1864, out of a total population of nearly 440,000, only 1903 persons were entitled to vote for the forty-seven members of the House of Assembly, and the greater part of these voters were white men. There seem to have been one or two negro or negroid members of the House of Assembly elected (from amongst the free people of colour) during the thirties of the nineteenth century, but these cases became rarer during the fifties, although the white population was only in the proportion of one to thirty-two coloured. The Duke of Newcastle when Colonial Minister in 1864 drew the attention of Governor Eyre to the fact that "the bulk of the population of Jamaica are not represented in its Assembly."

228. THE RUINS OF JAMAICA
The remains of a once noble mansion of the eighteenth century, abandoned by its ruined owner after 1846

[1] Some writers in the forties and fifties thought that the British Government, in spite of its new devotion to Free Trade principles and cheap food, might have discriminated in its custom-houses between sugar and cotton grown by slaves and the same products resulting from free labour.

During the middle of the nineteenth century the Acts which were passed by this white House of Assembly were frequently of such an oppressive and even outrageous character that they were constantly refused the approval of the Queen. "Of forty Acts actually passed by the Assembly in 1861–2, and allowed by the Colonial Office, only one in the slightest degree touched the well-being of the labouring classes—an Act about Industrial Schools. All the rest related to increased taxation, the increase of paid offices, Immigration Bills, which in no respect could be said to be beneficial to the labouring classes, and the like. Not one gave direct attention to the wants of the coloured people. Some were actually injurious to their welfare. The planters and the white population were careful of their own interests alone."[1]

229. A NEGRO PEASANT RETURNING FROM MARKET, JAMAICA

This denunciation of the Assembly was endorsed by several white members of that body, who referred to the rest of their colleagues as the "forty thieves."

The state of affairs grew worse during the long illness of Governor Darling, and Mr. Edward John Eyre (who had previously been administering the affairs of Antigua) was sent to Jamaica in 1862 as Lieutenant-Governor. His first achievements were certainly those of a reformer, and in consequence he was soon at issue with the corrupt House of Assembly, whose proceedings he characterised in terms of the strongest condemnation. In 1864 the House of Assembly forwarded a memorial to the Queen in which they declined to do any further business with Governor Eyre. Nevertheless he was in that year appointed Captain-General and Governor of Jamaica.

And yet Mr. Eyre seems not to have grasped the true causes of Jamaican unrest and commercial failure, viz. the outrageous over-taxation of the poor people (£300,000 had been added to the public taxes during the first two years of Eyre's administration, and that "not for the public benefit, but for the profit of private individuals"), the denial to them of the barest justice in the law courts, the unchecked exactions of land agents and white landlords. Eyre himself, in a despatch to the Colonial Office in March, 1865, wrote: "The young and strong of both sexes, those who are well able to work, fill the gaols of the colony." The American Civil War then raging added in various ways to the misery of Jamaica and the grinding poverty of 75 per cent of its population. But Eyre, though he was quick to detect and denounce the licentiousness, drunkenness, and political dishonesty of the white minority, could devise no plan for bettering the condition of the

[1] These remarks are quoted from a book of great interest dealing with the Jamaica of the sixties—*The Tragedy of Morant Bay*, by Edward Bean Underhill, LL.D., then Honorary Secretary of the Baptist Missionary Society. (London: 1895.)

black peasantry but to punish them for their complaints and imprison them for their idleness.

It was under these circumstances that Dr. Edward Bean Underhill, the Honorary Secretary of the Baptist Missionary Society of Great Britain, who had travelled through Jamaica in 1859–60, decided to write to the Secretary of State for the Colonies. [The Society whose affairs he directed had in 1864 felt it necessary to send a considerable sum of money to relieve the famine and distress amongst the negroes of Jamaica, and had received from the pastors of its church in that island a detailed description of the misery of the black populace and its causes.] His letter went to the root of the matter.[1]

Mr. Cardwell, then Secretary of State for the Colonies, sent a copy of this "Underhill" letter to Governor Eyre. Somehow the contents of the letter leaked out from the Governor's office (though not in any way through the Baptist Missionary Society); in fact it had become public property in Jamaica by the 28th February, 1865. Early in March of that year publicity was given by the Governor himself to the letter, through its being sent with an accompanying circular to almost every official, great and small, throughout the island, and to the clergy of all denominations. Consequently it was reprinted in all the newspapers and made known to everybody, rich and poor, black and white.

The result was an extraordinary ferment amongst the negroes and mulattoes, a ferment to a certain extent countenanced by such whites (even magistrates) as were inclined to deal fairly with the coloured population.

A great public meeting was called for the 3rd of May, in the city of Kingston. The mayor of that city was to have presided, but was prevented at the last moment by illness. His place was taken by George William Gordon,[2] a mulatto or octoroon citizen, who represented Port Morant district

[1] It is quoted in full on page xiii in the book already alluded to, *The Tragedy of Morant Bay*. It recapitulated the extreme poverty of the Jamaica negroes, and state of intermittent starvation; the excessive taxation, unemployment owing to decay of sugar industry, and the unjust tribunals. It made some most sensible and "modern" recommendations as to curative measures. It was, in fact, a statesmanlike document.

[2] Dr. Underhill describes George William Gordon as "a half-caste by birth, but a man of property, of good education and standing in society, married to an English wife, and of a religious habit of mind . . . a staunch and an unfailing advocate of the interests of the negro . . . and often an opponent of the Governor's measures in the Assembly." He was latterly a member of the Baptist Church and interested himself a good deal in Baptist missionary work, as well as in an attempt to solve the land disputes with fairness to the coloured people. He was described by Governor Eyre as "the most consistent and untiring obstructor of the public business in the House of Assembly." He had long held a commission as a magistrate, but this was taken from him by Governor Eyre. Although the Secretary of State for the Colonies did not restore the commission, he nevertheless required Governor Eyre to apologise to the "Honble. George William Gordon" for harsh terms used in correspondence. (Gordon's magistracy was taken away from him because he had spoken angrily to a brother magistrate as to the insanitary condition of a certain gaol, for which the latter was responsible.)

A year or so before the outbreak at Morant Bay, Gordon, though elected, had failed to secure appointment to the office of churchwarden, and attributed this disappointment to the hostility of Baron von Ketelhodt and the Rev. Mr. Herschell, a clergyman-magistrate. His desire to sit as a churchwarden arose from his wish to criticise the expenditure of public funds by the Church of England clergy of Morant Bay Parish.

Gordon was in serious financial difficulties at the time of the outbreak, owing as much as £35,000; but he had a great deal of landed property. His financial stress seems to have been due to failure of crops and the inability of many of his tenants to pay their rents.

Gordon attacked the administration of Governor Eyre in the press and freely criticised him in private conversations. He was wont, after the manner of coloured people of that period, to ventilate his private and public grievances rather windily, with many invocations of the Deity, and vague aspirations that a special Divine vengeance would fall on the oppressors of the coloured man and of himself in particular. His recorded utterances were just as much—and no more—provocative of an armed rising as are the daily diatribes of politicians at the present day against the party in power, in England or the United States.

of St. Thomas's Parish in the House of Assembly. At this first meeting in Kingston, Mr. Gordon, though chairman, said scarcely anything.

A good many other meetings were held at all the principal centres of the population about the island, usually presided over by white members of the House of Assembly who agreed with the terms of Dr. Underhill's letter and were in favour of general reform. In April, 1865, the negroes of Northern Jamaica (the Parish of St. Ann) drew up themselves and forwarded through the Government to Queen Victoria a humble petition, describing their destitute state and their inability to pay the heavy taxes now demanded, and equally heavy export duty on their produce. Unfortunately the reply to this petition (obviously drawn up by Governor Eyre himself, though sent from the Colonial Office in London) was needlessly unsympathetic and harsh, in fact, a State blunder. When made known to the black people of Jamaica it caused the profoundest dissatisfaction, and for this condition of their minds blame was venomously thrown back by Governor Eyre on the Baptists and the intervention of Dr. Underhill. The Colonial Office in London called Dr. Underhill's attention to Governor Eyre's reports, and Underhill then advised that a Royal Commission should be sent out to Jamaica at once to report impartially on the condition of the country. Had this advice been adopted and notice of it sent out to Jamaica, there would have been no tragedy of Morant Bay, and the subsequent career of Governor Eyre might quite possibly have ended happily. But the Colonial Office did nothing except continue its conferences with Dr. Underhill.

On the 12th August, 1865, a public meeting was called at the little seaside town of Morant Bay (St. Thomas in the East) by the Custos of the parish, Baron von Ketelhodt, to discuss the "Underhill" Letter. G. W. Gordon, who, as already stated, represented this district in the House of Assembly, took the chair; and a number of resolutions were unanimously adopted calling attention to the unsatisfactory condition of Jamaica. Although the Custos (a German planter-magistrate) called the meeting, he disliked Mr. Gordon, and vainly attempted to prevent the meeting taking place when he learned who was asked to preside over it. After the meeting was over a deputation walked forty miles to Spanish Town (then the capital) to lay the resolutions before the Governor. He refused to receive the deputation.

At that time much dissatisfaction was felt over land and trespass questions round about Morant Bay, where a certain Church of England clergyman-magistrate and the aforementioned Baron von Ketelhodt had made themselves disliked by their "oppressive and unjust conduct." Baron von Ketelhodt presided at a Court of Petty Sessions on the 7th October. It was a market-day, and a large number of negro peasants were collected in the vicinity of the Court. A case of assault was brought by a woman against a boy, who was convicted and fined four shillings. But the Court added to the fine costs amounting to twelve shillings and sixpence. A negro who was present in Court advised the boy to pay the fine only and not the costs. A rumpus ensued, the negro being arrested for contempt of court and rescued by the bystanders. A far more important case was about to be tried dealing with land disputes at Stony Gut (a place five miles north of Morant Bay). This was a case which should have been put before a judge and jury. In dealing with this the Court of Petty Sessions was acting *ultra vires*.

The land about Stony Gut was claimed by several whites, including a curate, the Rev. Mr. Herschell; but the negroes in the vicinity declared it was

Crown land and that they were at liberty to squat on it. Foremost among these squatters was a negro, Paul Bogle, who assumed a very truculent tone with the authorities in his communications. He was also an ardent Baptist and a friend and correspondent of G. W. Gordon. But both he and Gordon may have thought they were defending the legitimate rights of the peasantry against white land-grabbers. In the matter of Stony Gut it does not follow that they were, and Paul Bogle and his brother Moses were not precisely

230. THE BACK YARDS OF NEGRO HOUSES IN A SMALL NORTHERN TOWN OF JAMAICA

peasants, but educated men somewhat inclined to work up grievances and turn them to profit. In fact in the two brothers Bogle—especially Paul—we have the only two culpable ringleaders concerned in this Morant Bay rising. Paul Bogle (who was afterwards hanged) was certainly guilty of stirring up the people to attack and plunder without provocation the plantations and houses of the whites. But no evidence could be adduced of the Bogles being urged by G. W. Gordon to deeds of violence or to anything worse than contentious litigation.

The trouble following the riot of the 7th October and the anxiety about the issue of this land-suit led to the usual appeal to Governor Eyre, met by the usual rebuff. On the 12th October, 1865, a large crowd of dissatisfied negroes assembled in an open space facing the Court House. Baron von Ketelhodt called upon them to disperse, but as they began to throw stones he very shortly afterwards ordered the volunteers to fire on the crowd, several of whom were killed. There was instantly the cry of "war." The volunteers were disarmed, a few white men were killed [amongst them Baron von Ketelhodt[1] and the Rev. Mr. Herschell, "whose oppressive acts of injustice had especially roused the passions of the people"[2]], but not a single white woman or child was injured. During the two following days, however, several plantations were attacked, houses burnt, and one or two planters killed. The total number of persons (only a few of whom were white) *murdered* by the rioters amounted to *eighteen*, and the wounded whites and blacks were *thirty-one*. Two or three of the whites were killed by being beaten to death, the others were slain with guns or knives in the general mêlée or in the attacks on the plantations. A few buildings were burned at Morant Bay, including the Court House and school. That was the entire extent of the "Morant Bay Rebellion." No white woman was outraged. Many negresses and a few negroes intervened at the risk of their lives to save white men from death.

So much for the crime. This was the punishment. Mr. Eyre and a sufficient military force were soon on the scene, and martial law was proclaimed on the 13th October, the day following the outbreak. The number of persons executed by the order of this and other courts-martial was ascertained to have been 354; but in addition there were shot, hung, or killed without trial 85—a total of 439 negro men and women. Of these, 147 were put to death on the 25th October, at least ten days after the extinction of anything resembling riot or disorder. One thousand negro houses were burnt to the ground, and literally thousands of negroes were more or less cruelly flogged or mutilated. The Maroons who were called in to aid in punishing the peasantry of Eastern Jamaica killed children by dashing their brains out, and ripped open pregnant women. The Royal Commissioners—finally appointed to deal with the Jamaican situation at the close of 1865—described these floggings as "reckless and positively barbarous."[3]

But this was not all. Mr. Eyre seems almost to have parted with his reason and to have believed without any proof in a "diabolical conspiracy to murder the white and coloured inhabitants of Jamaica," a conspiracy which he boasted of having crushed within the first three days following the preliminary outbreak.[4]

He then returned to Kingston on the 16th October and issued a warrant at that place (*which was not under martial law*) for the arrest of George William Gordon, determining to hold him responsible for the outbreak at Morant Bay, though he had not visited that place since presiding at the "Underhill" meeting of August 12th, 1865. Gordon, who resided near Kingston, being warned by friends before the issue of the warrant that owing to unguarded expressions

[1] It should be noted that when the situation seemed hopeless Baron von Ketelhodt offered to give himself up to the rioters if they would let the other white men go free.

[2] Dr. Underhill.

[3] The floggings were sometimes inflicted with a cat in the strings of which piano-wire was interwoven. Sometimes two hundred lashes were administered: frequently one hundred. Women were flogged (with the cat, but not with piano-wire) and received from fifty to ten lashes. *Vide Report of Royal Commission*, 1866.

[4] Nevertheless, though the insurrection was so speedily at an end martial law was maintained, and the iniquitous Assembly (happily near extinction) passed repeated Acts interfering with the liberty of the subject, and authorising the local authorities to flog for almost every offence in the calendar, while other legislation attempted to interfere with the freedom of religion.

which had fallen from the Governor at Morant Bay, he, Gordon, would be held answerable for the circumstances of the riot, nevertheless refused to go away or to hide himself, saying that to do so would look as though he was guilty. Hearing that the warrant was issued, he actually proceeded alone to the office of the commander of the troops and gave himself up. He was placed under arrest by the Governor in person, even though the city of Kingston had been specially exempted from the operation of martial law. Eyre then took his

231. SUNDAY IN A SMALL JAMAICAN COUNTRY TOWN
Note the policeman, whom the author found subsequently to be a most intelligent civil-spoken guide

captive on a steamer to Morant Bay and committed him to the custody of a man who was to become notorious for cruelty, Provost-Marshal Gordon Duberry Ramsay.[1] The Governor had from the moment of the arrest prohibited all access to Gordon. He was not even allowed to receive a letter from his solicitor advising him as to the line of defence he should take up. This letter was read and destroyed by Brigadier-General Nelson, in command at Morant Bay. Here General Nelson formed a court-martial composed of two young lieutenants of the Royal Navy and a young ensign of the 4th battalion, West India Regiment. It assembled at two o'clock on Saturday the 21st, and "care was taken to exclude all

[1] Ramsay had fought bravely as a soldier in the Crimea and had won the Victoria Cross.

persons friendly to the prisoner." The whole description of the trial, as subsequently published by the Royal Commissioners, is on a par with the worst doings of the revolutionary tribunals in Paris during the reign of terror. Five witnesses were put forward by the prosecution, and the Provost-Marshal Ramsay "taught them their evidence with a rope round their necks and giving them a lash with a whip in between every sentence to enforce their false evidence on their minds."[1] Even though most of these wretched witnesses were under sentence of death and might have hoped to save their miserable lives by their perjury, yet no fragment of recorded evidence could be brought forward to implicate Gordon with this abortive rising. He was actually *prevented* from calling any witnesses on his own account. After being allowed for an hour to speak in his own defence, in which he resolutely pleaded "Not Guilty," the Court adjourned for a brief interval of deliberation. It then reassembled to pronounce Gordon guilty and to sentence him to death.

The finding of the Court and its sentence were at once referred through General Nelson to Governor Eyre for confirmation. The Governor lost no time in writing that he quite concurred in the justice of the sentence and the necessity of carrying it into effect. Gordon was forthwith hung (October 23rd, 1865), by two or three sailors, from the centre of the ruined arch of the Court House at Morant Bay. It is difficult to read unmoved the letter which he wrote to his wife a few minutes before his judicial murder took place, a murder entirely and absolutely the work of Edward John Eyre, Captain-General and Governor of Jamaica.

Any one wishing to revel in horrors, or, let us say, to appreciate how wicked white men can be, as well as black, should read the many documents collected and published in the Blue Books of 1866 regarding what went on in Jamaica between the 7th October, 1865, and the cessation of Eyre's reign of terror by the arrival of a Royal Commission on January 6th, 1866.[2]

It is sufficient to say, in conclusion, that it is one of the few really shocking episodes in the recent history of the British Empire. Before the Commission, however, could be appointed and got to work, Eyre did two things which saved him possibly from a criminal sentence. In the first place, he caused the House of Assembly to pass on his behalf an Act of Indemnity; and in the second place he induced this corrupt Legislature to pronounce its own demise, to surrender the Constitution granted by Oliver Cromwell, and make it easy for the Government of Queen Victoria to deal with Jamaica unfettered by any local privileges.

The evidence collected by the Royal Commission and its report on that evidence were inevitably so damaging to Governor Eyre that a strong feeling was created in England, and attempts were made to punish Eyre, at any rate for the judicial murder of George William Gordon, if not in a general way for the atrocities committed without reproof on his part by such agents of the Government as Provost-Marshal Ramsay. But the British Government of the day contented itself with merely dismissing Mr. Eyre from his post and from all future employment in the civil service of the Crown, though acknowledging at the same time the obligation of the Government towards him "for effecting an entire change in the system of the government in operation in Jamaica." Mr. Eyre retired, I believe, on a pension. A private prosecution

[1] Dr. Underhill.

[2] Sir Henry Storks was appointed the head of this Royal Commission and also Governor of Jamaica, to supersede Mr. Edward John Eyre.

was subsequently instituted in the county of his residence (Shropshire) by a member of the Jamaica Committee, but the bench of magistrates dismissed the case. Similarly abortive was the attempt to bring to justice Brigadier-General Nelson and Lieutenant-Commander Brand, who had respectively created and presided over Gordon's court-martial, though it must be admitted that in their case they did not bear the entire responsibility, since they submitted the verdict and sentence of their court to the consideration of the Governor, who confirmed it. Provost-Marshal G. D. Ramsay, who shot several harmless, innocent negroes with his own hand in time of peace, who hanged others without trial, who whipped and abused witnesses, who flogged with frenzy till the flesh of his victims bespattered the ground, was tried for murder in Jamaica and acquitted by a white Grand Jury.

232. A JAMAICA CONSTABLE OF THE RURAL CONSTABULARY

If bare justice had been dealt out without consideration of race or colour, there is little doubt that Governor Edward John Eyre would have been adjudged guilty of the manslaughter of George William Gordon, and have had to suffer a term of penal servitude. He is dead now, and, if there be a life beyond the grave, has perhaps made his amends to the many who suffered so cruelly through his wild, unbalanced delegation of the power of life and death; and some of my fellow-countrymen who read this book may think my raking up the ashes of this old tragedy a piece of wanton mischief-making [though they may probably approve with hearty acquiescence the denunciation of French crimes in Haiti, or the frightful cruelties perpetrated on the negro in the United States]. But in reading all the voluminous mass of official and private literature concerning Jamaica between 1850 and 1866, one feels it scarcely a sufficient comment to dismiss the deeds of the House of Assembly, of Governor Eyre, and above all of Provost-Marshal G. D. Ramsay and other subordinates, as "regrettable incidents," and to ask that bygones may be bygones. If such episodes of bad government are lightly glossed over in any history of the past, it is an encouragement for their recurrence in the future whenever a Government or an individual falls into a state of unreasoning panic, supervening on a long and stupid denial of justice or abuse of privilege.

In 1866 Jamaica became a Crown Colony without elective government. A new semi-military police on the lines of the Royal Irish Constabulary was set on foot at the close of 1866, and has proved in course of time to be the best and most efficient police force in America south of the Canadian border. It is composed entirely of negroes, except in regard to officers, and these are mostly selected from the Royal Irish Constabulary.[1]

Yet during the Dismal Period of Jamaica's history—from 1838 to 1868—a period in which the sugar industry was wellnigh killed, in which there were visitations of cholera and yellow fever, the usual allowance of storms and hurricanes, toll-bar riots, and State bankruptcy, there was really a steady advance towards material and mental improvement on the part of the negroes and mulattoes. Especially remarkable throughout the island was the work of the Baptist and Presbyterian ministers and missionaries, and this led to Jamaica actually having some effect on the subsequent history of West Africa. A movement was begun in 1838–40 under the auspices of the Baptist Missionary Society of Great Britain for the transference to Africa of such Jamaica negroes and mulattoes as might be discontented with their lot in the West Indies. Something of the kind also was attempted by the United Presbyterian Church Missionary Society (commencing in Jamaica), which founded the potent mission stations of the Old Calabar and Cross River district. As the result of this work (and similar institutions at Sierra Leone under the Church Missionary Society) not a few Jamaicans—negroes and mulattoes, men and women—embarked for West Africa between 1840 and 1870. To Sierra Leone, Liberia, Old Calabar, Fernando Pô, and the Cameroons they brought some degree of civilisation not to be overlooked in describing the history of that period in West Africa. They introduced the bread-fruit tree, West Indian cultivated bananas, West Indian oranges, guavas, bamboos, cacao, and other useful shrubs and plants. They founded (practically) the present agricultural prosperity of Fernando Pô, where some of their descendants still remain.

In 1868 came the first suggestion—unrecognised at the time—of a brighter era dawning in Jamaica. In that year the captain of a small American steamer had taken a cargo from New Orleans to Port Antonio (Jamaica), and not wishing to go back empty, filled up his ship with bananas. He found a ready market for this fruit in the Southern States, and thus began the fruit trade of Jamaica, which is now atoning for the slump in sugar and coffee (though these latter exports are reviving), and bids fair, with the cultivation of cacao, the breeding of cattle and horses, and the cultivation generally of tropical products (together with the exploitation of some of the loveliest tropical scenery in the world), not only to revive the fortunes of Jamaica but to make that island wealthy and prosperous as it has never yet been in its past history.

In 1884 a considerable measure of elective government was restored to the country. Nine of the members of the Legislative Council of Jamaica were to be elected on a low property and literacy franchise, which was to be distributed without distinction of race or colour. Provision was however made for securing a very positive official majority in case of need.

The political constitution of Jamaica, as finally shaped by the law of 1886 and the Order-in-Council of 1895, consists of a Governor, a Privy Council, and

[1] This constabulary is a credit both to the race which supplies the raw material and to that which furnishes the officers. The uniform is very like that of the Royal Irish Constabulary, on which, indeed, the whole force is modelled, while most of the officers are drawn from Ireland. The urban police wear a white helmet and a different, perhaps less soldierly-looking, uniform, but they resemble their comrades of the rural district in politeness and efficiency. I formed a high opinion of the negro constabulary throughout all those portions of the British West Indies which I personally visited. Its efficiency and good behaviour have enabled us to withdraw the greater part of the white troops who were formerly maintained in Jamaica and other islands at such a severe cost in money and health.

233. THE NEW WEALTH OF JAMAICA: A BANANA PLANTATION

a Legislative Council. The Privy Council consists of the senior military officer in the island, the Colonial Secretary, the Attorney-General, and eight other persons (or less) nominated by the Sovereign (these councillors are usually provisionally appointed by the Governor, and the appointment is then submitted to the approval of the King). The tenure of office of the Privy Councillors appointed by the King is limited to five years. The Governor of the island, however, though he is required ordinarily to consult with the Privy Councillors, is nevertheless authorised to act without such consultation or to act in opposition to their advice and decision if he deems his independence of action necessary for the welfare of Jamaica or of the Empire; but, of course, in taking such

234. THE HOME OF A PROSPEROUS NEGRO PLANTER, JAMAICA
Note the telephone wire running past the house, ugly but practical

a step he must satisfy the Secretary of State for the Colonies that he was right in doing so.

After the Privy Council, which is a kind of Ministry and Senate in one, comes the *Legislative Council*, which is presided over by the Governor, and contains *five ex-officio* members, *ten* who are *nominated* by the Crown (or provisionally appointed by the Governor), and *fourteen elected* members. The President (the Governor) has no deliberative vote, but only a casting vote. But assuming that the ten nominated members vote with the five ex-officio councillors, there is already a majority of one over the elected members.

But the votes of the ex-officio and nominated members of the Council may not be recorded in support of any law, vote, or resolution imposing any new tax or appropriating any public revenue, if not less than nine of the elected members have voted against any such law, vote, or resolution, or unless the Governor declares his opinion that the passing of such law, vote, or resolution is of paramount importance to the public interest, and this provision applies to any other measure or law discussed by the Legislative Council where the whole of the fourteen members cast their votes unanimously in one or other direction, that is to say, they may not be opposed by the official vote unless the Governor compels them to any such opposition by the declaration of his opinion. The Governor has also the right to veto legislation (by refusing his assent to a Bill) which would affect the Imperial position of Jamaica, Imperial regulations regarding marriage and divorce, commercial treaties with other Powers, the equal rights of all the inhabitants of Jamaica, without distinction of race or colour.

The qualifications of an elected member of the Legislative Council are that he shall possess the franchise, and that he shall not be holding any office of emolument under the Crown or Government of Jamaica, and that he shall either have resided in the electoral district for at least twelve months preceding the day of election, *or* be in possession of an income of at least £150 (in his own right or that of his wife) arising from land belonging to him or to her within the electoral district, *or* of a minimum of £200 arising partly from land and partly from any other source or business, *or* of a minimum of £300 annually accruing from any source whatever, *or* being able to show that he pays annually in direct taxes or export duty at least £10 per annum.

The franchise qualifications are limited to male persons of over twenty-one years of age, not legally incapacitated; British subjects by birth or naturalisation; and householders and ratepayers to the extent of the poor-rates and tax-payers of at least 10s. *per annum*, or parish taxpayers of at least 30s. *per annum*, or else in receipt of an annual salary of at least £50; provided that no person shall be registered as a voter who has been in prison with hard labour or for more than twelve months, or has been recently in receipt of public or parish relief. [The former condition of being able to write has been abolished.]

Nevertheless, in the returns of 1906 there were only 8607 registered voters in the whole of Jamaica out of a total population then standing at 820,437. The number of registered voters in 1901 was 16,256. It would really seem as though, having the right to vote by law, the Negro population of Jamaica was content with that assurance and did not care to register as voters.

On the Legislative Council of to-day only *four* of the elected members are of *unmixed* Nordic-European descent; *four* are of well-known Jamaican-*Jewish* families descended from the Spanish and Portuguese Jews of Guiana and Brazil;[1] *one* member is an absolute negro (of Bahaman birth), and the remainder (*five*) are octoroons and mulattoes of Jamaican birth.

As regards religion, the Roman Catholic Church, since 1860, has been gathering a large following in Jamaica, and has thirty-one or more churches in the island; but its work lies more among the whites and half-castes than the negroes. It also has under its charge about nine thousand Catholics from Cuba and Haiti. The Church of England is not only holding its own, but has had a marked increase of influence under the energetic administration of the present Bishop of Jamaica (Archbishop of the West Indies), whose views, teaching, and attitude toward the negro question are all that a *practical*

[1] This is the reason why at the present day not only are Spanish and Portuguese names very common amongst the apparently white and English inhabitants of Jamaica (chiefly along the south coast), but why not a few rather handsome Moorish-looking negroes (recalling sometimes with strange vividness the luxuriant-bearded, prominent-nosed, full-eyed Assyrians of 3000 B.C.) equally bear high-sounding Spanish names. The Jews, since the beginning of the seventeenth century, have played a most important part in the development of the British, French, Dutch, and Danish West Indies.

philanthropist could desire.[1] The Presbyterians are strongly represented in Jamaica, and among the other Free Churches the Baptists occupy a deservedly prominent position, and have become an essentially native Church—that is to say, they have few, if any, white pastors; whereas the clergy of the Anglican Church are *all* white men and nearly all of them from the United Kingdom. The Congregationalists (London Missionary Society), Wesleyans, Methodists, and "Quakers" (Society of Friends), and the Moravians are all strongly represented in Jamaica and have played a notable part in the education of the negro. There should also be mentioned the admirable work of the "Church of the Disciples of Christ," which has ten teaching districts and twenty-three churches in Jamaica. Since the days of emancipation many wild sects have

235. A JAMAICAN NEGRO FARMER AND BEE-KEEPER

arisen amongst the negro Christians of Jamaica, the beliefs advanced by these being often unconsciously a recurrence to African superstitions. The most prominent of these local sects at the present day is that of the Bedwardite Baptists.[2]

This movement was started by a tinsmith named Bedward, whose wife kept a bakery in the suburbs of wide-spreading Kingston. Bedward some twenty years ago started the idea that he had special power in baptism and was to be regarded as a prophet. Water, after being blessed by him, had the power of curing all diseases, moral as well as physical.

His preposterous claims were (as occurs in the history of all new religions) supported by a few coincidences and genuine occurrences of faith cure, and he soon built up a considerable following. Once a month he is said to hold

[1] Archbishop Nuttall has been parish priest, Bishop, and Archbishop in Jamaica from about 1865 to the present day; Bishop since 1880. *Ut floreat!* He has written a remarkable essay, "The Characteristics of the Negro," in *Mankind and the Church* (Longmans: 1907)

[2] For further details regarding the Bedwardites see Mr. Ralph Hall-Caine's book *The Cruise of the "Port Kingston,"* p. 97.

a baptismal ceremony at a place on the Hope River about ten miles from the capital. Bottles of his blessed water are sold at a shilling each, and at each of his monthly functions his wife prepares a meal for those who participate.

Apparently the sum of one shilling covers the cost of the baptism and the picnic feast, and the small profit on this enterprise, together with the less defensible sale of the magic water, constitute Bedward's gains out of his trade as Prophet. How far it is wholesome or sanitary for hundreds of negroes and negresses to be immersed at the same time in a pool which gradually becomes of very filthy water I cannot say; these "communions" are perhaps insanitary in their results. But if the local government at the present time were to intervene and forcibly put down Bedward's movement it would increase his sect to a gigantic following. This and other foolish superstitions are best left to be dissipated by the spread of education.

236. A STREET IN KINGSTON, JAMAICA

At the present day only about one-quarter of the total coloured population of Jamaica can read and write. In literacy the Jamaica negro is much behind his brother in British Guiana, Trinidad, Barbados, and the United States. Education, though free (and somewhat generously assisted by Government grants and splendid philanthropic institutions), is not, as it ought to be, *compulsory*[1] or sufficiently practical in relation to Jamaican needs. But more attention is being given now (since 1900) to the teaching of Agriculture, Horticulture, Bee-keeping, Poultry-rearing, etc.

Prior to 1834 there was practically no education given to negroes, except a pragmatical and useless oral disquisition on the religion which the White man so unctuously preached and so flagrantly malpractised in his dealings with the Black. Indeed, as late as 1823 it was forbidden to teach slaves to read or write. Money was frequently bequeathed by repentant Christians in the island for the instruction of the children of freed slaves, but it was generally embezzled for some other purpose. The Moravian Brethren did what they could, especially after 1823, but it was not till Emancipation year (1834) that the flood-gates of education were really thrown open.[2]

In that year the first Sir Thomas Fowell Buxton did a smart stroke

[1] By the law of 1892 the Governor is empowered to declare elementary education compulsory, but no Governor has yet done so.

[2] From 1838 to 1843 the British Parliament made a special education grant to Jamaica (for teaching negroes) of £30,000 per annum; and from 1843 to 1848 of about £15,000 per annum. But this generous provision was misapplied by the wicked and corrupt House of Assembly. Sir John Peter Grant was the first Governor of Jamaica who in 1866-7 took any active interest in education.

of business. He discovered the dormant "Lady Mico Charity" trust, and induced the Government of the day to authorise the diversion of these locked-up funds from the purpose for which they had been bequeathed and, supplemented by a Treasury grant of £17,000 a year for five years, their application at once to the "promotion of education among the black and coloured population of British Guiana and the West Indies."

How he snatched this prize out of the clutches of the Court of Chancery or of the Trustees of Lady Mico's bequest it is difficult to understand.

Dame Jane Mico was the widow of Sir Samuel Mico of the Mercers' Company in London. She died in 1666, and bequeathed a sum of one thousand pounds in trust, the interest on which was to be applied "to the redemption of poor Christian slaves in Barbary." Apparently it was not so applied, or British slaves in Algeria, Tunis, and Morocco had become scarce. At any

237. A COUNTRY SCHOOL (4,000 FEET ABOVE SEA-LEVEL), CENTRAL JAMAICA

rate, the original thousand pounds and its interest went on increasing automatically for a hundred and fifty years, until eventually the Chartered charity established by the British Government at the instance of Fowell Buxton had £120,000 to deal with in its educational enterprise in the West Indies and British Guiana. Jamaica has been the principal seat of the Mico Charity's educational work and is now its sole sphere; its schools in the Leeward and Windward Islands, Bahamas, British Guiana, Trinidad, and the archipelagos of the Indian Ocean having been made over to local educational systems.[1]

In 1892 the Legislative Council of Jamaica began its first effective measures to assist and enforce education, especially amongst the negro and coloured nine-tenths of the population. The number of scholars throughout the island rose in 1895 to the respectable total of 104,149; after that there was a falling off. But the worst blows to education in Jamaica were dealt by the Devil of unconquered and reactionary Nature, the Devil which is outside as well as inside

[1] Though the part these Mico schools have played in the early education of the Negro in Guiana, Barbados, and Trinidad should not be forgotten, for they were the first pioneers of sound, undenominational education in those regions.

poor struggling, martyred, yet undefeated Humanity. In 1903 there came a cyclone which blew down a number of the newly constructed schools. In 1907 the Kingston earthquake destroyed completely the new training-college of the Mico Charity outside Kingston—a building which had just cost £12,000. The floods of the autumn of 1909 have destroyed many other school buildings. Prior to this last disaster there were about 690 schools and colleges in Jamaica with an approximate attendance of 50,000 scholars.[1]

A notable personality during the past fifteen years in furthering elementary and secondary education in Jamaica has been the Most Rev. Enos Nuttall, Archbishop of the West Indies, to whom I have already referred.

The total population of Jamaica for the year 1908 was approximately 840,500. Deducting the 15,000 pure whites (in round numbers) and the 13,800 East Indians and about 700 Chinese (29,500 non-negro people) we are left with a total of 811,000 negroes and negroids as the main element of the Jamaican population at the present day. From this total, to arrive at the number of pure blacks one must deduct approximately 157,500 negroids—ranging from brown mulattoes or half-castes to octoroons (counting the "near-whites" as whites)—and there remain about 654,000 people of unmixed negro stock in Jamaica.

The conjectured increase in the whites between 1891 and 1908 is ascribed more to the immigration of British and Americans for business purposes (and a terminable stay) than to actual colonisation. Yet the resident whites look healthy and vigorous, and to judge from what one sees at "going-to-school" hours in the suburbs of Kingston, Port Antonio, St. Ann's, and the inland and western towns, there seems to be plenty of young white Jamaicans growing up likely in body and mind to be creditable examples of the white race.[2] The white birth-rate, however, seems to be small, partly owing to the large proportion of bachelors among the whites and the tendency of white women in the tropics to bear fewer children. Nevertheless, with our increasing mastery over tropical diseases there is no reason why a white population of at least half a million should not grow up alongside a negroid race of four millions in a perfectly cultivated Jamaica, provided the whites were allotted land in the central, cool, mountainous part of the island: such as the delightful country between the Blue Mountains in the east and the Nassau Mountains in the west, of which the Moneague district is an example.

The birth-rate among the negroes is about 38 per 1000, that of the "coloured" people a little lower. The death-rate for 1907 was about 26 per 1000. There is at the present time an annual surplus of births over deaths of 10,000.

[1] Most of the school buildings I visited seemed to me large, commodious, clean, and in good repair, and the instruction which was being given by coloured masters or mistresses was at least tolerably good. Some of these teachers are half-castes, and are quite as efficient as the ordinary school teacher of a country town or village in England. But, of course, the curriculum contains far too large a share of the Old Testament and of history and geography much more suited to the British Isles than to the centre of the West Indies. Industrial and agricultural education for the mass of the negro population lags much behind that which is offered to all and sundry in the United States; and this is probably why so many ambitious young Jamaicans go to Tuskegee for their higher education. Amongst educational factors of importance in Jamaica, however, should certainly be mentioned the Hope Botanical Gardens, and all the instruction in botany and horticulture which radiates therefrom and from the Castleton Hill Gardens; and secondly, the Institute of Jamaica, with its museum and its excellent public library of nearly 12,000 volumes, so readily and pleasantly accessible under Mr. Frank Cundall's direction.

[2] The proportion of Jamaicans (of Anglo-Saxon race) in the Civil Service of the Crown (England and Colonies), in the Church, the Army, Medicine, and other careers is quite remarkable. Sir E. Maunde Thompson, who has just retired from the control of the British Museum, is a Jamaican by birth.

238. IN THE BLUE MOUNTAINS OF JAMAICA
Tree fern in foreground

But the birth-rate is slowly diminishing and the death-rate among negroes slightly increasing.

All over America it is said that where the negroes have long settled down as a free people, living under natural conditions, there is a preponderance of female births over male. This is certainly so in Jamaica, wherein the female population among negroes and negroids is about 23,000 in excess of the other sex. In the extreme west of Jamaica the proportion of men to women is as fifty to a hundred. This disproportion of the sexes does not conduce to morality. No negress could bear the idea of growing to old age without being a mother: she would deem herself slighted. Therefore the negro and mulatto men are much run after; the marriage rate is not only low, but tends to decrease (it is just now about 3·8 per 1000 persons), and with its decrease rises the percentage of illegitimate births, which now stands at the figure of sixty-five children out of every hundred (year 1906). The absence of the marriage contract matters less than might be supposed; because the spouses in this mere concubinage are just as faithful to one another as those that get married before priest or registrar and, if they are not happy, get a divorce or separate without one. But the really serious feature in irregularity of sexual union is the effect it has on *infant mortality*. "Lightly come, lightly go": the child born of concubinage is treated (usually) with far more neglect than the legitimate offspring. In either case the mortality amongst young negro children in Jamaica is large. Out of the last record of deaths—21,732 in 1907—over 14,000 were the deaths of children *under five years* of age; but it has been found that in Kingston during 1907 the ratio of deaths among young children was sixteen legitimate to twenty-six illegitimate. Mr. Ralph Hall Caine, from whose work[1] I have taken some of these figures, further points out that nearly eighty per cent of the infants' or children's deaths (among the negroes and negroids) are registered without the certificate of a qualified doctor.

239. A TESHI WOMAN, EASTERN GOLD COAST COLONY
A type of negress often seen in Jamaica

240. A MOSHI WOMAN, NORTHERNMOST GOLD COAST
The Moshi people, of rather high civilisation, have some distant kinship with Benin

The Jamaican negro was recruited entirely from West Africa. The Maroons probably came from Guinea (the rivers between the Gambia and Sierra Leone) and the Gold Coast; the Koromantis likewise from the Gold Coast;[2] then there was a

[1] *The Cruise of the "Port Kingston,"* Messrs. Collier, London, 1908 (one of the best books written on Jamaica).

[2] Koromantin was the first and greatest of the British slave-trade depôts on the Gold Coast. It was situated about sixteen miles to the east of Cape Coast Castle. See page 207.

Either the larger proportion of the slaves was drawn from the Gold Coast, where the principal

large importation from the Congo and Angola, the Calabar district (Mokos), the Niger Delta (Ibos), and some thousands from Lagos (Akus), Yoruba (Nagos), and Dahomé (Pōpōs). Several hundred Mandingos from Senegambia, and perhaps an occasional Fula or Moor leavened the lump and imparted to some of the negro types handsome features and a clearer bronze or copper tint to the skin. Good living, civilisation, and a steady increase of

241. THE OMANHIN OF INSUAIN

A negro chieftain of the borders of Togoland, belonging to the Pōpō or Dahoméan group of West African peoples. His forefathers sold many Pōpō slaves to the Portuguese, British, and Danes

refinement in life have given to some of the negro men and women of the towns a refinement of feature and a beauty of figure which is not always revealed by

slave-trading depôts of the British were established between 1680 and 1807, or this ethnic type (Fanti, Ashanti, and their kindred) prevailed over the others. This is shown by the greater part of Jamaican folklore being traceable to the Gold Coast and its hinterland, and to the fact that the fragments of African speech still lingering in the Negro-English dialect of Jamaica are derived from the Chwi language of Ashanti-Fanti. The popular "Nancy" stories are so called for their taking "Anansi," the spider, as the chief figure. *Anansi*=spider in Ashanti. See the valuable work by Mr. Walter Jekyll, *Jamaican Song and Story* (London, 1906).

the clumsy clothes or the unnecessary skirts which they may wear. Mr. Ralph Hall Caine, in his work *The Cruise of the "Port Kingston,"* describes so aptly the young woman of this race brought up under favourable surroundings, that I cannot do better than quote his words:—

"At sixteen years of age she is a perfect example of the physical woman, and nowhere in the whole of the wide world can she be excelled in beauty of form and grace of carriage. Hard labour in field and mill, and in the interminable task of keeping her skin, no less than her clothes, in a state of immaculate cleanliness, has given to each muscle that sufficiency of exercise which shall reveal its presence in all suppleness, smoothness, and grace of outline, while the soft shiny skin, as the natural reflex of her food, is a matchless picture of healthful functional activity. Her teeth are pearly white, with a cleanness and a perfection of regular moulding that is the happy legacy of an unstinted appetite for gnawing at the close sinewy fibre of the sugar cane. Her head is poised with that nice accuracy which has been gained by balancing loads, heavy but within her strength. Her neck is neither long nor short, nor fat, nor lean, but shoulders, neck, and chest are all revelations of the woman who is leading a life close to primitive nature, clothed in fulness of flesh that shall show no ugly Adam's apple, or protruding clavicle, while the breasts are firm and full without a trace of that elongation that is at once her own pride and our despair."

242. A JAMAICAN NEGRO ARTISAN

But amongst the peasantry the men are ordinarily better looking than the women; and it must be admitted that some of both sexes display negro features of the coarsest and ugliest type, while their dress is neither so tidy nor so picturesque as that of the Cubans or even the Haitians.

Educated men and women of this race dress as nearly as possible like the white people of Jamaica, smartly and becomingly.[1]

As regards the "Colour Question" in Jamaica I should like to quote some passages from Sir Sydney Olivier's volume in the Socialist Library, *White Capital and Coloured Labour* (Sir Sydney has been for some years Acting-Governor and is now Governor of Jamaica):—

In Jamaica there is beyond question an aversion on the part of white Creoles to intermarriage with coloured families, and this aversion may be relied on, at any rate for a long time to come, to check any such obliteration of race distinctions as is foreboded by negrophobists in the United States as the necessary result of the admission of social equality.

In the lower social ranks of employees in stores, mixed marriages between wholly white and coloured people may frequently be met with.

[1] Mr. John Henderson and Mr. A. Forrest give in their book on *Jamaica* (Messrs. A. and C. Black, 1906) excellent descriptions of well-dressed Jamaicans.

The effects of a first cross between black and white are no doubt constitutionally disturbing, and many persons of mixed origin are of poor physique, but the phthisis and other diseases from which they suffer are equally common amongst the West Indian population of apparently pure African blood, and arise among these from the over-crowding of dwellings, bad nutrition, insanitary habits, and other preventable causes. There may naturally be aversion and a strong social objection on the part of the white woman against her marriage with a black or coloured man. There is no correspondingly strong instinctive aversion, nor is there so strong an ostensible social objection to a white man's marrying a woman of mixed descent. The latter kind of union is much more likely to occur than the former. There is good physiological reason for this distinction. Whatever the potentialities of the African stocks as a vehicle for human manifestation—and I myself believe them to be, like those of the Russian people, exceedingly important and valuable—a matrix of emotional and spiritual energies that have yet to find their human expression in suitably adapted forms—the white races are now, in fact, by far the further advanced in effectual human development, and it would be expedient on this account alone that their maternity should be economised to the utmost. A woman may be the mother of a limited number of children, and our notion of the number advisable is contracting; it is bad natural economy, and instinct very potently opposes it, to breed backwards from her. There is no such reason against the begetting of children by white men in countries where, if they are to breed at all, it must be with women of coloured or mixed race. The offspring of such breeding, whether legitimate or illegitimate, is, from the point of view of efficiency, an acquisition to the community, and, under favourable conditions, an advance on the pure-bred African. For notwithstanding all that it may be possible to adduce in justification of that prejudice against the mixed race, of which I have spoken, and which I have myself fully shared, I am convinced that this class as it at present exists is a valuable and indispensable part of any West Indian community, and that a colony of black, coloured, and whites has far more organic efficiency and far more promise in it than a colony of black and white alone. A community of white and black alone is in far greater danger of remaining, so far as the unofficial classes are concerned, a community of employers and serfs, concessionnaires and tributaries, with, at best, a bureaucracy to keep the peace between them. The graded mixed class in Jamaica helps to make an organic whole of the community and saves it from this distinct cleavage.

A very significant light is thrown on the psychology of colour prejudice in mixed communities by the fact that, in the whites, it is stronger against the coloured than against the black. I believe this is chiefly because the coloured intermediate class do form such a bridge as I have described, and undermine, or threaten to undermine, the economic and social ascendancy of the white, hitherto the dominant aristocracy of these communities. This jealousy or indignation is much more pungent than the alleged natural instinct of racial-aversion.

It is interesting to note in Jamaica (as in the United States) how the cross between Nordic White and Negro endows the half-breed so frequently with yellow or red hair and blue-grey eyes: though the texture of the hair may be woolly and the complexion brown.

Since 1866 and the new order of things which followed the Storks Commission and the governorship of Sir John Peter Grant, the criminality of the Jamaican negroes and negroids has been slight. That is to say, as regards any crime of a serious nature. Unfortunately, as elsewhere in the Negro world, the peasants are dishonest in very small things; in petty thieving which books of reference refer to portentously as "Prædial larceny"—the stealing from one another (mostly) and from white people of poultry, fruit, vegetables, etc. In twelve months of 1907–8 there were 12,118 summary convictions (but this record refers also to low-class Europeans and East Indians) for theft, bad language, drunkenness (the negro is not so nearly cured from the alcohol habit in Jamaica as he is in the U.S.A.), common assaults, and other minor breaches of the law. In the same period there were 7290 convictions for serious crimes. On an average day in 1908 there were 1695 prisoners in jail, about 1500 of whom were negroes or negroids.

Indecent assaults by negroes on negro women or children are not uncommon, a little more common, possibly, than they are among people of the same social status in England and in some Scotch towns.[1] But it is scarcely too sweeping an assertion to say that there has been *no* case in Jamaica or any other British West India island of rape, or indecent assault or annoyance on the part of a black man or mulatto against a white woman since the Emancipation of the Slaves. Sir Sydney Olivier, reviewing this topic as regards Jamaica, says with truth: "A young white woman can walk alone in the hills or about Kingston, in daylight or dark, through populous settlements of exclusively black or coloured folk, without encountering anything but friendly salutation from man or woman. Single ladies may hire a carriage and drive all over the island without trouble or molestation. . . . Whatever may be the cause, it is an indisputable fact that Jamaica, or any other West India island, is as safe for white women to go about in, if not safer than, any European country with which I am acquainted." The same statement might be applied with equal truth to all parts of Negro Africa.

Personally I found with one exception all classes and all colours in Jamaica exceptionally civil and obliging to the stranger: even a stranger like myself who was (with the best intentions) prying into back yards, photographing many things and many human types, and often in too much of a hurry to request permission or explain the motive. It was a real pleasure to ask the way or the name of a plant, bird, estate, or village because of the politeness of the response. The exception was in the case of the Maroons of north-eastern Jamaica, whom I found insolent and disobliging, and inclined to levy blackmail on any one who passed through their villages or plantations and wished to photograph the scenery.

I should say [so far as I can judge by one visit to Jamaica, by conversation with many Jamaican negroes and mulattoes, and by a study of the local Press and contemporary literature] that at the present day there is no people more loyal to the British Crown and Empire than the coloured Jamaicans. Gradually the old evil effects of slavery and forced labour have died out. The kuli and the Chinaman have inspired the lower classes of negroes with a desire to work, to amass money, to acquire land, to live in better houses and in better style. Education spreading yearly amongst the coloured people, especially those with an element of the Caucasian, has suggested to them careers in and outside of Jamaica, comforts, luxuries, and delights to be obtained through work of some kind or another. The Jamaican negro, in fact, has become almost an apostle of work in revivifying Central America. By thousands—almost hundreds of thousands—he has gone to labour on the Panama Canal from the time of its inception by De Lesseps to its resumption by the Americans. If you hear of a particularly enterprising negro in Haiti he is sure to be a Jamaican.

[1] In Sussex, for example, and in many parts of Hampshire, it is dangerous for a young woman to walk alone on the downs or in woods. She would run a great risk of being assaulted indecently by tramps, "masterless men," and those strange monsters that haunt the precincts of pleasure cities or garrison towns. One hears little of these cases because, as in George Moore's story in *Celibates*, the assaulted woman strives in horror and shame to keep the dreadful incident a secret.

Jamaican pastors, teachers, and preachers are bringing the negroes of Cuba into the fold of the Protestant churches. Jamaicans also come over to Africa and work there with excellent results.

The negroid in this island enters into all the professions and careers and fills nine-tenths of the posts under Government. The coloured population, besides residing as cultivators in the country, frequents the towns and earns a living as doctors, dentists, ministers of religion, teachers, waiters, tradesmen, skilled artisans, clerks, musicians, postal employés, press reporters,[1] the superior servants of the State railways, overseers of plantations, hotel-keepers (and very good ones); in fact, they fill all the posts required in a civilised community (and Jamaica has *tous les agréments de la vie*) which are below the white man's high standard of salary and above the grasp of the, as yet, uneducated negro. The pure negro in Jamaica is mainly a peasant and a countryman. It is computed that there are 700,000 negro and negroid Jamaicans—men, women,

243. A NEGRO HOMESTEAD IN NORTH JAMAICA

and children—who live on the land, in the proportion of about 620,000 blacks to 80,000 half-castes.

Out of the 113,000 holdings of property on the Valuation Roll of the Island in 1905, 91,260 were below £40 in value and belonged to the black peasantry. The acreage of these holdings varied from less than an acre to a hundred acres. (Sir Sydney Olivier).

The Jamaican peasant for the most part is a freeholder with no superior landlord above him. He has squatted on virgin land and gradually obtained it in fee simple; he has purchased land or been given land. It is complained, indeed, that in many directions he has been too leniently dealt with, in that he has acquired (mainly by squatting) nearly three-quarters of the cultivable area of Jamaica; and this he has cultivated most wastefully on African methods, has destroyed the forest by fire, practised no alternation of crops or system of manuring. He is, I can add on my own observation, a merciless gunner, shooting for the sale of the plumage or for food every bird within his reach. So

[1] The press of the island, which is quite as good as the good provincial press of the United Kingdom, s almost entirely "run" by negroids, though its proprietors are probably white men.

great has been the destruction of bird-life in Jamaica—partly through the negro gunner, and partly through the mongoose introduced by the white man to kill the rats—that with the disappearance of so many forms of insectivorous birds there has been a damaging increase in numbers of insects and ticks,[1] to the prejudice of the cattle and poultry and the discomfort and even disease of human visitors or settlers.

The negro peasants (as I have pointed out in other writings) are recklessly destroying the beauty spots of Jamaica, by deflecting waterfalls for temporary and rather futile irrigation, by digging up ferns of priceless beauty to plant twopenny-halfpenny cabbages and bananas, and hacking down trees of monumental splendour to obtain a honeycomb or a few orchids for sale to tourists. Well might the Nature Study which has passed into the curriculum of the

244. ONE OF THE FIVE HUNDRED WATERFALLS OF JAMAICA

Negro's elementary education in British Guiana be taught to every child in Jamaica, so that he may realise the wonders and the unsurpassed beauties of his own island, and realise them as a *commercial asset;* for there is no better way of making people good than that of pointing out how goodness "pays" in the long run.

Every child or student should be presented with that classic *The Birds of Jamaica*, by Philip Gosse; and it should become a Negro ambition to restore the bird fauna of Jamaica to what it was in Gosse's day: to bring back the vanished Macaw, subsidise the scarlet-bellied Trogon, shoot the man who shoots a Tody or a Humming-bird, preserve the Rosy Mountain-Dove, whisper to the

[1] The tick now prevailing throughout Jamaica is said to have been introduced as recently as 1855 with cattle that were brought over from Mexico. At first it was not noteworthy as an addition to the island's plagues, but during the last ten years, since there has been such a notable decrease in the birds of Jamaica, the tick has become the curse of the island. Many a tourist has had his supreme pleasure in Jamaican scenery modified or spoilt by the severe bites of these ticks, which often bring on a serious inflammation of the arms or legs, and even lead to eczema.

Flamingo, "All is now safe; come here and nest along our southern coast," lynch the plumage-hunter who pursues the Snowy Egret, let the black and lemon-crested Tyrant-bird become in very sooth a tyrant, and give perpetual harbourage and licence to the True Buzzards (eagle-like, but in spite of their nobility now nearly extinct), and to the Turkey-buzzard, *the* bird of Jamaica (which is no buzzard, neither a turkey, but a miniature Condor, and an elegant incident in every Jamaican landscape).[1]

245. FERNS IN JAMAICA

It is the sight of the birds, the marvellous-coloured fish and crabs and crinoids of the honeycombed limestone coast, the harmless Crocodiles[2] of the

[1] The Turkey-buzzard (*Cathartes aura*) can in certain lights and aspects become a picturesque feature in the landscape. The culmen of the sharp-hooked beak is a brilliant ivory-white, but the whole rest of the face and neck of the adult bird is a bare scarlet-crimson. The thickly feathered neck is a glossy bluish black, as are also the tail and under parts. The wings are of a dark sepia-brown, but the under surface of the pinions is a satiny white; and this is a particularly noteworthy feature when the bird is soaring in the air, the smooth greyish white of the under surface of the outspread pinions contrasting finely with the velvety black of the body and neck, the bold pink of the legs, and the brilliant crimson-scarlet of the bare head.

[2] There is one species of Crocodile (*C. americanus*, sometimes called *C. acutus*) in Jamaica and the rest of the Greater Antilles. There is *no Alligator* in America, *except in the Southern States of the Union*, from the Rio Grande to North Carolina. The only other Alligator in the world is in East China. The so-called Alligators of Central and South America are Caimans, a different genus. Since the senseless destruction of the Alligator in the United States, the Mocassin Snake has increased considerably

southern rivers (why shoot them, you senseless tourist, you unreasoning sportsman? You are not one-quarter so interesting), the ring-tailed Iguana lizards, (also nearly extinct. . . . Why?), the sea-birds of the Tropics nesting on the

246. A JAMAICAN PEASANT WOMAN OFFERING AUTHOR A LARGE BUNCH OF ORCHIDS

guano-whitened "cays," which will attract the crowds of educated tourists who will in future visit Jamaica as a living museum, where they may see the

and caused many deaths (I am so glad) by its bites. The Musk-rats, formerly kept under by the Alligator, are now multiplying fast in Louisiana, and are (I am delighted to know) burrowing into the levees and embankments along the Mississippi, and causing many thousand pounds' worth of damage. Jamaica, take warning!

wonders and beauties of the American tropics with the accompaniment of first-rate roads, excellent hotels, comfortable railways and steamers, and perfect security of life, outside the hurricane season, and except for an earthquake once in fifty years.

But apart from the money to be made out of the exhibition of Jamaica's beauties and marvels, there is the consideration of the future intellectual development of the Neo-negroes themselves. Some day they will awaken to the intrinsic importance of scenery, of other manifestations of Nature's energy than Man—the present culmination of living forms, so far as intellectuality is

247. CRINOIDS FISHED UP ON NORTH COAST OF JAMAICA

When first taken out of the water they are an exquisite mauve-pink, and though the full beauty of this colour fades, enough remains for several years to make them very decorative objects

concerned. They will miss the Tree Fern if the present ignorant generation destroys it to plant the Bread-fruit or the Yam. They will endeavour to preserve such Orchids as remain with as much zeal as they plant Rubber Trees or Pineapples, and will cultivate the Wild as well as the Edible Banana.

The Negro—like the British sportsman; and the unthinking coster who sallies forth from our towns in early spring to catch the goldfinch or ravage the country-side for saleable roots and flowers—is instinct with a spirit of destruction. In Africa—as in Jamaica—he is never happy unless he is killing something. Well, let him turn his attention to the rat, the fly, the flea, the bug, the jigger, the tick, and above all, the mosquito. Jamaica, like Barbados and nearly all the British West Indies, remains extraordinarily ignorant (here again its present curriculum of education is to blame) of the theory of the propagation of so many tropical diseases by insect or arachnid agencies: the theory suggested by Sir Patrick Manson, invented by Professor Ronald Ross, and supported by the investigations of so many modest, quiet, ofttimes poor saints of the New Hierarchy in British India, Italy, the United States, England, France, and Germany. Carrying out this theory unfalteringly, even to the sacrifice of noble martyrs (some day to be beatified by the New Church of Humanity), the American Government has extirpated the *Stegomyia* mosquito from the towns of Cuba and of the Panama Canal Zone, of Louisiana, Florida, and Porto Rico, and has thereby destroyed Yellow Fever from any refuge under the American flag. The British Government might now be well on the way towards eradicating the Plague from India by eradicating the rat and the flea: were it not for the crassly stupid opposition of Brahmins and Muhammadans; who would sooner see a million people die of Plague than allow temporarily the abrogation of the Purdah in the harem or the profanation of a temple, rotten with disease-breeding filth. Still, even in India we are making progress by applying the theory of Ronald Ross [who in that region tracked down the *Anopheles* that has destroyed far more people with Malarial Fever than have ever been killed by tiger or snake]. Somehow our Governors in the West Indies (with the exception of his present Excellency of Jamaica) thought all these newfangled ideas had nothing to do with the islands under their government; the churches and the missionaries went on teaching the negro a lot of perfectly useless stuff about the ten plagues of Egypt, the Israelites in a very wearisome wilderness [which is now being crossed by a railway promoted by Israelites], and some antiquated Noah's Ark natural history, and never said a word about the Fly, the Flea, the Gnat, the Rat, the Tick, the Bug, the Nematode Worm, the Trypanosome, Micrococcus, and Treponeme, about the preventability of nearly all disease by the extermination of disease-carrying insects.

248. A WILD BANANA (HELICONIA PSITTACORUM), JAMAICA

In Barbados, where, so far as climate is concerned, every one should live to be bicentenarians, the expenditure of public moneys on the extirpation of the *Stegomyia* mosquito has been resisted by Negro Assemblymen and coloured journalists (their faulty education is to blame, poor things); in Jamaica, so far, the authorities Colonial and Parochial (with the exception of the Governor) have done *nothing*—and the citizens, black, white, and yellow, have been acquiescent in their torpor—to get rid of the dangerous mosquitoes from the vicinity of human settlements, and so relieve this island entirely of the risk of Yellow Fever. Further drastic action on the same lines might eradicate the Malarial Fever which still makes portions of the coast-lands unhealthy for the native-born, as well as for the passing tourist who departs from the beaten track.

249. LOGWOOD TREES IN THE JAMAICA SPRING

Jamaica is a paradise which should have no *preventable* dangers. Earthquakes slay their thousands in tropical America and hurricanes their hundreds; but mosquito-carried diseases wipe out millions of human beings, and render those that are not killed unfitted to be the parents of healthy children.

With a view to enabling the untravelled reader better to understand the environment of the Negro in Jamaica, I venture to append a few descriptions of Jamaican scenery from my note-book :—

In the roadstead of Kingston. The spit of Port Royal is a flat tongue of land accentuated at its extremity by tallish buildings—earthquake-shattered—and casuarina

250. THE LOVELY GLIRICIDIA ("RAT-CATCHER") TREE OF JAMAICA IN BLOOM IN THE WINTER MONTHS

Its lilac-pink clusters of blossoms decorate nearly every garden and roadside

trees and coco-palms; but it partially encloses like a huge natural breakwater a vast lagoon—one of the best natural harbours in the world. Beyond this and the narrow green plain, hazy with the smoke of Kingston, rise the majestic Blue mountains, tier after tier, till their summits are often lost in the clouds. They are very different to the clear-cut, brightly and diversely coloured mountains of Cuba, or the bare blue ridges carved and scarped by water and crested with scattered pine forest in Haiti. The mountains of Jamaica are so densely clothed with diversified forest that their outlines are softened, while the prevailing tint in a distant view is indigo or purple. Jamaica at first sight looks like an exaggerated edition of Madeira. . . .

251. A "POOR RELATIONS" TREE

Most of the trees, large and small, in Jamaica and the southern West Indies bear a heavy burden of epiphytic growth: aroids, ferns, bromeliaceous (i.e. pineapple-like) plants, cacti, and orchids

January is the opening of spring in Jamaica, and the flower-shows of fields and gardens then transcend any reasonable description. Particularly remarkable is the honey-scented, sulphur-yellow blossom of the logwood-trees, and an almost Japanese effect is produced along the roadsides and in garden fences by the *Gliricidia* with its sprays of lavender-pink bean-blossoms, laburnum-like in growth. Verandahs and out-houses are covered by the immense white or smalt-blue flowers of the Thunbergias, by the scarlet-orange Bignonia from Brazil, white Jasmines, yellow Allamandas, and magenta Bougainvillea. Orange-trees loaded with golden fruit border every suburban road.

Away from the handiwork of man, the forested mountains constitute beautiful natural botanical gardens. The copses of tree ferns on the lower and middle slopes of the Blue mountain range are alone worth the twelve days' journey from England. Then there are the handsome upright fronds of the wild bananas (*Heliconia*) with blue-green stems and scarlet and yellow spathes; the foliage of the eight species of palms indigenous to Jamaica; a naturalised myrtle with large creamy-white flowers: the extraordinary cacti, trailing, arborescent, and stumpy; the handsome papyrus-like rush in the coast swamps, and the king of the reeds (*Gynerium*) with an immense plume of fawn-coloured blossom: the lofty bamboos with their yellow-green foliage and bottle-green stems; the banyan fig trees with innumerable depending roots and trunks of immense girth; the silk-cotton trees with their glabrous mauve-white trunks and horizontal branches towering one hundred to two hundred feet into the air; and several other giants of the forest, which might be nicknamed "poor relations' trees," since their main trunks and huge horizontal branches support an extraordinary family of divers parasitical plants—aroids, bromeliaceæ, cacti, and ferns. A feature of the Jamaica hedgerows at this season (January) which is grateful to the eye of the English or American tourist is the large white wild rose (*Rosa lævigata*), with its centre of golden stamens.

252. A BROMELIACEOUS EPIPHYTE (HOHENBERGIA) GROWING ON TREE TRUNK, JAMAICA
A familiar object in the southern West Indies and Equatorial America

Along the north coast of Jamaica there are about three hundred miles of road following closely the seashore, with forested, verdure-clad cliffs or mountains (broken occasionally by river-valleys) on one side, and on the other, palm groves and limestone rocks or coral reefs, over which the blue sea breaks in fountains of snowy foam when the northern breeze blows stiffly. Amid these reefs there are marvellous sea-gardens, wherein from the road parapet immediately above you can descry sponges, anemones and polyps, sea-lilies, crabs, and parrot-coloured fish, through a film of blue-green water in times of flat calm.

One element of the picturesqueness of Jamaican scenery is the limestone formation which is characteristic of so much of the coast and the lower mountain ranges. Rainwater has carved the limestone into remarkable amphitheatres, known locally as "cockpits" (Kingston harbour is really a submerged cockpit), or has washed out large and small caverns—many a one of which along the north coast must have been seen by Shakespeare with the intuition of genius when he described the island home of Prospero. Or there are natural bridges; strange tunnels through which a stream disappears underground to emerge on the other side of a mountain as a full-blown river. The entrances to these caverns, worthy of Prospero or Merlin, are hung with fantastic curtains of trailing aroids and cacti, draperies of maidenhair ferns, and matted tangles of pink begonias. On the white limestone rocks lizards of blended ultramarine, grass-green, and dull red bask in the sun. Humming-birds with emerald gorgets and long black plumes to their tails flutter in the sunlight round the tubular blossoms—orange, blue, mauve, rose-pink, waxy-white, purple, lavender, and sulphur-yellow—of a hundred different kinds of creepers, lianas, or rock-dwelling plants. Some caverns might be arranged for Sycorax rather than Prospero and Ariel. Their portals are wreathed with snaky cacti or are defended by stiff *Bromeliaceæ*, whose sharp-pointed leaves are armed with the teeth of a saw. The limestone bottoms of the tranquil streams and still pools where the overflowing waters of Jamaica rest after precipitous descents from mountain peak to valley, give a lovely tone of blue-green to the clear water which is a frequent interlude in the landscapes to the limestone crags, cliffs, boulders, and caverns.

The splendidly made, limestone-surfaced, parapeted roads of the Jamaica coast-line

253. A ROAD IN WESTERN JAMAICA

lead the delighted traveller past one romantic harbour after another—harbours partly enclosed by fantastic Capri-like islands, where picturesque sailing craft (the hulls often painted bright red) lie in still waters of purple and green, alongside piers of bamboo and palm, at which they unload or receive brightly coloured cargoes of fruit or foreign produce. The harbours mostly bear Spanish names, and are frequently reminders of some episode in the history of Jamaica during the sixteenth, seventeenth, and eighteenth centuries. Here was a pirate stronghold; there was the last stand of the Spaniards. From that ruined fort, half overgrown by palmetto palms, may have been witnessed the decisive defeat of a Spanish or French attack, or the capture of a contraband slave ship. The ruined dwelling-houses and sugar-mills tell of a less distant past when, under the changing industrial condition of Jamaica—the transition from slavery to eventual free labour and the competition of beet-sugar—many an old free-living family of British Jamaicans came to financial grief. The old home was abandoned, and the sugar plantation gave way in course of time to coffee, oranges, cacao, or bananas. The ruins may not be more than sixty to a hundred years old, but they have sometimes the dignity of a mouldering castle or monastery. The climate of Jamaica has coloured the walls of stone or brick with brilliant lichens and thick green moss-ferns in every cranny, and perpendicular fringes of the *Rhipsalis* cactus, like mistletoe in its growth.[1] Lofty trees grow from the desecrated alcoves or the bow-windowed front of a drawing-room. The unheeded leat of water which once played some important part in the industry of the sugar-mill now drips away to form a magnificent pool of water-hyacinths. The crumbling masonry tank that was once a refreshing plunge-bath has become the dry playground of brilliant-coloured lizards.

Yet in close proximity to these ruins are spick-and-span verandahed houses of painted wood, mounted high above the ground on pillars or blocks of concrete, approached by flights of steps and terraces of stone or brick, bright with flowering shrubs or roses. There are ruined churches—why ruined no one can tell me, since they were abandoned long before the recent earthquake—and within sight of them new chapels of wood and corrugated iron. Corrugated iron, indeed, enters somewhat too lavishly into the modern architecture of Jamaica, from the negro cottage to the Government building. A much

254. A TINY HARBOUR ON THE NORTH COAST OF JAMAICA
Once a pirate stronghold in the early eighteenth century

more picturesque form of roofing is the American shingle of pine wood. The Spanish tile seems to be unused. As a rule, however, the Jamaican towns and villages are pleasing to the eye. There is no uniformity in the style of houses, and they are usually gay with colour or dazzling white with limewash; and, of course, every dwelling is surrounded by magnificent foliage and brilliant flowers—*Hibiscus*, *Thunbergia*, *Bignonia*, *Petræa*, and *Bougainvillea*; by the red, yellow-green, and purple leaves of the crotons; and by glossy orange trees hung with their golden balls or thickly set with odorous blossom, *Citrus racemosus* with its lemon-yellow globes, the crimson-fruited akees, and the purple-and-green star-apples.

Though a constant destruction of bird-life has been going on at the hands of the European and negro gunners, partly to supply the plumage market, wild birds are still a feature in Jamaican scenery. Besides the two or three species of humming-birds, there is another exquisite form in the green tody, the "robin" of the Jamaican negroes. This is a tiny bird distantly related to the kingfisher group, with long flat yellow beak and a plumage of emerald-green, shading here and there into green-blue, and in addition a splendid patch of scarlet feathers on the throat and breast. The orange quits (*Glossoptila*) are worthy of remark: their plumage is deep smalt-blue, with orange throat,

[1] For an illustration of this epiphytic *Rhipsalis* see page 320.

Then there are the black *Crotophaga* cuckoos with parrot-like beaks, the tyrant birds with crests of black and lemon-yellow and shouting cries, the copper-coloured, rosy-tinted mountain pigeons, the tiny little ground-doves, the green pink-cheeked parrots, the large buzzards (almost the size of eagles), and, above all, the vulture-like turkey buzzards (*Cathartes aura*), whom the Jamaicans call "John Crows."

So as to include in this survey all portions of America which are mainly inhabited by Negroes or Negroids, it is necessary to make a brief reference to the Cayman Islands, which lie to the west-north-west of Jamaica. The largest of the three, Grand Cayman, is 178 miles distant from the western extremity of Jamaica, and is about eighty-five square miles in area. Altogether the group

255. CAYMAN ISLANDERS, GRAND CAYMAN

of three islands (Grand Cayman, Little Cayman, and Cayman Brac) has a habitable land surface of 100 square miles.

Geographically they belong to Cuba, though they may not have had any actual land connection: politically they have never been anything but British, though they were an early resort of the Anglo-French Buccaneers who, when harassed by British warships, fled thence to Louisiana. Since the latter part of the seventeenth century they have been under the British flag and the government of Jamaica. From this island they were colonised by Englishmen, who brought with them several hundred negro slaves. Besides this a number of derelict English seamen settled here during the nineteenth century. The population to-day numbers in all about 6000, 700 or 800 of whom are white, 2000 coloured, and the remainder negro. The people of all shades are vigorous, moral, and are increasing somewhat in numbers, though there is much temporary emigration. The proportion of illegitimate births is only 12·7, a great contrast to the rest of the West Indies, and to Jamaica especially.

"There is no pauper-roll and little actual poverty. All the colonists are freeholders: a rented house is practically unknown."[1] The homesteads are quoted as remarkably tidy, and although the islands are well furnished with courts and jails, there is hardly any crime. "My experience of the Negro here is that he is a law-abiding, respectful and honest man. He does not ape European customs and manners, except so far as his clothes are concerned" (*G. S. S. Hirst*). Education is described as "neglected." In 1905 a law was passed in the island's legislature establishing elementary schools in each district. Of course, as soon as the Devil heard of this, he sent a devastating hurricane (in 1907) and blew down nearly all the schools. The parents then —perhaps wisely—gave up a futile struggle with the Evil One and relapsed into apathy on the subject of reading and writing.

The local legislature referred to is styled "Justices and Vestry." It is composed of magistrates appointed by the Governor of Jamaica and vestrymen elected by the people. Its laws are subject to the sanction of the Governor of Jamaica, who also appoints the Commissioner who directs the affairs of the three islands. The people in Grand Cayman belong mainly to the Presbyterian Church, and in Little Cayman and Cayman Brac to the Baptist Church.

The Cayman Islanders are chiefly seafaring in their occupations. Those to whom a sea life is distasteful usually emigrate to Nicaragua or the Southern States, but return home to spend the money they have earned. Indeed, were it not for a hurricane once in ten years (the islands are low in many parts, nowhere reaching to more than 150 feet above sea-level, and therefore very unprotected) one cannot imagine their wishing to live anywhere else: for they are very slightly taxed, and their three islands teem with the romance of buried pirate-treasure; with natural curiosities in the way of stupendous caves under the sea, subterranean passages, and an immense natural cistern in the middle of a cliff of solid flint, together with dense coco-nut groves on the two little islands and, on Grand Cayman, splendid forests of mahogany, cedar (*Juniperus*), and most of the timber and dye-woods of Jamaica and Yucatan. There are remarkable orchids, found nowhere else; and there is a pretty species of Chrysotis parrot peculiar to Grand Cayman.

The principal industries are the export of coco-nuts, shipbuilding from the timber of Grand Cayman; the working of phosphates, the capture of Green turtle and Hawk's-bill (tortoiseshell) turtle on the rocks and in the shoal water to the north-east of Nicaragua; the making of basket-work, etc., out of the young leaves of the *Inodes* palmetto palm; the breeding and export of cattle, ponies, goats, rabbits, and poultry; and lastly, most fascinating of all occupations! the fishing for pink pearls obtained from the large conch shells.

[1] Mr. Frank Cundall, F.S.A., from whose *Handbook of Jamaica* some of this information is drawn, the remainder being supplied by His Honour the Commissioner (G. S. S. Hirst, Esq.).

CHAPTER XI

SLAVERY UNDER THE BRITISH—*Continued*

(BAHAMAS, WINDWARD ISLANDS, TRINIDAD, BRITISH HONDURAS, AND BRITISH GUIANA)

THE BAHAMAS are the vestiges of an archipelago of large, flat islands stretching between the vicinity of Northern Hispaniola and the coast of Florida, connected most nearly (so far as shallowness of water is concerned) with the north coast of Cuba, separated from Hispaniola by a narrow, but very deep trough, and from Florida by a strait of water which has an average depth of three thousand feet. The Great Bahama Bank (of which the Islands of Andros, New Providence, and Eleuthera are fragments) was once a huge island larger than Hispaniola. Its upper surface is entirely composed of and overlaid by a sedimentary limestone composed of coral and other calcareous detritus. Apparently the archipelago is again rising above the surface of the sea. It offers now, excluding mere rocks, an area of 4241 square miles.[1]

256. AN OLD FORT, DATING FROM THE EARLY EIGHTEENTH CENTURY
Near Nassau, New Providence Island

The Bahamas were the first portion of the New World reached by Columbus, who landed at Watling Island on October 12th, 1492. They were found to be inhabited by a friendly race of Amerindians, named by the Spaniards "Lucayans," and obviously related in race and language to the Arawaks of Porto Rico, Haiti and Cuba.

[1] About half the size of Wales, and larger than Jamaica; but this estimate is now disputed and the total land surface of the 29 islands, 661 "cays" or islets and 2387 rocks, is placed at 5450 square miles.

During the fifty years following Columbus's landfall the Spaniards lured away the Lucayans to service in Hispaniola, Cuba and the American mainland, or, if they would not come willingly, took them away by force. It is generally assumed that none of these Amerindians remained in the Bahamas when the British began to settle here after 1629; but a few may have lingered till the eighteenth century in the island of Andros.

A few English colonists came out in 1629 under a patent of Charles I and settled on the little island "New Providence,"[1] but twelve years afterwards the Spaniards descended on them and wiped them out. In 1649 a band of English people from the Bermuda Islands, expelled from that colony for their religious dissent, settled on the Bahaman island of Eleuthera and apparently brought some negroes with them. In 1666 New Providence was recovered from the Spaniards and settled anew, and in 1670 Charles II gave a Charter for

257. A STREET IN NASSAU, SHOWING CHRISTCHURCH CATHEDRAL

the Bahamas to the Lords-Proprietors of the newly created Carolina territory, through whose efforts in 1672 the total population of the Northern Bahamas was raised to about five hundred persons.

But even before this date the archipelago with its intricate channels, reefs, sand-banks, sheltered harbours, supplies of salt for meat and fish-curing, springs of fresh water, its facilities for whale hunting, and treasures of washed-up ambergris, its shipbuilding timber (*Juniperus barbadensis* or "cedar") and dye-woods,[2] and above all its splendid healthiness, had become the chosen resort and stronghold of the pirates and buccaneers of the Gulf of Mexico and Caribbean Sea. From these islands the piratical ships of the English, and sometimes the French and Dutch, preyed on Spanish commerce and attacked rich Spanish-American coast towns. Many of the seamen on these pirate ships were negroes.

Consequently the Spaniards again in 1684 and in 1703 seized and held the

[1] This name was not given to the island till 1667.

[2] Logwood and Braziletto. "Braziletto" (*Cæsalpinia vesicaria*) is a near relation of Brazil wood. It produces a bright red or orange dye.

settlement of Nassau and carried off the English pirate-colonists. But the place was soon regained, and at last the British Government took its duties seriously. The Lords-Proprietors of North and South Carolina surrendered their Bahaman charter to the Crown,[1] and King George I sent a gallant sea-captain—Admiral Woods Rogers—to govern the Bahamas and exterminate the pirates. Also the Hanoverian king was instrumental in obtaining for New Providence Island a potent addition to its white population—a band of Germans from the Rhine. By 1770 the British settlements in the Bahama Islands had a population of two thousand whites and one thousand negro slaves. About this time the cultivation of cotton had been introduced from Georgia, the seed being of the Persian variety. More slaves were imported to work this cotton, and over four thousand acres had been planted by 1783.

258. THE GOVERNOR OF THE BAHAMA ISLANDS ON HIS WAY TO OPEN HOUSE OF ASSEMBLY, 1908

After the close of the American War in 1783 (in the course of which war Spain had seized and garrisoned the island of New Providence, and had been turned out of it by a small force of British-American Loyalists from South Carolina and Florida), the Bahamas seemed to offer a welcome refuge to those subjects of Great Britain in the Southern States of the new Union who had taken the part of the British Government in the struggle, and now found it difficult to settle down under the Stars and Stripes. Accordingly, between 1784 and 1786 about four thousand white British-Americans and six thousand negro slaves arrived in the Bahamas, where the white men were given free grants of land. The new-comers went to work vigorously to plant cotton, and in a few years had added three thousand acres to the area already under cotton. Unfortunately they also brought with them a spirit of harshness in their "slave-driving" and their general treatment of negroes which had not hitherto been characteristic of the Bahaman whites. At first the new colonists were not well received by the old-established settlers, and attempts were made to deny them

[1] Their proprietary rights were bought up by the British Government in 1787.

the right to the franchise and membership of the House of Assembly. But by about 1790 all this sentiment had passed away, and all white planters, whether of American or European origin, were united in opposing any humane measures which were put forward by the Governor for ameliorating the condition and treatment of the slaves. The Governor, on his part, was constrained to move in the matter because of the growing feeling in the British House of Commons relative to the wrongs of slavery, a feeling which put pressure on the Government of the day, and caused the Secretary for War and the Colonies to urge on the colonial legislatures new and more humane slave laws.

In the Bahama Islands an Act was passed in 1796 dealing with the treatment of slaves, which was obviously based, like much contemporary legislation in the British West Indies, on the provisions of the Spanish Code of 1789 (see pp. 43–6). Slaves above ten years of age were to be provided with the following food allowance: either one peck of unground maize or sorghum, or twenty-one pints of wheat flour, or seven quarts of rice; fifty-six pounds of potatoes or yams per week, over and above a sufficient quantity of land for the slave to cultivate and use as a kitchen garden or orchard. Children were to receive half this food allowance. No infirm or aged slave was to be abandoned by the owner, but to be properly provided for. Two suits of proper and sufficient clothing were to be granted to each slave in the course of every year. Slaves were to be instructed in the Christian religion and to be baptised. Mutilation of slaves was to be severely punished, and if necessary the slave was to be freed by the court. Moreover, the law was not to direct slaves to be mutilated for any offence. The killing of a slave wilfully and with malice aforethought was to be adjudged murder, and to be punished with death without benefit of clergy. Any person wantonly or cruelly whipping or otherwise maltreating, imprisoning, or confining without proper support a slave, was to be punished by fine and imprisonment. No slave was to receive more than twenty lashes at any one time or for any one offence, unless the owner, or the keeper of a gaol, was present; and under no circumstances was the flogging to consist of more than thirty-nine lashes. "And whereas a mischievous practice hath prevailed in some of the colonies of punishing ill-disposed slaves and such as are apt to abscond, by fixing iron collars with projecting bars or hooks round their necks; be it enacted and declared that such practice is utterly unlawful."

259. A GOOD TYPE OF NEGRO SEAMAN

Capt. B——, a shipmaster of the Bahama Islands

Equally unlawful was the loading of the body of such a slave with weights and iron chains, except such as were absolutely necessary for securing the person of a slave in confinement. Every slave was to be allowed Christmas Day and the two following working days as a holiday. Free people of colour shielding or concealing runaway slaves might suffer loss of freedom as a punishment. A slave offering violence by striking or otherwise to any white person might be punished with death. Any slave who played at dice or cards, or was guilty of any kind of gaming, would be publicly whipped.

From the very commencement of the nineteenth century to the abolition of slavery in 1833, the House of Assembly which debated and passed the laws for this scattered archipelago was in constant conflict with the Governor or the Attorney-General or the British Colonial Office over the treatment of slaves. The members of the Assembly—needless to say—were all white, and were elected until 1834 by a purely white electorate, perhaps averaging in numbers about two thousand men.[1] The slaves numbered about ten thousand during the first quarter of the nineteenth century. There were three or four

260. A GROUP OF NEGRO PEASANT WOMEN AND CHILDREN, BAHAMA ISLANDS

thousand free negroes and mulattoes, but (until 1834) they possessed no civic rights.

Perhaps nowhere in the West Indies did the white planters fight more doggedly to maintain the abuses of slavery than in the Bahamas. The flogging of women slaves was regarded as a very Ark of the Covenant. Once take away from the Bahaman cotton-planter this legal right to be vilely inhumane, and the prosperity of the Bahama Islands would crumble and disappear. The oft-times ferocious and lubric flogging of female slaves did not come to an end until the abolition of slavery in 1834. Negro men and women were not infrequently whipped to death. One typically horrible case is recorded in

[1] The sum total of whites as late as 1831 was only 4240.

1833 by Lieut.-Governor B. T. Balfour as having just occurred on Watling's Island (Columbus's landfall). A slave was suspended from a beam by the hands and feet, face downwards. Another slave was placed across the suspended body and whilst in that posture a merciless flogging was administered, with the result that death ensued (apparently to both).

Before 1796 there was practically no legal limit to the number of lashes which might be laid on the quivering body of a male or female slave, but in that year a law of the Assembly grudgingly limited the number to thirty-nine; a limitation contemptuously disregarded in practice, and with safety, as slaves might not testify against their masters; planters, with one or two exceptions, never told tales of each other, and white juries never convicted white men of cruelty to negroes. Some slight reforms, however, were effected in 1824. In that year a law was enacted permitting a slave to purchase his freedom at current prices from his master. In 1829 the slave laws of the Bahamas were consolidated and further improved as regards humane treatment of the slave, though the legislators still clung to the privilege of whipping women as well as men. Nevertheless they stuck into the new Act the usual sickening humbug about religious instruction being given to the men and women whom at their own wicked will they might, in savage moods, torture and kill with virtual immunity.

261. A NEGRO DWELLING ON A COUNTRY ROAD, NEW PROVIDENCE ISLAND, BAHAMAS

At last in 1834 came abolition of slavery, followed by four years of enforced apprenticeship. The slave-owners were compensated from the pocket of the British taxpayer to the extent of a little over £20 per slave. In 1838 the last cargo of African slaves had been landed on the Bahama Islands (for the *trade* in slaves with Africa did not really receive its death-blow in the British West Indies until slavery itself was abolished); and from about 1840 onwards the Bahama archipelago entered on a new and more prosperous life.

During the last hundred years the white element in the population has risen from about 4000 to over 16,000,[1] and the negro or coloured element, from

[1] Excepting for about seven thousand, the bulk of the white people of the Bahamas (many of them derived from the United States between 1783 and 1868) are rather a poor lot physically and mentally.

an approximate 12,000 to 44,000. The negroes of the Bahamas have been derived from the Niger delta, Dahomé, the Eastern Gold Coast, and the Congo. They have fused into a stalwart type, and a healthy one, except for leprosy, which is the curse of some of the islands. An interesting point about the Bahama negroes is the relative frequency of polydactylism—six fingers and six toes.

262. A CORNER OF THE EXTERIOR OF THE "COLOURED" PEOPLE'S CHURCH OF ST. AGNES, NASSAU

The Bahamas have possessed since their more definite establishment as a British Colony in 1719 a Constitution based on an Elective House of Assembly. From 1834 the franchise to elect and the right to be elected to this Assembly have been shared by negroes and negroids with the white race. There is a Legislative Council of nine members nominated by the Crown, among whom are one or two coloured men; and there is the nearly two-hundred-years-old House of Assembly. This consists of twenty-nine members, elected by male British subjects who have resided at least a year in the Bahamas, and who possess land of at least £5 in value, or occupy premises at a minimum rental of £2 8s. (in New Providence Island, or £1 4s. in the other islands). The qualification for membership is the possession of an estate or of personal property worth not less than £200. At present there are *six* negroes or men of colour in the House of Assembly.

Education in the Bahamas seems to be somewhat lacking according to the criticisms, public and private, which have come under my eyes. A Government system of primary education commenced in 1847. A Board of Education now supervises the instruction given in the colony by Government or subsidised schools. There are now 46 undenominational primary Government schools with nearly 7000 scholars on the roll; and 16 partly aided schools. In addition, 26 schools are supported and directed by the Church of England and are attended by about 1600 scholars. Three Roman Catholic schools (chiefly for girls, with 500 pupils) are maintained by the Roman Church. Further there are 16 private schools for the tuition of the children of parents who can afford to pay for a superior education. Government primary

263. INTERIOR OF ST. AGNES' CHURCH, NASSAU

This is said to be due to much in-and-in breeding, and the results are evident in the large percentage of blind, deaf and dumb, deformed, paralysed, idiot, scrofulous, tuberculous, and leprous people. "Close intermarrying without the elimination of abnormalities has been productive of a shocking condition of degeneracy." See for details *The Bahama Islands*, by George B Shattuck (New York: 1905). But it is clear from subsequent researches that many of the "poor" whites and the negroes of the Bahamas are suffering from anæmia caused by the "Hook-Worm" disease. See p. 17 *et seq.*

education is free, and education is compulsory in New Providence and the larger islands.

A good secondary education is given almost gratuitously in the Nassau Grammar School and St. Hilda's School (for young women), both of which are conducted by the Church of England. There is also Queen's College, a teaching institution supported by the Wesleyan Church.

The complaints generally uttered about the style of education given in the Bahama Islands would seem to concentrate on this point: that the instruction is not sufficiently shaped to meet the immediate modern needs of the Bahamans; is not practical enough.[1] In 1905 (partly in consequence of the utterance given

264. A SPONGE-DRYING YARD, NASSAU

in the foot-note), a "Young Men's Intellectual and Industrial Institute" was founded on the lines of the American Hampton and Tuskegee; and this has

[1] The remarks on this subject made by a former Governor (Sir Gilbert Carter) in 1904 are worth quoting:—

"I fear that in this colony the type of education provided under the auspices of the Government is not that which is best suited to the needs of the masses, and if any real progress is to be effected, a radical alteration must be made in the present system. It may be said that none of the boys reached by the Education Act proceed with their studies after leaving school. As a rule, the main object of the parents is to get them away from school, so that their services may be utilised on board a sponger or in some form of manual labour. In the very unlikely event of a boy showing an aptitude for book-learning, and making the best use of his training, his great ambition is to become a clerk in a store, or possibly to enter the Government service. But the demand for this form of labour is extremely limited and very poorly remunerated, whereas there is need for a good class of artisans. At present there is not one master carpenter, blacksmith, or mason in the colony, and no means of training these and possible exponents of other industrial arts. There are men who build houses and small craft, and fashion wood and iron into various shapes; but it is the 'rule of thumb' which reigns, and there is little of the precision which comes of the trained hand and eye in conjunction with a trained mind. What is wanted here is a system based on that so ably conducted by Mr. Booker Washington at Tuskegee, Alabama, United States of America, and until that or some similar scheme based upon industrial training as the main factor in the educational method is adopted, I fear that no improvement in the condition of the large native population in this colony will be manifested. It is easy, however, to make a destructive criticism; but although an alternative system may be advocated, it is almost impossible in a colony like this, where the revenue is never sufficient for the calls upon it, to make the radical change which would be necessary in order to place this question upon a proper foundation, and unfortunately so far little disposition has been shown by the Legislature to assist the Government in its efforts to encourage practical agriculture, which, after all, is the industry upon which the mass of the people must rely, and about which at present they know next to nothing."

now become the "The Baynton Normal and Industrial Institute," duly incorporated.

The supreme industry of the Bahamas is sponge-fishing: an enterprise which employs over 6000 negro men and boys, a few negro women, and a hundred or so white men. Nearly 300 schooners and over 300 sloops of a total tonnage of about 7000 tons, and about 2700 open boats, form the fleet of the sponge-fishing industry. The search for sponges (by diving) and "pink pearls," and the capture of turtles for "tortoiseshell," besides the catching and curing of fish and the collection of beautiful shells, are maritime pursuits which have made the Bahaman negro a seaman of daring, resource, and instinctive local knowledge.

Another important industry carried on principally by negro labour is the cultivation of "Bahama hemp" or "Sisal." This is a fibre-producing agave (*Agave sisalia*) introduced from Yucatan to the Bahamas in 1850. Excellent pineapples, oranges, and the huge delicious *Citrus racemosus* (perversely called by Americans "grape-fruit"—there being nothing about it to suggest a grape) are cultivated now and exported chiefly to the United States. The thin soil overlying the coral-limestone rock has become (except in the interior of the larger islands) too exhausted for cotton-growing. A good deal of salt is still manufactured for West Indian consumption from the stagnant pools and lakelets of intensely salt water on the more southern islands of the group.

265. A SPONGE CART IN THE STREETS OF NASSAU

In the better-populated islands the Bahamans may be described as industrious, besides possessing many other good qualities. The women in their homes manufacture table-cloths, napkins, materials for dresses, etc., out of fine linen in what is called "Spanish drawn-thread work." This is eagerly bought up by American tourists, who are increasingly resorting to the Bahama Islands to spend the winter months.[1] The Bahaman women (negress or coloured) are deft and tasteful as dressmakers; to such a degree that many American women-visitors take advantage of their winter stay in New Providence to get smart dresses made for summer wear.

The negro men are chiefly engaged in husbandry[2] and seafaring pursuits. Those that are town-dwellers go in for almost every avocation that attracts the white man. They are (unskilled) masons, carpenters and joiners; storekeepers, engineers, blacksmiths; lawyers, doctors, ministers in chapels; clerks, minor officials, postmen, policemen, firemen, volunteer soldiers, and musicians. Wages are very low: ranging from 3s. to 18s. a week; 10s. being the average.

[1] Among the other assets of this group, and a great attraction to the tourists, are the lovely natural aquariums among the white coral rocks, and the breeding-places of thousands of rosy flamingoes and pelicans.

[2] Most of them work for white employers on the various plantations; but every negro family living outside the towns has its own orchard and kitchen garden, looked after mostly by the women. Curiously enough, however, Governor Carter reported a few years back that the negro peasantry think it much more stylish to eat canned fruit and vegetables from abroad. and provisions generally that are grown on the spot and not imported and preserved are considered to be "low down."

There is not much serious crime in the Bahamas ; such as there is, is more common, proportionately, among the indigenous white population than among the coloured. The Bahaman negro bears a good reputation in this American Mediterranean. He is honest in big things, exceedingly good-tempered, brave, law-abiding, and hard-working. Perhaps rather superstitious; for Obia practices still linger amongst the peasantry and fetishes are still hung on the fruit trees to protect them.

Among themselves the negroes of the Bahamas are charitable and even provident. Except in the semi-barbarous, sparsely-populated, outlying islands they all belong to mutual help societies which provide funds for burying the dead, for relief in sickness, and also act as savings-banks. The affairs of these benefit associations are conducted with remarkable shrewdness and

266. A SISAL FIBRE PLANTATION, BAHAMA ISLANDS

honesty. Noteworthy amongst them is that of the "Congo United Society." This has an adult membership of more than six hundred, besides a juvenile branch. It was founded by Congo slaves towards the close of the Slavery period. Although many of its members are illiterate the affairs of the society are administered honestly and wisely.[1]

Another method of promoting thrift is apparently of Yoruban origin. Little associations called "Asu" are formed of one or two dozen people who agree to contribute weekly a small sum towards a common fund. Every month (?) the amount thus pooled is handed to a member, in order of seniority of admission, and makes a little nest-egg for investment or relief. These "Asu" have no written statutes or regulations, no regular officers, but carry on their affairs without fraud or miscalculation.

Altogether the outlook for the Negro in the Bahamas is hopeful. The present population—over 60,000—is ridiculously small for a habitable area of 4000 square miles enjoying a perfectly salubrious climate and free from most tropical diseases. Though the cultivable soil is thin and has been

[1] Dr. A. R. Holly, in letter to author.

exhausted in many places, it can easily be renewed by local manures—phosphates, guano, dead fish, etc. The average annual rainfall is fifty inches, and vegetation is so abundant on the larger islands (in the interior) as to create serious obstacles to exploration. It is indeed a fact that the whole surface of Andros Islands[1] (about 2300 square miles in extent) has not yet

267. THE "GRAPE-FRUIT" (CITRUS RACEMOSUS)

been examined by a white man; and down to a hundred years ago Lucayan aborigines were believed to be lurking unseen in the dense forests. These forests contain mahogany, pines, fan-palms, junipers ("cedars"), wild cinnamon (canella bark), the handsome Quassia tree (*Simaruba*), Gum-elemi, numerous splendid flowering trees (native or introduced), and others valuable for their dyes, drugs, perfumes, timber, bark, or fruit. Many of these trees are

[1] It is really one huge island 109 miles long by 22 miles broad, but pierced through the middle by a number of shallow channels of salt water.

low-growing, sturdy, and gnarled (as compared to their congeners in the more mountainous West India Islands), because one of the drawbacks of the Bahamas is their low elevation (the highest hills are scarcely over 250 feet), and the fierce winds from the open Atlantic sweep over them unopposed.

The mean track of those awful Hurricanes[1], which are the supreme curse (balanced by an otherwise superb endowment) of the West Indies, lies fre-

268. AN INCIPIENT HURRICANE

quently across the *easternmost* islands of the widespread Bahama archipelago, and these perhaps will never be desirable sites for colonisation. But hurri-

[1] The West Indian hurricanes for the most part originate in the seas around the Lesser Antilles, or to the eastward of that chain. The rare cyclones of June and July usually spring up in the Caribbean Sea near the north coast of South America or in the vicinity of Trinidad. The course of all the hurricanes is *invariably* from the south and east to the west and north, with a curve, slight or abrupt, in the middle of their course. Violent winds occur off the Georgian and Florida coasts occasionally in May, but not in the West Indies. Cyclonic winds in this region or in the Caribbean may commence in June and are more frequent in July. But *August* is pre-eminently *the* hurricane month. September and October are bad. November shows an occasional, rare cyclonic wind. After that there is peace and safety till June or July. The mean track of the worst August-October hurricanes lies from the chain of the Lesser Antilles, along the north coasts of Hispaniola and Cuba, through either the north-west or south-east of the Bahamas to Florida. Jamaica has frightful thunderstorms accompanied by incredible deluges of rain, but is not often ravaged by a cyclonic wind. The Lesser Antilles, and especially the Leeward Islands, suffer most frequently from devastating hurricanes.

These disturbances are more frequent, and cause more loss of life and damage to property than earthquakes. From earthquakes, Trinidad, the Windward Islands, Barbados, and all the Lesser Antilles (except St. Thomas) are practically free. Hispaniola and Jamaica have suffered much, Cuba a little, the Bahamas not at all. It ought to be within the limits of Man's science in the next hundred years to acquire a control over the meteorological causes which create violent disturbances of the air and so put a stop to hurricanes and cyclones. When this comes about, and disease is also eliminated by the extirpation of insect pests, then, indeed, will the West Indies become the Earthly Paradise!

canes also afflict the north-western islands of the group. Yet the Bahamas are not so often or so severely ravaged by these cyclonic disturbances as the continent of North America, the Greater and Lesser Antilles. Moreover, the Bahama Islands are outside the Earthquake area, and thus enjoy an enormous advantage over the Greater and Lesser Antilles, Central and South America.

The British WINDWARD ISLANDS of to-day consist of St. Lucia, St. Vincent, Grenada, and the Grenadines (an area of 524 square miles). During the seventeenth century these islands were mainly given up to the Caribs by the French and English pirates as some compensation for turning these fierce Amerindians out of the Leeward Islands.

269. THE LITTLE "PITON" (ONE OF TWO ENORMOUS PERPENDICULAR ROCKS), ST. LUCIA ISLAND

All through the period from 1627 to 1803 the island of St. Lucia was alternately French and British; St. Vincent from 1627 to 1796, and Grenada and the Grenadines from 1762 to 1796, were likewise the battle-ground of the two Powers, being captured and recaptured, surrendered after successful naval engagements to be restored after treaties of peace. Since 1796 or 1803 they have all been British possessions.

Negro slaves were either brought hither from the British Leeward Islands or from Barbados (when the British got the upper hand), or came with French planters and adventurers from Martinique. On the whole the French-negro element has predominated, and the slaves (now the peasantry of these islands) speak a French jargon like the "Creole" tongue of Haiti, Guadeloupe, Dominica, and Martinique.

Between 1675 and the beginning of the eighteenth centuries several slave-ships were wrecked on the south coast of St. Vincent or on Bequia Island; the captive negroes escaped and made their way into the woods of the interior. Other fugitive negroes also fled to St. Vincent from Barbados and Martinique, and all found hospitality and shelter with the Caribs, who still possessed the interior of St. Vincent. The first instalment of negro immigrants (wrecked on Bequia in 1675) were "Mokos," or people from Old Calabar, the Cross River, and the vicinity of the Cameroons.

The Amerindian Caribs at first placed the negroes in a mild serfdom, but were annoyed at the frequency of their cohabiting with the Carib women, who readily conceived children by negro husbands. The Carib men at first plotted to kill these dark-skinned half-castes; but the negroes were now numerous.

270. KINGSTON, ST. VINCENT, WINDWARD ISLANDS

They rose against the Amerindians and drove them into a small part of north-west St. Vincent. The French from Martinique sought in 1719 to gain some advantage by taking the part of the Red Caribs (as the unmixed Amerindians were called) against the Black Caribs (Maroon negroes and Negro-Carib half-castes). But they were worsted in the attempt and driven off the island by the warlike blacks. Then came the English in 1723, but with no better if more peaceful results. After that for forty years the struggle between Carib and Negro went on, till the "Black" Caribs numbered several thousand and the "Red" Caribs two or three hundred. By the end of the eighteenth century the Red Caribs had become extinct, but the Black—about two-thirds Negro and one-third Carib—had developed into a very interesting and handsome type which must have resembled strongly some of the tall Melanesians of New Guinea and the Solomon Islands.

The British took definite possession of St. Vincent in 1763. By this time the Black Caribs had adopted French as their medium of communication, and some of their chiefs spoke French with elegance and aptness. They were inclined to protest against the partition of "their" island among British planters, denying to any European Power the claim to possess it. "We were cast ashore here or fled here from our oppressors. We intermarried with the original owners, the Caribs, then fought with and subdued them. It is our island now."

The Black Caribs were in 1773 (after much stiff fighting) induced to sign a treaty of peace and friendship, and about one-third of the island (at the north end of St. Vincent) was allotted to them as their exclusive property. But they continued to maintain some friendship for the French, and in 1779 assisted them to ravage British St. Vincent and conquer the island. St. Vincent was restored to Great Britain in 1783, but once again in 1795 it was

271. THE CARENAGE, GRENADA, WINDWARD ISLANDS

overrun by the Black Caribs. Sir Ralph Abercromby restored order in 1796, and to punish the Black Caribs for their unprovoked aggressions and many murders of white people the survivors among them (more than five thousand) were deported to the large island of Ruatan, off the north-east coast of what is now the independent republic of Honduras.[1]

The Caribs of Grenada had been brutally exterminated by the French between 1650 and 1656. From about 1670 a few hundred negro slaves were introduced into that island, and after 1713 until 1762 (when the island became definitely British) the French planters obtained considerable supplies of negroes

[1] In those days Britain maintained sovereignty over Ruatan and the "Bay" Islands, as part of the Honduras or "Mosquito" district where British adventurers went with negro slaves to cut mahogany. Other negro hybrids—independently of the Black Caribs—had somehow arisen in these coast districts of Northern and Eastern Spanish Honduras. They were known as the "Sambos," and gradually made common cause with the Black Caribs, as did some of the Amerindians of Honduras and Guatemala. The Carib negroids from St. Vincent now number some twenty or thirty thousand, and are the dominant people in this coast belt of Honduras. The negro element is dwindling under repeated crossing with the local Amerindian, but to this race they have imparted fertility and vigour and a superb physique. The descendants of the Black Caribs still retain the use of a French jargon (mixed with Carib) and adherence to Roman Catholic Christianity.

through the Dutch, so that by 1762 the number of slaves in the island (and the string of little islets known as the Grenadines) amounted to about 30,000. Under subsequent British and French rule (for France reoccupied Grenada in 1779–83) the amount of slaves decreased and a number of free blacks and mulattoes became landholders and planters. These retained their French sympathies. Indeed throughout the history of the West Indies and the Southern States of the North American Union it is remarkable—with the *sole* exception of St. Domingue—what a great hold the French quickly obtained over the negro and how loath the latter was to be transferred to the rule of the Anglo-Saxon. When that scourge of Britain in the Leeward and Windward

272. BY THE GRAND ÉTANG, INTERIOR OF GRENADA ISLAND, WINDWARD ISLANDS

Islands, Victor Hugues,[1] sent emissaries to Grenada (as to St. Vincent) in 1795, the French negroes and mulattoes rose against the British settlers under a mulatto leader named Jules Fédon and massacred without pity all the British on whom they could lay hands. Sir Ralph Abercromby suppressed the insurrection fifteen months afterwards.

St. Lucia was invaded by both British and French adventurers and settlers between 1635 and 1674, followed by alternate war and peace with the Caribs. The French intermarried with these Amerindians, who, by also mingling with the negroes that were introduced after 1674, became gradually absorbed into

[1] Victor Hugues was born of poor parents in France and went to Guadeloupe as apprentice to a hairdresser, afterwards becoming innkeeper, master of a small sailing-vessel, and then lieutenant in the French navy. Returning to France, he was elected a deputy to the National Assembly and attached himself to Robespierre, who in 1794 sent him as Commissioner to Guadeloupe. He was Governor of Cayenne from 1802 to 1809.

the parti-coloured community and by 1700 had ceased to exist as a separate people. The island was almost abandoned between 1666 and 1722 owing to its unhealthiness and the conflicting claims of France and England, but after that date, even though St. Lucia was declared neutral, the French and their negro slaves from Martinique began to colonise it in ever-increasing numbers until it was

273. THE NEGRO SOLDIER
A corporal of the British West India Regiment

definitely declared French in 1763. Thence to 1803 it remained French, except during brief British military occupations. During all this time the thirty or forty thousand negro slaves became thoroughly Frenchified in language and traditions. There were also wild maroon negroes in the mountains descended from the earliest slaves introduced in the seventeenth century and much mixed in blood with the Caribs. The French also had not disdained to interbreed with these two races, so that at the present day we are confronted with a very mixed type of negroid in Dominica, St. Lucia, and St. Vincent, speaking a French patois and obviously compacted of European, Amerindian, and Negro. St. Vincent Island had much to do with the formation of the West India regiments at the beginning of the nineteenth century during the Napoleonic wars. Even now this island furnishes recruits for the consolidated West India Regiment. An example of one is given here for the additional reason that it illustrates the fine-looking negroid type growing up in the Windward Islands.

In 1797 a Consolidated Slave Act was passed by the House of Assembly of Grenada (? and also of St. Vincent), which was of similar purport to the Bahama Act of 1796 (see p. 297). This improved the conditions of slave labour. The political constitutions of Grenada and St. Vincent were until 1876 similar to those of the other British West India islands (except St. Lucia), namely, consisting in part of elected legislators dependent on a popular franchise. To this franchise, after the abolition of slavery in 1834, negroes and men of colour were admitted on the same terms as white men. St. Lucia, however (held more or less under martial law until 1815), was never given a Constitution, and has always been a "Crown Colony." In 1876 the Constitutions of Grenada and St. Vincent (the two islands between them control the Grenadines) were surrendered to the Crown and replaced by Crown Colonial government: that is to say, the non-official members of the Legislative Council are nominated by the Crown, and are *not* elected on a franchise.

All things considered—the small size of the islands, the very diverse and mixed elements in the population[1]—this simplified character of the administration is best suited to their present requirements, though here and there a grumble may be heard from the educated men of colour of Grenada as to their exclusion from active political life and the too great preponderance in the Government of the white official element.

In 1778 a French colonist resident in Grenada, Monsieur Roume de St. Laurent, paid a visit to TRINIDAD, and was so struck by its many and great natural resources and the extraordinary fertility of the soil that he decided not only to settle in the island himself, but to do all he could to induce his countrymen and others to follow his example. The result of his efforts was a scheme of colonisation which was approved by the Court of Spain and chartered at Madrid on the 24th November, 1783. A new Spanish Governor, Don José Maria Chacon (speaking both French and English), was sent out to Trinidad in 1784 to put the new charter (printed simultaneously in Spanish, French, and English) into circulation and operation. The result of this liberal action on the part of Spain was the colonisation of Trinidad up to 1789 by nearly 11,000

[1] In St. Lucia there are now about 55,000 people, composed of 50,000 negroes and negroids, some 800 East Indian kulis, and 4200 whites and creoles, mostly of French descent.

In St. Vincent and Bequia there are 52,000 people—about 1000 British, 500 East Indians, 3000 Portuguese, and the remainder negroes and negroids, some of whom are slightly tinged with the old Carib intermixture.

In Grenada there is a population of about 70,000, out of which some 3000 are white or creole, and the remainder negro or negroid. Grenada is one of the most precious jewels in the West Indian chain. It is healthy, free from hurricanes, marvellously beautiful, and singularly fertile. Consequently it seems to be creating a special type of negro—good-looking and intelligent.

Almost the entirety of the negroes in the Windward Islands are Roman Catholic in religion and speak a French patois. St. Vincent is the most English of the lot. French culture, manners, and traditions have left a very strong impress on the 163,000 negroes and negroids of the Windward Islands.

French immigrants, mixed with a few Spaniards and Irish Roman Catholics. In 1793 more French came hither from Saint Domingue, and later on from other French West Indian islands after their seizure by the British forces. But in 1797 Trinidad was captured by a British fleet, and Don Chacon was succeeded as Governor of the island by Lieutenant-Colonel Picton. At this time there was a population of about 18,000 whites, two or three thousand negro slaves, and 1082 Amerindians, the survivors of the large "Indian" population originally inhabiting the island at the time of its discovery in 1498. As soon as Trinidad had been occupied by Great Britain many negroes were imported from Africa; but the slave-trade having been declared illegal in 1807, the labour supply for the sugar-planters was very inadequate. In 1851 only 8000 of the Trinidad negroes had been born in Africa, and there is scarcely any survivor at the present day of the ex-slave population not born in Trinidad, though there are a

274. OFF THE NORTH-WEST COAST OF TRINIDAD: THE "MOUTH OF THE DRAGON"

few free immigrants from West Africa. The negroes now inhabiting Trinidad are immigrants from Barbados, Jamaica, the Windward Islands, and Demerara, or the descendants of the negroes imported by the French and British prior to 1812.

In 1823 a series of resolutions was passed by the House of Commons of which the following is a summary, and these resolutions formed the basis of new legislation in the West Indian colonies, more especially in Trinidad, which being then, as now, a Crown Colony, had no elected Legislature to be consulted.

1. The flogging of female slaves was to be discontinued.

2. Effective and decisive measures were to be taken for the amelioration of the condition of slaves in order that they might be gradually fitted for participation in the rights and privileges of British citizenship, so that emancipation

might take place at the earliest period compatible with a fair consideration of the rights of private property. The Trinidad Order-in-Council which gave effect to these resolutions was published and put in force in 1824. Its more important provisions were as follows:—

A Protector of slaves was to be appointed to reside at the capital of the colony, there to have an office which should be free of access at all times to slaves, whose complaints were to be carefully noted; the Protector was not to be interested in slave property by ownership or management, or by guardianship of the owners of slaves; he was to keep the records of the operations of the slave laws, was to attend all trials affecting the lives or property of slaves; and in all his functions he was to have the assistance of the commandant of the military forces of the colony.

275. A FRUIT-SELLER, PORT OF SPAIN, TRINIDAD

Sunday markets were to be abolished throughout the colony; slaves were not to be allowed to work between sundown on Saturday evening and sunrise on Monday morning. The use of the whip or "cat" as a mark of the authority of the slave-driver was to be prohibited; only limited punishments restricted to twelve lashes were to be allowed to be inflicted on any one day; the flogging of females was altogether forbidden; and strict records of all punishments inflicted were to be kept on each plantation. With the consent of the owner, the commandant of the colony could issue licences for the marriage of slaves; husbands and wives were not to be separated from each other, nor children under fourteen years of age from their parents. Slaves were to enjoy property rights, householding and inheritance, etc.; savings-banks were to be established for the security of the property of slaves. The tax on manumissions was to be abolished; slaves were to be allowed to purchase their own freedom, or that of their wives or children; manumissions by private contract were to be in writing and made to the Protector. Slave evidence on oath was to be admitted to the courts in all cases; and ministers of religion were to certify as to the qualifications of slaves to be put on oath. Cruelty to a slave was to cause the right of the owner to hold the slave to be put at the discretion of the courts; a second conviction forfeited the right of the owner to hold any slave at all, or of the manager of a plantation to hold the position of a manager of slaves. In slave trials the burden of the proof was on the master. The Protector was to make an annual report of the conduct of his office, and the number of cases that came under his jurisdiction. This Order-in-Council represented the high-water mark of slavery legislation before the edicts of abolition; and if it had been copied and adopted in the United States forty years of suffering among four millions of people might have been avoided.

In 1837 some excitement was caused in Trinidad by a mutiny among the negro soldiers of the 1st West India Regiment, headed by a huge negro named Daaga or Donald Stewart.

Daaga was a slave-trader of the Pōpō country of Western Dahomé. He had raided the lands west of the Dahomé kingdom, had brought his captives to the coast and sold them to the Portuguese, when he himself and a few companions were lured on board a Portuguese ship, overpowered, and chained with the rest of the captives. On the journey across the Atlantic the slave-ship was captured by a British cruiser and taken with her cargo to the Wind-

276. A NEGRO HUT, TRINIDAD

ward Islands. Here Daaga and some of his companions were invited to join the 1st West India Regiment as recruits. They really wished, of course, to return to Dahomé, but had no option than to follow the wishes of their new captors. Still, after entering the British army and reaching Trinidad, Daaga and the other Pōpōs and many of the kindred Yorubas of the regiment plotted to rise against their white masters, and after overpowering them to march back to Guinea by land!

This mutiny of homesick slaves cost the life of one loyal black soldier, but no white man was killed or even wounded; indeed, Daaga intervened to prevent a white officer being injured. But thirty of the mutineers were killed in the fighting, six committed suicide, three were shot as a sentence of the court-martial (one of these was Daaga), and one was killed trying to escape.

Since those days, with the exception of a little negro rioting at the close of the nineteenth century (due to jealousy of the Indian kulis and discontent with the institution of a water-supply at Port of Spain), Trinidad has been tranquil and prosperous. There is a negro or negroid population now of about

277. A NEGRO COCONUT-SELLER IN TRINIDAD

150,000, together with 90,000 East Indians, about 5000 Chinese and unclassified hybrids, and nearly 50,000 whites of British, French, Corsican, German, Spanish and Portuguese descent. In the adjoining island of Tobago (which has been British since 1763 save for two intervals of French occupation) there are about 10,000 negroes or negroids out of a population of 19,000, the remainder being mainly whites descended from French colonists, from Courlanders or Baltic Finns, from Dutch and English.

In Trinidad the white population consists of about 10,000 unstable British [who—apart from the officials—have here no abiding city, but keep at the back of their minds a retirement to the United Kingdom when they can

278. INDIAN KULIS, TRINIDAD

afford it] and a staying Creole population to whom Trinidad is a lovely and a permanent home. With the French Creoles have mingled the descendants of the Spanish, Irish, and German settlers. The prevailing language is French or Creole French, and the religion of the majority is that of the Roman Catholic Church. There are now no pure-blooded living descendants of the Amerindian inhabitants, which even in the eighteenth century were still fighting with the Spaniards. As elsewhere they were largely exterminated by smallpox. In 1798 there were computed to be 1082; in 1830 about 700, and these were concentrated in and around the town of Arima in Northern Trinidad. From this period onwards the Amerindians melted rapidly into the negroid majority. Negro women manifested a preference for Amerindian husbands, and the females of this latter race preferred to mate with negroes, both proving the more fertile for the change.

The abolition of slavery and compulsory apprenticeship was fully effected in Trinidad by 1838, and in this same year the British Government was arranging in Calcutta with the Government of the East India Company for the recruitment of kulis to cultivate plantations in Guiana and the West Indies. For the first impulse of the Negro in Trinidad and elsewhere was to do nothing now that he was a free man. Scarcely a strange turn of mind on his part after being so long compelled to labour six or even seven days a week from dawn to sunset for another man's profit! Moreover, the natural tendency of the negro and negress is towards commerce, not agriculture. Digging and weeding the ground so bores the unregenerate, average negro that in his own continent he usually (though not always) turns over to his submissive women the toil of agriculture, and addicts himself to hunting and fishing, to warfare, to herding and tending flocks, and to trading. He likes a sea life, likes soldiering, likes palavering, law, politics, preaching, postman's work, domestic service, tailoring, shaving, building, timber-cutting, road-making, mining, porterage, engineering, hotel-keeping, horse-racing, quarrying, coal-heaving, diving for pearls, climbing for coconuts, and letting off fireworks. He dislikes most of all the very work he was brought specially to do in the New World—agriculture. Though, if he chooses, he can become a very good planter and field-hand, can attain to much and do much that the East Indian may never accomplish or even contemplate.

279. A CACAO TREE BEARING PODS OF COCOA BEANS

But between 1838 and 1845 the Trinidadian negro was taking things easy. Also there were not at that time, perhaps, more than 40,000 negroes in Trinidad. So in 1845 came the first batch of East Indian kulis to Trinidad. They were a success; and although many have returned with their savings to India, many out of the 144,000—in approximate numbers—who have reached Trinidad between 1845 and 1909 have remained there permanently. As they bring a considerable proportion of their women with them, they are not tempted to mix much with the negroids. In their new home they are developing into a very fine race from a physical standpoint, though they are much more backward in education—above all, world education—than the negro. But the importation of the Dravidian indentured labourer from the Panjab, from Eastern and Southern

India, was an excellent stimulus for the Negro. It was calling the Old World in to redress the balance of the New. Otherwise the Black man in British Tropical America had the White man at his mercy, and whilst the Negro took a hundred years to educate himself in true political economy (two-thirds of which is agriculture), the West Indies would have gone bankrupt.

Now such islands as Jamaica, Dominica, Grenada, and notably Trinidad (which last is specially endowed with its wonderful, inexhaustible supplies of asphalt-making, semi-fossil "pitch") are advancing towards permanent prosperity, because they possess in perfection—especially Trinidad—the right soil and climate for growing the Cacao tree. The world's demand for chocolate

280. THE SHALLOW COASTS OF WESTERN TRINIDAD

and cocoa, in spite of some fluctuations, is of necessity on the increase; and the parts of the earth's surface suited climatically to the growth of this product are very limited.

Trinidad[1] is a sumptuously beautiful country of 1754 square miles in extent.

[1] Jottings from my note-book on arriving at Port of Spain, Trinidad:—

The majestic cliffs and pierced, fantastic islands, crowned and draped with forest—above them storm clouds of superb shape with snowy, cauliflower crowns and fawn-grey, blue grey bodies and skirts. Extraordinary, stagy rainbows, often doubled, and the outer edge of the iris shading into rose pink. Sea glassy, reflecting everything in a softened satiny fashion. The awesome heights of frowning Venezuela (Trinidad beside this inky, jagged country looks the happy, graceful paradise it is). There is Patos Island, lying under the lee of Venezuela; fertile in disputes as to customs and contraband, for it is under the British flag by a wrench of geographical affinities

The steamer stops two miles from the shore of Port of Spain! The vast harbour is silting up. The shallow sea here is full of rising and sinking lavender-coloured Siphonophora, shaped like cups with a bunch of organs or tentacles at the top. These jelly-fish look like wonderful achievements in Venetian glass. . . .

On shore. Clean, straight streets and well-furnished stores. Electric trams. Stand-pipes with

It is one of the many earthly paradises which Fate has allotted to the control of Great Britain. There is a certain amount of malarial fever, especially along the

281. TREES IN TRINIDAD FESTOONED WITH THE RHIPSALIS "MISTLETOE" CACTUS

An epipbyte cactus which extends its range from tropical America to tropical Asia

supplies of pure water at frequent intervals. Everything looks very prosperous; the shops remind one much more of England than of America. The Indian kulis and the charming costumes of their handsome nose-jewelled women. On the quay there was a group of these Indian women clad in pure, undiluted orange robes. Against a background of pale azure, satin sea, and purple-green mountains it made a superb scheme of colour.

The negroes look much as they do in Jamaica, with perhaps a larger element of "white" in their composition and a slightly more Spanish appearance. I like to see them going about selling demure green-and-red parrots, a little in the style of pages carrying hawks on the fist. The parrots are all docility till they have been purchased; then they BITE!!

Outside the town there are spreading trees of immense size draped with the Rhipsalis cactus, which so strangely resembles the utterly unrelated Spanish moss. I looked hurriedly into the Lepers' Asylum. It is surrounded by a tall, pointed corrugated-iron fence, but inside there is a superb park. . . .

On the slopes of the mountains the forest with its immensely tall, white-stemmed trees and lavish inflorescence of the lower-growing trees and shrubs—scarlet, grey-white, pale mauve, pink, cream-colour, magenta—reminded me of the high woods of Sierra Leone in January.

coast and in the low-lying parts of the island where mosquitoes abound. The land rises, however, sufficiently into hills and even mountains to provide many cool places for the invigoration of the white man, and I cannot say that I thought the indigenous white people showed much sign of physical degeneration. They are, of course, a dark-haired, dark-eyed people, because of the considerable element of French and Spanish blood. But they are by no means a negligible quantity in the future politics of tropical America.

Partly, perhaps, owing to the clearly defined parti-coloured occupation of the island by a white race, a black race, and a yellow people (the East Indians), Trinidad has less in the way of representative government than any other British West India island, though as its conditions are very similar to those of British Guiana (where there *is* representative government which seems to work smoothly and satisfactorily) it is not easy to understand the long-continued tutelary condition of Trinidad; except that it is justified by its exceeding prosperity. The Legislative Council includes eleven unofficial members who are nominated (for five years) by the Governor. Amongst them, I believe, at the present day there are two persons of negro or negroid race. Two of the smaller towns have elective municipal councils; but the capital, Port of Spain, with nearly sixty thousand inhabitants, is managed by a board of thirteen persons nominated by the Governor, and including one or two negroes.

The large colony of BRITISH HONDURAS (7562 square miles), which lies on the east coast of Central America between Yucatan and Guatemala, began early in the seventeenth century by the attempts of the English buccaneers [under the leadership of a legendary Wallis[1]] to establish themselves. In 1638 an English ship was wrecked on the eastern coast of Yucatan, and such of the crew as escaped drowning settled there and somehow conveyed the news to the crews of other pirate ships that it was a goodly country. In 1642 English adventurers seized the island of Ruatan and held it for eight years, till a very large Spanish force compelled evacuation.

The Spaniards had already started a great industry in timber-felling, more especially to obtain logwood,[2] which had come into use in Europe as an invaluable deep black or purple dye.

For various reasons the Government of Queen Elizabeth and of the first two Stuarts were prejudiced against logwood (as a dye) and penalised its use. This prejudice, however, passed away, and about 1657 the British pirate-adventurers discovered, firstly, that logwood was worth £100 a ton, and

[1] Wallis or Wallace is said to have been a Scottish pirate-adventurer who harried the coasts of Yucatan at the beginning of the seventeenth century. The Spaniards corrupted his name into Valis or Balis, and this became later Balise and Belize Certainly in the eighteenth century the river on which this settlement was formed was called the "Wallis or Belize." But another and more probable explanation derives the name of this principal settlement near the mouth of the River Belize from "balise," a beacon or light-signal: a French term in use among the British-French buccaneers.

[2] Logwood, sometimes called Campeachy wood, is the timber of a beautiful tree of the bean order which is known to botanists as *Hæmatoxylon campechianum*. It grows freely on nearly all the West Indian islands, as well as in its original home, Central America. From its wood is obtained a powerful dye, which ranges in colour from blue-black to rich purple and pale mauve. It was much used at one time for colouring ink and adulterating port wine. The tree itself is always grateful to the eye, with abundant, graceful, evergreen mimosa-like foliage; and yellow blossoms exhaling the most delicious honeyed scent. When in full blossom each graceful tree or tall bush is completely covered with the mass of pale gold or straw-yellow flowers. It is one of the most beautiful sights in tropical America to see a grove of logwood trees in full blossom. Logwood is a distant relation of "Brazil-wood," the timber which yields a brilliant scarlet or crimson die, and is derived from trees of the leguminous genera *Cæsalpinia* and *Peltophorum*.

secondly, that it grew in profusion along the coasts facing the Bay of Honduras. About 1662, coming from Jamaica, they settled about the mouth of the River "Wallis" or "Belize," and also on the western side of Yucatan, from which they were eventually expelled by the indignant Spaniards, who carried off many of them to slave in the mines of Mexico. But on the south-eastern coast of Yucatan they stuck fast, and in 1670 the Spanish Government indirectly recognised their right, at any rate to cut logwood, in this region.

Nevertheless, having got rid of these obnoxious English heretics in the Campeche district of Yucatan, the Spaniards made a serious attempt in 1718 to abolish the Honduras settlements, and renewed their attacks at intervals throughout the eighteenth century whenever Spain was at war with Great

282. THE BELIZE RIVER, BRITISH HONDURAS

Showing motor-boat against the shore: this has become the most important means of transport in this colony

Britain. Nor can this obstinate clinging to the political rights of the King of Spain to all Central America be wondered at, when it was seen that the British, officially and unofficially, were aiming at occupying Central America themselves, and *as early as 1740* had projected an inter-oceanic canal through Nicaragua which would be under British control.

The Spaniards had neglected or abandoned this eastern side of Central America; and the Amerindian tribes along the coasts of Honduras and Nicaragua—"Mosquitia" or the Mosquito coast, as this low-lying, unhealthy region was called—received the English pirates, buccaneers, and timber-cutters with great friendliness, especially during the eighteenth century. British ships passed up the River San Juan into the great Nicaragua Lake, and realised then that it only needed a canal of about twenty miles to complete a through water route to the Pacific. The great Nelson took part in an invasion of Nicaragua by British ships in 1780.

Spain made her last warlike attack on the Belize settlements in 1798; after that, and the treaty-making which followed the close of the Napoleonic wars, the claim to British sovereignty over this south-eastern portion of Yucatan was fully recognised.

In their long struggle against the formidable Spanish power in Mexico and Guatemala the British settlers had undoubtedly been helped by their warlike negro slaves. Negroes were first introduced into this region about 1718 from Jamaica and the other West Indian islands, not direct from Africa. The value of a slave on importation was at least £120—a much higher price than ruled elsewhere at the same period. After being trained to the work of timber-cutting the value of the expert negro rose to as much as £300. Men of this price were not to be treated inconsiderately; they must be well fed, well clothed and housed, and given good reason to prefer servitude under a white master to a wild life in the woods, or flight to some Spanish settlement where they would be indulgently received. It was impossible to treat the select slaves of British Honduras with the restrictions on personal liberty necessary or customary on a West Indian plantation. The life of the woods was a life of liberty. "The slave was not driven in a gang to his daily toil, but worked side by side with his master, sharing with him the unrestricted life of the back-woods . . . performing the noble work of the axeman, which in itself has a smack of freedom about it . . . his cutlass . . . always by his side."[1]

During the greater part of the eighteenth century the average number of negroes in the Hondo, Belize, New River and Old River, and Sibun settlements scarcely exceeded 2000. By 1805 there were 2540 slaves, and 1098 free negroes and mulattoes.

Early in the eighteenth century the cutting of mahogany[2] had begun, and the export of this splendid timber gradually became a more important feature than logwood. The Spanish Government had never admitted (till the nineteenth century) that British Honduras was withdrawn from Spanish sovereignty: it only agreed (in between its different wars) to allow the British to settle in this region for the purpose, first, of cutting logwood; and it was not till the Convention of 1786 that mahogany was added to dye-woods as a legitimate article of export by the British. Even as late as this date the British were not allowed to establish any plantations: they were merely to fell timber.

Great Britain had at different times assumed a right to dispose of the Bay Islands and Ruatan, off the north coast of Spanish Honduras. Hither were sent in 1796 the insurgent Black Caribs of St. Vincent. [It is curious to note that the French in November, 1791, transported to Ruatan the Negro militia or "Suisses" employed against the victorious rebel mulattoes of Haiti;[3] and again in 1814, under the restored Bourbons, thought of capturing by some ruse the mulatto leaders in Haiti and deporting them to the same string of islands in the

[1] *British Honduras*, by Archibald Robertson Gibbs (London: 1883).

[2] Mahogany—*Swietenia mahogani*—is a tall, particularly handsome tree native to Central America and the larger West India islands. The tallest and biggest trees come from Southern Mexico, and those furnishing big timbers of the best average quality from British Honduras. "Spanish" mahogany for cabinet-making came from Santo Domingo (Hispaniola), but the mahogany forests in that island have been almost completely destroyed. The tree still grows (rarely) in Haiti, and much more abundantly in Cuba and Jamaica.

[3] These unfortunate Negro soldiers marooned on Ruatan were transported by the British to Jamaica and sent back to Haiti, where they were massacred in cold blood by the mulattoes and French.

Gulf of Honduras.] The Black Caribs landed here in 1796 have prospered greatly, and are extending their trading range actually into the confines of British Honduras and all along the northern coast-line of the Honduras Republic. The whole of this coast-line down to the confines of Nicaragua is much "negrified" by British importations of negroes or by runaway slaves.

But although in 1852 the Bay Islands (including Ruatan) were created a

283. A MAHOGANY TREE

British Colony dependent on Jamaica, the influence of the United States under the Clayton-Bulwer Treaty of 1850 (a singularly futile and self-denying ordinance on the part of Great Britain) constrained Great Britain to abandon her very definite and legitimate protectorate over the Nicaraguan Mosquito Coast (1856), and in 1859 to cede the Bay Islands and the control over the Black Caribs to the Republic of Honduras.

Representative institutions and orderly government came into existence in British Honduras during the second half of the eighteenth century,[1] and long before this possession was finally acknowledged by Spain as being part of the British Empire. During nearly two-thirds of the nineteenth century these institutions continued, and, of course, after the abolition of slavery in 1834 and the extinction of apprenticeship a few years later, the negro or negroid inhabitants of the colony were as much eligible—on a property qualification—to elect and to be members of the Legislative Assembly as persons of unmixed European descent. But during the 'sixties the colony was much harassed by the raids of Amerindian tribes, and constant quarrels on matters of finance and police occurred between the Lieutenant-Governor and the Legislative Assembly. Following the precedent of Jamaica in 1865, the settlers of British Honduras in 1869 were induced to agree to the surrender of their political Constitution, which took effect in 1870. From that time onwards the country has been governed as a Crown Colony by a Governor, an Executive containing the Governor, three officials, and two non-officials; and a Legislative Council of the Governor, three official members, and five non-official, who are nominated by the Governor and who usually include one or more representatives of the coloured people.

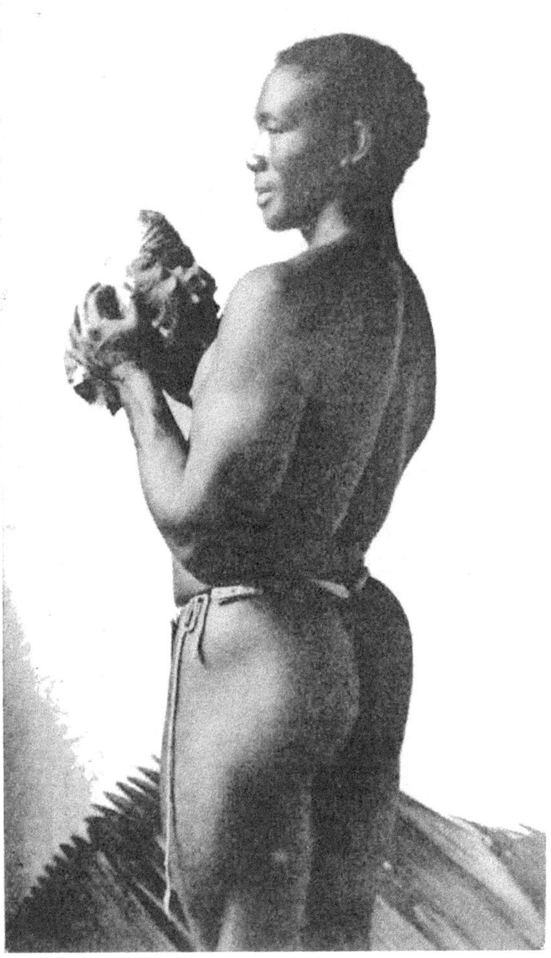

284. A HYBRID BETWEEN NEGRO AND AMERINDIAN OF BRITISH GUIANA

Resembling closely the "Black Caribs" of the Bay Islands and British Honduras

In 1880 the colonists became very restive under the somewhat despotic administration of the Lieutenant-Governor and petitioned the Secretary of State for the restitution of self-government, but Mr. Gladstone's

[1] A. R. Gibbs in his excellent *History of British Honduras*, published in 1883, gives 1670 as the date at which "free representative institutions" came into existence. But these do not seem to have taken a definite or continuous shape until after the visit of Vice-Admiral Sir William Burnaby in 1765. In 1862 British Honduras was elected to the status of a colony depending on Jamaica, and in 1884 to the rank of an independent colony.

Cabinet could not see its way to granting their request. Since the year 1884, the Governors of British Honduras having usually been carefully selected, there has been no outward sign of discontent with the present method of administration, which, though it may seem arbitrary as applied to a country of nearly 8000 square miles, is perhaps in the long run the more efficient and economical when the still small population of this region—42,300—is taken into account. Of this population at the present day 37,000 (approximately) are negroes or negroids, about 3000 are Amerindian half-breeds with the negro—Mosquito Indians (Waikña) and Black Caribs—or pure-blooded Amerindians of the Santa Cruz, Icaiche, Maya, and Peten tribes. Of the remainder 2000 are whites or near whites, European or of European descent, a few being derived from the Southern States of the Union. There are said to be relatively few pure-blooded negroes in British Honduras, the coloured population of that colony—the Creoles—being much mixed with white blood.

There is a continuous feud going on between the Waikñas and Black Caribs on the one hand, and the pure-blooded Amerindians on the other, who are styled Ladinos, and, of course, are Spanish-speaking in contrast to the Carib (who talk Carib mixed with French) and Mosquito half-breeds (who talk jargons compounded of French, English, Carib, Toltec, and negro languages). But there are also a few East Indians who have migrated from Jamaica, and an increasing number of Chinese. It is remarkable, in fact, how the Chinese are mingling with the Maya Indians of south-east Yucatan, finding beside the evident physical affinity some mental sympathy as well.

"There is no class feeling here," writes a correspondent of the author in British Honduras. "The complete mixture of races has done away with that. Negroes or negroids have occupied some of the highest positions in the colony without giving rise to ill-feeling. There has been a negro captain in the police.

"But we suffer from lethargy, as they do in the West Indies. Our people, while willing to take an infinitude of trouble in discussing matters, and revelling in polite argumentativeness, nevertheless shirk the responsibility of a definite decision. The negro element loves politics, but is badly educated and easily led by 'talkers.' The negro here has taught himself to think that British Honduras is in all matters ahead of other parts of the world and of the British Empire, including England; and that this proud position is due to the intelligence of the Honduran negro.

"Our local education is only primary[1] and is given chiefly by religious bodies in forty-two elementary schools. Well-to-do people send their children to the United States or to Scotland to school. Eighty per cent of the coast-town negroes are *illiterate*, and ninety-five per cent of the timber-cutters. . . . This might be a rich as well as a beautiful colony; but some change in our present methods of development is needed. We have lived long on our mahogany and the supply of this timber is very limited, while past administrations have taken no heed of forestry regulations or of replanting. The labourers are so used to the roving life of the woods,[2] with its liberal allowance

[1] Perhaps this explains and excuses the ignorance mentioned in the preceding paragraph.—H. H. J.

[2] "The mahogany labourers of Honduras are capable of severe physical toil, but prefer to be relieved by idle spells and indulgence in feasting and merry-making. They are as excitable as negroes generally are, as frivolous and unreliable, as good-humoured, easily pleased, vain, passionate, and variable in all their humours and inconsequent in their ideas. They are insincere, and if not consciously untruthful are given to great exaggeration in their statements. . . . The labourers care chiefly for rum, music, dancing,

of holidays—a month to six weeks at Christmas!—that they dislike settling down to agriculture It will therefore be necessary to import field labour from some other source, probably East Indian kulis. Much of the coast country is extremely fertile."

The writer goes on to advocate the creation in British Honduras of considerable colonies of East Indians.

Nevertheless, though the Honduran negroes or negroids shirk agriculture—as the negro of the passing generation does everywhere—this particular type, the new Honduran, is very intelligent if given a chance of becoming well educated. But as a rule educated Hondurans do better for themselves outside British Honduras, mostly in Louisiana, Texas, and the Greater Antilles.

One coloured citizen of this colony by birth is Dr. Ernest Lyon, the present United States Minister-Resident in Liberia, at one time a schoolmaster and a member of the Baptist ministry. But he received the education which permitted him to occupy such positions in the United States; where, of course, the mulatto or negro—however he may be maltreated socially—has a splendid education offered him at very little cost. Several of the Honduran negroes have received medical diplomas enabling them to practise as physicians.

The Honduran police force and volunteers are nearly entirely composed of negroes and negroids with white officers.

Though the British and French had often attempted, as one of the episodes of warfare raging in America, to occupy Dutch GUIANA wholly or in part, neither of these Powers did more than hold for a short time the Dutch settlements west of the Corantyn River. But these temporary occupations of the Dutch Chartered Company's possessions did much to upset the conditions of slavery. After the Peace of 1783 the Dutch Government took a more direct interest in the management and government of these regions, in anticipation of the time when the charter of the New West India Company would come to a close and not be renewed. In October, 1784, the reorganised Dutch Government of the colonies of Essequibo and Demerara issued regulations for the treatment of servants and slaves. As regards the latter, the punishment of flogging was to be restricted to twenty-five lashes at any one time and "not to be inflicted until the offender had been laid on his face and tied between four stakes." Slaves were to be properly supplied with provisions, and ground on which they might plant. They might be allowed to dance once a month, but not later than two o'clock in the morning. "If any one wanted to place the head of a negro suicide on a pole, as a deterrent to others," he was to apply to the nearest authority, the Burgher officer. It was forbidden to work slaves on Sundays and holidays; negroes were not to be allowed to sing their usual songs on board vessels where there were whites, on pain of arbitrary correction, etc.

and sexual pleasures. Their wants are easily supplied. Their dwellings are little better than outhouses even in the towns; their food is coarse and ill-prepared, consisting for the most part of salt fish, plantains, yams, flour, pork, tropical fruits, vegetables, fresh fish, rice, and maize. Their favourite drink is coffee." [Not a dietary to be complained of.—*Author.*] "Their clothing when at work is a shirt and trousers for the men, a skirt and bodice for the women, with a handkerchief round the head. But they spend a large proportion of their wages on dress and finery for holidays and Sundays. They are usually cleanly in their persons and habits. They are healthy and active, yet when an infectious disease is introduced the mortality amongst them is very high, as they 'crumple up' at once and are without the resisting power of the tougher European. They are not so superstitious as the average West Indian negro; and this in spite of education being singularly backward among these timber-cutters and peasants."—From another correspondent.

This ordinance was received with anger and contempt by the Dutch planters (because it was considered too mild); and apparently it was not vigorously enforced.

Already the western part of Dutch Guiana had become very English, partly owing to the British occupation of 1781, partly to the throwing open of these regions by the Company for general settlement in 1730 and the consequent attraction thither of English, Scottish, and Anglo-American planters. The English language seems to have been more used by the negroes than Dutch or French, and in the latter part of the eighteenth century, newspapers, pasquinades, and public notices were, as often as not, printed in English.

In 1792 the charter of the Dutch West India Company came to an end, and for three years Dutch Commissioners introduced considerable improvements into the government of all Guiana. But all this time the Bush negroes were increasing in numbers and constantly attacking the planters' settlements.

285. A TYPICAL "BOVIANDER" OR UP-COUNTRY SETTLER
Half Amerindian, quarter Dutch, quarter Negro

The invasion of Holland by France precipitated the long-contemplated action of the British Government, who after the great American War of 1777–83 had made up its mind on two points: that it wanted the Cape of Good Hope and the rivers of Guiana. In May, 1795, a British naval force appeared off the Demerara River. Soon afterwards the Bush negroes rose. The Dutch enlisted slaves and Amerindians, and after one or two serious disasters in which the Dutch troops were cut to pieces, this mixed force (in which a Scottish officer took a prominent place) succeeded in inflicting severe punishment on the Bush negroes. Thirteen of these who were taken prisoners were broken on the wheel, and one of their leading chiefs was burnt at the stake "with the horrible accompaniment of having his flesh pinched out with red-hot tongs." But in 1796 a force under Sir Ralph Abercromby took possession of Demerara, practically with the agreement of the local Dutch authorities, who yielded to overwhelming force, and soon afterwards the whole of Dutch Guiana was in the possession of the British. Between 1796 and 1801 the British seem to have pacified the slaves of Dutch Guiana by kindlier treatment, and as every one believed that the British occupation would be permanent and that there was increased security for order and good government, large numbers of slaves were brought over from Africa. But after the Peace of Amiens the British forces evacuated all Guiana, one of the conditions of that treaty being that the Dutch settlements were to be nominally restored to Holland, but that the French Colony of Cayenne was to be allowed to extend its hinterland behind Surinam and Demerara to the Essequibo River: in other words, Napoleon intended eventually to secure for France the whole of Guiana, probably up to the Orinoco River.[1]

However, this withdrawal did not last long, for in advance of the formal

[1] So that through his insane ambition in the Old World he lost the one possible chance of making France a great South American power.

declaration of war in 1803 in the West Indies against France and Holland, the British forces had once more taken possession of the Dutch colonies, and although the region that is now called Surinam was restored to Holland in 1814, the colonies of "Demerary," Essequibo, and Berbice were purchased from the Dutch and united to form the colony of BRITISH GUIANA, which by subsequent extension westwards and southwards over a no-man's-land now covers an area of 90,277 square miles [or nearly 3000 square miles larger than the whole of Great Britain].

In 1823 a great ferment began amongst the negro slaves in what was now British Guiana. They had heard through the conversation of their masters of the great Anti-Slavery agitation being carried on in London, and of the 1823 resolutions of the House of Commons as to the better treatment of slaves. Moreover, from the beginning of the nineteenth century, missionaries of the London Missionary Society had come out to British Guiana as they had gone to Cape Colony; and in both directions they had taken up the cause of the Negro.

286. A BOVIANDER
Same as No. 285

One of their missionaries in Guiana was the Rev. John Smith, who had established a chapel and attracted a large slave congregation, to whom he talked vaguely, but strenuously, of the approach of a time when they might all be free. Gradually the idea spread amongst the negroes of the coast region of British Guiana that King George IV had ordered their freedom, but that the planters kept this order from their knowledge and refused to carry it out. The result was a slave insurrection, in which two or three white men lost their lives, and some houses were burnt and property destroyed. As a matter of fact, the remarkable feature of this outbreak was the loyalty of many of the slaves to their masters and mistresses, and the way in which even when the large bands of armed negroes were temporarily victorious they refrained from pushing their victory to the extent of murdering any of the white people in their possession. However, the Governor took prompt measures with the military and naval forces at his command (being also helped by loyal Amerindians),[1] put down the revolt, executed a number of prisoners by hanging, issued a proclamation to appease the slaves still in rebellion, and arrested the Rev. John Smith. To overawe the negroes who did not join in the revolt, the bodies of rebels after execution were hung in chains, or were decapitated and their heads stuck about on poles in the towns and on the plantations.

The Rev. John Smith was tried by court-martial, and on the 24th November, 1823, was found guilty and sentenced to be hanged. As far as can be ascertained, no clear evidence of any kind was brought forward to involve Smith in *any* complicity with this nearly bloodless revolt against servitude; the utmost that could be alleged against him with truth being that by his preaching, and

[1] It is noteworthy through a century and a half of Guiana history how often the Amerindian tribes, especially the Caribs, came to the assistance of the whites to enable them to keep the negroes under control.

perhaps writing, he had led the negroes to believe that a day was coming when they would obtain their freedom at the hands of the British Government.

Fortunately, the death sentence of the court was accompanied by a recommendation to mercy, and still more fortunately the Governor of the colony was not an Eyre. General John Murray submitted the minutes of the trial and the sentence for the consideration of the Crown, but meanwhile the Rev. John Smith died in prison on the 6th February, 1824, from tuberculosis. He had long been sickly, but it was alleged by his brother missionaries that his death was hastened by the agitation of the trial and his treatment in prison.

The British Government, alarmed at the ferment amongst the slaves in Guiana and other parts of British America, made statements in Parliament and issued royal proclamations in 1824 denying rather ambiguously that measures for a general emancipation were under consideration, and enjoining on the slaves that they should render due obedience to their masters and entire submission to the laws.

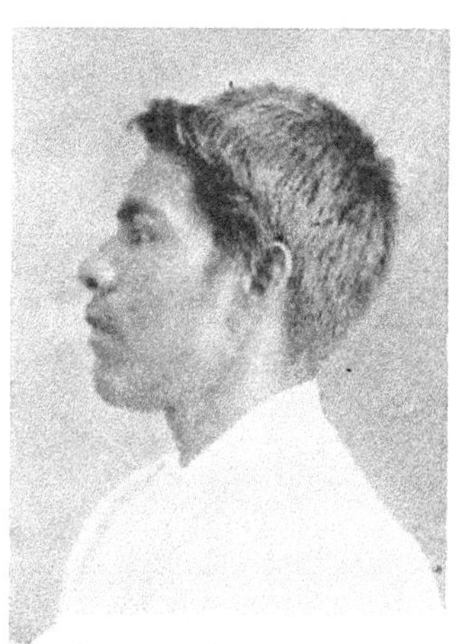

287. A BOVIANDER OF BRITISH GUIANA

Quarter Negro, three-quarter Amerindian

In 1831 the three separate colonies of Demerara, Berbice, and Essequibo were united into the one colony of British Guiana; in 1834 the status of slavery was abolished by law, as elsewhere in British America, and by 1838 even apprenticeship had come to an end. In that year it became necessary to import kuli labour from India to work on the Guiana sugar-plantations in lieu of the negroes, who, now being masters of their own actions, turned away from field labour with disgust, except so far as to cultivate their own plots of land and supply themselves with food-stuffs. In 1853 Chinese labourers were introduced in addition to the kuli traffic. About this time also there began to arrive numerous Portuguese settlers.

This colony possessed representative institutions even under the Dutch, and these were guaranteed and continued from the first British occupation. As amended by the Act of 1891, the Legislature known as the Combined Court has the power of imposing the colonial taxes and auditing the public accounts, and discussing freely and without reserve the items of the annual estimates prepared by the Governor in Executive Council. A kind of senate exists under the name of "the Court of Policy," which consists of the Governor, seven official or ex-officio members, and eight *elected* members. These members and the additional financial representatives of the people, which together with the Court of Policy form the Combined Court or General Legislature, are elected by the direct vote of the people on a franchise limited to males over twenty-one years of age (British subjects or naturalised subjects), and based on a property qualification, but without any conditions of literacy, race, or colour. The qualification of a membership of the Court of Policy or of the Combined Court is likewise the possession of property combined with the status of British citizenship or British naturalisation. There are therefore no race or colour disabilities in the Constitution of British Guiana; therefore nothing but the preliminary condition of possessing a reasonable amount of property prevents the negro from electing or being elected to membership of the Guiana Parliament.[1] As a matter of fact, half the number of seats in the Legislature are held to-day by negroes or negroids; and the negro element wields much power in the Guiana State, yet cannot be said down to the present time to have abused his position.

In British Guiana, both under Dutch and British rule, the Amerindians were well treated, and if they have diminished in numbers to any extent it was not in any way the fault of the Europeans, but of some inherent want of racial stamina. As in Brazil, they now seem to be recovering, and their birth-rate is high. The early Dutch settlers married Amerindian wives, and there is a considerable riverside population, called the "Bovianders," of sturdy half-castes derived from these unions. At no time, apparently, has there been any racial prejudice against these unions or the half-caste results. The mother of George Augustus Sala is said to have been the daughter of an Amerindian Guiana chief, and the naturalist Waterton married an Amerindian half-caste. Male Amerindians of Guiana are sometimes described[2] as selfish, grasping, improvident, lazy, sullen, and revengeful, though not hasty in temper. But they are usually inoffensive, capable of great endurance in work if they work at all, though still unfortunately much addicted to intoxication from native-made alcohol (*piwarri*), which when persisted in gives them a serious disease of the intestines.

Whilst slavery prevailed in the seventeenth, eighteenth, and early nineteenth centuries the Amerindians of Guiana were subsidised by the Dutch and British to assist in capturing runaway negro slaves, and in consequence a deep-set ill-feeling has grown up between Amerindians and Negroes. Nevertheless, there has been much racial intermixture between the two in the interior

[1] "By the constitution of 1891 direct representation in the Legislative Council has been granted to people who have shown eagerness to avail themselves of their privileges. For the first time in its history the Court of Policy in 1894 was entered by a pure-blooded African, who as representative for his native country filled his place with modesty and dignity. Once grant the principle of representation, and its logical outcome must be a preponderance of the coloured element in the Legislative Assembly. The African races are more numerous than any other, as they number more than half the whole population of the Colony. The East Indians come next in point of numbers, and ought to be represented by some educated babu; whilst the Portuguese, who although not very numerous have a large pecuniary stake in the Colony, should endeavour to obtain the election of one of their number to champion their particular interests in the Chamber." (*Twenty-five Years in British Guiana*, pp. 286, 287, by Henry Kirke, M.A., B.C.L., Oxon. Formerly Sheriff of Demerara.)

The property qualifications for the suffrage and the membership of the Court of Policy and Financial Representatives are rather high for America.

Voters (if they live in the country) must own three acres of land under cultivation, or be tenants of not less than six acres under cultivation, or own a house worth £20 a year, or occupy a house worth £40 a year, or have an annual income of £100, or have paid direct taxes of at least £4 3s. 4d. for at least a year previous to registration, and have resided in the district at least six months. In the towns the qualification is ownership of a house worth at least £104 3s. 4d. (one would think legists who fix these quaint odd sums must be suffering from a perverted sense of humour), or occupation of a house on a rental of £25 a year or an annual income of £100 coupled with residence in the town, or residence and payment of a year's previous taxes of at least £4 3s 4d.

I suppose these totals of pounds, shillings, and pence instead of plain pounds are intended to be a further arithmetic test!

There are at the present time about 3100 registered electors throughout British Guiana.

The qualification for membership as above is to own 80 acres of land of which at least 40 are under cultivation, or to own property worth £1562 10s., or a house, etc., worth an annual rental of £250. If you wish to be eligible for a Financial Representative you must in addition to all this possess a clear annual income of at least £300.

[2] Mr. A. E. Aspinall in his excellent West Indian *Pocket Guide* (Stanford) gives a much more sympathetic description of the Carib on page 93. The great authority on the Amerindians of Guiana is Sir Everard Im Thurn, G.C.M.G., now Governor of Fiji.

parts of British Guiana. But under normal circumstances the Amerindian [though he or she exhibits no repugnance to an association with either the European or the East Indian] detests and despises the Negro. The East Indian kulis sometimes intermarry with the Amerindians, and the result is quite a handsome type of humanity.

When, in 1853, the first attempt was made to introduce Chinese labourers into British Guiana, instead of a respectable class of labourer being recruited, the Chinese Government officials sent prisoners from the jails, beggars, and vile persons. But in later attempts (1859 and subsequently) a very good class

288. EAST INDIAN KULI WOMEN

of Chinese kuli was imported, and many of these after their arrival not only became Christians, but have remained such, and constitute a sound element in the Guianan policy.

The Negroes are afraid of the Chinese, and do not behave to them in the bullying manner they sometimes adopt toward the East Indian. The Chinese, on the other hand, without hesitation, take to themselves mulatto or negro concubines, and a considerable number of hybrid types are arising between the two races, which, as in Jamaica, look like very vigorous, stalwart Amerindians.

That the climate is well suited to East Indians is shown by the fine healthy appearance of the kulis; the men are stronger and the women fairer than their parents in India. In fact a fine race of people is springing up in Guiana, the offspring of these Indian immigrants, who may, it is hoped, in time form an important element in the resident population.[1]

The Portuguese immigrants in British Guiana (mainly from Madeira, the Azores, and Southern Portugal) now number about 16,000.

At no time have they made any difficulty about intermarrying with the mulatto or negro people of the colony. Yet perhaps the two races are at present drawing apart, partly from an increased self-respect which is growing up in the negro community, added to difference of religion, the bulk of the Negroes or Negroids belonging to the Protestant churches. The Portuguese, though very industrious, have not perhaps altogether upheld the high standard of conduct that the white man should maintain.

289. EAST INDIAN KULIS, BRITISH GUIANA

[1] "We have now seen the Indian peasant in his old and in his adopted home. Let us compare the two positions. On the one hand, misery and poverty, debt and starvation; on the other, comfort, food, and moderate labour, leading to independence and even wealth. Let any one compare the immigrant when he first lands in Demerara with the same man a year or two afterwards. At first he is a poor, cringing creature, bowing to the earth before every white man he meets; apologetic for his very existence. You meet the same man in two years' time, strong, clean, erect, passing with an indifferent stare, or if he knows and respects you with a hearty 'Salaam, sahib,' and a wave of his hand towards his turban. What is the cause of this change? Because the man has found out that he is some one; that he has a value and position of his own; that in the eyes of the law no one is better than he; because he is free from debt, and making money. All these things combine to make him hold up his head, and give a spring to his step. But I will go further than this, and say that the position of the Indian immigrant in Guiana can be compared favourably with the position of the agricultural labourer in the Southern Counties of England." (Henry Kirke, 1898, *Twenty-five Years in British Guiana.*)

Writers on British Guiana usually discriminate between the "Creole" negroes, who are descended from the former slaves, imported or smuggled into the country down to 1824, and the free African immigrants who have entered the colony much more recently, have, in fact, been born in Africa. Amongst these there are a number of Krumen, engaged chiefly in seafaring or seaside occupations, and easily identified by their chipped upper incisor teeth and "blue" noses. The other "African" negroes are obviously wanting in education compared to those born in the colony, but they are more useful in agriculture.

The Negroes indigenous to British Guiana are a fine race physically, and in size above the average not only of the East Indians, Chinese, and Amerindians, but of the Europeans, while the women (as is often the case in America) are nearly as big and powerful as the men. They are accused racially of petty dishonesty, but in faithfulness and devoted affection towards Europeans are superior to any other race in the colony. They are improvident, somewhat inclined to drunkenness, but very good-tempered and seldom revengeful. They are stated to be entirely "unmoral" in their sexual relations, but to be less inclined now to unite with low-class Europeans. They have no sexual dislike for the East Indians, but the natives of India, on the other hand, have the greatest antipathy for the blacks, and there is probably little sexual intermixture of the races for this reason. An Indian kuli would ordinarily prefer to live unmarried sooner than cohabit with a negress: they are not perhaps so squeamish about marriage with mulattoes.

290 A YOUNG WOMAN OF BRITISH GUIANA
Three-quarter Negro, quarter Chinese

The Negro surnames in Guiana are often ridiculous and inappropriate, being derived from old Slavery days, when they either took the patronymic of their estate master or proprietor—possibly some name great in the annals of England, or one thrust upon them by their facetious owner, such as Adonis, Hercules, Napoleon.[1]

Elementary education seems to be well advanced among the negro and coloured population of British Guiana. It is said among those of the present generation between the ages of ten and thirty at least 85 per cent can read and write.

No school for negroes existed in this colony until 1824, when as a result of the 1823 House of Commons' Resolutions two free schools for boys and girls were started in Georgetown, Demerara.

The first Colonial Government grant for public education was £130 given in 1830. In 1834 the "Lady Mico Charity" (referred to on page 271) estab-

[1] "There are a large number of highly educated black or coloured people who, except in colour, differ not at all from a similar class in England or Scotland. Some of the black barristers who practise in our courts are singularly polite and courteous in word and manner. Of course there are others somewhat the reverse, but none of them worse than the coarse, brow-beating practitioner at the Old Bailey. . . . As a race the Negro is much more courteous than the Briton. The coarseness and brutality of the miner and labourer of Briton are absent, and his manners and language are generally pleasing and decorous." (Henry Kirke, in *Twenty-five Years in British Guiana.*)

lished six schools in different parts of the colony. By 1840 there were seventy-four denominational schools conducted by the Church of England, the Presbyterians, Wesleyans, Congregationalists, and Baptists, which had a roll of nearly five thousand negro scholars and received a Government grant-in-aid of £3159.

In 1876 an admirable Education Ordinance was passed by the Legislature and brought into force. By this attendance at school was made compulsory (oh, Jamaica! why did you not follow suit?). Parents or guardians of children which failed to attend school might be punished. The employment of children under the age of nine was forbidden, and every child of nine years old and upwards to fourteen years was required to attend school for at least two and a half hours each day the school was open. The establishment of private industrial schools was authorised, especially in regard to imparting instruction to children in practical agriculture, a proportion of the money thus earned to go to the child or its parents. This Ordinance with some amendments and additions is in force at the present day.

The following is the curriculum of the Government and private Primary schools in British Guiana: reading, writing, arithmetic, school gardens, trades or industries, Nature study, English, geography, elementary hygiene, sewing, singing, and physical drill. In all these schools there are, of course, no colour or race disabilities.

Special attention is given to the teaching of agriculture by school gardens, lectures on agricultural chemistry and botany, the education of native pupil-teachers and demonstrators, apprenticeship under the Government Botanical Department, and other rewards and inducements. But it is said that the Guianan negro still shows himself averse to tilling and planting as compared to other avocations, though of late he has evinced a disposition to compete with the East Indian as a rice-grower.

In 1909 there were 223 primary schools in British Guiana and 32,085 scholars on the books (a muster on inspection of 27,526);[1] 23,979 were examined in 1908–9, and in the same twelve months the local Government grant towards primary education was approximately £25,000. Education equal to that of a public school is provided for boys at Queen's College, a Government institution (undenominational and very highly equipped). The education here, though not quite gratuitous (and admittance is dependent on success in entrance examination), is very cheap—in the highest grades only £12 a year. There are at present 126 negroes and negroid students at this college, together with a few Europeans and East Indians.

The Government and private benevolence have established a number of important, well-furnished scholarships which would enable the gainer of them (in a competitive examination) to complete his studies at a foreign university. Out of twenty-five scholarships recently bestowed eight have been won by negroes or negroids. It is gratifying to note (despite the gloomy predictions once emitted by the dying planter aristocracy) that this spread of education in Guiana is coincident with a diminution of crime. A correspondent in Guiana, who is in a position to know, writes to me as follows: "Crime is decidedly on the decrease. The suicide of a black man or woman is nowadays almost unheard of, though so common an occurrence in slavery days. Negroes and negroids are very rarely charged with murder or serious felony. The

[1] Out of a total population of 304,549 in 1908.

negro is a clumsy plotter, and is not vindictive or morose: he has more bark than bite in him. Since the final emancipation of the slaves in 1838 there have been only three riots in the colony, and each of these was carried on principally by women and children."

The daily average of prisoners and convicts in jail or penal settlements throughout British Guiana for the year 1908–9 was only 501·26 (out of a population of 304,549). Of these, two-thirds were negroes or negroids. In 1905–6 the same average was 618·2; in 1884, 739; in 1881, 958. The population in 1881 was approximately 252,186. But irregularity in morals still dogs the negro's upward advance in Guiana as elsewhere; or it may be that he is less cunning a hypocrite, his faults are more eagerly laid bare by the white statistician, and he is also frankly philoprogenitive, and likes begetting and bringing forth children. The man is seldom simultaneously polygamous, and his consecutive adulteries arise mostly from the innate desire of the pregnant negress to withdraw from her husband's society till the child is born and weaned. The percentage of illegitimate births in the negro population of British Guiana was 58·4 per cent in the year 1907.

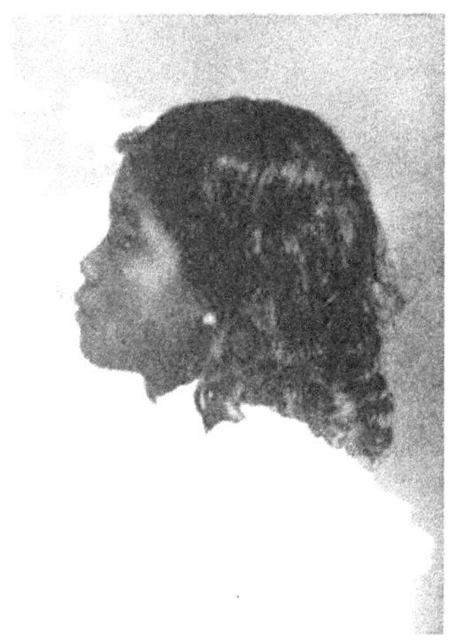

291. A HYBRID BETWEEN NEGRO AND EAST INDIAN (GUIANA)

Some remarkable figures as to the birth-rates of the various races in British Guiana have recently been transmitted to me by Mr. J. van Sertima. In the year 1907 the birth-rate among the Europeans of "Nordic" type was 13·6 per thousand, as against 12·2 in 1906; the Portuguese birth-rate was 22·9 (in 1906, 28·8). The East Indian birth-rate for 1907 was 24·4 (32·5 in 1906); that of the Chinese, 32·9 (in 1906, 31·2). Of the semi-civilised Amerindians (Caribs, Arawaks, Warraus, etc.) the birth-rate, strange to say, is the highest in the community, from 50 to 52 per thousand. [See page 107 for birth-rate in Brazil.] That of the negro is 32 to 34 per thousand, and of the half-castes (mainly negroids), 32 to 28 per thousand.

Of the total births registered during 1907, 438 per thousand were amongst the negroes, 115 per thousand represented the mixed negroid element, and, in the same proportion, 360 the East Indian, 40 the Amerindian, 29 the Portuguese, 9 the Chinese, and 6 the Nordic Europeans.

The total population for 1908 was 304,549; of which approximately 117,798 were negroes (1413 of African birth); 34,325 mixed race, largely negroid; 7500 Amerindian;[1] 123,326 were East Indians; 4000 Chinese; 4,600 Nordic Europeans, and 13,000 Portuguese.

The bulk of the negroes and negroids are Protestant Christians and the remainder Roman Catholics. There is scarcely a single Muhammadan amongst them, and nowadays fetish worshippers or believers in Obia are rare, especially as compared to the West India Islands. The language commonly used by the Guiana negroes is that Creole dialect of all Guiana and of the British, Danish,

[1] The estimate for the Amerindians is, of course, much under the total number in the colony, as so many groups of this people still lead a semi-nomad existence in the forests, and keep aloof from all connection with the colony.

and Dutch West Indies, which has English for its basis, mixed with African, Carib, French, and Dutch words. Of course, all the even slightly-educated negroes and mulattoes can speak good English, much more easily understood by a Londoner than the dialects of Scotland and Northern England.

As has been repeatedly mentioned, the Guianan negroes (like those of Trinidad, Honduras, and several West India islands) have shown themselves very averse, since the abolition of slavery, from agriculture as a calling, especially in the case of the descendants of former slaves. The Negro had such a sickener of this pursuit from having cultivated the White Man's plantations for nearly two hundred years under the lash that he seems instinctively predisposed against this most praiseworthy of all callings. And he has now such a sense of his own importance that he asks for work in the fields a higher wage than the modern planter or company can afford to pay with the more patient, careful, silent, industrious kuli at hand. The place of the negro men, women, and children on the sugar estates has now been completely taken by the East Indian family. On the other hand, the negro is still disposed to cultivate rice, and suffers less from mortality in that most unhealthy pursuit than the other peoples of Guiana.

But it is in the trades, industries, and professional careers that the Guianan negro or coloured man comes to the front. He is not a good man of business, and though successful as a pedlar or petty market salesman (or woman), he seldom keeps a shop in this colony; in all Georgetown (the capital) there is only one negro grocer. As a shopkeeper, large or small, he has been ousted by the Chinese and Portuguese. But, on the other hand, almost all the carpenters, joiners, upholsterers, painters, masons, engineers, machinists, pan-boilers, timber-cutters, printers, bookbinders, and plumbers are negroes or coloured men. From this race is drawn nearly all the thirteen thousand miners who do the rough work in the gold and diamond mines of the interior.

Negroes are employed to collect rubber, balata gum,[1] the fibres, barks, timber, and other products of the interior forests. They are certainly not, therefore, an idle or an unimportant people in the economy of British Guiana. They furnish nearly all the police and soldiery; they or their half-caste relations are the clerks, the book-keepers, and petty employés of the commercial houses of the towns. They provide most of the lawyers and doctors, the pastors, school-teachers, press reporters, several of the magistrates, most of the lesser Government officials. In all these posts they are pronounced (as in Dominica) to be "just as honest as the Whites." Indeed, in following the recent criminal records of this colony one might go farther and state that the negroes and negroids of Guiana bear an excellent character for honesty in all serious responsibilities where money and valuable property are concerned.

There is a slight "colour question" in Guiana, but the sensitiveness lies rather between the "near-whites" of pale ivory complexion and the darker-tinted mulattoes or negroes. There is now practically no intermarriage between whites and blacks; on the other hand, numerous unions take place between whites, especially Portuguese, and the lighter-skinned negroids, many of whom would almost sooner perish in celibacy than intermarry with the negro or mulatto.

[1] A substance like caoutchouc, derived from a tall *Mimusops* tree.

CHAPTER XII

THE ABOLITION MOVEMENT IN GREAT BRITAIN

THE following brief recital of the events and personages connected with the abolition of Slavery and the Slave-Trade in America may be of use to the reader of this book :—

The earliest revulsion of feeling in the minds of Englishmen regarding the righteousness of condemning fellow human beings to transportation and servitude arose concurrently with the vigorous development of the African Slave-Trade, in the last forty years of the seventeenth century. At first British sympathies were mainly extended to the wretched apprentices, convicts, or political prisoners who were sent to the plantations in America from London, Bristol, and other English cities, from Scotland, and from Ireland. But before this British philosophers had grown sentimental over the wrongs inflicted by the Spaniards on the Amerindians ; and had even denounced the treacherous treatment of the Caribs by the early English settlers in the Leeward Islands.

From the idealised Carib or Arawak, sympathy gradually turned towards the negroes. It was observed that rich West Indian planters bringing negro slaves with them to England frequently treated these slaves with great cruelty and harshness. As early as 1670 (?) the Rev. Morgan Godwyn, a clergyman of the Church of England, wrote a treatise entitled "A Negro's and Indian's Advocate," based on the sufferings of slaves in the Island of Barbados, of which he had been a witness. He dedicated his treatise to the Archbishop of Canterbury. He was succeeded as an author by many other Church of England or Nonconformist divines during the seventeenth and eighteenth centuries, notably Richard Baxter (? 1675), the Rev. Griffith Hughes, Rector of the church of St. Lucy in Barbados (1750), Dr. Hayter, Bishop of Norwich (1755), Bishop Warburton (1766), John Wesley (1774), Dr. Porteus, Bishop of Chester (1776), and the Rev. James Ramsay [1] (1784).

In 1729 the question of whether a negro was or was not a free man within the limits of the United Kingdom was decided by a joint opinion of the Attorney-General and Solicitor-General then advising the Government. They were of opinion that a slave coming from the West Indies into Great Britain or Ireland did not become free whether or not he was baptised, and that his master could legally compel him to return again to the plantations.

In 1765 a much-mishandled West African Negro from Barbados—Jonathan Strong—applied to a London surgeon for advice. The brother of this surgeon—the afterwards celebrated Granville Sharp—took up this man's case, enabled him to recover his health ; and when his former master—a drunken ruffian called David Lisle—attempted to kidnap and sell him, Sharp defended the wretched slave by an appeal to the Lord Mayor, who set Strong free. Nevertheless the captain of the ship delegated for the purpose by Strong's new purchaser attempted to seize the ex-slave by force, and Sharp intervened

[1] Referred to on page 229.

with great courage before the rather vacillating Lord Mayor, and carried off Strong triumphantly, afterwards putting him in a secure refuge.

He then determined to take up the case in a decisive manner, and eventually—in 1769—after a tremendous research into the laws and customs of Great Britain and Ireland, he produced a book entitled *A Representation of the Injustice and Dangerous Tendency of Tolerating Slavery in England.* He rescued various other slaves from re-transportation to the West Indies, and finally the question was fought to an issue over James Somerset, a slave who had been brought (apparently from Africa) to England by his master, Charles Stuart, and who was to be sold as a slave and sent to Jamaica. The case of James Somerset was argued before Lord Chief Justice Mansfield, who finally, in the name of the whole bench, on the 22nd June, 1772, pronounced the decision that as soon as the Slave set his foot on the soil of the British Islands he became free. After this decision Granville Sharp wrote to the principal Secretary of State, Lord North, urging him most earnestly to abolish immediately both the trade in and the slavery of the human species in all the British Dominions, as being utterly irreconcilable with the principles of the British Constitution and the established religion of the land.

In 1776 David Hartley, M.P. for Hull, moved in the House of Commons "That the Slave-trade was contrary to the laws of God and the rights of man." But his motion met with little sympathy, as did several subsequent petitions to Parliament from English towns. Amongst these was a petition from Bridgewater, Somerset, presented in 1785, which was well to the fore in this movement against Slavery and the Slave-trade, not entirely, however, without the desire to cast a slur on Bristol.[1]

In 1785, however, Dr. Peckard, Vice-Chancellor of Cambridge University, who had conceived a strong dislike to the principle of Slavery, composed as a subject for a Latin prize essay the question "Is it lawful to make slaves of others against their will?"

292. GRANVILLE SHARP

The "Senior Bachelor" of Cambridge—Thomas Clarkson—Saint Thomas Clarkson, I hope he may some day be called among the beatitudes of an universal Christian Church—had already taken prizes for Latin essays and resolved to compete for this one. To fit himself for the task, he determined to read a remarkable book, *An Historical Account of Guinea,* by Anthony Benezet[2] This book contained the sum of the writings and observations of the explorers Adanson, Moor, Barbot, Bosman, and others.

As the result of his studies, Clarkson became body and soul devoted to the cause, first, of abolishing the Slave-trade between Africa and America, and secondly, of getting rid of Slavery altogether. But although an enthusiast, his zeal was splendidly tempered by judgment and discretion, as is occasionally the case with the great men of Britain and America. He realised that the first battle to be fought was over the abolition of the Slave-trade. If that could be won, the status of Slavery itself might next be tackled. At any rate, if the planters could no longer look to Africa for the recruitment of fresh negroes year by year, they might be disposed to treat more kindly and considerately the slaves already in their possession. He resolved to devote his life to this cause,

[1] Bristol and Liverpool were the great strongholds of the British Slave-trade. No doubt Bristol had in some way annoyed Bridgewater—just as Manchester then and thenceforth posed as the antithesis and antidote of Liverpool.

[2] See p. 354.

and his Latin essay (which obtained the prize) was expanded into a book on Slavery and the Slave-trade, published (in English, of course) in 1786. This led to his making the acquaintance of William Dillwyn, who had been born in North America, but who had settled in Essex and had thrown himself for years past vehemently into the cause of the slaves, he having caught this enthusiasm from (Saint) Anthony Benezet, whose book on Guinea had also inspired Clarkson.

Granville Sharp about this time was commencing his interest in the Sierra Leone Chartered Company, which was to acquire land on the west coast of Africa for the repatriation of homeless freed slaves. He soon heard of Thomas Clarkson. Both of them now came into contact with William Wilberforce, who after a wild youth had settled down into an eager philanthropic Member of Parliament. Wilberforce (after one or two others had failed) promised to bring up again the question of the Slave-trade before the House of Commons.[1]

The first committee to collect evidence and move for the abolition of the Slave-trade was formed on the 22nd May, 1787, under the presidency of Granville Sharp. Wilberforce found in the great minister William Pitt, a sympathiser in this movement against the Slave-trade, and Pitt appointed in 1788 a Committee of the Privy Council to inquire into the question. Wilberforce got this changed into a Committee of the whole House, which commenced to consider the matter in May, 1789. The discussion of Wilberforce's twelve resolutions continued till 1791; but the Bill to put a stop to the British Slave-trade which was brought forward on April 18th, 1791, was prejudiced by the negro insurrections already commencing in San Domingo, Martinique, and the British island of Dominica, and was defeated in the House of Commons by a great majority. Finally, after one or two partial successes, Wilberforce carried a resolution on the 1st January, 1796, that the British Slave-trade should come to an end. But in the final stage of the Bill the measure was lost by four votes.

293. THOMAS CLARKSON

Between 1796 and 1807 Wilberforce stuck to his object with splendid tenacity, helped whole-heartedly by the Prime Minister Pitt, and by his almost equally great opponent Charles Fox.[2] However they might disagree

[1] A good many dinners and social meetings occurred at this period and drew together most of the representatives of light and learning to discuss with Clarkson, Wilberforce, and Granville Sharp the rights and wrongs of Slavery and the Slave-trade. The great painter Sir Joshua Reynolds was an ardent Anti-Slavery man; so also through the influence of Dr. Samuel Johnson was for a time James Boswell, Johnson's biographer, who made one or two rather happy remarks. To those who repeated the planters' preposterous argument that "Africans were made happier by being carried from their own country to the West Indies," Boswell remarked, "Be it so. But we have no right to make people happy against their will." But with his customary fickleness, Boswell afterwards turned round and derided the Anti-Slavery movement.

[2] The details of this long and exciting struggle must, of course, be read in *The History of the Abolition of the Slave Trade*, by Thomas Clarkson. But a passage from the speech of Mr. Huddlestone in 1805 deserves special quotation.

"He asked how it happened, that sugar could be imported *cheaper* from the *East* Indies, than from the *West* Indies, notwithstanding the vast difference of the length of the voyages; was it on account of the impolicy of slavery, or that it was made in the former case by the industry of free men, and in the latter by the languid drudgery of slaves?

"As he had had occasion to advert to the eastern part of the world, he would make an observation upon an argument which had been collected from that quarter. The condition of the negroes in the West Indies had been lately compared with that of the Hindoos. But he would observe that the Hindoo,

on other policies, great and small, Pitt and Fox rivalled one another in the remarkable eloquence and pith of their attacks on the Slave-trade (and inferentially on Slavery). But Pitt died at the beginning of 1806, and Fox died in the following October of that year. The mantle of Fox fell on the shoulders of Lord Grenville, who by a clever move first of all carried the Bill for the abolition of the Slave-trade through the House of Lords.

Finally, on the 16th March, 1807, the third reading of the Bill was passed without a division, to the effect that no vessel should clear out for slaves from any port within the British Dominions after May 1, 1807, and that no slaves should be landed in British colonies after March 1, 1808. This meant, of course, the abolition of the Slave-trade under the British flag. It only remained that this great measure should receive the renewed assent of the Lords (since it had been amended), and finally the Royal sanction. The crisis was one of palpitating anxiety to the supporters of the measure, because the petulant King (George III, not known to sympathise very strongly with the Anti-Slavery movement) had intimated that he was about to dismiss his ministers over the question of justice to Roman Catholics. However, Lord Grenville carried the Bill with extraordinary despatch through the House of Lords (helped by the Duke of Norfolk and all the Church of England Bishops),[1] the measure was submitted to the King, and "as the clock struck twelve, just when the sun was in its meridian splendour to witness this august act and to sanction it by its most vivid and glorious beams," the King's Commission was opened by the Lord Chancellor and the Royal assent to the abolition of the Slave-trade was completed. The Ministry then delivered up their seals of office to the King.

291. WILLIAM WILBERFORCE

As a young man (twenty-nine), when he began to take up the question of the Slave-trade

Amongst those who made themselves odious or ridiculous in history by a malignant or stupid opposition to this long-debated act of justice were the Duke of Clarence, afterwards William IV, who was, however, balanced in the House of Lords by his brother the Duke of Gloucester;[2] a certain General Gascoyne (who, as usual, appealed to Scripture to sanction the Slave-trade and Slavery in its utmost extent), Lord Hawkesbury, Sir William Yonge, the Lord Chancellor Eldon, and the Earl of Sheffield; the principal or the most effective supporters of Mr. Wilberforce in the Legislature were (besides those persons already mentioned) Mr. Barham, a planter in the West Indies, Henry (afterwards Lord) Brougham, the Earl of West-

miserable as his hovel was, had sources of pride and happiness to which not only the West Indian slave, but even his master, was a stranger. He was, to be sure, a peasant; and his industry was subservient to the gratification of a European lord. But he was, in his own belief, vastly superior to him as one of the lowest caste. He would not on any consideration eat from the same plate. He would not suffer his son to marry the daughter of his master, even if she could bring him all the West Indies as her portion. He would observe, too, that the Hindoo peasant drank his water from his native well; that if his meal were scanty, he received it from the hand of her who was most dear to him; that when he laboured, he laboured for her and his offspring. His daily task being finished, he reposed with his family. No retrospect of the happiness of former days, compared with existing misery, disturbed his slumber; nor horrid dreams occasioned him to wake in agony at the dawn of day. No barbarous sounds of cracking whips reminded him that with the form and image of a man his destiny was that of the beast of the field. Let the advocates for the bloody traffic state what they had to set forth on their side of the question against the comforts and independence of the man with whom they compared the slave."

[1] Notably the Bishop of London (Dr. Porteus) and the Bishop of Llandaff.

[2] The Duke of Gloucester—the best of George III's sons—made a most effective speech against the Slave-trade in the final debate in the Lords.

morland, Sir Samuel Romilly, Richard Brinsley Sheridan, Lord Henry Petty, and Mr. Canning.

It was recognised on all hands that this parliamentary struggle which began in 1776 with the motion against the Slave-trade by David Hartley and closed in 1807 with the theoretical abolition of the British Slave-trade, really involved the much greater issue of the abolition of the status of Slavery on British soil, and this, of course, was why the former was so long and bitterly opposed by those who had vested interests in America. In 1807 the African Institution was founded in England with a view to keeping a vigilant watch on slave-traders, and to procuring the abolition of the Slave-trade by other European nations. Further, it was to promote the instruction of the Negro races and to diffuse information respecting the agricultural and commercial possibilities of Africa; so as to create a legitimate commerce in that continent which should remove all inducement to trade in human beings. This African Institution led to great results both in West Africa and the West Indies.

295. SIR THOMAS FOWELL BUXTON, BART.
First Baronet: died 1845

In 1811 (Lord) Brougham carried through Parliament a Bill which declared the traffic in slaves to be a felony punishable with transportation; and this measure, coupled with the vigorous action of British warships, to a great extent brought the British Slave-trade to a close. And the negotiations with the British Government at the close of the Napoleonic Wars induced most of the European nations with commercial fleets (as also the United States) similarly to abolish and punish slave-trading.

But so long as Slavery existed in America it was impossible to bring the Slave-trade completely to a close. Moreover, the cessation of large and free supplies of slaves accentuated the cruelty of slavery conditions in the United States and in the British, Danish, and Dutch West Indies. Wilberforce and his friends Thomas Fowell Buxton, Zachary Macaulay, Dr. Lushington, and Lord Suffield recommenced in 1821 their activities in Parliament for the abolition of Slavery, and in 1823 established the Anti-Slavery Society. [Sir] Thomas Powell Buxton[1] relieved the aged Wilberforce of the stress of fighting in the new movement. On the 5th May, 1823, he moved in the House of Commons a measure for the gradual abolition of Slavery. But the Prime Minister, Canning, saw this measure foredoomed to failure, and instead carried through the House of Commons several resolutions dealing with the amelioration of Slavery conditions and recommending these to the attention of the Colonial Legislatures, at the same time bringing them into immediate effect in the Crown Colony of Trinidad. These were the celebrated 1823 Resolutions which took whole or partial effect throughout the West Indies and Guiana in 1824, and which, though they did a good deal to help the slave, only made his desire for freedom more acute.

In 1828 the free people of colour in most (but not all) of the West Indian colonies were placed on a footing of equality with the whites. But in 1830 the agitation in Parliament for the complete abolition of slavery was renewed. The movement was delayed by the contemporary excitement over the Reform Bill; but when that became law, the

[1] He was made a Baronet in 1840, not so much for his great work in bringing about emancipation as for his strenuous efforts and expenditure of funds to create a legitimate commerce in West Africa which might take the place of the Slave-trade. See *Memoirs of Sir T. F. Buxton*, etc., by his son Charles Buxton (John Murray, 1877): a book of exceptional interest, for Buxton was concerned with many other things besides Slavery. His relations with Pope Gregory XVI and his descriptions of the Rome of 1839-40 are well worth recording. Pope Gregory was a keen anti-slavery reformer.

great Reform Ministry under Earl Grey adopted abolition as a Government measure. It was carried through the House of Commons and the House of Lords with little difficulty, and received the Royal Assent on the 28th of August, 1833. By this measure all children under six years of age were at once emancipated, but as regards the rest of the slaves, they were required to remain as apprentices to their masters for seven years, during which they were to give their labour for three-fourths of the working day and were to be liable to corporal punishment if they failed to do so. On the other hand, they were to be supplied with food and clothing gratis.

But this long apprenticeship was displeasing to the Anti-Slavery Party, and was reduced eventually to four years from 1834 instead of six. In Antigua, and perhaps one or two other West Indian islands, the planters made the best of a bad business, and all the slaves were liberated within the year 1833. But in any case, on August 28, 1838, Slavery ceased to be a legal status throughout the British Dominions in America, Africa, and Asia.

A sum of £20,000,000 was voted by the House of Commons from the British taxpayers' money as compensation to the slave-owners in the British Dominions, and also, no doubt, as a kind of "conscience money" in expiation of national wrong-doing. About £16,000,000 of this went to the British West Indies, Guiana, and Honduras; the rest to the Cape and Mauritius.

William Wilberforce died in 1833, a month before the Emancipation Bill received the Royal Assent. Clarkson lived to 1846 (he was eighty-six at the time of his death), having had the supreme satisfaction of commencing this struggle in 1786, following its course for sixty years, and seeing every item in his programme carried into effect.

In the last quarter of the eighteenth century the annual import of negroes into America was:—

By the British, 38,000; French, 20,000; Dutch, 4000; Danes, 2000; Portuguese, 10,000; total, 74,000.

Of these [it is calculated by Bryan Edwards], 700 came from the Gambia, 1500 from the Isles de Los and adjacent rivers, 2000 from Sierra Leone, 3000 from the Grain Coast (Liberia), 1000 from the Ivory Coast, 10,000 from the Gold Coast, 1000 from Quita and Pōpō (Togoland), 4500 from Dahomé, 3500 from Lagos, 3500 from Benin, 14,500 from the Niger delta, 7000 from Old Calabar and the Cameroons, 500 from the Gaboon, 14,500 from Loango, the Lower Congo, and northernmost Angola, 7000 from São Paulo de Loanda and Benguela (Central Angola).

After the Napoleonic Wars were over, in spite of the Slave-trade having been forbidden by several of the leading European nations and by the United States, the export of negroes from Africa to the Southern States, Cuba, Porto Rico, and the French West Indies went on increasing in volume till the annual average in (say) 1820 was about 100,000. The British Government took up its self-imposed duty of preventive service in 1819, and from that year to about 1878 it employed a considerable squadron to patrol the sea between Cape Verde, Brazil, the Cape of Good Hope, and Fernando Po [besides a similar work off the East African coasts and Persian Gulf, which was continued till 1895].

Its principal rendezvous in West Africa was Sierra Leone. This peninsula had been acquired by a philanthropic Chartered Company in 1787 as a refuge for Negro emigrants, notably those who had drifted to England after the American War. Later on, most of the rebellious Maroons from Jamaica were sent here. In 1808 the Imperial Government annulled the Charter and took over Sierra Leone as a colony. Soon after 1811 it became the principal place where the British Government maintained courts to condemn slave-ships and to land released slaves.

Between 1819 and 1828 the British cruisers captured and landed at Sierra Leone 13,281 slaves, an annual average of about 1400. Between 1828 and 1878 an approximate 50,000 negroes released from slave-ships were disembarked here; but the history of this interesting colony after 1808 belongs to the history of Africa.

CHAPTER XIII

SLAVERY UNDER THE DANES, ETC.

OTHER northern powers besides the Dutch and English were drawn by the demand for sugar and spices to acquire a West India island or two for their "plantations," and some establishment on the west coast of Africa for the recruitment of slaves to cultivate the sugar and cull the spice. In 1641 a Duke of Courland—the Teutonic ruler of a little Baltic duchy long since merged in Russia—obtained the grant of the island of Tobago[1] (near Trinidad) from Charles I of England [who had no more right to dispose of it than the King of France]. But the rival attempts at settlement on the part of the Dutch made things very disagreeable for the Courlanders, and eventually the Duke who reigned over Courland in 1681 disposed of his title to a company of London merchants.

In 1681 the "Great Elector" of Brandenburg (Frederick William) formed a company to trade in slaves from the Gold Coast to America, and not being able to obtain a West India island of his own, made common cause with the Danish Chartered Company of Guinea and the West Indies. Brandenburg ships from Stettin, and East Friesland vessels from Emden (the Prussian Company) proceeded to the Gold Coast, where in 1682 and 1685 they built forts (Grossfriedrichsburg and Dorotheaburg), and traded for gold dust and slaves. The Great Elector even purchased from the Dutch the little island of Arguin, near Cape Blanco (North Senegal coast), but this North German irruption into the slave-trade led to nothing. By 1720 the African and West Indian enterprise was abandoned.

The Swedes commenced to trade in slaves about 1640, and built in 1645 the well-known fort of Christiansborg, near Accra, on the Gold Coast. This was taken from them by the Danes in 1657. In 1784 Sweden bought from France the small West Indian island of St. Bartholomew, where with the aid of negro slaves the Swedes endeavoured to grow sugar for the Swedish market.[2]

In 1813 Sweden abolished the slave-trade as a lawful enterprise for Swedish ships, and in the same year acquired the French island of Guadeloupe from the British Government. But this transfer only took place on paper, and in 1815 Guadeloupe was restored to France.[3]

[1] The island of Robinson Crusoe described by Defoe.

[2] This island was repurchased by France in 1877.

[3] Amongst other curious ruling powers introduced into the West Indies and the inevitable slave-trade during the seventeenth century was the Order of the Knights of St. John of Jerusalem, which had become a sovereignty in the Mediterranean by their occupation of the islands of Malta and Gozo. In 1651 they are said to have purchased or been granted by France the islands of St. Christopher, St. Martin, St. Bartholomew, Tortuga (off the Haitian coast), and St. Croix. Their interest in these islands lapsed to France a few years afterwards. The idea of Louis XIV in drawing the Knights of St. John to the West Indies was to get them to war against the pirates who infested the Caribbean Sea in the last half of the seventeenth century.

The connection of Denmark with the slave-trade and negro slavery was more important and lasting. In 1657 the Danes captured Christiansborg Castle (on the Gold Coast) from the Swedes; and although they then sold it to the Portuguese, they repurchased it three years afterwards, and thenceforth set to work vigorously to establish the Danish power on the Gold Coast. The Danish West India and Guinea Company was formed in Copenhagen in 1671, and built forts along the Gold Coast between Christiansborg and the eastern side of the Volta River.

In 1666 the island of St. Thomas in the West Indies (about thirty-three square miles in area and situated at the eastern extremity of the long line of the Greater Antilles) was occupied by the Danes and taken over by their West

296. CHRISTIANSBORG CASTLE, NEAR ACCRA, GOLD COAST

India Company in 1671. Slaves were first introduced here from the Danish Gold Coast in 1680. The adjoining island of St. Jan (twenty-one square miles) was occupied in 1684, but not definitely annexed till 1717. The much larger island of St. Croix (Santa Cruz, forty miles south-east of St. Thomas, eighty-four square miles in area) was purchased by the King of Denmark from France in 1733 for over £30,000.[1]

Although on the coast of Africa the Dane was rated as a kindly master, only second to the Spaniard and Portuguese, yet even the Danes went through their period of cruelty.[2] In the island of St. Jan, as the result of ill-

[1] Before that purchase Santa Cruz had been Dutch, English, Spanish, and French. It was the Porto Rican Spanish massacre of the Santa Cruz English colonists in 1650 which provoked Cromwell to declare war and seize Jamaica in 1655.

[2] Besides the usual floggings, cutting off of ears, hands, and legs, and final hangings (when there was nothing more to torture), the Danes—till the influence of the Moravian missionaries bettered things—were in the habit of "pinching" recreant slaves with red-hot iron pincers, or for heinous offences "pinching pieces of flesh out of them." This pastime spread to the United States, and was not unknown there in the nineteenth century.

treatment there was a terrible slave insurrection in 1733. All the whites were killed, except a few who gathered round an old English planter and one surgeon spared by the negroes to dress wounds; and the Danish authorities were obliged to appeal to the French in Martinique to assist them in putting down the rising. Then when the last three hundred of the revolted slaves were surrounded and offered their lives if they would surrender, they preferred committing suicide to giving themselves back to slavery.

Between 1755 and 1764 the Danish Crown bought from the Danish West India Company St. Thomas and St. Jan, and then governed directly all the Danish West Indies. For nine years during the first fifteen of the nineteenth century the Danish West Indies were under British control—a circumstance which implanted very firmly the English language amongst the negro slaves. Even now English, and not Danish, is the common speech of the islands.

The Danish slave-trade left this mark on the west coast of Africa: the Danes introduced in the eighteenth and early nineteenth century a special type of long-barrelled gun, known to the trade as "long Danes." To this day the type of long-barrelled musket is in request in remote parts of West Africa, and it was with "long Dane guns" that the Ashanti people made such desperate war on the British.

In 1792 the Prince Regent of Denmark (afterwards Frederick VI) issued a decree prohibiting the slave-trade to Danish subjects from and after the year 1802. Although, as it were, ten years' grace was allowed for the cessation of the traffic, this action afforded a powerful stimulus to the anti-slave-trade movement. It set an example which put other civilised nations on their mettle. The United States felt obliged to follow suit in 1794 and 1807; Great Britain also.

In 1792 the charter of the Danish West India Company came to an end and was not renewed, the Crown (as previously in the West Indies) taking over the direct management of the Gold Coast forts. These last grew during the first half of the nineteenth century into quite a large domain, including a Danish protectorate over the Akwapim country and the Lower Volta River. In spite of the Danish prohibition of the slave-trade, however, one cannot help thinking that a clandestine traffic in slaves must have continued from the Danish Gold Coast,[1] for when the Danish Government *abolished the status of slavery* in all its oversea possessions in 1848 (especially in the West Indies), the four Gold Coast forts and the Volta River protectorate were soon found to be of little value or interest to Denmark; so that these African possessions were sold to Great Britain in 1850 for the modest sum of £10,000, and have constituted since a very important part of the British Gold Coast Colony.

In 1733 there was a slave insurrection in the Danish island of St. Jan, which was only subdued by the help of the French Governor of Martinique, who sent a force of four hundred soldiers to the assistance of the Danish Governor. Otherwise the condition of the negroes under Danish Government in the West Indies was a better one (in slavery days) than under other flags. The Moravian missionaries were encouraged during the middle of the eighteenth century, beginning in 1732, to teach and Christianise the slaves. A good example of the type of negro which grew up under Danish rule is a remark-

[1] As late as 1830 slave-ships under the Danish flag were captured by British cruisers.

able personality at the present day: Dr. Edward Wilmot Blyden, born in St. Thomas in 1832.[1]

The substitution of the direct rule of the Danish Crown for that of a Chartered Company did not at first improve the commercial development of these three islands, as their trade was strangled by a protectionist tariff entirely in favour of the Crown revenues. But by degrees the Danish sovereign relaxed the monopoly, until in 1766 he went—very wisely—to the opposite extreme and declared St. Thomas a free port. This policy led to an enormous increase in the value of the Danish Antilles, especially as St. Thomas possessed a splendid natural harbour, particularly well situated as a refuge for sailing-vessels entering or leaving the Caribbean Sea. Sugar cultivation covered every square mile of utilisable soil on St. Croix, and the slave population of this island in 1792 must have risen to sixty thousand. Not many Danes came to settle either here or at St. Thomas; the European planters were chiefly French Protestants—Huguenots—who were unable to live then in any French possession; Jews of various nationalities; English, Spaniards, and Swedes. During the war of the French Revolution, from 1793 to 1801, St. Thomas and St. Croix brimmed over with prosperity, because as Denmark was then a neutral power, much colonial produce could sail safely under the Danish flag.

297. DR. EDWARD WILMOT BLYDEN
A former Secretary of State and Diplomatic Envoy of Liberia: born in St. Thomas

After the Napoleonic Wars were over, St. Thomas and St. Croix continued so prosperous that the Danish Government seems to have regretted its condemnation of the slave-trade in 1792, and to have been reluctant to add to that measure a complete emancipation of the slaves. But Britain's action in setting free the slaves of the British West Indies between 1834 and 1838 made it necessary for the Danish Government to put an end to slavery. Early in 1847 a decree of King Christian VII was promulgated by which all children born in the Danish Antilles after July 28th, 1847, would be born free. Yet this measure was wholly insufficient for the angry slaves of St. Croix, who forthwith rose and dominated the island. The Danish Governor could only recover possession of St. Croix by declaring slavery to be completely at an end. Since the year 1848 slavery ceased to be recognised as a legal status in Danish Africa or America. But even then, the rebellion having spread to St. Thomas,

[1] Dr. Blyden went to Liberia at the age of nineteen, and became first a professor in Liberia College, then an explorer, and latterly a minister of state and a diplomatic representative of Liberia in England and France. Dr. Blyden has also served the (British) Sierra Leone Government as a superintendent of Muhammadan education. He is deeply versed in Arabic and Hebrew, Greek and Latin, and is the author (amongst many other works) of a well-known book entitled *Christianity, Islam, and the Negro Race.*

the Danes would have been driven from their Antillean possessions had it not been for the intervention of the Spanish Government, who feared to see the spirit of successful revolt spreading to Porto Rico and Cuba. A Spanish force landed in St. Thomas and restored Danish authority (1847-8).

The free negroes now returned to work, and laws were framed to assist the planters by introducing a method of apprenticeship, according to which children, vagrants, and petty offenders were apprenticed for a term of years to European planters. Although the apprenticing took place before a magistrate and for a nominal payment, the system was little else than forced labour and caused great indignation among the negro population. Yet it served to maintain the prosperity of St. Croix as a sugar- and rum-producing island.

But combined with the refusal of the local Government to allot lands in

298. CHARLOTTE-AMALIA
The capital of St. Thomas, Danish West Indies

St. Croix to free negro settlers, it led to another serious revolt in 1878, which nearly ruined the island. Houses, factories, the whole town of Frederiksted, and many of the cane-fields were destroyed by fire; and in the suppression of this revolt several hundred negroes and thirty or forty Europeans were killed.

Since 1870, however, the prosperity of the Danish Antilles had been going downhill. It was not merely the decline in the price of sugar or the abolition of forced labour, but the growth of steam navigation which has made St. Thomas far less important as a port of call for steamers than it had formerly been for sailing-ships. The negro population has been steadily decreasing for the last thirty years, the young men emigrating in search of better opportunities to other West India islands and to Panama. There are now several thousand more women in the three islands than there are men. In St Jan the population has decreased from 2475 in 1835[1] to 925 at the present day, and

[1] In 1802 there were 2000 whites, 1000 free negroes and negroids, and 2500 slaves.

the total population of the three islands (of which about a thousand are Europeans) is now under 30,000, whereas in 1835 it was 43,178. The population of St. Thomas is nearly all confined to the capital town of Charlotte-Amalia. This island is without springs or wells, and has a very poor and uncertain rainfall. Yet the scenery is said to be lovely,[1] and the island enjoys increasing favour with tourists because of its good roads, its clean, beautiful capital of Charlotte-Amalia, its glorious views of azure sea and distant islands and islets, its own pretty hill scenery and romantic, ruined "pirate castles" (which, however, were really built by the Danish Company).

The island of St. Jan is used for rearing horses, cattle, and poultry. It is the home of the "bay-leaf" tree (*Pimenta acris*), which is used for making "bay-rum." This aromatic toilet requisite is manufactured in St. Thomas.

St. Croix has a better rainfall than the other two islands and a fertile soil, but no good port. Like St. Thomas, it has admirable roads; indeed, the road-system of St. Croix is said to be the best and the most complete of any island in the West Indies.[2] Sugar-cane cultivation and the manufacture of sugar are still its principal industry, although fruit-growing and cattle-breeding are becoming important.

The present government of the Danish Antilles is that of a Crown Colony with partially representative institutions. The Governor is assisted in his functions by two colonial councils, one for St. Thomas and St. Jan and the other for St. Croix. In the first there are four members nominated by the Crown and eleven elected by the people; in the second, five councillors are nominated and thirteen are elected. In both suffrage and councillorship there are no colour distinctions.

It is said that a project is on foot for developing with Danish funds the resources of these islands, whose inhabitants will be allowed to elect one or two representatives to sit in the Danish Riksdag. If this plan is to be carried out and similar facilities are offered to Danish Greenland, we may live to see the quaint spectacle of a Negro from the West Indies and an Eskimo from the Arctic Circle sitting side by side as Danish subjects in a Danish Parliament.

It seemed a more likely outcome of the difficulties in which the Danish Antilles found themselves at the commencement of the twentieth century, that the three little islands might be sold to the United States and the Danish negroes be merged into the English-speaking community of Aframericans. But the United States by taking up and making the Panama Canal has itself greatly enhanced the value of the Danish Antilles, with their splendid harbours of Charlotte-Amalia (St. Thomas) and Coral (St. Jan).[3] These once again as free ports on the direct line of route from northern and western Europe to Colon may recover their old importance, especially as a *point-de-repère* for Scandinavian and North German shipping. So that the African Negro, who already speaks English, French, Spanish, Portuguese, Dutch, and three or four separate Creole jargons, may have to add Danish to his curriculum.

But if for no other reason than that they gave the first harbourage and support to the pioneer Moravian missionaries (who made St. Thomas their West Indian head-quarters from 1732 to 1782), the Danes have played a notable part in the history of the Negro in the New World. For the Moravian

[1] A. E. Aspinall, *The Pocket Guide to the West Indies* (London: 1907).

[2] *Les Petites Antilles* (Les Antilles Danoises), par. P. Chemin-Dupont (Paris: 1908).

[3] Coral Bay is a harbour of refuge from hurricanes. The port of St. Thomas is sometimes swept by these terrible wind-storms.

Brethren "were the truest and best guides Europe has ever supplied to the African race," as was written of them more than thirty years ago by one not usually enthusiastic about Christian propaganda (W. G. Palgrave). To the miserably unhappy negro slaves in Danish, Dutch, and British tropical America, and to those labouring under even harder circumstances in North America, they brought the first ray of hope. And it must be remembered that the Moravians were supplied with funds by the Danish kings and travelled in Danish ships. But for this active support on the part of Kings Christian VI and Frederick V it is doubtful whether the Moravian Brethren would ever have got or maintained a footing in the West Indies, and all but the Danish possessions were closed to them.

Through the intercession of their powerful Saxon protector Count Zinzendorf (who had great influence at the Danish Court) they were allowed in October, 1732, to start for St. Thomas.[1] The two pioneers were Leonard Dober and David Nitschmann, and they were accompanied by a released slave—Anthony—from Denmark. Mission work was commenced in St. Thomas in December, 1732. In the year 1733 a terrible slave insurrection broke out on the little island of St. Jan, and for several succeeding years prejudice against teaching the negroes was very strong; but as it became evident that slaves drawn within the mission fold by the Moravians stood apart from the turbulent element and were far better workers (especially where the plea for kinder treatment from the master was listened to), the Moravians grew in favour with the planters, as they did also in the British colonies of North America and in Dutch Guiana, where they established themselves between 1735 and 1745. In Dutch Guiana the most noteworthy Moravian pioneer was Friedrich Martin.

299. LEONARD DOBER
One of the two first Moravian missionaries to settle in the West Indies

The news of the betterment of the Danish slaves in St. Thomas and St. Croix spread to Jamaica and Antigua; and the Moravian missionaries were invited by private planters or by the Governor to establish in those islands (Jamaica in 1754 and Antigua in 1760).

They could not, however, do very great things in the British West Indies, Dutch Guiana, or North America till all the slaves were emancipated (though their educational work among the freedmen was remarkable); but in these countries under Protestant Powers it was mainly through the Moravian and

[1] Count Zinzendorf (see later) came out himself in 1739 to see how the missionaries were getting on in the Danish islands, and raised them up out of crushing persecutions at the hands of jealous Lutherans and angry planters. Zinzendorf became a Bishop and head of the Moravian Church. He was one of the most remarkable persons of the eighteenth century, and really worthy of the twentieth century in his ideas. He founded Moravian missions among the Hottentots of South Africa, the natives of Ceylon (both these were ultimately destroyed by the clergy of the Dutch Reformed Church), of Lower Egypt, Algeria, Northern Russia, Greenland, Labrador, Pennsylvania, South Carolina, Georgia, Dutch Guiana, and Jamaica.

the Quaker that the door of hope was first opened to the despairing negroes, who at that period of the eighteenth century, in Georgia, the British West Indies, and Guiana, were committing suicide at a rate which alarmed even their callous owners.

The Moravian Church, whose educational work is now world-wide, from near the North Pole to Australia and South Africa, from Tibet to the coast of Nicaragua, arose out of Hussite reforms and religious warfare in Bohemia and Moravia. It was reconstituted as an episcopal Church in 1467, and its tenets were as nearly as possible (and are still) based on the plain teaching of Christ. Dogmatic formulation of creed counted for little, the main object of the *Unitas Fratrum* (as this Church styled itself) being to lead a simple, godly life and encourage industry as much as possible.

300. FRIEDRICH MARTIN
The first Moravian missionary who explored Dutch Guiana

During the sixteenth and seventeenth centuries the Moravian Brethren were persecuted horribly by the Holy Roman Empire and (sad to say) by the Roman Catholic Church. In Bohemia and Moravia they were almost exterminated. Towards the close of the seventeenth century they effected some community with the Church of England, which has never lessened, and even as early as 1739 we find an Archbishop of Canterbury assisting them to work in Georgia. In 1722 the remnants of the Moravian Church crossed over into Saxony, where a refuge had been offered to them by [Saint] Nicolaus Ludwig, Graf von Zinzendorf, on his estates. Here the town of Herrnhut was founded, the centre of Moravian mission work down to the present day. But it was really the Count of Zinzendorf who founded the true Moravian Church and imparted to it that largeness of view and sweet reasonableness in theology which make it remarkable in the narrow-minded Christianity of the eighteenth century. The original Moravians received by him were fanatical, ignorant peasants, who not long after his most generous and ample establishment of them at Herrnhut denounced him as the Beast of the Apocalypse. They were indeed—as fifty other sects have been from 900 A.D. to 1900 A.D.—half crazed with warped study of that dangerous and needless addition to the books of the New Testament, the Revelation of John; and it required the saving common sense of Zinzendorf—the General Booth of his century—to turn their fervour into the channel of perfect service to man.

CHAPTER XIV

SLAVERY IN THE UNITED STATES

IN 1619 the first negroes were landed in the English Colonies on the North American continent. In that year a supply of slaves was being brought by the Dutch from the west coast of Africa to serve in the Dutch settlements of Manhadoes and New Amsterdam (New York), and on its way thither the ship conveying the slaves called in at Jamestown, Virginia, and sold some twenty negroes to the tobacco-planters of that newly founded British colony.

The planting of tobacco from 1620 onwards became a most profitable enterprise in Virginia and was indeed the principal cause of the British "catching on" in North America, where hitherto their efforts had several times been checked or completely frustrated by inclemencies of climate, hostility of indigenes, and the absence of any easily obtained mineral, vegetable, or animal product which would enable people to get rich quickly so that they might stomach the dangers and discomforts of life in a savage land.

The white convict transport system began about this time through James I putting into execution laws that had been framed by Queen Elizabeth's Parliament for dealing with vagabonds; but until the reign of Charles II there was no great output of white convict labour from British gaols to serve as slaves or indentured apprentices in the American plantations.

Therefore throughout the seventeenth century from 1620 onwards there was an increasing demand in the States of the eastern seaboard of North America for negro labour. The white convicts when they did arrive, if females, were soon married and ceased to be useful as labourers; and if male, either struck against field labour of an exhausting kind or died from the effects of it. To do the dirty and the fatiguing work of opening up the temperate and sub-tropical regions of North America, the negro seemed a more useful immigrant.

The work of tobacco-planting was a healthy occupation, and the Virginian negroes throve and were not unhappy in their slavery during the seventeenth century. There was little or no temptation to run away because the fierce Indians haunted the backwoods, and to attempt to escape by sea was impossible. At the close of the seventeenth century, or actually in the year 1700, rice was introduced into South Carolina as a profitable article of export; but the cultivation of rice in swamps under the hot sun proved most unhealthy to the negroes, whilst it was an impossibility for a white man. Consequently the slave supply for South Carolina, and later still for Georgia, had to be constantly renewed by drafts from Africa.

The rush to get rich during the first half of the eighteenth century enhanced the value of slaves in North America and incited their white owners to get all the work they could out of them. In South Carolina the condition of the slaves was often one of great hardship and the slave laws were very cruel. The male slaves were almost deliberately worked to death in the pestilential rice swamps, as it was thought to be more profitable to get several years' continuous hard labour out of them, than to work them more gently and perhaps enable them to survive to an invalid old age in which they would have to be supported at the owner's cost. The result was that after 1710 slave insurrections were menaced. In 1720 a slave plot at Charleston was nipped in the bud and the negro conspirators were burnt, hanged, and banished. But a formidable revolt of slaves actually occurred at Charleston in 1740. On the first day of this same year,

301. COTTON

however, George Whitefield paid the second of his seven visits to North America, and after travelling through Georgia and South Carolina founded a school for negroes in Delaware under the Moravian Brethren.

By 1760 there was a slave population in Virginia, South Carolina, and Georgia of 400,000. A few thousand slaves in addition were scattered over Pennsylvania, Delaware, Maryland, New York, and New Jersey, more as domestic servants.

In 1770 the cultivation of cotton was begun in South Carolina and Georgia, and after the excitement and turmoil of the American War of Independence was over, cotton-planting in the Southern States increased enormously and created an immense demand for negro labour. A few of the United States negroes had fought in the British army as free soldiers against the American colonists, and after the Peace of 1783 some of these free blacks migrated to

Nova Scotia,[1] to England,[2] the Bermudas, Bahamas, and Jamaica; and some formed the nucleus of the 1st West India Regiment (Barbados).

By 1800 there were 1,002,037 negroes and negroids in the United States, about 200,000 of whom were freed men and women.

Slavery as an institution had, however, been condemned to public disapproval by the Quakers early in the history of North America. In 1671 George Fox, after a long journey in the previous year through the island of Jamaica, had denounced to the newly founded *Society of Friends* or Quakers of England the condition of slavery as iniquitous no matter to what race it was applied; and when compelled to leave England by religious persecution, or deported thence as felons, the Friends in North America, especially in Pennsylvania (1696), Delaware, Maryland, and Virginia (as well as in St. Kitts, Jamaica, and Barbados), set their faces steadily against negro slavery and endeavoured to do all they could to alleviate the lot of the slaves.[3] With them joined to a great extent the Puritan element in the New England colonies, together with all the Nonconformist bodies, beginning with the Baptists, who were finding it possible to exist independently of the Church of England in North America or in Britain.

The first great anti-slavery apostle who arose in the United States—whilst they were still under the dominion of Great Britain—was Anthony Benezet—Saint Anthony Benezet, as he will some day be called. He was born in Picardy (Northern France) in 1713. Being a Protestant, he and his father were expelled from France and settled in London. Thence Anthony Benezet moved to Philadelphia, in Pennsylvania.[4] He joined the Quakers, and under the influence of John Woolman became an eager but a reasoning, eloquent, and learned denouncer of slavery and the slave-trade. He wrote much on the subject, but the two most convincing of his works were published in 1762: *A Caution and Warning to Great Britain and her Colonies on the Calamitous State of the Enslaved Negroes in the British Dominions*; and *An Historical Account of Guinea, its Situation, Produce, and the General Disposition of its Inhabitants; with an Enquiry into the Rise and Progress of the Slave-trade, its Nature and Calamitous Effects.*

He had opened up relations with John Wesley and Granville Sharp in England so that they might co-operate in the common cause, and as late as 1783 he wrote in the simple "thou and thee" phrasing of the Quakers a letter to Queen Charlotte which probably secured her sympathy in the anti-slave-trade movement. But it was his *Historical Account of Guinea* which really set the forces of English philanthropy moving. Public opinion in England after the declaration of the law that there could be no slavery within the limits of the Kingdoms of Great Britain and Ireland had relapsed into toleration of what went on in the Colonies and in Africa. Another crusader was required. Benezet's book on Guinea turned the Cambridge student Clarkson to the one great purpose of his life.

[1] There are now about 6000 negroes and negroids in Nova Scotia. Most of these were the refugees or the children of refugee slaves who escaped from the United States and were only safe from recapture on British territory.

[2] Emigrated afterwards to Africa.

[3] In 1776 all Friends who would not emancipate their slaves and renounce the practice of slave-holding were expelled from the membership. Mention should also be made of the efforts in the same direction (in America) of the Lutheran Moravian missionaries and of the Huguenots (French Protestants).

[4] He lived here with his wife and three brothers, and made a modest livelihood by teaching French and writing books.

Benezet therefore (he died in 1784, a year before the conversion of Clarkson) deserves to rank with Harriet Beecher-Stowe as a writer who moved the world to great reforms. His influence was not merely confined to England: his correspondence with the Abbé Raynal and other Frenchmen of far-sighted philanthropy really created the anti-slavery movement in France. The influence of George Whitefield and of Wesley (invoked by Benezet) and of the Methodist Church which he founded, and which spread so quickly to America; and later on the new spirit of the Evangelical or Low Church section of the Church of England; joined forces, politically and spiritually, with the Quakers, Baptists, and Independents. And at the close of the eighteenth century the opinion in England and New England of all high-minded, virtuous, thinking, educated people was against the slave-trade and the status of slavery.

George Washington in his will gave freedom to all his own slaves, and it was well known that he had expressed an earnest wish that slavery (not specifically mentioned in the Constitution of the United States) might be abolished in every State of the Union. He several times expressed this wish in writing, and declared that he himself would vote for the emancipation of the slaves. On the 1st of March, 1780, the Assembly of the Commonwealth of Pennsylvania passed an Act for "the gradual abolition of slavery." Being largely a Quaker State, it had always opposed slavery in principle, and had wished in 1712 to forbid the importation of negroes; but in the following year (1713) the Government of "good" Queen Anne (who herself was a shareholder in the slave-trade) had disallowed the measure. During the first half of the nineteenth century, the Government of Pennsylvania felt unable to proclaim the inherent freedom of all persons of all colours on its soil, except they had *been born* within the State, or had *been brought thither voluntarily* by any one having a claim over them. Thus, if a master of slaves knowing the conditions of Pennsylvania voluntarily brought his slave there, that slave became free. Otherwise, slaves could not run over the border of Pennsylvania and become free; but no slave might be retained in Pennsylvania, as a slave, longer than six months. Slavery was also abolished in Massachusetts in 1780, in Connecticut and Rhode Island in 1784 under conditions which did not make its abolition wholly operative till some years later. New Hampshire excluded slavery from the scope of her Constitution in 1792, likewise Vermont in 1793. New York began the gradual abolition of slavery in 1799, and completed it on the 4th of July, 1827. New Jersey finished with slavery about 1829. Ohio,

302. ISAAC T. HOPPER
A typical early nineteenth-century Quaker and Anti-Slavery Reformer

Indiana, Illinois, Michigan, Wisconsin, and Iowa were organised as a Territory in 1787, and slavery was wholly excluded "for ever" from the lawful conditions of life. Maine was an offshoot of Massachusetts after that State had abolished slavery.

Maryland was the most northern Slave State of the Union, and remained such down to the early part of the great Civil War in 1863. The Federal District of Columbia (Washington) recognised slavery as of local validity until 1862, and runaway slaves from other States could be arrested on its small territory under the Federal Fugitive Slave Act. Slaves, however, were happy in and around Washington; they were so near head-quarters that ill-treatment would be punished.

The United States in Congress in 1794 forbade *the participation of American subjects in the Slave-trade* between Africa and foreign countries.

So far as it affected the coast ports of Georgia, that State in 1798 declared the trade in slaves between Africa and Georgia to be prohibited. North Carolina closed its ports to the importation of slaves from Africa as early as 1793. In 1819, however, the State of Virginia annulled as much as possible its anti-slave-trade prohibitions of the previous century.

On the 1st January, 1808, the Federal Government of the United States prohibited the importation of African slaves into United States territory. At the Peace of Ghent in December, 1814, the United States and Great Britain mutually pledged themselves to do all in their power to extinguish the slave-trade.

Nevertheless, in spite of these Federal laws and engagements, the slave-trade between Africa and the States of the Union to the south of the Mason-Dixon line went on with very little interruption of an official kind until the American Civil War. This was notably the case with regard to South Carolina and Georgia. Probably the southern coast of South Carolina was the last portion of the United States that received slave cargoes from Africa. There are negroes still living in this region (also in Virginia and Georgia) that were born in Africa.

Between 1780 and 1816 there had grown up in the United States (chiefly in Maryland, Pennsylvania, the District of Columbia, New York, and Virginia), a considerable class of free negroes or men of colour; mostly slaves who had been manumitted by their masters or allowed to purchase their freedom. Such freedmen were becoming a source of trouble to the white community in these States, because though not slaves, they were not allowed the ordinary privileges of citizens, and being more educated than their brother slaves, they began to ask awkward questions and inspire the slaves with a similar discontent.

So it was resolved by their well-wishers to ship them off (if they were inclined to go) to Africa, to create there a new home where they could live as freemen. Naturally it was the British experiment of Sierra Leone which suggested the idea.

At first it was decided to join forces with Great Britain and send these negro colonists to Sierra Leone; but the British Governor of that colony viewed the proposal suspiciously. Besides, he himself had begun to appreciate this important factor in the question of an American negro colony on the West African coast: namely, that West Africa belonged to the West Africans, who were not disposed to welcome any large colony of strangers.

So the American envoys passed on, in 1821, to the adjoining "Grain

Coast," and in that year founded the future Republic of Liberia by establishing its nucleus at Monrovia.

The history of the Liberian experiment has been so fully described in my book on that country[1] that I need say no more of it here, except to add that it did *not* solve the difficulties of the Free Negro question in the United States between 1820 and 1870. Firstly, the negroes in the United States preferred life in that Republic (especially after 1865) to life anywhere else; secondly, if they had been born in America they suffered from the West African climate and diseases nearly as much as a white man; and lastly, the native inhabitants of "Liberia" were fairly numerous and not at all inclined to make way for American strangers. They were also too warlike and well armed to be easily subdued.

The Liberian experiment will probably succeed in this way: that the thirty or forty thousand descendants of American negroes and the natives they have already affiliated to their government may form the nucleus of a future civilised, self-governed, independent Negro State; but the bulk of the citizens of that State will be of local African origin.

The outcome of the Liberian Colony has at any rate been too trifling in importance to have provided an "expatriation" solution for the American negro problem. Nothing that has been achieved in Liberia will encourage the American negro and negroid to emigrate in millions to Africa. If he has noticed Liberia at all, it is in the direction of deciding more emphatically than ever to stay in the New World, where he is—with all his disadvantages—far better off than he would be as a belated colonist of Africa. Moreover, in returning to Africa, he runs the risk of finding himself some day once more the subject of a European Power; and in these new and great Republics of the West he hopes that the lesson of equal rights and equal opportunities for all races of mankind has been better mastered than in the Old World.

Thomas Jefferson had proposed in 1784 that in the new territory to be acquired by the United States (especially the region divided into Tennessee, Alabama, and Mississippi), there should after the year 1800 be neither slavery nor involuntary servitude, otherwise than in punishment of crime; but he failed to carry this proviso, even though in 1787 at the Convention of Philadelphia the majority of those who framed the Constitution of the United States were opposed to slavery. South Carolina, however, Georgia most of all, and Virginia, less fiercely,[2] contended for the retention of the status of slavery in the Constitution of their respective States.

By the beginning of the nineteenth century the slave-holding States were divided from those in which all men, theoretically, were free, by the Mason and Dixon line; that boundary which was traced by two English surveyors, Mason

[1] *Liberia* (London: 1906).

[2] As early as the seventeenth century the Legislature of Virginia had enacted that "all persons who have been imported into the colony, and who were not Christians in their native country—except Turks and Moors in amity with His Majesty, and those who can prove their being free in England or in any other Christian country—shall be counted and be slaves, shall be bought and sold, notwithstanding their conversion to Christianity after their importation." About the same time, it was further laid down by law that a white man marrying a negress should be banished from Virginia, and the clergyman who performed the marriage service should be subjected to a heavy fine.

Between the years 1699 and 1772 the Legislature of Virginia passed numerous Acts to *discourage* the importation of slaves. The means resorted to was the imposition of considerable duty on imported slaves. But the King of Great Britain, as advised by his ministers, vetoed most of these Acts.

and Dixon, in 1763–7, originally for the purpose of dividing Pennsylvania on the north from Maryland and (West) Virginia on the south. This line in 1820 was extended westwards along the course of the Ohio River (the northern frontier of Kentucky) to the Mississippi, and across this river it mounted northwards so as to include Missouri within the area of States wherein slavery was permissible.

This was what is known in United States history as the "Missouri Compromise": a compromise, but at the same time the first definite acknowledgment of the scission between north and south.

First came the difference between Pennsylvania on the one hand, and Virginia and Maryland on the other, which in 1780 turned the Mason-Dixon line into the boundary between Slavery and Freedom. Then in 1787 an Ordinance of Congress adopted the Ohio River as the continuation westwards of the Mason-Dixon line between the Slave States and those which were contemplating or achieving cessation of slavery. This brought the distinction westward to the Mississippi. When Louisiana had been taken over from the French, the right of Slavery to continue on the west bank of the Lower Mississippi had been tacitly admitted. How far northwards and westwards was this licence of Slavery to extend?

The admission of Missouri into the Union as a State was to be the test. Missouri as a Territory had radiated from the old French settlement and town of St. Louis, founded in 1764. Under the subsequent rule of Spain negro slaves had been introduced by the French colonists. Missouri upheld the institution when it sought to be promoted in 1819 from a mere Territory to a self-governing State. Yet if it were admitted to the Union as a Slavery State it would disturb the balance of power in the Senate. A solution was found in 1821 by the admission of Missouri as a Slavery State and simultaneously the promotion to Statehood of Maine, which had been detached from Massachusetts. But the chief point in the Compromise was that the Slavery limit westward of the Mississippi, to the Pacific, should follow the degree of N. Latitude 36° 30'. South of that line it was tacitly, but not implicitly, admitted that slavery might continue.

On the strength of this Compromise, Arkansas was admitted as a Slave State in 1836; Florida and Texas in 1845. In both the two last of course slavery had existed theoretically since the early times of Spanish occupation. But Florida had really been "Indian" territory with the merest fringe of European colonisation (though it contains the oldest town in the United States, St. Augustine, founded in 1566) until 1827–35; when the whites of Georgia calmly, and defiant of Federal veto, removed most of the Seminole "Indians" and sent white emigrants and negro slaves to take their place.[1]

In 1822 there was alleged to have been discovered a plot at Charleston (S.C.) amongst the slaves and free negroes for an uprising of black against white, and the destruction of the whites, on July 4th of that year. The principal leader was Denmark Vesey, a blacksmith who had won a prize in a lottery twenty-two years before, and with the proceeds had purchased his freedom. His lieutenants were Monday Gell, a self-educated, talented negro harness-maker; and Gullah Jack and Peter Poyas, half-savage leaders among the

[1] The Amerindian tribe or nation of the Seminoles of eastern Florida kept negro slaves in the eighteenth and early nineteenth centuries. But it was remarked that they were very good and indulgent to these slaves, and never, under the greatest pressure of hunger and need, sold them if they were unwilling to go to a white master.

Angola slaves with whom South Carolina was then being so abundantly furnished by the Portuguese slave-trade.

As a result of the timely discovery of this conspiracy by the Charleston police, thirty-five negroes were hanged, a number were probably flogged, and others were transported or imprisoned. But the plot deserves mention because it was cited as the excuse for the greater harshness of South Carolina slavery laws after 1822, and for the sending off as many free negroes as possible to Liberia. Further excuse for the putting in force of cruel laws was afforded by the great rising of negro slaves under Nat Turner, in Virginia

303. WILLIAM LLOYD GARRISON

(Southampton County), on August 21, 1831. Some whites lost their lives in this revolt, which was suppressed with the usual ruthlessness.[1]

In 1833 the American Anti-Slavery Society was founded in Boston by a brave man, William Lloyd Garrison. Two years previously, in Boston, he had commenced to publish "without a dollar of capital" an anti-slavery journal, the *Liberator*; and had addressed the world in its first number, with these stirring words: "I am in earnest—I will not equivocate—I will not excuse—I will not retreat a single inch—and I will be heard." He lived till 1879 to see his rushlight grow to a blaze of illumination, his paper and his society terminated in their existence only by the full accomplishment of their programme: the complete abolition of slavery throughout the Union in 1865.

[1] For information on this and other incidents of the ante-bellum slavery times in South Carolina, see the articles in the *Political Science Quarterly* of Boston, Mass., by Ulrich Bonnell Phillips—especially "The Slave Labor Problem in the Charleston District" (Boston: 1907).

Meantime the year 1850 had brought another crisis and another compromise. The conquest, annexation, and organisation of California and Northern Mexico again raised the question[1] whether the first of the new States should be "Slave" or "Free." Congress, with the superior voting power now in the hands of the North, decided that California should be a Free State, but as a solatium to the South, avoided fixing the "Slave or Free" status of the future States of Utah and New Mexico, and declared that the Federal district of Columbia, though closed to the slave-trade, was a region in which slavery existed. It also passed the celebrated Fugitive Slave Law.

This Act provided for the arrest of runaway slaves in any State of the Union to which they had fled, and the handing of them over not to local magistrates or courts, but to United States Commissioners and other Federal officers of the law. Their claims to freedom were to be tried *without a jury*, and when their status of servitude was proved to the satisfaction of the Federal commissioner, they were to be handed back to the authorities of the State from which they had fled (equivalent in some cases to a sentence of death by flogging!).

304. JOHN P. HALE
One of the Anti-Slavery Kansas agitators of 1855. . . .
"Free soil, free speech, free labour, free men!"

The next excitement was over Kansas (1854–7), which, with Nebraska, was being prepared for Statehood from out of the north-western portion of "Louisiana." By the fair interpretation of the Missouri Compromise these new States must be "Free" in constitution; but the South was getting bold, and had adopted the theory of "squatter sovereignty," by which it lay solely with the new settlers of these Territories to decide under what Constitution they should live. If, therefore, the South could send men into Kansas in excess of the North, they might by a superiority of voting power turn Kansas, as New Mexico had been turned, into a slave-holding Territory and afterwards State. A regular local-civil war arose and the South was beaten.

A striking landmark in the progress towards civil war was the "Dred Scott" decision. Dred Scott was a negro slave who had been taken by his master from the Slave State of Missouri to reside with him in the Free Territory of Kansas. Afterwards he was sold in Kansas, and then sued for his freedom (no doubt put up to do so by Abolitionists as a "test case"). Of

[1] *How* bored a twentieth-century person, if he could have lived backwards into the nineteenth century, would have become with the one-ideaed Southern statesman! As late as 1850-1 they were discussing in Charleston the reinstitution of the African Slave-trade on the West African coast, knowing so little of the England of that period as to imagine that the British Government would have permitted such a reversal of progress. They simply could not conceive of any policy different to their own. All the world must shape itself to the mistaken needs of South Carolina. And these were the people so admired by Gladstone, Kingsley, Huxley, and Carlyle!

course, by the terms of the Compromise of 1820, Dred Scott was a free man. Scott brought his case before the Federal Courts, and finally the suit had to be decided on appeal in the Supreme Court of the United States.

The result was a staggering blow to the Abolitionists of the North and a signal instance in history of the inhumanity of pedants in the law; of judges to whom the administration of the law is not in the first place the enunciation

305. HARRIET BEECHER-STOWE
From a daguerreotype of about 1852, just after the publication of *Uncle Tom's Cabin*

of perfect justice but a fascinating puzzle-game, a kind of chess, with absolutely no regard for the feelings of the chessmen.

The Supreme Court had not been consulted in 1820 as to the Missouri Compromise; and when this arrangement was brought before its notice by the Dred Scott case in 1858 it decided that the 1820 Compromise had no standing in United States constitutional law; that slaves were by that Constitution recognised as "property," and that the Federal Government had no right to forbid any recognised form of property from being held on any part of the

United States territory. It further put Scott out of court as being a slave or descendant of a slave, and consequently not a citizen of the United States or having any standing in the Federal Courts[1]

This cynical and pedantic decision was the real provocation of the Civil War, a war which cost the lives by bullet or disease of 300,000 men and a National Debt of 8000 *millions* of dollars, and left behind a legacy of hatred between white and coloured in the south-east of North America which it may take another generation to heal. It is to be hoped that if any of these Supreme Court judges of 1858 are living who pronounced a decision clamping the United States Constitution to the maintenance of slavery as an institution, they still writhe in their senile consciences at the fruits of their pitiless pedantry, the worship of the letter and disregard of the spirit.

The Dred Scott decision made civil war inevitable. The South could now plead that they abode by the Constitution. The Abolitionists in the North were inflamed to fanaticism against Slavery. During the ten years[2] which followed the enactment of the Fugitive Slave Law of 1850 (which in its subsequent operations was the cause of incredible cruelties, fraudulent kidnappings, scandals, blackmailing, and frequent manslaughter), *the publication of "Uncle Tom's Cabin"*[3] *in 1852;* the civil war provoked by the South in Kansas (1854–6); the murderous assault on Charles Sumner,[4] who had made a series

[1] Yet, when it was a matter of getting a representation in Congress out of all proportion to the numbers of its free-white citizens, at the time of the framing of the United States Constitution, the Southern States had been allowed to count three-fifths of the slaves as having a right to indirect representation in the House of Representatives.

[2] In this splendid period of ten years, ever to be a glory in the annals of America, slavery was hotly and indignantly opposed by some of the greatest geniuses that the United States had yet produced, geniuses and apostles. William Lloyd Garrison, Wendell Phillips, Charles Sumner, William E. Channing, Ralph Waldo Emerson, John G. Whittier, Henry Wadsworth Longfellow, William Cullen Bryant, Walt Whitman, Abraham Lincoln, Frederick Law Olmsted, are a few amongst the names of the notabilities who attacked, with risk to life, limb, health, and fortune, the hydra-headed monster—a monster only scotched, remember, not completely killed, which may issue from its cavern yet again and again at the call of Mammon and racial arrogance. But in the eyes and minds of the general public, mostly of a generation now passing away, it will be felt that four persons more than any others in the United States (acting quite independently one of the other) abolished slavery. The first was William Lloyd Garrison, the second Harriet Beecher-Stowe, the third John Brown, and the fourth Abraham Lincoln.

[3] Mrs. Harriet Beecher-Stowe, whose novel *Uncle Tom's Cabin* set the whole world on fire, and ranged most Europeans and Americans (outside the United States and the West Indies) on the side of the slave, was born (1811) in Connecticut (like John Brown), and died in that State at Hartford in 1896. *Uncle Tom's Cabin* was almost literally true, based on such works as *The Narrative of the Life and Adventures of Charles Ball* (published at New York in 1837) and on its author's personal observations of Kentucky and Tennessee. A few years ago I was taken over Osborne House by a friend who had access to that residence of the late Queen before it had been completely thrown open to its present purposes. In the library I saw lying on a table, much as it had been left by the Queen before her death, a copy of *Uncle Tom's Cabin*, rather prettily bound in a pink and silver wrapper. Inside on the fly-leaf in the Queen's own handwriting were words much like these: "From my dear Mama, Xmas, 1859. This book has made a deep impression on me."

We all know that subsequently, when the actual decision of peace or war lay with Queen Victoria (most of whose Liberal Ministers were in favour of the recognition of the South and war with the North), the Queen resolutely decided on complete neutrality, moved thereto by the consciousness that the North stood for freedom and the South for an impossible continuance of slavery. There is little doubt in my own mind that the agency which made of Queen Victoria so resolute an Abolitionist was the novel written by Harriet Beecher-Stowe: one of the few instances in history of the pen being mightier than the sword.—H. H. J.

[4] Charles Sumner made a great speech on the 18th of May, 1856, against the conditions under which the slave lived in South Carolina and Virginia. A senator of South Carolina, Preston S. Brooks, no doubt born a decent man, but his mind twisted by the corrupting influence of slavery into the mind of an assassin, stole after Sumner till he caught him writing in the Senate Chamber. Coming up behind him unawares, he thrashed him with a heavy stick, till he left him for dead. Was he apprehended? (at Washington on the very borders of Virginia?). No. He walked about a free man and was pre-

or speeches in Congress denouncing the "Crime against Kansas" (the attempt of leading Southern statesmen to force Kansas, against the will of the majority of its settlers, to become a Slave State); the Dred Scott decision; and lastly, the pamphlet *On the Impending Crisis of the South*, by a poor white of North Carolina named Helper: all these events and influences bred uncontrollable fury in the North against the despotism of the South. Amongst the few whose excitement could not vent itself sufficiently in speech or written word was John Brown, a native of Connecticut, who had been one of the leading fighters in the civil war of Kansas. He entered the State of Virginia at Harper's Ferry with fourteen resolute men and seized a Federal arsenal in the dead of night, designing to distribute its store of arms and ammunition among such slaves as he could induce to revolt against their masters. It was a "raid" which, if moderately successful, would, he thought, precipitate the struggle between North and South and lead to the abolition of slavery.

His invasion was a flash in the pan, for he was soon overwhelmed, captured (twelve of his following likewise), and led to execution on December 2, 1859. "But his soul went marching on."

306. CHARLES SUMNER

Abraham Lincoln denounced Brown's violent effort as "absurd." With regard to its chances of success it *was* wildly absurd, besides being "quite unconstitutional." It was of the order of deeds which cannot be defended by appeal to any man-made law, and which, if they were not quite properly visited with the death penalty, would reduce civilised society to chaos. Very often the cause for which a John Brown may commit a raid or an isolated murder is a rotten, a selfish, or a lunatic one; and the raider richly deserves his execution. In one case out of five hundred a John Brown may be fighting (most irregularly) for some cardinal point of liberty, for something which will lead to the enhanced spiritual or physical welfare of mankind. If he succeeds and does not get killed, he is possibly made a cabinet minister, a dictator, or a privy councillor. If he dies he receives, or should receive, beatification, for he has earned it by giving up his life for the future welfare of many people.

The election of Abraham Lincoln was the last episode which decided South Carolina—protagonist of the Slave Powers, and rightly so called, for it had been from first to last the wickedest of the Slave States—to secede from the Union. As soon as the assembled Presidential electors of that State

sented by the grateful Virginians with a magnificent gold-headed stick to replace the one with which (so far as intention went) he had murdered the man who had dared to speak against slavery. Sumner partially recovered, and did not die till 1874, but owing to the blows of his would-be assassin having affected the spine, he was always semi-paralysed. His would-be murderer died in 1859.

heard by telegram in November, 1860, that Abraham Lincoln had secured a majority of votes in the Presidential electorate and was therefore certain to become President of the United States in the following March, they summoned

Your Friend
John Brown

307. JOHN BROWN'S PORTRAIT AND AUTOGRAPH

a State Convention. This body on December 20th passed an Ordinance seceding from the rest of the United States of America.

Lincoln had never advocated abolition of slavery throughout the Union. He merely stood for a bargain being kept. He hated slavery and wished to restrict the area in which this institution was to exist to the narrowest limits consistent with the pre-existing inter-state agreements or understandings. But a bargain being a bargain, he resented the attempts of the South to withdraw from the agreements of 1820 and 1850; and most of all he opposed any idea of secession.

As early as 1849 he had proposed to Congress to emancipate the slaves in the District of Columbia (against compensation); and in 1854 he came to the front as an opponent of the extension of Slave Territories or States. Despite his protestations of wishing to uphold the Union above all and everything, he had plainly said in 1858 that there could be no protracted compromise in the matter of slavery: "A house divided against itself cannot stand. I believe this Government cannot endure permanently, half-slave and half-free . . . it will become all one thing or all the other."

As it was incredible that the overwhelming voting power of the North and New West would declare itself in favour of slavery everywhere, this utterance from the favourite candidate of the North, and his subsequent election as the nominated new President by the Republican National Convention on a "No Extension of Slavery" ticket (May 16th, 1860), made the breach with South Carolina inevitable.

308. ABRAHAM LINCOLN
From a print published just before the signing of the Emancipation Edict

War was begun by the South in January, 1861, and the gage of battle taken up by Lincoln on April 15th, 1861. Half Virginia, and the other Slave States of Delaware, Maryland, Kentucky, and Missouri stood by the Union; the rest, from Texas to Eastern Virginia, confederated with South Carolina.

In the great struggle which ensued the Negroes and Negroids of all the former Slave States signalised themselves in history for two things: their considerate behaviour towards their defeated masters and their bravery in battle. They remained quiescent throughout the South, where active fighting was not going on; and although every white man may have been absent at the war, they respected strictly the property of their owners and the chastity of their owners' wives. Not even in the prejudiced history of the South can it be maintained that the negroes revenged themselves for their servitude and ill-treatment while those who had held them in bondage were away from their homes. Of course if a Northern army was near, many slaves would run away to obtain liberty or to enlist under its colours. Frequently they were turned back and ordered to return on their employers' plantations till the issue was decided. In some cases they were enlisted (if there was a justification) in the armies of the Federal Government (though its negro soldiers were usually obtained from Washington, Maryland, West Virginia, and the free negroes of the Northern States): in all such cases the negro troops fought under the Unionist banner with such bravery, and—if one may say so—such Christianity, that they won admiration from their white comrades and materially hastened the day of their emancipation by influencing public opinion in their favour.

On January 1st, 1863, Lincoln signed a Proclamation emancipating the slaves in the States of Arkansas, Texas, Mississippi, Alabama, Florida, Georgia, South Carolina, North Carolina, Tennessee, and certain portions of Louisiana and Virginia, giving liberty in theory (and two years afterwards in practice) to over four millions of human beings. Lincoln lived to see this "unconstitutional" measure ratified by Congress on January 31st, 1865, in the adoption of the Thirteenth Amendment to the Constitution of the United States; which provided that "neither slavery nor involuntary servitude, except as a punishment for crime, whereof the party shall have been duly convicted, shall exist within the United States or any place subject to their jurisdiction."

309. PRESIDENT LINCOLN'S SIGNATURE TO THE PROCLAMATION OF EMANCIPATION, 1863

310. A GRAVEYARD OF FEDERAL AND CONFEDERATE SOLDIERS, HAMPTON, VIRGINIA
Adjoining the grounds of the Institute for the higher training of the Negro

This was confirmed by a vote of twenty-seven States and proclaimed December 18th, 1865, as an integral part of the United States' Constitution: to be accepted, of course, by the seceded States as part of the war settlement.

This action was followed up by the triumphant and dominant Republican Party in the enactment of the Fourteenth and Fifteenth Amendments to the Constitution. The Fourteenth Amendment, which became part of the Constitution in 1866, provided (amongst other things) for full rights of citizenship being bestowed without distinction on all persons born or naturalised in the United States, as a whole, and in the State in which the person resided. The Fifteenth Amendment gave the Federal and State Franchise to all citizens of the United

States, independently of race or colour. This was adopted in 1870, and by 1871 all the seceded States were back in the Union, and had their local freedom of administration restored.

Then followed the trying period of Reconstruction. The slave was given a vote; his master was in an electoral minority. As the slave was too ignorant, in almost all cases, to come forward as a candidate for Congress or for the Senate, the "carpet bag" politicians of the North were the only Republicans who could be elected by the ex-slave voters. Between 1866 and 1876 the White South, according to its own account, "passed under the harrow," and is supposed to have suffered cruelly in its sensitive feelings and its property from the conjoint rule of ex-slave and Northern governor.[1] It endeavoured to right matters with violence. Negro voters were bribed to remain away from the polling-stations, or terrorised into not voting by violence or threats of non-employment. The Ku-Klux-Klan and other secret societies sprang into existence to make the Negro franchise inoperative and to drive away the Northern politician.

A small civil war broke out in 1874 (in Louisiana) which was suppressed by Federal troops; but the North was disinclined to take up the gauntlet or to risk another internecine conflict to enforce the strict carrying out of the Fourteenth and Sixteenth Amendments. It left the Negro in the old States of the Secession still in social bondage, an ill-treated, neglected ward instead of a slave: trusting to the sense of justice and humanity which would come in time to a better-educated South and lead it of its own free will to make expiation and atonement.

[1] For an excellent summary of the actually beneficial results of the conjoined Northern governor and negro voter, see the pamphlet *Why the Negro was Enfranchised*, by Richard P. Hallowell (Boston: 1903). The writer brings clearly into the light the admirable reconstruction work in South Carolina of Governor David H. Chamberlain.

CHAPTER XV

SLAVERY IN THE SOUTHERN STATES: II

BEFORE dwelling on the present difficulties yet generally happy condition of the Negro in the United States, South as well as North, it may be as well to realise his existence there as a slave between the beginning of the eighteenth century and the year 1860. He was not treated well by Dutch, English, or French settlers prior to 1700, but the contemporaneous behaviour of the free white colonists and the European officials towards the white convicts, apprentices, and religious dissidents, and towards the Amerindian aborigines, was so bad that their demeanour with the African slave attracts no special attention.

We have already seen[1] that the State of Virginia as early as about 1680 showed a determination to retain the negro in slavery, and was (perhaps wisely) intolerant of any mixing of the blood. But the negroes of "Ole Virginny" did not dislike tobacco planting and curing, and in many respects they were content and even happy down to the tightening of servitude in the nineteenth century. It was in South Carolina in the first quarter of the eighteenth century that life was made unbearable and short for the unfortunate African, and that, being driven to mad despair, the negroes broke out in the Charleston revolt of 1740 and attempted (small blame to them!) to slay the pitiless devils who were their masters.

This rising, repressed with ease by the white folk (and followed by atrocious punishments) gave a more stringent character to future slave legislation in the "Southern" States,[2] which then consisted of Maryland, Virginia, North Carolina, South Carolina, and Georgia. The remembrance of the Charleston revolt kept the American colonists on the alert for a hundred and twenty years afterwards to forestall and nip in the bud any possible negro rising.

But as a matter of fact, though the slave legislation was as cruel in the eighteenth as in the nineteenth century, there were fewer slaves to be afflicted by it, the mass of the slaves were too brutish to feel the iron entering into their

[1] In the foot-note on page 357.

[2] Already distinguished from the more Quaker, Puritan North as the region wherein white men directed and slaves laboured. North of the Mason-Dixon line the whites did every kind of work. In North Carolina there were many "poor" white labourers, and this State had a better slavery record than its neighbours.

Mr. James Bryce, in his *Study of the American Commonwealth* (p. 618), points out the striking contrast between the culture of the North and of the South from the very beginning. When in the early eighteenth century the English Commissioners for foreign plantations asked for information on the subject of education from the respective Governors of Virginia (a Southern State) and Connecticut (a Northern), the Governor of Virginia replied, "I thank God there are no free schools or printing-presses, and I hope we shall not have any these hundred years." From the Governor of Connecticut came the answer, "One-fourth of the annual revenue of the colony is laid out in maintaining free schools for the education of our children."

souls, and the colonial wars against France and England—and against the "Indian" tribes between 1750 and 1815—provided interesting distractions for them and for their masters. Fighting often brought freedom in its train, and a campaigning life or pioneering work in the backwoods could never be so heart-breaking as agriculture under the whip. Moreover, it must be remembered that down to about 1816 the British Americans were not really free to organise slave-labour effectively, and with the full application of the wicked laws they had made or were about to enact: Louisiana, Florida, Texas, Alabama had been

311. THE UNREGENERATE TYPE OF SLAVERY DAYS
A Virginian Negro

previously under the kindly sway (so far as the negro was concerned) of the French or Spanish, or were still strongly held by Amerindian tribes.

So that we need not waste time over the eighteenth century in drawing up our indictment against the Southern States: we can begin our survey with the commencement of the long peace following the far-reaching Napoleonic Wars; a period during which the United States grew (in occupation, not merely in paper agreements) from an area of about 960,000 square miles to one of nearly

24

three million square miles, extending not merely to the Mississippi, but to the Pacific, to Mexico, and to the Hudson's Bay Territory.

According to the law of Louisiana (down to 1865), "A slave is one who is in the power of the master to whom he belongs. The master may sell him, dispose of his person, his industry, and his labour: he can do nothing, possess nothing, or acquire nothing but what must belong to his master."[1]

In the laws of Maryland, slaves were frequently classed with "working beasts, animals of any kind."

The Supreme Court of North Carolina in 1829 laid it down that "The end of slavery is the profit of the master, his security, and the public safety. The subject is one doomed in his own person and his posterity to live without knowledge and without the capacity to make anything his own, and to toil that another may reap the fruits. . . . The power of the master must be absolute to render the submission of the slave perfect."

The penal codes of the slave-holding States bore much more severely upon slaves than upon white people. In the State of Virginia there were *sixty-eight penal offences* with the death penalty attached *in the case of slaves*, but of which only *one* (murder in *the first degree*) was punished with death in the case of a white person. In the State of Mississippi there were thirteen offences, including high treason, murder, robbery, rape, burglary, and forgery, for which a white person as well as a negro might be sentenced to death, but in addition there were thirty-eight offences for which the slave was to be executed, with or without "the benefit of clergy," but which in the case of a white person were punished by fine or imprisonment. In Alabama there was positively no offence for which the death penalty in the case of white people was rigidly prescribed, and there were only six offences for which it *might* be inflicted by the judge. But *in the case of slaves*, the fixed and *only* punishment was *death* for almost every offence known to the law, and the death penalty could even be inflicted on the mere accessories to the committing of trifling delinquencies, the only exception being, ironically enough, that any slave guilty of the manslaughter of a slave, "a free negro, or a mulatto," was only to be punished by stripes not exceeding thirty-nine, or by branding in the hand. In South Carolina, which had a very bloody code, there were capital sentences in connection with twenty-seven offences in the case of white people, and for thirty-six crimes committed by slaves. Simple larceny to the value of one dollar and seven cents was a capital offence whether perpetrated by a white person or a slave, without benefit of clergy! In this barbarous State (as it must have been until the conclusion of the American Civil War) for some offences even white women were to be publicly whipped after being branded with a red-hot iron, whereas men only received the branding.

In Tennessee the death penalty was inflicted on whites for murder, and being accessory to murder, but slaves were liable to death for eight crimes until 1831, when the capital offences for slaves were reduced to six. In the case of the other two, flogging, the pillory, and imprisonment were substitutable at the will of the judge. In Kentucky four crimes were capital offences amongst white people and eleven amongst slaves. In Missouri there was almost an equality in the allotment of death to the two divisions of society. In most of these Southern States murder in the case of the white people was described as being

[1] *A Sketch of the Laws Relating to Slavery in the Several States of the United States of America.* Second edition. By George M. Stroud. Philadelphia, 1856.

of the first or second degree, and only in the first case (which was very seldom proved[1]) was the death penalty inflicted.

Even as late as 1856 the Constitution of Maryland enacted that a negro convicted of murder should have the right hand cut off, should be hanged in the usual manner, the head severed from the body, the body divided into four quarters, and the head and quarters set up in the most public places of the county where such act was committed.

In several of the States slaves were forbidden, or might be denied the security of trial by jury for offences of a higher grade than petty larceny; and this was ironically countered by other laws stating that the slave was *not* to be tried by a jury save for offences "more serious than petty larceny"—that is to say, capital offences. In Maryland and the Northern States, however, the slave, like the free man, was entitled to "a speedy trial by an impartial jury."

A slave could not be a witness against a white person either in a civil or a criminal cause; he could not be party to a civil suit; he could not be educated; the law even discountenanced his receiving moral and religious instruction; he was required to give implicit submission to the will of his master only, but not to that of other white persons.

As early as 1740 the Legislature of South Carolina enacted that any person or persons whatsoever who shall hereafter teach, or cause any slave or slaves to be taught to write, or who should use any slave as a scribe in any manner of writing, should for such offence be fined £100 current money. In 1780 the same State declared any assembly of slaves, *free negroes,* mulattoes, or mestizoes . . . for the purpose of mental instruction in a confined or secret place, to be an unlawful meeting, and the persons taking part in such assembly might be punished with twenty lashes each. Another part of the same Act made it unlawful even when white persons were present for such negroes, free or enslaved, to meet anywhere for mental instruction. In 1834 the same State enacted another law which punished most severely any white person (by fines), free coloured people or slaves (with fifty lashes) for imparting instruction, or the keeping of school, or teaching any slave or free person of colour to read or write. Virginia made much the same laws down to 1849, Georgia also, North Carolina, and Alabama, with some variation, the fines being perhaps less, but on the other hand, reading being prohibited, together with writing, or any form of mental instruction.

North Carolina allowed slaves to be taught arithmetic! but sternly forbade reading and writing, or the giving or selling of any book or pamphlet. In Alabama slaves or any coloured persons, bond or free, might not even be taught to spell.[2]

The steady perusal of the many books and pamphlets published between 1830 and 1865, dealing with the maltreatment of slaves in the Southern States, as well as the speeches made in Congress by Charles Sumner and others, leaves even the hardened reader and the cynical with a feeling of nausea, perhaps even with a desire for some posthumous revenge on the perpetrators of this Outrage on Humanity, worse than anything recorded in the nineteenth century of the Turk in Europe or the European in Congoland. Until I went through this course of reading I vaguely thought of John Brown as a violent, half-crazy old man, of William Lloyd Garrison as a well-meaning fanatic, and

[1] Especially in regard to negroes or negroids, for slaves might not bear evidence against white people.
[2] In the State of Mississippi slaves who had learnt to write had their right thumb cut off.

the host of northern denunciators of the South between 1850 and 1860 as "inebriated with the exuberance of their own verbosity."

I only wonder now they kept themselves so much under control, that ten thousand men did not march behind John Brown to clear out this Augean stable.

Here are a few extracts from books and newspapers to show the type of cruelties perpetrated. These extracts could be multiplied a hundredfold, a thousandfold, it must be understood, if I had the space to devote to such a gruesome purpose and anything was to be gained by such a bloody recital.

The following is from the *Nashville* (Tennessee) *Banner*, June, 1834:—

"INTERESTING TRIAL.—During the session of the circuit court for Davison County, which adjourned a few days since, a case was tried of more than usual interest to the public. It was that of Meeks against Philips, for the value of a slave who had been killed by Philips whilst in the employ of Meeks as his overseer. . . . It appeared in evidence that the negro had disobeyed Philips's orders in going away one night without his permission, for which in accordance with his duty he undertook to chastise him. The boy proved somewhat refractory, and probably offered resistance, though there is no direct evidence of the fact. From Philips's evidence, which must be taken for, as well as against him, it seems he had a scuffle with the boy, during which the boy inflicted a blow upon him which produced great pain. Philips, with assistance, finally subdued him. While endeavouring to swing him to the limb of a tree he resisted by pulling back, whereupon Philips, who is a large and strong man, gave him several blows upon the head with the butt of a loaded horsewhip. Having tied him to the limb the rope gave way, and the boy fell to the ground, when Philips gave him several kicks in the side and again swung him to the tree.

"He then called for a cowhide (whip), which was accordingly brought and the chastisement was commenced anew. The suffering wretch implored for mercy in vain (there must be a Hell, for Philips *et huic generis omnes!*—H.H. J.). Philips would whip him awhile and then rest, only to renew his strokes and wreak his vengeance; for he repeatedly avowed his intention of whipping him to death!—saying, he had as good a negro to put in his room or remunerate his master for the loss of him. The sufferer writhing under the stinging tortures of the lash continued to implore for mercy, while those who were present interposed and pleaded too in his behalf; but there was no relenting arm until life was nearly extinct and feeling had taken its departure. He was cut loose, bleeding and weak, and died in a few minutes after."

The jury found for the plaintiff, and Philips was possibly mulcted in damages for the value of the slave, but there was no record of his having been tried and punished for manslaughter or murder; and the bystanders (whites presumably, since blacks would have incurred the same fate if they had interposed) merely remonstrated with Philips: did not knock him down or shoot him.

Here is an epitome of the *Souther* case quoted by Stroud[1] as having occurred on the 1st September, 1849, in Virginia:—

"The indictment contains fifteen counts, and sets forth a case of most cruel and excessive whipping and torture. The negro was tied to a tree and whipped with switches. When Souther became fatigued with the labour of whipping,

[1] *A Sketch of the Laws Relating to Slavery*, etc. Second edition. By George M. Stroud. Philadelphia, 1856.

he called upon a negro man of his and made him 'cob' Sam with a shingle. He also made a negro woman of his help to 'cob' him. And, after 'cobbing' and whipping, he applied fire to the body of his slave, about his back, belly, and private parts. He then caused him to be washed down with hot water in which pods of *red pepper* had been steeped. The negro was also tied to a log, and to the bed-post, with ropes, which choked him, and he was kicked and stamped upon by Souther. This sort of punishment was continued and repeated until the negro died under its infliction."

The slave's offences, according to the master's allegation, were "*getting drunk*," and dealing with two persons—*white men*—who were present, and witnessed the whole of the horrible transaction, without, as far as appears in the report, having interfered in any way to save the life of the slave.

"The jury found the master guilty of murder in the *second* degree." Which meant that it was punished as manslaughter by a short term of imprisonment.

The following remarks and story are quoted from F. L. Olmsted's *Cotton Kingdom* in relation to the northern and more hilly part of Alabama :—

"The whip was evidently in constant use, however. There were no rules on the subject, that I learned; the overseers and drivers punished the negroes whenever they deemed it necessary, and in such manner, and with such severity, as they thought fit, 'If you don't work faster,' or 'If you don't work better,' or 'If you don't recollect what I tell you, I will have you flogged,' I often heard. I said to one of the overseers, 'It must be disagreeable to have to punish them as much as you do?' 'Yes, it would be to those who are not used to it—but it's my business, and I think nothing of it. Why, sir, I wouldn't mind killing a nigger more than I would a dog.' I asked if he had ever killed a negro. 'Not quite that,' he said, 'but overseers were often obliged to. Some negroes are determined never to let a white man whip them, and will resist you when you attempt it; of course you must kill them in that case.'"

Mr. Olmsted visited (in the late 'fifties) an estate in central Alabama[1] and witnessed this episode :—

He had been riding over the estate with the overseer, and as they crossed on horseback a leafy gully his horse shied at something concealed in the undergrowth. It turned out to be a young Negro girl hiding there from the overseer because she should have been at work and knew it—at work not on any business of her own or to fulfil any contract into which she had entered of her own free will, but because another human being arrogated to himself the right to make her work for him all the year round.

The overseer questioned her: her explanation seemed to him unsatisfactory.

Whether her story were true or false, could have been ascertained in two minutes by riding on to the gang with which her father was at work, but the overseer had made up his mind.

"That won't do," said he; "get down." The girl knelt on the ground. He got off his horse, and holding him with his left hand, struck her thirty or forty blows across the shoulders with his tough, flexible, "raw-hide" whip (a terrible instrument for the purpose). They were well laid on, at arm's length, but with no appearance of angry excitement on the part of the overseer. At every stroke the girl winced and exclaimed, "Yes, sir!" or "Ah, sir!" or "Please, sir!" not groaning or screaming. At length he stopped and said, "Now tell me the truth." The girl repeated the same story. "You

[1] I have visited more or less the same district (1908) fifty years after Olmsted and have found the old estates divided up into thriving negro farms.—H. H. J.

have not got enough yet," said he. "Pull up your clothes; lie down." The girl, without any hesitation, without a word or look of remonstrance or entreaty, drew closely all her garments under her shoulders, and lay down upon the ground with her face toward the overseer, who continued to flog her with the raw hide, across her naked loins and thighs, with as much strength as before. She now shrunk away from him, not rising, but writhing, grovelling, and screaming, "Oh, don't, sir! oh, please stop, master! please, sir! please, sir! oh, that's enough, master! oh, Lord! oh, master, master! oh, God, master, do stop! oh, God, master! oh, God, master!"

A young gentleman of fifteen was with us; he had ridden in front, and now, turning on his horse, looked back with an expression only of impatience at the delay. It was the first time I had ever seen a woman flogged. I had seen a man cudgelled and beaten in the heat of passion before, but never flogged with a hundredth part of the severity used in this case. I glanced again at the perfectly passionless but rather grim, business-like face of the overseer, and again at the young gentleman, who had turned away. If not indifferent, he had evidently not the faintest sympathy with my emotion. Only my horse chafed. I gave him rein and spur, and we plunged into the bushes and scrambled fiercely up the steep acclivity. The screaming yells and the whip strokes had ceased when I reached the top of the bank. Choking, sobbing, spasmodic groans only were heard. I rode on to where the road, coming diagonally up the ravine, ran out upon the cotton-field. My young companion met me there, and immediately afterward the overseer. He laughed as he joined us, and said:

"She meant to cheat me out of a day's work, and she has done it, too."

"Did you succeed in getting another story from her?" I asked, as soon as I could trust myself to speak.

"No; she stuck to it."

"Was it not perhaps true?"

Any meeting of slaves "under pretence of divine worship" might be dispersed, and the slaves receive twenty-five lashes on the bare back without trial. No slave or free negro might conduct a religious service. In some States, in a very grudging way, within the hours of daylight, religious instruction might be imparted by white persons, and, of course, masters were free to take their slaves with them to church in attendance on them. It was repeatedly proclaimed that however much slaves might be baptised into Christianity, they did not thereby acquire a right to freedom; though in arguing the case of slavery, many of its apologists would profess to find sanction for it from the fact that Christianity only disapproved of the enslavement of Christians. It was pointed out by those who attacked slavery that the much-abused Turk, if the slave whom he captured in warfare became a Muhammadan, could no longer hold him as a slave.

Many of the State Legislatures profess to forbid—"save at the time of a sugar crop"—working on a Sunday. But the putting of this law in force was left entirely and solely to the conscience of the slave-owner or overseer, and all who travelled through the Southern States down to 1860 note in their journals and reports the constant working of slaves on that supposed day of rest, which, indeed, was allotted to them in law so that they might not rest but cultivate the plots of ground allotted to them and raise food for their subsistence. In Louisiana the law required that if a slave worked on Sunday he was to receive compensation by being given a subsequent holiday, but this, again, was purely a matter for the owner to arrange. In South Carolina and Georgia the slaves very seldom got any seventh-day rest, except in the slackest winter months.

Throughout the Southern States slaves could not redeem themselves without the acquiescence of their master, even though the latter had been cruel to them; with the doubtful exceptions of Louisiana and Kentucky, provided cruelty could be proved, which owing to the law of evidence was very seldom the case. The slave could make no contract, therefore could not be legally married, could not be punished for adultery, nor prosecuted for bigamy. Slavery was "*hereditary and perpetual*" in the Southern States, but the children of imported slaves were usually able in the Northern States to claim their liberty.

Referring to the general condition of the negro slave in the United States in 1855 and comparing it with the worst conditions of European peasantry, F. L. Olmsted writes: "Bad as is the condition of the mass of European labourers, the man is a brute or a devil who, with my information, would prefer that of the American slave."[1]

He and other writers[2] between 1833 and 1861 descant on the constant episodes of hunger in the life of the slaves of the Southern States. When they were kept at work of an important and lucrative kind from early morn to night time they were usually given large quantities of rough vegetable food; but in other times they were half starved. The slaves had an extraordinary craving for meat in some form, especially mutton or pork. It was very seldom that they were granted any meat but bacon, and that as a rule was only given to them occasionally. Louisiana was the only State in which meat was required *by law* to be furnished to the slaves. The required ration was four pounds a week (this law was afterwards described as a dead letter and unobserved by the planters in that State). In North Carolina the law fixed *a quart of corn per day* as "the proper allowance of food" for a slave.

Many of the thefts charged to the negroes were simply the stealing of vegetables, cereals, poultry, sheep or pigs, or fish from the weir by famished negroes; and the thefts were punished by the most frightful floggings, often ending in the slave's death.

Famines (as in eighteenth-century Jamaica) were of frequent occurrence in the Southern States, especially those in the Valley of the Mississippi, during the first half of the nineteenth century. Their existence was scarcely noticed in the Southern press during that period, and usually they were only recorded in local annals, which were subsequently published in some of the Northern newspapers. During these famines or periods of food-scarcity hundreds or even thousands of negroes died of sheer starvation.

As among the Arabs of East Africa or the Nubians, Arabs, and Hausa of the Sudan, so in tropical and sub-tropical America the institution (*pace* the late De Bow) created a lust for blood, and an indifference even to monetary loss if the vilest passions could have full fling. Not only were Southerners almost less concerned about the killing of a negro than they were over the killing of a

[1] *The Cotton Kingdom*, in two volumes, by Frederick Law Olmsted. (Second edition. New York, 1861.) Olmsted was a fine fellow, who on horseback, or if need be on foot, travelled all over the Slave States of the Union between 1850 and 1860. His books, four in number, are profoundly interesting. They are cool, calm, a series of photographs. He gives the reader a succession of sober word-pictures, and leaves him mostly to form his own conclusions. He can also depict the beautiful, unappreciated scenery of the sub-tropical South as no other writer of his period was able to do. His works (*Seaboard Slave States; Texas Journey; Journey in the Back Country*; and (*Journeys and Explorations in*) *The Cotton Kingdom of America* should be reprinted.

[2] Read on this subject *The Narrative of Charles Ball, a Black Man* (New York, 1837).

cow or a mule, but they rather liked killing them for fun.[1] Olmsted quotes a number of instances of this callousness in the Southern press of the 1850-60 period.

It had become almost proverbial in America that the feelings of affection for wife and children were not to be taken into account if the caprice of an owner or his bankruptcy or death required a negro or negress to be sold. In this respect the United States were more inhumane than the British West Indies, the Spanish or Portuguese, or the French (if they obeyed the Code Noir, which they did not). Thousands and thousands of instances in the nineteenth century (and earlier) occurred in the Southern States of husbands and wives (some of them mulattoes, octoroons, and "near-whites") being thus arbitrarily parted, never perhaps to meet again; or being forced for "stud" purposes to contract other unions. Little children were torn from their mothers' arms soon after they were weaned, to be kept perhaps as "a pet" by some languid Southern lady; treated as a pet till death, or a fit of ill-temper on the part of the owner sent the "pet" to toil under the lash of an overseer with a hoe or a sickle.

From this cause more than any other (I am not thinking of *Uncle Tom's Cabin*, but of the actual plain statistics on which it was founded), negroes and negresses would run away, knowing full well if they did so that there was one chance in a hundred of their reaching Mexico (where slavery was abolished in 1829) or Canada.

They might, if they got far enough North in the hundred or thousand miles of their flight, meet a Quaker, who showed them the way to the "underground railway,"[2] or friendly negro freedmen or fellow-slaves willing to risk tortures and imprisonment or death to help—at any rate, not to hinder—a comrade in distress. But they must first elude the bloodhounds put on their track. If they escaped these, they might die of starvation in the pathless woods, be frozen to death in the Alleghany Mountains, poisoned by rattlesnakes or "mocassins," drown in crossing wide rivers, or be shot at sight by a white patrol.

Better these things than recapture, when the master or overseer would feel it was preferable to lose an emaciated slave or a cadaverous ex-mistress than

[1] That this species of humour is not quite extinct in the reconstructed South may be seen by the enclosed extract, which I clipped myself from a Tennessee newspaper in 1908.—H. H. J.

SHOT THEM FOR FUN

A WHITE MAN KILLS THREE NEGROES, WOUNDS FOUR

A Cold-Blooded Murder Occurs in Memphis—What the Murderer said when he was Arrested

Memphis, Tenn., Dec. 11.—"I shot 'em, and that's all there's to it." Beyond this, which he mumbled as he was being led to a cell at police headquarters, William Latura, a white man of this city, proffered no explanation of the killing of three negroes and wounding four others at a saloon here early to-day.

According to the statement of bystanders, when Latura entered the saloon a group of negroes were about a pool table in the rear room, engaged in a game. As he walked into the room, it is declared, Latura, after surveying the crowd, leisurely unbuttoned his long overcoat and drew out an automatic pistol If any words were passed, those who escaped the rain of bullets which followed by dodging behind the furniture, declare they heard none. As Latura shot one after another of the negroes they fell. When the police arrived three were dead and four others were lying about the floor wounded. One of the latter was a woman. After his weapon was empty Latura threw it away, and walked to a neighbouring saloon, where he quietly submitted to arrest.

[2] The hiding and forwarding system which the Quakers concocted for sending runaway slaves to Canada.

to forego the exquisite delight of torturing a human being to death, unrebuked by public opinion. Public opinion indeed had, as likely as not, been evoked to "see the fun"; and had ridden over on its blood horses or driven with its fast trotters to see a wretched negro or negress, an octoroon or "near white" whipped to death or lunacy by hickory switches; or hung up by the thumbs and flogged

312. THE PERSIMMON TREE (DIOSPYROS VIRGINIANA), WHICH HAS SO OFTEN SUPPLIED FUGITIVE SLAVES WITH SUSTENANCE

The fruit is pulpy, sweet, and of delicious flavour, and the tree therefore serves the double purpose of attracting opossums

into a bloody pulp with cowhide thongs dipped into scalding cayenne pepper-tea before each stroke.[1]

As to the pursuit of runaways by dogs, the breed of dog employed was usually a cross between the Spanish bloodhound and some mongrel dog of good size and strength, perhaps with elements of the greyhound and the bull-dog. They were ugly-looking creatures, smaller than the ordinary bloodhound and most ferocious. They were, in fact, trained to hate negroes. Down to 1861 throughout the Southern States there were men who made it a profession to

[1] Every one of these allusions is drawn from accurate authorities.

keep "nigger dogs" and with them to follow up and catch runaway slaves, and packs of about a dozen were employed at a time. When the runaway was caught by the dogs they were usually allowed to bite and tear him to a certain extent, to satisfy their rage. "The owners don't mind having them kind o' niggers tore a good deal; runaways ain't much account nohow, and it makes the rest more afraid to run away when they see how the others are sarved."

313. THE TYPICAL "BAYOU" OF THE SOUTHERN STATES, IN THE STAGNANT WATER OF WHICH SLAVES WOULD LIE CONCEALED FOR DAYS

The payment for catching the runaway within two or three days was from ten to twenty dollars; but as much as two hundred dollars would be paid if the hunting occupied two or three weeks. It was not that the slave was then of any value to his owner, but an example must be made to deter others.

Of course, whenever the fugitive saw a tree, he endeavoured to climb it, but in such case a bullet or a charge of buckshot dislodged him.

This being the case, when a runaway realised that there was no escape from the dogs or the master, he frequently committed suicide, or fought with the dogs till he was killed by them, the white bystanders heartily enjoying the spectacle. As these scenes frequently took place in a bayou or by the banks of a river, the wretched negro when all was up would endeavour to drown himself.

As has been pointed out by numerous Northern writers or modern authors of the New South (for in many districts there is a New South growing or grown up which loathes and burns with shame for the wickedness of its ancestry or its predecessors), the immorality of slavery reacted on the nature and disposition of the White South. The poor whites were shockingly ignorant and were virtually slaves to the aristocratic planters, who treated them like dirt and withheld the franchise from them.[1]

Manners, morals, and speech were exceedingly coarse. The negro slaves were (at any rate until about 1850) often obliged, men and women, to work stark naked in the plantations and even alongside the miserably-made public roads. White children and young women were accustomed to such sights, such indecencies of speech and action as must have left them with no ignorance of the existence of filthy and refined sensuality. So crudely indecent in fact were the conditions of slave life that the slightly veiled concupiscence yet comparative lack of prurience in the eighteenth-century British and French West Indies —still more the grave Spanish propriety in clothing and personal demeanour in public life—seem positively a glimpse of wholesomeness compared to the condition of South Carolina, Georgia, Northern Alabama, Mississippi, Texas, and Northern Louisiana in the first sixty years of the nineteenth century. If this indictment is thought too strong, read the books published between 1830 and 1861, in the libraries of the United States and of Great Britain. Many of these quote from the files of Southern newspapers and those of the Northern States on the borderland, to illustrate by the reports of trials and scandals the state of morals in the South. Some no doubt are prejudiced or purposely exaggerate. But the evidence in the mass is damning; and includes frequent descriptions of duels between men, or even boys, which commenced with revolvers (to punish a saucy word) and finished up with a bowie-knife hand-to-hand combat—a slicing of the fallen man by the victor. There were, as we know, Southern vendettas which did not end till three or four households of men and boys had been wiped out by assassination. Scarcely a single instance is recorded of any one of these white duellists or murderers being punished even by a fine.

At the burning of a negro near Knoxville in Eastern Tennessee about 1852, the editor of a local paper (a white Methodist preacher) wrote of this punishment of a negro who had killed a white man: "We unhesitatingly affirm that the punishment was unequal to the crime. Had we been there we should have taken a part, and even suggested the pinching of pieces out of him with red-hot pincers—the cutting off of a limb at a time, and then burning them all in a heap."

[1] "And yet, as fine and well-disposed men, and as anxious to improve, are to be found in the South-Western States as are to be found anywhere. They are as honest as men ever are, and they will treat a stranger the best they know how. The trouble is, the large slave-holders have got all the good land. There can be no schools, and if the son of a poor man rises above his condition there is no earthly chance for him. He can only hope to be a slave-driver, for an office is not his, or he must leave and go to a Free State. Were there no Free States, the white people of the South would to-day be slaves."

"There are to-day . . . more than 30,000 people in Tennessee alone, who have not a foot of land or a bit of work to do. . . . I have seen hundreds of families living in log cabins ten or twelve feet square, where the children run around as naked as ever they were born, and a bedstead or chair was not in the house, and never will be. I have seen the children eat wheat and grass, growing in the field. I have seen them eat dirt."—Olmsted, *The Cotton Kingdom*.

About 1857 a negro of Georgia assassinated his master by felling him with a bludgeon. He was caught and tried; then sentenced to death and roasted at a slow fire on the site of the murder in the presence of many thousand slaves driven to the ground from all the adjoining counties, and when at length his life went out, the fire was intensified until his body was reduced to ashes which were scattered to the winds and trampled under foot. After this, *magistrates and clergymen* addressed appropriate warnings to the assembled multitude.

"The popular report of Southern hospitality is a popular romance. Every wish of the Southerner is imperative; every belief, undoubted; every hate, vengeful; every love, fiery. Hence, for instance, the scandalous fiend-like street fights of the South. . . . The Southerner seems crazy for blood. Intensity of personal pride and prejudice; an intense partisanship. . . . The talents of the South all turn into two channels, politics and sensuality. The ratio of illiterate citizens in the South was three times larger than in the North, and a proportionate difference in the libraries and publishers of the one division as compared to the other."[1]

Many Northern writers during the close of the Slavery period would point out the erroneous conception held by the South that white men who had to toil as artisans or mechanics in the North lived under miserable circumstances; and that the preferable ideal was a white aristocracy and negro slaves to perform all the manual labour. But as a matter of fact, the true state of the case was that the white masses of working-men and working-women in the North—even in the early and middle parts of the nineteenth century—lived on a very much higher scale of comfort and possessed far more of the amenities of life than most well-to-do Southerners.

The difference really lay in this, that partly owing to a more benign climate the Southern white man was content with very little, was willing to "pig" it sooner than take any trouble. Travellers through the Southern States (Northern Americans, Englishmen, and Germans) in ante-bellum days point out the miserable discomforts of Southern hospitality; the difficulty in obtaining a room to one's self or a bed to one's self; the filthy condition of the beds; the absence of couches or arm-chairs, of decent reading-lamps, of curtains and carpets, of windows that would open and shut or that contained any glass; the rarity of obtaining even a jug of hot water for shaving—much less a hot bath; the absence of flower gardens and fruit trees, decent cooking and varied food, good stabling and considerate treatment of horses. "From the banks of the Mississippi to the banks of the James River (Virginia) I did not [writes Olmsted] see, except perhaps in one or two towns, a thermometer, a book of Shakespeare, a pianoforte or a sheet of music, a decent reading-lamp, an engraving, or a work of art of the slightest merit. I am not speaking of what are commonly called "poor whites," but of houses which were the residences of cotton planters and well-to-do shareholders in cotton plantations."[2]

So much for the homes and vaunted hospitality of the South (for which, by the by, the traveller almost invariably had to pay one or more dollars a day). Of course, there were exceptions, "a dozen or so" between Virginia and the Mississippi, but they were chiefly in the old French districts of Louisiana or Southern Alabama.

[1] Extracts from various writers, 1854–61.

[2] Exceptions to these statements must be taken in so far as they refer to the area of Louisiana and Alabama under French civilisation.

As regards the value of slave servants in comparison with free domestics, all these writers on the ante-bellum South [and many of the Southerners themselves, when they were allowed to utter their thoughts freely] condemned the former in favour of the latter. "Their time isn't any value to themselves" was the constant cry of the Southern housewife in recounting the laziness and slovenliness of her domestic slaves. Again and again it is pointed out that as the negro derives no benefit from his work he takes no interest in it, only just gets through it sufficiently to escape a flogging. The slave-owners frequently hired out their slaves as servants to others, but the rate of hire was exorbitant, and it was soon discovered by the new settlers in the new lands that it was

314. A "GREAT HOUSE" OF FORMER DAYS AND ITS SETTING OF LIVE OAKS (LOUISIANA)

cheaper to get down German and Irish men and women from the North and pay them fair wages.

How the "lazy, brutish" negro could work and demean himself, if decently, sympathetically treated, is shown by the description given by Olmsted and others of their interviews with farmers in Northern Mississippi, Eastern Texas, Arkansas, and Virginia. Here, of course, new Northern ideas came into play. It seemed inherently so monstrous that these slaves should derive no profit whatever from their labour that Northern immigrants would give the slaves they owned or hired, tips and even considerable presents from time to time. Once the negro saw that he could earn money for himself by his labour (and with the money perhaps get to learn to read), he would work almost night and day and never dream of running away.

The hundred-thousand planter aristocrats who governed the South on behalf of twelve or thirteen millions of human beings shaped all the ends of government to the one sole purpose of upholding the filthy tyranny of their slave system. They permitted no free press, no free pulpit, no free politics. Religion must be specially prostituted to their liking or out it went. By the middle of the nineteenth century the Baptist church, the Independents, Methodists,[1] and latterly the Presbyterians had to split into two Churches, one for the North and West which denounced slavery, and one for the South which upheld or palliated it. The Roman Catholic Church and the American form of the Church of England remained undivided, but at the cost of condoning slavery or evading any pronouncement.

As the 'fifties progressed towards the 'sixties and the inevitable struggle between North and South grew nearer, the tyranny of the South grew greater and more stringent till it was in a worse condition than even the worst descriptions of the Russia of yesterday. There was a severe censorship of the press, a constant interference with mail-bags and private correspondence, and the rejection of all mail matter coming from England or from the Northern States which might spread views subversive of slavedom. School-books imported from the outer world were reprinted with alterations and emendations to distort all the teaching to a support of slavery. It was even proposed by responsible persons like J. O. B. De Bow[2] that *the circulators of books containing any criticism of slavery as an institution should be subject to imprisonment for life or the infliction of the death penalty!* The same writer described an excellent geographical compendium published by Appleton and Co., of New York (which slightly animadverted on slavery), as a work which would "encourage crimes that would blanch the cheek of a pirate," and other publications by the

[1] The *Methodist Protestant*, a religious newspaper edited by a clergyman in Maryland, where the slave population was to the free only in the ratio of one to twenty-five, printed in 1857 an account of a slave auction in Java (translated from a Dutch paper—slavery was not abolished in the Dutch possessions till 1863), at which the father of a slave family was permitted to purchase his wife and children at a nominal price, owing to the humanity of the spectators. The account concluded as follows:—

"It would be difficult to describe the joy experienced by these slaves on hearing the fall of the hammer which thus gave them their liberty; and this was further augmented by the presents given them by numbers of the spectators, in order that they might be able to obtain a subsistence till such time as they could procure employment.

"These are the acts of a noble generosity that deserve to be remembered, and which, at the same time, testify that the inhabitants of Java begin to abhor the crying injustice of slavery, and are willing to entertain measures for its abolition."

To give currency to such ideas, even in Maryland, would have been fatal to the support of a minister's white congregation; and accordingly (wrote Olmsted) in the editorial columns prominence was given the next day to the following salve to the outraged sensibilities of the subscribers:—

"SLAVE AUCTION IN JAVA.

"A brief article, with this head, appears on the fourth page of our paper this week. It is of a class of articles we never select, because they are very often manufactured by paragraphists for a purpose, and are not reliable. It was put in by our printer in place of something we had marked out. We did not see this objectionable substitute until the outside form was worked off, and are therefore not responsible for it."

[2] J. O. B. De Bow was a writer or editor of reviews, encyclopædias, etc., dealing with the Southern States. He was a native of Maryland and acquired a great reputation as a literary man. He was, however (in literature), a pompous ass, and his celebrated *Resources of the South and West*, in several volumes, though it is replete with interesting information, is throughout vitiated by his rancour against the Northern advocates of decent treatment to the Negro. Here is an extract from his great Review:—

"The Almighty has thought well to place certain of His creatures in certain fixed positions in this world of ours, for what cause He has not seen fit to make quite clear to our limited capacities; and why an ass is not a man, and a man is not an ass, will probably for ever remain a mystery. God made the world; God gave thee thy place, my hirsute brother, and according to all earthly possibilities and probabilities, it is thy destiny there to remain, bray as thou wilt. From the same great Power have our sable friends, Messrs. Sambo, Cuffee, and Co., received their position also. . . . Alas, my poor black brother! thou, like thy hirsute friend, must do thy braying in vain."—The braying seems to have been done by De Bow!

same firm as "ulcerous and polluting agencies issuing from the hot-beds of abolition fanaticism."

As late as 1852 in the revised statutes of Louisiana, it was set forth that "any one who might write anything with a tendency to produce discontent amongst the free coloured population of the State, or make use of such language from the bar, the bench, the stage, or the pulpit . . . might suffer *death* at the discretion of the court or be sentenced to imprisonment at hard labour for life." But in spite of these precautions, the tranquillity of the South (wrote Olmsted in his introduction to *The Englishman in Kansas*) was that of hopelessness on the part of the subject race. In the most favoured regions this broken spirit of despair on the part of the negro was as carefully maintained by the white citizens, and with as unhesitating an application of force (when necessary to teach humility) as it was by the army of the Czar in Poland, or the omnipresent police of the Austrian Kaiser in Italy. In Richmond and Charleston and New Orleans the citizens were as careless and gay as in Boston or London; and their servants "a thousand times as childlike and cordial, to all appearance, in their relations with them as our servants are with us." "But go to the bottom of this security and dependence, and you come to police machinery such as you can never find in towns under free government: citadels, sentries, passports, grape-shotted cannon, and daily public whippings for accidental infractions of police ceremonies. I happened myself to see more direct expression of tyranny in a single day and night at Charleston (South Carolina) than at Naples (under Bomba) in a week; and I found that more than half the inhabitants of this town were subject to arrest, imprisonment, and barbarous punishment, if found in the streets without a passport after the evening 'gun-fire.' Similar precautions and similar customs may be discovered in every large town in the South."

Yet in a fatuous conviction that no amendment was necessary to its polity the articulate[1] South went on year after year in the 'fifties boasting of its culture (which did not exist) and its immense superiority to the barbarian North; despite the absence of glass from many of its windows, bath-rooms, and sanitary appliances of at least 1850 civilisation from most of its houses, the seventy-nine per cent illiteracy of its women and forty-five per cent illiteracy of its men.[2]

[1] A large proportion of the white South was *in*articulate—could not read or write or vote, or speak intelligently, but was inherently intelligent enough to be *most* dissatisfied with its aristocratic government.

[2] These remarks do not apply to Virginia; still less to Maryland. The culture of these States bordering on the North had something of Northern thoroughness. The following extracts, however, will illustrate the Chinese complacency of the South prior to the outbreak of the Civil War:—

"The institution of slavery operates by contrast and comparison; it elevates the tone of the superior, adds to their refinement, allows more time to cultivate the mind, exalts the standard in morals, manners, and intellectual endowments; operates as a safety-valve for the evil-disposed, leaving the upper race purer, while it really preserves from degradation in the scale of civilisation the inferior, which we see is their uniform destiny when left to themselves. The slaves constitute essentially the lowest class, and society is immeasurably benefited by having this class, which constitutes the offensive fungus—the great cancer of civilised life—a vast burthen and expense to every community, under surveillance and control; and not only so, but under direction as an efficient agent to promote the general welfare and increase the wealth of the community. The history of the world furnishes no institution under similar management where so much good actually results to the governors and the governed as this in the Southern States of North America."—From an address on "Climatology" by Dr. Barton (New Orleans, 1856).

A well-known Southern newspaper, the *Richmond Enquirer* of Virginia, was in the habit of comparing the North to the South on the same analogy as the relations between Greece and Rome during the Augustan Æra. The South, of course, represented in the eyes of this journalist the dignity and energy of the Roman character conspicuous in war and politics, which could not easily be tamed and adjusted to the arts and industry and literature. On the other hand, the Northerners were compared to

And so the South drifted on to Secession and the Civil War, with, as its inevitable results, the abolition of Slavery and Reconstruction: a reconstruction not yet complete, nor will be, till the Negro and the Coloured man enjoy the same citizen's rights in the eleven seceded States as are accorded to the Amerindian, the White man, the Chinese and Japanese. So slight a retribution has this been to the South in comparison with its Slavery record that future historians will be greatly puzzled in picking up the chain of events in

315. COTTON BALES GROWN BY FREE NEGROES, COLLECTED FOR TRANSPORT TO ENGLAND (TUSKEGEE CITY, ALABAMA)

North America, and think there is a chapter missing somewhere; or be more than ever inclined to desert the old-fashioned view of God's judgments.

What vexes my sense of justice is to see that Brother North has stepped in and borne the greater part of the penalty; has sent his clever sons to construct or reconstruct many things—plantations, pilotage, ports, mining, smelting, and casting; sanitation, house-building, furniture-making, forest-preservation, rail-

the "degenerate and pliant Greeks, excelled in the handicraft and polite professions, who were the most useful and most capable of servants, whether as pimps or professors of rhetoric. Obsequious, dexterous, and ready, the versatile Greeks monopolised the business of teaching, publishing, and manufacturing in the Roman (as the Northerners in the American) Empire—allowing their masters ample leisure for the service of the State, in the Senate or in the field."

"It is by the existence of slavery, exempting so large a portion of our citizens from labour, that we have leisure for intellectual pursuits."—Governor Hammond in *Southern Literary Messenger*, South Carolina.

ways, press, and sound banking; that he has shouldered so great a proportion of the war debt; has provided about ten million pounds sterling to educate, civilise, convert the Negro, where the very-slightly-repentant South has (in thirty years) spent barely a million. And the North has not merely spent money, but has furnished just the right kind of Northern men and women to do this apostles' work.

And all the time the naughty South—the more-than-ever dare-devil, handsome South (for whom the plain Elder Brother has always had a certain weakness)—goes about with its panama or broad-brimmed felt hat cocked on one side, with a twinkle in the eye and an amused glance at the Negro institutes and colleges which are rising on every side, created or subsidised (for the most part) by the Puritan, Quaker, Christian North.

CHAPTER XVI

THE EDUCATION OF THE NEGRO IN THE UNITED STATES: HAMPTON INSTITUTE

PRIOR to the Civil War, and during the tightening of Slavery which followed the Peace of 1815 and lasted till the Secession from the Union, there were no avowed schools or institutes for educating the Negro in the fourteen Slave States. There could not be, of course, since it was illegal to educate him. Gradually the Moravians and Methodists had withdrawn their schools to the north of the Mason-Dixon line.

But in Pennsylvania the Presbyterian friends of the coloured race had established in 1854 a college named the Ashmun[1] Institute, which in 1864 and after the war was strengthened, enlarged, and renamed "Lincoln University." It remains devoted chiefly to Negro education. The white Methodists conjoined with the African Methodists began in Ohio in 1856 what became in 1863 (thenceforth wholly under the auspices of the African Methodist Church) the Wilberforce University.

In 1855 a Kentucky Abolitionist, John Fee, established a Negro college at Berea, in Kentucky, which still flourishes, but now has more white than coloured students.[2]

But these schools and institutions with a strange lack of foresight arranged their curriculum (then and indeed now) only to produce negro divines, lawyers, grammarians, and orators: the industrial, outdoor side of life was quite neglected. Students were and are taught a vast deal of wholly useless classics, of old-fashioned, incorrect history, and of the Old Testament and seventeenth-century theology.

However good the intentions which prompted the bestowal of this education, there was not in it the solution of the Negro problem in America either before or after the Abolition of Slavery. For this solution the civilised world will always be indebted to General S. C. Armstrong.

In the middle of the nineteenth century there were living in the island of Maui (Hawaii Archipelago) a missionary and his wife of the name of Armstrong, who were of Scotch-Irish descent. They had a son, who was named Samuel Chapman Armstrong, born and bred in Maui, who, as he grew up, took a very keen and practical interest in the educational work his parents were conducting amongst the Polynesian natives of the Hawaiian kingdom. Young Armstrong gradually realised that the missionary work—perhaps not of his

[1] Named after Jehudi Ashmun, the white American who founded Liberia (see my book on *Liberia*). He was a fine character and an attractive, handsome personality, in spite of his hideous fore-name.

[2] I am indebted for much information on the subject of Negro education to a publication of the Atlanta University Press, edited by W. E. Burghardt DuBois (Atlanta, 1900): *The College-bred Negro.*

parents, but of their colleagues—lacked the essential element of industrial teaching. The bewildered Melano-Polynesians were taught a vast deal about the Bible—the Old Testament especially—and the problems in Syria from three thousand to nineteen hundred years ago. They also learned the hypothetical doctrines concerning a future life, but very little about how to turn their present undoubted existence to advantage. Even whilst he studied the question as a youth, something better in this respect was being done, because the American

316. GENERAL SAMUEL CHAPMAN ARMSTRONG
The founder of Hampton Institute and of the modern system of educating Negroes and Amerindians

and British missionaries in the Pacific archipelagos were, after all, practical men and women, and not dreamy fanatics. In fact, Armstrong's father had taken decided steps towards the close of the 'fifties in the direction of industrial training, and the results were so satisfactory amongst his converts that they remained in his son's mind when the latter returned to the United States to pursue his own education to a finish.

Samuel Armstrong entered the United States army and eventually rose to be a major-general in the service of the North. During the Civil War he assumed command of Negro troops in Virginia and led them several times to victory. This was a peculiarly hazardous enterprise, because the generals of the South had declared that there would be no quarter given to white men who led Negroes against them in battle.[1]

During a lull in the war, after the Emancipation Edict of Lincoln, when Armstrong was in command in the northern part of Virginia, he had to keep order amongst ignorant multitudes of masterless Negroes, and conceived the idea of occupying their limbs and minds in industrial work of an educational character. When peace was finally made between North and South he was established in charge of a Freedman's Bureau for finding work for ex-slaves, Amerindians, and, if need be, poor whites, and was allowed to make use of his disciplined Negroes as settlers and teachers in an industrial colony.

317. COLONEL ROBERT GOULD SHAW

The land and buildings at Hampton—Old Point Comfort—a peninsula on the south side of Chesapeake Bay, had been confiscated by the United States Government, and in 1868 the American Missionary Association—a body which deserves the greatest credit for the persistence and patience with which, through long, thankless decades, it dealt with the task of saving the Amerindian and educating the Negro—acquired a large portion of this Hampton peninsula to enable General Armstrong to develop his plan for training the Negro and Amerindian in industrial and agricultural work. With the co-operation of the Federal Government, the Hampton Normal and Industrial Institute was founded, and grew under private and State subsidies till it had become a great college for the education of the Negro and Negroid (of all shades of colour) and the Amerindian. The institute is now under the control of seventeen trustees, of whom Mr. R. C. Ogden, of New York, is president. It has an annual income from investments of over £12,000 ($60,000). In addition to this, there is a further revenue derived from State grants, students' fees and other sources. It is able to spend perhaps £20,000 a year.

General S. C. Armstrong died in 1896, having had the satisfaction in his last years of seeing the uprise of Tuskegee and the success of Booker Washington's work. He seems to have been a peculiarly lovable type, not uncommon among the Anglo-Saxons of the New World, good without being pietistic, essentially manly, hard-gritted and practical, having no delusions about the Negroes' or the Amerindians' defects of character and racial drawbacks, but most large-hearted and universal in his sympathies—a foretaste

[1] The remembrance is still vivid in the States of the achievement of General Robert Gould Shaw, in command of the first Negro regiment at the battle of Fort Wagner in 1863, and the death of this gallant white general, whose body was found almost buried under the corpses of the slain. His march through Virginia has been commemorated by some of the beautiful sculpture of Augustus St. Gaudens.

perhaps of a type of more perfected human being that may exist all the world over at the close of the twentieth century; free from racial prejudices, and treating every human being on his or her merits and capabilities. If the United States succeeds in solving the Negro problem in a way that satisfies the best of the blacks and the best of the whites, the initial credit for this great achievement must be laid to the memory of Samuel Chapman Armstrong.

He was succeeded as director of the Hampton Normal and Agricultural Institute by Dr. Hollis Burke Frissell, an American of English descent, still speaking with a trace of the pleasant Northumbrian accent.

When, on such an autumn morning as I saw it, you reach Hampton from the north by steamer across the Chesapeake Gulf, you behold a region of narrow, scalloped peninsulas, enclosing blue lagoons and inlets of the sea. The land is perfectly flat, yet relieved to the eye by notable buildings and picturesque vegetation. Above the shore-line of the water there is a bordering of orange sedge; then the eye travels over good-tempered-looking forts, with no aggressive armament in sight, chiefly built, it would seem, to provide smooth green slopes for the use of nurses, children, and khaki-clad soldiers. These shaven lawns are made to look reasonably martial by occasional pyramids of obsolete cannon-balls.

318. DR. HOLLIS BURKE FRISSELL, OF HAMPTON INSTITUTE

Then as you travel out to Hampton Institute you observe in turn the sandy roads with their tram-lines, low wooden bridges over straits of water, fields of great yellow maize-stalks, weeping-willows, sycamores, rich green cypresses and dark green pines and cedars, flaming crimson oaks, hedges over which the wild vines noted by the Norsemen trail orange-russet foliage and display their pretty clusters of small, lead-blue grapes. In the clear air black turkey-buzzards are soaring.

The grounds of Hampton Institute offer an orderly beauty rarely to be seen in the United States. Noble trees flank stately buildings; grey-white pavement walks lead to and through cloisters of brick and stone; green lawns slope gently to the canals of blue water on which white-sailed yachts make a silent progress. There are occasional piers with green weedy steps advancing into the water from the formal flower gardens of the "old-time" mansions, now the residences of the teachers or the locations of students. There is a handsome red-brick church with a lofty clock tower and a cloister porch. The library is of pale pink brick, with white stone copings and columns, and a leaden dome of blue-grey. The schools for teaching trades are plain tall buildings of sufficient comeliness. I can only suggest one necessary addition to the collegiate centre of Hampton: there should be peacocks—birds rare even yet in the United States—trailing their beauty over the smooth green lawns and under the shade of the magnificent magnolia trees.

The grounds of Hampton surround a peaceful, walled, cypressed cemetery, where lie the remains of the soldiers of North and South, white man and negro, who fell in this part of Virginia fighting over the Slave issue. But Hampton, though attractive and inspiring in its outward appearance—perhaps one of the most beautiful amongst the many beautiful educational institutions in the United States—is thoroughly practical in its teaching resources. Besides a model farm at Shellbank, some five miles distant, there are fields for agricultural and horticultural experiments within the home area, together with greenhouses and hot-houses for the training of Negro gardeners, poultry runs to teach the students the principles of poultry farming; cowsheds and stables and yards for horse and mule breeding or training. There are shops for teaching bricklaying and masonry, waggon, cart, and carriage building, painting and lettering, tailoring and hat-making, millinery and dressmaking, printing and bookbinding, architectural designing and surveying. There are iron foundries

319. LATE FOR LUNCH: HAMPTON INSTITUTE, 1 P.M.

and electrical engineering works. Such of the students as show aptitude are trained in music, and there is a fine students' band.

To some extent, also, arts of design in addition to architecture are encouraged and stimulated. The Amerindians in this respect at Hampton outvie the negroes; their basket-work and mat-making are exquisite, and some of them have executed remarkable specimens of wood-carving. [The Amerindian is going to surprise the world yet by some genius in the plastic or pictorial arts before he becomes finally fused into the great American nation.] The Negro, however, takes the lead in music.

Indeed, one dimly perceives a musical solution of the Negro-culture problem, a possibility that in music the Aframerican—perhaps even the Negro of Africa—may achieve triumphs not yet attained by the White men. This race is sensitive to rhythm and melody to an extraordinary degree; it almost seems as though they were, or could be, ruled by music. At any rate, at Hampton, as at Tuskegee, music is the main discipline. The big and small children of the Whittier School, moving to and out of their class-rooms—a hundred or more at a time—to some inspiriting tune, and the adult students entering and leaving the church and lecture-hall in the same manner, hold themselves well, look up with bright, confident faces, and extort one's sympathy by their grace of movement.

In this undenominational chapel-theatre of Hampton (as also in the same building at Tuskegee) it is a wonderful experience to hear the singing of the Negro students and teachers, both in a mass and in solo parts. They really constitute an already made opera troupe; indeed the singing was more perfect in tune and time than one has heard in many an opera-house. There are Negro tenors at Hampton and Tuskegee that, were it not for the prejudice of colour, would be in immediate request by some impresario.[1]

The choral singing at Hampton is perhaps a little more finished in training than that of Tuskegee; but the choice of songs at both places (perhaps from the reason that all these performances take place in the building which is used as a chapel) tends too much to be monotonously religious and even doleful. The excuse at both institutes is the desire to keep alive the old plantation

320. THE PRINCIPAL'S HOUSE, HAMPTON
An old colonial mansion, dating back to the eighteenth century

songs. Until I visited America I had always thought that negro plantation songs were of the Christy Minstrel type, or even of the joyous "coon" variety, the really good melodies of which have relieved many a musical comedy of stupidity. But it is not so. With two or three rare exceptions I could not ascertain that a single one of the deservedly popular "nigger" songs which have come from America to England between 1860 and 1908 were ever initiated or composed by negro or coloured musicians. The plantation songs so well sung by these choruses in the States are hymns, the words of which were in most cases of negro invention during the old slavery days, while the tunes to which they are sung probably accompanied the Methodist hymns of the eighteenth century, and may be of English or French origin, several hundred years old. None of these melodies seem to be of African origin. The words are usually sad, wistful reminders of a land of glory or bright

[1] I think all who were present with me at Tuskegee in November, 1908, will agree as to the fine quality of the soprano voice of a mulatto teacher, who was formerly a student. It was really worthy of grand opera.

mansions beyond the grave, or very materialistic descriptions of the passage from life to death over the "River," and of the sober joys which will be experienced in Paradise.[1]

Beautiful as is the music to which these (usually silly) canticles are sung, it surely does not mark the limit of the vast capacity of these singers for music in its higher branches, or even in its more joyous workaday types? Why should they not be allowed from time to time to sing some rousing, rollicking "coon" song—decorous, of course, but inclining singers and listeners to rhythmic mirth? They need not shriek or trill in the themes of conventional Italian opera (thank goodness, they have not yet adopted the tremolo of our white sopranos, or the baaing or bellowing of stout Italian tenors !), but pending the emergence from among them of a first-class Negro composer, they could certainly be taught to render the music of Handel, Mendelssohn, Brahms, Gounod, Parry, Elgar, and Sullivan. At one place which I visited in the States I induced—for they are very quick to learn—a chorus of Negro singers to render that sextet out of Sullivan's *Patience*, "I hear the soft note of an echoing voice," and the effect was tender and delightful. (For the matter of that, the Williams and Walker Company, and other troupes of negro actors and actresses have shown what they can do entirely on their own account in comic opera.)

321. A REAL NEGRO MINSTREL, LOUISIANA

Although Hampton and Tuskegee are described as undenominational in religion (Hindu and Muhammadan students are received at both places without question), there is still a great deal of doctrinal religion enforced on the students, who besides scarcely ever singing any song or chorus that is not "sacred," are required to attend rather lengthy religious services in the chapel. At these times the singing is always a delight, and the organ-playing magnificent, while the prayers are short and sensible. But a good deal of the Old Testament is read and expounded, and the Bible almost entirely absorbs and limits the speculation, the poetry, the science, and the historical study of this remarkable race, trembling as it is (at least as I believe) on the verge of great possibilities of intellectual expansion. If a Negro student at Hampton or Tuskegee contributed an article to a review, it would probably be on the subject of Jephtha's daughter—was she sacrificed or not? the righteousness of the fate which overtook the children who mocked Elisha, or the trials of Job; as though any of these or similar problems are of the slightest practical utility in the Negro world of to-day, any more than the legends of Iphigenia, of Romulus and Remus, or other stories told in the infancy of history.

[1] Here is a specimen of the nonsense sung as a plantation song or hymn; nonsense excusable in poor, despairing, ignorant slaves, but unworthy of a growing-up race of hopeful men and women:—

"March de angels, march,
March de angels, march,
My soul arise in heaven, Lord,
For to see when Jordan roll,
De Prophet sat on de tree of Life
For to see when Jordan roll,
Roll Jordan, roll Jordan, roll Jordan, roll."

The Negro students in Africa and America, as those of the white and yellow races in civilised countries, might surely be initiated now into the knowledge of the newer Bible we are just learning to read, the Story of the Earth on which we dwell. Without carrying them too far away from practical and industrial studies, they might be initiated now into the elements of modern theories in geology and biology, if only to explain the difficulties and peculiarities of their own racial problem, the purport of the natural science they have to acquire in dealing with the cultivation of the fields, the breeding of live-stock, and the elimination of disease. I do not think for a moment that the highly educated, broad-minded men and women who direct the teaching at Hampton (and their colleagues of the coloured race at Tuskegee) are naturally inclined to give the Negro an instruction of too "Sunday-school" a character: the fault, if any, perhaps lies with the trustees, and the magnificently generous men and women of the Northern States who have so endowed these educational institutes, but who are not, all of them, quite in sympathy with the New Learning.

322. A NEGRO STUDENT OF HAMPTON

It seems to be expected by these supporters of the movement for the higher education of the Negro, that no matter what enlightenment may pervade the colleges and schools for the white people, a very strong element of dogmatic religion shall enter into the curriculum of the Negro and the Amerindian, with the idea, no doubt, that the unbalanced mind of these backward races requires the discipline of what we call "Christian teaching." Much of this last, as understood in the United States, is a wholly unnecessary attempt to combine Judaism and Christianity, to make a fetish of the Old Testament, which hangs as heavily round the neck of these young men and women going out to the battle of their existence in the world of the twentieth century, as does the actual Koran sewn up in its leather case, and slung round the shoulders of some misguided Arab or Negro dashing into a "holy war" against the civilisation of the Christian.

That the Negro students would be receptive of the wonderful gospel which has been revealed to us through the books of Darwin, Spencer, Charles Kingsley, Haeckel, Edward Clodd, Lindley, Huxley, Humboldt, Bates, Wallace, Agassiz, Lyell, Geikie, E. D. Cope, Henry Fairfield Osborn, and the great astronomers and chemists of the nineteenth and twentieth centuries is evident by the interest shown in the lectures of a Welsh professor directing the research department at Hampton,[1] and those of Professor Carver at Tuskegee (on botany).

But though attempts are now being made to deal in a scientific manner with

[1] Dr. Thomas Jesse Jones, who has written much in the *Southern Workman* on the Negro and other racial problems. Amongst his bound collection of papers is *Social Studies in the Hampton Curriculum*. The *Southern Workman*, established by General Armstrong in 1876, and now conducted by Mr. William Aery, is a remarkably interesting monthly magazine (well illustrated), published at Hampton Institute (price 5d., or 10 cents). It deals mainly with the ethnology of backward peoples all over the world.

sociology [so as to instruct the Negro in what may be called the practical policy of the Ten Talents], the teaching body at Hampton endeavours to steer clear of any burning political question, either State or Federal. It hopes to effect its purpose in the improvement of the Negro's social status by concentrating all its efforts on imparting a sound industrial training, and on the creation of a moral standard and a standard of domestic culture amongst the Negro students which may, by its spreading from this centre (and from Tuskegee), create in time a self-respect amongst the coloured people, a racial conscience which shall set up and maintain such high ideals of industry, talent, and morality, that these qualities, becoming at last characteristic of the Negro race in the United States, may dissipate the race prejudice of the Caucasian, and cause

323. HAMPTON STUDENTS AT THEIR MEALS

him to yield with a good grace a full recognition of the right on the part of his Negro fellow-citizen to absolutely equal treatment.

The teaching at Hampton aspires to make the Negro and the Indian student, male and female, not only an efficient artisan, agriculturist, tailor, dress-maker, gardener, architect, secretary, cook, or housekeeper, but also a person of reasonable refinement, abhorring dirt, tawdriness, and bad taste; appreciating not only clean but comely surroundings. The rooms of the boy and girl students (I found, on several surprise visits) are altogether such as might have been occupied gladly by a university student in England. The furniture (made, I believe, on the spot) was as good as all American furniture is nowadays—a surprise to the English visitor because of the absence of veneer and sham, and the beauty of the native woods. Flowers or foliage plants often decorated the rooms, each of which had its own little library of books. As at Tuskegee, so here, the students were taught in turn the appropriate and tasteful arranging of a house (proportionately to various incomes), and the manner of laying table for a meal. And as regards manners at table, it is thought that these are best generated by the practice of mixing the sexes at the meal hours. Girls and boys sit at the same table.

In fact, everything is done at Hampton (and Tuskegee) to give the Negro a good conceit of himself, a proper pride in dress and demeanour, and in comeliness of surroundings. The very cooking-stoves[1] in their experimental kitchens—even in the "boys'" cooking-place at the Shellbeach Farm—are bound with brass and ornamented with wrought-iron ornament, and (hackneyed as the phrase is) are fit for a drawing-room, are really beautiful specimens of metal-work in colour and form. In the larger kitchens these cooking-ranges burn anthracite coal, but the smaller and more modest cooking arrangements are carried out with gasolene burners. In all cases the students are taught to aim at perfect cleanliness and odourlessness in their cooking arrangements.

324. A NEGRO STUDENT IN HIS ROOM AT HAMPTON

The male students of Hampton (and Tuskegee) wear a blue-black, semi-military uniform, with an ultramarine stripe down the trousers. My photographs show the smart appearance the students present. Not only is the uniform worn by the male students of military cut, but a wholesome military tone of discipline, smartness, and bodily efficiency is given to the students of the Institute by a Negro officer, Major Moton, the military instructor. The boys at Hampton really receive a military education, which should fit them, if necessary, to become members of a citizen army if the United States were engaged in a great war. This training makes them patriotic as well as manly, self-respecting, yet respectful to superior authority. There is no aggressive waving of the Stars and Stripes at Hampton. Least of all is there the slightest attempt to revive the bitterness between North and South.

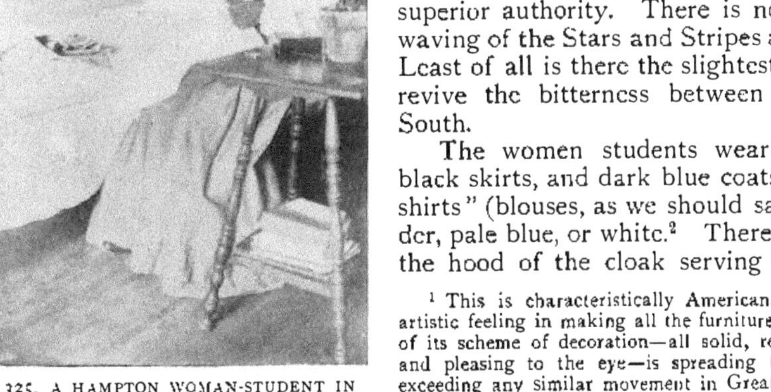

325. A HAMPTON WOMAN-STUDENT IN HER ROOM

The women students wear dark blue-black skirts, and dark blue coats and "waist shirts" (blouses, as we should say) of lavender, pale blue, or white.[2] There are no hats, the hood of the cloak serving the purpose

[1] This is characteristically American, where a truly artistic feeling in making all the furniture of a house part of its scheme of decoration—all solid, real, appropriate, and pleasing to the eye—is spreading to a degree far exceeding any similar movement in Great Britain.

[2] The college colours of Hampton are blue and white.

when necessary of a head-covering, a fashion which might be followed with advantage over the rest of the civilised world. The girl students dress their hair very carefully, and untidiness in personal appearance is treated as a misdemeanour, though occasionally it is a little difficult for the Indian girls to keep their long black wisps of hair under proper control. It is surprising, on the other hand, what sleekness and length the negresses can impart to their head-covering by the careful and persistent combing and brushing of the kinky tresses.

A noteworthy point about these Negro students at Hampton and Tuskegee is the pleasant, deep-toned, melodious voices of the men and the low-pitched voices of the women (also, to an Englishman, the absence of the "American" accent in the intonation of English). All the students at these institutions are taught to speak as clearly and distinctly as possible, and to be particularly careful as to their pronunciation. They are advised to speak from the chest, and not through the nose. Although the so-called American accent (which is largely the provincial pronunciation of the eighteenth century in Britain, and can be matched in several parts of England at the present day) is gradually disappearing from the United States under the unconscious admiration for the voice utterance of educated people in Europe, it still lingers in a more marked form with the whites than with the blacks. Yet there is a good deal of nasality in the pronunciation of several millions of American Negroes still uneducated. In the eastern coast belt of the Southern States I believe this to be due to the fact that so many of the Negroes came from the Guinea Coast region, where the native languages are extremely nasal.

326. AN AMERINDIAN WOMAN-STUDENT, HAMPTON INSTITUTE

An interesting adjunct of the Hampton Institute is the Whittier School for children, which begins with a kindergarten, and ascends through higher grades of instruction till the child is able (if its parents wish) to re-enter the Institute as a college student. It is pretty to see these children with their pearly-white teeth and gleaming white eyeballs, plump little bodies, and perfect satisfaction with their own personal appearance, marching into school to a musical drill, and singing with a fervour due rather to the tune than to the out-of-date words "An' befo' Ah'll be a slave, Ah'll be buried in ma grave, and ma spirit shall ascend to God on high." Alas! all this revolt against "slavery" must be tempered now by the feeling that we are nearly all of us slaves to the exigencies of civilised life. There are white slaves toiling in England and in America more unremittingly, more breathlessly, than any African who formerly worked on a cotton plantation or in a mine; not under the lash, it is true, but dreading to stop on the treadmill of life lest they should be caught by the cruel fangs of hunger, or the disrespectability which comes of not being able to pay your way.

It is surprising to note amongst these Negro children and students at Hampton, as at Tuskegee, the extraordinary prevalence, with dark eyes and a dark skin, of red, blond, or golden hair. There are even examples of blue-eyed, fair-haired Negroids, retaining, as the only trace of their African blood, the undulating curl in the hair and the pale olive complexion. Have we here a new race in the making? The features are fine, regular, and beautiful: it is only that terrible murky complexion which ties down this child, this man or woman, to the dark primeval days when the Negro rioted in the wealth of food provided by the Indian or African plains and forests, and hid his talent in a napkin.

What incident in his race-history relieved the Amerindian of this stigma of an ineradicable skin pigment? He led seemingly a life as feckless as that of the African black man; yet dressed in civilised clothes he at once sinks naturally into the white community, and when he mingles his blood with that of the white race, his descendants are handsome according to the white ideal, and the olive of his skin is permeated with a rosy blush.

CHAPTER XVII

THE EDUCATION OF THE NEGRO: TUSKEGEE

IN reviewing the new turn of the Negro problem in the States since the outbreak of civil war between North and South, namely, the attempt by education to fit the ex-slave and his descendants for citizenship, I should have given priority of place to the Penn School of St. Helena Island, off the coast of South Carolina.[1]

This work of redemption began as far back as 1861, though the Penn School was not actually founded and named till a few years later.

327. IN ST. HELENA ISLAND, SOUTH CAROLINA
The palms are *Inodes palmetto*, the "Thatch Palm"

Previous to 1861, the negroes of the island of St. Helena were considered among the lowest slaves of the South. They were ruled by black drivers, and, under the strictest overseeing, raised the finest of all cotton, that known as Sea Island, which takes a whole year's labour to perfect. Cleanliness or neatness were as unknown as the alphabet, and decent home-life was nowhere to be found among the plantation negroes, to whom the appearance of a white face was so rare as to frighten the children by its novelty.

The approach of the Federal naval forces in November, 1861, led to the abandonment of the island by its white families. Realising the necessity for prompt action, the Government and public-spirited Northerners sent down men and women to teach the negroes, to give them clothing, and to direct the working of the plantations, so that some cotton and at least provision crops might be raised. Gradually a new order of affairs was introduced, and out of the work of the Freedmen's Aid Society there has grown up a school which for forty years was under the headship of the first woman teacher to land in St. Helena,

[1] Unfortunately, pressure of time and uncertainty of health prevented my paying a personal visit to St. Helena Island; and my account of the negroes of this district and the work of the Penn School is derived from the information kindly supplied by Miss Rossa B. Cooley and Miss Grace Bigelow-House.

Miss Laura W. Towne. This able woman, who cheerfully gave her life and private means to the ignorant blacks about her, was the uncrowned queen of St. Helena Island. She conducted this "experiment station" with most gratifying results, and lived to see the Penn School (as it is now called) grow into a flourishing and incorporated institution under a Board of Trustees, with academic and industrial departments, and a school farm in charge of a trained agriculturist, who is a graduate of Hampton Institute.

During Miss Towne's long career she helped the negroes to grow out of the barbaric conditions of slavery into a law-abiding, self-respecting people. The heads of the families now own their farms. They have passed beyond the one-room cabin stage, some of them being proud possessors of "painted houses with glass windows"; and they are as temperate and moral as the average country communities in the North, and far superior to many portions of Rhode Island and Delaware. All this was facilitated by the sale in 1863 of the plantations, for unpaid taxes, their repurchase by the United States Government, and their subsequent resale in farms of ten acres, readily acquired by the negroes and jealously guarded. During all this time the objectionable poor white has been wholly absent; none the less, the negro has been constantly subject to political frauds, so that at present only about one hundred coloured men of the nine hundred qualified are permitted to vote. Although scourged by frequent epidemics of smallpox, and devastated by the cyclone of 1893, which cost three hundred lives, their isolation, land ownership, and freedom from interference have enabled the negroes to rise steadily, morally, and industrially, until the island promises to become a very well-to-do and successful community, as well as a striking object-lesson of the possibilities of growth among coloured people when intelligently guided.

The Penn School is now devoting itself to industrial training, for the methods of agriculture are still primitive, and scientific farming would double or treble the cotton crop. For the simplest ironwork the people must go to Beaufort, there being but two trained mechanics on the island. These, be it noted, are coloured missionaries from Hampton, come to teach carpentering, blacksmithing, and harness-making, and to give other instruction to the 275 pupils of the school. Eight public schools have been established, largely owing to Miss Towne, and they are reported to be much above the average Southern school in equipment and instruction, though of course far below the Penn School. The latter has among its varied departments one for "domestic science," for the teaching of home sanitation, comfort, comeliness of surroundings, and decent cooking.

In Beaufort County (with an area of perhaps 15,000 square miles) there is at present a population of some 5000 whites and 31,500 negroes and coloured. The school attendance among the white children by the last returns was an average of 260 for the year 1908; for the negroes and negroids it was 5618. Yet the allowance of State funds for the education of these 260 white children was an approximate £5000, and for the blacks £1750. This will give some idea of the South Carolinian sense of justice towards its negro citizens.

But by means of Northern generosity and the allotment of some educational funds distributed by the General Education Board of New York the work at Penn School is carried on with ever-increasing happy results.

Between 1864 and 1869 there came into existence thirteen Negro Universities, which were established by the co-operation of General Armstrong's Freedmen's Bureau and the co-operation of the American Missionary Association, the Baptists, the Friends, and even the Negro soldiers of the United States army.[1] Noteworthy among these are Howard University of Washington, D.C.; Fisk University of Nashville, Tennessee; Atlanta University[2] of Georgia; Biddle University of North Carolina; Southland College of Arkansas (first among the thirteen in point of age); the Rust University of Mississippi; Claflin University of South Carolina; and the Straight University of New Orleans.

Then, later in foundation, are the Leland University of New Orleans, created

328. TYPES OF NEGRO STUDENTS, ATLANTA UNIVERSITY, GEORGIA

and endowed by Mr. H. Chamberlain in 1870; the New Orleans University (Methodist Church, 1873); the Shaw University of Raleigh, North Carolina (Baptist Church, 1874); the Wiley University of Marshall, Texas (Methodists, 1880); the Livingstone College of Salisbury, North Carolina (Zion Methodist Church, 1880); the Virginia Normal and Collegiate Institute of Petersburg, supported and managed by the State of Virginia; the Georgia State Industrial College (Savannah, 1890); the Branch Normal College of Pine Bluff, Arkansas,

[1] Lincoln Institute in Missouri, though now a State-supported College, was founded on a donation of about £1500, subscribed by Negro soldiers of the 62nd and 63rd Infantry Regiments.

[2] Atlanta University is the home of the great writer on Negro questions, W. E. Burghardt DuBois.

founded by the State in 1875; and the Alcorn Agricultural University of Mississippi State.

This list still leaves unmentioned many notable Colleges and Universities specially founded and maintained for Negro instruction in the Seceded States[1] by the Free Churches (Methodists, Baptists, Friends, and Presbyterians).

It is noteworthy that the Roman Catholic Church and the Protestant Episcopal (Anglican) Church in the United States maintain nothing in the way

329. PROFESSOR W. E. BURGHARDT DUBOIS

of Negro education, have never at any time shown particular sympathy with or desire to help the Negro slave. Indeed, in slavery times numerous Bishops and Institutions of the Church of England—which afterwards became the Protestant Episcopal Church—held slaves. Yet the Anglican and the Roman Churches in the West Indies and South America have been the great opponents of Slavery, and the Anglican Church, especially for the last forty years, has been an ardent champion of Negro education in tropical America.

[1] It is not necessary to deal with Negro educational facilities in the rest of the United States, as besides the special Negro colleges such as the State College of Delaware and those others already mentioned, the Negro or Negroid child or student may be educated with the young white citizens.

From the point of view of the White man as well as the superior type of Negro it is a question still whether these universities founded by generous men or by generous religious communities are not too narrowed in usefulness by their imitation of eighteenth to nineteenth century English and Scottish Universities and Colleges. They still afflict the Negro and the coloured man (as their "white" sister institutions do the White American student) with an inordinate and wholly unnecessary amount of Greek and Latin grammar and literature,[1] the only essential good of which might be picked up by a clever student in a few days' reading at a modern encyclopædia. They give the negro of to-day John Bunyan and Milton (to excess); the *Evidences of Christianity* (the origin of nine-tenths of school and college disbelief); time-wasting rot about *Logic*—the best Logic is the accomplished fact, the fist, the dollar, the kiss, the vote—*Psychology and Metaphysics:* and Yellow Fever, Dysentery, Cancer, Tuberculosis, Malaria still unsubdued! And lastly there are courses of Bible study (quite apart from a sensible short exposition of the teaching of Christ and of Christ-like men) which in their elaboration and taking up of precious time are only defensible in the case of professional Orientalists and Ethnologists—which few of these negro students aspire to be.

Oh for the besom of a reformer, here and in Britain! Latin is profoundly interesting and is even important to the merchant and the statesman *if* taught as the parent of the seven living Romance languages, not otherwise; Greek might be briefly mentioned in general lectures on Philology; all that is of value in the literature of these dead tongues can be obtained in good English translations and its best essence is embodied in English poetry: the rest could be left to specialists. The Old Testament should be reserved for those who are making a particular study of the history of man and of religious beliefs, and cease to be the fetish of the Protestant Churches; "Rhetoric," "Logic," and "Metaphysics" should be penalised.

[1] Here is a list of the principal works in the Classics more or less forced on the students at these Negro Universities and Colleges, works included in the published curriculum (at any rate down to a few years ago):—

In Greek: Xenophon (*Anabasis*), Homer's *Iliad* and *Odyssey*, Thucydides, Demosthenes' *Oration on the Crown* and *Olynthiacs* and *Philippics*, Plato's *Apology*, the Tragedies of Euripides and Sophocles, the works of Aristotle and Herodotus (why not the travels of H. M. Stanley?), the Greek New Testament (and of course the Old Testament in Hebrew!), Æschylus (*Prometheus Bound*), etc.

In Latin: Cæsar's *Gallic War*, several books of Sallust, Virgil's *Æneid*, Horace in his *Odes* and *Epodes*, *Satires* and *Epistles*, Cicero on *Friendship* and on *Old Age*, and in his *Oration against Catiline* and other "old unhappy things of long ago"; Livy on the Second Punic War, Tacitus on the Germans of A.D. 100, etc. etc.

In the name of true religion and of common sense, of man's all-too-short life on this wonderful planet, of the necessity of teaching the principles of forest preservation and disease prevention, of respect for beautiful birds and beasts and other wonderful works of God, of all that should make the seven years of studenthood fruitful in real useful learning, cannot some termination be put to this fetishistic nonsense, this solemn cant, this abominable waste of time and brain-power? How many ideas are there in any of these classical writers except perhaps Plato, Aristotle, and Homer, which cannot be—for the ordinary man and woman—crystallised into a dozen quotations in English? But this mistaken passion for the Greek and Roman Classics seems peculiar to Protestant Christians in Britain, Germany, and the United States. It is as if when their ancestors boldly left some State Church to found another less regular sect of Christianity they were more than ever concerned to show themselves orthodox in the "Classics." So they carried the worship of Hebrew, Greek, and Latin to a mania.

Is it not time this nonsense was brought to an end in the rational United States?

From the foregoing diatribe I ought perhaps to except partially the Shaw University of Raleigh, N.C., in which Greek is stated to be "optional," and German is taught with some care, besides French. But WHY NOT SPANISH and PORTUGUESE? Here we have the United States with a population of nearly ninety millions impinging on and also ruling countries in which the language spoken (by many millions) is Spanish; and trading with and deeply concerned with a sister republic of equally vast area—Brazil—wherein the language of twenty millions is Portuguese; and I doubt whether there is a single School, College, or University in the United States, white or negro, in which either of these languages is taught or encouraged.—H. H. J.

Then, in place of these solemn pretexts for wasting precious time and youthful zeal, should come instruction of an inspiriting kind in the most modern presentments of History and Geography, of Anthropology, Zoology, Botany, and of that New Bible the Story of the Earth itself—Geology. Astronomy should be taught to all classes: Freshmen, Sophomores, and Advanced. Likewise Mathematics (very little Euclid), a reasonable dose of Geometry, much Chemistry, much Physiology, and the theories of the origin and prevention of disease; AND, besides an unpedantic illustration of the English Language and its history and application to thought-rendering, a thorough grounding should be given to all students in SPANISH, French, and German. Inducements should also be offered to study Portuguese and Italian. Persons eager about language study (a splendid source of enlightenment but made horrible to boys and youths by the wicked, fetishistic worship of Greek and Latin) should be encouraged to get an insight into Irish and Welsh, Dutch and Danish, Sanskrit and Arabic: just an insight to let them understand a little better how civilised man talks and thinks to-day as he does.

But of course it is to-day obvious to all intelligent people in America (as it was to General Armstrong forty-six years ago) that the Negro, Negroid, and Amerindian must be civilised not only in mind but in body; taught to be clean-minded and clean-skinned, adroit in the use of his hands above all: workers, not merely talkers, constructors, artists, inventors, mechanicians, intelligent agriculturists, doers of the Word, not merely listeners and cogitators. These colleges and universities are well enough—would be better still if my suggested curriculum were adopted; but they merely train clergymen, lawyers, politicians, petty officials, schoolmasters (to teach second-hand knowledge of no great value), third-rate writers, a few geniuses able, as geniuses are, to suck nourishment from marl or verjuice—but they don't solve the tremendous need of the United States for field-hands—INTELLIGENT field-hands; they don't turn out cooks—and cooks, as Booker Washington points out in pleasanter language than mine, are more necessary than preachers. They don't send out into Twentieth-Century-America machinists, inexpensive electricians, plumbers, builders, bricklayers, carpenters, cabinet-makers, gardeners, stockmen, sawyers, hydraulic engineers, printers, tailors, dressmakers, bootmakers, metal-workers, and laundry-hands.

Hampton having therefore proved a success in spreading this New learning, has been the parent institute, the model from which have sprung by direct transplanting or by imitation the many other Industrial Schools and Colleges in the United States for the training of Negroes, Negroids, and Amerindians to useful or beautiful handicrafts and to an appreciation of the amenities of civilised existence. The greatest of these is "The Tuskegee Normal and Industrial Institute for the training of coloured young men and women."[1]

[1] The following institutions have grown out of the Tuskegee Institute and have been chartered under the laws of the various States where they are situated. Not only have they been founded by Tuskegee graduates, but the officers and in many cases the entire faculty are composed of Tuskegee graduates:—

Mt. Meigs Institute, Waugh, Alabama; *Snow Hill Institute*, Snow Hill, Alabama; *Calhoun School* (for women), Alabama; *Voorhees Industrial School*, Denmark, South Carolina; *East Tennessee Normal and Industrial Institute*, Harriman, Tennessee; *Robert Hungerford Industrial Institute*, Eatonville, Florida; *Topeka Educational and Industrial Institute*, Topeka, Kansas; *Allengreene Normal and Industrial Institute*, Ruston, Louisiana; *Utica Normal and Industrial Institute*, Utica, Mississippi; *Christiansburg Institute*, Cambria, Virginia. The *Utica Normal Institute* is conducted by a well-known educational expert of the new school, Mr. W. H. Holtzclaw.

Tuskegee[1] town is a beautiful garden city of south-eastern Alabama, founded and unconsciously planned long before the notion of garden cities had been a matter of deliberate intention. Its name and its history show that it was once the head-quarters of the Maskogi (Muskogee) Indian tribe, all traces of which have long since disappeared from this locality, though a few still remain in western Alabama.

Founded about 1817, Tuskegee became quickly almost the "culture capital" of Alabama. It had (and still has) great schools for white girls and boys; solemn, handsome pillared houses, set in park-like grounds, neat villages of well-treated slaves or contented freedmen; and screened by its evergreen oaks, its cypresses and magnolias, it asked for no more contact with the hustling outside world than was necessary to sell its cotton, or occasionally to renew its labour force. So when the railway schemes of the 'forties and 'fifties were being laid out to connect New York with Montgomery and New Orleans, Tuskegee begged that it might be left alone and in peace, out of sight or hearing of this disturbing element of progress. It is therefore at the present day—but perhaps after all to its benefit—several miles off the great Southern Railway route, with which it is connected, however, by a branch line.

330. ONE OF THE FEW SURVIVING MASKOGI AMERINDIANS OF WESTERNMOST ALABAMA

In visiting Tuskegee, I had the great advantage of going there in the companionship of Mr. and Mrs. James Bryce. When we left the British Embassy at Washington very early on a mid-November morning, the broad avenues, the public gardens and waste spaces of that city, lay under four inches of snow. It was pleasant to leave these surroundings of chilly vastness for the snug comfort of an observation car, genially warm, yet bright with the daylight of its three glass sides. We were the guests of Mr. Robert C. Ogden, one of the Trustees of both Hampton and Tuskegee, and one of the best friends the Negro race has ever had in the history of North America.

This railway journey of seven hundred miles from the northern frontiers of Virginia to the middle of Alabama—a journey undertaken with that perfect comfort which can be found in America alongside the supremest *dis*comfort in railway travelling—was of itself a matter of keen interest to me. We trundled slowly through the western part of Virginia on the single line which is all the United States railway system can at present devote to its main Southern Route. As far as the eye could see, the country was in the grip of winter. The distant mountains of the Alleghany Range rose up blue and gaunt, covered or patched with newly fallen snow. The flat country was completely white, except for

[1] This name is pronounced as if written in phonetic English "Taskígi."

the black trunks and branches of the trees and the sides of buildings. The air, even at the end of the train on the car's open platform, was icy, and the foliage of the evergreen trees was heavy with its snow burden.

It was unmitigated winter till midday. Then the bright sun effected a partial thaw. This was checked by a frost in the late afternoon, and the result in the sunset glow was wonderful: we seemed to be passing through a land of glass. Telegraph wires were strung with glass beads, and all the twigs and branches of innumerable trees on the foot-hills were encased in glass. Glass forests, in fact, surrounded us on both sides of the valley through which the train slowly travelled. The woods on the eastern heights caught at one time the pink glow of the sunset, and shivered in amethyst tints. To the west, in the shadow, the ice film was a cold blue. In the following morning, passing through Georgia, there was a heavy rime on the ground and a cobalt tone about the distance, but we had returned to the autumn colouring of October as seen in more northern latitudes. Against a background of green pines with grey stems and blue-grey interspaces flamed the vivid crimson, orange purple, lemon of the diverse oaks, the birches, liquidambars, sycamores, and maples. In central Alabama it was still late summer or early September with, on our arrival, a humorous touch of frost in the air which made the banana clumps in ornamental gardens look seared and forlorn

331. MR. LEWIS ADAMS
The Negro tinsmith who helped to found Tuskegee Institute

Scarcely stopping at Tuskegee itself the special portion of our train destined for the Institute passed through the pretty, shady town of country-houses, stores churches, and cotton-ginneries and landed us comfortably at the entrance to the Tuskegee Institute. Here Mr. and Mrs Bryce were greeted by a large number of Negro students from the British West Indies and two or three East Indians (Hindus). At the entrance to the Institute estate we passed under a triumphal arch of evergreens, decorated with the American and British flags, and we marched in a procession to the music, alternately, of the National Anthems of both countries. Then we proceeded to our lodgings at the Principal's residence, and commenced our inspection of this great training-college and its affiliated schools the following day.

The idea of the Tuskegee Institute was partly conceived and initiated in 1879 by a Negro tinsmith named Lewis Adams, and by a white banker of the Southern aristocratic type, Mr. George W. Campbell. Both of them were residents at Tuskegee town. In the following year the State Legislature of Alabama, struck with the work already achieved in the education of Negroes, decided to grant an annual subsidy to the Institute. Messrs. Campbell and Adams therefore decided to apply to General Samuel Armstrong, the Principal of Hampton, for a coloured teacher who should be competent to direct the little school which had been founded on the site of unsuccessful cotton plantations, in the outskirts of Tuskegee. The man whom Armstrong selected was Booker Washington, and he commenced work in 1881 with two frame houses and a ruined chapel.[1]

The now celebrated Booker Taliaferro Washington, an ex-slave once valued at $400, the child of a poor negress of Virginia, and of a white or mulatto father, who possibly bore the Italian name of Tagliaferro,[2] was born about the year 1858. He has written his own Life, which has been translated into many languages, and to it I refer the reader who is interested in his personality. He managed by dint of extraordinary exertions and privations to become a student at Hampton in 1873, and here he attracted the notice of General Armstrong, who with much other encouragement gave him his chance at Tuskegee.

332. THE "FRAME-HOUSES AND RUINED CHAPEL" WHICH FORMED THE COMMENCEMENT OF THE TUSKEGEE INSTITUTE

First occupied in 1881, but now outside the grounds

Washington's work gradually attracted outside attention, and the amount of the small State grant was slightly increased; but the enormous work carried on by the present Institute could never have been effected without the really remarkable donations and subsidies of wealthy Americans. Noteworthy amongst these was Mrs. Mary E. Shaw, a Negro woman of New York, who left the whole of her fortune to Tuskegee. But there should also specially be mentioned Andrew Carnegie, who not only presented the Institute with a magnificent library, noteworthy for its wide range of literature and its beautiful architecture and furniture, but also endowed Booker Washington and his Institute so that he was henceforth free from all monetary anxieties. He has secured to him for life (with ultimate provision for his widow) an income which, though modest as incomes go in the United States, is equivalent to that of the well-paid principal of an English college. He is therefore able to devote the whole of his energies and resources to the work of the Institute, and has not now to think, as formerly, of earning enough money to support his wife and family. William H. Baldwin, Collis Huntingdon, Maurice Jesup, and Albert Willcox are other donors (all white men of the Northern States) who have not only endowed Tuskegee with large sums of money, but have personally put their ideas into the Institute and have seen that their money was spent to the greatest possible advantage.

The special feature of Tuskegee (as of Hampton) is industrial education; and the special importance of Booker Washington and his teaching lies in the fact that he has brushed aside all discussion of the political claims of the Negro,

[1] The chapel itself was subsequently removed, and is now set up in the grounds of Tuskegee Institute.

[2] Tagliaferro or Taillefer ("Cut Through Iron") was a common nickname in Norman and Crusading times which grew into an Italian, French, and British surname. The Telfers, Tallifers, etc., are English and U.S.A. variants. No doubt Englishmen bearing this Norman name emigrated to Virginia, for in a corrupted form it is still met with in that State. Booker Washington's white grandfather may, however, have reached Virginia in the late eighteenth century, when so many European adventurers followed the French troops thither in the War of Independence. It would be curious if the blood of some Crusader of mediæval Italy flowed in the veins of this regenerator of the Southern Negro!

and the justice or the injustice of his treatment by the South, to concentrate his own attention and that of his listeners on the supreme necessity of making the Negro a valuable citizen of the United States. He has probably said to himself over and over again, "Satan finds some mischief still for idle hands to do." He wants the Negro to become the most industrious race in the United States, to be as avaricious of *time* as Jews used to be of *money*, to live as well as possible,

333. BOOKER TALIAFERRO WASHINGTON, LL.D., HARVARD UNIVERSITY
Founder of Tuskegee

eat well-cooked, wholesome food set forth daintily; to build no house that has not got a bath-room, to be fastidiously clean in person and neat in dress; to be able to do everything, but most of all to be accomplished masons, architects, carpenters, cooks, dressmakers, tailors, hatters, ploughmen, gardeners, cotton-cultivators, tobacco-growers, poultry-keepers, horse breeders and trainers carriage-builders, bootmakers, botanists, typewriters, shorthand clerks, and electricians.

Neither at Hampton nor Tuskegee is the education of a "charitable" description. At both places the student must make a small deposit on being admitted, and an annual payment (in Tuskegee merely for board), though there are scholarships to be gained by the industrious which may relieve him or her of the entire cost of their education.

The instruction given by these two great institutes, and through their now numerous daughter-schools and affiliated colleges, is intended to create, by dispersed tuition, a great middle class of educated coloured people, who shall gradually replace the illiterate, unskilled, dirty, improvident Negroes of the South and East, and yet not unduly swell the ranks of the negro lawyers, doctors, and clergy. You could not, for example, come to Tuskegee and engage one of the female students as a parlourmaid (though after seeing their work in this line of life you might well wish to do so). The young woman who has shown that she thoroughly understands how to lay a table attractively, how to wait at table, how to answer a door and announce visitors, and such other duties as are theoretically those of a parlourmaid, is to go out into the world not necessarily to become a parlourmaid herself straight off, but to radiate this instruction from smaller schools and institutions, or, if she marries, as she probably will, to know henceforth how the house and household of a decent-living person should be kept. Of course many of the male and female students obtain immediate employment in different careers as soon as they leave Tuskegee (or Hampton), but a large proportion of them really go out into the world as well-equipped, all-round, educated teachers in other schools; and it is their pupils who are destined to fill the industrial ranks.

334. A TUSKEGEE STUDENT

It should perhaps again be insisted on that Tuskegee, like Hampton, is very large-hearted as to the nationality of its students. Both places are becoming an *alma mater* not only to the Negroes of the British West Indies, to Amerindians and Filipinos, to Cubans and Portoricans, but even to natives of British Africa. I saw several Zulus either at Hampton or Tuskegee, also Liberians, and natives of Sierra Leone and the Gold Coast.

This tendency, if it grows, and if concurrently the whites of the Southern States treat the American Negro with greater fairness, cannot fail to spread "American" influence amongst the coloured peoples of the world, perhaps to the advantage of the United States.[1]

During my stay of ten days at Tuskegee I visited in detail all the departments of education. Especially interesting was the Kindergarten for the tiny children, in which there were golden-haired, blue-eyed babies; red-

[1] I doubt if it be realised fully in Great Britain what a commercial gain has accrued to the United States by the establishment of American missionary schools in the Turkish Empire—Rumelia, Asia Minor, Syria, Armenia, and Egypt. This result was certainly not intended by the pious and philanthropic persons who, with singleness of purpose, devoted either their money or themselves to spreading knowledge and civilisation amongst the backward peoples of the Near East; but nevertheless this is one way in which their nation is being rewarded.

haired, brown-eyed children; and brown-black negrolets. In the case of the seemingly-white children there was the dull sallow complexion, or some other detail which might have revealed the drop of Negro blood in their ancestry to some cunning and possibly cruel person, who by proving the fact in their case might have raised a clamour had such a child been sent to a white school for superior education. But whether brown, yellow, or white, black-haired, red-haired, or blonde, these children danced and sang and went through their exercises with a grace and an adroitness which brought them the hearty plaudits of Mrs. Bryce and other visitors.

335. THE CARNEGIE LIBRARY, TUSKEGEE INSTITUTE

The Children's House is the Public School of the Institute community, to the maintenance of which the county of Macon (in which Tuskegee is situated) contributes a small annual grant. Besides the Kindergarten there is a regular school for boys and girls, which gives them a thorough education, and if they wish it, prepares them through preliminary classes to enter as students the College of the Institute.

It is of course the Industrial Education that makes Tuskegee specially worth visiting. There is a School of Agriculture and a chemical laboratory, and a museum where specimens of the very varied vegetable products of the South are preserved for illustrating lectures, and where the animals (including insects) of the South-eastern States are illustrated. Attached to this Agricultural

School are hot-houses, classes for practical horticulture and floriculture, and even for landscape gardening. On the large farm attached to the Institute, and in the experimental plantations, almost every crop known to the Southern States is cultivated by the students under instruction. Particular attention is given to the cultivation of fruit and vegetables.[1] A department of Bee culture was started in 1887 by Mr. J. H. Washington, the brother of the Principal.[2] On the experimental farm ten years' work has shown that a poor, worn-out soil such as was that of the sandy grounds of Tuskegee can by careful tillage and manuring produce excellent crops, especially of cotton. The effect

336. THE LIBRARIAN AT TUSKEGEE AND HIS ASSISTANT

of this teaching has spread far and wide throughout this part of Alabama, where, of course, cotton is now grown at a considerable profit.

The live-stock industry of the School of Agriculture has gradually built up a dairy herd of 264 head of cattle, of which at least 106 were milch cows at the time of my visit. The milk they furnish supports a vast creamery and system of dairies in which instruction is given in what may now be called the "science of pure milk" and of butter-making. An additional herd of 159 head were being reared for meat production. There were also at the time of my visit 518 pigs, kept according to the latest ideas of sanitation, disease prevention, and the

[1] At the time of my stay there were said to be 13,000 peach trees, 125,000 strawberry plants, 2924 grape vines, and 198 fig trees in the experimental orchards of the School of Agriculture.

[2] John Washington's work in connection with Tuskegee and with other attempts to uplift the Negro has been almost as remarkable as that of his better-known brother, Dr. Booker Washington.

producing of good pork. At the same time the poultry yard contained 548 fowls of choice breeds, and a large number of geese, ducks and turkeys. Particular attention was being given to egg production and the use of incubators, and the fattening of pullets. The Horse-barn contained 137 horses and mules.

Sound instruction is given in Veterinary science, in the matching of sires (donkeys and horses) and mares for mule-breeding. In going round these veterinary schools, it is interesting to see horses, bulls, and cows—sometimes of a considerable size—being led into a demonstration pound in the middle of

337. A PRACTICAL FIELD LESSON IN AGRICULTURE BEING GIVEN TO NEGRO FARMERS IN ALABAMA BY THE FARMERS' INSTITUTE OF TUSKEGEE

the lecture hall, so that they may illustrate various points in anatomy or in perfection and imperfection of breed.

In the vast Slater-Armstrong Memorial Trades Building, mechanical industries are taught in an effective and practical manner. There are saw-mills, boiler-houses, and shops for instruction in carpentry, cabinet-making, carriage-building, wheelwrighting, harness-making, blacksmithing, plumbing, tinning, house- and carriage-painting, engineering, electric lighting, architecture and mechanical drawing, shoemaking, tailoring, ropemaking, basket- and mat-making, and printing. A thorough course of instruction is also given in brickmaking, bricklaying, and masonry. I noticed particularly what excellent boots and shoes—shapely and strong—were being turned out by the students of the shoemaking department. It seemed to me, in fact, that in all these sections of the Institute the instruction was of the very best, and of the most up-to-date character. The schools and shops were supplied with the most recent technical literature on the subjects taught, obtained, not only from the United States, but also the United Kingdom, Germany and France.

With regard to the special instruction for women, there are the "Girls' trades," which are taught in a great, commodious building called "Dorothy Hall." They comprise laundry-work, cooking, dressmaking, millinery, basket-work, mattress-making, and soap-manufacture. When passing through the well-equipped dressmaking establishment I listened to a part of a lecture on the juxtaposition of colours. The lady professor proved as an article of the Religion of the Modes, that the placing side by side of mauve and helio-

338. THE CREAMERY AND MILK-TESTING SCHOOL, TUSKEGEE

trope on a hat was a crime of peculiar heinousness. Personally I could not agree with her diatribes, for the delicious samples of these two exquisite tints which she held up side by side that we might be duly shocked seemed to me to blend as delightfully as they do in many a flower, and the arrangement, together with white, was a fitting contrast to the tawny skin of a handsome mulatto student who was wearing a gown in which they were temporarily combined.

This department was conducted by women of colour; but although the work was exceedingly tasteful, it all seemed to be designed more with reference to a white skin; and no special attempt was made to meet the requirements in shape and colour of dress appropriate to dark-complexioned, dark-haired women. The models and *mannequins* on which the costumes or the hats were fitted all seemed to be dazzling blondes.[1] This, it seems to me—the special designing of costumes for educated colour women—is a point that Tuskegee has not quite grasped, and which it should go into most thoroughly and perhaps lay down the law of taste, to be spread far and wide through America by its pupils.

Of course, the farcical side of the colour question in the States is that at least a considerable proportion of the "coloured people" are almost white-skinned, and belong in the preponderance of their descent and in their mental associations to the white races. These, of course, require to dress as do European men and women. But it is undeniable that for people of dark skin—amongst the women, at any rate—a special standard of appropriate taste awaits the definition of a genius.

This, indeed, is, it seems to me, a matter of crucial importance to the civilised Christian Negro. As regards the Muhammadan, it is solved at once in Africa and Asia by the exceedingly picturesque, dignified, and suitable costume of the men, and perhaps also of the women, in the Muhammadan world. Dress a Negro like an Arab, or like a Hindu, and you really forget that he is a Negro: he passes almost naturally into that Eastern world where people have far less right or tendency to mock at a coloured skin, where, indeed, the brown tint of the epidermis seems more in keeping with these tropical surroundings than the pale or red-mottled hands and face of the European.

Who that visited Sierra Leone, say, ten years ago, or Liberia at the present day, can have failed to contrast unfavourably the Negro in high white collar, black coat and tight waistcoat, trousers, patent leather boots, and an ugly black "chimney-pot" or hard-straw hat; or a negress in a green silk blouse, very tight waist and voluminous skirt (her exaggerated mop of woolly hair crowned, possibly, with some extravagance in millinery worthy of a typical coster girl), with the Muhammadan people passing by, aptly clothed in costumes that were cheap, cool, dignified, and yet very picturesque?

On the other hand, I am quite ready to admit that the latest developments of European fashions for men suit the Negro's appearance remarkably well—the panama or straw hat, the Tyrolese or squash hat, the motoring cap, look well on a Negro's head, as do the shorter jacket, fairly loose, straight trousers on his well-shaped body. The collars need not be too low-necked (as they used to be till quite recently in America), nor need they be Gladstonian and consequently limp and stained with perspiration. All over the States now Negro men from the artisan to the college professor are as a rule not only as well dressed as the average white American, but are nicely dressed, so that they present nothing to gird at. This is also the case to-day in Sierra Leone and in some Liberian coast towns, especially among the Kru-boy element.

Dr. Booker Washington and his sons dress well in appropriate clothes that are of good cut. I am almost inclined to hope and believe that he possesses no frock-coat and silk hat in his wardrobe. I certainly trust that he and other leaders of the Negro people will not fail to inveigh against these garments, which only look well on two white men out of ten, and never look other than ugly and inappropriate on a person of dark complexion.

But it is in regard to the Negro women of civilisation who are not Muhammadans that some special effort should be made in the way of dictating a law

[1] In a great "white" dressmaking establishment at Birmingham (Alabama), I saw that the proprietors had the moral courage to set up amongst their dummies quadroon and octoroon types to show off such of the firm's costumes as were more suitably worn by women of colour.

of taste and suitability in costume. The right notion is a difficult thing to seize, but I have had glimmerings myself. I remember once in New York stopping for a moment to look at a mulatto woman standing on the pavement to await a tramcar. She had a golden-yellow skin, dark, mournful eyes, rather a long, thin face, with projecting cheek-bones. Except for her eyes she was an ugly woman, and in an inappropriate costume would have been frightful. As it was, one felt she could only be done justice to, in her *pose* at that moment, by a Carolus Duran. Her figure was beautiful, and she wore a modification of the Directoire costume, the waist *svelte*, but not pulled in, the hips not enhanced. The dress was all black, and the small hat, partly veiled, was dull black also. She was the embodiment of elegance, and the dark, long-lashed eyes, the sad face, with its yellow skin partly revealed under the gauze of the hat, had a poignant note of romance. One felt she was a fine creature, and respected her for knowing how to clothe herself.

339. AN OCTOROON PARLOURMAID TRAINED AT TUSKEGEE

At a large evening party which took place at Tuskegee whilst I was there, I passed in review some two hundred female costumes. Only a few were tasteful. Some negresses of almost black skin came in dresses of snowy white, or cream colour, which simply made them unendurably grotesque. Others were in pale blue, bright pink, or vivid green. On the other hand, those that dressed in *écru*, in varying shades of brown, dark blue, or the greenish blue of the indigo dye; in grey-green, ash-grey, or crimson, looked exceedingly nice.

In treating of this most delicate question of costume, on which people are more sensitive than they are on religion, I might repeat some remarks made to me by Mr. Roosevelt at the time of my visit to America. He was referring to those passages in my book on Liberia, wherein I had ventured to criticise the American Negroes of that country for wearing black frock-coats, black silk hats, high collars, and tight trousers, in a temperature seldom less than eighty degrees in the shade. In discussing the matter, I referred as usual to the singularly picturesque costume adopted by the Muhammadan Negroes in Liberia.

His comment was, "Yes; and I have often heard people recommend the "very picturesque uniform of the British West India Regiment. But does it "not occur to you that the Negro is sensitive about making a side-show of "himself when he dresses up in what we think to be fantastic garments? If "he does not wish to become a Muhammadan, why should he dress like one? "Why should he introduce the spirit of the Ghetto? It was the special "costume forced on the Jew in the Middle Ages—the costume which at any "rate was to be markedly different from that of the Christian or the Muhammadan—which did so much to keep the Jews as a separate and despised "caste. Never, for example, would you get the coloured people of the United

"States to dress differently to their white fellow-citizens; but if they did so, "even though they might be picturesque in the eyes of painters, they would "be objects of ridicule to the rest of the community."

All the girl students who pass through Tuskegee are expected, without exception, to master a certain amount of cooking and of domestic science (the work of housemaids, parlourmaids, and children's nurses). It is deliberately intended thus, that no matter what rôle they may fill in life, they should be competent to direct the affairs of a home, and that they shall realise all the responsibilities of motherhood. The boys are likewise taught the elements of cooking. And all this teaching has to be put to a practical test by the students serving in turn as cooks to their own and the teachers' dining-rooms. There are, therefore, no salaried cooks at Tuskegee merely for the preparation of meals, though there are special instructors in the art of cooking.

340. AN OCTOROON STUDENT AT TUSKEGEE

As at Hampton, great stress is laid on the æsthetic surroundings of a home. Dr. Washington is perpetually preaching the gospel of cleanliness—of the person and of the house in which he or she is to live. Constant bathing is insisted on at Tuskegee, and a good deal of attention is given to teaching swimming amongst women as well as men. I did *not* find all the students' quarters as immaculately clean and tidy as they were at Hampton, and it will take time before this passion for cleanliness and scrupulous order has seized hold of the Negro race as it has over a small portion of the Caucasian (chiefly the people of Northern and North-western Europe and their descendants in the United States). But to the eye of the casual observer there is no difference in the outer aspect of Tuskegee and of Hampton. Every girl student seems to be well dressed and with tidy hair; and the boys wear the well-cut, handsome military uniform already described. And their bearing matches their uniform, for they are assiduously drilled by a staff of military officers of the United States Army attached to the service of the Institute.

I never entered a class-room that did not seem faultlessly clean and sweet, and with windows always open. Many of these rooms are bright with flowers from the gardens of the Institute. To all the students (who, of course, come mainly for industrial training) a simple academical teaching is given in geography, the English language, the history of the United States and of Great Britain. Visitors to Tuskegee, both expected and unexpected, have a feeling that the teachers of these classes are ladies and gentlemen in the best sense of these terribly abused words. They may be so "near white" as to be mistaken for teachers borrowed from the white world, or they may be of unmixed Negro race,[1] like Professor Carver, who teaches scientific agriculture, botany, agricultural chemistry, etc. He is, as regards complexion and features, an absolute Negro; but in the cut of his clothes, the accent of his speech, the soundness of his science, he might be professor of Botany not at Tuskegee, but at Oxford or Cambridge. Any European botanist of distinction, after ten minutes' conversation with this man, instinctively would deal with him "*de puissance en puissance.*"

I have met in my journey through America and the West Indies not a few Negroes of the type of Professor Carver (most of all in the States); after meeting them I have felt inclined to resent with militant bitterness the outrageous attacks on the Negro in general, emanating from a few rampant platform orators of Mississippi, Georgia, and South Carolina, who in education and manners are not fit to associate with some of the men and women who teach in the Institute at Tuskegee. One of the officials of this college, in appearance and mainly in descent, is a good-looking Irishman of six feet one. He is a "near white," and his wife is, I believe, altogether of the white race. They once ventured to travel on a Tennessee railroad in a car intended for "white" people. Some malicious individual spread the news that this individual travelling with his wife was only a "near white," had a little of the Negro race in his composition. Whereupon a large party of white railway passengers dragged this man from the car in the presence of his wife and lashed him with whips before the railway officials could intervene. Needless to say, he got no redress.

341. DR. ROBERT E. PARK

Who has written much on the Negro question in North America, has worked a good deal with Booker Washington at Tuskegee, and has supplied the author of this book with information and statistics

These are not subjects, however, on which Dr. Booker Washington desires to dwell, either personally or vicariously. He realises fair and square the difficulties of the Negro's position, and the root of it all, the root of it which must be logically traced back, on the lines of the parable of the Ten Talents, to the Negro's age-long neglect of his opportunities in Africa. He does not pretend that he is dealing with ideal Americans like the white and coloured philanthropists who have founded Hampton and Tuskegee, have spent millions of dollars and lifetimes of work to help his people. He has got to appease the violent prejudices of at least 15,000,000 Southern whites, and the indifference or hostility of perhaps another 15,000,000 white people in the rest of North America. He has got to correct, battle with, acknowledge, and apologise for the backwardness, silliness, laziness, weakness of resistance

[1] I believe I am right in saying that there is but one man of pure "white" descent in the *personnel* of Tuskegee Institute, and that is Dr. Robert E. Park, who in an honorary capacity assists Dr. Washington in some of his work. I have been much indebted to Dr. Park for varied information on the American negro.

to alcohol and sensuality of perhaps 4,000,000 of his own people in the United States.

He knows that the overwhelming majority of the white people in the States are opposed to any further mixture in blood, are angrily resolved to keep the white race white. Booker Washington—I believe—would have the existing types of Negro and Negroid (from octoroon to undiluted black) reunite and interfuse, thus possibly creating a new race altogether; which by its industriousness, sobriety, wealth, and good manners, may win for itself such a place in the regard of white America that it may be accorded in practice what is at present only granted in principle—equal suffrage with the other educated peoples of North America. He takes courage from the review of the Jews' position in the world to-day and the condition of the Jews fifty to a hundred years ago—without the franchise, shut out from the social circles of Christians or Muhammadans, almost without protectors, and affected racially by this boycotting: obliged to live, possibly, in the unhealthy quarter of a town, and under most unhealthy conditions; unable to own land, compelled to dress differently, massacred in times of popular excitement, swindled, and exiled. He sees them to-day not only on a parity with the Christian and superior to the Muhammadan, but even playing a very large part in the direction of the world's destinies. He knows that such and such a Jew really determined the British occupation of Egypt, that another made it possible for Britain to reconquer the Sudan, that a third may have stepped in to prevent the needy Republic of Liberia from becoming French or German; that a group of Jews probably holds in its hands at the present day the decision as to whether there is to be war in Europe between the ambitions of Germany, Russia, and the Western Powers.

342. PROFESSOR G. W. CARVER
A great Negro Botanist and Professor of Agricultural Chemistry

He believes that the course to be followed by the Negro will be far more arduous and lengthy than that which has at last placed a small and very mixed caste of Syrian people among the great races of history, and in the most arrogant and secret of the world's great councils at the present day. But the power needed to do for the Negro what has been accomplished for the Jew, for the Parsi, the Armenian, the modern Greek, and the Japanese is *money*. And money can only be produced by industry. And it is no good making money by the sweat of your brow or the keenness of your brains, if you have only an ill-nourished, unwashed, badly dressed, ugly body to make use of that money, and to defend the possession of it. So that physical development, the social and economic well-being of the Negro, are as much his preoccupation (and that of many others like him, now teaching in the States) as the introduction of the Negro into habits of ceaseless industry. His is a gospel of *work.* He hates having to speak, though he talks to great effect when he does. But he realises how much of the Negro's energy and time is wasted in palaver, that the passion for talking is as much of a snare and a drawback to the Negro as it is to the Celtiberian in Ireland and Wales, in France and Portugal, and in Latin America.

How far he will be justified of his faith and hope for the Coloured People depends at the present time on how much longer he lives to direct with energy the "Tuskegee movement." The University of Harvard has made him a Doctor of Law; a President of the United States publicly received him as his guest at the White House, sat down to break bread with him, and thus removed the tabu placed on the Negro by the narrow-minded South. This action of Mr. Roosevelt's produced an uproar in the States which probably amused and astonished the late King Edward; who, as ruler of the British Empire, frequently sat at meat with other rulers, vassal princes, men of science, councillors, or simple citizens of Negro or Asiatic race.

343. MAJOR J. B. RAMSAY

The coloured military instructor at the Tuskegee Institute. A typical "near-white" of distinguished record who would be insulted if he attempted to travel with "white" people in the Southern States, or to enter a "white" church or theatre

But until recently the mass of the people of the United States were singularly narrow in their outlook. They might have splendid thews and sinews, healthy minds for their own society and their own work, and be the germ of the mightiest people yet to come; but their outlook was that of the village; far narrower even than an ordinary English village, for amongst the rustics of the remotest English county there is one who has served in many parts of the world as soldier or sailor, mechanician or miner. It is an amusing instance of this paltry-mindedness that although the United States created Liberia, it did not definitely recognise the independence of that Negro Republic for nearly twenty years after other civilised Powers had done so, because of the awkward situation which would arise if Liberia sent a coloured man to represent her at Washington, and this negro or mulatto had to be asked to an official banquet! The same worry has constantly affected the United States' relations with Haiti or with Brazil, with Abyssinia or with Zanzibar. The negro tram conductor or railway official may—and does very often, unnecessarily—sit down beside you and enter into conversation unasked, and the white American replies civilly, and sees nothing to take exception to in such familiarity. But Professor Carver, or Booker Washington, or W. E. DuBois may not travel as a passenger in the same compartment with *you*, the white man, and *you* are socially tabued in the South if you take a meal with them!

This nonsense has got to be uprooted if the United States is logically to extend its beneficent governing influence beyond its actual geographical frontiers. If it is to direct the destinies of Filipinos, Cubans, Portoricans; perhaps also Haitians, Liberians, and Spanish Americans in Central America or in Venezuela; it must take a larger view of skin colour, and exact as its only tests of full rights of citizenship, *educational attainments*, *morality*, and to a slight extent *property*.

The earner and producer of nothing—the drone—has no right to a voice in the destinies of any country he or she may inhabit. Booker Washington is the last person in the world to advocate adult suffrage for the Negro (or for the white man, for the matter of that). Perhaps, even, in view of the present backwardness of the Negro, the friends of that race in the United States would consent—unwillingly—to a slightly greater property qualification than might be exacted from the Caucasian (provided that the same restriction applied equally to the Amerindian or Asiatic); but not even the most placable and moderate-minded amongst the educated Negroes of the United States at the present day can acquiesce in the present situation, in which through the prevalence of mob-law in nearly all the eleven Southern States of the Secession, the Negro or coloured man is practically without a voice in either municipal or political affairs. Theoretically he has that voice, but practically he is restrained by the threat of mob violence from exercising it, or using it to any effect.

344. A PROSPEROUS NEGRO FARMER OF ALABAMA WHO HAS BEEN INSTRUCTED THROUGH TUSKEGEE

However, once again Booker Washington deprecates excitement about this grievance. His main object is to get the Negro to WORK, and to stop talking. He wants at least to achieve this before he dies (and when I say "he," it must be borne in mind that I am obliged to regard him as a type of thinker, and that his thoughts and work are shared by other Negro or coloured leaders), and during his lifetime to succeed in raising the mass of ten million men, women, and children of the Negroid races in the United States above the slough of immorality, alcoholism, and sloth, in which many of them exist undoubtedly at the present time. Many of his people—he realises—are tempted to commit crimes of violence not only in the mania caused by whisky or cocaine or other forms of alcohol or drugs, but in the rough justice of revenge—revenge for brutal and unjust treatment by the whites: and even from lack of interest in life. If alcohol breeds quite half the Negro crime in the United States, and injustice is responsible for a quarter, one-eighth at least is caused by lack of occupation for the mind and body, the remainder being due to unchecked, inherited impulses. He hopes that the States and the Federal Government, as well as private philanthropy, will maintain and extend institutions like Hampton and Tuskegee, and notably the work which is carried on from New

York and Washington through the General Board of Education and the Department of Agriculture. The present results—he points out—and those to come, cannot but be beneficial to the commercial and industrial development of the States of the Southern Confederation: States which, with their benign climates, their endowments of coal, iron, mineral-oil, and hard-wood forests,

345. A NEGRO FARMER OF ALABAMA EXHIBITING AT A COUNTRY FAIR

their abundant rainfall, innumerable rivers, and fertile soil, their tobacco, cotton, sugar, rice, maize, and fruit, seem destined in course of time, and after the opening of the Panama Canal, to become the most important section of the American Republic. Every acre of land in the South can be turned to advantage; and if at the present day the Negro population of these eleven States is something like 7,500,000; the white population, handsome, vigorous, and prosperous, is 20,000,000.

CHAPTER XVIII

THE NEGRO IN ALABAMA

THE byways and many of the highways in the State of Alabama are as shockingly bad for wheeled traffic as elsewhere in the United States (away from the highly civilised east and north). I thought I had never travelled over such bad roads anywhere in the world as those of Georgia and Alabama until I came at a later date to try the roads of Mississippi. Of course, in the rapid development of these new countries it has been much more practical and profitable to make railways than to lay out macadamised roads. The influence of the motor will, however, bring this last adjunct of civilisation into existence. In curious contrast to the awful condition of the country routes, the streets of many a small and large town in the States of the American Union are better paved, furnished with better side-walks, are freer from dust and mud than is the case with English cities. But except for one or two great highways, the country roads of Alabama are of loose sand; on either side runs a deep ditch, the breadth of the road is small, and when one vehicle attempts to pass another there is a risk that one of them will heel over into the deep trench on the side of the road.

346. THE DREADFUL ROADS OF ALABAMA

But an American buggy and the driver thereof, especially if he be a Negro, is apparently independent of made roads and can be driven without an accident through pine woods, across swamps and brakes of bamboo, and into running streams. Until one becomes convinced by experience that an American buggy almost never upsets and can climb and descend steep banks and thread its way through forests, a journey of the type which I made over so much of this State or of Eastern Georgia (to visit the agricultural settlements of negroes) seemed to me an experience of peculiar peril. The scenery, moreover, of the woodlands is often distractingly beautiful; and between the terror of a disaster to life or limb on the one hand, and enthusiasm for the landscapes on the other, it was not always easy to pursue a careful statistical inquiry. Occasionally I obtained relief from this "trick" driving by a spell of smart progress along a red clay high-road of less variegated surface, one which had been a famous slave-route of the past, along which the slaves were marched in chains from coast-port to interior-market.

In these journeys I wished more particularly to see not only the average homestead of the better class of Negro planter, but also to ascertain to what extent the teaching emanating from Tuskegee during the last twenty years had affected the well-being of the agricultural negroes.

In no case did I see any negro dwellings so poor and "African" in appearance as in some of the country districts of Virginia. The log-huts on the borders of the beautiful pine forests were picturesque and not at all slovenly. Their general aspect is sufficiently illustrated by my photographs. Affixed to each dwelling-house would be a chimney of clay to serve the kitchen hearth. Occasionally, the interior of the house was rather rough. But the beds were ample, comfortable, and seemed to be spotlessly clean (with most artistic patchwork quilts). These large log cabins were surrounded by outbuildings also of logs, erected for live-stock—cows, horses, mules, donkeys, poultry, and pigs The boundary of the home enclosure was usually marked by a zigzag fence of split pine stems or by strands of barbed wire strung from post to post.

347. MR. T. M. CAMPBELL
Agricultural instructor, who accompanied the author on some journeys in Alabama

In the better class of negro homestead the dwelling-house was neatly built of grey planks, the roof of grey shingles, with glass windows, green shutters, and green verandah rails. The house, of course, was mounted on brick piles a few feet above the ground—it was very rare to see any negro or other dwelling in the States which had not a space between the ground floor and the earth beneath. The front garden of these negro houses was always fenced off from the road by a plantation, and nearly always divided into flower-beds. These at the time of my visit (November) were still gay with chrysanthemums and bordered by violet plants in full bloom, scenting the air deliciously. The garden might also contain a rough pergola of pea-vine and ornamental clumps of tall pampas grass, or of the indigenous *Erianthus* reed; there would almost certainly be wooden beehives, and beyond the flower-beds a kitchen garden containing cabbages, pumpkins, sweet potatoes, gourds, and other vegetables. In the back premises there was an abundantly furnished poultry-yard of fowls, guinea-fowls, turkeys, and geese—the latter being licensed wanderers, requiring no supervision. There was sure to be a pigsty, for the pig is as necessary to the Negro farmer as to the Irish peasant. Then there would be stables for mules and horses, cowsheds, barns, and stacks of "hay" (various kinds of fodder). A plantation of cotton might extend for ten to a hundred acres round the homestead.

The interior of these houses was almost always neat and clean, and divided into at least two bedrooms, a hall, a kitchen, and a parlour. The big wooden bedsteads not only had clean linen, but were spread with handsome quilts of gay colours worked by the mistress of the house. Some of these patchwork quilts—as in Liberia—exhibited real artistic talent. [Indeed, if the women of

348. IN LOVELY ALABAMA

The roads are often shallow watercourses, but never mind; the beauty of the scenery makes full amends for man's neglect

Liberia or Negro America would only make these bedspreads on a large scale, there should be quite a market for them in Europe. They design patterns, usually of conventional groups of fruit, foliage, or flowers, and obtain the colours for their design by cutting out and applying patches of various calicoes, cloths, or silks to the quilt.]

There are usually many pictures on the walls: chiefly coloured prints from newspapers. It was almost invariable to see in these negro homes (all over America) portraits of Booker Washington, Frederick Douglass, and W. E. B. DuBois; of Presidents Lincoln and Roosevelt, and even of the late King Edward VII and Queen Victoria. The last-named is a great favourite in American-Negro circles. There are also photographs of negroes and mulattoes,

349. MR. T. M. CAMPBELL,
An instructor of the American Board of Agriculture, giving advice to a negro farmer on maize growing

relatives or friends of the household. In several farmhouses the housewife would show me with pride her china cabinet. This would be a well-designed piece of furniture fitting into a corner, and here would be stored dinner and breakfast services in china or earthenware, together with a certain quantity of real or imitation cut-glass. Indeed, the furniture of these dwellings was often surprisingly good, as it is throughout America—a fact that never seems to me to have been sufficiently noted by British travellers.

The illumination of these country dwellings of the Negroes was usually petroleum lamps with candles in addition; but the poorest people sometimes use nothing but rough lamps or saucers apparently filled with some form of turpentine obtained from the pines. Besides a large family Bible there might be quite a number of other books, some of which were manuals dealing with the cultivation of cotton or maize or the fertilisation of soils. Usually both husband

and wife could read, write, and keep accounts. If there was lack of education it was generally with the man and not the woman. The husband might be an absolute negro and the wife a pale-skinned quadroon or vice versa, but very often in the best-appointed homes both husband and wife were negroes without any white intermixture. The children of the home when not at school assisted their parents in the management of the small estate. Most of the farmers I visited had a substantial sum in the local bank.

Some of them had a large tract of magnificent pine forest as their freehold property and part of their estate; perhaps as much as three hundred acres. This would be enclosed with a neat fence of barbed wire to keep out strollers, who might by carelessness start a forest fire. In some places the forest was being cut down extravagantly to obtain a little ready money by the sale of the

350. A NEGRO'S LOG CABIN (THOROUGHLY COMFORTABLE AND TASTEFULLY FURNISHED INSIDE), ALABAMA

timber. But Tuskegee ideas of forestry were making way, and in addition much excellent tuition as to the conservation of forests, the judicious thinning and replanting was being given by instructors sent out from the American Board of Agriculture, which has its head-quarters at Washington.

Nevertheless, none of the Negroes with whom I conversed seemed to have acquired as yet any feeling for landscape beauty. Some of them with whom I spoke were quite well enough off for themselves and their descendants not to cut down a patch of forest at all, but to keep these magnificent pines, magnolias, and evergreen oaks for the gratification of their eyes; and in like manner to appreciate the beautiful wild flowers of the uncultivated tracts—mauve asters, the brilliant yellow golden-rod, the wild roses, the magenta-coloured berries of the "French Mulberry,"[1] the creamy-white tufts of the sage brush, and the pinkish-green foam of the dog-fennel (*Eupatorium perfoliatum*).

[1] The *Callicarpa americana*, a striking object in sub-tropical American landscapes as the thickly clustered berries are a rich magenta-purple. It is of course neither French nor a mulberry, but America is the land of misnomers.

Truly, there is beauty in the South: the sleepy South. A sense of well-being, a quiet satisfaction with the climate, the food, the temperature, the lovely surroundings, the absence of all external worry which should go far not only to appease race quarrels, but to make the natives of Alabama, Southern Georgia, Northern Louisiana sensible of their privileges in being the citizens of such a delightful region. Here there is just enough of winter, just a sufficient touch of frost in the air between January and March to keep the resident vigorous and to check the excessive growth of vegetation. Then comes the spring with a riot of loveliness in wild flowers, which must surely touch the heart even of the stolid Negro. The summer may be very hot, but it is dry and there is always the shade of the ineffably beautiful woods, with the magnolias two hundred

351. A NEGRO WAGGONER, ALABAMA

feet in height, starred with their huge creamy-white flowers, while the aromatic scent of the pines pervades the whole State with a wholesome and pungent perfume.

Then comes the autumn, the pageant of the American year; when some of the many species of oak turn to tints of crimson, purple, orange, and russet, while others remain a glossy bottle-green; when the beeches become lemon-yellow, and the liquidambars, orange-chrome; while the young pines stand out in purest emerald and their giant parents of three-hundred-feet altitude offer a fine contrast to the glowing red and gold by their foliage of deep blue-green. There is also the glaucous tint of the sleek palmetto palms which give an oriental dignity to the underbrush, and this again is varied with the yellow-green of the dwarf bamboos (miscalled "canes"). Here and there the monotony of the forest is broken by a clump of Erianthus reeds, with tall, cream-coloured blooms. Like fairies flitting through a vast and splendid transformation scene, the birds enliven the forest glades. There are azure-and-russet Bluebirds

(*Sialis*), scarlet and brown Tanagers (the *genius loci* in these autumn woods), crimson-scarlet Cardinals, and the blue-black and white American Jay.

The fields of cotton are gay in spring and summer with the reddish or lemon-yellow, black-centred flowers; but as I saw them in the autumn they were equally striking (even though their foliage was withered) because of their great masses of pure-white cotton-wool.

In the hollows between the cotton plantations there were stagnant swamps or bayous; though swamp is an ugly name to apply to what is, in columnar trees and their still reflections, a vegetable Venice. The water, no doubt, is not really stagnant, but flows slowly towards some outlet through the stems of the gigantic trees. It was in these stretches of deep water and dense forest that the slaves would hide and often escape detection until the pursuers abandoned their chase. Here, in far earlier times, there were deer wading deep into the water and jaguars or pumas lying in wait for them on the fern-tufted limbs of the gnarled water-oaks.

352. A NEGRO'S COW, ALABAMA (OF THE GUERNSEY BREED)

Besides cotton, the country negroes of Alabama grow sugar-cane or sweet sorghum, and crush the cane in a rather primitive mill worked by a mule or sometimes by an up-to-date steam-engine with boilers and elaborate machinery. More often than not, the syrup flowing like muddy water from the cane or reed was guided into wooden troughs and then passed through cloth strainers and boiled, so that quickly and in a rough-and-ready fashion the family obtained an ample supply of syrup for their own yearly use, but not of sufficiently good quality for sale.

353. A NEGRO SCHOOL AND CHURCH: BACKWOODS OF ALABAMA

Of course, vegetables are much cultivated in a climate so suited to their growth. Sweet potatoes, maize, pumpkins, and cabbages are taken to market, and in the vicinity of towns, salad-vegetables are grown all the year round. For a vegetarian, the Southern States of North America are a paradise: there are so many appetising, nourishing forms of vegetable food: lentil beans, haricot beans, green corn, cucumbers, pumpkins, rice, Chili peppers, egg-plants, okroes, sweet potatoes, ground nuts—all of them to be met with in these negro households, and many of them bringing the water to one's mouth as one thinks reminiscently of how hunger has been stayed by the good things of an American country kitchen, and more often than not prepared by a cook of that negro race which seems to have an innate genius for the preparation of food.

How often I contrasted in my mind the life of these Negroes in the Southern States with that of our English poor: how often I felt it to be greatly superior in comfort, happiness, and even in intellectuality: for many of these peasant proprietors of Alabama had a greater range of reading, or were better supplied with newspapers, than is the case with the English peasantry, except in the home counties.

And in their dress they compared equally or favourably with the same class in England in being neatly and becoming clothed. Of course, when the men were engaged in very rough field work they wore coarse clothes, or merely shirts and trousers; but as often as not they—as do all white workmen throughout the United States—would don a clean blue cotton overall covering trousers and waist. The men wore the rather picturesque Southern hat of black felt with the high crown and the broad brim; the women the flounced and plaited white or lilac sun-bonnets, once characteristic of rural England and still so common and so picturesque in provincial America. When dressed in their best they were costumed in good taste, with well-fitting, smart-looking boots, Panama (or squash) hats for the men, and neat straw hats for the women. The women's clothes seemed to me well made and neat and free from glaring eccentricities in colour or outline.

354. A SMALL COUNTRY SCHOOL FOR NEGRO CHILDREN, ALABAMA

The postal service throughout Alabama is apparently excellent, and most of these negro farmsteads had their own post-box for the receipt and despatch of letters on the high-road or by-road nearest to the house.

Of course the keeping of live-stock is a very important feature in the life of the agricultural Negroes of this and other States, and has of late been remarkably encouraged and benefited by the teaching of Tuskegee. On most of the holdings there were good milch cows descended from Guernsey or Holstein stock. Many a negro farmer kept mares and a jackass for mule breeding. I was surprised at the excellence of the poultry. There were Leghorns, Buff Orpingtons, Plymouth Rocks, and other good breeds for laying and for the table. Turkeys, of course, were kept on a very large scale; also geese and guinea-fowl.

355. A NEGRO MINISTER AT A CAMP MEETING

At intervals of a few miles, travelling through Alabama and Eastern Georgia, one encounters a neat church of timber (raised on brick piles) and an equally neat school-house, both of them intended for and entirely maintained by the negro population. These buildings are usually painted white with green roofs. Even if there is a State grant for the *school* the *church* is entirely maintained by Negro subscriptions, several churches being usually served by the one itinerant pastor, himself probably a farmer in his spare time. Such of these men as I met seemed intelligent and reasonable, and I was told that the type of religious teacher in Alabama (largely through the influence of Tuskegee) has greatly improved within the last few years. There are the usual revival meetings, and in any case annual church festivals which are turned into pleasant picnics by public custom. The whole set of the influence amongst the leading pastors *now* is *against* religious hysteria, and these camp meetings are said no longer to be characterised by the curious mixture of raving religious ecstasy and sexual laxity which was, no doubt, rightly attributed to them a few years ago, and which perhaps still exists amongst the less civilised Negroes of the Eastern States.

The teachers in the country schools are invariably *women* and usually graduates of Tuskegee, of Hampton, of Calhoun, or of some other educational institute mentioned in chapter XVII. The school-house is usually bright, clean,

356. THE FORMER RESIDENCE OF A GOVERNOR OF ALABAMA (TUSKEGEE CITY)
Now owned and inhabited by a coloured merchant born a slave of the said Governor

and well ventilated, and there was no nasty smell in it from the crowding of children such as too often characterises the inferior Church or country schools in England. The well-kept plastered walls were hung with maps of the most modern and up-to-date character, with good pictures and diagrams. The teachers not only spoke correct English (without a marked American accent), but were striving to make the Negro children speak in the same way. I observed that many of these Negro peasants or peasant proprietors talked amongst themselves a dialect scarcely to be understood by an Englishman, and the old people (ex-slaves) never used any other forms of speech and were difficult of comprehension. But the middle-aged and younger folk could, if they wished, speak a more correct English (from the London standpoint) than might be met with in the country districts of the remoter parts of Great Britain.

Out of a Negro population in the State of Alabama of about nine hundred thousand, there are some *twenty thousand households*—say one hundred thousand persons—engaged in farming *on their own account*, not as the paid servants of white planters. These agricultural Negroes either own their farms as freehold, rent them from white landowners, or work the farm on the system of half the produce going to the landowner.

In the Macon county of Alabama 421 Negro farmers (in 1908) owned amongst them as freehold 55,976 acres of land, or more than one-seventh part of the land of the county. Some of the "old time" colonial mansions of the ante-bellum period are now owned by negroes or mulattoes, in one or two instances actual descendants of the slaves on the estate which the "great house" dominated. In one instance pointed out to me the handsome old dwelling with its avenue of live-oaks had been purchased from his former white master by the slave boy, grown up to be a prosperous farmer.

CHAPTER XIX

THE INDUSTRIAL SOUTH

I DO not know why the eleven Southern States of the old Confederacy are (apparently) so little visited by British tourists who have crossed the Atlantic (or if visited, then by people who leave their impressions unrecorded), any more than I understand why the artist-painters of the United States have failed to see *what* a field of inspiration lies before them in the *gorgeous landscape beauty* (I must underline the words) to be found in South Carolina, Georgia, Florida, Alabama, and Louisiana—possibly also in Texas. In the first place there is a great deal of the world's history of the eighteenth and nineteenth centuries illustrated in the coast towns of the Southern States (most of which are beautiful, and many extremely picturesque). There is also a romantic interest attaching to Montgomery, the State capital of Alabama, and once the Federal capital of the seceded Confederacy. From the capital of Montgomery was launched the declaration of the independence of the South from the dictation of the Northern States. Here was elected the President of the new Confederacy, and from this centre went forth some of the best blood, the finest fighting-men of the white South, to fight in a perfectly hopeless cause, to display valour, heroism, chivalry, and brilliant tactics in defence of a rotten social system.

The Capitol at Montgomery is an imposing building, though here and there is a suggestion of stucco, characteristic no doubt of the bad middle nineteenth century, but singularly rare amongst the honest and sumptuous architecture of modern America. But the place is penetrated with a certain dignity and sad romance, forbidding one to smile at any particle of homely rubbish, Berlin-wool-antimacassar culture that may linger in the corners of the gaunt rooms [which are now unmeaning in their majestic proportions since they have ceased to belong to the central palace of a nation]. About the Capitol are quiet gardens, and of course in this region there is very little winter, so that though the month of my visit was December, I could see that the violets and roses picked for me, unasked, with that delightful instinctive courtesy of the American, would certainly not be missed out of the wealth of flowers that made the place fragrant and full of colour.

The library of the Capitol has become a sort of museum, which illustrates in an exceedingly interesting way the history of the hopeless struggle of the South. There are innumerable portraits—paintings (execrably bad, but yet, one feels, strong likenesses of the subjects), daguerreotypes, enlarged photographs, crayon drawings, steel engravings—illustrating handsome, manly men and beautiful women. The badness of the art cannot efface this impression of physical beauty, neither does it wholly conceal the unbalanced mentality of the women. The men look hard-gritted, some of them a little cruel, but on the whole Englishmen of a fine type, with a mixture here and there of the fiery French or sullen Spaniard, still, mostly English in look.

The women are too beautiful to have been altogether useful : it is a beauty such as one could match immediately at the present day in the "Society" of England and Ireland. Their natures must have been spoilt by being the mistresses of slaves. They were not sobered by domestic service. Somehow, in looking at these hundreds of portraits one feels that it was the women who precipitated and maintained the struggle between South and North, the women who were to blame (a rare episode in the history of the world). And it is still mostly the women who maintain the perfectly nonsensical and out-of-date scission of brotherly feeling between North and South, so far as it is maintained at all. It is the women who keep alive the false sentiment which still permeates Southern circles, and still attempts to band together the cream of Southern society in associations for perpetuating memories of that criminal Civil War,

357. IN THE PINE WOODS OF ALABAMA

instead of relegating it to the limbo of losses that are cut, blunders which we wince at remembering. So we have (in Alabama especially) the *United Sons of Confederate Veterans*, and the *United Daughters of the Confederacy*.[1]

The men, of course, are shaking themselves free of much of this stale nonsense. They want to make money, and fortified with money, to marry beautiful women and rear a large family of beautiful children in homes which, in

358. "SPANISH MOSS," IN THE MYSTIC DREAM WOODS OF MAGNOLIA, PINE, AND PALM IN THE INCOMPARABLE SOUTHERN STATES

their architecture and decoration, their pictures and statuary, their gardens and motor garages, shall not be inferior even to the splendours of the North-Eastern States.

[1] I would venture to suggest that if the Masonic feeling which permeates all America cannot be resisted, and the women must band together into clubs and societies instead of acting individually, they should maintain their present *beneficent* organisations and rename them: call themselves "Dryads of the Spanish Moss," the "Companions of the Cypress," "Magnolia Maidens," and devote their energies, amongst other aims, to the preservation of the Southern forests and the wonderful landscape beauty of the South, which is too much threatened now by an industrialism not always profitable.

One sees no sign of race decrepitude *here*. As already stated, the absolutely white population of the eleven ex-slave States is at least twenty millions, as against seven to eight millions of coloured people. Mineral oil has been discovered in Louisiana, and perhaps also elsewhere in the South. The northern counties of Alabama are extremely rich in coal and iron; there is still a million acres or so of hard-wood forest scattered about the Southern States; so that in addition to the agriculture which still produces the world's largest crop of the best-quality cotton, an enormous supply of oranges and grape-fruit, of apples, peaches, grapes, and strawberries, and a maize which is perhaps the best in the world, the South now looks to derive great wealth from its industries, so that it will no longer be dependent on the North and North-East for manufactured goods.

And this outlook is making the Southern men more tolerant of the Negro, who is so valuable to them as a labour force that they can no longer afford to treat him badly. As it is, there are laws in existence—and if they are unwritten in the Statute-book, they are nevertheless just as much in vigour—which would be appealed to should any person attempt to induce Negroes in large numbers to leave the Southern States, or even one Southern State for another. Public feeling in Alabama, in Louisiana, for example, will not allow the Negroes of those States to be recruited for service on the Isthmus of Panama or on the railways of Mexico. This is why the American Government, in constructing the Canal and other public works in the State of Panama, is compelled to obtain its labour force from the British West Indies, from Spain and Italy, Central and South America. Surely this is a sufficient answer to the foolish negrophobe writers (chiefly hailing from Virginia and the North-Eastern States) who advocate the expulsion of the Negro *en masse* from North America? Why, if this idea were even formulated, the South would rise once more in rebellion against it, for as things stand at the present, the South would be ruined if the Negro left it.

Of course, the Southern Negro is a free agent, and if uninvited he chose to leave the Southern States for anywhere else, he could not be restrained. Therefore the fact that he stays where he is shows that he is not on the whole badly treated, but it also means that if he were, he would migrate to other parts of America and leave the twenty million Southern whites dependent on their own hands and arms, or on such foreign white labour as they could recruit from Europe. No doubt they could obtain this labour force from the white peoples of the Old World, and eventually it might become as strong, as hard-working, and as efficient as the most modern type of Southern Negro; but in the interval that would ensue during the replacing of the Negro by another type of labour most of the Southern whites would go bankrupt.

I was strongly advised to visit Birmingham, in Southern Alabama, if I wished to realise the meaning of the "Industrial South."

This great city, the population of which (including suburbs) is about 100,000, is not unlike the British Birmingham in its outward appearance; for though it lies twenty degrees nearer to the Equator, it stands on rather high ground (at the southern termination of the Appalachian chain), and it has a winter nearly as tart as that of its English godmother.

Birmingham, Alabama, is in close touch with the great iron and coal mines—the iron, coal, and limestone which are going to make Alabama as important in American industries as it already is in American agriculture. On the outskirts of the town there are already uncountable hundreds of tall, big chimneys, puffing out night and day, with scarcely a Sunday rest, volumes of black or white smoke. But in the centre of the town shops and buildings are handsome, commodious, and modern.

Negroes form a large proportion of the population, for in the adjacent iron mines about ninety per cent of the labour is negro, while the same race furnishes fifty-five per cent of the coal miners and fifty per cent at least of the men employed in the great steel works and iron foundries (it might be mentioned incidentally that throughout the Southern States seventy-five per cent of the men employed in constructing and repairing the railroads are negroes).

359. "L'HOMME À TOUT FAIRE"
A negro bootmaker, trained at Tuskegee

In Birmingham there are several negro banks. I visited one of them which was lined with marble and upholstered with handsome woods. There are, as in the other towns of Alabama, negro doctors, dentists, haberdashers, modistes, shoemakers, barbers, grocers, druggists, and general storekeepers. There are theatres for coloured people at which only negro actors and actresses perform. Excellent are these performances, usually in musical comedy—how excellent, amusing, and of good taste may be known by those who have witnessed (for example) the performances of the Williams-Walker travelling company in England or America. There are Negro churches which have cost from $10,000 to $30,000 to build. There is a Negro press, and there are numbers of young negro or mulatto men and women who are expert stenographers and typists.

But the main object of my journey to this industrial region was to see the great steel works and iron foundries of Bessemer and Ensley (in the distant suburbs of Birmingham), where a large number of negroes are employed conjointly with white Americans in work involving intelligence, strength, courage, and a just appreciation of the dangers involved in the harnessing of the forces of fire, steam, and electricity.

To an imaginative person the journey was not unlike a visit to some marvellously realistic reproduction of Dante's Hell, such a reproduction as might conceivably have been constructed by some eccentric American multi-millionaire as a realistic warning to that strange American public, white and black—two-thirds of which probably believes more strongly in this phase of an after-life than in any other detail of the Christian cosmogony.

We travelled—my companion[1] and I—in tram-cars which rushed along the roads as quickly as trains. The outskirts of Birmingham are diversified with low red hills covered with a sparse wood of low growth which might be pleasingly picturesque but for the blasting effects of smoke. In and out of the trees are placed many villas of diversified design, some of them really pretty and no one of them of shoddy construction. We changed cars outside a great Stadium where at the moment a football match was proceeding before an assembly of many thousand miners and factory hands (this and everything else about Birmingham was astonishingly like England of the North-Western Midlands). Then again, careering northwards in the rapid tram-car, we passed through suburbs of thickly packed artisans' houses, till at last the tram-line

360. "L'HOMME À TOUT FAIRE"
A coloured storekeeper, Alabama

came to an end and we were on the verge of the Forbidden City, the labyrinth of which may not be entered save by special permission, or by those who are of the calling.

Against a splendid sunset stood up rows of tall black chimneys in close rank, belching incredible volumes of black smoke, while here and there arose solitary chimneys pouring out white smoke. The greater part of the foreground was occupied by vast, gaunt antres[2]—colossal iron buildings, painted red and enshrining Hell. Towards these, bewildering railway lines converged, detraining the damned at the portals of Inferno; the night shift, that is to say,

[1] Mr. J. O. Thompson (Collector of Revenues), to whom I owe much kindness. He and his cousin of Tuskegee travelled over much of Alabama with me, by train, on horseback, in buggies, and on foot, so that I might see many things in a short space of time. In Birmingham I was the guest of Mr. Belton Gillreath, one of the trustees of Tuskegee and a prominent citizen of Birmingham, who has made practical study of the Negro question.

[2] "Antres vast and deserts idle."—Shakespeare.

for the great steel works. We, being of another world, were stopped at the entrance, but a short colloquy furnished us with a one-armed, silent Virgil. With him we passed through the great red iron gate, and then more by gesture than by speech, were warned of all the chances of immediate death on every side —from locomotives, if we walked between the railway tracks, from electricity if we stepped here, boiling water if we ventured under this, or a rain of golden molten metal if we gazed up at that.

Never have I walked more circumspectly, or at first felt more reluctant to intrude. But the irresistible fascination of the wonderful sights led us on, led

361. A POSTER ADVERTISEMENT OF A TRAVELLING NEGRO THEATRICAL COMPANY, MISSISSIPPI

us through a region of machinery hung with mystic blue, mauve, and red lights into a vast space, the roof of which seemed as high as the firmament, where the increasing roar of steam and flame nearly stunned one to insensibility. Yet this universality of deafening sound was cut from time to time by still more insistent, agonising yells, as of tortured spirits, and one occasional, awful, alto voice—the Devil himself, no doubt.

Mercifully the volume of sound lessened just as I was feeling I could no longer retain consciousness, yet dared not sit down for fear of being burned up. Then I began to notice there was method amid this madness, that clever Negro devils were at work cutting and shaping, with huge machinery, an endless succession of white-hot iron bars, fish-plates, rails, and cylinders; acting apparently under the direction of a golden-haired, blue-eyed youth—an archangel, no doubt, fallen from the Heavenly Host. Some of his attendant devils, coal-black with soot or grime, climbed perpendicular ladders out of sight into the vastitude of the roof, visiting as they went casements (containing as it were imprisoned souls) into which they plunged instruments of torture. Each step they took up the rungs of the ladders was marked by blue electric flames.

We climbed iron bridges, descended iron steps, and sidled between hideous dangers till we reached the central Hell of all, a building longer and higher than the eye could follow. Speech was an impossibility in the awful persistence of sound, and sight was occasionally blinded by the activities of a volcano which irregularly sent up showers of molten stars and clouds of awful luminosity. Turning my back on this pulsating flare, I was aware of negroes travelling to and fro on chariots of blue flame, directing the infernal couplings of gigantic pistons which lunged continually at cells and fed them with molten metal. Each thrust was followed by shrieks and shrieks. . . .

362. "L'HOMME À TOUT FAIRE"
A negro electrical engineer (trained at Tuskegee and employed in Birmingham)

At last we reached, half blinded, a cooler region, lit by lamps of violet and blue. Here lay sullenly cooling masses, cylinders, rods and rails of red iron and steel, which at times would scream and gasp under jets of steam, as though expressing uncontrollable agony. Negroes and a few white men (though their complexions differed in no way, and one only discriminated by the hair) banged, hammered, cut, and shaped these crude substances into finished implements.

And then, at the end of our sight-seeing, we emerged into the cold, fading daylight, into an amphitheatre of blasted hills, quarried and scarred in the search for iron and limestone. Near at hand were the pit mouths of the coal mines, and thither were trooping white and negro miners in their working clothes, while others strode homewards to their brick cottages to wash and change and enjoy the respectable amusements of Ensley.

CHAPTER XX

THE MISSISSIPPI SETTLEMENTS

FEW regions, I imagine, would seem more dismal to the homesick Englishman than trans-Appalachian America in the late autumn, more especially the region of the Mississippi plains, in what is called the Yazoo Delta, which occupies so much of the area of the State of Mississippi up to the borders of Arkansas and Tennessee. It was somewhere in this region, I imagine, that Dickens located his settlement of Eden, made proverbial through *Martin Chuzzlewit.*[1]

To any one fresh from the splendid pines, the magnolia and oak forests of

363. UNTIDY AMERICA
This is a characteristic representation of the ugly disorder of the towns along the Mississippi railroads

southern Alabama, or the diversified hill-and-stream country of north-western Alabama and eastern Tennessee, the Mississippi plains—except perhaps for a month at spring-time—must be for a long while to come one of the dreariest countries in the world. The low, scrubby, oak forests are (I am told) soon browned by the summer heats. They are tinted grey in the late autumn, with a miserable streak or patch of yellow foliage here and there. The undergrowth is of dead creepers or lifeless bushes, parched to a whitish grey, and the ground is of cracked mud. The stubbly fields at this time only exhibit brown-grey withered maize stalks. The cotton is chiefly represented by a few dark brown plants, while many of these plantations have been cleared by fire, and are reduced to black charcoal or grey ashes. This region is too far to the south to be more than snow-flecked in the worst part of the winter; otherwise much of

[1] Probably Eden was higher up the great river, nearer to its junction with the Ohio.

its off-season ugliness would be veiled under that beautiful mantle of white which lends so much dignity in the winter-time to North American landscapes.

Towns along the railway line are numerous, but they are the ugliest settlements so far that I have seen in America. The frame houses are usually unpainted, and with shingle roofs of cold grey, nearly as depressing as corrugated iron. The churches—never absent from the smallest settlements—and likewise the schools, are often the only comely buildings in the place. The interiors of the houses (you find on examination) are well furnished and comfortable, but the surroundings of the dwellings are often actually squalid. There is little or no garden about the home, and no attempt at a tidy fence round each domain. The waste land between the cottages is strewn with paper, straw, empty tins, and rusting iron. The stores (shops) are garish in their allurements, and any hoarding or blank wall is covered with violent advertisements. The ill-defined, excessively muddy or dusty streets are the wandering-ground of cows, dogs, hogs, scabby mules and horses with drooping heads. To keep out these cattle, the untidy cotton plantations are fenced in by stakes of different lengths, linked together with rusty wire.

364. ISAIAH MONTGOMERY
Ex-slave of the Jefferson Davis family; founder of Mound Bayou Negro settlement, Mississippi

The white people who inhabit these settlements are, however, very different in appearance from the ague-stricken, lank-haired creatures described by Dickens. The men are tall, essentially virile, and often handsome. The women are so usually good-looking that a female with a homely face is a startling exception. Both men and women are well and tastefully dressed, and apparently as close up to the fashions of the day as in New York. The children are spoilt and ill-mannered, while the otherwise charming women require missionaries from the north-east and south to teach them voice production. At present they speak with an exaggerated accent and range of tone which to a twentieth-century American or a Britisher are jarring and discordant.

Yet it must be admitted that the modern Edenites are, like the rest of the Americans, of unbounded civility and kindness to a stranger. One can but admire their cheerfulness in a region of dismal, monotonous ugliness. No doubt it is more tolerable in the spring-time, when the scrubby, paltry forests burst out into fresh verdure, and the untidy fields are fresh with new corn, or gay with yellow and red cotton blossoms. But it is a land without the dignity of a snowy winter, without the splendour of semi-tropical forests; almost absolutely flat, yet with the horizon constantly limited, and the view circumscribed to an untidy foreground by the ugly scattered trees growing in featureless forests of uniform height.[1] Twenty years ago there remained considerable

[1] Mr. Roosevelt, discussing Dickens and *Martin Chuzzlewit* in my hearing, pointed out very aptly that Dickens had missed the moral he should have drawn, if not in the preface to *Martin Chuzzlewit*, at

areas of land to the west and the east of the Mississippi Valley (principally what is called the Yazoo Delta), between Memphis and Vicksburg, in which it seemed impossible to establish a settled population. The district was too aguish for the whites. It occurred therefore to the management of the railroads of the Mississippi Valley to attract Negro colonists who might turn this region to some end, and produce cotton or other crops for the freight trains to carry. Relations were entered into with Mr. Isaiah T. Montgomery, as the recognised leader among the negro people in northern Louisiana. Montgomery explored the vacant lands which the railway company were able to offer for settlement and came with a few followers in 1888 to what is now called "Mound Bayou." (In this flat, low-lying region there is a large mound which may

365. THE CHURCH AND PART OF THE TOWNSHIP, MOUND BAYOU, MISSISSIPPI

possibly be the burial-place of some vanished tribe of Indians: close by it is a winding creek, sometimes filled with water.)

Isaiah Montgomery is one of the remarkable personalities among the ten million coloured people in the United States at the present day. He is a pure-blooded Negro, originally of Virginia origin, and must now be about seventy years of age. It is a pity that whilst he retains such a clear memory of the distant past he does not employ a stenographer to take down his experiences from his youth up. He has a remarkable command of the English language, and to listen to him is like hearing the recital of a sequel to *Uncle Tom's Cabin;* for his account of his father's, mother's, brother's and his own experiences of slavery from about the time that *Uncle Tom's Cabin* leaves off until the close of the Civil War would finish the work of Mrs. Harriet Beecher-Stowe. (It is interesting, by

any rate in the amends made to the American public twenty-five years after its publication. The people whom Dickens holds up for our sympathy all ran away from the heart-breaking difficulties of opening new grounds in the basin of the Mississippi. Those whom posterity might possibly admire the more were the few who stuck to "Eden" and the "New Thermopylæ," and little by little painfully conquered this dismal wilderness, at any rate from the point of view of healthfulness and prosperity. The making of beauty has to follow.

the by, to hear him relate how, when he was a young man, a contraband copy of *Uncle Tom's Cabin* was smuggled into the slave village in which he resided; how the one or two educated negroes like himself read it aloud to the others by stealth —for it was a penal offence to introduce this book into any of the Southern States: how the kind master—a brother of Jefferson Davis—heard that somebody had got the book and told his wife, and how the "Madam" begged that it might be lent her by her own slaves, read it, and became more than ever an Abolitionist!)

If Mr. Montgomery sees these words in print and is induced to record his experiences of slavery, he will be able to give to the world a picture of slave-holders at their best. His father was the favourite slave of a Mr. Davis, brother to the President of the Confederated States. Though a negro of

366. LOADING WAGGONS WITH COTTON GROWN BY NEGRO FARMERS AT MOUND BAYOU, MISSISSIPPI

unmixed origin, like his son, Isaiah must have been exceptionally clever, for in spite of the laws which forbade the education of a slave, he was enabled to learn, more or less by stealth and from his master, not only how to read and write and keep accounts, but how to become a very accurate land-surveyor, architect, mathematician, and manager of an estate. He, in his turn, taught his little son to read. Isaiah Montgomery relates how, when accompanying his master once, as a groom, to some market town where there was a great assemblage of aristocratic planters and their wives, the fact that he was able to write was accidentally revealed. Whereupon the case was discussed by a neighbouring slave-owner and his wife. Said the lady to Mr. Davis, "If he were *my* nigger, I should cut off his thumbs." "No, no, my dear," intervened her husband. "Egad, that would never do, because then he could not pick cotton."

All the Davis slaves, without exception, were treated by their master and mistress with unwavering kindness and consideration. And as a result, when emancipation was declared and the Davis family was temporarily impoverished by the result of the war, all their plantation slaves under the leadership of Montgomery remained on the estate *without pay*, worked it and managed it entirely without any white direction, and punctually forwarded the revenues to the Davis family in the North. Twenty years later the estate was sold, and Isaiah Montgomery with a few of his neighbours formed a settlement of negro farmers in the Mississippi Valley.

When they first colonised the Yazoo Delta, about 1888, it must have been exceedingly like Dickens's "Eden." For portions of the waters of the Mississippi, circulating through the land in a network of depressions, turned it into a sickly swamp. Such grounds as remained above water were swarming with rattle-snakes. The low, thick woods contained pumas and bears to an inconvenient extent, and to the constant depletion of the settlers' small stock of cattle and poultry. Alligators came wherever there was water to float them or even

367. A NEGRO HOMESTEAD, MOUND BAYOU, MISSISSIPPI

crossed dry land from creek to creek; but they were far less dreaded than the swarms of mosquitoes, which, until the forest and the coarse grass were abated, made life intolerable. On the other hand, deer and wild turkeys were so abundant that they atoned for the loss of domestic live-stock.

Gradually in the course of twenty years the region around Mound Bayou has altered to an astonishing extent. There are vast cotton plantations where there was once thin forest; there are streets of well-built houses, three or four of which are really remarkable for their architecture and handsome furniture. There is a Negro bank—the "Delta Bank"—there are one or more cotton-ginneries, and a large oil-mill is under construction for the manufacture, on the spot, of cotton-seed oil. Within the principal settlement of Mound Bayou there are four churches and as many schools. The largest of the churches serves—as do most of these edifices—as church, lecture-hall, theatre, council-hall, and centre for a debating society. Its interior is entirely lined with varnished pine planks exceedingly well fitted, and giving the interior a handsome appearance, especially when lit up at night by oil lamps and chandeliers. Two of the handsomest houses in the town were constructed by a firm of white builders, but all the rest of the houses, the bank, churches, and schools, were erected by negro masons and carpenters. There are good stores in the town, selling most things except alcohol.

The only criticisms I have to offer apply properly to the whole State of Mississippi and almost all the towns therein—black or white—namely, the shocking condition of the roads and the general untidiness which prevails outside the houses. Hogs, dogs, mules, thin cows, geese, turkeys, and fowls wander about the streets seeking their living. The hogs and the dogs are the most objectionable.

A few of the Mound Bayou houses had neatly fenced-in gardens. One of these was smart enough for a Bournemouth villa, with lawns and flower-beds, which at this season were bright with rose bushes in full blossom, chrysanthe-

368. "PALACES AND MUD"
A characteristic of Greenville and of many Mississippi townships: splendid public and private buildings, shocking roadways

mums, and borders of violets. But the roads are so bad that driving in any vehicle is both ludicrous and painful. The soil, of course, is nothing but deep mud after rain, or loose dust in dry weather. The difficulty here, as elsewhere in America, seems to be the expense of transporting stone and breaking it up for macadam. Where the road becomes an absolute slough or a dust-pit, short lengths of the stems or boughs of trees are laid across it, but these either rot or get dislodged by the hoof-beats of the mules. The innumerable creeks are roughly bridged, but with such insecurity that only foot passengers cross the bridge, and waggons and carts prefer to struggle through the mud and water.

In Greenville, Mississippi (a prosperous country town about twenty-five miles south of Mound Bayou), the contrast between handsome buildings and squalid roads is seen at its most exaggerated. The very heart of the town, it is true, has its broad streets neatly paved with encaustic brick—an idea, it is to be hoped, which may, for many reasons besides æsthetic ones, extend by degrees over the whole town and be copied by all the other prosperous settlements of the Mississippi States. But in the handsomest quarters of Greenville, with noble churches and really beautiful dwelling-houses, surrounded by charming gardens, the main roads and the cross roads are disgusting sloughs of mud or unwholesome tracts of filthy dust. In this town, however, the neat side-walks of cement slabs extend for many miles. Mound Bayou might make bricks and tiles to any extent out of the excellent clay which it possesses, and as its prosperity increases its side-walks should be made with blocks of cement and not with mouldering, slippery planks. In all of these Mississippi towns also

369. COTTON BALES AWAITING SHIPMENT ON THE BANKS OF THE MISSISSIPPI

(to say nothing of Alabama and Louisiana) no measures are taken to enforce such laws as limiting the pouring forth of coal smoke from manufactory chimneys. This is an additional cause of dirt and discomfort.

Apart from these defects there is an air of marked prosperity and busy life about the Mississippi towns, and in this respect, as in its outward aspect, Mound Bayou does not differ from its white neighbours. The people seem to be too busy to loaf or to quarrel, and, according to the white sheriff of the town, there is very little crime there.

On the other hand, a white man temporarily sojourning in Mound Bayou, in charge of a gang of railway workers, did not entirely endorse my optimistic impressions. He spoke in the highest terms of Mr. Isaiah Montgomery and the leaders of the community, who are mostly old men or men of middle age, and who are hard-working, trustworthy, and moral; but he declared the young people to be the reverse. Away from the immediate precincts of the town he spoke of crime, of robbery with violence being constantly committed, and of much immorality amongst the young men and women. The young people, he said, were spoilt by book education, cared nothing for farming, and wished to drift away to life in the towns.

The crimes of violence—murder for robbery—by negroes against negroes in Alabama, Mississippi, and Louisiana are unhappily very frequent, though perhaps proportionately not so numerous as they are among the Italian settlers. The immorality among the younger people seems also to be on the increase, but it arises partly from the excessive dullness of their lives. The more extended education which the new generation has received has awakened a keener appetite for pleasure, and this must be met and satisfied to a greater extent than at present through the churches. These, it seems to me, were becoming alive to their importance as centres of social activity. Many of the negro pastors are now educated men, students of well-equipped negro colleges or universities. They are encouraging musical performances and reading exercises amongst their people. (The champion speller of the whole of the United States in a 1908 competition was a little negro girl of Tennessee!) The danger which lies before the work of Hampton, Tuskegee, and Mound Bayou is lest agriculture may not prove sufficiently attractive to the younger people now growing up, and that they may thus drift away into careers and professions of the towns, already overcrowded, or of a character which brings them into abrupt competition with the whites, while the whole community is in a transition period of race conflict.

CHAPTER XXI

LOUISIANA

NEGRO life in Louisiana at the present day is probably more like the old slavery times of the ante-bellum period than is the case with the other Southern States. Though there are many towns and villages peopled exclusively by Negroes, there do not seem to be—or I have not discovered them—Negro farmers on a large scale as in Mississippi and Alabama. The general surface of the State of Louisiana—which is much more pleasing in appearance than grey, scrubby Mississippi—seems to be divided into large plantations and estates owned by white American people, and worked by Negroes as hired labourers or tenants: or small holdings in the possession of French Creoles or Acadians, Spaniards of ancient establishment, or Italians recently arrived. A vast deal of employment, however, is given to coloured labour on the levees of the Mississippi, and the railways, canals, wharves, and other public works of the State. Apparently the coloured people of Louisiana are exceedingly prosperous, but they strike one as being of a lower class intellectually than those of Mississippi, Alabama, and Georgia. They are more definitely Negro (often very illiterate), and the mulatto or octoroon class is not so obvious as in the other Southern or Eastern States. The women of this mixed type have in the past too often drifted away into a career of prostitution, and are consequently dying out without leaving descendants, while the male mulattoes or octoroons evidently find a more attractive sphere for their energies in the regions further to the north or east.

The Negroes of southern Louisiana are, like the whites, strongly impregnated with French civilisation.[1] They are the descendants of the slaves of old Creole families, which had settled and prospered between the commencement of the eighteenth century and the date at which Louisiana was purchased by the United States from the French Republic (1803). Louisiana (see p. 137), of course, had been founded as a European colony by the French at the close of the seventeenth century, but it was afterwards ceded to Spain, together

[1] I extract an interesting commentary on this aspect of Louisiana by F. L. Olmsted, written fifty years ago.

"The people after passing the frontier changed in every prominent characteristic. French became the prevailing language, and French the prevailing manners. The gruff Texan bidding, 'Sit up, stranger; take some fry!' became a matter of recollection, of which 'Monsieur, la soupe est servie,' was the smooth substitute. The good-nature of the people was an incessant astonishment. If we inquired the way, a contented old gentleman waddled out and showed us also his wife's house-pet, an immense white crane, his big crop of peaches, his old fig-tree, thirty feet in diameter of shade, and to his wish of 'bon voyage' added for each a bouquet of the jessamines we were admiring. The homes were homes, not settlements on speculation; the house, sometimes of logs, it is true, but hereditary logs, and more often of smooth lumber, with deep and spreading galleries on all sides for the coolest comfort. For form, all ran or tended to run to a peaked and many-chimneyed centre, with here and there a suggestion of a dormer window. Not all were provided with figs and jessamines, but each had some inclosure betraying good intentions."

with its aspirations for a vast north-western hinterland ; and the Spaniards left their impress on the coast country to a very marked degree. They imported hundreds—even thousands—of Spanish convicts, mainly from the Canary Islands. To a certain limited extent both the French and the Spanish mingled with their Negro slaves. The French cross-breeds have very largely died out or gone elsewhere; but there are still colonies of Negroes in the south-west coast-lands of Louisiana that are tinged with Spanish blood. They are a rather

370. THREE GENERATIONS OF LOUISIANA NEGROES
Grandmother can only talk Creole French; mother talks French and English; boy only talks English

truculent lot, and live a good deal away from close contact with civilisation, as hunters and fishermen. It is remarkable to note, however, that the descendants of the original Spanish colonists are still in appearance exactly like the natives of the Canary Islands, or the Spaniards of Spain (according to the district from which they come), and that for the last fifty years or so they have kept themselves to themselves, and have been as much opposed to miscegenation as the Anglo-Saxons.

Among the other strange human elements to be found in the interesting population of this State are small colonies of Malays in the western part of Louisiana, on or near the coast. It is possible that these may be the descendants of prisoners of war and others brought by the Spaniards from the Sulu Archipelago or the Philippine Islands.

On some of the great sugar estates there has been a continuity of service, pleasant to note, from the days before the Civil War down to the present time; that is to say, that slaves, when freed, remained on the plantation as paid labourers, and their descendants work there, or in the domestic service of the house, to the present day.

A few of those amongst the domestic servants are mulattoes. Like so many of the coloured people of Southern Louisiana, they are bilingual: as familiar with French as with English. Indeed, a good many of the Louisiana Negroes, as well as the white descendants of the Creole colonists, are trilingual, speaking equally well English, French, and Spanish. Some of them even add a fourth language—Italian or Sicilian: for the Italian or Sicilian emigration into Louisiana has produced another racial element which cannot be overlooked in its importance. These hard-working people, still slightingly known by the Anglo-Saxon inhabitants as "Dagos,"[1] form an important skilled-labour element on the plantations, and as kitchen gardeners or horticulturists. Their tendency is, however, to save hard for a few years, and then establish themselves in towns as fruiterers, greengrocers, and restaurateurs. They cannot be regarded as a permanent element in field culture, and it is probable therefore that the sugar and rice planters in Louisiana will never be able to afford to part with the invaluable labour of the Negroes: especially when the opening of the Panama Canal doubles the value of the Southern States.

371. A NEGRO CENTENARIAN, LOUISIANA

The Italian (it is as well to observe) absolutely refuses to mingle sexually with the Negro in Louisiana, whatever may occur elsewhere. I have seen it stated that the opposite was the case, and that the Negro element in the United States would eventually become fused into the white American community through the obliging medium of the Italian. Apart from my personal observations of the attitude of the one race towards the other, I am assured by several sound authorities that Italian miscegenation with the Negro is almost non-existent. On the other hand, the Italians blend readily with Spaniards, Germans, Irish, and Slavs.

A sight well worth seeing is an old-time Southern mansion, the "great house" of some aristocratic family of planters. As often as not the present owner of such a house is, on the father's side, of Northern descent, and the estate came into his family at some date since 1815, by intermarriage between some hardy Northern pioneer and a Creole heiress of French descent. This mixture of peoples (with here and there a touch of Spanish blood) has pro-

[1] A silly term, derived from the common Spanish name Diego, which might well be abandoned by common consent, as much for the dignity of the United States as for consideration due to the Italian people.

duced a Southern aristocracy which is certainly one of the comeliest peoples of the world.

Such a house as I am about to describe may have been built at any time between 1830 and 1840. There is a vague suggestion about it of East Indian influence, but this may be only a case of adaptation to a similar climate. The "great house" of the plantation is usually built close to the banks of the Mississippi River or one of its branches or affluents, and is usually placed on an artificial mound. Even then the roof of the house may be barely on a level with the Mississippi water. Between it and the river rises a grassy embankment—the "levee," about twenty feet in height. Sometimes the wilful river has eaten away the ground in the course of time, until the levee almost

372. THE "GREAT HOUSE" OF A LOUISIANA SUGAR PLANTATION, ABOUT 100 YEARS OLD

abuts on the house itself; elsewhere the Mississippi may have left a mile of land between itself and the mansion once built upon its banks.

There is a certain splendour about these houses—lofty rooms, colonnades of white painted columns along the front (something like the stucco palaces of Regent's Park). The furniture is massive and handsome, and is usually of English or French origin, some of it dating back to the seventeenth century. On the lofty walls of the superb sitting-rooms hang portraits of the Dombey period—1830 to 1850; Dombeys with black silk stocks, strapped trousers, and square-toed boots, toying with watch-chains, while the left hand indicates rolls of documents; Mrs. Chicks or Edith Dombeys, with flat black hair and square-cut, snowy necks and bosoms, shawls held captive by taper fingers, and a suggestion of accomplishments on the harp or the tapestry frame. Occasionally there is a picture of a volatile young man in a gorgeous waistcoat, who might be the original of Harriet Beecher-Stowe's *Augustine St. Clair*. Yet with all their pomposity, these huge pictures have a dignity and a history about them; and the descent (on the walls of the lesser rooms) to the crayon or tinted enlargements of photographs that marked the 'seventies, 'eighties, and 'nineties of America is painful to the eye.

In these old-time plantation houses the service and the cooking of the coloured people are perfection. The silver and napery are beautifully kept, the table is exquisitely decorated with flowers, the dishes are served "au point"; and the presentation of each viand to the favourable notice of "Mas'r Henry," "Mas'r John," "Miss Julia," or "Miss Sophie" is rather the affectionate respectful tender of an offering than the performance of a salaried duty.

373. THE NEGRO AND HIS MULES
Carting the sugar cane, Louisiana

Horses and carriages may be had for the holding up of a finger, and there are at least ten negrolets ready and anxious to do one's bidding.

Yet withal there is a sad look of abandonment about these once beautiful and stately homes. The old-fashioned bath-rooms are often out of repair; the books in the library are seldom of later date than 1885; the geographical globes which once ministered to a sheltered, tutorial education exhibit an Africa innocent of Stanley. The proprietors usually prefer life in a palatial villa in the suburbs of New Orleans, or a home in the distant North; they may revisit the ancestral plantation for an occasional picnic or a business inspection, but during the other eleven months of the year the "family" is represented by some bachelor cadet, constantly in the saddle or the sugar factory.

374. A NEGRO PLANTATION FOREMAN, LOUISIANA

This last—the main object of my excursion into Louisiana—has no languor about it, no faded fragrance of the 1840 period, no arrested development of invention. It is ferociously modern, cut-price, labour-saving, by-product-using, and test-tube regulated. The unpunctuality, petty thefts, indolent postponement of small repairs tolerated in the house-servants "de vieille souche" at the mansion, half a mile away, would be met here with prompt dismissal. Yet here again the Negro plays a notable part. It is true that the scientific and high engineering work is conducted by white Americans, Spanish or French Creoles, or an occasional German; but the whole of the rough labour and two-thirds of the skilled work are performed by coloured men, pure negroes for the most part.

The field work in the vast plantations of sugar-cane is also mainly in the hands of negro men, women, and children, who toil for good wages under the supervision of negro and white overseers. A few Italians or Sicilians work alongside the black people, without quarrelling, but without social intermixture. By negro labour the cane is attended throughout the year. In November-December it is cut, stripped of leaves, and carefully laid on the ground in parallel rows, ready to be picked up mechanically by machinery—huge iron arms and fingers cleverly directed by negroes or mules (working in a merry accord which seems unattainable between mules and white men)—and deposited in large waggons. When the cane is first laid low with great knives, it lies—with its unnecessarily luxuriant leaves—in many acres of hopeless confusion about the sturdy limbs and bulky petticoats of the negro women. But

375. OUTSIDE A SUGAR MANUFACTORY, LOUISIANA

—as if by magic—it is deftly lopped, pruned, and laid in absolutely straight rows while you stand and watch. The colour of the cane being mainly light purple, these lanes of cane-stalks constitute, with the alternate intervals of rejected foliage (up and down which the mule waggons and machinery are driven), ribbons of mauve between broader bands of yellow-green. Thus the flat plains of Louisiana at this season resemble vast silken skirts in two gay colours, slashed and trimmed, here and there, by white roads and dykes of pale blue water, and fringed along the distant outer-edge with grey-green forest. Trains of trucks or miniature railways, mule waggons, and even ox-carts convey the cut cane to the crushing-mills. It is only between November and February that the great factories where the sugar is made and refined are working with all hands and at high pressure, and perhaps in November and December only that an unremitting seven-days-a-week, night-and-day labour of black men and white men is carried on. This is the critical period. The cane must be cut and carried before any frost can cause deterioration; and as soon as it is cut it must be crushed. Machinery working with a furlong of "endless" chain transfers the cane from the carts and railway trucks up an ascending trough into the grinding-mills on the upper storey of the factory. Here the cane is passed through three sets of steel mills until its refuse fibre comes out absolutely flat and dry, and is carried automatically into the giant furnaces which create the steam power of the establishment.

These furnaces thus are mainly fed by the refuse material of the sugar-cane, while the dirty, turbid, mud-coloured juice pours away in streaming

376. THE PLIOCENE, EVERGREEN DREAM-WOODS OF LOUISIANA
Cypress and palmetto, live oaks and laurels

cascades and rivulets into vacuum boilers, skimming-vats, cooling-vessels, and receptacles where the thickening juice is treated with lime and sulphur. (Sickly indeed are the resultant smells!) Finally, after treatment by the centrifugal process in awe-inspiring copper machinery working at shrieking speed (wherein an imprudent gesture of the workman may tear off a limb or a finger), it emerges in the form of brown or moderately white, granulated sugar—the degree of whiteness being mainly due to the extent to which the sugar is washed and freed from the taint of molasses. As to the dear old friend of our childhood—treacle, molasses—it seems in these American factories to be a disappearing by-product: the cunning of chemistry can now tùrn nearly all the liquid element of the sugar-cane into sugar of three or four qualities. The residue of sheer muck is subjected to tremendous pressure, and issues therefrom in large cakes of dry mud. This is broken up into a manure, and is spread over the cane-fields, together with the ashes of the fibrous refuse burnt in the furnaces.

Thus there is now practically no waste in the sugar production of a well-managed Louisiana plantation. The cane is cut down close to the ground, but springs again from the roots. Meantime the stumps are shielded from winter frosts and the ground around them is eventually manured by their being covered over with the refuse leaves and tops of the cut cane. The furnaces are fed by the fibrous refuse of the crushed cane, the ashes of which, combined with the irreducible compressed "muck" of the juice, form the manure for the next year's crop. To this is added the digging-in of the decaying swathes of leaves which have protected the spring shoots, and there you have the almost endless cycle of the sugar crops—assisted occasionally by the importation of newer seedling canes from Demerara, or the sprinkling of the soil with "fertilisers"; or broken temporarily by outbreaks of boring insects, or some unwontedly cold winter or unmitigatedly dry autumn.

And through all this cycle, with its varying cares and responsibilities, negro labour seems to be the one unfailing resource of the Louisiana planter. The white men have strikes, are called away by higher ambitions, or are stricken by occasional epidemics of disease. The Negro is there all the time He is a spendthrift, yet loves to have money to spend. There are the sugar or the rice planters and the fruit growers, the railway companies, builders, and shipping firms always ready with work at good wages. The Italians, Hungarians, and Slavs save and often transmit to Europe the payment for their labour. The Negro is at home, and spends his money locally as soon as he earns it.

Great indeed is the debt which the Industrial and Agricultural South owes to the co-operation of the Negro.

CHAPTER XXII

THE NEGRO AND CRIME

I WAS told in New Orleans that I took too favourable a view of the Negro in the South. The usual stories were related about the vicious conditions of his life, his drunkenness, fondness for gambling, excessive addiction to sexual pleasures, the insulting attitude he assumed towards white women, and the danger they ran from Negro assaults in lonely places, and so forth.

Through the kindness of some American friends—a charming lady amongst

377. THE AUTHOR ON THE MISSISSIPPI

the number, herself a widely travelled woman and a native of Tennessee—I was enabled to visit a number of outlying Negro villages along the Mississippi River near its mouth; and again, later, other Negro villages in the western part of Louisiana. The people here were certainly "saucy" to a stranger, inclined even to be insolent; but it may have appeared impertinent to them that a "foreigner" (as I was at once declared to be) should walk about photographing houses and people, even when apologies were tendered or permission requested. But whenever this Tennessee lady appeared on the scene, or any other of my American guides more or less known to the people, the surly attitude was at once dropped.[1] The best solution of any trouble which might arise through my putting questions or taking photographs was always found in an appeal to the local minister of religion (sometimes in origin a British West Indian). These men were invariably polite, and quick to appreciate my purpose.

The negresses of the country districts in Louisiana, especially those who talk Creole French, wear a very ugly head-dress, as may be seen by the photographs. With some of the old women this bundle of rags and false hair is arranged so as to simulate a great backward projection of the skull, and gives them a hideous, ape-like appearance. Some of the men, however, are good-looking, and with a refined version of the negro features.

Neither men nor women give the impression of idleness: true, I encountered one wandering minstrel playing plaintive airs on a guitar; but even he was working for his living.

As to drunkenness, there was little or no sign of it, possibly because the new prohibition laws were producing their effect.

I believe, however, that the men gamble excessively; but although this is very regrettable from their own point of view, it is a stimulus to industry rather than otherwise, since the loss of their money compels them to keep steadily at work, while if they gain in lotteries, by betting, or at cards, they spend their gains on smart clothes and good living, which is beneficial to trade.

378. THE HIDEOUS HEAD-DRESS OF THE LOUISIANA NEGRESSES

To see the Negro at his worst, I visited those parts of the vast city and suburban area of New Orleans where the coloured people of the lower classes mostly congregate. I was escorted by an official of the police force; no restrictions were placed on where I went, but no doubt I was unconsciously guided, and possibly the worst parts of the town were withheld from my view, though, as a matter of fact, my very obliging guide seemed anxious to give me a truthful impression, and to show me the worst aspects he could find of Negro life.[2]

I came out from this inspection of "bad" New Orleans scandalised at what I had seen, but not so far as it affected the negroes; I was merely amazed at the shamelessness of the whites. Here and there, it is true, I saw a tipsy negro. In one saloon they were playing cards, but every one seemed to be in a good humour. There were no angry voices (there was a marked absence of obscenity in speech, I should state), and no one complained of being cheated. In another saloon, to the music of a gramophone, some twenty Negro men were dancing, but not indecorously. Here there was not the slightest sign of

[1] I noticed amongst the Negro men near New Orleans not the slightest resentment towards the United States, or the State of Louisiana in particular, for any racial trouble which might have arisen affecting the Negro's position; on the contrary, an intense "American" patriotism, a desire to vaunt the institutions of the United States in season and out of season, and to compare them favourably with those of Great Britain or the British colonies.

[2] Though he was far from being unfair to the coloured people, and on the contrary had much to say in their favour.

drunkenness. Moreover, all these "bad" places seemed to be far cleaner than similar haunts in England.

But at last we reached the streets of strange sights. We passed through a quarter of the town inhabited by negro and coloured prostitutes, and entered some of their houses; but none of the black or yellow women thus encountered

379. LOUISIANA NEGROES

gave any sign in their outward appearance of the manner in which they earned their living. There was nothing immodest in their speech, gesture, or clothing. In fact, they might all have been the keepers or tenants of respectable lodgings (furnished with almost Puritan respectability, with old prints and lithographs illustrating Scripture subjects, portraits of notabilities between 1850 and 1870, illuminated texts, Longfellow's poems, *Uncle Tom's Cabin*, horsehair sofas, and Berlin-wool antimacassars), but for the information of the police officer that they were women of the town, and visited, by the by, by white men as well as black.

We next entered a district in the vicinity of the great prison and of the police head-quarters: the region under police supervision specially assigned to houses of prostitution. This quarter (besides its special Negro subdivision) was, in the arrangements of the police and in the manners of the people, divided into geographical areas: here was the street of Jewish brothels; there two or more streets would be given up to the Italians or the Slavs (generally called Polaks or Bohemians); and lastly there were the establishments of English-speaking women—Anglo-Saxon Americans, Canadians, English, and Irish (I did not notice any admission of Scottish nationality).

This was one of the great sights of New Orleans, and should be—if the

380. NEW ORLEANS FROM AN HOTEL ROOF

The outskirts of this vast city are beautiful; but the heart of the town is spoilt by the smoke nuisance

white race has any proper pride—one of the most disgusting, dishonourable sights in the world. The houses were usually of only two storeys (interspersed with an occasional fine mansion). On the outside of the small dwellings the name of the woman-tenant was painted up in large letters—Nelly Corbet, Lizzie Devant, Sadie Buskin, and so on. It was night, and the large windows of the ground-floor rooms were open. Between it and the street hung a Venetian blind, with the slats turned horizontally, so that it was easy to look through this slight screen at the painted, half-naked woman within, lying on a bed or sofa. She could distinguish equally well the face of the gazer, and address to him plain-spoken invitations to enter.

I noticed negro men as well as white men looking through the blinds in the long array of mean houses. I wondered if the sights they could see—in the highest degree indecent—were calculated to inspire them with a lofty idea as regards the sacredness of the white woman. Any person without let or hindrance can reach and perambulate these streets, just as one can pass at any time of the day or night from Regent Street to Soho;[1] it is apparently one of the amusements in vogue among the lower classes and strangers in New Orleans (and in one or two other great Southern towns) to stroll round the prostitution quarter after ten p.m. "just for the fun of it," just to have this spectacle of lascivious, more than half naked, painted, and grotesquely costumed white women spread before the passer-by or those who like to tarry. Every now and then the women, tired of playing the spider, would walk out into the street or sit in their doorways accosting men. [It was pathetic enough to see some of these poor things "off duty," as it were, repairing to coffee-stalls. They then dropped their smiles and leers—though they appeared painfully incongruous in their ballet-girls' skirts and excessively low-cut bodices, the paint under the flaring light of the naphtha lamps looking such very obvious paint. It might even be streaked and furrowed with tears—tears that flowed at some little word of kindliness from a bystander that was not a brute; or at neglect; at some feminine quarrel; or from some passing shudder of disgust at the loathsome life they had compelled themselves to lead.] The most shameless among these women were of our own race—Anglo-Saxon Americans, or girls from the Old Country who had somehow strayed across to the States.

The whole thing seemed to me like a nightmare, half horrible, half supremely ludicrous and inconsistent. For instance, one very smart house, with a Turkish Parlour, a Hall of Mirrors, a Louis Quinze salon (no mere tawdriness, but everything extremely well done), was the property of a retired negress or mulatto woman of the town, almost world-famous in her day—why, only a psychologist could determine, for her numerous framed, enlarged photographs resembled more than anything else an obese female gorilla. This person, I believe, is just deceased, but for years prior to her death was famous in New Orleans and in Louisiana for her splendid donations to charities, especially for hospitals. The greater part of the money she raked in from her numerous houses of prostitution she spent on or bequeathed to institutions of the noblest character![2]

She employed [or the syndicate which had taken over her business, employed] to keep this particular house that I am describing, a New England lady of great personal distinction so far as outward aspect went—a woman of slightly stern features, with fine eyebrows and an intellectual brow, surmounted by well-dressed grey-white hair, wearing pince-nez which of themselves bespoke a rigid chastity and a cultivated mind, while the well-cut and modest evening dress of black and white enhanced the look of somewhat frigid distinction. This woman, as soon as she abandoned her professional oaths, talked with a shrewd kindliness, a convincing respectability that was in strange contrast to her manner of earning her living. She spoke of the numerous young women present with a motherly interest, describing how she had married their predecessors to wealthy clients, and hoped in time to pass on all she had now to a similarly prosperous and wholesome middle-age.

I believe that although such establishments as this are often kept by a negress, a mulatto, or a quadroon, the racial distinction is maintained here as in other departments of life, and only "white" clients are admitted to the society of the white women of the town.

[1] Though Soho is now respectability embodied, given up to pianos, publishers, and old-print shops.
[2] Who probably knew nothing of the character of their benefactress.

But I repeat (and what I have described with absolute truthfulness regarding New Orleans I know to exist with regard to several other large Southern towns), does such a spectacle as this tend to enhance the negro's respect for white women?

If he argued about the subject at all (but his own literature is far too prudish to do so), he might say, "Well, at any rate, the brothels dedicated to my own people are conducted with such outward decorum that their vicious character is not apparent to the casual observer." The fact is that much of the negro's vice is excessive uxoriousness, unlimited adultery, and that here, as in Africa, there is a standard of decorum as regards actual physical and verbal decency maintained by the Negro which is absent from many of the white peoples of the world.

It is such spectacles as may be seen at night in New Orleans by any negro passer-by which may tend to inflame the imagination of Negro men; and when to these is added the maddening influence of drugs (the sale of which is still unchecked by law) and of bad alcohol—and here the law of the State *has* stepped in and effected supremely good results—it is scarcely wonderful that Negro men have occasionally made attacks on the virtue of white women. Before they can be blamed without reserve for such vile actions, the White South should at any rate suppress all public indecency affecting the prestige and honour of the white woman.

As far as I could ascertain—though it is very difficult to obtain reliable information—within those Eleven States of the South, which contain an approximate coloured population of seven and a half millions, and in which there is special social legislation affecting the Negroes, there were twenty-four cases of proved indecent assault or rape by Negroes on white women during the year 1907. I could not learn that any statistics were compiled, or at any rate published, as to *white* criminality in regard to this particular offence. Either it was not thought to matter, since the worst result would simply be another white baby added to the vigorous and handsome white population of the South, or it may be that white men here, as elsewhere in America, are much more moral in their relations with women of their own colour and nationality than they are in Europe.

In the Eleven Southern States marriages between Negroes and Negroids and White people are illegal. Cases are frequently cited in magazine and newspaper articles of the cruel intervention of the law in this respect. A man with just the slightest drop of Negro blood in his composition—a mulatto grandmother, perhaps—falls in love with a poor girl of wholly white ancestry and offers her a home, or she may equally be drawn to him by his personal attractions. They cannot marry. If they live together as husband and wife (possibly with children as the result), the law when it discovers the fact intervenes and punishes them for indecency. Yet they have only to cross the line, which is now entirely ignored by the Federal Constitution of the United States—the Mason and Dixon Line—to be free to marry or to cohabit with the recognition of the law and without punishment for an act which in the legislation nowadays of most countries is regarded as one affecting only the personal conscience. Yet the most inconsistent South does not apparently intervene in the public brothels I have described in this chapter, and appoint a professed anthropologist to determine the exact racial composition of the prostitutes or their clients.

According to Ray Stannard Baker and other white authorities on the Negro problem in the States, a good deal of immorality still exists (more particularly as regards youths of the white race and coloured women in a dependent position as domestic servants) in the south-eastern third of the United States, especially in the plantations of the country districts. I cannot say that I met with obvious traces of this myself. It seemed to me that such unions now have become as repellent to white racial pride as to the growing self-respect of the coloured community. The mulatto element certainly appears to be on the increase in the North and North-East, but that, I think, is due to the tendency of Negroes in the coloured regions of the United States (as in the healthier parts of South Africa) to develop a lighter tone of skin colour; and no doubt the half-white women are now marrying back into the Negro community, carrying with them their quota of Caucasian blood.

There is, I am convinced, a deliberate tendency in the Southern States to exaggerate the desire of the Negro for a sexual union with white women, and the crimes he may commit under this impulse. A few exceptional Negroes in West and South Africa, and in America, are attracted towards a white consort, but almost invariably for honest and pure-minded reasons, because of some intellectual affinity or sympathy. The mass of the race, if left free to choose, would prefer to mate with women of its own type. When cases have occurred in the history of South Africa, South-West, East, and Central Africa, of some great Negro uprising, and the wives and daughters of officials, missionaries, and settlers have been temporarily at the mercy of a Negro army, or in the power of a Negro chief, how extremely rare are the proved cases of any sexual abuse arising from this circumstance! How infinitely rarer than the prostitution of Negro women following on some great conquest of the whites, or of their black or yellow allies! I know that the contrary has been freely alleged and falsely stated in histories of African events; but when the facts have been really investigated, it is little else than astonishing that the Negro has either had too great a racial sense of decency, or too little liking for the white women (I believe it to be the former rather than the latter) to outrage the unhappy white women and girls temporarily in his power. He may have dashed out the brains of the white babies against a stone, have even killed, possibly, their mothers, or taken them and the unmarried girls as hostages into the harem of a chief (where no attempt whatever has been made on their virtue), but in the history of the various Kafir wars it is remarkable how in the majority of cases the wives and daughters of the British, the Boers, and the Germans, after the slaughter of their male relations, were sent back unharmed to white territory.

There are depraved white women in the States as in England,[1] as in France, as in Germany who have invited the attentions of Negroes or Negroids, and have even been base enough when discovered to accuse the coloured man of the initiative. There are also undoubted cases of criminal negro lust: horrible cases, as bad as those that can be found year after year in the English or American criminal records of white men assaulting white women and young girls. But not only can no excessive preponderance in this crime or misdemeanour be laid to the charge of the Negro, but he certainly sins less frequently, as regards white women, than is the case with the Caucasian. And even his attitude towards his own womenkind in the United States very rarely

[1] Witness the behaviour towards the black contingents that have visited London within the last twenty-five years, and the crop of subsequent police court or Divorce Court cases; the desire to marry a Zulu prince or an Ashanti noble on the part of young women of the lower middle class.

offends against public decency, which is not always the case with the white peoples.

A shocking case occurred in 1907, in Georgia, of rape and mutilation inflicted by a Negro on a white girl fourteen years old. The girl did not die, but the details of the case were sufficiently abominable to make any decent man, black or white, grind his teeth and "see red" as he thought of the vengeance which should be inflicted on this unspeakable brute. But this solitary instance in the annals of 1907—singular, I mean, in its revolting character—was repeated and reiterated under slightly varying forms in the press, in magazine articles, and in the conversation of white Americans, until the stranger might well believe it was a weekly occurrence in the State of Georgia, instead of being an abnormal episode of horror.

381. "UNEDUCATED SEMI-SAVAGES"

In various sober-minded analyses of recent cases of assaults on white women by Negroes it has been shown by white writers as well as Negro journalists that the bulk of these crimes were due to the maddening influence of vile whisky and cocaine snuff; and a proportion of the assaults resulted from the temptations of proximity [negro men being allowed to work on the farms of poor whites alongside white women-drudges, the same temptation leading, admittedly, to a good deal of immorality among the white field labourers]. One or two episodes were acts of revenge for the seduction of coloured girls by whites, and the remainder were attributable to dementia. I cannot recall a single recent instance of indecent assault or rape on the part of a Negro against a white woman in which the criminal came from the educated negro classes, or was a settled agriculturist, a well-established tradesman, or any kind of citizen with a stake in the country. The only cases quoted in the press and in books are those of artisans, farm hands, loafers, and uneducated semi-savages.[1]

The elimination of spirit-drinking and unchecked drug-selling will, together with extended education, go far to remove the cause of these rare and occasional attacks by the coloured man on the honour of the white woman. But meantime the municipal authorities in the cities of the South should do all they can to elevate the white woman in the respect and estimation of the Negro by suppressing those public exhibitions of white debauchery described in this chapter. It is a coincidence worth noting that in several recent cases of assaults on white women in country districts the negro convicted of the assault came from one or other of the seaboard cities that maintain these public brothels.

[1] I do not believe, as already stated, that there is any inherent tendency on the part of the Negro in America or Africa to dishonour the white woman: rather the contrary. I have already quoted the fact that in the most densely "Black" parts of the United States white women can live alone in perfect safety. There is not a complete absence of danger to lonely white women and girls anywhere in the United States (or in many parts of England, Germany, and France), but the danger may arise even more frequently from white tramps and social outcasts than from negroes.

The origin of "lynching" negroes for murder, attempted murder, rape, or other serious crime against the white community goes back to Slavery times, but becomes most prominently noticed by American and English historians after 1845, when an increasing regard for civilisation and decency was sending the slave accused of a capital offence for trial before a properly constituted court. Allusions to the rape or attempted rape of white women or girls by negroes or mulattoes are rare in the literature of the United States prior to 1870. Occasionally in such a book as the *Narrative of Charles Ball* stories are told of slaves who mainly from a mad spirit of revenge have carried off their master's daughter, sister, or wife into the woods and have outraged the unhappy woman. But for very shame the crime has been hushed up and the negro criminal has been executed privately by the men of the white family concerned, generally with a savagery too horrible for description. In the case

382. TIRED WAYFARERS
Negro labourers tramping in search of employment

of mere murder or attempt to murder the execution was apparently a public event in which any one might participate and add to the horror or the humour of the legal process.

But—the Ku Klux Klan atrocities being merely looked upon as a reverberation of the Civil War—it was not till about 1870 that free negroes were charged openly with making attacks on the modesty or virtue of white women. These allegations at that period were confined to Tennessee, Mississippi, and Georgia; and lynchings occasionally followed either the charge or the condemnation. It is, however, really only since the last twenty years that the question as a racial indictment of savage lust on the one side and equally savage punishment on the other has become acute. And there is more than a suspicion that the negro is sometimes falsely accused, and more than a dread that the "lynching" with its mediæval tortures is less a grave punishment for vile erotomania or lawless violence on the negroes' part than the indulgence of a lust for cruelty and even nasty depravity on the part of the white people.

Many an unoffending wayfaring negro has been injured or killed during the last fifteen years because white women and even children have become panic-struck by the foul stories spread as to negro propensities, and have wildly accused coloured men of intentions which they never entertained, or they have misconstrued perfectly innocent acts and gestures. In the recent literature dealing with this subject the evidence of several negro notabilities has been collected—mostly ministers of religion—to the effect that when running through a lonely suburb to catch a tram-car, some silly fool of a woman has started up from their path and begun to shriek for help. In some cases the negro notability relating the story has stated that his only chance of safety was to stand perfectly still and to rely on his known name, position, and antecedents. But it required great courage and presence of mind to do this. Others fled for their lives to avoid even the risk of identification.

Justification for Lynching has been pleaded in that the accused culprit might be declared innocent by a jury or might be given an inadequate punishment if found guilty. It has been maintained that the only way to strike terror into the whole negro community was to have the man accused of assault on a white woman (and captured under incriminating circumstances) immediately executed by the mob, often in a most cruel and barbarous fashion. Sometimes, to satisfy the mob conscience, the wretched negro has been tortured till he confessed his guilt, and photographers have been present and been permitted to photograph[1] the torture during its infliction either in broad day- or flash-light if the proceedings were conducted in comparative darkness. The fact that these numerous photographs and "picturesque" descriptions of lynchings, executions, tortures, or the physical or mental agony of the accused or of the victim of the crime should have been allowed without let or hindrance, even—one might judge—*arranged* for the special benefit of the photographer, illustrates sufficiently the depravity of the uneducated white South. Can one even say with truth uneducated? The crowd seems to consist frequently of well-dressed men and women who—the United States being what it is—were presumably well able to read and write.

Lynching, of course, and those unreasoning outbreaks of mob violence against the negroes in Georgian, Carolinian, Tennessee, and Maryland cities, which result in serious loss of life and property (and are a disgrace to the civic authorities) are of course a remnant of the cruel Slavery days prior to 1863. The South knows at the bottom of its national heart that it has injured the negro anciently and hates him for that reason, as well as the irrational one that he is a negro! "Twoad, be 'ee? I'll larn thee to be a twoad," says the country boy in a clever number of Mr. Punch some years ago; and forthwith bashes the toad to death. This is the spirit that animates many a mob and many a writer, pressman, and pamphleteer in their attacks on the unfortunate Ethiopian, who can only change the colour of his skin by miscegenation or by a thousand years of evolution.

But that this lynching spirit will in time affect the interests of White America is well shown in the following extracts from a New York newspaper (summarised), which appeared in the late autumn of 1908, at the time of some quarrels about land ownership in Tennessee:—

"Let me call your attention to the fact that this 'Night-Rider' business is essentially an ominous development. It is the first-fruits of the mob spirit reaching higher with its

[1] These photographs and much other information on lynching are given in *The Negro*, by R. W. Shufeldt, M.D. (Boston, 1907).

lawless hand. I have no doubt but that the two prominent lawyers in Tennessee, who have just suffered horribly at the hands of a mob, have many a time shrugged their shoulders nonchalantly over the lynching of negroes. When the mob spirit begins, as it is beginning, to 'hoist the Colonels by their own petard,' the dominating forces of public opinion are going to see what some of us have been pointing out all the time, that the mob that lynched the negro for rape is father to the mob that lynched him for *other* and lesser crimes, and grandfather to the mob that now lynches him for *no* crime, and great-grandfather to the mob that lynches the white man and burns his property."

This summary of a letter from a prominent Southerner goes true to the mark. For years we have maintained that the lynching of negroes in the South must be put down, if for no other reason than that lynchings of whites were sure to follow. No mob of excited, irresponsible, whisky-inflamed men, North or South, can be trusted to enforce lynch law with discrimination. Some tried it in Springfield, Illinois, only to find out afterwards that the man originally accused was innocent; they did not confine themselves to seeking him out, but killed, robbed, and destroyed at random. The forces of evil once unleashed, no one can direct and no public sentiment can control, whether in Illinois, or in Tennessee, or in Mississippi. Granted, if you please, for argument's sake, that there is a higher Anglo-Saxon law, which compels short work with the criminal where rape or an indecent assault is committed, it is a long-proved fact that its self-appointed instruments never stop there. They go from hanging to burning; from killing for rape to slaughtering for an impertinent remark; from lynching men to torturing women; and then, the spirit of lawlessness being well rooted, they kill whites who have offended them, or who sell their tobacco where they please.

The descent of this road to barbarism is facile and swift. Examples of it are more frequent in the South because that region, misled by the cessation of the Ku Klux horrors, believed that lynching could be held in sufficient check. We have in mind a community in northern Alabama where the lynchings and burnings of innocent and guilty alike became so menacing that the neighbouring sheriff at Wetumpka found it necessary to form a posse and round up the entire crowd, whose "defence of white womanhood" had created a new sport—nigger-killing—superior to any other local amusement. Twelve white men were sent to the chain-gang or driven away, and there has been peace between the races and obedience to the laws ever since. We reported two years ago a horrible case where a negro woman in Mississippi, accused only of being the wife of a man alleged to have done wrong, was tortured as by savages, fine splinters being driven into her flesh and set fire to. Nobody was punished. Now, how could any community tolerate such a crime and not sink in the scale of civilisation? We guarantee that if the law were similarly permitted to fall into disrepute in New York or Massachusetts we should have our Night-Riders too. There is no such thing as saying to lynchers: "Thus far and no further."

It is so essential that lynching and mob-law should be put down in what is in some respects the foremost country of the world (and should therefore be the world's exemplar); that, when next there is a lynching outbreak in any district (and the State authorities do not promptly suppress it, track down and punish the white ringleaders and their followers), if the President of the United States despatched a large force of Federal troops to the offending county of the misgoverned State, and levied a war contribution on the White or the Black inhabitants of that county (whichever was the first to begin the trouble), and distributed the overplus of this heavy impost (after paying *war* expenses) among the people of the injured race, I believe that President would be elected to a second or a third term of office. The Americans may elect their rulers, but they love a chief magistrate who rules.

The great racial weakness of the Negro is dishonesty of a petty kind. The European, and to a certain extent the Asiatic, has got a stage farther than the Negro, and is honest in small things; but possibly dishonest towards the general community in great matters. The Negro is rapidly following in these footsteps. No doubt in the best-organised Negro communities in the United States one's fowls and turkeys, melons and oranges would be perfectly safe, but there would be considerable "graft" in municipal matters, or dishonesty in the collection of taxes or the administration of private and public funds.

Great is the petty dishonesty (I am informed) in Haiti. One European finds it impossible to keep peacocks. Another loses all his ducks. A third catches negroes stealing his vegetables by night with the intention of selling them in the public market the next day. Yet the victims of Haitian thieves will tell you, and I should think with perfect truth, that you can send large sums of money by negro messengers from one part of Haiti to another. Neither the messenger nor the people of the villages through which he will pass would dream of dipping their hands into the money-bags.

383. "POSSIBLE PETTY LARCENY"

There is undoubtedly much petty dishonesty amongst the poorer uneducated Negro people of the United States, but it is directed more against their black brothers and sisters than against the white community.

The same may be said with regard to their crimes of violence, which are certainly excessively numerous from all accounts. The killing of a *white man* by a *Negro* is an extremely rare occurrence, though a good proportion of the burglars in the United States are coloured men. The killing of Negroes by Negroes is a very common event, and does not excite that horror throughout the Negro community which it should do. While I was staying in Tuskegee a negro farmer—a respectable, hard-working man with a thriving cotton plantation—was stabbed in the back and otherwise mutilated by another negro, who flung his body on to the road (a great blood patch still remaining as I drove by). The crime was committed simply with the idea of robbing the farmer of a few dollars in silver which he had brought back from the market. The murderer accosted the farmer as he drove back from the town and asked for a lift in his buggy, and when they were well clear of the settlement killed him in the manner described.

Whilst I was in the States episodes of this kind might be read several times a week in newspaper paragraphs. But although this is an outrage on the Negro community, it does not directly affect the white man, and it should in the first instance be complained of and preached against by negroes. On the other hand, the white men of the United States, especially in the Southern States and Ohio, are reckless in their attacks on the Negro. Europe seems to have passed unnoticed massacres following on anti-Negro riots which have taken place in great American towns within —let us say—the last ten years, several of which have almost equalled in atrocities and number of killed the massacre of Saint Bartholomew or a Russian pogrom.[1]

What the United States wants is a good Rural Constabulary, white and coloured: best of all a Coloured Police, mounted and unmounted, under White Officers, a Police to be under the orders of the State Governor. If she had such a constabulary as that of Jamaica (or of her own devising in Cuba and in Panama) crime would diminish enormously, and insecurity of life and property diminish to as low a figure as in the British West Indies or the Canal Zone.

[1] See for details the works of Ray Stannard Baker and W. E. Burghardt DuBois.

CHAPTER XXIII

THE NEGRO AS CITIZEN

IN Florida I found the Negroes in an advantageous and creditable position (a position demanding probity and marked ability), largely through the result of Tuskegee and Hampton teaching. A high State post has been held at Jacksonville (the capital) by a negro, Mr. Joseph E. Lie, who is also a Solicitor in Chancery. In Jacksonville also negroes have been elected by their fellow-citizens as municipal judges and have served their term satisfactorily.

In the north-western part of Florida the rougher class of negro works a good deal in the pine forests, collecting turpentine. I had a glimpse of some of these camps in the pine woods, but thanks to that blessed spread of Prohibition in the South and the restrictions on the sale of alcohol, these camps seemed — and are, I am told — orderly and without crime, although the country Negro of Florida, like his brother of the other Southern States, still lies under the stigma of being a petty thief, prone to carry off at night the fowls, turkeys, or vegetables of some homestead in his vicinity.

384. "L'HOMME À TOUT FAIRE"
Negroes laying down a tramway in Florida

Yet there seemed to me, travelling through Florida, a singular lack of ill-feeling between the whites and the "Nigs." Nearly all the rough work of Florida was being done by good-tempered negroes under the direction of white foremen or engineers. Negroes entirely, under white supervision, are building that wonderful East Coast of Florida railway, from Miami to Key West—one of the world's wonders, a railway which crosses the shallow, open sea for miles on low viaducts, and carries you from one fairy-like coral island to another till you are brought within ninety miles of Cuba.

In Florida the Negro seems to be preferred to Italians or other "foreign" whites. It is probably in northern Florida, western Georgia, Mississippi, Arkansas, eastern Texas, Louisiana, and Alabama (most of all) that the American Negro is seen at his best as peasant, peasant proprietor, farmer, artisan, professional man, and member of society. Here I detected no bumptiousness of manner amongst the educated, and experienced little or no rudeness from the uncultivated.

My visits to the cities or towns of Georgia and South Carolina were so few and so fleeting that I could form no personal impressions of the negro worth recording. From the publications which issue from the Atlanta University (and are written or compiled by Negroes and negroids) one would say—with other evidence—that there was a good deal of intellectuality among the town-dwelling coloured people in this and in Augusta and the other inland towns of this large State. But the student for a comprehension of this now complex question of the extremes of negro life and culture in Georgia, of prosperity and the ruin of hopes (after white riots), of well-directed State industrial education, of the abuses of the penitentiary and the leasing-out of convicts (which brought a new slavery into existence), is advised to study the works of Mr. Ray Stannard Baker, W. E. Burghardt DuBois, Edgar Gardner Murphy, and William Archer.

385. ONCE A SLAVE: VIRGINIA

There is much in the city life of negroes in these two States which requires the attention of white and coloured philanthropists. But it is specially in Savannah and Charleston that the charge of excessive immorality and crimes of violence are laid on the negroes by the press of Georgia and South Carolina. But the "poor" white population of the sea-coast cities also bore a bad reputation, and in both cases immoderate consumption of bad spirits was the root of nearly all the evil. Increasing habits of temperance or abstinence fostered by State legislation and Church influence are rapidly making these accusations stale.

In the Sea Islands off the coast of South Carolina (between the rivers Santee and Savannah) there are negroes living at the present day who were born in Africa and landed here as slave youths or children in the 'forties and 'fifties. Others are descended from runaways, and very early in the conflict between North and South control was temporarily abandoned over the negro population of these almost tropical, swampy, flat islands, separated from the mainland by broad tidal creeks.

From these and other reasons, these amphibious South Carolina island negroes are in some places leading a wilder, more primitively African existence than anywhere else in the United States except it be in remote swamps of south-west Louisiana. Many of the Sea Islanders retain a remembrance of their original African language (which in the few words I have seen in print appears to be of the Yoruba stock or from the Niger delta). They retain their belief, or their parents' belief—in witchcraft and fetishes, they maintain their medicine-men—"guffer doctors"—and their fetish temples are called "Praise Houses." It is here that their religious dances—called very appropriately "shouts"—take place. In the less-visited islands the "English" of these negro squatters and fishermen is scarcely recognisable as English, and contains

386. A DEAR OLD NEGRO NURSE OR "MAMMY" OF THE IDEAL TYPE: VIRGINIA

many African words and a few Portuguese expressions current once on the West Coast of Africa. Also they are when away from white influence inclined to sparsity of clothing—not nowadays a common trait in the United States negro. They are also pure negroes, entirely without any infusion of white blood.

Crime is very rare among them. They are almost all peasant proprietors, many having bought their holdings from the State out of confiscated and abandoned white plantations. From these islands once came the celebrated Sea Island cotton; and it comes still, and in increasing quantity, but grown now by free negro estate owners. I have already referred to the educational work done in this region by the Penn School.

There is a relatively small Negro population in North Carolina, which in comparison to its neighbours north and south is a very "white" State which was settled originally by English, Scotch, and Irish settlers—colonists of a good stamp.

As regards the country life of the Negroes in Virginia, it is probably on a lower level than in the great States of the South. The coloured people—mainly pure negroes—away from the influence of Hampton, seemed to me rather stupid peasants, and their houses were often miserable, dirty huts. On the sea coast of Virginia the fishermen are nearly all negroes, either pursuing their calling in their own fishing boats or engaged by white proprietors to guard and superintend the oyster fisheries. In parts of the coast they have relapsed into a semi-savage existence, so easily nourished are they on the oysters, clams, and sea-fish they obtain for the taking.

387. "L'HOMME À TOUT FAIRE"
A negro mason, Virginia

In the old slavery days of the eighteenth and nineteenth centuries, Virginia proverbially turned out the smartest and most intelligent negroes. Nearly every prominent negro in history or fiction prior to 1863 came from Virginia, and no part of the United States was more passionately loved by the black race in actuality or tradition than the State of Virginia. Here indeed, in spite of ferocious slave laws, they were more kindly and paternally treated, became more closely associated—feudally—with the great white families.

Yet though Virginian towns and schools still turn out clever negroes and mulattoes, one has a feeling as one passes through the towns of this aristocratic State that the educated negro has here no abiding city, that things are made hard for him, and he finds it better to carry his ambitions farther South or West: for, curiously enough, West Virginia, so without negroes in its population at the outbreak of the Civil War that it was Abolitionist in policy, is now receiving or breeding negroes in ever increasing numbers, no doubt in connection with its mining industries.

In Maryland there is a very intolerant feeling in white circles against the coloured population, still very considerable in the towns. Here and in the eastern part of Pennsylvania there are many thousand negroes engaged in industrial pursuits.

In Baltimore and in Philadelphia there are Negro quarters which certainly were foul-smelling slums, nearly as bad as the ordinary London slum. Here the conditions of Negro life might cause the passing visitor to shake his head if he did not stop to reflect that these conditions had been deliberately brought about by white men. So much has this been realised by the better class of white men in these cities, that probably before these lines are printed the worst of the Negro slums in Baltimore, Philadelphia, and Richmond will have been swept away by the civic authorities. They have been the property of wicked white landlords, and have lain under the thumb and the spell of the vile saloons wherein the Negro has been maddened by poisonous alcohol. Certain other economic conditions, moreover, have almost compelled a section of the Negro community to develop vicious conditions of existence for the gratification of sexual passion in the dissolute sections of the white community.

These questions were fully investigated after the terrible anti-Negro riots which prevailed in Baltimore a few years ago. The respectable members of the Negro community faced the situation with splendid courage. The ringing earnestness of their appeal for fair play touched the hearts even of the city "bosses" among the whites, even of the corrupt municipalities of these great American cities of the east. The result has been a co-operation between the well-thinking and the right-doing of both races, and an immense recent improvement in the conditions of Negro life in the cities of Maryland, Pennsylvania, and northern Virginia.

388. "L'HOMME À TOUT FAIRE"
A negro coachman in Washington

It is often a grievance to the indignant Southerner that the Federal Capital should contain such a large Negro population—about one hundred thousand. The coachmen are nearly all negroes, the men who attend to the streets are negroes, so, of course, are all the lesser employés on the railways and at the railway stations; many of the clerks, typists, shorthand writers; barbers and shop assistants. In addition there are numerous coloured doctors, dentists, lawyers, and surveyors, engineers, electricians, builders, and architects. Not a few of the excellent officials in the great public offices, museums, galleries, are negroes or negroids. I heard here no stories of negro violence or tendency to crime which would contrast this section of the Washington population with that of pure "White" origin.

Then look at Washington. There is a poor Negro population certainly in the environs, and even scattered about the main thoroughfares of that City of the Future, which does live in a condition of ramshackle poverty—perhaps one may say dirt—which would not be tolerated in New York. Though it does not conduce to the appearance one would expect of the Federal Capital, still it is evidence of a kindly treatment of the coloured race to see ridiculous little Negro tenements of one—and at most, two—storied frame houses [sometimes grotesquely countrified, built of a strange patchwork of material and overgrown with creepers] interspersed in Washington between beautiful villas, grand houses, or actual palaces. The stranger feels inclined to suggest[1] that some stimulus should be applied to the coloured people inhabiting these grotesque survivals of the life of the 'forties and 'fifties to induce them to build their houses more in relation to those of their neighbours, or else to sell plots which become very valuable, and move away to the environs of the city, where they can put up a log cabin and be as untidy as they like.

Before leaving England for America I had studied a good deal of the literature extant on the American negro and negroid. The preponderating impression left on my mind by the works published prior to 1898 (after which less

389. "L'HOMME À TOUT FAIRE"
Negro street attendant, Washington, D.C.

pessimistic conclusions began to be formed) was that the United States negro and coloured people were hopelessly sunk in vice, crime, and squalor; that the blacks would never be fitted for any position better than hewers of wood and drawers of water, that the half-caste women invariably drifted into a life of prostitution, and the half-caste men into poorly-paid posts of drudgery beneath the notice of cheap whites.

I was therefore surprised after my arrival in New York to realise that in that city there were about a hundred thousand blacks, mulattoes, and octoroons who seemed to be very useful, contented, and creditable members of the community. I visited possibly over a hundred negro homes in New York, some of them independent houses or villas; others flats, two-roomed or one-roomed apartments. As regards the houses of the well-to-do negroes or mulattoes, everything was in good taste. The houses were clean. The

[1] It is curious what an influence the United States has over the incoming "foreigner," so that the foreigner soon identifies himself with the interests and outlook of this grand country, and discusses her affairs with an almost proprietary interest.

furniture was solid, well-designed, and tasteful. The appointments of the dining-table were such as the most fastidious English man or woman could not object to. There were well-furnished libraries, and all the new appliances of civilisation at their highest perfection—such as telephones, bathrooms, dinner-lifts, electric fans, heating apparatus—in regard to which New York is so much in advance of London. The poorest part that I visited, in what was declared by the police to be the worst existing tenements in the negro quarter, was clean, wholesome, and attractive as compared to the dwellings of many respectable, hard-working Londoners.

The staircases, for example, were always clean and well lit; there was none of that horrible odour of the *indiscrétions du chat* (as the French delicately phrase it) which is so characteristic of the frowsy, early-nineteenth-century houses of respectable lower-middle-class London; there were no disagreeable smells of bad cooking; the sanitary arrangements appeared to be quite up-to-date and devoid of offence. The people I visited of the poorer class were cooks (of both sexes), long-shore men, railway porters, and car attendants; tram-conductors, seamstresses, washerwomen, and so forth. Their rooms seemed to be comfortably furnished, and were superior in every way to the worst slums of London.

390. BROBDINGNAGIAN NEW YORK
Beyond the scope of a snapshot camera!

The educated class apparently supplied school teachers, shorthand writers, typists, dressmakers, tailors, and an infinitude of other small tradespeople and professionals to New York's hive of industry. I could really see no difference in surroundings, in culture, in decorum between the lives of these absolute Negroes, or of the many different degrees of Negroids, and the lives led by Anglo-Saxon white people earning the same wages in New York; while there was a balance in favour of the Negro if you compared his life with the lowest class of recently arrived Irish or Italian emigrants, Bohemians and Hungarians; and it was by many degrees superior to the Asiatic squalor and unwholesome mystery which surrounded even the police-inspected Chinese dwellings. In fact, the best way to appreciate the community of feeling between the Negro and the White man in the United States is to compare this interchange of sympathy and this community of culture with the condition of the American Chinese. *They* are aliens, if you like.

In the States of Ohio, Missouri, and Indiana there is little or no country population of negroes, except in the south-eastern part of Missouri. The Negroes and Negroids congregate in the great towns, where they are on much the same social and industrial footing as has already been described in reference to New York. There are, of course, Negroes in the railway services of the North-Eastern,[1] North-Central, North-Western, and Western States, but in all this

[1] There are practically no Negroes, except just as domestic servants, in the North-Eastern States outside the towns. They are prominent, however, as residents in Boston and in some of the suburbs of that

part of North America the Negro is sporadic, and does not fill a very important place in the social economy. In the regions of Kentucky and Tennessee, below the mountains sloping to the valleys of the rivers, he is present here and there as a country settler, sometimes a descendant of a freedman of the old slavery days, while he is very abundant in the Kentucky and Tennessee towns, and not necessarily in a very inferior position. But the country-folk of these two States is now mainly white, and in the mountains perhaps the lowest type of the American white, *mentally*, though ordinarily of good physical development. Much of the lynching and of the trouble in connection with the Negro problem originates in Tennessee and Kentucky, especially in such a place as Nashville. In the eastern part of Kansas the country Negro is making considerable progress as a cultivator and farmer.

North of the old States of the Secession, the coloured people—some 2,500,000 in number—not only have the electoral and municipal vote like any other citizen of the United States, but exercise their voting privileges without let or hindrance. In New York City, for example, there are nearly 19,000 Negro voters, and in Philadelphia at least 20,000. But the Negro, like the Jew, nowhere votes uniformly in the North, where he has absolute justice. It is only in the South (where in a measure his very existence is at stake) that he votes "solid" and "Republican."

By 1880 the White South had entirely regained power over the administration of all the States of the Secession.[1] The Negro had been shouldered away from the polling-booth, and as regarded the new generation born out of Slavery, Election or Registration-of-Franchise Acts were being passed by the White legislators which made it difficult for the coloured man to obtain a vote. These difficulties do not appear on paper. The bald statement of the

beautiful city. Here they even hold professional posts. It is complained by some critics of the Negro that he is a spoilt person in Massachusetts. It is in this State more than in any other that marriages have taken place between full-blooded Negroes and white women, and it is alleged that the results of these marriages have often been unhappy. Although Harvard again and again asserts its superiority to race prejudice by receiving Negroes amongst its alumni, or conferring degrees on Negroes, and although many of the more notable philo-Negro philanthropists, male and female, hail from the Athens of the United States, there has been a tendency lately rather to tire of this enthusiasm and to profess to find the educated Negro a bumptious and irksome personage in Boston society, from which, indeed, he is being politely but firmly excluded. Those persons who discussed this matter with me at Boston cited a number of instances where social encouragement offered to educated people of colour had resulted in their becoming—to put it plainly—a bore. They were not content (it was said) with the interchange of social civilities, but tried to force themselves into the intimacy of the whites. In fact they are already classed in the English slang, which, together with other British tendencies, is making Boston less foreign to London than is Edinburgh or Dublin, as "bounders." This tendency of thought, whether it be just or unjust, is worth regarding, as it is slightly affecting already the attitude of Massachusetts towards the colour question.

[1] To make these questions clearer to my English readers, I would remind them that down to 1863 there were FOURTEEN States which upheld Slavery as a lawful institution: VIRGINIA, MARYLAND, NORTH CAROLINA, KENTUCKY, TENNESSEE, SOUTH CAROLINA, GEORGIA, FLORIDA, ALABAMA, MISSOURI, MISSISSIPPI, LOUISIANA, ARKANSAS, and TEXAS. There were, however, only ELEVEN States which seceded in 1861: Virginia, North Carolina, South Carolina, Tennessee, Georgia, Florida, Alabama, Mississippi, Louisiana, Arkansas, and Texas. The other three on the northern borderland between Slave and Free either remained faithful to the Union or were controlled by the Executive at Washington. The western part of Virginia was also detached from the Slave and Secession cause, and therefore after the Civil War was begun was made in 1863 into a separate State, and never having possessed many slaves or negro inhabitants took henceforth the side of the North in its public policy towards negroes. But the *Eleven States of the Secession* have remained to this day apart from the rest of AMERICA in their domestic policy towards the negro and people of colour with any drop of black blood in their veins. Here alone—except perhaps in the Transvaal, Orange State, and Natal of British South Africa—does the racial composition of a citizen (and not mere dirtiness, drunkenness, or inability to pay) exclude him or her from municipal or national privileges and public conveniences otherwise open to all and paid for by all.

qualifications required for the registration of a voter in the Southern States does not seem to exclude any slightly educated negro or negroid, and few people would plead for the vote to be given to an absolutely illiterate man. In Mississippi the vote is refused to persons who have not paid taxes, who "cannot read or understand the United States Constitution"; and no doubt this last test can be strained to exclude many Negro citizens. In Louisiana an applicant for the vote must be able to read and write or possess $300, or be the son or grandson of a person qualified to vote on January, 1867. The first two alternative conditions, coupled with a knowledge of the U.S.A. Constitution, are conditions of the vote in South Carolina. In Virginia the applicant must be able, *six months before the date of the election*, to show that he has paid all his State poll-tax for the three preceding years—a "tiresome," meticulous condition which no doubt serves as a useful sieve to exclude many Negro would-be voters.

391. AWAITING THE SUFFRAGE
Which, if hard work counts for anything, the negress richly deserves

Still in the published text of voting qualifications of the Southern States there is not much to explain why in the year 1909 there are so few Negro voters on the franchise-roll of these States.

In the same way the Coloured man is shut out almost entirely from the municipal franchise in the Southern States. Therefore he has no effective say as to the manner in which public moneys (to which he is a contributor) are expended. He can put in no effective protest against the utterly indefensible system of the boycotting of one race by another—the forcing of negroes or any person with the least (supposed) drop of negro blood in their veins to ride in special railway-cars or in a railed-off part of the tram-cars; their being unable to go to the same church, theatre, hotel, public library, and often public park, as the white man.

Surely this procedure, which prevails throughout the whole Slave States, is a breach of the Fourteenth Amendment of the United States Constitution? However that may be, it persists; and it is sought to excuse it by the plea that the common use of all public buildings, vehicles, etc., might lead to social intercourse between the sacred white people and their coloured fellow-citizens. And social intercourse might lead . . . not to intermarriage, for that is forbidden by law in most of the seceded States, but to the concubinage of the white with the black. Further argument leads to a reference to that obsession of the South: attempts at rape or indecent assault on the part of negroes against white women.

Yet with all these imperfections in the social acceptance of the coloured people of the United States—imperfections which with time and patience and according to the merits of the Neo-negro will disappear — the main fact was evident to me after a tour through the Eastern and Southern States of North

America: that nowhere in the world—certainly not in Africa—has the Negro been given such a chance of mental and physical development as in the United States.

Also that nowhere else has the Negro so greatly availed himself of his opportunities. Intellectually, and perhaps physically, he has attained his highest degree of advancement as yet in the United States. Politically he is freer there, socially he is happier than in any other part of the world.

From the point of view of happiness this statement may be called in question. I may be reminded that the negroes of the British West Indies, or of Haiti, or of Brazil are theoretically happier than their brethren in the United States, because it is imagined by people who do not know intimately tropical America, or who are not good observers, that the banana and certain other food products grow luxuriantly and without the assistance of human labour, that the negro enjoys an intensely hot climate and under such tropical conditions has the best of health. This is not the case. Food perhaps in some parts of the West Indies is easier come by than in North America: it is certainly cheaper, but then, on the other hand, the public wealth is much less. But it is not so varied or so good as it is in North America, where the whole resources of a continent ranging from the Arctic to the Tropic are by a network of railways and thousands of steamers placed at the negroes' disposal, so that fresh or preserved he can with the money at his command live far better not only than his brethren in tropical America and Africa, but even than the European artisan, with the exception of the people of France and the United Kingdom. In America, moreover, he has his own excellent theatres and many opportunities for hearing music, good, bad, and indifferent. He has access to some of the finest and most conveniently appointed libraries in the world. The climate also is more reasonable. It is a mistake to assume the negro is fond of the sun's heat or of a muggy atmosphere. He endures these discomforts better than we do and is physically much better suited than we are to exist in a perpetual Turkish-bath atmosphere. But just as his ideal of beauty is the same as ours, so probably is his ideal climate. No region of Africa, however elevated, has proved too cold for negro habitation. By a curious coincidence some of the plateau regions and high mountains in that continent are at the present time uninhabited and open to the white man, but this has arisen more from intertribal feuds and struggles for the possession of them than dislike to the cold climate of these altitudes. In North America the negro probably stands cold as well as the white man does, and in North America and South Africa his race is as much stimulated to better physical and mental development by a temperate climate as is the case with the Caucasian.

392. A TYPICAL MULATTO FARMER OF THE SOUTHERN UNITED STATES

Shrewd, virile, and thrifty

The present Negro and Negroid population of the United States is about 10,000,000. The pure white population is about 79,000,000. Another million of Amerindians, Mongolians, and other non-Caucasian types makes up the approximate present total of 90,000,000.

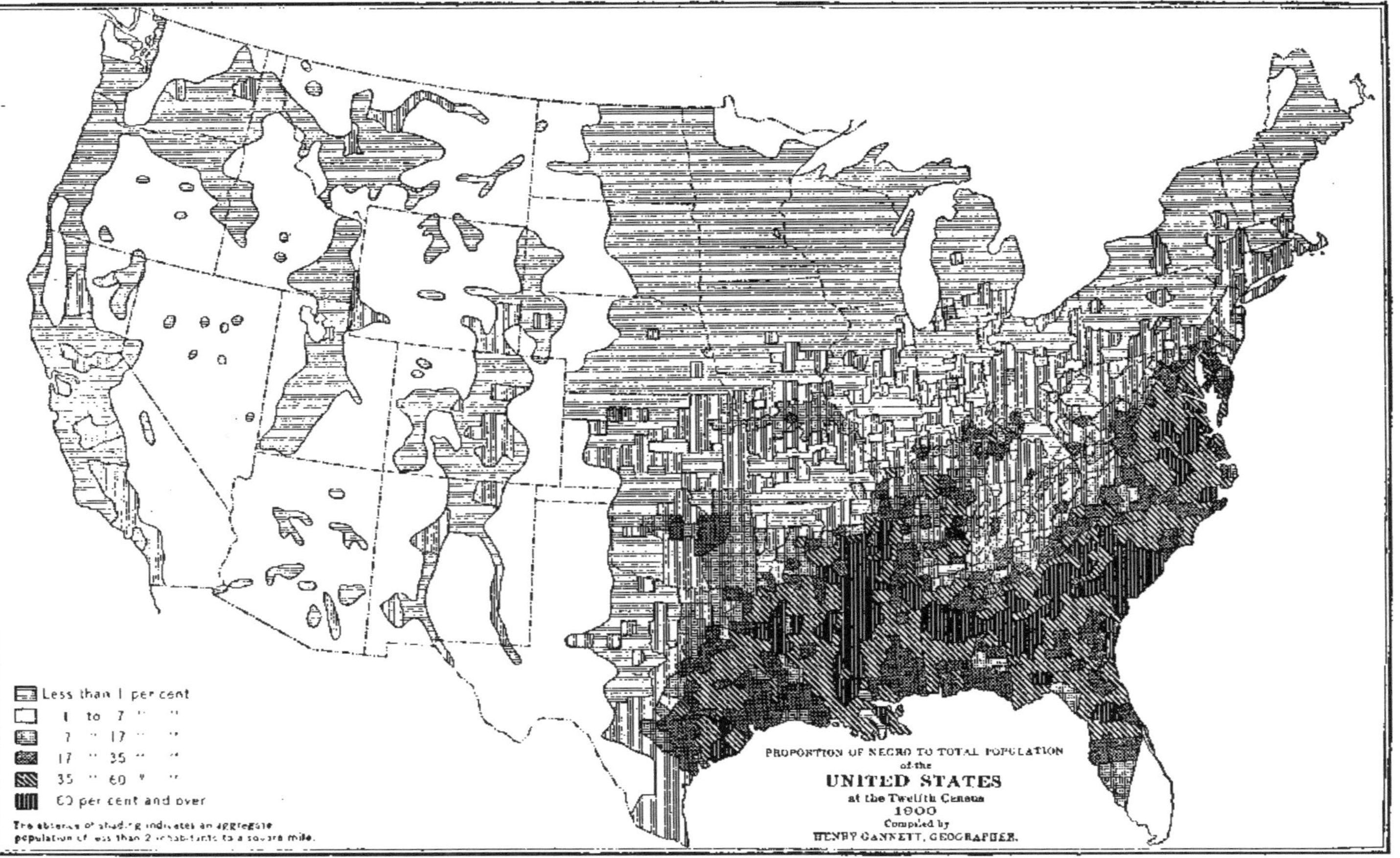

393. A SKETCH-MAP SHOWING APPROXIMATE DISTRIBUTION OF NEGROES AND NEGROIDS IN THE UNITED STATES

The "white" element in this assemblage of peoples increases monthly by leaps and bounds, by immigration, by a very fair birth-rate, and by the absorption of the Amerindian (who is almost of the "White-man" sub-species). The Negroes and Negroids are not increasing in North America at anything like the same rate. They yearly lose a fringe of their race—the "near-whites" by their absorption into the white community—in the West, perhaps, or the North Centre, where the newer peoples are not so particular about racial tabu. Death (from neglect, improper food, infectious diseases) still takes twice as heavy a toll from negro babyhood as from the white nursery. Mulattoes are less prolific (ordinarily) than pure whites and pure blacks. Phthisis kills annually as many negroes or mulattoes as it does Caucasians; pneumonia is still more deadly in the negro community. Except a few thousand West Indians and Central American people of colour, the Dark race receives no recruits from the world outside the United States.

394. THE NEGRO AND THE STARS AND STRIPES

In 1790 the Negro element formed 19 per cent of the total population of the United States [757,208 Negroes as against 3,172,006 Whites]; in 1880 the percentage had dropped to 13·1, in 1900 to 11·6. In Delaware, Maryland, the District of Columbia, Virginia, North and South Carolina, the (native) White population was increasing between 1890 and 1900 at the rate of 29·2 per cent, and the Negro in the same States at the rate of only 19·9 per cent.

On the other hand, in West Virginia, Florida, Alabama, Mississippi, Oklahoma, and Arkansas the Coloured people are increasing faster than the Whites.

And the solution will probably be that the two races—white-skinned and brown-skinned—will co-exist in amity and common American citizenship on the 3,000,000 square miles of the United States. Whilst ten millions of Aframericans are slowly increasing to twenty millions between Florida and Alaska, two, three, four, five millions of Euramericans will be leaving the North American continent for Central America and South America and the paradises of the West Indies.

For in cleansing Cuba and in making the Panama Canal, the white American has learnt the secret of the Tropics: of how to live under an Equatorial sun amid torrential rain, and yet by exterminating or avoiding insect poisoners to keep his health and vigour.

In the larger Imperialism of to-morrow, when the influence of the English, French, and German-speaking White man extends from Cape Columbia (in Grinnell Land) to Cape Horn, there will be room in between his stride and his thrones for brother peoples of darker skins but equal brains. In that day, when the white American meets his brown-skinned brother on equal terms in the mart, the exchange, the university, and the theatre, he will, if he comes across them in some old book of the early twentieth century, smile at the rude diatribes of a Vardaman and frown at the discourtesy of a departed Dean of a Missouri Medical College.

CHAPTER XXIV

THE NEGRO IN THE NEW WORLD

THE following is an approximately correct summary of the numbers and distribution of the *Negroes* and *Negroids* in the New World at the close of 1909:—

Dominion of Canada (about)		30,000
UNITED STATES (say)		10,000,000
Bermudas		12,500
British Honduras		37,000
WEST INDIES—		
Bahamas	44,000	
Jamaica and Dependencies	810,000	
Cuba	609,000	
Hispaniola (mainly Haiti)	2,900,000	
Porto Rico	375,000	
British Leeward Islands	125,000	
Danish Islands	30,000	
Dutch Islands	30,000	
French Islands	330,000	
British Windward Islands	163,000	
Barbados	180,000	
Trinidad and Tobago	160,000	
		5,756,000
Panama (40,000) and the rest of Central America (say 40,000)		80,000
Venezuela and Colombia (say)		60,000
British Guiana		118,000
Dutch Guiana		85,000
French Guiana		22,500
BRAZIL (about)		8,300,000
Remainder of South America (say)		90,000
	TOTAL	24,591,000

Only round figures are employed in this calculation, and a slight reduction has been made on all estimates that were vague. The total, therefore, is scarcely likely to be an over-estimate of the proportionate importance of the negro peoples in the two Americas.

This *24,591,000* of the *African* race in the New World (including its ten millions of hybrids with the White peoples) may be contrasted with the

110,540,000 Whites of European origin or descent, the *20,855,000 hybrids* between the White and the Amerindian; the *16,000,000* of pure-blood *Amerindian* and *Eskimo;* and the *393,000 Asiatics* (216,000 East Indian, 150,000 Chinese, 27,000 Japanese) which combine to form the population of the New World. It will be noticed that in point of numbers the *Negroes* and *Negroids* come *second* in the list, though they are hard pressed by the yellow peoples of mixed Amerindian and Caucasian blood. The last-named can with difficulty be kept long from fusion, political and social, with the White race in the Americas—the distinction even now is rather fanciful—and this union would materially increase the proportial importance of the whites, an importance to be further augmented, as time goes on, by the ranging of the Amerindian on the side of the Caucasian. To the White man's community again will surely gravitate the descendants of at least four millions out of the ten million mulattoes, octoroons, and "near-whites" (the negroid hybrids) which are at present classed with the "coloured" or negro people of the United States, West Indies, Brazil, and Spanish-speaking America. Then if this Caucasian-Amerindian-Octoroon fusion be already assumed (producing as an ultimate result a series of racial types extremely like those of modern Europe), we shall find ourselves discussing a New World with a population divided into two racial groups: (1) the *White* or *Caucasian* (mingled with the Amerindian and tinged as are the Mediterranean peoples with a little Negroid intermixture) amounting at the present time to nearly *140,000,000;* and (2) the dark-skinned *Negro*, now over *20,000,000* in numbers, if in our calculations we class with him the negroid mulattoes. For reasons to be found in contemporary literature (some of which are quoted in this book) it would seem probable that the rate of increase is likely to be the same in both groups for a considerable time to come; so that we may not see during the first half of the twentieth century any displacement of the relative strength in numbers of the "White" and the "Coloured" people in the Western Hemisphere.

INDEX

www.ingramcontent.com/pod-product-compliance
Lightning Source LLC
Chambersburg PA
CBHW041929260326
41914CB00009B/1232
* 9 7 8 1 6 3 9 2 3 8 6 9 9 *